STARCRAFT
WINGS OF LIBERTY

TABLE OF CONTENTS

SINGLE PLAYER

MULTIPLAYER

"4TH ANNUAL HYDRALISK DERBY, 1ST PLACE BABY!"

THE STORY SO FAR

The original StarCraft story covered events among the Terran, Protoss, and Zerg races.

As the story begins, a Terran Confederate marshal, Jim Raynor, responds to the threat of strange Zerg forces arriving on Terran colonies. Later, word of Protoss forces eradicating colonies infected with Zerg spreads throughout Terran space.

During his attempts to battle the Zerg infestation and reason with the Protoss, he is initially allied with, and then later betrayed by the eventual ruler of the new Terran Dominion, Arcturus Mengsk.

The betrayal nearly causes the death of Raynor, and results in the destruction of the former Confederate capital of Tarsonis, as well as the sacrifice of Mengsk's second in command, the Ghost Sarah Kerrigan to the Zerg.

The Protoss, attempting to battle the threat of the Zerg, are eventually grudgingly reunified with their outcast Dark Templar brethren, and with their aid, they defeat the Zerg Overmind, which had invaded their homeworld, Aiur.

As a direct result of these events, and the death of the Zerg Overmind, the human Ghost Sarah Kerrigan is eventually transformed by the Zerg, becoming a dangerous fusion of human Psionic and Zerg.

As StarCraft: Brood War opens, the shattered remnants of the Protoss race flee Aiur to the Dark Templar homeworld of Shakuras. The Zerg have pursued them, and through a cautious alliance with the transformed Kerrigan, the Protoss succeed in using ancient Xel'Naga technology to wipe out the Zerg forces on Shakuras—but as a direct result, Kerrigan is able to then gain control of the leaderless Zerg Swarm.

The events in the Terran portion of Brood War were complex, but the heart of the situation was the return of human forces from the United Earth Directorate—forces not allied with the Terran Dominion led by Arcturus Mengsk.

Through a series of betrayals and battles, eventually Jim Raynor, Arcturus Mengsk, and the Protoss in the region become allied against the UED incursion, as the UED assault the Zerg world of Char and gain control of a gestating Zerg Overmind on the planet.

The final events play out as Kerrigan leads Zerg and a very reluctant alliance of Protoss and Terran forces to annihilate the United Earth Directorate who are in control of the new Zerg Overmind.

At the very end of Brood War, Kerrigan eventually betrays her temporary allies, slaying the Overmind and gaining full control of the Zerg Swarm, and assuming the mantle of the Queen of Blades. With the power of the UED fleet broken, and Terran Dominion and Protoss forces in the sector damaged, it remains to be seen what the future holds in the battle against the Zerg…

SINGLE PLAYER

The StarCraft II Campaign was designed to introduce the game to players new to the StarCraft universe then gradually ramp up the difficulty level. The early missions are tutorial-like and forgiving; the endgame missions are sprawling, and quite challenging. Many missions set tasks that prepare you for the multiplayer experience you may crave after completing the Campaign.

Thus our Single Player Basics section focuses on giving guidance to a wide range of players, from novice to expert. Truly hardcore StarCraft players, especially veterans of the Battle.net wars, may want to jump ahead to "Part Two: Multiplayer" to explore the more esoteric fine points of mastering StarCraft II.

DEVELOP A HOTKEY SYSTEM!

The most important gameplay skill you can learn for StarCraft II is this: create your own hotkey system, and then master it. And by "mastering" a hotkey system we mean burn it into your unconscious mind so it haunts your dreams.

Always assign hotkeys to critical units and groups and structures. But just as important, always be consistent about these hotkey assignments from mission to mission, game to game, scenario to scenario. Set it up any way you want, but do it *consistently*.

Some examples are listed below:

- Always hotkey your Orbital Command so you can instantly access the structure for a quick scanner sweep when cloaked units attack your forces out in the field.

- Always set the same hotkeys for specific training facilities, such as Barracks or Factory or Starport.

- It is particularly important to hotkey any units you send out as scouts. Scouts are usually weak, expendable units who die fast when they stumble into the lethal trouble they are looking for. You want to get a glimpse of what the scout has discovered before the poor guy gets obliterated.

- Always assign the same hotkey to your special ability units such as Wraiths or Siege Tanks so you can quickly select and activate their special ability (e.g., cloak Wraiths or toggle tanks between siege and mobile modes).

- Always assign the same hotkey to specific unit groupings. For example, always hotkey your primary ground assault force (usually a balanced mix of units) to the same key every game or mission.

- Do the same with any other sort of group you like to form regularly: your primary flying squadron, your mobile base defense force, your reconnaissance team, and so forth.

TERRAN TACTICS

You control Terran forces in the "Wings of Victory" Campaign, so Part One focuses primarily on the Terran race.

BASIC TERRAN STRATEGY

Overall, Terran strategy tends to be more defense-oriented, especially in the early going, with an emphasis on solid base development and orderly expansion. But the race is balanced enough that you can adapt Terran forces to almost any style of play, conservative or aggressive.

GAME PHASES

Most single-player missions unfold in recognizable phases. Generally, the early phase is about base development and reconnaissance; the middle phase is about expansion; and the endgame is about crushing your foe in a final showdown.

However, not all missions conclude with the destruction of your enemy's base or force. Some feature less conventional objectives: mining a certain amount of minerals, or escorting civilians safely down a Zerg-infested road, or simply holding out against an endless stream of enemy forces until a friendly ship can extract your team. Sometimes you'll have to adapt to changing objectives on the fly.

Note also that aspects of each game phase apply to other phases, and that phases overlap. All that said, let's take a look at how a typical mission unfolds.

EARLY GAME: DEVELOP & EXPLORE

Command decisions made in a mission's first five minutes can mark the difference between a clean, efficient victory and a long, painful slog marked by setbacks, or even failure. Good early choices certainly make things much easier in later phases.

For Terrans, the typical early focus is to establish a productive, well-defended base buoyed by a robust resource-gathering operation. We also recommend some early recon work.

Our tips for the early going:

- Immediately order any pre-existing SCVs to mine nearby mineral deposits.

- Place your Command Center's rally point in the midst of those deposits so that newly trained SCVs automatically start mining when they emerge. Then train as many new SCVs as your initial funds will allow. You can never have too many SCVs!

- Most Campaign missions start with a pre-existing Barracks in place. If not, order an SCV to build a Barracks as soon as you mine your first 150 minerals.

- Important: Add another Supply Depot to raise your unit cap. Keep one SCV dedicated to the task of building additional Supply Depots over the course of the mission.

- Start training Marines at the Barracks. In groups, Marines are tough all-purpose troops who can target both enemy ground and air units with good punch. But you need a fair-sized squad (minimum 8-10) for Marines to be effective; they must have enough concentrated firepower to take out more powerful enemies quickly. In smaller groups Marines are easily overwhelmed because their firepower doesn't compensate for each individual Marine's relative weakness.

- Start building Bunkers on your base perimeter. Your goal is to put at least one Bunker in each obvious approach route to the base.

- As your first Marines emerge from the Barracks, send them to garrison your Bunkers. Keep this up until every one of your Bunkers has a full complement of Marines.

- Put an SCV in auto-repair mode behind each Bunker cluster for quick repair work when Bunkers are damaged.

- Add 2-3 more Supply Depots in the very early going

- After your Bunkers are full, keep training Marines until you have a squad of 8-10 of them grouped in the center of your base. Assign a hotkey to this squad.

At this point you've got a solid defense in place for fending off enemy raiders in the early stages of a standard mission. But your base isn't fully secure or developed yet, and you need infrastructure in place for the expansion that lies ahead in the mid-game phase. Plus you should start getting a sense of what's lurking out there in the fog of war.

- Send out a few cheap scouts (Marines or even SCVs) to get a peek up the road. Try to locate new resources (mineral fields and gas geysers) as well as enemy bases and deployments.

- Tip: Assign a hotkey to each scout so you can switch your view to him quickly, especially if he's getting attacked. A lone scout will die fast if he wanders into an enemy assault team or a bustling base. Double-tap the hotkey to get a good glimpse of the area before he goes down!

- Build Refineries atop nearby Vespene Gas geysers and assign SCVs to work each Refinery. (Any SCV that finishes construction of a Refinery automatically begins gas delivery from that structure.)

- Keep training new SCVs for mining and gas delivery. You want at least 2-3 SCVs for every mineral patch and 3 for every Refinery.

- Add a Tech Lab to your Barracks so you can start producing Medics, Marauders, Reapers, and Firebats. (Note: In the Campaign, you gain the ability to train Reapers and Firebats in optional missions. Firebats first appear in "The Evacuation" and Reapers in "The Devil's Playground.")

- Build an Engineering Bay so you can construct Missile Turrets. This structure detects the enemy's cloaked units. Tip: Build new production buildings behind your Command Center.

- When the Engineering Bay is done, build a Missile Turret just behind each Bunker cluster around the base perimeter. (Make sure it's *behind* the Bunkers!) Put at least one turret near your Command Center too, just in case enemy air units slip past your perimeter defenses.

- Get a Factory in place so you can start producing your vehicles (Hellions and Siege Tanks).

MID-GAME: EXPANSION

Once you've got a well-established, well-garrisoned base and a good idea of what's happening out on the map, it's time to start expanding your operations.

- Locate any expansion sites that you can secure and send a military force to protect it while a Command Center is established. Remember you can create a Command Center in a fortified area and then fly it to an expansion site.

- Track down any bonus resources or hidden goodies on the map. Make use of your fast moving or flying units for this purpose.

- Scout out enemy positions and figure out an avenue of attack, or, if you can't attack, set up a solid defense.

- Continue to build your military and research new upgrades. Unless you are limited by the mission, you should always continue to build up your military forces!

- Evaluate any special military needs that are necessary for victory during the mission, be it a specific tech or a large number of a specific type of unit.

ENDGAME: THE SHOWDOWN

Once you have fully established your economy and built up your military as much as possible in terms of size and technology, it is time to finish off your opponent.

Note that some missions do not follow a standard 'build up base, expand and attack' model at all, and there may be very significant environmental hazards that must be dealt with.

Be sure to see the specific mission entry for more information on special missions.

- Move a massed force of units to tackle each objective area. Strike with maximum force so that you take minimal losses.

- Leave enough of a defensive force at threatened bases or areas to hold the line.

- Rebuild lost forces and rally them to a position where they can soon rejoin your offensive army.

- Focus on each objective in order, unless you have a critically pressing need to split up your force.

- Tackle any special or bonus objectives that require specific action to complete before you finish a mission.

BASE BUILDING

In general, good base building techniques are always the same for the Terran—establish a sturdy defense making use of your defensive structures, get your economy running, and build up your military production.

On missions where you do not have access to your defensive tools or a restricted economy or military, you must make do with what you are given, and making use of your units more carefully becomes more important.

Remember to make use of SCVs ability to repair structures and units, it is always cheaper to repair a unit or building than to build a new one, and you can also use SCVs set to Autocast repair to help hold the line on especially difficult defensive missions.

RESOURCE GATHERING

- Every mission is a production race at some level: Whoever cranks out more and better units usually wins, regardless of combat skill. But your production outflow depends on the inflow of raw materials. Creating an efficient mineral/gas collecting operation is perhaps the most fundamental skill to master in StarCraft II.

- Expand your SCV corps until you have at least two and preferably three units mining each mineral cluster.

- Build a Refinery on every defendable Vespene Gas geyser near your base. Assign three SCVs per Refinery to the task of gas delivery.

- Protect your SCVs. Their labor is the bedrock of your economy. Put garrisoned Bunkers along the supply route from resource-rich sites to your base. Keep a mobile force nearby ready to fend off raiders.

- Assign a single hotkey to all of the SCVs working a specific resource site, and keep it updated to include any new SCVs you deploy to that site. If the enemy launches a major raid on that supply line, you can select the entire SCV crew with a single button press and quickly pull them back behind your base defenses. Once the raid is repelled, you can reassign your SCV squad back to collection with a single hotkey press and click. Don't forget to reassign SCVs to gas!

- In a pinch, SCVs can fight. But remember that they're very fragile and easy to kill. Use them against only small squads of weaker enemies like Zerglings or a handful of Zealots. Otherwise, send them fleeing into your base or toward other units that can defend them.

- Try to disrupt the enemy's supply line. Send swift raiders or powerful units with area-of-effect attacks like the Siege Tank to decimate your foe's weak resource gatherers. Sacrificing a single Siege Tank to take out a large batch of enemy gatherers is almost always a very good trade.

- Always be on the lookout for new mineral and gas resources. Send out scouts until you've revealed the entire map.

- If you find a rich, defendable source of minerals and/or gas, it's worth the money to build an expansion base nearby, starting with a Bunker or two for defense and then a new Command Center to reduce travel time for your gatherer corps. Be sure to construct a well-defended base around the Command Center, in the same way that you built your original base.

- At each new expansion base, train another full crew of SCVs (3 per mineral patch, 3 per Refinery).

COMBAT TIPS

Taking damage does not decrease a unit's firepower. A near-dead Marine with only one red health bar inflicts the same amount of damage as a Marine with full health. So it makes sense to keep your units engaged in combat as long as possible, pulling a unit back for repair/healing only when its overall health dips dangerously into the red zone.

Repairing/healing existing units is considerably cheaper than training new units. Remember that SCVs can repair any Terran mechanical unit (Hellions, Siege Tanks, etc) including flying units. You can also deploy Medics and eventually Medivacs that can heal wounded biological units (Marines, Marauders, Firebats, and Ghosts/Spectres).

Always deploy Medics in teams of two! That way they can heal each other after healing your combat units. The same goes for SCVs: deploy teams of two for repair purposes, so they can fix each other after repairing damage to the structures and/or mechanical units to which they're assigned.

DAMAGE MATCHUPS

Remember that some units deal bonus damage to other units. You can see this information easily in-game by mousing over a unit's weapon on its information pane.

When facing large numbers of enemy units that are all of one unit type, you can build up a counter force by creating units that have bonus damage against that specific unit type.

COUNTER UNITS: KNOW THEM COLD!

There are a few special cases where units don't just deal bonus damage—they can flat out kill other units without retaliation. The two special cases for this are air units and cloaked units.

Air units can attack ground units without an anti-air attack without fear of retaliation. If you have air to ground units, feel free to beat up on your opponent's ground forces.

Cloaked units are similar. If you have cloaked units and your enemies forces have no units that can detect them, you can freely inflict damage without worry of retaliation. Just be careful about approaching enemy bases with cloaked units, they often have structures that can detect your units.

If your enemy does show up with anti-air or detection units, evaluate the situation. If you have a very large mass of air or cloaked units, you may be able to destroy the offending enemy units or structures and continue with your rampage. If the situation doesn't look favorable, withdraw!

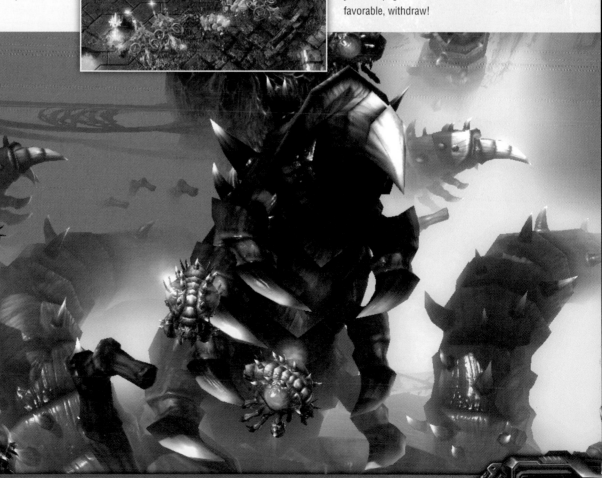

ATTACKING

Always use the Attack Move command to move troops across an active battlefield unless you're ordering an all-out retreat. When you issue a simple Move order, your troops stop shooting and move to the selected spot, ignoring any hostile forces along the way. Units deployed with Move won't fight again until they arrive at the designated spot.

If you use the Attack Move command instead, your units work their way to the same spot, but aggressively engage any enemy units they encounter on the way. Group your units into large squads and concentrate ranged fire on single dangerous targets to eliminate them quickly.

Let your Siege Tanks spread their fire but beware your own splash damage! Don't rush units into close range with enemy forces if you have friendly Siege Tanks firing onto the field. They quickly become very *un*friendly.

Make use of fast moving or aerial units (or scanner sweeps) to scout out ahead of your army and figure out which units should engage to suffer minimal losses.

DEFENDING

The Terran forces have many powerful defensive advantages. Be sure to make use of them all.

- Bunkers are awesome. Units inside Bunkers are completely shielded from damage and automatically gain +1 range. Always keep an SCV behind each Bunker for swift repair.

- Use your Command Center to protect SCVs. Command Centers can only carry SCVs.

- The Neosteel Frame research upgrade adds 2 more slots to each Bunker and 5 more slots to your Command Centers.

- Your various turrets and their upgrades researched throughout the campaign are very helpful for defending your base, expansions, and key chokepoints.

- Siege Tanks are amazing on defense, and a few stationed near a chokepoint behind Bunkers and turret can destroy many times their cost in enemy forces.

RECON & RAIDING

Aerial units and very fast moving ground units are the perfect units for recon, and aerial units and cliffjumpers are excellent for raiding.

When setting out on a recon mission, accept that you may take some losses, that's okay—the cost of the information gained is always worth a few lost units (though they might disagree with that assessment).

For raiding missions, be sure to strike with a small, highly mobile force, eliminate your target quickly, and then withdraw before the enemy can retaliate.

If you are striking with a large force, it is no longer a raid, it's an offensive!

Aerial units or cliffjumping Reapers make the best raiders, as they are unbothered by most terrain, and you can hit your target from its least defended area.

"TECH-UP" & UPGRADES

- *More* guns is preferable to *better* guns, especially in the early going. In other words, don't sacrifice your troop production to the activity of upgrading your equipment. Spend the bulk of your early funds on basic defensive structures and a strong garrison of troops. Weapon and armor upgrades are valuable in the long run, but also expensive and very time-consuming.

- A corollary of the previous tip is this: Wait a while before constructing an Armory. Your Armory is "upgrade central"; it has no other purpose other than researching better weapons and armor. Save it for later.

- Identify which upgrades complement your style of play. If you're a fan of raiding with cloaked units, by all means buy any upgrade that enhances cloaking ability (energy boost, etc)

EXPANSION TIPS

In a typical Campaign mission, your initial forces start out in a base with plentiful resources nearby. But in many cases, you must find new mineral fields and gas geysers and then outpace the enemy in extracting their raw materials. Indeed, a faster inflow of resources can offset weaknesses in combat skill. If you can build more stuff than your foe, you can be an inferior tactician and still kick his ass.

- Don't worry about aggressive expansion until your initial base is secure and its resource-collecting operation is humming along at high capacity. Higher-level players often ignore this suggestion, of course; they may go on the attack the moment their first grunts hit the field. But in general, it's best to focus on development first.

- But scout early for other mineral/gas sites on the map. Try to keep an eye on them as you develop your home base. Don't let your enemy drain resources from auxiliary sites without a fight!

- Keep an eye on what your foe is doing, too. His expansion efforts directly affect yours.

CAMPAIGN

Depending on your experience with Real Time Strategy Games in general, or StarCraft in particular, you can make use of this guide in several ways. For newer players, or for those of you that are feeling a bit rusty, we strongly recommend you begin with the Campaign.

As you encounter decisions or difficult spots, consult the Campaign Walkthrough chapters for advice and information to smooth your ride. The Walkthrough covers all possible mission branches, as well as all secrets and hidden goodies throughout the campaign.

Once you have completed the Campaign, or when you want a break, check out the Challenges, which are training maps designed to teach you some basic skills that are useful in multiplayer matches. At this point you may also want to play a few Skirmish games against the computer to practice.

When you are ready for multiplayer, skim through the Early Game portion of the multiplayer section for some basic advice to incorporate into your play, and when you want to really dig into the heart of multiplayer, check out the full Multiplayer Strategy section for much more detailed advice on all aspects of multiplayer in StarCraft II.

Finally, the racial sections cover units, structures, and abilities for the Terran, Protoss, and Zerg.

CAMPAIGN WALKTHROUGH

WINGS OF LIBERTY

INTRODUCTION

The StarCraft II "Wings of Liberty" Campaign features a rich, complex Terran tale that unfolds over the course of 29 missions. At most points in the story, the Campaign's unique structure offers you a choice of missions, sometimes as many as five. This lets you branch off to follow storylines associated with different characters.

Note, however, that at three specific points in the Campaign story you must make a choice between two paths of action. For example, at one point you decide whether to save an infested civilian population or to "purify" the planet. Each choice leads to a different mission with a different outcome. Once you choose a path and then complete the ensuing mission, you can't play the other one unless you load a game that you saved before the story branch, or you can play alternate missions via the Mission Archives but your main storyline will be locked based on your initial choice.

Thus you can't play all 29 Campaign missions in a single pass without backtracking. (A completed Campaign lets you play 26 of the 29 total missions available.) Again, you can save your game before making the mission choice, play out one course of action, then reload and play the other one if you want.

NO WRONG CHOICES

Here's a tip that may save you some hand wringing: there is no "incorrect" choice at any of the story-path branches. Whichever mission you choose unfolds in a way that validates your choice as correct.

THE CAMPAIGN FLOWCHART

Each Campaign mission features a pre-mission briefing by a specific character called the "mission contact." Because you can play missions in many different orders, we've organized our walkthrough into mission strands associated with the seven mission contacts: Jim Raynor, Dr. Ariel Hanson, Gabriel Tosh, Matt Horner, Tychus Findlay, Zeratul, and Valerian. (The mission contact in the Raynor mission strand is actually a cybernetic adjutant.)

Note that you can't always play all of the missions in a particular strand right in a row. To unlock certain missions you must complete not only the previous mission in the strand, but also jump to another strand to complete a specific number of missions or complete a prerequisite total number of missions first.

For example, in order to unlock "Safe Haven" in Ariel Hanson's mission strand, you must complete "Outbreak" (the previous mission in the Hanson strand) AND also fulfill one of the two following conditions:

* Complete at least two missions in another strand after you complete "Outbreak"

OR

* Complete a grand total of 12 missions (including "Outbreak").

The StarCraft II Campaign structure lets you play "Outbreak" as the fifth mission of the Campaign if you so choose. If you do that, you'll have to complete "Outbreak" plus at least two more missions from other mission contacts before you can unlock "Safe Haven."

THE JIM RAYNOR MISSIONS

LIBERATION DAY

THE OUTLAWS

ZERO HOUR

TERRAN MISSION FLOW

Here's the full mission structure of the Campaign, organized in an easy-to-follow flowchart:

THE ARIEL HANSON MISSIONS

THE EVACUATION

OUTBREAK

THE TYCHUS FINDLAY MISSIONS

SMASH AND GRAB

THE GABRIEL TOSH MISSIONS

4

THE DEVIL'S PLAYGROUND

WELCOME TO THE JUNGLE

8

A: BREAKOUT
B: GHOST OF A CHANCE

THE MATT HORNER MISSIONS

6

THE GREAT TRAIN ROBBERY

CUTTHROAT

ENGINE OF DESTRUCTION

MEDIA BLITZ

7

A: SAFE HAVEN
B: HAVEN'S FALL

THE ZERATUL MISSIONS

WHISPERS OF DOOM

A SINISTER TURN

ECHOES OF THE FUTURE

IN UTTER DARKNESS

8

THE DIG

11

THE MOEBIUS FACTOR

PIERCING THE SHROUD

14

SUPERNOVA

THE VALERIAN MISSIONS

MAW OF THE VOID

THE GATES OF HELL

A. BELLY OF THE BEAST
B: SHATTER THE SKY

ALL IN

AN IMPORTANT NOTE ABOUT OUR "SOLUTION PATHS"

Our walkthrough offers well-tested strategies including some tips for better performance that come directly from Blizzard design and QA experts. However, all StarCraft II missions are designed to yield success to multifarious approaches.

This guide's Campaign walkthrough tends to be conservative and deliberate, with an emphasis on exploring fundamental aspects of the game. We encourage you to experiment and adapt our suggestions to your own preferred style of play. Try alternate tactics. Be bold and slashing. Split your forces and multitask. See if you can find more elegant solutions than ours.

Don't worry: it won't hurt our feelings.

KEY

Mission

Story Branch

X — Requires # Missions

LIBERATION DAY

MISSION OVERVIEW

This is a straightforward, tutorial-like mission in which you simply guide your troops along the road through Backwater Station, gunning down whatever attacks you. As Raynor succinctly declares, "Alright, boys, let's show the locals they don't need to fear the Dominion."

PREREQUISITES

Begin the campaign.

OBJECTIVES

MAIN

- Destroy the Logistics Headquarters.
- Raynor must survive.

BONUS

- Destroy all 6 Dominion Holoboards.

CREDIT REWARD

None

ACHIEVEMENTS

ACHIEVEMENT		PTS	REQUIREMENTS
	Liberation Day	10	Complete all objectives
	Raynor's Back	10	Kill 5 enemy units in the mission with Raynor
	Down with Mengsk	10	Kill every enemy unit in the mission on Hard difficulty.

LOCATION: MAR SARA

Mar Sara was the eighth colony-world settled by the old Terran Confederacy. Though considered a backwater, its mining industry was once seen as a key strategic asset.

ADJUTANT'S BRIEFING

Backwater Station is the center of Dominion logistics on Mar Sara. Destroying Dominion authority here will cripple Emperor Mengsk's operations throughout the planet.

MISSION

You start with Jim Raynor and five Marines in the southwest corner of the map (1) on the outskirts of the Backwater Station mining operation. The Dominion outpost is nestled in the map's northeast corner (at 10), darkly visible through a hole punched in the map's fog of war. The rest of the map is obscured.

GOOD GRUNT

The Terran Marine is a well-balanced unit, inexpensive to train and effective against almost every foe you face, land or air. Marines are particularly effective when massed into squads.

FOLLOW THE MAIN ROAD.

Drag a selection box around your full squad, assign them a hotkey, and send them east along the cracked asphalt road. Just a few meters ahead, you run into a colonist who warns you not to go up the road. Continue east to the roadblock (2) and eliminate its crew of Dominion Marines.

NEW TECHNOLOGY

MARINE

Light infantry unit. The Marine is a versatile trooper who can attack both air and ground units.

LEGEND

PRIMARY

1. Start

2. Roadblock

4. Dominion guard

8. Dominion Transport

10. Dominion Compound

11. Logistics HQ

SECONDARY

3. Holoboard

5. Holoboard in the center of Backwater Station

6. Holoboard

7. Holoboard

8. Holoboard

9. Holoboard

BONUS: DESTROY THE DOMINION HOLOBOARDS.

Keep following the road north until you reach the Dominion Holoboard (3) broadcasting the Emperor's propaganda. This is one of six such Holoboards on this map; if you destroy all six you complete the mission's bonus objective. Destroy this one and continue north until you run into another Dominion Marine. Take out the enemy trooper and proceed.

ATTACK MOVE

The regular Move command orders troops to ignore all combat engagements until they reach the spot you designate, whereas Attack Move lets the moving units stop and engage foes en route which helps you deal with surprise enemy forces. In general, always use the Attack Move command unless you're rushing reinforcements to a hotspot or pulling damaged units out of the fray for healing/repair.

CLEAR THE TOWN CENTER.

Around the bend, you reach a full squad of Dominion Marines standing guard around another Dominion Holoboard in the center of Backwater Station (5). (Some Vikings fly overhead as well. The Viking is a new unit introduced in StarCraft II, but this squadron flies off; you don't fight Vikings until later in the mission.) Here, Raynor automatically calls in a "special delivery" of three drop pods that deliver more of Raynor's Marines right on top of the enemy. To minimize damage, quickly move your first squad to assist these reinforcements and mop up as quickly as possible.

Group the new arrivals into your squad. Destroy the Dominion Holoboard then move south a few steps to find another Holoboard (6). Be ready! Attacking this one triggers a surprise ambush by Dominion Marines. Turn your guns on them immediately; you can finish off the Holoboard after the skirmish. Now head southwest into the abandoned enclosure to find yet another Dominion Holoboard (7) broadcasting the Emperor's propaganda. Blast it to scrap: four down, only two to go.

⊖ DESTROY THE DOMINION COMPOUND.

Advance all of your troops northeast into the Dominion compound (10). The Mar Sara colonists swarm inside the compound with you, throwing flaming projectiles at the last Dominion Holoboard (9) then at the guards in an angry assault. Direct your initial fire at the enemy troops; anything that shoots back at you should be targeted first.

When your Marines or your colonist allies approach the Logistics Headquarters (11), a pair of big armored Vikings suddenly drops in to defend it. Concentrate fire on them until they fall, and then turn all guns on the HQ building until it finally goes up in flames.

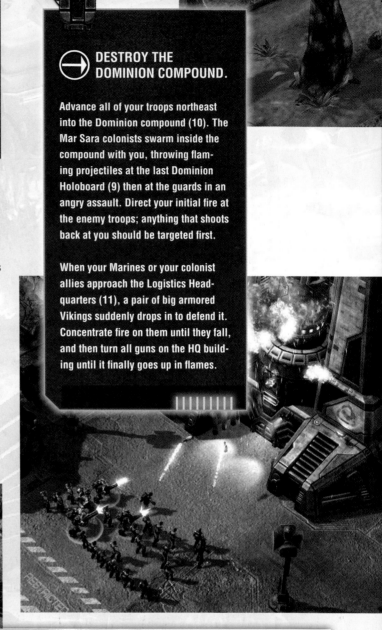

Follow the road northwest to another Holoboard (8) and witness signs of local restlessness, as well as Dominion brutality. Rush in to wipe out the oppressors; after you gun down the enemy Marines, destroy the armed Dominion Transport that fires on you. As you proceed, note that the locals are gaining hope and begin to voice support for Raynor's efforts. You also learn that a contingent of local hostages is being held up ahead.

INTERLUDE: JOEYRAY'S BAR

Your victory triggers a cut-scene: back in Joeyray's the next day, Tychus Findlay arrives with a friendly business proposition for his old war buddy. Raynor is intrigued, and agrees to give it some thought.

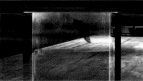

Afterward, click on Tychus for another dialogue exchange and then explore the room. Note that Joeyray's is an interactive environment with plenty of backstory-rich items you can click on to activate.

CHANGE IS THE ONLY CONSTANT

Check for new interactive "stuff" posted on Joeyray's corkboard every time you complete a mission. Not only does the corkboard provide you with some history, it's also a window into the future. Be sure to watch the TV news broadcast too.

When you're finished exploring the bar, click on the "mission case" that sits open on the bar (the console with the hologram of the adjutant's head floating above it). This brings up the Mission Selection screen for the adjutant's next mission briefing.

THE OUTLAWS

MISSION OVERVIEW

This mission introduces you to the basics of building structures, gathering resources, and training units. Your overall objective is once again uncomplicated, however: Destroy the Dominion's excavation outpost and confiscate the alien artifact.

PREREQUISITES

Complete "Liberation Day."

OBJECTIVES

MAIN

- **Destroy the Dominion base.**

BONUS

- **Rescue the Rebels.**

CREDIT REWARD

45,000

ACHIEVEMENTS

ACHIEVEMENT	PTS	REQUIREMENTS
The Outlaws	10	Complete all objectives
Cash Reward	10	Collect all Mineral and Gas Pallet pickups
Be Quick or Be Dead	10	Complete the mission on Hard difficulty in less than 10 minutes.

LOCATION: MAR SARA

Much of Mar Sara's surface was incinerated by the Protoss during the last war. However, many colonists have returned to rebuild their world's once robust mining industry.

ADJUTANT'S BRIEFING

Thanks to your actions, Mar Sara is now in a state of open revolt against Arcturus Mengsk. Ex-convict Tychus Findlay has revealed the Dominion came to Mar Sara to excavate an alien artifact. Seizing the artifact will strike another blow against the Dominion and generate funds from selling it to Findlay's mysterious contacts.

MISSION

GATHER RESOURCES AND TRAIN NEW TROOPS.

You start in a base (1) with a Command Center, a Barracks, a Supply Depot, and some Marines and SCVs. Immediately set all but one of your SCVs to work in the mineral fields; order the remaining one to build a Refinery atop the nearby gas geysers. Select your Command Center, set its Rally Point directly atop the mineral fields, and use your first minerals to train more SCVs (cost 50 apiece).

The moment the Refinery is finished, assign 1-2 more SCVs to that structure for faster collection of refined Vespene Gas. Once your resources are built up, put a few more SCVs in your Command Center build queue and order one to build a Supply Depot to increase your Supply cap by 8 units. Then start cranking out Marines from your Barracks.

BUILD A TECH LAB AND TRAIN MEDICS.

Click on your Barracks and add on the Tech Lab. A Tech Lab lets you produce a special new support unit, the Medic, who can heal wounded biological troops. Train a couple of Medics and add them to your group of Marines. You'll want to add another Supply Depot soon as well. Continue training Marines and the occasional Medic at your Barracks to keep roughly a 5:1 ratio of Marines to Medics, and send these new units out to join your main strike force.

NEW TECHNOLOGY

MEDIC

Advanced support infantry unit. The Medic heals nearby biological units and is trained at a Barracks with a Tech Lab add-on.

LEGEND

PRIMARY

1. Start

2. Mining camp

4. Enemy Hellions attack

5. Spawn cave

6. Enemy Bunker

7. Dominion Command Center

SECONDARY

3. Rebel base

 EXPAND.

Once you've gathered a strike force of 8-10 Marines and a pair of Medics, send this squad due north toward the small mining camp (2). Scoop up the Gas Pallet and Mineral Pallet en route by directing any troop to walk over them for an instant resource boost. Continue up to the camp to find more Mineral Pallets. Your adjutant reports that Dominion troops are attacking a rebel base to the southwest (3).

CACHE PICKUP

Remember: *Any ground unit can pick up resource caches such as Mineral Pallets.*

BONUS: SAVE THE REBEL BASE.

Push southwest to engage the Dominion Marines attacking a Colonist rebel base (3). Quickly assist to catch your foes in a deadly crossfire. Move any unit into the glowing green beacon to take control of the remaining rebels. You also gain control of the Barracks inside the Rebel base. It has a Tech Lab add-on, so you can start training more Medics right away.

Rebel Base

Until you liberate the Rebel base, the Dominion will send wave after wave of its Marines to attack it. Each wave is spawned from a cave to the northwest (5) and heads straight for the base. Once you liberate the base, the Dominion waves stop emerging from the cave.

DESTROY THE HELLIONS.

Send your massed Marine/Medic squad north to attack the two Dominion Hellions (4) that rush south to meet you. Their flames can take a toasty toll, so make sure you're still producing a good ratio of Marines and Medics from your Barracks as replacements.

RUN THE SPREAD OFFENSE VS. HELLIONS

The Hellion flamethrower shoots in a straight line with a "rail-gun" type attack, meaning it burns through *everything* in that line, including units stacked behind other units. To minimize damage from Hellion attacks, spread out your units!

DESTROY THE DOMINION BASE!

Mass your assault force of Marines with Medics in support. Push them all north into the Dominion base where the massive crane is poised to remove the alien artifact from the excavation pit.

The base is full of other Dominion structures: a dangerous manned Bunker (6), a Barracks training Marines, a Factory training Hellions, a Command Center (7), and several Supply Depots. Numerous Marines and Hellions form the base defense. You must destroy all Dominion structures to complete the mission.

Concentrate your massed Marines' firepower on the deadly Bunker (6) to destroy it as fast as possible. Once the Bunker is gone, nail the enemy Marines that emerge. Then focus on the Hellions and mop up the remaining troops. Target the Barracks and Factory to eliminate the enemy's troop production then blast the other buildings and SCVs. When the last Dominion structure or unit falls, watch Raynor's crew nab the alien artifact.

INTERLUDE: JOEYRAY'S BAR

After the mission, you end up back in Joeyray's. Talk to Tychus. You learn that his mysterious buyer is the Moebius Foundation, a legitimate scientific research group anxious to get its hands on alien artifacts.

Spend some time exploring Joeyray's again, clicking on all of the interactive objects for some pungent new commentary. Look for new items on the bulletin board, and be sure to click on the Zerg skull hanging on the wall to get Raynor's perspective on fighting the menace. Don't forget to check the TV for the latest news as well. When you're ready to move on, click on the mission case and trigger the next adjutant briefing.

MONEY FOR LATER

You earn 45,000 credits as a mission reward for winning "The Outlaws." But you can't spend these credits until you get access to the Armory aboard Raynor's flagship, the Hyperion, after the game's third mission, "Zero Hour."

ZERO HOUR

MISSION OVERVIEW

Get ready to face the relentless, slavering menace known as the Zerg. Your main goal here is survival. The primary objective is to fend off wave after wave of swarming Zerg until Raynor's flagship, the *Hyperion*, can arrive to extract your crew and ferry you offworld. But the Zerg have burrowed in and cut off three squads of rebel fighters who could use a hand.

PREREQUISITES

Complete "The Outlaws."

OBJECTIVES

MAIN

- Hold out for evacuation.

BONUS

- Rescue the Rebel fighters.

CREDIT REWARD

55,000

ACHIEVEMENTS

ACHIEVEMENT	PTS	REQUIREMENTS
Zero Hour	10	Complete all objectives
Hold the Line	10	Complete the mission without losing or salvaging a building.
The Best Defense...	10	Destroy 4 Zerg Hatcheries in the mission on Hard difficulty.

LOCATION: MAR SARA

With the resurgence of Mar Sara's once lucrative mining industry, the Dominion was quick to swoop in and establish military control over the growing colony.

ADJUTANT'S BRIEFING

With the artifact secure, you need to wait for transport at Backwater Station before you can leave Mar Sara. Transportation is on the way. Caution is advised. Dominion security forces may succeed in tracking the artifact to the station.

MISSION

FORTIFY THE BRIDGES.

You must hold out until the *Hyperion* arrives. (A timer counts down the seconds in the upper right corner of the screen.) Survival hinges on your ability to defend the two bridges that lead into your base area.

Fortunately, each bridge already has a Bunker in place with a squad of Marines posted nearby. But a single Bunker may not be enough to hold off the Zerg swarms that hunger for your flesh.

Immediately send one existing SCV to the northwest bridge (at 2) then put all other SCVs to work in the mineral fields. Quickly garrison the existing Bunkers guarding the bridges; you start with enough Marines nearby to do this. When the SCV arrives, have it build a second Bunker at the bridge, and then garrison that Bunker with Marines as well.

Leave the SCV in Auto-Repair mode (its default setting) behind the Bunker at the bridge for quick, automatic repair when Zerg rushes damage the structure. Don't dally, because the first Zergling assault hits your northwest bridge not long after the mission starts.

NEW TECHNOLOGY

BUNKER

Defense structure able to garrison and shield infantry units. It can hold up to four Marines, providing excellent protection while still allowing them to fire at targets in range.

LEGEND

PRIMARY

1. Start (Base)
2. Northwest bridge (build Bunkers)
3. Northeast bridge (build Bunkers)

SECONDARY

4-6. Trapped rebels

??. Port-O-Potty

CHOKING THE ZERG

The key to beating large Zerg ground swarms is to avoid getting surrounded by them. To do this, try to force the attacking Zerg through narrow choke-points that you can block off and/or concentrate heavy fire into.

In "Zero Hour," the two base bridges (2 and 3 on our mission map) form natural chokepoints. Control them with Bunkers and massed troops on your side of each bridge so the Zerg swarm cannot get through cleanly to spread out.

After the first Zerg wave is crushed, Raynor automatically sends an SCV to the northwest bridge. Direct it to move to the northeast bridge and build a second Bunker at that bridge mouth. As you do this you get a distress call from some stranded Mar Sara rebels. (For more on this, see the bonus objective later in this mission walkthrough.)

BEEF UP GROUND AND AIR DEFENSES.

The Marines you start with can easily fend off the first few Zerg rushes, especially if your boys are bunkered. But subsequent Zerg attacks grow increasingly more intense and include bigger swarms of Zerglings escorted by powerful Hydralisks. If you lose a Bunker, be sure to rebuild it immediately. Mass any extra troops around the bridges: don't let the Zerg punch through!

Soon Tychus reports seeing aerial attackers on the move: Mutalisks that start drifting down from the Zerg base. You begin the mission with several Missile Turrets already in place along your northern perimeter, so these will target the flying Zerg. Keep SCVs repairing your defensive structures and add extra Missile Turrets, including one or two closer to the base center near your Command Center.

Deploy a mobile reinforcement squad of 8-10 Marines plus a few Medics in the center of the base, ready to rush to hotspots if defenses are being overwhelmed or are nonexistent.

CREEPY TIPS

Zerg units move faster on creep, so engage them on untainted terrain whenever possible. If Creep Tumors spawn to spread creep, find and destroy them (they're burrowed and thus "cloaked") if they're within scanning range of your Missile Turrets.

BONUS: RESCUE THE REBEL FIGHTERS.

Three separate groups of rebels will appear on the map during the course of the mission and request rescue operations. The first group appears to the northeast (4) near Backwater Station; the second just north (5) of your leftmost bridge ; and the third up on a plateau (6) northwest of the base. Each stranded squad has Mineral Pallets that you can scoop up as additional reward for the rescue.

THE BUNKER BARRICADE

You can completely block the Zerg's ground access to your base by building Bunkers that seal off the two bridges. Of course, Bunkers can't be raised; you can't send your own forces around them either. But you can garrison a Bunker and then unload those units on the far side; you can then re-load new garrison troops from your side. This crafty technique lets you seal off the advancing Zerg yet still send out rescue units.

To rescue each rebel group, you need only walk to the beacon to trigger the rescue. Once your unit arrives, you automatically gain control of the rebels. At that point we recommend you rush them back across the nearest bridge into your base to join in the defense effort.

Some particularly nasty Zerg forces surround the third rebel group (at 6). Send a rescue party of at least 8-10 Marines supported by 2-3 Medics, and you should reach the trapped rebels with little problem.

HOLD OUT UNTIL HORNER ARRIVES!

Brace yourself for an insane last couple of minutes before extraction. Huge columns of Zerg swing down and frenetically rush the bridges, trying to smash into the base. Only one of your base structures needs to be intact as the timer hits 00:00, so don't panic if your defenses get overrun in the waning moments. If your Command Center is at full health with 50-60 seconds left, chances are good you've got the mission licked.

VICTORY!

Successful completion of "Zero Hour" triggers the movie cutscene "Escape from Mar Sara." Raynor discovers that he's facing an old nemesis.

INTERLUDE: THE *HYPERION*

Welcome to the *Hyperion*, flagship of Raynor's Raiders. After the cinematic you end up on the Bridge with Horner, Tychus, and a nerdy looking fellow named Egon Stetmann, the ship scientist. Talk to these folks to pick up more of the story so far.

Use the movement bar at the bottom of the screen to explore the other parts of the ship. For now you can go only to the Armory to buy permanent upgrades for your units. After the next mission you can stop in the Cantina to relax, hire mercenaries, and check out the latest news updates in the galaxy. Completing another mission after that unlocks the Laboratory, where you can see what items you must acquire during missions for more upgrades.

FIRST ARMORY PURCHASES

We highly recommend that you start with Marine Stimpacks. Then when you get a few more credits add the Stabilizer Med Packs for your Medics so they can heal 25 percent faster using 33 percent less energy per heal. A strong force of Marines with Stimpacks and a support group of upgraded Medics is a formidable force indeed. Later, when you can afford the Marine Combat Shield as well, your massed Marine squads will be remarkably tough against nominally superior units.

When you're ready for the next mission, return to the Bridge and click on the Star Map in the center to bring up your mission options. In this case, you have two choices.

NEW MISSIONS!

After you complete "Zero Hour" you can answer the distress call of Dr. Ariel Hanson and head to the besieged fringe world colony of Agria for "The Evacuation." Our walkthrough takes you there next. New unit available: Firebat.

Or you can continue to pursue Tychus Findlay's search for alien artifacts and visit the Protoss shrine world of Monlyth for "Smash and Grab." New unit available: Marauder.

BRIDGE

This is the command center of not only the *Hyperion* but also Raynor's entire rebel force. Use the Star Map to select new missions, or use the Mission Archives console to replay old missions. You'll always find Jim Raynor and his captain, Matt Horner, perusing the Star Map. On occasion, visitors such as Tychus Findlay, Dr. Ariel Hanson, and Gabriel Tosh appear on the Bridge. Be sure to talk to them when they do!

MATT HORNER

Matt Horner is the *Hyperion's* captain and Jim Raynor's right-hand man. He provides input on all strategic and tactical planning; in fact, Raynor often defers to his judgment. You'll always find Horner looking over the Star Map on the Bridge.

LABORATORY

The Hyperion's Laboratory serves two important purposes. Here, Egon Stetmann conducts his eccentric research projects using rare Zerg or Protoss samples you acquire during your missions. When you accumulate enough samples, Stetmann turns them into valuable new units and upgrades that you can select for your forces at the Research Console. The Laboratory is also where you store a special Ihan Crystal acquired from an old ally. This powerful artifact gives you access to new missions.

EGON STETMANN

Stetmann may not be a bona fide PhD scientist, but he has a knack for turning Protoss or Zerg samples into useful new technology.

THE HYPERION

CANTINA

The ship's Cantina is where personnel go to unwind, have a drink, play a videogame, or just chat with comrades. At various times during the Campaign you can talk to Raynor's old war buddy Tychus Findlay or the mysterious miner/pirate Gabriel Tosh to get their unique perspectives on things. This is also where Graven Hill does business, selling contracts for mercenary troops. Be sure to catch the latest UNN news report on the TV as well.

GRAVEN HILL

Graven Hill brokers contracts for some of the toughest mercenary outfits in the galaxy. He's always at his regular table in the Cantina. Check his laptop computer to see what guns-for-hire are available.

ARMORY

Visit Rory Swann in the Armory and use his Armory Console to spend your hard-earned credits on buffing up your troops and equipment. Select units appear in their full-sized glory in the Armory's vehicle bay behind the console. Click on them to view their specs and other interesting tidbits of info.

RORY SWANN

Swann just may be Jim Raynor's most valuable associate. He keeps all of your battle-tech primed and up to date, and if you provide enough credits he can acquire the latest upgrades for every unit. Swann is a mechanical genius; he can reverse-engineer almost anything he gets his hands on.

THE EVACUATION

MISSION OVERVIEW

This is a classic escort mission. Your job is to provide protection for successive convoys of Agria colonists as they flee up the highway to the colony starport from their base at Larks' Crossing. Once they arrive safely, the colonists can board an escape craft for evacuation from the Zerg that are rapidly infesting the planet.

PREREQUISITES

Complete "Zero Hour."

OBJECTIVES

MAIN

- Reach Dr. Hanson's settlement.
- Escort 50 colonists to the colony ships.

BONUS

- Harvest 3 Chrysalis DNA (+3 Zerg Research).

CREDIT REWARD

100,000

ACHIEVEMENTS

ACHIEVEMENT	PTS	REQUIREMENTS
The Evacuation	10	Complete all mission objectives
Handled with Care	10	Complete the mission without losing a Transport Truck.
Sacrifice Nothing	10	Complete the mission on Hard difficulty without losing or salvaging a building.

LOCATION: AGRIA

Founded by renowned terra-former Dr. Bernard Hanson, the Agria fringe world colony has been one of the Dominion's principal botanical and wildlife preserves.

DR. ARIEL HANSON'S BRIEFING

...any ship receiving this transmission...the Zerg are invading Agria. The Dominion abandoned us here. We're just a small farming colony. We've got to evacuate before we're overrun. If you can hear this message, please help us.

MISSION

Two huge Zerg hive colonies (11, 12) sit one on either side of the main highway that the colonists are using to escape from Larks' Crossing (3) north to the colony starport (6). These creep-filled areas have only three narrow access routes (4, 5, 7) onto the highway. The key to success in this mission is to plug those three Zerg access routes with well-garrisoned Bunkers.

FIND HANSON'S SETTLEMENT.

You start with some Firebats and Medics (1). Burn your way west through the Zergling swarms until you reach the glowing green beacon on the outskirts (2) of Larks' Crossing, the colony base. Though few, the Firebats are grimly effective against Zerglings.

CASH CROPS

Nab the Gas Pallet and Mineral Pallet in the farm fields north of the road as you approach Hanson's settlement (2) from the start (1).

NEW TECHNOLOGY

FIREBAT

Specialized anti-infantry attacker equipped with flamethrowers. The powerful flame attack can damage multiple ground units in an area. This heavy infantry unit is particularly effective against Zerglings.

RESEARCH OPPORTUNITIES

- +3 Zerg Research

NEW UPGRADES AVAILABLE AFTER MISSION

- Incinerator Gauntlets: Increases flamethrower attack area by 40 percent.
- Juggernaut Plating: All Firebats gain +2 armor.

LEGEND

PRIMARY

1. Start
2. Beacon
3. Main base
4. South bunker
5. North bunker
6. Starport

SECONDARY

7. Build new Bunker here
8-10. Zerg Chrysalis
11-12. Zerg hive colonies

BEEF UP YOUR ESCORT.

When you arrive, Dr. Hanson gives you control of the main base structures (3). Immediately increase your SCV corps, make sure they're all working, and pop a Refinery atop the Vespene Gas geyser. The Barracks already has a Tech Lab add-on, so you can start training Firebats, Marines, and Medics right away.

NO MARAUDERS

If you chose to complete "Tooth and Nail" before "The Evacuation," you have Marauders available too. But Marauders are weak against Zerglings, whereas Firebats blister the beasts quickly. So focus on training Marines and Firebats with Medics in support.

ESCORT THE COLONIST CONVOYS.

Before you can get very many Marines trained, Dr. Hanson announces that the first convoy from Larks' Crossing is preparing to move out. Soon a handful of colonists load into a transport truck. Before the truck starts heading up the road, select your original Firebats and Medics plus any new combat units you've trained, then right-click on the transport truck to assign your troops to escort it up the highway to the colony starport (6).

Protect those colonists! If you lose 20 on Hard or Brutal difficulty, you fail the mission. When you reach the starport ramp, note the strange object (7) by the side of the road. This is a Zerg Chrysalis Egg. For more on this, see the bonus objective section below.

Later, when you have more troops trained, you can split your escort force into two squads. (Be sure to add Medics to each squad.) Assign both to escort the transport truck; when Zerg attackers appear, rush one squad into the teeth of the assault. The other squad stays with the truck to intercept Zerg thrusts from other directions.

PALLET PICKUPS

Keep an eye out for Gas and Mineral Pallets stashed across the map. Look for them along the edges of the highway and in the off-road clearings. These packages give your economy a quick infusion of much-needed resources.

GARRISON THE ROAD BUNKERS.

Shortly after the first convoy pulls out, Raynor notes the unmanned Bunkers sitting along the road. These sit strategically in the mouth of two approach routes that the Zerg use in assaulting colonist convoys. Send the first four Marines from your Barracks directly to the Bunker at (4). Then send the next four Marines further up the road to garrison the Bunker at (5).

These two Bunkers provide invaluable fire support as you escort colonists up the road during the mission. Remember to keep at least one SCV (and preferably two so the SCVs can repair each other) next to each one in Auto-Repair mode for ongoing repairs. Keep a few Firebats near each Bunker as well. Eventually, you want to build a second Bunker at each location.

BONUS: HARVEST DNA SAMPLES FROM THREE ZERG CHRYSALIS EGGS FOR STETMANN'S LAB RESEARCH.

The first time you escort a convoy to the evacuation ships, Raynor notices a Zerg Chrysalis Egg on the roadside near the starport ramp (8). Stetmann wants Zerg DNA for his research back on the *Hyperion*. Any unit can collect it from the Chrysalis, but send along a Firebat or two to fend off the three burrowed Zerglings who pop up nearby!

Once you've garrisoned your Bunkers and trained a variety of other troops, create a separate search squad that includes Marines, Firebats, Medics. Send this crew off to extract DNA from the other two Zerg Chrysalis Eggs on the map (9 and 10). Careful though! Burrowed or flying Zerg units guard each of the eggs.

ADD MORE BUNKERS AND AN AIR DEFENSE.

You can win this mission with just the initial two road Bunkers in place plus two strong squads of Firebat-heavy escorts for the convoys. But you can make things much easier if you add one or two fully garrisoned Bunkers in the Zerg approach route on the right (east) side of the road (7) as well.

If you want more security, add a Missile Turret next to each Bunker to take down the Zerg Overlords that float around and drop creep on everything. Watch out for burrowing Roaches that pop up suddenly, and Nydus Worms that emerge in creep areas, and Zerg drop pods that fall from the sky to disgorge swarms of Zerglings and Hydralisks.

Keep escorting the transport trucks from Larks' Crossing up to the starport until 50 colonists have been loaded aboard the evacuation ships. Each truck hauls about 8-12 passengers per trip. If a truck is destroyed, the colonists hop out and continue on foot; you can still escort them, but they're more vulnerable now. When the fiftieth colonist boards the ship, the mission is a success.

INTERLUDE: *HYPERION*

Afterwards, Dr. Hanson joins the team as the *Hyperion's* new Science Officer. Talk to her on the Bridge to learn about the dire situation in the refugee camps on Meinhoff. Talk to Matt Horner to see what an idealistic guy he is. Then go explore the newly available areas of the ship.

Visit the Cantina to meet Mr. Hill, a broker for mercenary soldier contracts. Mercenaries are enhanced squads; you purchase an initial contract from Hill in the Cantina, then produce the hired mercenaries from the Merc Compound in the field during a mission. This production is not cheap in minerals and gas, but mercenaries are powerful units and emerge *immediately* from the structure when you click their production button. Thus they can give you a quick boost of firepower in tough situations.

You automatically get the War Pigs contract for free; the Pigs are a squad of four elite Marines with enhanced vitals that include +65 percent Health and +35 percent Damage. We recommend that you spend the 25,000 credits for the services of the Devil Dogs as well, a squad of two enhanced Firebats. These will be especially valuable in the Hanson missions versus the Zerg. After all your business with Hill is transacted, talk to Tychus.

Merc Compound

After you meet Mr. Hill, the Merc Compound automatically appears in your base when each new mission opens (but only if you start with a base). Any mercenary squad whose contract you purchased from Hill is available after a "cooldown" cycle of time elapses.

Go to the Armory and click on the new Firebat suit in the bay for some interesting background data. Then access the upgrades panel to see what's new. We recommend you go for the Firebat Incinerator Gauntlets for a wider area of flame attack. Also consider the Neo-Steel Bunker upgrade, which increases the number of Bunker slots from 4 to 6. Strong Bunkers are very important against Zerg swarms.

MISSION BRANCH!

After you complete "The Evacuation" you unlock the next mission for Ariel Hanson, called "Outbreak." Dr. Hanson asks Raynor to investigate the deadly epidemic sweeping through the refugee camps on Meinhoff. Our walkthrough takes you there next. New unit available: Hellion.

If you're following our walkthrough order, you've completed a minimum of four missions at this point. This unlocks the first mission for the black market trader Gabriel Tosh. Now you can visit the Kel-Morian mining planet of Redstone III to attempt "The Devil's Playground." New unit available: Reaper.

You still have the option of pursuing Tychus Findlay's search for alien artifacts by heading off to the Protoss shrine world of Monlyth for "Smash and Grab." New unit available: Marauder.

OUTBREAK

MISSION OVERVIEW

Meinhoff is overrun with colonists infested by a Zerg virus. Your task is to build a tightly defended base and then purge the planet of all infested buildings. Venture out only in daylight, however. Infested folk swarm at night. By day, the unfortunate mutants must remain burrowed to avoid UV radiation.

PREREQUISITES

Complete "The Evacuation."

OBJECTIVES

MAIN

- Cleanse the infestation: destroy all 144 infested structures.

BONUS

- Kill the 2 Zerg Infestors: Night Only (+2 Zerg Research).

CREDIT REWARD

110,000

ACHIEVEMENTS

ACHIEVEMENT		REQUIREMENTS
Outbreak	10	Complete all mission objectives
28 Minutes Later	10	Complete the mission before the 5th night.
Army of Darkness	10	Destroy 15 infested buildings at night time on Hard difficulty.

LOCATION: MEINHOFF

This planet is known for its rich, abundant mineral deposits. The Kel-Morian Combine has controlled Meinhoff for many years. Recently, however, it's become a haven for refugees escaping the invading Zerg.

DR. ARIEL HANSON'S BRIEFING

Jim, refugee populations from across the sector have been using Meinhoff as a staging point. But with so many people in close proximity, an epidemic of some kind has started sweeping through the camps. Please, my people need help! We've got to do something before it's too late.

MISSION

This mission requires good planning just to survive, much less succeed. Your twin goals are to secure your base well enough to fend off massive swarms of Zerg and infested humans at night, and then send out strike teams to incinerate all 144 infested structures during daylight hours.

SEAL OFF THE OPEN CHOKEPOINTS.

Night is nasty on Meinhoff, and when the mission opens you have just 2:00 until your first sunset. (An onscreen timer in the corner counts down each cycle of day and night.) Immediately follow Raynor's order and hustle an SCV to each of the open passages (2 and 3) leading into the base, then build a Bunker in each chokepoint.

As the Bunkers go up, get your other SCVs working the mineral fields. Move all available combat troops supported by Medics into the gaps on either side of the Bunkers. Be sure to post an SCV in Auto-Repair mode just behind each Bunker. Issue the Hold order to all combat troops; you don't want them wandering too far from the Bunker.

NEW TECHNOLOGY

HELLION

Fast skirmisher vehicle with a flame attack. Very effective versus Zerglings.

SENSOR TOWER

Lets you spot enemy units within its sensor sweep radius; they appear as red blips on your minimap.

RESEARCH OPPORTUNITIES

- +2 Zerg Research

NEW UPGRADES AVAILABLE AFTER MISSION

- Twin-Linked Flame Thrower: Doubles width of the Hellion's flame attack.

- Thermite Filaments: Hellions do an additional +10 damage to Light Armor.

LEGEND

PRIMARY

1. Start

2-3. Primary chokepoints

SECONDARY

4. South passage

5-6. Zerg Infestor locations

NO TURRETS NECESSARY

You face no enemy flyers in this mission so don't waste money building Missile Turrets.

Hurry! The moment darkness descends, swarms of infested Terran refugees and Marines try to stagger into your base through the two chokepoints. Garrison the finished Bunkers with Marines.

Note that a ramp (4) leads up into the base from the southwest as well. Some "Destructible Debris" blocks this passage. Your infested foes will smash through the debris eventually, opening a new attack route into the base. Luckily, that won't happen for a while (unless you clear a lot of the map quickly, which triggers the debris attack), so you can ignore it for the first few days. A good trick is to build a Bunker up against the debris to give you map visibility beyond the pile. This lets you monitor any enemy activity on the far side. Putting a Bunker here also gives you a head start on defending the gap later.

NEW SENSOR TOWER!

Your Sensor Tower (placed on the ramp at the front of your base) makes all enemy units within its sweep radius appear as red blips on your minimap. This gives you an early warning system, alerting you to large enemy advances.

DEPLOY YOUR NEW HELLIONS!

Toward the end of the first night, Swann delivers a quartet of Hellions plus a Factory with the tech to build more. Immediately plug these agile flame-spewing vehicles into the gaps you're defending. Again, give Hellions the Hold command once placed so they don't move away from the Bunkers; you don't want them rushing out and getting cut off from the main defense squad.

BUILD A LETHAL STRIKE FORCE.

As your well-positioned defenders fight off the grotesque attackers, turn your attention to unit training. The next goal is to amass a battalion of troops that can quickly raze infested Terran structures during your brief windows of daylight. Your best bet is a strong corps of the speedy Hellion flamethrower units plus some SCVs for repair. Consider adding a Reactor to your Factory so you can start producing two Hellions at once.

HELLIONS OR MARAUDERS?

If you completed "Smash and Grab" before "Outbreak" you have Marauders available from your Barracks. Marauders are good at demolishing regular Zerg structures (which are armored) with their armor-busting Punisher grenades. But the Zerg-infested Terran structures in this mission are "organic" rather than armored, so flame-throwing units such as Firebats and especially your new Hellions are much better for razing those buildings.

Use Marauders against the "real" Zerg structures (such as Spine Crawlers) in the southern part of the map. Marauders are also effective against the centaur-like, heavily armored Aberrations that occasionally attack you.

Hellions are also ideal for fending off the furious Zerg Broodling packs that burst from each infested building that you burn down. Broodlings are speedy melee attackers who close very fast but are weak against flames.

DEFEND BY NIGHT, PURGE BY DAY.

When darkness finally ends, any infested creature caught outside is consumed by the daylight. Now you can send out your strike force and start blasting buildings. You won't face any opposition except for the Spine Crawlers rooted in some areas and the aforementioned Broodlings who emerge from destroyed buildings.

Destroy as many buildings as you can during the daylight hours. Keep your base growing and keep training new units; deploy newly trained troops to both of your chokepoint defenses as well as to your "purge force" out in the field. As your strike force grows you can split it into multiple groups to speed up the razing process.

If you can afford it, build an Engineering Bay and an Armory then start buying any available upgrades for your infantry and vehicle weapons and armor. You automatically start with a Merc Compound in your base. Get those troops out into the field too. You need all the help you can afford!

FIRST TARGETS

Always start by shooting things that fight back! Thus your initial targets in each new infested area should be any Spine Crawlers you encounter.

Watch out for Aberrations!

Large, heavily armored units called Aberrations begin to assault your base after a few nights or if you've made swift progress razing infested structures. Be aware that Hellions fare quite poorly against Aberrations.

Keep a small squad of armor-busting Marauders hotkeyed in your base; rush them to engage any Aberration that tries to punch through your chokepoint defenses. If you don't have Marauders available, counter Aberrations with massed Marines backed by Medics.

The Adjutant informs you whenever 30 seconds of daylight remain. When you hear this warning, immediately cease any demolition activity and hustle your troops back into your base. If you get caught outside the base after dark, the emerging swarms can easily swamp your strike force.

Night Dangers

If you attack any building at night, the structure instantly spawns a horde of enemy troops. Stay out at night only if you have vastly superior forces.

PLUG THE SOUTHWEST GAP.

By Day 3 you should have things under control enough to plug the southwest passage (4) with defenders. Build a Bunker and place Hellions and Firebats, supported by Medics and at least one SCV on Auto-Repair. Again, give all combat units the Hold command so they don't get pulled from their posts. Eventually an Aberration-led infested column smashes through the debris blocking the once-safe southwest passage.

QUICK PLUG

Keep a small convoy of Hellions in your base center, ready to rush to reinforce any of the three chokepoints.

BONUS: KILL THE TWO INFESTORS! (NIGHT ONLY)

Early on the second night Horner reports the bio-signature of a previously unknown burrowing Zerg creature: an Infestor. He pinpoints two of them on the map, one in the east and one in the southwest.

Killing these provides research samples for Stetmann in the Lab and earns you more Zerg Research Points. But they emerge from the ground only during the dangerous night hours. The best tactic is to go to the area where they nest during the day and clear out the infested buildings, then wait until the Infestor pops up. Kill it quickly and then send your troops on a beeline for the protection of your base!

MOP UP THE LAST INFESTED STRUCTURES.

When only a few structures remain, the ever-helpful Horner up on the *Hyperion* reveals the remaining infested buildings on your minimap radar. This lets you spot any structures you may have overlooked in the corners of the map. When the last infested building is razed, the mission is complete.

INTERLUDE: *HYPERION*

Afterwards you end up in the Hyperion's Cantina where Raynor watches a news report on TV. A new area of the ship is now open: the Laboratory. Go there to meet Egon Stetmann and learn about research opportunities, then click on the Research Console to spend the Research Points you've earned so far. If you completed all of the research-based bonus objectives so far, you have enough Zerg Research progress to choose between two great Bunker upgrades. Either one is valuable; we prefer the Fortified Bunker option (Bunkers gain +150 health) but the Shrike Turret is nice too. You can pick only one: once the choice is made, the other option is no longer available.

After you check in at the Armory and buy an upgrade or two, go to the Bridge where Ariel Hanson speaks to Raynor. Her refugee people have found an unclaimed planet called Haven near the edge of Protoss space. Talk to Horner to learn of his fears about the infestation in the Haven settlers.

Finally, click on the Star Map to select your next mission. The next Ariel Hanson mission, "Safe Haven," isn't available until you either complete a total of 12 missions (including "Outbreak") or complete at least two other missions after you finish "Outbreak."

SAFE HAVEN

MISSION OVERVIEW

When you launch this mission, Raynor asks Horner to open a channel to the Protoss. The Protoss Executor Selendis presents a compelling case for the "purification" (incineration) of the Haven colony. This would halt the infestation of the Zerg virus, but wipe out the remnants of Ariel Hanson's people. In response, Dr. Hanson pleads for time to cure the infestation herself. And thus you face a terrible choice.

PREREQUISITES

Complete "Outbreak" plus 11 other missions (total of 12), or complete at least two other missions after completing "Outbreak."

Select PROTECT THE COLONY after you launch the "Safe Haven" mission.

OBJECTIVES

MAIN

- Destroy the 3 Protoss Nexuses.
- Destroy the Purifier mothership.

BONUS

- Stop the first terror fleet.
- Stop the second terror fleet.
- Stop the third terror fleet.

CREDIT REWARD
125,000

ACHIEVEMENTS

ACHIEVEMENT	PTS	REQUIREMENTS
Safe Haven	10	Complete all mission objectives
You Shall Not Pass	10	Save 4 Colonist Outposts.
My Precious!	10	Save 3 Colonist Outposts on Hard difficulty.

LOCATION: HAVEN

Despite its idyllic conditions, Haven's close proximity to Protoss territory has deterred most Terran colonization attempts. Until now.

DR. ARIEL HANSON'S BRIEFING

My people established a new colony on Haven. It was going well but now the colony's gone dark. They're not responding on any frequency. We need to get there and see what the situation is. They might have been exposed to the Zerg virus, and they are on the verge of Protoss space. Jim, I'm worried that something has gone very wrong.

THE HAVEN DECISION

PROTECT THE COLONY: Do you choose to save the Haven colonists from purification by fighting the Protoss? This choice triggers the mission "Safe Haven."

PURIFY THE COLONY: Or do you undertake the colony purification yourself instead of letting the Protoss do it? This choice triggers the mission "Haven's Fall."

MISSION

Swann delivers a squadron of Vikings and adds its schematic to the Starport in your base. Vikings are very useful in this mission. The Haven colonists are loading onto evacuation ships in advance of the Purifier's approach. The massive mothership/destroyer has an impenetrable shield at first; you can't hurt it at all until you destroy the three Nexuses in the field that generate its shield, so don't waste your time targeting the Purifier in the early going.

NEW TECHNOLOGY

VIKING

This durable support flyer can transform into a ground vehicle.

RESEARCH OPPORTUNITIES

- +3 Zerg Research

NEW UPGRADES AVAILABLE AFTER MISSION

- Jotun Boosters: Increases attack range +2.
- Ripwave Missiles: Viking missiles do area damage.

LEGEND

PRIMARY

3-5. Protoss Nexus locations

6-10. Colony settlements

SECONDARY

1-2. Put Bunker & Turrets here

DESTROY THE FIRST NEXUS.

The first Nexus (3) is not far, just east of your base. Get your production ramped up quickly, and then place a Bunker and a Missile Turret at the top of each access road (1 and 2) leading into the base. After you get a few garrison troops in the Bunkers , crank out 3-4 more Vikings immediately and group them with your initial Viking squadron.

If your Factory can train Goliaths (available after the Tosh mission, "Welcome to the Jungle") or Diamondbacks (available after the Hanson mission, "The Great Train Robbery"), or if your Barracks can train Marauders (available after the Tychus mission, "Smash and Grab"), get some in the queue. These units are all very good in match-ups against armored units such as Protoss Stalkers. Otherwise pump out Hellions and plenty of Marines with Medics plus several SCVs in Auto-Repair mode for support. Start grouping these units into an assault force.

When your assault force has at least four Vikings, a few Hellions (or other vehicles) and 10-12 Marines, push off for the nearest Nexus (3). Hellions are particularly lethal against both the Protoss Zealots and Sentries on the ground guarding this Nexus. Meanwhile your Vikings and Marines can target the enemy aircraft at the site. Knocking out the flying Warp Prisms has the added bonus of cutting off power to the annoying Photon Cannons on the ground.

Once the enemy air units are eliminated, the Vikings can drop down in Assault Mode and help mop up any remaining Protoss ground forces. Finally, blast the Nexus into dust.

LOST SETTLEMENT

The Purifier arrives shortly after the mission opens and destroys the southernmost settlement (6). There's nothing you can do to stop the massive ship so early in the mission, so don't even try.

VIKING: AIR AND GROUND

Keep cranking out Vikings to create one big Viking squadron. Consider adding a Reactor to your Starport so you can double-queue them! Hotkey the entire squadron but then put half the group on a separate hotkey as well. This way you can quickly select that half and drop it down into Assault Mode (i.e., make it a ground-based unit) if your ground forces are getting overwhelmed. The other half of the squadron can continue with air-to-air combat.

Note that this engagement triggers the advance of a trio of Protoss Stalkers that rush up the rightmost road to raid your base. If you placed your Bunker and a few other defenders in the approach route (2), you can fend off this attack easily. You can rush your speedy Vikings back and put them on the ground if you need additional help with this small incursion.

BONUS: STOP THE FIRST TERROR FLEET.

Once the Purifier lays waste to the first colony settlement (at 6), its air escort, a small Protoss "terror fleet" of two Carriers, jets up to attack the southwest settlement (7). Scramble some Vikings from your assault force and rush them over to defend the colonists. The Viking's Lanzer Torpedoes are very effective against capital ships such as Carriers. Five Vikings ought to do the job just fine.

After you destroy the Carriers, the colony evacuation ship takes off, leaving several pallets of Gas and Minerals behind. Put your Vikings into Assault Mode so they drop to the ground and gather the abandoned goods, then elevate again and fly your boys directly back to base.

EXTRA TURRETS

Chances are good that the Purifier will survive long enough to hover eventually toward your base. Put up a few extra Missile Turrets (at 1) to hammer the deadly mothership if it arrives.

DESTROY THE SECOND NEXUS.

Soon the Purifier is on the move again! Now it heads for the evacuated base at (7). Again, leave it to its task. Your assault force's next target is the Nexus in the southeast (4). This one has a tougher bunch of protectors, including Stalkers and Colossi on the ground.

Fortunately, Vikings can actually hit the towering Colossi from the air. (Yes, the Colossus is a ground unit, but it's so tall your flyers can target it.) By all means send plenty of those counter units to the Nexus. (Stalkers are weak against Marauders or Diamondbacks, but you may not have those units available yet, as noted before.) Just a reminder: Make sure you include support troops (Medics and SCVs) in your force. Wipe out the defenders and destroy the Nexus. Now the Purifier has only one last Nexus powering its shields.

BONUS: STOP THE SECOND TERROR FLEET.

After the Purifier nukes the settlement at (7) it sends off two more Carriers and a Scout to harass the Haven colonists trying to evacuate the settlement at (8). Hustle your Viking squadron to knock this terror fleet from the sky. Again, Vikings are very good against Carriers, so the task should be fairly easy. Once the evac ship takes off, remember to drop your Vikings to the ground and pick up the resource crates it leaves behind.

DESTROY THE THIRD NEXUS.

Now the Purifier moves to its next target, the colony base at (8). Beef up your assault force with any new units you've produced at your base and launch your attack on the final Nexus (5). This one adds powerful psionic units called Archons to the Zealots on the ground, plus a Photon Cannon. In the air, Carriers produce nasty, buzzing swarms of interceptors, and a Void Ray inflicts heavy damage to your armored units with its Prismatic Beam attack.

Once again, you're fortunate in that your Vikings are quite effective against Carriers and Void Rays. The Archons are another matter, however. The splash damage from their Psionic Shockwave attack is very lethal to biological units like Marines. Hit them with Marauders or Goliaths, if you have any. If your Vikings can clear the skies quickly, get them down on the ground to help against the Archons too. When the defenders are finally eliminated, destroy the Nexus to finally take down the Purifier's shields.

BONUS: STOP THE THIRD TERROR FLEET.

After the Purifier obliterates the settlement at (8) it unleashes another fleet to harass its next target, the settlement at (9). This fleet is comprised of three Carriers and a Scout. Once again, speed your Vikings (you want at least 7-8 of them here) to save the colonists. Don't forget to scoop up the goods left by the departing evacuation ship.

DESTROY THE PURIFIER.

Now you're free to hit the Purifier. Do so with everything you've got! It's vulnerable now without its shields, but its colony-eradicating death ray is still operating at full power. By now the Purifier is most likely on its way to the last Haven settlement (10), the one behind your base. (It heads there after destroying the colony settlement at (9).) Select every combat unit at your disposal that can hit air targets (Vikings, Marines, and if you have them, Goliaths) and sick them on the Purifier until it goes up in a cloud of purified smoke.

INTERLUDE: *HYPERION*

Victory triggers a final scene between Dr. Hanson and Raynor entitled "Good Man."

You end up in the ship's Cantina. Watch some TV and check with Mr. Hill for new mercenary contracts; he's got a tough Viking squadron available called Hel's Angels. Chat with Tosh, who's heard some interesting rumors, and talk to Tychus. Then make all the other usual visits around the *Hyperion* before heading to the Bridge for your next mission selection on the Star Map.

HAVEN'S FALL

MISSION OVERVIEW

If you agree with the Protoss Executor Selendis and believe that many more lives can be saved via a painful but necessary purification, you have a grim task ahead of you. The Zerg are well entrenched and their Virophages are infesting the countryside. As in "Safe Haven" you have Vikings at your disposal now. They will prove particularly useful in this mission.

PREREQUISITES

Complete "Outbreak" plus 11 other missions (total of 12), or complete at least two other missions after completing "Outbreak."

Select PURIFY THE COLONY after you launch the "Safe Haven" mission.

OBJECTIVES

MAIN
- Destroy all Zerg infestations.

BONUS
- None.

CREDIT REWARD
125,000

ACHIEVEMENTS

ACHIEVEMENT		PTS	REQUIREMENTS
	Haven's Fall	10	Complete all mission objectives
	Outpatient	10	Protect 3 settlements from the Zerg infestation
	House Call	10	Protect 5 settlements from the Zerg infestation on Hard difficulty.

LOCATION: HAVEN

Despite its idyllic conditions, Haven's close proximity to Protoss territory has deterred most Terran colonization attempts. Until now.

DR. ARIEL HANSON'S BRIEFING

My people established a new colony on Haven. It was going well but now the colony's gone dark. They're not responding on any frequency. We need to get there and see what the situation is. They might have been exposed to the Zerg virus, and they are on the verge of Protoss space. Jim, I'm worried that something has gone very wrong.

MISSION

GET THE BIGGER PICTURE.

This can be a brutal war of attrition. The Zerg are well established in the area, with three big Hives (4, 5, and 6) in place that you must destroy. All three are extremely well defended. And a Virophage with support units has fully infested a colony settlement (7).

NEW TECHNOLOGY

VIKING

This durable support flyer can transform into a ground vehicle.

RESEARCH OPPORTUNITIES

- +3 Protoss Research

NEW UPGRADES AVAILABLE AFTER MISSION

- Phobos-Class Weapons System: Increases missile range +2 and cannon range +1.
- Ripwave Missiles: Viking missiles do area damage.

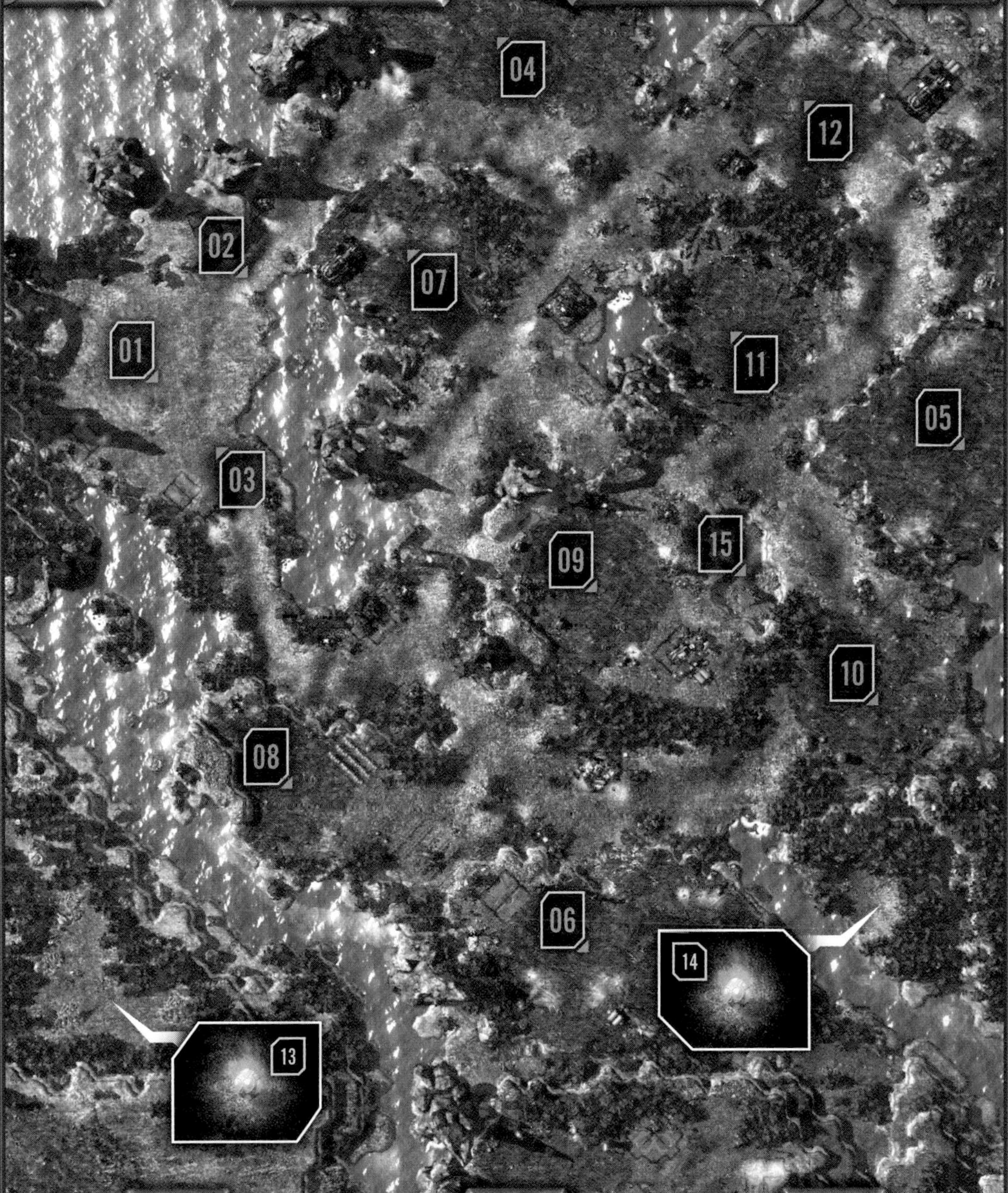

PRIMARY

1. Start

2-3. Chokepoints

4-6. Zerg Hive complexes

7. First infested settlement (Virophage)

8-12. Threatened settlements

SECONDARY

13-15. Gas pods

But it gets worse: the Zerg are swarming toward other local settlements (8 to 12) too. At each one an Overlord will eventually drift in and drop a Drone that slowly morphs into a big Zerg Virophage. This foul monster then spews its green vomit on settlement structures until the entire place is infested. Once infested, the settlement starts producing Infested Terran colonists who rise from the vile goop and stagger in a steady stream to attack your base.

If you don't halt this creeping advance early on, the tide is difficult to reverse. As Horner reports, "The more of them [Virophages] there are, the more infested we'll have to fight." Every time another settlement falls, a new stream of Infested Terrans is added to the one already flowing. Eventually, no matter how fast you produce troops, the ever-growing flow of Infested Terrans will wear down your defenses.

BLOCK THE ACCESS ROUTES!

This first step is critical. You must set up an airtight base defense immediately, blocking the two base access roads at their chokepoints (2 and 3) and putting defense on the high ground overlooking both chokes. Build two Bunkers just a few feet down each road, spacing them tightly so no Zerg can get through without destroying a Bunker first. Garrison each Bunker with Marines and at least one Firebat then post a couple of SCVs in Auto-Repair mode nearby. Add more Firebats and some Hellions parked just behind the Bunkers. Remember, the flame attacks of Firebats and Hellions are your most effective weapons against Infested Terrans and Zerglings. As resources become more plentiful, add more of these fiery units at the chokepoints.

Important: Put at one or two Vikings in the air directly over each pair of Bunkers as well. Flying heavy assault units known as Brood Lords are in the area, and as Horner reports, "they're lethal against ground targets." But Brood Lords cannot hit air targets, so your Vikings can feast on them with air-to-air strikes. You'll need to counter Brood Lords quickly, before they can spit an overload of Broodlings at your ground troops. Later you can add a Missile Turret at each chokepoint, after you've built an Engineering Bay and your Viking attack group (see the next step) is out in the field wreaking havoc.

BUILD A WING OF VIKINGS.

Once your base is secure, your best bet is to rush to each newly threatened settlement and destroy the Zerg Virophage before it can fully infest the settlement. One stout squadron of 8-10 Vikings can do this job admirably for you. You must use them carefully and efficiently, of course, and rush them back for repairs after engagements. But if you use Vikings well, you can spend the bulk of your precious resources on defending your base, and then to build up a juggernaut army for the final push. Just build occasional Vikings to replace any you might lose from this main attack squadron.

DESTROY THE FIRST INFESTED SETTLEMENT.

Build 4-5 more Vikings and group them with the ones you got at the start. Send this squadron to attack the infested settlement at (7). You'll encounter no anti-air Spore Crawlers nor any Zerg ground units such as Hydralisks that can shoot down flyers except for a few Infested Marines, so keep your Vikings aloft at first and have them clear out the hovering Brood Lords. Keep an eye out for Mutalisks roaming the map as well.

DO THE VIKING HOP

The Viking dual ability is handy. Typically you want your Viking squadron to eliminate enemy flyers (Mutalisks and Brood Lords) first, and then drop down to fight on foot. But if your flying Vikings come upon an anti-air Spore Crawler or Hydralisk, immediately drop the squadron to the ground, focus all firepower on the anti-air foe to eliminate it quickly, and then lift off again.

Once that's done, switch the Vikings to Assault Mode so they drop to the ground. Let them fight off any ground attackers then turn their attention to the Virophage. After that, start blasting the infested Civilian Biodome and Huts that were spawning infested folks. Keep your Viking guns blazing until every structure in the settlement is razed.

Use the same tactics: clear the air first, then drop to the ground in Assault Mode to splatter the Virophage and any other Zerg ground units and infested buildings. Remember to hop your Vikings back up into the air if things get hairy on the ground, and fly critically damaged flyers back to base for repair. Once you completely clear the settlement of anything resembling Zerg-ness, rush the entire squadron back to your base for a tune up. Then send them after the next Zerg infestation attempt.

Once you completely clear the settlement of infestation, the Zerg won't be back. You end the flow of Infested Terrans and Marines from that camp for good, too. Fly your Vikings straight back to the base for repairs. Add 2-3 more Vikings to this group if you can.

Again, every settlement you save from infestation means one less stream of Infested Terrans attacking your base. So in this case, the best defense is a good offense!

Watch Your Flight Path

Don't fly your Vikings over any of the three Zerg Hive bases! They're full of Spore Crawlers that will shoot your guys from the sky.

KEEP PURIFYING SETTLEMENTS WITH YOUR VIKINGS.

Okay, that's one down and a lot more to go. The Zerg will start trying to infest the five other civilian settlements. But they attack only one settlement at a time, so you can keep your mobile Vikings moving from hotspot to hotspot. Don't worry if you can't reach a settlement before it is officially "infested" (as reported by Horner). If the Zerg succeed in fully infesting a settlement, just wipe it clean from the map with your Vikings. Destroy everything!

Aberration Alert

Watch out for the occasional centaur-like Aberration spawned from infested settlements. They're very powerful armored units, so your best counter is Marauders, Diamondbacks, or Goliaths.

GET GAS

Don't miss the Gas Pods scattered amongst the large animal bones in two locations (13, 14). Send a single Viking to each site, drop it to the ground, and walk it through all the pods for collection.

BUILD A GROUND ASSAULT GROUP.

Your Vikings are masterful against the Virophage teams trying to infest villages, but Vikings alone will have a tough time taking out the three Zerg Hive complexes. So meanwhile, back at the base, keep expanding your production and slowly build up a powerful corps of Firebats, Hellions, Marines, and any other ground units available for training. (Goliaths are great if you have them; they can knock Brood Lords right out of the sky.) This will give you a nice one-two punch later when you move into the big Hive areas (4, 5, and 6).

GO AFTER THE NORTHERN HIVE COMPLEX.

When your corps is ready, send it up the northeast road from your base. Keep your Viking wing directly above the ground column; don't let your flyers zoom ahead to the Zerg complex or they'll get decimated. A number of Hydralisks give anti-air support to the Spore Crawlers around the base's creep perimeter, so your Vikings can't just fly in to hit the base. Instead, let your ground army start the engagement and take out the first line of anti-air Zerg. Then move your Vikings forward.

Keep up this approach as you sweep across the base: ground troops first to target Spore Crawlers and Hydralisks, then swoop in the Vikings to blast Mutalisks from the sky. When you finally eliminate all enemy flyers, drop your Vikings into Assault Mode and complete the evisceration of the Zerg base. Destroy every structure.

Important: As you attack Zerg structures, be ready to hit your Viking group hotkey and quickly order them back to airborne status whenever a building's health bar nears zero. When destroyed, Zerg buildings can release a brief but deadly swarm of Broodlings. Your Vikings can rise up safely out of range and wait until the Broodlings self-destruct in a few seconds, then drop back down again to continue the ground destruction.

INTERLUDE: *HYPERION* LAB

Afterwards, watch the result of Ariel Hanson's vaccine experimentation in the disturbing cutscene entitled "Infested." After the cinematic, make the usual rounds of the ship, then get back to the Bridge for the next mission selection via the Star Map.

→ SMASH THE OTHER TWO HIVES.

The eastern and southern Zerg Hive complexes are tough but similar challenges. Replenish your army with fresh troops before you make each move. Use the same tactics as in the northern Hive: ground troops first to take out anti-air structures, then Vikings flying in close support. Remember to destroy every single structure in each Hive complex.

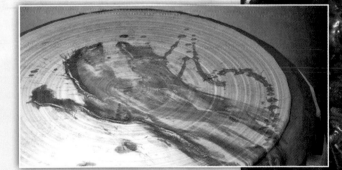

THE DEVIL'S PLAYGROUND

MISSION OVERVIEW

This mission pits you against both the Zerg and the unique geology of Redstone III. Your goal is to mine 8,000 minerals, but the planet's volatility keeps you on your toes. Regular volcanic eruptions send lava surging across the low basins, so be ready to hustle your units to high ground.

PREREQUISITES

Complete any four missions.

OBJECTIVES

MAIN
- Gather 8,000 minerals.

BONUS
- Kill the Brutalisk (+3 Zerg Research).
- Locate Tosh's miners.

CREDIT REWARD

110,000

ACHIEVEMENTS

ACHIEVEMENT		PTS	REQUIREMENTS
	The Devil's Playground	10	Complete all mission objectives
	Red Lobster	10	Kill the Brutalisk with lava
	Reaper Man	10	Locate all of Tosh's Crew on Hard difficulty

LOCATION: REDSTONE III

Redstone III is a Kel-Morian hazardous mining planet. Rights to exploit Redstone's mineral fields were the flashpoint for conflicts between different mining guilds prior to the start of the Terran Guild Wars.

GABRIEL TOSH'S BRIEFING

I hear the mighty Jim Raynor's on the move, but short on funds. The planet Redstone's got the most valuable minerals around, and with the Zerg invasion the Kel-Morians packed up and left it all behind. Some enterprising men could turn a big profit there. Meet me at Redstone if you want a piece of the action. The place is a little unstable; the low ground gets flooded with lava every few minutes. But that's also where the richest mineral nodes are found.

MISSION

This mission introduces a new unit, the Reaper. Trained at your Barracks once you add a Tech Lab, Reapers can hop up walls and low cliffs. This special ability brings you a number of rewards on this map. Keep an eye out for collectible items up on small platforms around the map that only Reapers can reach.

GET THE LAY OF THE LAND.

This is what the game designers call a "greed" mission: The more resources you spend, the further you get from winning the mission. Let's start with a quick overview: Take a peek at our mission map. The darker areas are high ground, safe from the volcanic eruptions that recur throughout the mission. The lighter reddish areas are the low ground periodically flooded by the deadly lava surges.

Your Terrans start out on the manmade raised platforms (1 and 2) to the northwest, with a few more units you can unlock scattered across the map. Four sprawling Zerg bases, two very large (4 and 6) and two smaller (3 and 5), hunker on the natural plateaus overlooking the mineral-filled basins that dominate the rest of the map. A few Zerg are burrowed in other locations across the map, but only in small numbers. Finally, note that a Brutalisk, a terrifying Zerg monster, roams a small area (10) in the extreme southwest corner of the map.

NEW TECHNOLOGY

REAPER

This fast moving light infantry raider is capable of jumping up and down cliffs. Reapers carry pistols and explosive devices called D-8 Charges. They cannot attack flying units.

RESEARCH OPPORTUNITIES

- +3 Zerg Research

NEW UPGRADES AVAILABLE AFTER MISSION

- G-4 Clusterbombs: Anti-personnel charge with a large blast radius. Ejects smaller payloads in a radius for increased damage.

- U-238 Rounds: Attack range increases +1. Reapers do an additional +3 Damage to Light Armor.

LEGEND

PRIMARY

1. Your base
3. Small Zerg base
4. Large Zerg base
5. Small Zerg base
6. Very large Zerg base

◉ = "Reaper reward" platform

SECONDARY

2. Tosh's men
7-9. Rock ramps
10. Brutalisk!

Unfortunately, all of the mineral fields sit in the low basins and thus are bathed in lava every few minutes. A large number of resource pickup items (Mineral Shards and Gas) sit up on the ground in the back of the teeming Zerg bases up on the plateaus, but obviously, these are jealously guarded. Getting access to them will be somewhat difficult. But you can also find plenty of these pickups sitting atop Reaper-accessible raised platforms in less hostile areas.

CREATE HOTKEY GROUPS AND START MINING.

A volcanic eruption begins just seconds into the mission, raising the lava level. Quickly drag a selection box around your SCVs (who automatically start out working the small mineral field north of your base), assign them a hotkey, and rush them up the ramp onto the platform where your base sits (1).

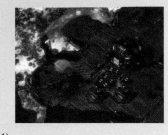

Any unit or building caught on low ground during one of these lava surges will be engulfed and incinerated. Each surge lasts just a few seconds before the lava recedes. The lava level stays low until the next eruption five minutes later. A countdown timer in the corner lets you know how long until the next eruption.

Success in this mission is much easier if you include all of your units in hotkey groups. When the alarm horn sounds, you won't have time to scan around the map, looking for individual units on low ground and moving them one by one to safety. Group units any way you like; follow your own hotkey system. But just do it! Whenever the alarm warns of seismic activity, you can simply punch a few hotkeys and click on high ground to rush your troops uphill and keep them from getting barbecued.

RICH MINERALS

Mineral crystals are yellow on Redstone III. This indicates "rich mineral fields" that yield 7 mineral units per SCV trip instead of the usual 5.

PROTECT YOUR HARVESTERS.

The mineral field to the north gives out eventually, so you'll have to move your SCVs (grouped and assigned a hotkey!) downhill into the large basin to the south of your base platform. Small Zerg swarms occasionally descend from the southern plateaus and attack your workers in the basin. Luckily, Tosh offers you a squad of four Reapers early in the mission: perfect escorts for SCVs. These Reapers automatically hop up onto a small platform at the front of your base and score some pickup items. This is a simple illustration of their value in this mission. Send them to nab the goods atop the small platform on the other side of the entrance ramp too.

Deploy these Reapers near the center of the basin so they engage any Zerg raiders before the enemy can reach your mining operation. After you have a Tech Lab you can train more Reapers at your Barracks. Also add Medics and other troops to your basin protection squad as you expand production.

BONUS: FIND TOSH'S CREW.

Tosh reports that he left one of his mining crews behind on the planet but doesn't know where his men are. One bonus objective is to find them. Fortunately, they're not far, just over on the other platform to the north (2). Send at least 3-4 Reapers to rendezvous with Tosh's men because Zerglings are burrowed en route near the top of the ramp. Afterward, send the Reapers to clear out a second pack of burrowed Zerg (including a Hydralisk) on the eastern end of the platform. Keep an eye out for a Reaper to rescue and some pickup materials as well. This rescues some more Reapers, who join the fight, and clears the northern platform of all Zerg units. Afterwards, have your Reapers gather the gas and mineral items on the two nearby small platforms.

Tosh's crew includes some SCVs that you can put right to work in the mineral field just down the ramp. Remember to group them and assign a hotkey. Move your Command Center across the platform, closer to the top of the ramp. This way the SCVs have a far shorter distance to travel when delivering minerals.

FIELD HQS

To significantly cut down SCV travel time, you can move your Command Centers right next to mineral fields in the low basins. When the lava alarm sounds, just click the Command Center's Load button to pack five of the nearby SCVs inside, then click Lift Off to raise the structure safely above the lava level. Be sure to move any SCVs you couldn't load into the Command Center to high ground!

SEAL OFF THE ZERG APPROACH ROUTES.

Although the Zerg-infested plateaus cover a large area of the map, only three rock ramps (7, 8, 9) lead down from the plateaus into the big central basin. Of these, only two (8, 9) come from Zerg bases. Seal off these two approach routes! If you place a fully garrisoned Bunker and 4-5 more good Zerg-killers (Reapers, Firebats, Hellions, all placed with the Hold command) plus some support units at the top of each rock ramp, you can intercept every Zerg raiding party before it wanders down from the plateaus. This lets your SCVs harvest the basin with no worries other than the lava surges.

And because your Bunkers and troops are posted on high ground you don't have to move them at all during eruptions. Again, it's important to have a Medic and two SCVs in Auto-Repair mode posted near each of these Bunkers as well.

MORE FREE REAPERS

The small platform just northeast of (9) holds some nice collectibles plus three more of Tosh's Reapers. They join your forces when you find them.

BE PATIENT!

In the early going it may seem like you're getting nowhere in your effort to amass 8,000 minerals. But you must expend resources in the early going to set up a robust, efficient, and well-protected mining operation. Once your security perimeter is in place, your SCVs can mine unmolested by the Zerg, and your mineral count will start to climb dramatically. Also remember that you can salvage Bunkers in areas you've already cleared or mined out. This adds minerals back into your total, bringing you closer to your goal of 8,000.

BONUS: KILL THE BRUTALISK.

Again, a powerful Brutalisk lurks down in the southwest corner (10). Start rallying a combat group at (7). Be sure to include a few Marauders for their carapace-busting grenade attacks. Remember that mercenaries from the Merc Compound are always quite lethal too, so consider buying a crew-for-hire and adding them as well. When you have a good strong force, go for the Brutalisk.

BROIL THE BRUTALISK

Lure the Brutalisk to low ground with Reapers then have them jump up the cliff just as the next lava surge begins. The lava destroys the big beast.

Defeating the Brutalisk completes a bonus objective and gives Stetmann more material for his research in the *Hyperion* lab. But the Brutalisk on Redstone III is also guarding some precious Mineral Shards and Gas. Send any unit to nab these nice gifts and boost your minerals total.

START RAIDING THE ZERG BASES.

Eventually the central basin runs out of mineral resources and you must expand into Zerg-controlled areas. The two smaller Zerg bases (3 and 5) have a number of Mineral Shards and Gas ready to be nabbed; the two bigger bases (4 and 6) have considerably more pickups.

INTERLUDE: *HYPERION*

After the mission, you learn that Tosh is a renegade Ghost with a deep hatred for Mengsk and the Empire. Tosh is on the Bridge, and you can talk to him. The former Dominion assassin has another lucrative project for Raynor. Go to the Cantina and talk to Tychus for another perspective on this Tosh fellow. (Don't miss the latest TV news broadcast; it's a hoot.) Then head to the Laboratory and talk to Ariel Hanson about a rare crystal called jorium.

While in the Laboratory, be sure to check if you can research new projects, then stop in at the Armory to buy more upgrades with your newly acquired credits. When you're ready to move on, return to the Bridge and click on the Star Map to bring up the next mission selection screen.

A good tactic is to conquer the smaller, easier Zerg bases first, then see how close your mineral count is to 8,000. Start with the southernmost base (3); when you finish, you also gain access to some previously inaccessible mineral fields down the ramp to the southeast. Then smash the base at (5) and nab the pallets. Meanwhile, add a few more Reapers and (if available) Hellions and Marauders for the push into the bigger bases. Remember to keep plenty of Medics and (if you have mechanical units) SCVs in your strike force too.

MISSION BRANCH!

Completing the first Gabriel Tosh mission unlocks the next one in Tosh's mission strand, "Welcome to the Jungle." New unit available: Goliath.

Again, if you've completed any six missions you can try Matt Horner's first mission, "The Great Train Robbery." New unit available: Diamondback.

It is possible to reach the 8,000 mineral mark without invading the bigger, nastier Zerg bases (4, 6). But if you're shy of 8,000 by just a few hundred minerals, you can attack either big base and try sending fast units (Hellions and Reapers) to quickly nab the Mineral Shards. The instant you nab a shard, its mineral count of 100 goes to your total, even if the unit that acquired the shard is destroyed. Careful, though: the shards are well defended.

VICTORY!

The moment you hit the 8,000 minerals mark, you win the mission and jump off the planet.

WELCOME TO THE JUNGLE

MISSION OVERVIEW

This mission is a race with the Protoss to the terrazine gas geysers on the map. Your goal is to extract gas from a minimum of seven geysers. Meanwhile, the Protoss wants to seal the altar around each geyser, denying you access. Once an altar is sealed, you cannot penetrate its Protoss force field and reach the terrazine canister. With only 13 gas geysers on the map, the first one to seven wins.

PREREQUISITES

Complete "The Devil's Playground."

OBJECTIVES

MAIN

- Extract terrazine gas from 7 geysers on Bel'Shir.
- Don't let the Protoss seal 7 altars.

BONUS

- Find the 3 Protoss Relics (+3 Protoss Research).

CREDIT REWARD

120,000

ACHIEVEMENTS

ACHIEVEMENT		PTS	REQUIREMENTS
	Welcome to the Jungle	10	Complete all mission objectives
	Appetite for Destruction	10	Prevent the Protoss from killing a SCV
	It's So Easy	10	Prevent the Protoss from capping a Terrazine Node in the mission on Hard difficulty

LOCATION: BEL'SHIR

Dotted with ancient shrines and ruined temple-gardens, Bel'Shir was once held as a sacred spiritual retreat for the Protoss Templar.

GABRIEL TOSH'S BRIEFING

There's a rare gas on Bel'Shir the Protoss call "The Breath of Creation." They think it be a gift from their gods. [Laughs.] We call it terrazine, and it be worth a fortune to the right bidder. Of course those Protoss'll kill us if they catch us on their holy ground. Or, at least, they'll try.

MISSION

You start with a small but solid base (1) near an ancient Protoss fortress built over Bel-Shir's lush jungle landscape. A massive Protoss base sprawls across the top of the map (10), so don't blunder north into its lethal fire. Smaller Protoss expansion bases (3 and 4) are active just north and northwest of your starting position. You can avoid them too, but it isn't as easy. The Protoss have built altars around all 13 terrazine gas geysers (A to M) spread across the map.

GOLIATH UP!

Keep up a steady production flow of Goliaths in this mission. You need their Hellfire Missiles to take on the waves of Protoss flyers (Scouts and Void Rays) that hit your gas-raiding party.

NEW TECHNOLOGY

GOLIATH

Heavy fire support unit. This well-rounded assault walker can hit ground targets with its Twin Autocannons, but its Hellfire Missiles are particularly lethal against flyers.

RESEARCH OPPORTUNITIES

- +3 Protoss Research

NEW UPGRADES AVAILABLE AFTER MISSION

- Ares-Class Targeting System: Goliaths gain +3 missile range and +1 cannon range.
- Multi-Lock Weapons System: Goliaths can fire anti-ground and anti-air weapons simultaneously.

LEGEND

PRIMARY

A-M. Raw Terrazine

1. Start

5. Move Goliaths here

8. North corridor

10. Main Protoss base

SECONDARY

2. Protoss Relic

3-4. Small Protoss bases

6. Ramp

7. Protoss Relic

9. Protoss Relic

GATHER TERRAZINE TO THE NORTHWEST.

Tosh paints your radar with the locations of the Protoss altars. Your early goal is to raid four of these nearby geysers (A, B, C, D), which are unguarded or only lightly guarded at first. So make a bold move: Immediately rush out two SCVs, one to each of the nearest unguarded altars (A, B) to nab your first canisters of gas.

CANISTER DELIVERY

After your SCV extracts the terrazine canister from a Protoss altar, it automatically returns to your nearest Command Center to deliver the gas. Keep an eye on its route: you may want to redirect it away from the Protoss expansion bases. The SCV must complete this delivery before it can move on to the next geyser. If an SCV dies while carrying a terrazine canister, he drops it. But, another SCV can come along and pick it up finishing the delivery!

At the same time, deploy the Goliaths you start with plus an SCV for repairs directly to the spot (at 5) just north of the first two geysers to protect your two terrazine-poaching SCVs. Use your initial resources to send another Goliath there as well. The Protoss soon take offense at your incursion and send a small but deadly force of flying Scouts to retaliate, so you want at least 3-4 Goliaths defending the spot.

Get your base humming too while your SCVs tap the terrazine at (A) and . Train more SCVs to work the mineral field and Refinery. Keep adding troops (including Marauders if you have them, plus Marines, Medics, and a second SCV) to your assault squad at (5) when you can, but be sure to leave a few units defending your base perimeter as well. The Protoss will send raiders at your base from time to time. Put one garrisoned Bunker at the top of your base access ramps.

THE ANTI-STALKER

If you've already completed "Smash and Grab" on Monlyth (the first Tychus Findlay mission) you have Marauders available from your Barracks once you add a Tech Lab. As you may recall from that mission, Marauders are particularly potent versus Protoss Stalkers.

It's a very good idea to interdict this first Protoss sealing effort if possible. Then send SCVs to collect gas simultaneously from each of the two geysers (C and D). If you can collect terrazine canisters from all four of the closest geysers (A to D) in the mission's opening minutes, you're in good shape; you need only three more gas canisters to win the mission, so your operations are much easier to manage down the stretch. The squad you placed at (5) should be in perfect position to intercept and destroy the Protoss Probe and escorts.

WARNINGS

Whenever a Protoss Probe moves from its base to target a terrazine altar for sealing, the targeted altar flashes red on your radar map and you get a verbal warning from your Adjutant.

STOP THE PROBES FROM SEALING NEARBY GEYSERS.

Soon a Protoss Probe escorted by other units (Scouts and Stalkers) heads south from the main Protoss base to one of the nearby terrazine geysers (C or D, depending on your progress). The Probe's task is to

activate the altar's force field generators. Once activated, the generators can create an impenetrable seal around the geyser in about 45 seconds.

FORTIFY YOUR BASE!

Protoss raiders hitting your base get increasingly more powerful as the mission progresses; eventually, these attackers will include a lethal flying Void Ray. So be sure you keep deploying new Goliaths to the northern perimeter of your base. Their Hellfire Missiles can knock down Protoss flyers quickly. Add another Missile Turret on the northwest perimeter as well, if you can afford it.

TAP THE GEYSERS ALONG THE EAST BOUNDARY.

After you finish raiding the four closest terrazine geysers (A to D), your best bet is to retreat into your base and spend a few minutes beefing up your assault team. Add at least two SCVs in Auto-Repair mode for Goliath repair as well. You can't wait too long, however; the Protoss are still sending out Probe-led squads to seal off more altars, sometimes even two at a time.

When you've got 6-7 Goliaths to fight flyers, a few Marauders (if available) to stave off Stalkers, some Firebats or Hellions to target Zealots, and a good support team of Medics and SCVs, send this party down the northeast ramp (6). Sneak one unit carefully north to nab the Protoss Relic at (2) but then turn east to skirt around the Protoss expansion base that sits just north of the Relic (3). Target the altars along the eastern edge of the map (at E, F, G, and H). Some of these are likely sealed shut by now, but you should find at least two available for gas collection.

Keep two SCVs dedicated to collecting the terrazine. When one SCV finally fills and unhooks a gas canister, let the unit go alone back to the base with just a couple of escort troops; chances are good it will deliver the canister unmolested. (Make sure it takes a safe route!) Then have the bulk of your assault force fight your way to the next geyser with your other gas-collecting SCV.

BONUS: NAB THE PROTOSS RELICS.

Another good reason to move up the east side of the map is to find the pair of Protoss Relics stashed there (2 and 7). The first Relic is unguarded and easy to nab as long as you don't wander into the Protoss base just north of it. but you'll have to fight through some Protoss defenders including a Photon Cannon to reach the second Relic.

The third Protoss Relic (9) is more problematic to reach. We suggest you avoid the Protoss expansion bases (3 and 4) by heading up the east passage (6) and then swinging around to reach the Relic via the northern corridor (8). Do this with a strong force, however: chances are good you'll run into a Protoss squad or two en route. You may want to save this Relic hunt until you've got your seventh terrazine canister secured but not delivered. Just manually halt the SCV carrying that last canister next to your Command Center so the mission isn't completed yet. Then send out your Relic raiding party.

MOVE TO THE MIDDLE

Another strategy is to wipe out the Protoss base in the middle (at 3) and expand there. Putting in a Command Center gives your SCVs a shorter trip to deliver terrazine canisters.

PROTECT THAT LAST CANISTER!

When your SCV finally unhooks the seventh gas canister from an altar, remember that the job isn't done until he delivers it to your Command Center. Guard him well! The moment he arrives, you win. So throw every available unit into the task of escorting that final canister back to your base. If you still have Protoss Relics to find, you can manually halt the SCV with the final terrazine canister right next to your Command Center until you complete the bonus objective. When ready, just select the gas-carrying SCV and right-click on the Command Center to complete the mission.

INTERLUDE: *HYPERION*

Back on the Hyperion Bridge, Horner reports a mysterious transmission about something called Project Shadowblade.

Afterwards, you end up in the Cantina. Talk to Tosh and Tychus, then check in with Mr. Hill who has some new mercenaries available: an elite Goliath squad called Spartan Company. Then make your rounds of the rest of the ship. Be sure to chat with Dr. Hanson if she's still in the Lab. And check out the new Go-

liath upgrades available in the Armory.

When you're ready, return to the Bridge and talk to Horner to hear his thoughts. Then use the Star Map to pick your next mission. The next Tosh mission, "Break-out," won't be available at this point unless you've either completed a total of 13 missions or completed at least two missions since finishing "Welcome to the Jungle."

BREAKOUT

MISSION OVERVIEW

Tosh's revelation about the Dominion's secret Spectre program soon brings up a dilemma. Another secure transmission comes into the Bridge from a Ghost named Nova who claims that all Spectres are psychopathic killers; those captured are held in New Folsom and must not be released. She wants you to destroy Tosh's Spectre Program facilities on Avernus Station. Tosh denies the charge and claims that Nova is merely a Dominion assassin; the imprisoned Spectres will become loyal allies against the Emperor if you help him set them free.

PREREQUISITES

- Complete "Welcome to the Jungle" plus 12 other missions (total of 13), or complete at least two other missions after completing "Welcome to the Jungle."
- Select HELP TOSH after you launch the "Breakout" mission.

OBJECTIVES

MAIN
- Destroy the Main Prison Base.
- Tosh must survive.

BONUS
- Kill guards at Cell Block A (25,000 credit bonus).
- Kill guards at Cell Block B (25,000 credit bonus).

CREDIT REWARD
125,000

ACHIEVEMENTS

ACHIEVEMENT	PTS	REQUIREMENTS
Breakout	10	Complete all mission objectives
Cool Hand Tosh	10	Complete the mission without Tosh going below 100 life
Jailhouse Rock	10	Complete the mission on Hard difficulty in less than 25 minutes

LOCATION: NEW FOLSOM

New Folsom is a notorious political prison where enemies of the Dominion are kept on ice. Its remote location and inhospitable landscape makes escape virtually impossible.

GABRIEL TOSH'S BRIEFING

New Folsom is ripe for the taking, man. Every voice that was ever raised against Mengsk is penned up inside those walls. We let all them prisoners loose an' he'll never know what hit him. Just let me know when you're ready to pull the trigger.

THE SPECTRE DILEMMA

HELP TOSH: Do you want Tosh to bring his Spectres to the cause against Mengsk's Dominion? This choice triggers the mission "Breakout" at New Folsom Prison.

HELP NOVA: Or do you want Nova to bring her knowledge of Ghost training to your team? This choice triggers the mission "Ghost of a Chance" at Avernus Station?

MISSION

This mission is short, sweet, and fun. Its primary purpose (aside from wrapping up the Tosh story) is to let you test drive the new Spectre abilities introduced in StarCraft II. Your task is to safely guide the permanently cloaked Gabriel Tosh through  the wild, bloody mayhem of a raid on the heavily guarded New Folsom prison.

The key: Avoid and/or destroy Missile Turrets plus the cloak-detecting Ravens on the map. Note that completing the bonus mission objectives of killing the guards in Cell Blocks A and B not only earns you a cool 50,000 credits but also makes your overall objective considerably easier.

NEW TECHNOLOGY

SPECTRE
Enhanced stealth assassin and saboteur.

NEW UPGRADES AVAILABLE AFTER MISSION

- Psionic Lash: Grants special psionic attack to Spectres. Deals 200 damage to targeted unit.
- Nyx-Class Cloaking Module: Spectre cloak no longer requires energy.

BONUS OPPORTUNITIES

- 50,000 credits

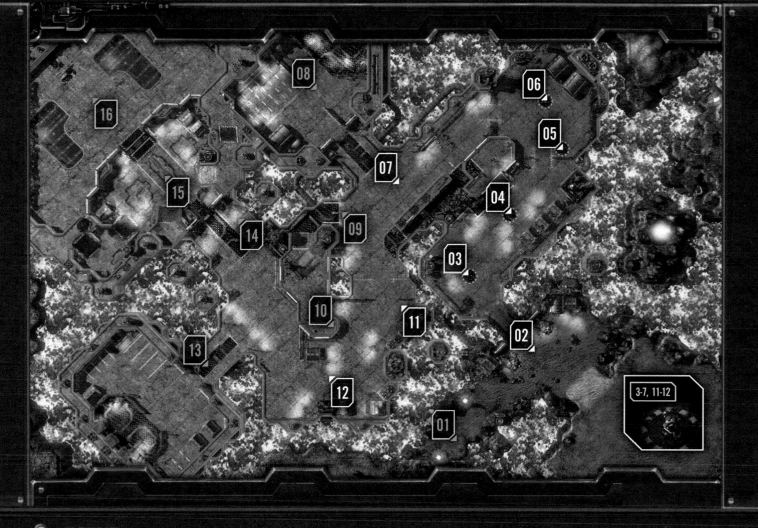

LEGEND

PRIMARY

1. Start
8. Cell Block A (turret)
9. Ramp
10. Raven
13. Entrance to Cell Block B
14-16. Enemy troop concentrations

SECONDARY

2. Dominion bridge guards
3-7, 11-12. Missile Turrets

USE MINDBLAST AND PSI SHIELD TO INFILTRATE THE PRISON.

Gun down the Dominion Marines just ahead; they can't see Tosh so you can approach and fire with impunity. Move toward the bridge and use Mindblast on the Marine squad at the near end (2). The psionic explosion stuns and deals damage to most of the squad members, making it easy to finish them off with Tosh's AGR-28 Gauss Rifle.

Cross the bridge but stop outside the red detection radius of the Missile Turret (3) up ahead. Missile Turrets can't attack you, but they reveal cloaked units, so you must maneuver cautiously. Use Mindblast twice on the Marines in front of the turret to finish them off. One more Marine is posted behind the turret. Use Mindblast on him too then quickly nail him with your rifle. Now you can safely destroy the Missile Turret.

NO HEAVY LIFTING

You have an unlimited flow of allies working with you so don't take wild chances. When in doubt, retreat! Let Raynor's Raiders move up and take the heat in hectic firefights.

A Siege Tank and a few Marines guard the next Missile Turret (4). Activate Tosh's special Psi Shield ability that protects him from all damage for 10 seconds, or until the shield has absorbed 300 damage. This gives you enough protection to take out this guard post. Destroy the dangerous tank first, then shoot the Marines. Finally, destroy the Missile Turret.

Beware the Splash!

Enemies won't shoot at Tosh if he's undetected. However, he still takes splash damage from explosive devices such as Siege Tank shells that explode nearby. Keep Tosh away from allies being shelled by Siege Tanks!

This triggers the first advance of Raynor's troops. From here on out, squads of Raynor's Raiders will push forward into each new area of the prison that Tosh unveils. The fighting is intense at times, but Tosh will remain unharmed as long as he avoids being detected. Your primary focus must be to keep Tosh outside of the white detection radii of each Missile Turret as you figure out a way to bypass or destroy the turret. Don't be distracted by the carnage all around you. Focus on the white circle!

CONTROL TOSH WITH "HOLD POSITION"

Tosh will automatically pursue enemies he's attacking, even if it leads him into a detection radius. Use the Hold Position command to keep Tosh from wandering across that white circle of doom.

Up ahead, two Bunkers and a Siege Tank bracket a Missile Turret (5). Use Psi Shield and take out the turret. Another Missile Turret is just up ahead (6) so don't let Tosh advance far. Use Hold Position to keep him between the striped lines and take out everything within range: Bunkers, Siege Tank, and other enemy troops. When these defenses are cleared, use Psi Shield again and go take out the next turret (6). Now Tosh can help destroy the Dominion Factory and clear the area for Raynor to drop in an advance base.

Here Tosh introduces his Consumption ability, which lets him drain both Life and Energy from friendly units. Use this liberally in the upcoming action. Friendly Medics can restore Tosh's health, but using Consumption is the best way to quickly restore critical Energy.

Head southwest from Raynor's new base to find another Missile Turret (7) supported by a Bunker and Siege Tanks. Use Psi Shield and KO the turret then hurry around the sandbags to avoid catching splash damage when the tanks bombard Raynor's advancing troops. Take out the tanks and other units; Horner points out the Cell Block nearby.

BONUS: KILL THE CELL BLOCK A GUARDS.

Head northwest through the open security doors and stop at the edge of the red detection circle. A large platoon of guards paces back and forth, and a Siege Tank is parked nearby. Move as close as you can outside the red circle and select Hold Position; let Tosh pick off as many pacing guards as he can. Then use Psi Shield, kill the Missile Turret (8), and mop up the block to release the prisoners and earn your first 25,000 credits bonus.

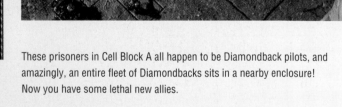

These prisoners in Cell Block A all happen to be Diamondback pilots, and amazingly, an entire fleet of Diamondbacks sits in a nearby enclosure! Now you have some lethal new allies.

KILL THE RAVEN.

Exit the Cell Block area and head south very carefully. A flying Raven (10) and a Missile Turret (11) provide overlapping detection radii in this deadly passage, with Siege Tanks lobbing in shells left and right. First, move up the ramp to the left (at 9) and use Psi Shield to approach and shoot the Raven. When it flees out of range, immediately destroy your main threat, the Siege Tank directly below. The Raven will patrol back and forth; stay at the upper platform railing to shoot the bird every time it comes back. Eventually you destroy it.

Now you can go back down the ramp and use Psi Shield to approach and kill the next two Missile Turrets (11 and 12) and clear the southern area. This lets Raynor push up his forward base of operations and also frees your approach to Cell Block B (13).

BONUS: KILL THE GUARDS IN CELL BLOCK B.

Carefully approach the open security door (13) to the heavily guarded Cell Block B. Inside, another detector Raven patrols back and forth across the entrance. Wait until it gets furthest away; you can slip past its detection radius and hurry over to the rightmost corner of the enclosure, where you're safe.

Every time the Raven patrols away from you, step out and nail whatever you can while undetected. Use Psi Shield to destroy the last Siege Tank, and then shoot down the Raven. This frees the Cell Block prisoners who run to the nearby fleet of Siege Tanks. More powerful new allies! It also earns you another 25,000 credits payday.

NUKE YOUR WAY TO THE PRISON ENTRANCE.

Here's where everything seems to go insane. A bristling encampment of Dominion forces is arrayed in the three enclosures (14, 15, and 16) leading up to the prison entrance door. This includes a huge base filled with unit-producing Factories and Barracks and Starports. We're talking dozens of Dominion Marines, Hellions, Vikings, Marauders, Banshees, a handful of Siege Tanks and Bunkers, and even a pair of massive Thor walkers planted in a passage. The kicker is that you must destroy every single unit and building in the prison to complete the primary objective.

It looks very daunting. But here's a tip: as wild and raucous as the battle may seem, your only real concern as a Spectre is the status of the Missile Turrets in the three areas. (Fortunately, you encounter no more pesky Ravens in the prison.) The trick, of course, is figuring how to take out turrets without getting detected and slaughtered. But Raynor gives you a trump card: four tactical nukes. A Tac Nuke Strike spreads destruction over a wide area, so you can get close enough to each Missile Turret to call in a strike on it without stepping into the turret's detection range. Once the turrets are dead, Tosh can tear through the remaining Dominion masses with impunity (as long as he avoids taking splash damage, of course). When the last of the prison guard falls, the Spectre prisoners are released.

INTERLUDE: *HYPERION* BRIDGE

You get a nice new cantina decoration out of the deal. Afterwards, make your rounds of the ship. Talk to Swann in the Armory to learn that Spectres are now available to your fighting force.

GHOST OF A CHANCE

MISSION OVERVIEW

If you believe Nova, then you believe that unfortunately you've been helping Tosh conduct his evil plan. The Rich Minerals you helped him extract from Redstone combined with the terrazine gas you helped him poach from Bel'Shir have literally fueled his Psi-indoctrination project that converts Ghosts into Spectres.

PREREQUISITES

- Complete "Welcome to the Jungle" plus 12 other missions (total of 13), or complete at least two other missions after completing "Welcome to the Jungle."
- Select HELP NOVA after you launch the "Breakout" mission.

OBJECTIVES

MAIN

- Destroy Jorium Stockpile.
- Destroy Terrazine Tank.
- Destroy Psi-Indoctrinator.
- Nova must survive.

BONUS

- Kill 10 enemy Spectres (5,000 credits each)

CREDIT REWARD

125,000

ACHIEVEMENTS

ACHIEVEMENT	PTS	REQUIREMENTS
Ghost of a Chance	10	Complete all mission objectives
Dominate Tricks	10	Complete the mission with your Dominated units killing 15 enemy troops
Total Protonic Reversal	10	Kill every enemy unit in the mission on Hard difficulty

LOCATION: AVERNUS STATION

This is Tosh's space platform, where Spectres are "born."

NOVA'S BRIEFING

Tosh's Spectre facilities are on Avernus Station. Join me there and we can shut it down for good. I've identified three facilities that are vital to his operation. Our first target will be the jorium stockpile. Next will be the terrazine tanks. And finally the psionic waveform indoctrinator Tosh uses to complete the Spectres' activation process. I can penetrate most of his defenses, but I'll need your backup to get through them all.

MISSION

If you chose to believe Nova you now must use her to go after Tosh and his Psi-indoctrination facilities. The defenses include ten of Tosh's psychotic Spectre buddies scattered across the three platforms of Avernus Station. You can pick up an extra bonus of 5,000 credits per Spectre kill, so watch for them.

PHASE 1: DESTROY THE JORIUM STOCKPILE

OPEN THE GATE.

Group your Marines and Medics and send them to destroy the Bunker just ahead. Then clean out the rest of the area, including the Missile Turret up the ramp to the east, above the gate. Knocking out turrets makes life easier for Nova, your Ghost. Your Marines can't proceed any further until Nova opens the gate (2).

Move Nova east just halfway across the rampart. Use her Snipe ability to fire a long-distance Psi Round at the enemy Marauder further east down the rampart. (Remember that mechanical units are immune, so Snipe doesn't work on turrets or tanks.) Then continue to the gate control (3), gunning down the few Marines en route. Destroy the mechanism to open the gate.

NEW TECHNOLOGY

GHOST

Sniper with great Psionic ability.

NEW UPGRADES AVAILABLE AFTER MISSION

- Ocular Implants: Ghosts gain +2 range and +3 sight radius.
- Crius Suit. Ghost cloak no longer requires energy.

BONUS OPPORTUNITIES

- 50,000 credits

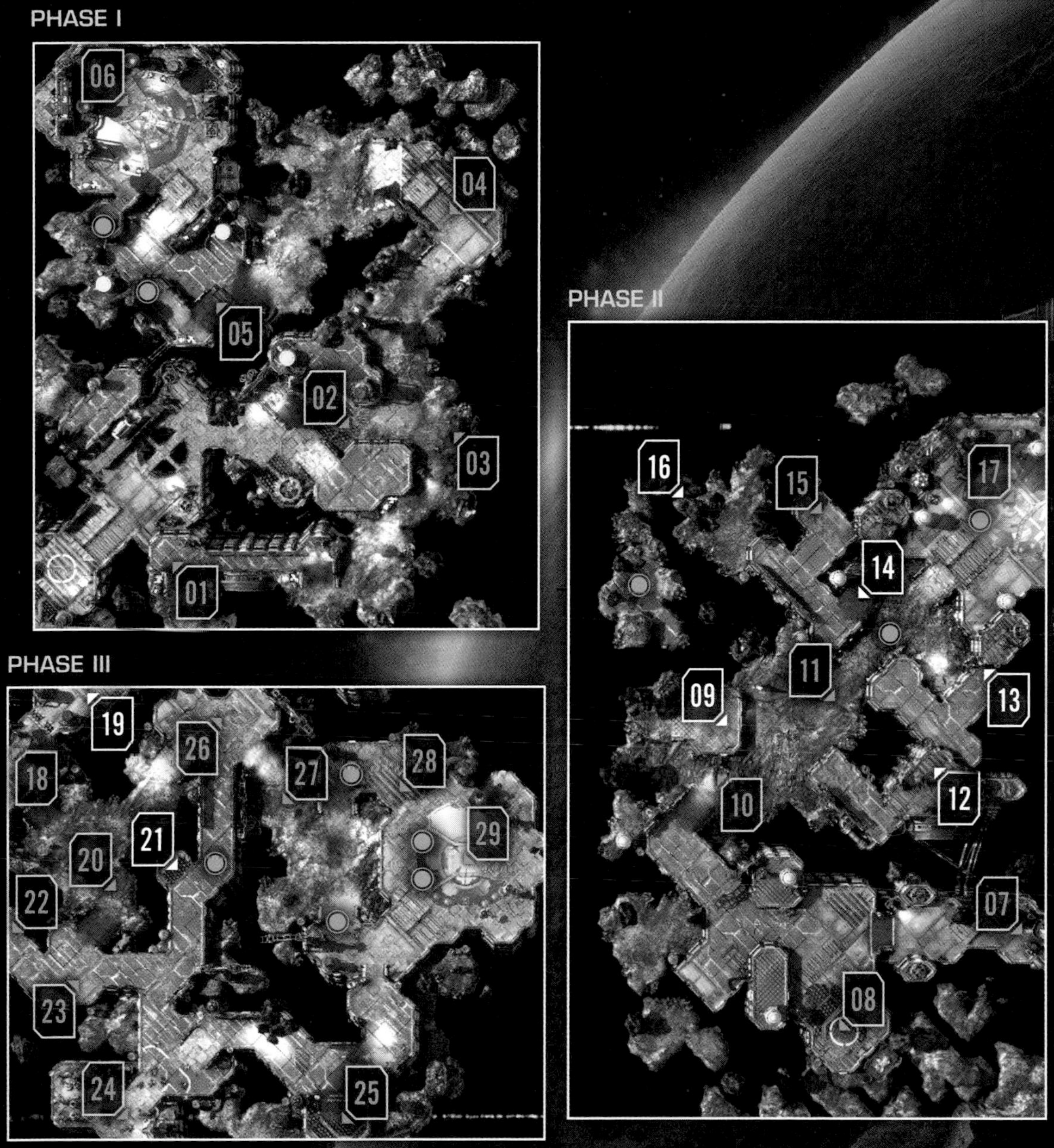

PHASE I

PHASE II

PHASE III

LEGEND

PRIMARY

1. Start: First platform
2. Gate
3. Gate Control
4. Turret guards
5. Snipe Spectre from here
6. Jorium Stockpile
7. Start: Second platform
8. Vikings
10. Place tanks here
11. Tosh's Nuke hits here!
15. Nuke Silo
17. Terrazine Tank
18. Start: Third Platform
20. Move Nova here
22. Attack with Banshees/Vikings
23. Missile Turret
24. Ultralisk
25. Stolen Thor
26. Nuke Silo
27. Tosh's nuke hits here!
28. Nova calls Tac Nuke Strike
29. Psi-Indoctrinator

SECONDARY

9. Siege Tank
12-13. Missile Turrets
14. Ramp
16. Rock ramps (Reapers only)
19. Siege Tank
21. Siege Tank
◎ = "Tosh's Spectre

CLEAR THE EASTERN TURRETS.

Move your Marines through the gate but don't advance any further north. A pair of enemy Marauders and a Medic are posted to the north. Let Nova step just past the gate and Snipe both Marauders. Then your Marines can push forward to gun down the poor Medic. Move the Marines just to the top of the ramp and destroy the Missile Turret, but hold position there.

A second turret sits not far away, guarded by Marines and Marauders (4). Let Nova snipe all of them with Psi Rounds for quick kills. Then have your Marines destroy the second Missile Turret.

Flying Detectors

Just like Missile Turrets, Ravens can detect cloaked units. But Ravens are more dangerous because they're mobile and airborne.

DOMINATE THE SIEGE TANK.

Use Nova's Domination ability to take charge of the enemy Siege Tank. (Careful! A nearby Raven will detect you, so do the Domination fast, before the tank can nail you with rounds.) Cast it on the tank and then direct

the vehicle southwest to tangle with a squad of Tosh's troops just south of the turret's location down the slope. They will destroy the Siege Tank for you, but the tank will inflict some damage on them as well.

Watch out for that flying Raven! Nail it as soon as possible to keep Nova invisible. Then start sniping the enemy soldiers at the bottom of the slope, but keep your Marines nearby just in case.

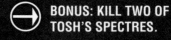

BONUS: KILL TWO OF TOSH'S SPECTRES.

Ten of Tosh's Spectres are scattered throughout this mission, and killing them all is a bonus objective worth 5,000 credits per kill. The first two are just up ahead. Send Nova a few careful steps up the ramp to the southwest (5) until you spot the enemy Spectre up on the platform. Use Snipe to nail him. Then go to the spot where he stood and pick off the second Spectre on the opposite platform to the northwest.

PSIONIC RADAR

Nova has a passive ability called Psionic Radar that displays all unrevealed Psionic units (such as other Spectres) within its sensor radius.

DESTROY THE JORIUM STOCKPILE.

Now things get tricky. The Jorium Stockpile, one of your main objectives, sits on the big platform to the north (6). A pair of Missile Turrets flank the stockpile and a massive Battlecruiser hovers above it, guarding the treasure.

You can use Nova's Domination ability to take control the Battlecruiser. The moment she takes control, the Missile Turrets open fire on it, mistaking it for their enemy! Meanwhile, the Battlecruiser fires back at them. It's beautiful, man. You can even turn the big ship's Yamato Cannon on the turrets, killing them instantly. Once both turrets are toast, turn the dominated Battlecruiser's guns on the Jorium Stockpile.

Once the stockpile is destroyed, Nova gets dropped onto the next platform area (7) where the Terrazine Tank is located.

PHASE 2: DESTROY THE TERRAZINE TANKS

CLEAR THE LANDING ZONE.

Creep a couple of steps west. A squad of Tosh's men with a cloak-detecting Raven overhead suddenly pops out of the darkness, revealing Nova.

Two different approaches can work here; take your pick. You can quickly use Snipe on the big Marauder for a one-shot kill. That way, even with the Raven detecting you, you can easily dispatch the two remaining Marines in a simple firefight. Or better yet, immediately use Domination to control the Raven, which makes Nova undetectable again. Select the Raven and drop an Auto-Turret on the ground. The turret blasts the Marines and Marauder as you attack them too, wiping them out.

If the pesky Raven manages to flee before you kill it, it glides south to join a pair of Vikings (8). Move west first and gun down the two Marine gate guards. Then find the Raven at (8) and use Domination on it. The two Vikings immediately blast it from the sky, and now Nova is invisible again. Use Domination on either one of the Vikings; now they fight each other! Finish off the winner with your rifle.

This clears the landing zone, and Raynor drops in a couple of Siege Tanks, a Raven of your own, and thankfully, a squad of Reapers.

OPEN THE GATE.

The gate contol is on the other side of the gate and is guarded by a Siege Tank plus Marines. Your Reapers can hop right over the wall, but we suggest you ease your Raven forward and drop an Auto-Turret on the platform just above the tank. Pull the Raven back quickly after it plants the turret to avoid damage from the enemy Marines. Then you can move your Reapers forward to finish off the Siege Tanks, nail the nearby Missile Turret, and then blast the gate mechanism.

CLEAR THE CENTRAL TURRETS.

The next defense emplacement is a Bunker and a Missile Turret just down the rampart. Bombard these from a safe distance using both of your new tanks in Siege Mode. Then send Nova up the rock ramp to the north and use her Domination on the enemy Siege Tank in Siege Mode there (9). It will start to bombard its own forces below it, a cluster of Hellions and Vikings surrounding a Missile Turret. Some of them move out of range. After the turret is demolished, take the tank out of Siege Mode and drive it down the ramp to continue the attack until its own forces destroy it.

Now set up your own Siege Tanks in Siege Mode (at 10) to bombard the remaining turret guards; be sure to support your tanks with your Reapers and Nova, because Tosh's men might rush them. Important: Don't move any units forward beyond (10)! Tosh has an unpleasant surprise waiting for you up ahead at (11).

DODGE THE NUKE!

Send Nova forward alone to mop up any units still at (11), near where the turret stood. Tosh suddenly calls in a Tac Nuke Strike on that spot. You have a few seconds until it hits, so immediately rush Nova back to (10) to avoid the explosion. It will wipe out any of Tosh's own units still in the rock basin.

BONUS: KILL THE SPECTRE.

Now move Nova back up to where the turret stood. One of Tosh's Spectres stands in the gap up ahead. Snipe him down.

CLEAR THE AREA.

Here are some suggested steps for clearing the area for your approach to the main platform where the Terrazine Tank is stored:

- Send Reapers up the platform to the right to destroy the Missile Turret there. Then direct your Raven carefully to (12) and drop an Auto-Turret to destroy the enemy Siege Tank just below.
- Now send your Reapers to the spot at (12) and let them destroy the nearby Missile Turret to the northwest.
- Put your tanks in Siege Mode at (11) to nail the Bunker on the platform to the right. Move your Reapers in to mop up any Marines who emerge from the Bunker.
- Direct Nova forward to spot the soldiers up on the platform to the left. As she does so, your emplaced Siege Tanks blow them to shreds.
- Send your Reapers to destroy the Marines and Missile Turret at (13). Easy pickings.
- Put your tanks in Siege Mode at (14) to bombard the guards near the Nuke Silo (15). Then send them up to the top of the ramp and repeat Siege Mode to hit the Missile Turret at the end of the ramp and any remaining guards.
- The way is now clear for Nova to reach the Nuke Silo.

HACK THE NUKE SILO.

Move Nova to the glowing green circle next to the Nuke Silo (15). Once she hacks in, you're ready for a launch. The silo is already armed with a nuke.

BONUS: KILL TOSH'S SPECTRE.

This is a fun one. One of Tosh's Spectres is posted on an outcropping east of the Nuke Silo. The best way to reach him is to send your Reaper squad hopping along the rocky peninsula (16) that leads to him.

DESTROY THE TERRAZINE TANK.

The Terrazine Tank (17) sits atop the big northeast platform, guarded by a strong contingent of troops (including the last Spectre in this sector) and surrounded by Missile Turrets, with a Raven hovering out front too. If you want, you can park your tanks in Siege Mode partway up the approach ramp and eliminate most of the guards.

Better yet, just walk Nova exactly halfway up the approach ramp and call in a Tac Nuke Strike right in front of the Terrazine Tank to end it quickly.

BONUS: KILL TOSH'S SPECTRE.

The nuke will kill the Spectre too, adding to your total for the bonus objective. (If you're following this walkthrough, you've now plugged 5 of the 10 enemy Spectres in this mission.) If for some reason you don't have a Tac Nuke Strike available, you can bring up Nova and use her Snipe ability to kill the Spectre. He is camped directly in front of the Terrazine Tank.

PHASE 3: DESTROY THE PSI-INDOCTRINATOR.

You deploy on a new platform (at 18), this time with a wing of Banshees and Vikings at your disposal. This last platform is loaded with a strong enemy presence, and it can be very difficult. But if you deploy and strike thoughtfully, you can reach your final target with remarkably few losses.

WORK NOVA TOWARD TOSH.

Take little steps here. First, send Nova east to (19), snipe the two Marines there, then use Domination on the Siege Tank. Put it in Siege Mode on the far right side of platform so it destroys the Bunker and Missile Turret on the opposite platform. Keep the enemy tank blasting at those targets until it dies.

SEIZE THE SOUTHERN RAMPARTS.

Now group your Banshees and Vikings together and send them west a bit (over open space), then south to hit troops at (22). One is a grounded Viking that hops up into the air, but your Vikings will nail it fast. Don't push any farther forward (southeast) because of the enemy Missile Turret lurking ahead at (23). Instead, keep your full aircrew to just northwest of the platform until the Banshees can finish off the other units below.

Land your Vikings and walk them forward in Assault Mode to blast the turret. Now you can bring Nova up onto the rampart. Move her very carefully east to the edge of the detection circle put out by a Raven hovering above more of Tosh's troops, including some mercenary Marauders. Snipe them one by one until only the Raven remains, then raise your Vikings back into the air and kill it.

TAKE OUT THE ULTRALISK.

Send Nova alone to the barricades at the top of the ramp and let her shoot through them. Then walk Nova down to a science enclosure where a huge Zerg Ultralisk (24) wanders around. (Another Ultralisk is restrained nearby.) Your Ghost is cloaked, of course, so the beasts can't see her. You can gun down the roaming Ultralisk and head back up the ramp, or Dominate the Ultralisk for an extremely powerful ally and some fun.

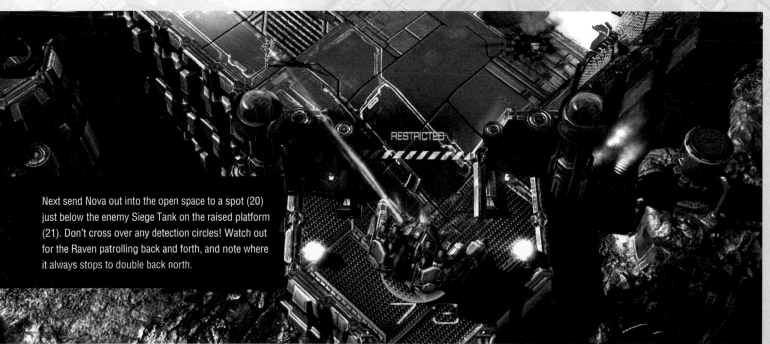

Next send Nova out into the open space to a spot (20) just below the enemy Siege Tank on the raised platform (21). Don't cross over any detection circles! Watch out for the Raven patrolling back and forth, and note where it always stops to double back north.

WORK NOVA TO THE STOLEN THOR.

Now send Nova further east to spot a big squad of Marines deployed near some Missile Turrets. Nova can patiently run forward, use Snipe on a Marine, then run back out of the detection circle when the other Marines pursue; repeat this multiple times until you Snipe the entire squad. Or Nova can just thin out the Marine squad a bit with some sniper work and then put your Vikings on the ground to engage the Tosh's Marines. After the last enemy Marine goes down, clear out the Missile Turrets so Nova is undetected. Then have Nova use Domination on the stolen Thor (25) parked on a platform below.

Now comes the fun part. Walk the Thor to the central rampart (21) and follow it north, hammering through Missile Turrets and Tosh's goons along the way. Don't miss the Spectre! Keep the Thor fighting all the way to the Nuke Silo at the other end if you can. Bring in your Vikings (on the ground) and Banshees for support. When you secure the silo, walk Nova into its green glowing beacon. She hacks control of one tactical nuke.

DODGE TOSH'S NUKE!

If you wander down the ramp heading southeast from the Nuke Silo you find out that Tosh still has a tactical nuke of his own. He drops it right at (27) so run back up the ramp to avoid annihilation.

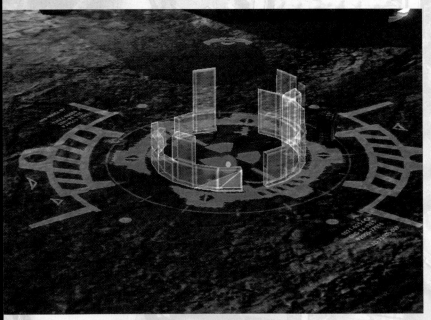

BONUS: KILL THE LAST FOUR SPECTRES.

After Tosh's nuke misses you, send Nova back down the ramp to Snipe two more Spectres, one on each ramp leading up to the Psi-Indoctrinator. (See our map for their exact location.) Watch out for the Raven overhead; send in flying Vikings for a quick strike to knock it out then pull them back. Note: Two more Spectres are posted over the Psi-Indoctrinator, but they're about to get incinerated.

NUKE THE PSI-INDOCTRINATOR.

You're almost done. Send any remaining Banshees and/or Vikings (kept on the ground here) up the north ramp to hit the Missile Turret; they can clean up other threats too, but the key is to KO the turret so Nova can get up the ramp unmolested. It's worth sacrificing units here to clear that safe spot (28), because once Nova gets there, it's all over. Just call in the Tac Nuke Strike right on top of the highlighted target and the mission is won.

INTERLUDE: *HYPERION*

Tosh hails in on a channel to gloat and threaten Raynor from six light years away.

After the cinematic, make your ship rounds. Nova delivered Ghost tech for Swann in the Armory, so you have Ghosts available from this mission on.

THE GREAT TRAIN ROBBERY

MISSION OVERVIEW

As Swann suggests, the way to destroy the Dominion trains is with a good Diamondback squadron. However, it's difficult to factory-build enough of the hover-tanks in the time allotted. Fortunately, a number of abandoned Confederate Diamondbacks are scattered around the map. Find and commandeer them to make your job much easier.

PREREQUISITES

Complete a total of 6 missions.

OBJECTIVES

MAIN

- Destroy 8 Dominion trains.
- Don't miss more than 3 trains.

BONUS

- Commandeer all 6 Confederate Diamondbacks hidden on the map.
- Unearth the Defiler Bone Samples (+3 Zerg Research)

CREDIT REWARD

110,000

ACHIEVEMENTS

ACHIEVEMENT		PTS	REQUIREMENTS
	The Great Train Robbery	10	Complete all mission objectives
	Bully the Bullies	10	Kill the Marauder kill team
	Silver Streak	10	Complete the mission without letting a train pass by on Hard difficulty

LOCATION: TARSONIS

Once the shining capital of Terran space, Tarsonis now stands as a ravaged, sobering monument to the fallen Confederacy.

MATT HORNER'S BRIEFING

We've received reports of a new Dominion salvage operation on Tarsonis. They're running a large number of supply trains with minimal security. If we intercept the trains and "liberate" their contents before they can be shipped offworld, we could make a serious profit.

MISSION

UNDERSTAND THE LAYOUT.

Check out our mission map. You base (1) sits up on a central plateau surrounded by ruins. Two access ramps (6 and 7) run up to the base from the northwest and southwest. Two sets of train tracks approach the access ramps (at 3 and 5) then split to circle around opposite sides of the plateau. A third set of tracks (4) winds along the southern part of the map. The Dominion trains will travel along these three tracks accompanied by increasingly fierce escort units.

Be aware that a *lot* of Dominion units and buildings are clustered around the edges of the map. To avoid run-ins with these forces, don't intercept trains too early or too late on their journey. The best places to engage are near the access ramps (at 3, 4, and 5). You want to destroy each train before it gets too far east of the central plateau.

UNDERSTAND YOUR OBJECTIVES.

You must destroy eight Dominion trains to win. The mission features increasingly difficult "train scenarios." Each scenario features a specific number of escorts or other complicating factors that may include the speed of the train, retaliatory attacks on your base, or other Dominion units appearing on the map.

NEW TECHNOLOGY

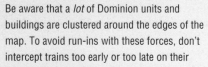

DIAMONDBACK

Fast, high-damage hovertank. Effective versus mobile targets because its powerful Eviscerator Railgun can fire while the Diamondback is moving.

NEW UPGRADES AVAILABLE

- Tri-Lithium Power Cell: Diamondbacks gain +1 range
- Shaped Hull: Diamondbacks gain +50 health

RESEARCH OPPORTUNITIES

- +3 Zerg Research

LEGEND

PRIMARY

1. Start
2. Pallet stash
3. Tracks from NW tunnel
4. Tracks from SW tunnel
5. Tracks from W tunnel
6-7. Build Bunkers here

SECONDARY

○ = Abandoned
Diamondback

8-10. Defiler Bones

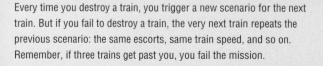

Every time you destroy a train, you trigger a new scenario for the next train. But if you fail to destroy a train, the very next train repeats the previous scenario: the same escorts, same train speed, and so on. Remember, if three trains get past you, you fail the mission.

BONUS: FIND ALL SIX DIAMONDBACKS.

You start with a small base and a few Marines and SCVs. Here's a mission where completing your bonus objective is critical to your overall success. As the mission opens, put your SCVs to work and add a Tech Lab to your Barracks. Soon Horner reports that "Confederate vehicles" (Diamondbacks) are hidden in the hills. Send out your initial Marines to commandeer the abandoned hover-tanks; check our map for the Diamondback locations (marked as blue circles). Hurry! The first Dominion train arrives just minutes after the mission starts.

WATCH FOR PALLETS!

Mineral and Gas Pallets are scattered across the map. Explore the enclosures where you find the abandoned Diamondbacks, and look around the perimeter of your base. Don't miss the nice stash up in the northeast corner (2) of the map!

BONUS: UNEARTH THE DEFILER BONE SAMPLES.

Three piles of Defiler Bone Samples, valuable for research, are hidden on the map (8, 9, and 10). Send Marines to scoop them up as they commandeer Diamondbacks and gather other goods.

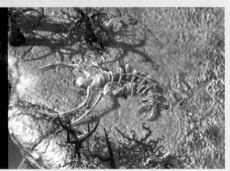

CREATE A SUPPORT SQUAD FOR YOUR DIAMONDBACKS.

The first Dominion train rolls alone, so it's easy to destroy, but every sub-sequent train travels with escorts. These escort squads grow larger and more varied as the mission progresses. You want your Diamondbacks free to focus their full firepower on the train, if possible. Thus it helps to develop a strong support corps to tangle with the Dominion train escorts and provide a screen for your hover-tanks.

When your Barracks has a Tech Lab, start producing the Marines, Firebats and Medics you'll need to counter the first few columns of Dominion escort troops; if you have Marauders available, get a few in the works to help face all the armored units escorting the later Dominion trains. Your Factory, meanwhile, should produce nothing but Diamondbacks for this mission. Be sure to assign a separate hotkey to this infantry group! You want to keep their control separate from your Diamondbacks in the heat of battle.

KEEP YOUR BASE PRODUCTION HUMMING.

Early production is very important in this tightly timed mission. As always, get plenty of workers collecting minerals and gas, and keep one SCV busy building Supply Depots from the get-go. Note that the Dominion won't take kindly to your train attacks and will soon retaliate by striking at your base, so you'll need a base defense too.

One other point: A squad of 7-8 Diamondbacks can easily destroy a Dominion train before it reaches its destination. But you may lose a few of your hover-tanks to the enemy train escorts, so keep a Diamondback in your Factory production queue at all times.

DESTROY THE FIRST DOMINION TRAIN.

Group all commandeered Diamondbacks into a single hunter-killer squadron and assign it a hotkey. Add a couple of SCVs to this group. The hover-tank is perfect for hunting a train because it can fire its railgun while on the move. Place this Diamondback group on the northernmost set of train tracks (3). The first Dominion train comes through the north-west tunnel and travels along that track.

Map Arrows

Check your mini-map when you hear the Adjutant announce the approach of each train. Flashing arrows indicate the exact route of the current train.

As mentioned earlier, the first train travels without escort, so it's a sitting duck for your Diamondbacks. Once the train is destroyed, it drops a bonanza payload of goods; scoop them up to boost your gas and mineral funds. Then send your Diamondback squadron down to (4) to wait for the next train. Send your support squad (8-10 Marines plus a few Firebats and Medics) as it emerges from your Barracks to that spot as well.

BUILD A BASE DEFENSE.

You need a good base defense in place as soon as possible. Use your new funds to build a Bunker in each approach route to the base (6 and 7), and garrison them with Marines. Don't forget to post an SCV or two near the Bunkers for quick repairs.

DOUBLE-DUTY BUNKERS

Consider building Bunkers at the bottom of your base access ramps (near 3 and 5). Well-garrisoned Bunkers in those spots not only defend your base but also thin out Dominion troops who escort the trains passing along the nearby tracks. Drop a Bunker between the two tracks at (4) as well.

DESTROY A SECOND DOMINION TRAIN.

The second train comes through the west tunnel and follows the center set of tracks past (5). The Dominion has learned from its previous loss; a squad of Dominion Marines escorts this second train.

Important: Your Diamondbacks are weak against Marines, so send in your support squad first! Let your own Marines engage the enemy escorts as the train continues onward. Note that a Firebat's armor can withstand a lot of damage from enemy Marines, so put any Firebats you have in the front line. Now you can punch your Diamondback group's hotkey, target the train, and forget about them. Turn your attention to the battle between your Marines and the train escorts. Use the hotkeys to keep your teams focused on their respective tasks.

COUNTERING THE TRAIN ESCORTS

You need a strong support squad to protect your Diamondbacks from Dominion train escorts. Start by assembling massed Marines with a few Firebats and Medics for Trains 2 through 5. Add Marauders (if you have them available) for Train 6 and beyond.

DEFEND YOUR BASE!

Moments after you destroy a second train, the Dominion sends a small raiding party of Marines and Firebats to attack your base. They head for the access ramp at (6). A fully garrisoned Bunker on the ramp can repel this raid, but if your base defense is still weak, rush your train-killer Diamondbacks and the support squad of Marines to intercept the raiders.

Once you wipe out this small incursion, send your main force of Diamondbacks and its support squad of Marines/Medics down the ramp to (4) to wait for the next train.

Note: You should also have 2-3 Bunkers filled with Marines guarding your base by now. If you don't, you'd better get them up soon. Dominion forces will continue to make occasional runs up the plateau from here on out. Start cranking out more Diamondbacks from your Factory too. Time to add their heavier firepower to both your support group and your base defense.

TRAIN SCHEDULE

The countdown timer for each train's arrival starts the moment the previous train exits a tunnel. So the sooner you destroy a train, the more time you'll have to prepare for the next train.

Note: It's pretty difficult to clear *all* of the Bunker construction sites before the next train arrives. Focus on clearing the path along the center track first (used by trains emerging from the western tunnel) since that's where the next train will travel.

DESTROY A THIRD TRAIN.

The third Dominion train exits the southwest tunnel and follows the southern set of tracks past (4). If you destroyed the first two trains, this one features Dominion Hellions as escorts, along with a few Marines. As before, use your own Medic-supported Marines to target these escorts while your Diamondbacks unleash their full fury on the train. When the train is destroyed, gather its dropped goods again.

CATCH A TRAIN WITH STIMPACK MARINES!

Marines enhanced by activated Stimpack move fast enough to keep pace with a moving train. They must stop to fire, but they can catch up again quickly.

INTERDICT THE ENEMY BUNKER CONSTRUCTION.

After you destroy a third train, the Dominion starts sending out SCVs to build a series of Bunkers (locations marked by green circles on our mission map) along the tracks. Rush your fastest troops to take out these SCVs if possible. (Hellions are speedy.) Try to nail the enemy SCVs before Bunker construction is completed.

The reason: The Dominion soon deploys infantry to each of these Bunker construction sites, whether the Bunker is built or not. Four Marines and a Firebat go to each site. The enemy Marines will garrison the Bunker at the site once the Dominion SCV finishes it. But if you manage to destroy the enemy SCVs and Bunkers first, the Dominion troops arrive with no structure to garrison, so they remain out in the open where they're much easier to kill.

Stray Train Escorts

Once you destroy a train, any of its remaining escort units peel off and head for your base unless engaged in a fight.

DESTROY A FOURTH AND FIFTH TRAIN.

If you destroyed the first three Dominion trains, the fourth train also exits the western tunnel. (Check the flashing arrows on your mini-map for its route.) Now the train escort squad consists of Firebats and a stronger contingent of Marines. Wipe them out with your full force, focusing your armor-busting Diamondback fire on the enemy Firebats to decimate them more quickly.

DIAMONDBACK VS. ARMOR

Although a Diamondback struggles against massed Marines, its armor-piercing railgun is very effective against armored units such as Firebats, Marauders, Siege Tanks, and Goliaths.

Then turn your Diamondbacks loose on the train. Afterwards, direct your hover-tanks and support troops to clear the northern track of Dominion Bunkers if you have time before Train 5 arrives.

When the fifth Dominion train exits the northwest tunnel, rush your Diamondback group and its support corps to the best intercept point (3) along the northernmost rail line. If you destroyed the previous four trains, Train 5 adds a pair of Marauders to the Firebats and Marines you saw guarding the previous train. Again, wipe out the escorts with your combined force, focusing your Diamondbacks on the armored Firebats and Marauders. Then unleash your hover-tanks on the train.

KEEP BEEFING UP DEFENSES.

In the lull between trains, continue your ongoing effort to add units to each of your three main forces: the Diamondback tank-killer group, its mobile support corps, and the base defense group. Add a couple more Bunkers to your base too. The Dominion will start sending more powerful units to attack your base, including Goliaths, Siege Tanks, and even flying Banshees. Be ready for them. Add your own Goliaths along with more Marines to knock down the flyers.

BEWARE THE MARAUDER KILL-TEAM.

Once you destroy five trains, the Dominion has had it with your shenanigans and sends out a powerful Marauder "kill team." Horner helpfully marks this kill-team with a flashing red death's-head icon on your minimap. He also recommends that you avoid it. Good advice, Matt! Tangling with an angry Marauder may leave you too weak to effectively intercept subsequent Dominion trains. This enemy Marauder patrol loops around the map, following the tracks. They may also attack your base.

KILLING THE KILL-TEAM

If you have a strong base defense set up, you can send out a fast unit to lure the patrolling Marauder kill-team up to its doom in your base. Eliminating it makes life much easier for your Diamondbacks and other troops out in the field.

DESTROY YOUR SIXTH AND SEVENTH TRAINS.

After you've destroyed five trains, the Dominion also boosts the speed of its trains somehow, so you have less time to destroy them. Diamondbacks can keep up, but you may need a few extra hover-tanks to knock out each train before it escapes to the east. (Marines with active Stimpacks can give some help here too, though not as much as on the slower trains.) Fortunately, the next train emerges unescorted, so if you can avoid the Dominion Marauders and attack the trains with enough Diamondbacks, you can make your sixth train kill without suffering too many losses.

Once you nail your sixth train, the next train also features the speed boost but no escort. Once again, give chase and overwhelm it with Diamondback firepower. But keep an eye on the Marauder "kill-team" icon on the map and launch your final train attack when they do not threaten your position.

DESTROY THE FINAL TRAIN.

After you destroy your seventh Dominion train, Tychus reports that the speed boost has been disabled so the trains return to normal speed. However, the train escort squad becomes very powerful, with Goliaths and Siege Tanks joining the usual Marines.

Remember, your objective is to destroy eight Dominion trains and not let more than two get past you. If you've eliminated seven trains but already missed two, then fling every combat unit you have at the next train. Empty your base if necessary. Throw your SCVs at the enemy escort troops as fodder! Do whatever it takes to concentrate all your firepower on the train. The moment it explodes, you win the mission. If it gets past, you lose.

However, if you have any trains to "give"…that is, if you can still let one or two trains get past without losing the mission…consider retreating to your base. Let the next train go and use those precious minutes to pump out more train-killing Diamondbacks and support troops. Then descend on the following train with your beefed-up force

The eighth train's destruction reveals the curious artifact that the Dominion has been seeking: a battered Confederate adjutant designated 23-46.

INTERLUDE: *HYPERION*

Why is the Dominion so interested in digging up an old Confederate adjutant? It must harbor some very valuable data.

Go to the Bridge and talk to Horner. In the conversation, Raynor recalls a fellow at Deadman's Port named Colonel Orlan who could decrypt anything. If you want to find out what's locked inside adjutant 23-46, you might want to pay Orlan a visit.

CUTTHROAT

MISSION OVERVIEW

Sure enough, Colonel Orlan decrypts the adjutant found on Tarsonis, but there's a little problem: he plans to double-cross Raynor and sell the decrypted info to the Dominion. Your only option now is to team up with a mercenary named Mira Han who can help Raynor stop Orlan and retrieve the old Confederate adjutant. Of course, being a mercenary, Mira has a price.

PREREQUISITES

Complete "The Great Train Robbery."

OBJECTIVES

MAIN

- Acquire 6,000 minerals before Orlan does to buy Mira Han's mercenary contract.
- Destroy Orlan's mercenary fortress.

BONUS

- Find 3 Protoss Relic contraband items (+3 Protoss Research).

CREDIT REWARD

120,000

ACHIEVEMENTS

ACHIEVEMENT	PTS	REQUIREMENTS
Cutthroat	10	Complete all mission objectives
Minesweeper	10	Kill 25 total units with Vulture Spider Mines
Solitaire	10	Don't train additional SCVs before purchasing Hans contract on Hard difficulty

LOCATION: DEADMAN'S PORT

Deadman's Port has long been a refuge for smugglers and pirates seeking to avoid the guns of the vigilant Dominion Defense Fleets.

MATT HORNER'S BRIEFING

We still need to access the Adjutant we retrieved from Tarsonis. Our old mercenary associate Colonel Orlan is an expert in Confederate code decryption. If our intel's right, he should still be based at the merc-haven at Deadman's Port. He's not very trustworthy, but he's our best bet of breaking that encryption.

MISSION

You start with 400 minerals versus Orlan's zero, but he's already set up four mining operations. It's a mining race: first one to 6,000 minerals wins. But you'll find it impossible to simply mine the minerals you need. Fortunately, as Horner points out, pirates have been stripping down ships at Deadman's Port for years, and valuable scrap is plentiful. You'll need to scavenge tons of scrap (labeled "Salvageable Scrap" in the game) to add to your mineral count. The hitch is that you'll have to spend some of your resources to create a strong scavenging party and to fortify your base against Orlan's occasional attacks.

Take a quick look at our mission map to get the lay of the land on Deadman's Port.

SECURE YOUR BASE.

Get your initial SCVs mining the meager mineral fields in your base (1). Add a Refinery atop one of the gas geysers (not both). Send a Marine to snag the Salvageable Scrap stacked nearby. Build just one Bunker in each of the chokepoints (2 and 3) leading into your base area; get Marines garrisoned inside both Bunkers as soon as possible. When Mira delivers some Vultures, lay their Spider Mines in an arc beyond the Bunkers.

NEW TECHNOLOGY

VULTURE

Fast skirmish unit. Can lay Spider Mines.

NEW UPGRADES AVAILABLE

- Replenishable Magazine: Allows Vultures to replenish mines in the field. Mine cost: 15 minerals.
- Cerberus Mine: Increases Vulture's mine blast radius by 33 percent and mine trigger radius by 33 percent.

RESEARCH OPPORTUNITIES

- +3 Protoss Research

LEGEND

PRIMARY

1. Start

2-3. Place Spider Mines here

4. Shredder

6. Shredder

7-8. Platforms with scrap

10. Orlan's base

11. Mira Han's base

13. Shredder

14. Circular grate

15. Orlan's expansion center

SECONDARY

5. Protoss Relic

9. Protoss Relic

12. Protoss Relic

THE MATT HORNER MISSIONS

Bunker Spot

Be sure to build a Bunker closer to the *far end* (3) of your base's southwest exit. If you build it at the near end instead, a Dominion Siege Tank eventually parks at the far end, out of your range, and hammers your defenses in Siege Mode. Lay Spider Mines in that area for insurance.

Meanwhile, get your base production in gear so that you can crank out the few troops you need. You have to strike a careful balance between spending too much (and thus falling too far behind Orlan in the race to 6,000) and not spending enough to protect your base. Add a Tech Lab to your Barracks so you can train some Medics.

Eventually you want each of your two Bunkers fully garrisoned and supported by one Medic and one SCV for repairs plus one Vulture to lay mines and add good punch versus enemy infantry.

ASSEMBLE A SCAVENGING PARTY.

You don't need a big party, but be sure to add support units. Start with the four Vultures that Mira delivered. Add two SCVs for repairs plus a squad of 3-4 Marines and a Medic. Also consider adding 2-3 extra SCVs that you'll leave at a couple of spots along the route. (More on this later.) Send this group north to wipe out the Command Center in Orlan's expansion base (15). Destroying any of Orlan's expansion centers gives you minerals as a reward and slows down his mineral extraction rate, so it is doubly advantageous to do so.

FAST SCAVENGING

It is entirely possible to beat this mission without producing any new offensive troops. Try sending out just three Vultures (plus SCVs) to scavenge and keep the remaining Vulture in the base to lay mines and defend both chokepoints. Build the chokepoint Bunkers and garrison fully, then group a few more Marines with the defending Vulture to fend off Orlan's base raiders.

SCAVENGE THE LOOP!

Check our mission map. Your short-term goal is to scoop up all the Salvageable Scrap you can find. Your scavenging party's route should follow a rough loop (see the map arrows) that carefully avoids Orlan's base (10), veers south past Mira Han's base (11), then curves back north toward your base (1).

Avoid Orlan!

Don't let your scavenging party venture too close to Colonel Orlan's main base up in the northwest. His troops will tear your force to shreds.

The key is to explore *every* nook and cranny along the way. Valuable scrap is stacked in corners and atop raised platforms (7 and 8). Pick up every box of scrap salvage and every gas pallet you find. Small squads of Orlan's forces, mostly Marines and Auto-Turrets, guard the scrap piles. Wipe them out in each new area and then grab all the Salvageable Scrap you can find.

BONUS: GATHER THE PROTOSS RELIC CONTRABAND (3 ITEMS).

Along the loop you can find three large piles of "Salvage-able Scrap" (5, 9, 12) with health bars above them. Open fire to destroy each pile and reveal a Protoss Relic hidden inside. Send a unit to nab the relic and gain one Research Point. Note that one of them (5) is right outside your base via the southwest exit.

Don't miss the shredder areas (4, 6, 13) where two big scrap blocks worth 150 minerals apiece rise up regularly on the lifts. If you brought extra SCVs with you (as we suggested earlier) you can leave an SCV at each shredder to nab new blocks as they appear. If you have no extra SCVs, another trick is to have a Vulture lay a Spider Mine near each shredder so you have map visibility. When you see scrap blocks restock, send a unit to scoop them up.

Occasionally, Orlan sends out patrols to attack your base. Make sure your scavenging party avoids these; let your base defenses handle the incursions. You need your scavengers to focus entirely on scrap collection. A couple of scrap areas down south have enemy Goliaths posted as guards, so be ready for them.

You should surpass Orlan's total and hit the 6,000 mark fairly quickly if you're thorough in your exploration along the loop. But if you're still trailing Orlan's Minerals count (upper right of screen) when he hits the 4,000 mark, consider sending a second scavenging party out of your base's southwest ramp (3). You'll find two lightly guarded stashes of scrap near the big circular grate (14) just west of the ramp. Gun down Orlan's Marine guards there and scoop up scrap boxes worth several hundred mineral units.

GET MIRA HAN'S BASE UP AND RUNNING.

Once you hit 6,000 minerals, you automatically pay off Mira Han and she offers you control of her entire base and forces. However, she personally pockets the payoff, so you start from scratch with zero minerals. Send out troops to raze Orlan's three outlying Command Centers (not the one in Orlan's base!) and start mining the nearby mineral fields.

By now the mineral field near your original base (1) is probably tapped out. You can move your original Command Center and SCVs up to work the mineral field at (15) after you demolish Orlan's old center there. Don't forget to check the shredders every minute or so for the two 150-point scrap-box pickups as well.

BUILD AN INVASION FORCE.

Now gear up all of your production facilities and start massing troops for an all-out assault on Colonel Orlan's base. He defends with a variety of light and armored units plus a few flying units, so you want a good mix to counter. Vultures/Hellions are good versus light units (Marines), and Diamondbacks provide good anti-armor punch versus enemy Siege Tanks, Goliaths, Bunkers, and so forth. Produce a good contingent of Goliaths for their anti-air ability as well; Orlan has Starports that produce the occasional Wraith, but more importantly, a big Dominion Battlecruiser (16) hovers above his base and will attack your forces when you arrive. Finally, make sure you add SCVs and Medics for repair.

Rally all troops produced from Mira's base to a spot just north of the base's exit ramp. Orlan continues to send raiding parties south from time to time, so you can meet and crush them there. Orlan's raiders sometimes include Wraiths or Siege Tanks, so be ready for those.

ASSAULT ORLAN'S BASE.

Advance warning: Shortly after you penetrate Colonel Orlan's base, he will try to call in a Tac Nuke Strike on your position. We'll discuss this shortly, but it's good to know the danger *before* you plunge into the base.

We like a two-pronged attack, sending one force north from Mira's base and another one from your original base, hitting Orlan from the east. First, group your anti-air units and assign a hotkey. Then bring both forces up the two base ramps simultaneously. But don't rush all the way into the base yet!

INTERLUDE:
HYPERION

Orlan returns the now-decrypted adjutant. The unit plays a shocking intercepted transmission, exposing Mengsk.

DODGE THE NUKE!

When one of your units moves into the circular grate (10) at the top of the ramps, Orlan appears onscreen to taunt you and call in a tactical nuclear strike. The targeted spot is the center of the grate. You have 20 seconds to pull your troops back down the ramps to a safe distance.

After the nuke hits, hammer your way into the northwestern part of the base. Destroy every structure! But watch your right flank, as Orlan keeps sending down units from the upper level of his base. Watch out for his Siege Tanks planted in Siege Mode up on the high ground at the top of the ramp. Eliminate those immediately.

Once the lower platform is cleared, replenish your forces and charge up the ramp to the upper platform, the heart of Orlan's base. This is where you find the Dominion Battlecruiser. Hit your anti-air hotkey and immediately target the big ship before it can inflict painful damage. Try to lure it away from Orlan's Mercenary Fortress, which has its own guns that inflict splash damage; try to avoid battling both the cruiser and fortress at the same time. Once you destroy the Battlecruiser, mop up enemy combat troops and attack the Mercenary Fortress, keeping your forces spread out to minimize the splash damage. Reduce the fortress's health to near zero to complete the mission.

ENGINE OF DESTRUCTION

MISSION OVERVIEW

This mission features the flying Wraith. You learn how to escort, scout, and wreak havoc with this cloaked starship. Your task is to find and commandeer the Dominion's powerful new war machine called the Odin. Once you capture it, Tychus Findlay takes its controls. Then you must escort him on a wild rampage through the Valhalla complex, silencing all five bases there.

PREREQUISITES

Complete "Cutthroat."

OBJECTIVES

MAIN

- Escort Tychus to the Odin.
- Tychus must survive.
- Destroy all five Dominion bases.
- The Odin must survive.

BONUS

- Find 3 Devourer Tissue Samples (+3 Zerg Research).
- Find and destroy the Loki.

CREDIT REWARD

120,000

ACHIEVEMENTS

	ACHIEVEMENT	PTS	REQUIREMENTS
	Engine of Destruction	10	Complete all mission objectives
	Kicking Asgard	10	Destroy the Loki
	Ragnarok & Roll	10	The Odin cannot lose more than 30% of it's total life on Hard difficulty

LOCATION: VALHALLA, SIGMARIS PRIME

Valhalla is a top secret Dominion research center hidden on a small moon of Sigmaris Prime. Hundreds of vehicles and weapons systems have undergone final testing here, including the Viking multi-role Combat Walker and the Minotaur class Battlecruiser.

MATT HORNER'S BRIEFING

The decrypted Adjutant contains records proving Mengsk ordered the massacre on Tarsonis. Now we just need to broadcast those records. Mira Han gave us a tip that might help. The Dominion is unveiling a new war machine called the "Odin" on Korhal. If we hijack the Odin, we can use it to gain access to the UNN studios and broadcast the records of Mengsk's war crimes. The Odin is currently in the testing facility on Valhalla.

MISSION

Here's the key to this mission: The Odin is a very formidable unit, but it isn't indestructible. You must create a strong assault team to escort the Odin from base to base, and include enough SCVs to keep the big unit in good repair. Each base features a specific combo of units in its defense group. Your new Wraiths can scout ahead to each successive base to reveal those units. With that knowledge, you can create the most effective counter units to escort the Odin.

Of course, our walkthrough tells you what lies ahead as well. But Wraiths are also useful for attacking and softening up the enemy defenses before the Odin arrives. Note that none of the Valhalla bases have cloak-detection structures or units, so your Wraiths can operate freely.

NEW TECHNOLOGY

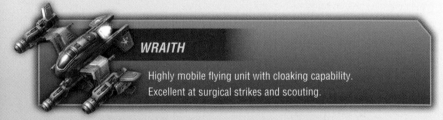

WRAITH

Highly mobile flying unit with cloaking capability. Excellent at surgical strikes and scouting.

NEW UPGRADES AVAILABLE

- Tomahawk Power Cells: Wraiths start with +100 energy.
- Displacement Field: Wraiths evade 20 percent of attacks when cloaked.

RESEARCH OPPORTUNITIES

- +3 Zerg Research

LEGEND

PRIMARY

1. Start
2. Odin
3. Your base
4. Infantry base
5. Infantry base
6. Build bunkers here
7. Vehicle base
8. Battlecruiser & Siege Tank!
9. Mixed base
11. Air base

SECONDARY

10. Loki
12-14. Devourer Tissue Sample Tubes

CAPTURE THE ODIN.

You start with a handful of Marines and Medics. Your job is to escort Tychus Findlay and keep him alive long enough to reach the Odin. He leads the way, so just hotkey your squad and follow, hitting any targets that emerge from the fog. Don't worry if Tychus runs off without you; if he gets too far ahead, he stops and waits.

TISSUE BONUS

Don't miss the Devourer tissue sample tube just inside the first doorway to the left. It's worth a Zerg Research point.

Frankly, Tychus barely needs your help, but get up there with him and pick off a few Dominion threats anyway. Just around the first bend, the Dominion activates a pair of Perdition Turrets that pop up out of the ground. Once Tychus reaches the glowing marker (2), a cutscene shows the Odin being assembled. Tychus takes control and blasts his way right through the security doors into the next area. Raynor drops in a set of base facilities for you to control, including a Starport.

Add Tech Labs to your Factory and Barracks right away. You barely have time to get your SCVs to work when another scene is triggered. Two Dominion Battlecruisers suddenly drop in to attack the Odin. But Swann quickly deploys a squadron of a new flying unit, the Wraith. Your agile Wraiths, the lumbering Odin, and your gritty Marines make quick work of the big capital ships. Swann also drops in a Starport. Add a Tech Lab immediately so you can start producing more Wraiths. Along with the Odin, the Wraith is the star of this mission.

CLOAK MANAGEMENT

A Wraith expends the battery energy of its cloaking generator while cloaked; the generator slowly recharges once you decloak the craft. To conserve and recharge battery energy, be sure to decloak your Wraiths whenever they're not in the fray.

Another good tactic is to create two separate squadrons of Wraiths, pulling one back to recharge while the other one cloaks and fights/scouts. This way you always have cloaked Wraiths available. You probably won't need to use that tactic in this mission, however.

BONUS: NAB THE DEVOURER TISSUE SAMPLES.

Keep your eyes peeled for three Devourer tissue sample tubes in Valhalla's research areas. One is in the corner (12) just inside the first building you enter after mission start. The next Devourer sample is against the northeast wall (13) of the second Dominion base. Another sample is in corridor (14) just outside the fourth Dominion base.

HELP THE ODIN CLEAR THE FIRST VALHALLA BASE.

Tychus cannot receive outside communications in the Odin, so he goes rogue and decides to start wiping out the Valhalla bases on his own. He immediately heads north to the first base (4). Assign a hotkey to your new wing of cloaked Wraiths, rush them out in front of the Odin, and bring your Marines up beside it. Send out 2-3 SCVs from your base as well; you want them in your support group to repair the Odin as it inevitably takes damage.

The first base (4) is garrisoned with infantry, with just a couple of Barracks guarded by a handful of Marines, Firebats, and Marauders supported by a few flying Medivacs. This is a piece of cake for the Odin, but take the opportunity to practice leading with your awesome Wraiths. Since Wraiths can hit both ground and air units, they're able to target anything in the base. Be sure to decloak the Wraiths once all enemy shooters are dead so the craft can recharge.

ASSEMBLE A DOUBLE-PURPOSE FORCE.

Raynor's a shrewd soldier, and that's why he drops a Bunker in the northeastern gap (6) leading into your base. Defending that gap is a big key to success in this mission. Dominion troops will challenge your base at that gap several times, deploying a variety of units including aircraft. For now, fill the Bunker with Marines, put two SCVs behind it for repair, then add a couple of armored mech units such as Goliaths when you can.

That's just a start. It's about all you can do before Tychus impetuously pushes the Odin into the next Valhalla base (5). But you should keep an ongoing production flow of troops to your base's chokepoint. This not only gives you an impregnable defense there, it also rallies the strong force you'll need to support the Odin as it moves into the more heavily defended bases later in the mission. From that gap (6) it's just a short march to those bases.

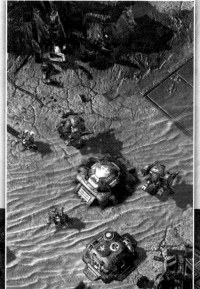

WIPE OUT THE SECOND BASE.

The second base (5) is another infantry area similar to the first but larger with a couple of defensive Bunkers and an ongoing mineral mining operation. Its guard units include Firebats as well as Marines and Marauders. Several Medivacs fly above in support.

Your best bet for Odin escort here is still a good mass of Marines supported by Medics. But once again, unleash your cloaked Wraiths on the enemy base before the Odin arrives. Direct your Wraiths to hit the more lethal targets first: the enemy Bunkers are a good start. After the Odin and your Marines arrive, focus the Wraiths on knocking the enemy Medivacs out of the sky so the Dominion troops below have no healing support.

Once the targets that shoot back are eliminated, decloak the Wraiths to recharge. But let them participate in the razing of base structures. Hey, they deserve it. Don't miss the Zerg sample (13) against the northeast wall, and don't forget to have SCVs repair the Odin during its downtime before Tychus stomps off to the next base.

BOLSTER YOUR WING

Add 2-3 more Wraiths to your initial squadron of four for a very lethal group. Concentrated fire from six Wraiths can take out targets very quickly.

WIPE OUT THE THIRD BASE.

The third Valhalla base (7) is primarily a vehicle depot that features a number of Factories guarded by mech units: Diamondbacks, Vultures, and a Siege Tank. Hovering above the traffic is another Dominion Battle-cruiser. A platoon of Reapers joins a few Marines and Marauders in the base defense as well. Hovering in the corner is a pair of nasty Banshees.

NAIL THE TANK EARLY!

The Siege Tank (8) in the vehicle base is devastating versus your massed Marines, so be sure your cloaked Wraiths make the tank a priority target when they scout ahead into the base.

Send in your cloaked Wraiths first to scout and knock out the Battle-cruiser. Next, have them hit the Bunker and Marines, eliminating the last of the base's meager anti-air capability. Now your Wraiths have reign over the area; decloak them and target the defenseless Banshees next. (Banshees have no air-to-air weapons.) Then turn your Wraiths loose on the Siege Tank (8).

Send in your cloaked Wraiths first. You have a choice: you can go after the Loki (10) right away (see the next section) or skirt around it and soften up the base for your ground troops first. Six or more Wraiths can take out the Loki in a fairly short time, leaving your squadron enough cloaking time to inflict some pain to the base too. But if your Wraiths' cloaks run out of power in the base, pull them back! You don't want to lose any Wraiths now. You'll need a strong squadron of Wraiths in the final Valhalla base.

BONUS: DESTROY THE LOKI.

A massive capital ship called the Loki (10) is docked in fourth base. Find it with your cloaked Wraith squadron and then turn them loose on it. As mentioned in the previous section, six Wraiths can chew up the Loki with surprising alacrity.

Bring a strong squad of Marines plus a few Goliaths to counter the Dominion Reapers. (You can start sending up some of the troops you've been rallying in the gap to your base.) Massed Marines can take out Diamondbacks quickly, too. Careful: if the enemy Siege Tank still lurks in Siege Mode over on the eastern edge of the base (8), it will make mincemeat of your Marines.

When the third base is destroyed and Tychus halts his advance for a few seconds, get your SCVs repairing him. Also make sure your Wraiths are decloaked and recharging. You'll need them ready for the next base.

WIPE OUT THE FOURTH BASE.

The fourth Valhalla base (9) has a mix of troops protecting the Loki, a huge experimental capital starship. Guards here are more numerous and range from infantry (Marines, Firebats, Marauders) near the entrance to a few flying units (Banshees and Vikings) elsewhere in the complex. As always, Marines are a good bet for your Odin support team. But a good mix of units helps.

WIPE OUT THE FIFTH BASE.

After the fourth base goes down, be sure to get the Odin fully healed up with your SCVs. You don't want to lose it now, with victory so close! The fifth base is a flight-oriented installation featuring a deadly Dominion Battlecruiser plus a stout wing of Banshees and Vikings.

⊖ WRAITH DETECTORS

Enemy Missile Turrets (15) sit along the far (southwest) edge of the Dominion air base. These can detect your Wraiths, so keep your cloaked flyers away!

You *really* need your cloaked Wraiths to engage strong and fast here. As Horner points out, the Odin's one weakness is its anti-air capability. If you send 7-8 cloaked Wraiths ahead of the Odin you can take out not only the Battlecruisers but most of the other enemy air units as well, making the ground assault almost a stroll in the park for Tychus. Bring in a handful of Goliaths to help your Marines gun the menace from the sky too. When the base is completely decimated, the mission is over.

INTERLUDE: HYPERION

Afterwards, talk to Horner on the Bridge to learn some interesting info about Tychus.

MEDIA BLITZ

MISSION OVERVIEW

Tychus marches the Odin like a Trojan horse right into Korhal's capital. The show starts with a Godzilla-like rampage as you unleash the Odin on Dominion troops protecting UNN transmission towers in three separate sectors of the city. After the initial carnage, you must build up a strike force to finish the job by seizing control of the towers. The mission is a success only after you upload your incriminating transmission of Mengsk to all three UNN towers.

PREREQUISITES

Complete "Engine of Destruction"

OBJECTIVES

MAIN

- Launch a surprise attack.
- Access the three UNN broadcast towers.

BONUS

- None.

CREDIT REWARD

125,000

ACHIEVEMENTS

ACHIEVEMENT		PTS	REQUIREMENTS
	Media Blitz	10	Complete all mission objectives
	Seek & Destroy	10	Destroy an enemy Barracks, Factory, and Starport during the sneak attack
	Blitzkrieg	10	Complete the mission on Hard difficulty in less than 20 minutes

LOCATION: KORHAL

Arcturus Mengsk's homeworld of Korhal was once a prosperous colony until it was obliterated by Confederate nukes. Vast fortunes have been lavished on the planet's reconstruction since Emperor Mengsk took the throne four years ago. Now it is the Terran Dominion's capital planet.

MATT HORNER'S BRIEFING

We have the Odin. Now we can use it to spearhead our takeover of the UNN studios on Korhal. Once the Odin has taken out their defenses, we'll broadcast our evidence against Mengsk. Figure they'll throw everything they have at us. They'll be talking about this one for years.

MISSION

Your overall objective is to fight your way to three beacon markers (5, 6, 7) glowing in front of the UNN broadcast towers. Each of the three towers sits at the back of a heavily fortified Dominion base. You must camp a unit atop each tower's glowing beacon until you gain control of that tower's transmission. When you control all three towers, you win.

TRIGGER THE SECRET MISSION!

Destroying a specific building on this map unlocks a special extra mission.

This mission can be a real slugfest, with the stolen Odin and your new Thor heavy assault mechs hammering through heavy Dominion defenses. Cloaked Wraiths can be useful too, but only if you first clear out the Missile Turrets that can detect them in each base. (We marked all Missile Turret locations on our mission map.) The three main bases differ from each other in their defense garrisons, so your counter unit choices should differ from base to base as well.

NEW TECHNOLOGY

THOR

A heavy assault mech that can attack both ground and air units.

NEW UPGRADES AVAILABLE

- 330 mm Barrage Cannon: Improved Thor bombardment cannon stuns targets and does area damage of 500 over 6 seconds.

- Immortality Protocol: Special ability that lets destroyed Thors be reactivated in the field.

PRIMARY

◎ = Missile Turret

1. Start

2. Your base

3-4. Place Bunkers and defense units

5. UNN Tower Beacon (Sector 1: airbase)

6. UNN Tower Beacon (Sector 2: tank base)

7. UNN Tower Beacon (Sector 3: mobile base)

8-9. Dominion mining operations

SECONDARY

10. Science Facility (Secret Mission!)

PHASE 1: THE ODIN'S RAMPAGE

WRECK THE PARADE.

This first phase of the mission is on a timer. You get 5:00 to go crazy in the Godzilla of war machines, the Odin, until the Dominion is alerted and the second phase of the mission begins. You start out surrounded by Dominion troops that consider you "friendly." It's fun to disabuse them of this silly notion. Enemy units won't attack the Odin until you fire the first shot, so make sure that first shot is a good one.

Here's how: The Odin has a special attack called "Barrage" which drops a salvo of shells that devastate an entire targeted area. (It affects only ground forces and structures.) Drop a nice Barrage right on top of the Marines and Hellions lined up directly behind the Odin. As the civilians scatter, knock out the remaining Dominion troops surrounding you.

WREAK ODIN'S DESTRUCTION ON THE ENEMY BASE(S).

The clock is ticking, so hurry to take advantage of your time in the Odin. During this period you control only the Odin, and you should inflict as much punishment as you can on the surrounding Dominion bases. Your goal is to soften the defenses for Raynor's troops so they have an easier time reaching the beacon markers in front of the UNN broadcast towers later. (Raynor drops in base facilities for you as the mission begins, but you can't control them until the 5:00 timer runs out.)

Take your pick of strategies during this period. You can use the Odin to destroy a specific base or try to soften up all three bases, focusing on major defensive installations such as Bunkers, Missile Turrets, Auto-Turrets, and Siege Tanks in Siege Mode, then blasting any production facilities such as Factories, Barracks, or Starports. Or you can try to focus on wiping out all Missile Turrets to give your cloaked Wraiths safe passage later.

Take a look at our descriptions of each base below and then formulate your plan of attack.

SENDING THE ODIN TO SECTOR 2

Remember, the Odin is weakest against air units, but it is a fearsome anti-armor platform. So our favorite Odin rampage is to wipe out all defenses and production facilities in Sector 2, the tank-heavy base in the northeast (6). The battalion of Siege Tanks, Diamondbacks, and Goliaths deployed there can be brutal on any regular assault force coming up the ramps, so take delight in chewing it to pieces with the Odin.

In fact, you can terminate almost every unit and structure in that base before the "Dominion Alert" timer rans out. This allows you to focus on assembling a strong anti-air assault force in the next phase to KO the air-heavy Sector 1 base up in the northwest (7).

PHASE 2: THE BUILDUP

FORTIFY YOUR BASE.

Immediately set an SCV to work healing your banged-up Odin. Dominion troops including flyers make aggressive forays into your base regularly during this mission, so you want each entry gap well defended. Build Bunkers in the two chokepoints (3 and 4) leading into your base; get the Bunkers garrisoned right away, with SCVs nearby for repairs. Soon after you gain control of your base, Swann drops in a Thor plus the Factory plans for building new ones. Nice! Put one Thor near each Bunker.

Immediately construct an Engineering Bay so you can put up a Missile Turret in each chokepoint as well. Then start rallying the troops you want for your main assault force near the two Bunkers. This keeps your base safe until you launch your big offensive.

ASSEMBLE A HEAVY ASSAULT FORCE.

You can custom-assemble an attack group based on what you destroyed during your earlier Odin rampage. But if you just want a good all-purpose crew, you can't go wrong with Thors and massed Marines, with Medics and SCVs in support. You can get through all three bases with this group. With those two unit types and the Odin you can handle anything the Dominion throws at you, air or ground.

THOR COUNTERS

The Thor is a beast, but it is quite weak against massed Marines or multiple Marauders. Keep a shield of other units between your Thors and enemy infantry squads!

PREPARE FOR EXPANSION.

Whichever direction you launch your assault force (via 3 or 4) leads to a Dominion mining camp (8 or 9). Wipe out all facilities and support units at the camp you approach, scouring the mineral field free of activity. Later, if your own base's mineral field gets tapped out, you can move your Command Center and SCVs over to the camp you just liberated for continued harvesting.

PHASE 3: THE ASSAULT

GAIN CONTROL OF TOWER 1.

Sector 1 (5) is the enemy's airbase. Other than Missile Turrets and a couple of Auto-Turrets, the bulk of this base's defenders are Banshees and Vikings. No Bunkers or other ground forces are posted here, although of course Vikings can fight well whether on the ground or in the air.

If you choose to attack this base with your main assault force (including the repaired Odin, of course), the best units to train are a large mass of Marines with Medic support plus a 3-4 Thors; both units are very good versus Banshees and Vikings. If you can knock out the Missile Turrets early with your ground forces, you can bring in cloaked Wraiths to help in the mop-up operations. But don't miss the single Raven hovering over the field. It, too, can detect cloaked Wraiths.

Once you clear the area around the Sector 1 UNN Tower beacon (5), move any unit onto the glowing beacon and keep it planted there until the onscreen "Upload Progress" display shows that the Sector 1 tower is 100 percent complete.

GAIN CONTROL OF TOWER 2.

Sector 2 is the Dominion tank base, filled with big Siege Tanks and mobile Diamondback hover-tanks, plus a few Goliaths guarding the base entry ramps. Although the base has five Missile Turrets, only two are near the front entrance (see our map), so if you can knock those out early you can bring up cloaked Wraiths to help clear the front half of the base.

Your best assault group here is the Odin and 4-5 Thors plus a sizeable squad of Marines with Medics. The Thor is weak versus massed Marines, but in this base you encounter few enemy Marines: just one garrisoned Bunker near the side entrance plus a couple of extra soldiers. Your own Marines are very good at taking out the enemy Diamondbacks, but the enemy Siege Tanks can decimate your massed Marines quickly. Whenever you notice shells incoming from a Siege Tank, rush your Thors forward to engage it. A Thor can cut right through an enemy Siege Tank in just seconds.

Once you clear the area around the Sector 2 UNN Tower beacon (6), move any unit onto the glowing beacon to start the broadcast upload. Keep the unit there until the "Upload Progress" display shows that the Sector 2 tower is 100 percent complete. During the upload you must fight off several waves of assault teams sent at you by General Warfield.

SECRET MISSION UNLOCK: FIND THE SECRET DOCUMENTS AT THE SCIENCE FACILITY

Behind the Dominion mining base at (9) you find a bridge that leads out to a Science Facility (10) on a separate platform. Move a few Marines across the bridge. Select the Marines and click Attack Move on the building to force an attack. When the Science Facility explodes it leaves behind a console with documents that reference a secret Dominion lab. Walk a Marine over the console to pick up the documents. This information will trigger a secret mission available next time you bring up the Star Map on the *Hyperion* Bridge.

GAIN CONTROL OF TOWER 3.

Sector 3 features a large and speedy defense force of Reapers, Hellions, and Vultures. Again, a handful of Thors plus a good platoon of Marines/ Medics is a good combo for your base assault team. A Thor is particularly devastating against both Vultures and Hellions, and massed Marines can shred Reapers quickly. Firebats are also good against this base's defense force due to their armor, high HP, and overall effectiveness versus light units like Reapers, Vultures and Hellions. So add a few Firebats to your assault group as well.

After you clear the area around the Sector 3 UNN Tower beacon (7), move any unit onto the glowing beacon to start the upload. Leave the unit on the beacon until the "Upload Progress" display shows that the Sector 3 tower is 100 percent complete. As at the other beacons, you must fight off several waves of assault teams sent at you by General Warfield during the upload. When the third transmission is uploaded, you win the mission.

INTERLUDE: HYPERION

Afterwards, watch Raynor and Horner celebrate in the cinematic, "Hearts and Minds." Make your ship rounds and spend your new loot, then check the Star Map on the Bridge. If you destroyed the Science Facility and nabbed the secret documents pickup, you have a special new mission available on the planet Castanar.

PIERCING THE SHROUD

SECRET MISSION!

MISSION OVERVIEW

The documents you found on Korhal when you destroyed Mengsk's Science Facility (in the mission "Media Blitz") have led the *Hyperion* to a top-secret Dominion bio-weapons lab on an asteroid registered as a Beryllium storage warehouse, orbiting the planet Castanar.

PREREQUISITES
Complete "Media Blitz"

OBJECTIVES
MAIN

- Investigate the Dominion lab on Castanar.
- Destroy the fusion reactor.
- Escape from the Hybrid.
- Raynor must survive.

BONUS

- Find the 4 Protoss Relics (+4 Protoss Research).
- Kill the Brutalisk (+3 Zerg Research).

CREDIT REWARD
125,000

ACHIEVEMENTS

ACHIEVEMENT		PTS	REQUIREMENTS
	Piercing the Shroud	10	Complete all mission objectives
	Lock and Load	10	Locate all 13 weapon pickups
	Not so Brutalisk	10	Kill the Brutalisk without losing a unit to the Brutalisk on Hard difficulty.

LOCATION: CASTANAR

Located near the Dominion's fringe, Castanar is a small, nondescript world with little in the way of natural resources. The only notable feature of the planet is the massive Beryllium Storage facility orbiting the planet on a captive asteroid.

MATT HORNER'S BRIEFING

The classified documents we found on Korhal imply the Dominion has a top-secret bio-weapons lab on an orbital platform at Castanar. If the Dominion is cooking up a big surprise for us, I'd like to know about it.

MISSION

This a "hero mission" played as Jim Raynor, with just a handful of troops at your disposal. Your task is to investigate a sinister Dominion bio-lab built into an orbital asteroid. As you progress, Raynor can pick up special weapons. In the mission prelude, Horner mentions that you have security codes that may let you hack into lab systems. These allow you to make interesting tactical choices at certain junctures.

NEW TECHNOLOGY

- None.

NEW UPGRADES AVAILABLE

- None.

RESEARCH OPPORTUNITIES

- +4 Protoss Research
- +3 Zerg Research

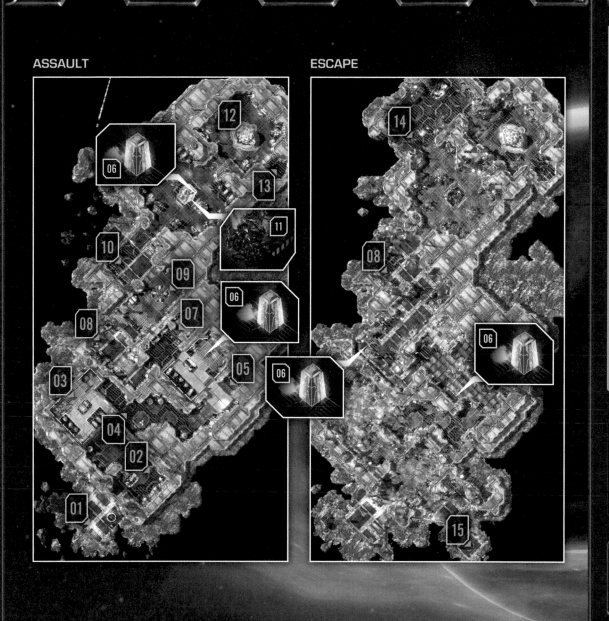

ASSAULT

ESCAPE

LEGEND

PRIMARY

1. Start

2. Beacon: Security control panel

3. Zerg holding pen

4. Grenades

5. Beacon: Security control panel

7. Plasma gun

8. Beacon: A.R.E.S. warbot control panel

9. Vehicle bay

10. Beacon: Brutalisk lab camera

12. The Hybrid

13. Fusion reactor

14. Chrono Rift Device

15. Hercules escape vessel

SECONDARY

6. Protoss Relic

11. Brutalisk containment chamber

HACK THE SECURITY CONSOLES.

You start with Raynor and a small squad of Marines and Medics (1). Plant a Breaching Charge on the main entry door and step back. After the door blows, enter the lab and walk onto the glowing beacon then click the "Security Camera" button that appears onscreen. You get a view of the next room, where you see two types of enemy troops deployed.

Now make a choice: If you want to eliminate the Firebats and fight the Marines, click on "Activate Left Side Guns." If you want the reverse, click "Activate Right Side Guns." It's up to you. Neither choice is particularly better, so just go with your personal preference. After the poor guards finally destroy the floor turrets, enter their room with guns blazing.

FIND THE GRENADES AND PLASMA GUN.

Follow the corridor down to some Marines guarding a stash of six grenades (4). Take them out and nab the grenades. Fight your way further down the corridor, tossing a grenade at the big enemy squad ahead. When you climb the ramp at the corridor's end toss another grenade at soldiers guarding a control console marked by a glowing beacon (5). Take out the guards and step into the beacon.

Click "Activate Security Camera" for a peek at the hefty force in the next room. You're given another tactical choice: you can release 17 Zealots, 65 Zerglings, or 4 Ultralisks. Whatever you choose to release will attack the lab guards. When their fight is over, go through the door with a Breaching Charge and wipe out whoever or whatever remains. (Toss in a grenade or two before you enter to make the job easier.)

DESTROY THE ZERG HOLDING PEN.

Proceed up the ramp into the next area, Lab 1. You find some Zerg-Protoss hybrid creatures, and then the security team locks you in and releases a Zerg swarm. Pick off attackers but try to maintain a steady stream of fire on the Zerg holding pen; once it's destroyed, it stops spawning Zerg. For good measure, destroy the shackled Ultralisk over in the corner too. Then use another Breaching Charge to blast through the next door to the northeast.

Here you discover more of the creepy hybrid creatures in cloning tanks. Raynor decides the entire place needs to be nuked. Fortunately, Horner has detected a big fusion reactor nearby. That ought to do the job. Before you move on, nab the bonus Protoss Relic item (6), worth +1 Protoss Research, in the containment chamber marked by the hazard stripe just off the main room.

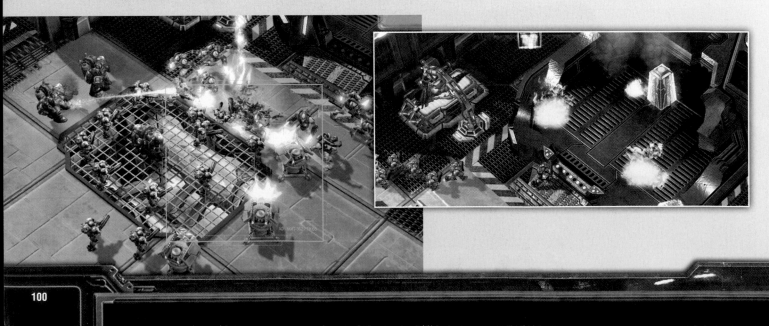

Continue into the next room where a handy health/energy power-up restores you to 100 percent. Set a Breaching Charge on the door to the right to find an experimental Plasma Gun (7) holding six rounds in its energy chamber. This weapon is very powerful; it can get a one-shot kill on a Siege Tank, a fact that will prove useful soon enough. Raynor equips the Plasma Gun automatically when he walks through it. Backtrack out of the room and head southwest down the next corridor.

DON'T BE TOO FRUGAL

Don't worry too much about hoarding your grenades or plasma gun rounds. You will find more of each as you move through the facility.

USE THE A.R.E.S. WARBOT TO CLEAR THE VEHICLE BAY.

Around the corner you encounter a Viking followed by a patrolling Siege Tank. Nail both with single Plasma Gun shots. Proceed into the open bay and step into the glowing beacon (8) to activate another security camera. You see a powerful force of Siege Tanks and Vikings plus Marines in the next bay (9). But your console also gives you control of a big A.R.E.S. warbot. Take your pick of weapon type: we like the Anti-Armor Missiles to take out the heavy units.

EXPLODING BARRELS

Immediately target the barrels in the vehicle bay for explosive results. You can inflict lots of extra damage on the Dominion units in the bay.

Click on the A.R.E.S. warbot to take control and fight with it until it dies. (It's on a destruction timer so you'll lose it anyway.) Then send in Raynor and his squad to mop up the rest. Use grenades and the Plasma Gun to speed up the proceeding.

BONUS: KILL THE BRUTALISK.

Keep fighting into the next bay where one last Viking stands near another beacon (10). Blast the Viking with a plasma round, step into the beacon, and activate another security camera. Raynor calls for reinforcements because something big and ugly is in the next room: it's a Brutalisk (11) in a containment chamber.

Take your pick of the reinforcement choices; it's quite a range. Then set a Breaching Charge on the door to the northeast and start your assault into the next room. Work your way around the Brutalisk chamber, clearing out the entire room first. Don't miss the additional Plasma Gun rounds up in the northern corner, plus some more grenades, a health/energy power-up and a Protoss Relic (6) (+1 Protoss Research) at the other end of the room.

When the room is secure, go to the beacon at the control panel in the northwest part of the room and activate the Brutalisk Security Cam. You get the choice to release and kill the Brutalisk (worth +3 Zerg Research) or leave it be. Assess the health of your squad and make the decision.

TAKE OUT THE FUSION REACTOR.

Now proceed to the heavy security door with the red flashing lights marked "Do Not Enter." Use a Breaching Charge to get through into the next room, where you discover Mengsk's prized research project: a living, deadly Zerg/Protoss hybrid monster (11). Clear out the few Marine guards in the room then head for the reactor (12). You automatically attack it. When the reactor explodes, the containment field holding the hybrid weakens and the monster revives. This is bad news.

RUN!

Now you must work your way back through the collapsing lab to a transport vessel. The map changes due to collapsed structures, but just keep running. There are several debris barriers you must blast clear to move on. In these situations, make sure you deal with any immediate threats before planting the explosives.

Don't use Attack Move at all; you can't afford to waste time attacking the hordes of Zerg along your way out. In fact besides the debris, the only thing that should slow you down are the last two Protoss Relics (6) for bonus Protoss Research points. Both are on your route out, so they shouldn't take long to nab. You can also grab the Chrono Rift Device (14) that you can set behind you as you run, blocking passages to keep pursuers off your tail.

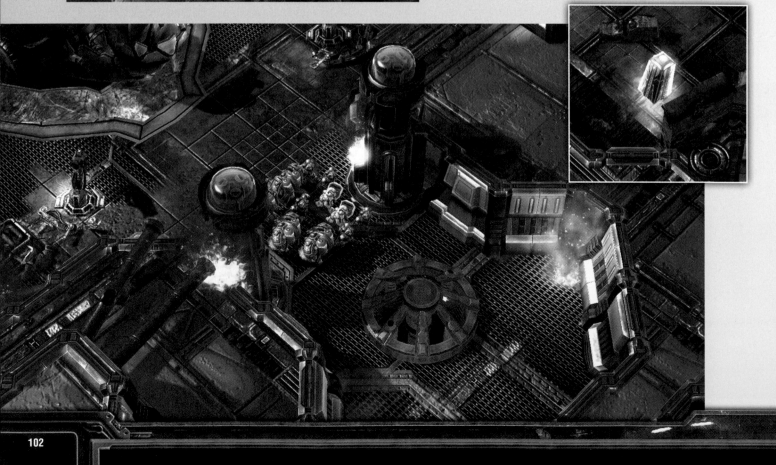

Run past attackers! Use your mini-map and keep looking for the next passage out. Use the Plasma Gun and grenades to speed up that process.

Don't fight the Hybrid under any circumstances! You can't kill him. He disappears and reappears at will. He is only meant to distract and delay.

The Hercules escape vessel (15) is in the bottom right of the map. The moment you reach the glowing transport beacon and load Raynor aboard, you win, so don't be distracted by anything.

INTERLUDE: *HYPERION*

Click on the mission case on the bar to trigger the next mission briefing.

SMASH AND GRAB

MISSION OVERVIEW

An imposing Protoss force is arrayed around the alien artifact on the eastern platform, but a massive Zerg landing to the west creates a sense of urgency. This mission is a gripping race with the Zerg: who can slash through Protoss defenses to reach the artifact first? Your new Marauders help you hammer the Protoss efficiently, but you must also defend your base against the occasional Zerg foray from the west.

PREREQUISITES

Complete "Zero Hour."

OBJECTIVES

MAIN

- Secure the alien artifact before the Zerg can reach it.

BONUS

- Find 4 Protoss Relics (+4 Protoss Research).

CREDIT REWARD

110,000

ACHIEVEMENTS

ACHIEVEMENT	PTS	REQUIREMENTS
Smash and Grab	10	Complete all mission objectives
Rock Solid	10	Complete the mission without losing a unit to a Protoss Stone Guardian
Hit & Run	10	Complete the mission on Hard difficulty in less than 15 minutes.

LOCATION: MONLYTH

Monlyth is a Protoss shrine-world largely abandoned centuries ago—and little is known about the few Protoss who chose to remain there. These Tal'darim and their ancient shrines still remain a mystery to Terran researchers.

TYCHUS FINDLAY'S BRIEFING

The Moebius boys think there's another artifact on a world called Monlyth. Supposedly there's Protoss guarding it—a group of fanatics that call themselves the Tal'darim. Now don't get all sentimental thinking these Protoss are buddies of yours… 'cause they ain't.

MISSION

A glance at our map shows you the big picture: The Zerg swarm claws eastward along the corridor at the top of the map from its massive base (2) toward the Protoss-guarded artifact (3). Meanwhile, your Terran force must follow a parallel route to the artifact, moving east from your base (1) across the southern corridor.

SECURE YOUR BASE.

Shortly after the mission opens, your Adjutant reports a squad of Protoss Stalkers on the perimeter; Swann quickly drops in four Marauders to counter. Your new Marauders tear through the Stalkers with ease. This is the last Protoss incursion you'll face, but Zerg packs will start probing from the west soon, so spend a few seconds securing the top of the ramp (4) leading up to your base.

NEW TECHNOLOGY

MARAUDER

Heavy infantry with a powerful grenade attack. Slows down targets that it hits.

NEW UPGRADES AVAILABLE AFTER MISSION

- Concussive Shells: Marauder attack slows all units in the target area.
- Kinetic Foam: Marauders gain +25 health.

RESEARCH OPPORTUNITIES

- +4 Protoss Research

LEGEND

PRIMARY		
1. Start	4. Chokepoint	10. Protoss base
2. Zerg base	7. Sentry Force Fields	
3. Artifact Fragement	9. Sentry Force Fields	

SECONDARY	
5-6. Protoss Relics	11. Protoss Relic
8. Protoss Relic	

UNIT AVAILABILITY

If you've chosen to complete "Smash and Grab" before "The Evacuation," you have neither Firebats nor Hellions available yet. Although these flame-spewing units are particularly effective versus Zerg swarms, your main foe in this mission is the Protoss.

Remember that the best anti-Zerg tactic is to funnel the beasts into narrow chokepoints so the swarming hordes can't spread out and surround your units. Build a Bunker and array other defenders (including a couple of Firebats, if you have them available) at the top of the ramp, not the bottom. This gives you the high ground and squeezes Zerg raiders into a narrow column as they climb the ramp, making it easy to concentrate deadly fire on their tightly clumped squads. It also prevents the Zerg from fanning out and hitting your troops from all sides.

Keep your base humming along, training Marauders for your strike force, and hiring any mercenary troops available from the Merc Compound when you can afford it. Build an Engineering Bay so you can upgrade the hitting power of your Marauders. This also lets you build a Missile Turret next to your Bunker; later in the mission, the Zerg will send a few flying Mutalisks toward your base.

BONUS: SCORE THE FIRST TWO PROTOSS RELICS.

One Protoss Relic (5) is just a few yards from the bottom of your base's exit ramp, so it's easy to nab. Just send any unit to grab the item. The next relic (6) is tucked right next to your base, but it sits on a platform that you can't reach unless you leave the base, head east through some Zerg creep past a pair of Spine Crawlers and some burrowed Zerglings, then double back through Protoss Stalkers and two Photon Cannons. Don't make your move on this relic until you have 5-6 Marauders, a couple of Firebats (if available) and various support troops.

CROSS THE ENERGY BRIDGE.

Keep developing your base and massing a strike force with a central core of Marauders. Don't wait too long to make your move to the east, however; the Zerg are making inexorable progress up north! Your Adjutant reports the Protoss won't last long.

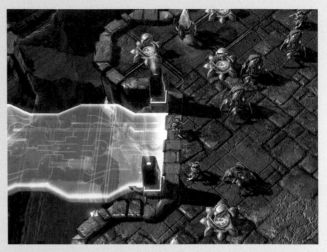

Push your strike force east and fight your way to the shimmering energy bridge. Careful here: when you try to cross, two Protoss Sentries (7) block the span by generating impassable Force Fields. Crossing the bridge is much easier if you neutralize the eastside Photon Cannons first.

POWER OUTAGE

Protoss structures such as Photon Cannons rely on glowing, crystal-like Pylons nearby for power. To neutralize the Photon Cannons on the east side of the energy bridge before they can shoot, move some Marauders halfway across the bridge and blast the two Pylons on the opposite turrets.

BONUS: NAB THE OTHER TWO PROTOSS RELICS.

After you cross the energy bridge the next Protoss Relic (8) is easy to acquire. It sits on a platform guarded by two Photon Cannons powered by a single Pylon. Target the Pylon to quickly neutralize both cannons then send a unit to nab the relic behind them.

The final Protoss Relic is a bit more difficult to reach. You must fight your way across a moderately-guarded Protoss base (10) then send a unit down a narrow corridor to the relic (11).

FEND OFF THE ARTIFACT GUARDIANS.

Be sure your strike force is strong (8-10 Marauders plus some Marines and support units) for the final push to the alien artifact (3), because a nasty surprise awaits you. At first glance, the Protoss final line of defense seems light. Two Sentries spew out Force Fields to block the passage (9) while two Stalkers open fire, but if your strike force is strong you overcome this easily. Move any unit into the glowing green beacon on the ground.

However, just when the artifact seems within reach, a strange thing happens. Stone barriers suddenly rise from the ground, blocking access to the artifact. The towering statues that surround the artifact come to life, turning into massive Stone Zealots! You need a lot of firepower to bring them down. Concentrate fire on each target, one at a time.

When the final Stone Zealot falls, Swann sends in a dropship to pick up the artifact. Watch the finale as the frustrated Zerg reach the platform too late … and Raynor has an exchange with the Queen of Blades herself.

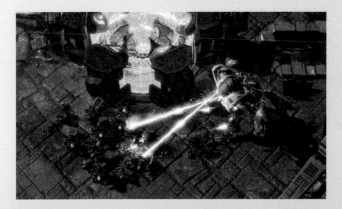

VICTORY!

Successful completion of "Smash and Grab" triggers the cinematic, "The Queen of Blades." Tychus views some database footage on the fearsome Zerg queen and learns some of her troubling background from Horner.

INTERLUDE: *HYPERION*

Your victory also opens the Cantina (if it isn't already open), the social center of the ship. Drop in to chat with Tychus and/or Tosh, watch the latest news on the TV, and meet with Mr. Hill to check out his mercenaries for hire.

If you've completed a total of five missions at this point, you can visit the Lab where you can access, review and choose science upgrades. The excitable Stetmann explains that he needs samples from your planet-side missions in order to complete research projects that can make big improvements to your weapon systems and tactics. If you've already completed "The Evacuation" and but not all of the Dr. Ariel Hanson missions yet, you can chat with her in the Lab as well.

When you're ready for a new mission, return to the Bridge and click on the Star Map to bring up your mission options.

MISSION BRANCH!

You can't move on to the next Tychus Findlay mission, "The Dig," until you've completed a total of eight missions. So you'll most likely have to move on to another mission strand for a while.

At this point you've completed a minimum of four missions, so you can attempt "The Devil's Playground" for Gabriel Tosh. New unit available: Reaper.

Completing a minimum of six missions unlocks the first mission for the *Hyperion*'s intrepid captain, Matt Horner. Now you can visit the ex-Confederacy capital planet of Tarsonis for "The Great Train Robbery." New unit available: Diamondback.

THE DIG

MISSION OVERVIEW

Rumor has it that Mengsk believes alien technology can destroy the Zerg, which explains why his Dominion troops so vigorously seek the alien artifacts. Perhaps this also explains why the Queen of Blades is so interested in the artifacts as well. Your job on Xil is to take control of a massive Drakken Laser Drill, and then use it to burn into an ancient vault that holds another piece of the puzzle. Unfortunately, a rabid sect of Protoss called the Tal'darim Guardians vigorously defends the mysteries of the ruins.

PREREQUISITES

Complete "Smash and Grab" and at least seven other missions.

OBJECTIVES

MAIN

- Recover the Drakken Laser Drill.
- Destroy the Xel'Naga Temple door.
- The Drakken drill must survive.

BONUS

- Find 3 Protoss Relics (+3 Protoss Research)

CREDIT REWARD

120,000

ACHIEVEMENTS

ACHIEVEMENT		PTS	REQUIREMENTS
	The Dig	10	Complete all mission objectives
	Drill Hard	10	Kill 20 enemy units with the laser drill
	Yippee-ki-yay...	10	Destroy all the Protoss structures in the mission on Hard difficulty

LOCATION: XIL

Xil is a dead world, scoured of life long ago. Excavated ruins suggest that the planet's indigenous alien culture was wiped out virtually overnight.

TYCHUS FINDLAY'S BRIEFING

Moebius wants us to go after another artifact on some dead world called Xil. Apparently they sent in a specialist team but they lost contact with 'em two days ago. Their bad luck, I guess. Figure we'll get hazard pay for this one.

MISSION

Scan our mission map for a quick overview of the situation. Raynor drops your small strike team into a canyon (1) west of the base (2) abandoned by the Moebius expedition. The Drakken Laser Drill (3) sits nearby. Two huge Tal'darim Protoss bases (10, 11) sprawl across the top of the map on either side of the massive Xel'Naga Temple (4) where the artifact you seek has been entombed. Your first task is to seize the base and commandeer the laser drill. Then you must fight off waves of powerful Protoss attackers as you use the drill to slowly crack open the Xel'Naga Temple.

SEIZE THE ABANDONED BASE.

You start with a few Marines and a Marauder (1). Head south down the canyon and eliminate the Protoss Zealots and Stalker. The Tal'darim consider this to be sacred ground, and regard you as "terran thieves." Don't worry if your squad loses members in this first skirmish; help is coming. Continue south until you trigger the arrival of Swann's gleaming new Siege Tanks.

NEW TECHNOLOGY

SIEGE TANK

Heavy tank. Transforms into long-range artillery in Siege Mode.

NEW UPGRADES AVAILABLE AFTER MISSION

- Maelstrom Rounds: Siege Tank do +40 damage to primary target. (Splash damage remains the same.).
- Shaped Blast: Siege Tank Shock Cannon does 75 percent less damage to friendly units.

RESEARCH OPPORTUNITIES

- +3 Protoss Research

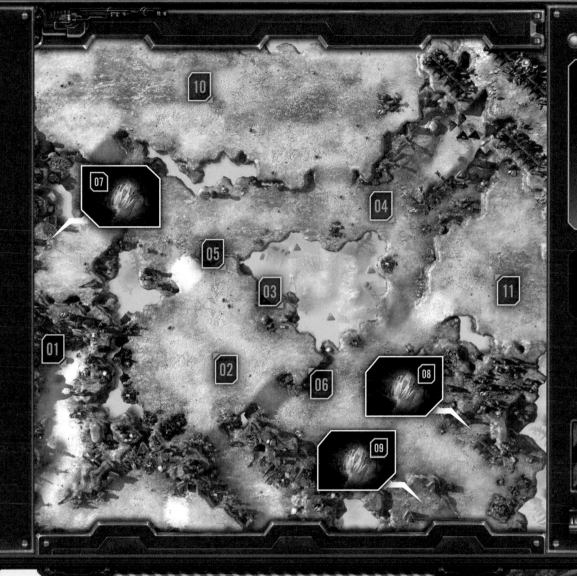

PRIMARY

1. Start

2. Base

3. Drakken Laser Drill

4. Xel'Naga Temple

5-6. Put Siege Tanks here

10-11. Protoss bases

SECONDARY

7-9. Protoss Relics (inside Xel'Naga Shrines)

After your tanks automatically go into Siege Mode and wipe out the battery of Photon Cannons, select them and switch into Tank Mode so they're mobile. Push them forward until Raynor reports. Follow his order; move the tanks into the highlighted spot on the high ground and put them back into immobile Siege Mode. They will bombard the Protoss Stalkers below, clearing your way to the abandoned Moebius base (2).

Once your troops climb the ramp into the base, Raynor's adjutant decrypts its security overrides and transfers control of its structures to you. The nearby Drakken Laser Drill automatically starts cutting into the Xel'Naga Temple door. As Tychus says, "One hundred and seventy four gigawatts, the power of the sun at your fingertips." But the Temple's access portal is formidable with 100,000 hit points. It takes quite a while to burn through its barriers, and the Protoss won't sit around waiting for you to finish.

⊖ SET UP YOUR PERIMETER DEFENSE.

Horner soon reports that the Tal'darim are mobilizing against you, and Raynor helpfully points out the chokepoints and high ground on the base perimeter. Now quickly do the following:

- Get your SCVs harvesting and start building more Siege Tanks at your Factory.
- Build a Bunker at the top of each main access ramp and move one Siege Tank to each of the overlook locations (5, 6). Put the tanks in Siege Mode to increase their power and range.
- Garrison your Bunkers and rush additional tanks to the chokepoints as soon as they roll off the Factory floor.

As you do all this, Horner manages to access part of the Moebius expedition's sensor net. This makes more of the map visible, including the approach routes from the Protoss bases. As the Tal'darim begin sending strike teams to hit your base, you can see them coming. This gives you an important tactical advantage.

USE THE DRILL OFFENSIVELY.

Here's why: The Drakken Laser Drill is a deadly marvel of technology. When the first Protoss Archons appear (with a dire warning), Horner announces that you can select the laser drill and use it to hit targets. Its range is essentially unlimited in this mission; you can hit any target you can see on the map. Of course, you can't shoot things you *cannot* see, so the additional visibility provided by the Moebius sensors lets you use the Drakken laser to destroy powerful Protoss units long before they reach your base.

In particular, use the drill to eviscerate Archons and the big Colossus walkers that lumber to the attack. You can "fire and forget" if you want, because whenever the big laser finishes off a target, it automatically returns its attention to the Xel'Naga Temple door.

DRILL TARGETS FLASH RED

Priority targets like Archons and Colossi flash red on your mini-map. Nail them with your Drakken Laser Drill! Assign the drill its own hot-key so you have quick access to its awesome power. You can also queue multiple targets by holding down the Shift key as you select them; the drill will move from target to target automatically.

PROTECT THAT DRILL!

Consider dropping in an extra Missile Turret on either side of the Drakken drill. These can engage the waves of Protoss Scouts and Prisms that start to attack, typically flying in across the open pit in the middle of the map. Meanwhile, keep cranking out Siege Tanks and parking them on the high ground to bombard the approaching Protoss columns. Add another Marine-filled Bunker atop each approach ramp too.

THE FINGER OF GOD

The Drakken Laser Drill can hit anything on the map and destroy it quickly, but only if you can see the target through the fog of war. Here's a crazy tip courtesy of the Blizzard team. To reveal Protoss base targets for extended periods of time, construct a Barracks or Factory or even a second Command Center, levitate it (it's loaded with hit points!) and fly it into an enemy base. Then use the laser drill to wipe the newly visible Protoss units and structures off the map! Be sure to focus the laser first on things that can target your flying building.

BONUS: RETRIEVE THE PROTOSS RELICS FROM THE XEL'NAGA SHRINES.

Three ancient shrines (7, 8, 9) hold Protoss Relics that earn you Research points. But you can't access the relics until you blast open the shrine doors. Unfortunately the shrines cannot be blasted away with conventional weapons, only the immense power of the Drakken Laser Drill can melt through their armored exteriors. (The shrine must be within the sight radius of one of your units before the drill can target it, however.) Once the shrine is destroyed, send in any unit to nab the relic.

HOLD ON UNTIL THE TEMPLE IS BREACHED.

Fight off the Protoss waves, nailing only Archons and Colossi with your laser drill, until the Xel'Naga Temple's inner sanctum is finally breached. Your troops pick up the artifact, ignoring the threats of the Tal'darim Executor, and the mission is complete.

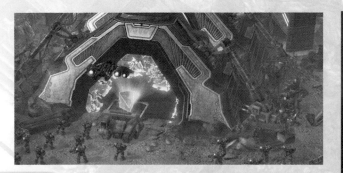

INTERLUDE: *HYPERION*

Your success on Xil triggers a scene back aboard the Hyperion. In a deserted corridor of the ship, Raynor runs into an old ally. Raynor places the Ihan Crystal he receives on a podium in the ship's Lab where it becomes your portal to a new strand of four missions.

You control Zeratul in those missions, and although they are not part of the Campaign's central story line, they do reveal some important information. We suggest you play through the Zeratul mission strand before you move on to the next Tychus mission, "The Moebius Factor."

Before you do anything else, though, make the usual rounds of the *Hyperion*. Make upgrades and check research progress, hire new mercenaries if you can afford it, and talk to everyone for advice and perspective.

MISSION BRANCH!

You can't advance to the next Tychus Findlay mission, "The Moebius Factor," until you've completed a total of eleven missions. So you may find it necessary to explore another mission strand for a while.

Here you can use the Ihan Crystal in the Lab to access the first mission in the Zeratul strand, "Whispers of Doom."

THE MOEBIUS FACTOR

MISSION OVERVIEW

The Queen of Blades has arrived on Tyrador! Dr. Narud of the Moebius Foundation tells Raynor he's ready to evacuate the planet, but none of the teams sent to purge the Foundation data cores have reported back. You task is to destroy these cores before the Queen of Blades finds them; they reveal the coordinates of the remaining artifacts. Narud insists the fate of the entire Sector hangs in the balance.

PREREQUISITES

Complete "The Dig" and at least ten other missions.

OBJECTIVES

MAIN

- Destroy the 3 data cores.
- Kerrigan must not access any data core.

BONUS

- Kill the Brutalisk (+3 Zerg Research).

CREDIT REWARD

150,000

ACHIEVEMENTS

ACHIEVEMENT		PTS	REQUIREMENTS
	Moebius Factor	10	Complete all mission objectives
	Alive Inside!	10	Locate all Moebius Survivors
	Hard Core	10	Complete the mission before Kerrigan destroys 6 Abandoned Buildings on Hard difficulty.

LOCATION: TYRADOR VIII

One of the first "planned" worlds of the old Confederacy, Tyrador is famous for its centers of higher learning, its orderly streets, and its sanitary parks.

TYCHUS FINDLAY'S BRIEFING

Seems your Queen of Blades figured out who's been payin' us to snatch up all them artifacts. Moebius' head honcho Dr. Narud claims the Zerg are attacking his main Research Campus on Tyrador. He can't evacuate his people until all their artifact research is safe.

MISSION

This is an "island-hopping map": that is, your ground troops can reach other parts of the map only via airlift. It also challenges you to build a well-defended base plus an expedition force at the same time that you're racing the Queen of Blades to a set of three data cores. Vikings and Siege Tanks, as well as your new flying Medivac transport, will be valuable units in this mission.

SECURE YOUR BASE.

Yes, the Queen of Blades arrives shortly after the mission opens and begins her hunt for the first Foundation data core. But you've got plenty of time to get your base in order first. Aside from the three actual data cores, Moebius has nine *false* data cores scattered around the map. These draw Kerrigan's attention for minutes at a time, giving you space to operate. Check the countdown timer labeled "Kerrigan Data Access" in the upper right corner to see how long you have to destroy the data core highlighted in green on your mini-map.

NEW TECHNOLOGY

MEDIVAC

Air transport. Heals nearby units.

LEGEND

PRIMARY

1. Start
2. First data core
3. Helipad (Moebius squad)
4. Helipad (Moebius squad)
5. Second data core
7. Landing zone
8. Third data core
9. Helipad (Moebius squad)
10. Helipad (Moebius squad)

SECONDARY

6. Brutalisk

NEW UPGRADES AVAILABLE

- Advanced Healing AI: Medivacs can heal two targets at once.
- Rapid Deployment Loadout: Medivacs deploy cargo almost instantly.

RESEARCH OPPORTUNITIES

- +3 Zerg Research

THE TYCHUS FINDLAY MISSIONS

GAINING MOEBIUS ALLIES

Moebius Security forces are trapped in several locations (marked as yellow icons on the mini-map) around the city. When you move any of your units next to one of these isolated squads, the Moebius boys happily join Raynor's Raiders, giving you control of their units.

The entire squad opens fire on the data core. You have until the Kerrigan timer hits zero to destroy the structure. After the core explodes, quickly load your troops into the Medivac and fly them back to your base to escape Kerrigan's fury. Spore Crawlers are particularly lethal to Medivacs, so be careful when transporting troops across the map. If a Medivac gets shot down you lose all troops aboard too.

Avoid the Queen's Wrath

Kerrigan, the Queen of Blades, is invincible and vastly powerful in this mission. Do not try to tangle with her!

BEAT KERRIGAN TO THE SECOND DATE CORE.

Load up your initial Medivacs with a "demolition team" including at least one Siege Tank, a couple of Goliaths, and some Marines and Firebats. Be sure to add 2-3 SCVs for repair too. Get 4-5 Vikings and two empty Medivacs ready too; group them with the two loaded Medivacs and fly due west to the helipad (3) where more Moebius Security units wait to be liberated.

Quickly install a fully garrisoned Bunker at the top of the lone entrance ramp leading up to your base. Start an Engineering Bay (for Missile Turrets) and add a Tech Lab to your Factory (for Siege Tanks). The area below the ramp is a creep-filled pit, and Zerg raiders make regular runs at your base. These can include Mutalisks and vicious Brood Lords, so get a couple of Vikings and a Missile Turret near your Bunker. Put a turret up on the northwest perimeter of the base too.

Fly to the lower left corner of the helipad; your flyers want to avoid the Spore Crawler rooted in the ground just beyond the upper right corner. Drop just one unit to "liberate" the Moebius squad then scoop them up into the empty Medivac.

Be ready for Nydus Worms that occasionally pop up near the bottom of the ramp. When the Tech Lab is done, roll a Siege Tank off the Factory floor, then park it in Siege Mode at the top of the ramp next to the Bunker; it can pound any worm below into pulp. Finally, add a couple of Firebats or Hellions to round out your base defense.

MERC HEAVIES

If you have a Merc Compound with the Hel's Angels (3 Vikings) and the Siege Breakers (2 Siege Tanks) available, buy both mercenary groups as soon as you can afford them!

Now send your flotilla northwest to the next helipad (4) where another stranded Moebius squad waits for help. Drop all troops here, put your Vikings on the ground, and start hammering through the Zerg toward the data core (5). When you reach it, destroy it. Two down, one to go.

BEAT KERRIGAN TO THE FIRST DATA CORE.

Kerrigan appears on the mini-map as a pulsing death's-head icon, and her path to the first data core (2) is marked in red arrows. Load a Siege Tank onto one of your Medivacs then fly southwest to the helipad, located just behind the data core structure. Your arrival liberates the Moebius security squad there (Marines and a Goliath). Drop your tank onto the helipad.

CREATE A SAFE PATH TO THE THIRD DATA CORE.

The last data core (8) is on an island packed with Spore Crawler batteries, but here's a good route in. Reload the Medivacs, raise the Vikings, and fly everyone southwest a bit (see our map). Now fly your Vikings only, sending them west to the waterfront (7). They fly right into a spitting Spore Crawler, so immediately drop your Vikings to the ground and let them slice it up. Now you've created a safe landing zone for your Medivac transports. The designated path is only safe if you killed the Brutalisk.

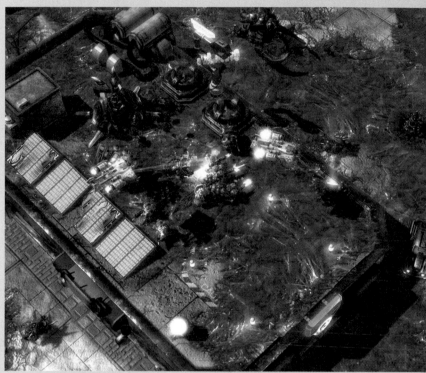

BEEF UP

Don't ignore your base while your demolition team hits the data cores. Keep pumping out Siege Tanks, Vikings and a couple more Medivacs so you have backups ready to bolster your field team.

BONUS: KILL THE BRUTALISK

Reload all troops onto Medivacs and make the short flight to the raised platform behind the monstrous Brutalisk. Drop all troops, lower your Vikings, and unload all guns on the beast. You will take damage, most likely, but your Medivac and SCV repairs help minimize losses.

Fly in the Medivacs and dump your full load of troops on the ground at (7). Fight your way northwest to the data core. The Zerg will throw plenty of aggression your way; Nydus Worms burst forth, and flyers move to the attack. But try to keep your Siege Tanks focused on the data core structure. When its health bar gets low, focus every gun you have on the data core. The moment it explodes you win the mission, so don't worry about losing a few units by ignoring the Zerg.

INTERLUDE: HYPERION

Your success on Tryador triggers a pair of cinematic sequences. You end up in the Cantina.

SUPERNOVA

MISSION OVERVIEW

This can be a frightening mission. You start out wedged between an all consuming wall of fire sweeping across the map from the west and several encampments of a huge Protoss Tal'darim expeditionary force to the east. The firestorm serves as a mission timer. The artifact you seek for the Moebius Foundation is shielded in a heavily defended vault on the far eastern edge of the map. Your new Banshee tactical strike craft makes things a bit easier, however.

PREREQUISITES

Complete "The Moebius Factor" and at least 13 other missions.

OBJECTIVES

MAIN

- Clear the landing zone.
- Destroy the artifact vault.

BONUS

- Find 4 Protoss Relics (+4 Protoss Research).

CREDIT REWARD

120,000

ACHIEVEMENTS

ACHIEVEMENT		PTS	REQUIREMENTS
	Supernova	10	Complete all mission objectives
	Cool Running	10	Complete the mission without losing a unit to the flame wall
	Shock N' Awe	10	Complete the mission with 75 cloaked kills on Hard difficulty

LOCATION: TYPHON XI

This remote world is part of an extremely old system, as indicated by its increasingly unstable sun. This, combined with sparse mineral deposits, has always made Typhon a bad candidate for colonization. Nonetheless, a significant Tal'darim expeditionary force is present.

TYCHUS FINDLAY'S BRIEFING

Moebius have got themselves set up again since the Zerg chased 'em out of their old place. They say they've worked out a way to find another artifact: a lovely little place called Typhon.

MISSION

This is a "mobile base" mission. Your task is to relocate your base buildings eastward several times to stay ahead of the relentless supernova firestorm. The trick is to be on the ground long enough to mine minerals and gas so you can keep producing troops. The Protoss are encamped at each good base location, so you must drive them out before you can fly in your buildings.

Overall, the key to success is to be smart about your expenditures. Other than cheap, quick Tech Labs and Refineries over new gas geysers, you shouldn't spend on structures you cannot move or salvage. Also note that as you move east, you can snag four Protoss Relics (4, 5, 6, 10) for Research points.

SECURE THE FIRST LANDING ZONE.

You start with a squadron of Banshees (1). A full wing of 8-10 Banshee bombers is devastating against ground targets, but you must keep them cloaked in combat or anti-air guns will chew them up. Cloak and fight your way up to the clearing (2) and destroy the nearest Photon Cannon, which detects your Banshees. Then knock out the Pylon to cut power to the second cannon, thus hiding the Banshees from enemy sight again.

NEW TECHNOLOGY

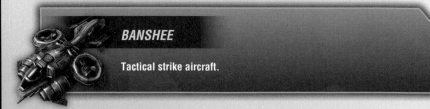

BANSHEE

Tactical strike aircraft.

NEW UPGRADES AVAILABLE AFTER MISSION

- Shockwave Missile Battery: Banshee attack fires multiple missile bursts in a straight line.
- Cross-Spectrum Dampeners: Banshees can remain cloaked for twice as long.

RESEARCH OPPORTUNITIES

- +4 Protoss Research

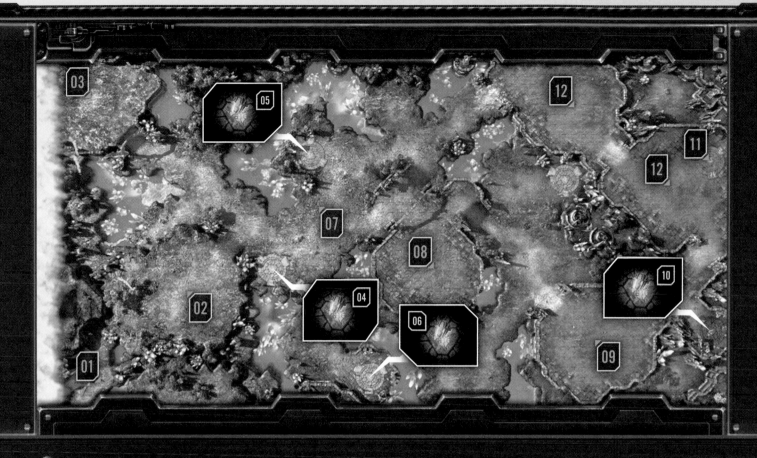

LEGEND

PRIMARY

1. Start
2. Your base
3. Protoss base NW

7. Interim move
8-9. Large Protoss bases
11. Artifact Vault

12. Large Protoss base

SECONDARY

4-6, 10. Protoss Relics

CLOAK/DECLOAK

Cloak Banshees during combat and immediately decloak them once the fighting stops to conserve energy. If detector units (Photon Cannons in this mission) are present but you want your Banshees to fight anyway, leave them decloaked to save energy until the detector is destroyed, then immediately cloak.

BUILD A BANSHEE STRIKE FORCE.

With the landing zone secured (2), Raynor drops in your base. You start with a Command Center, Barracks, Starport (with Tech Lab attached), Factory, and a pair of Refineries. Other than adding Tech Labs and Refineries in later locations, you don't have to build any other structures in this mission. With a fixed supply cap of 200, you don't even need Supply Depots!

Start resource gathering: the mineral/gas count is low, and time is short. Add more SCVs to suck up as much income as possible here. Build one Bunker in the northeast gap leading into the base and put your existing Marines inside. Add a Medic. Then start cranking out new Banshees from your Starport. Add a Medivac and a couple of Vikings to the queue as well. But keep your main spending focused on Banshees.

BONUS: RETRIEVE THREE PROTOSS RELICS.

Send your Banshees followed by a couple of SCVs (for repairs) through the base exit and just around the corner to the right to get the Protoss Relic at (4). No detection units exist here, so keep your SCVs well back, cloak the Banshees, wipe out the few relic guards, then decloak and send in an SCV to scoop up the relic.

Now send your Banshees south to get the Protoss Relic at (6). Again, no detector units are deployed here, so when the Banshee squadron engages the first defender, cloak up and sling the pain. Wipe out all Tal'darim right up to the relic without getting a shot fired in return. Then proceed to nab the relic.

FIRE STARTER

Stay away from the Protoss base in the northwest (3)! It's only real purpose is to show you how the supernova can devastate a base.

Finally, send this same group northeast to nab the relic at (5) too. Keep the Banshees well out front and cloaked to wipe out the Protoss squad (7) on the path. Decloak and continue up to the relic platform guarded by Photon Cannons. They detect your Banshees, so just stay decloaked and concentrate fire on the Pylon powering the cannons. When that goes down, send in an SCV again to nab the relic.

MAKE A MOVE EAST.

By now the firestorm is approaching your base (2). Unload your Bunker, salvage it, and send all troops forward to secure an interim point (7). Lift off your Factory, Starport, and Barracks and fly them over to the meager mineral field next to where you got the Protoss Relic at (6).

Load your SCVs into the Command Center, fly it to (6) as well, then immediately unload and start harvesting the new field. Add a Tech Lab to your Starport and build more Banshees. Put a Factory on the lone Vespene geyser and start collecting more gas.

SALVAGE YOUR BUNKERS

Bunkers can be salvaged for 100 percent of their mineral value, so don't let the flames consume them. Salvaging a Bunker takes five seconds though: don't wait too late!

ELIMINATE THE CENTRAL PROTOSS BASE.

Wait until you have 7-8 Banshees with full energy. Then send them east into the central Protoss base (8). Cloak as you enter the base and target the two Pylons to cut power to the Photon Cannons. (Or you can just hit the Photon Cannons directly.) A Banshee squadron this big can take out targets quickly. Once the Protoss detectors are disabled, your Banshees can wreak holy havoc on the other ground units. Be sure to target Stalkers first; they're the only anti-air threat remaining. Keep an eye on Banshee cloak energy and pull back any units on the verge of decloaking.

Once the area is cleared of Protoss, fly in your buildings from (6) and fire up production again. Build a Bunker at the north entrance and fill it with Marines to fend off any Protoss raids. Start building more Banshees: you'll need them for the next Protoss base. Add a couple more Vikings too.

BE QUICK, NOT HASTY

This mission is set up such that the faster you move, the faster the fire wall moves, so rushing your expansion too fast into the middle point (8) doesn't actually buy you much time. If you hurry into a big Protoss bases with too small a strike force the defenses will cripple you.

ELIMINATE THE SOUTHEAST PROTOSS BASE.

Send your Banshee wing (at least 10 units) with Viking support plus a few SCVs southeast toward the next Protoss base (9). Watch for two powerful Archons en route; be sure to cloak before you destroy them, then decloak afterwards to save energy. When you reach the base entrance, leave your SCVs safely back. Fly your Banshees/ Vikings around the perimeter of the base targeting Photon Cannons. (The base power sources are all floating Warp Prisms; these are air units, so your Banshees can't hit them, but your Vikings can.) The Vikings can fend off the enemy Scouts in the area too. Fly badly damaged craft back to your SCVs for repairs. The defense features Immortals and Stalkers on the ground, Scouts in the air. Whenever your Banshee cloaking starts to wane, fly back to the SCVs for repair and recharge.

BONUS: RETRIEVE THE PROTOSS RELIC IN THE SOUTHEAST.

Send your replenished Banshees east from the new base and veer southeast to find the fourth artifact (10) in a courtyard with light defense.

Once each detector cannon is eliminated, target the anti-air Stalkers then bring in your Vikings to hit the Scouts and Warp Prisms. Once all defenders are destroyed, demolish the Protoss buildings and bring over your own base. Remember to bring down your Marines and salvage their Bunker.

MAKE THE FINAL PUSH TO THE ARTIFACT VAULT.

The Protoss base (11) guarding the Artifact vault has a full mix of tough units: Archons, High Templars, a few Stalkers, some Phoenix and Scout fighters, and plenty of Photon Cannons. But you don't have to beat them all to win; you just need to destroy the Artifact vault. Build up a mass of 10-12 Banshees and send them up toward the southernmost perimeter of the Protoss base. Follow with a squad of SCVs plus all your other troops; park them at the bottom of the ramp leading up to the base.

Send the decloaked Banshees to take out the two Photon Cannons at the southern end of the base. Alternately, you can park a Siege Tank in Siege Mode or two on the ramp and let it bombard the Photon Cannons. The moment the second cannon explodes, immediately cloak (the Banshees are undetected now) and start wreaking havoc on the surrounding ground troops. Hammer your way east to one more Photon Cannon sitting just south of the vault.

By now your cloak energy is almost expended, so destroy the cannon and pull your Banshees back to your SCVs for recharge and repair. If any Protoss troops follow you down, send your ground troops forward to meet them. When your Banshees are ready, send them back cloaked to hit the vault. A full wing of 10-12 Banshees can destroy the target quickly.

North Base

Another big Protoss base sits to the northwest (13) of the vault area. Stay away from it! It's not necessary that you engage it.

INTERLUDE: *HYPERION*

Mission success triggers the spectacular cinematic, "Heir Apparent." Raynor meets the mastermind behind the Moebius Foundation and learns the significance of the alien artifacts.

Check out every area of the ship and talk to everyone to get the full story. In particular, visit the Armory to see another cinematic, "Trouble." Talk to Swann afterward to get clarification.

WHISPERS OF DOOM

MISSION OVERVIEW

The first time you use Zeratul's Ihan Crystal in the Hyperion's Lab, you trigger a spectacular memory: his facedown with the Queen of Blades in a cinematic entitled "Old Rivals." Zeratul tells you of his search for an ancient prophecy that may be a harbinger of doom for the entire known universe. The prophecy is said to be on the planet Ulaan and divided into three fragments, each kept at a separate Xel'Naga shrine.

PREREQUISITES

Use the Ihan Crystal after completing "The Dig."

OBJECTIVES

MAIN

- Guide Zeratul to all 3 Xel'Naga shrines on Ulaan (+3 Protoss Research).
- Zeratul must survive.

BONUS

- Destroy all 3 Zerg Hatcheries (+3 Zerg Research).

CREDIT REWARD

None

ACHIEVEMENTS

ACHIEVEMENT		PTS	REQUIREMENTS
	Whispers of Doom	10	Complete all mission objectives
	Stalker Delight	10	Complete the mission with 3 or more Stalkers
	Merely a Flesh Wound	10	Complete the mission on Hard difficulty without suffering Health Damage to Zeratul

LOCATION: ULAAN

Legends hint that Ulaan is the resting place of tablets inscribed with a prophecy that reveals the will of the ageless Xel'Naga. No living creature has touched its surface for millions of years … until now.

ZERATUL'S BRIEFING

Raynor! The hounds of the void are closing in! I impart my memory, my very essence, into this Ihan Crystal, so that you will see what I have seen, and that the future may yet have hope.

MISSION

This mission features small group tactics and introduces you to some basic Protoss units. Your goal is to guide Zeratul along a winding path to three separate Xel'Naga shrines, then escape to his Void Seeker. Zerg infest the area; you're only given a few units to work with, so you can't smash through with brute force. You must be frugal and clever.

NEW TECHNOLOGY

PROTOSS STALKER

This ranged support unit can attack both ground and air units. It is strong against flying Mutalisks but vulnerable to Zergling rushes.

RESEARCH OPPORTUNITIES

- +3 Protoss Research
- +3 Zerg Research

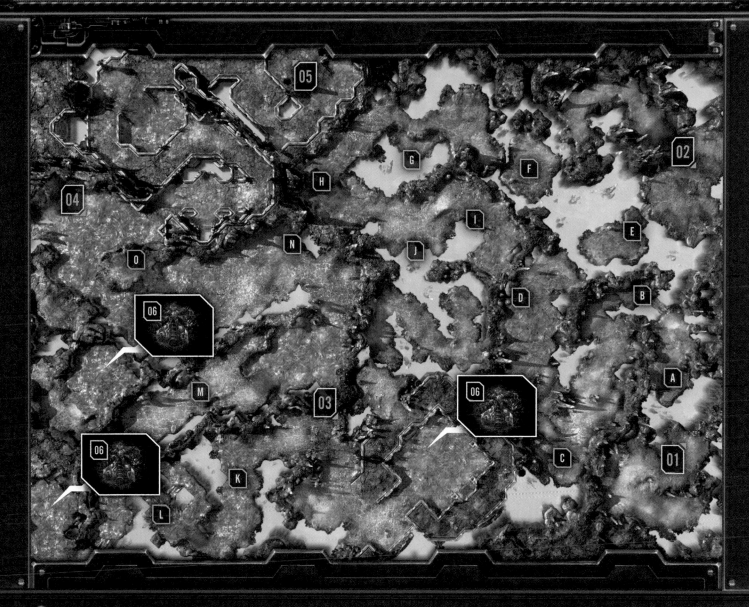

LEGEND

PRIMARY

1. Start
2. Xel'Naga Shrine
3. Xel'Naga Shrine
4. Xel'Naga Shrine
5. Ship (Finish)

SECONDARY

6. Zerg Hatchery

FOLLOW THE PATH TO THE FIRST XEL'NAGA SHRINE.

You start on a rock ramp (1) with only Zeratul. The Dark Templar is permanently cloaked, so he can operate with impunity as long as no Zerg detection unit (Overseer or Spore Crawler) is nearby. Follow the path as it veers up into a patch of creep and wipe out the Zerg. When you reach the chasm (A), you can use Zeratul's Blink ability to "phase through the shadows" (i.e., teleport) to the other side. Just move Zeratul into the first marker, select Blink, and click on the marker across the chasm.

Continue up the path to the collapsing bridge (B) and Blink across that chasm. Proceed to the pile of rocks (labeled "Destructible Rocks") and either bash through or Blink past them. Keep following the path until Zeratul automatically stops and notes the Spore Crawler (C) ahead. Use Zeratul's Void Prison power on the Crawler to stun it and suppress its detection capability. It stays stunned long enough that you can rush up and kill it before it recovers.

DETECTION TIP

When Zeratul is selected, you can see the detection radius of Zerg Spore Crawlers and Overseers marked as a circle of purple arrows. This telltale indicator disappears if you select units other than Zeratul, however, so be careful.

Proceed up the path until you reach the edge of the next patch of creep. Another Spore Crawler (D) sits up ahead, and a massive Ultralisk patrols up and down the path. Wait until the big Zerg turns from Zeratul and marches away, then quickly cast Void Prison on the Spore Crawler. Hurry to kill the Zerg detector before it recovers.

Continue to the edge of the next creep patch. You see another detection radius: another Spore Crawler (E). But this one is across a chasm! Cast Void Prison on it, immediately Blink across the chasm, and slay the abomination quickly.

Walk to the next chasm where an Overseer patrols side to side with a nasty swarm of Hydralisks beneath it. Zeratul cannot attack a flying unit, but his special ability can stun it. Move Zeratul to the edge of the chasm and nail the Overseer with Void Prison. Immediately Blink across the chasm and rush north to the glowing beacon (2) at the Xel'Naga shrine. Zeratul recovers the first fragment of the prophecy and a nearby gate opens.

FOLLOW THE PATH TO THE SECOND XEL'NAGA SHRINE.

Head through the gate and follow the path to the next chasm (F). When you Blink across, it appears to be a trap; an Overseer with a swarm of flyers including deadly Mutalisks descends on Zeratul. But suddenly a squadron of Protoss Stalkers warps onto the rock platform! Stalkers are lethal against enemy flyers, and these take down the Zerg menace quickly and chase off the Overseer.

THE PROTOSS SHIELD

Protoss units have shields that absorb damage and slowly regenerate when not in combat.

Stalkers can Blink too, so group the whole squad with Zeratul and teleport everyone west across the gap; you can Blink multiple units at once. Follow the path until the Overseer approaches then use your Stalkers to gun it from the sky, then pull them back out of the range of the pack of Hydralisks patrolling a platform just below (G). The Hydralisks are close enough to inflict ranged damage on your Stalkers if you try to pass on the high ground. Blink the cloaked Zeratul down to attack them. The Hydralisks burrow to escape. Now you can move your whole squad safely past.

The next encounter is tricky. See the edge of the detection radius up ahead? There's a Spore Crawler (H) just around the next bend in the path. Carefully direct Zeratul to wipe out the Spine Crawler just outside the detection radius, then pull Zeratul back. Move your Stalkers forward to engage and destroy the flapping Mutalisks. Now you can push your combined group forward to blast the Spore Crawler.

STALKER RESTOCK

Any Stalker lost during the mission is replaced by another warping in as you move forward from hazard to hazard.

Continue until Zeratul comments on the dangerous Brood Lords (I) up ahead. An Overseer patrols up and back over a chasm, so Zeratul can be exposed. The key is to engage only one Brood Lord at a time. Wait until a Brood Lord is close enough so Zeratul can cast Void Prison to freeze it (stopping it from spitting Broodlings) while the Stalkers blast it to pieces. Then repeat on the second Brood Lord.

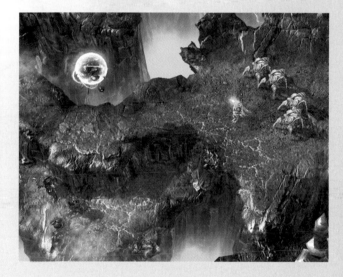

You may lose a Stalker or two to this exchange. But after the battle, just follow the path and Blink across the next chasm: there, new Stalkers warp in to replace any lost ones so you still have a total of four.

Continue along the path until Zeratul warns of an aerial assault! As your Stalkers take on the Zerg flyers (J), make sure Zeratul is ready to cast Void Prison on the Overseer that floats in during the ambush. This keeps Zeratul safely cloaked as he engages the ground Zerg that attack. When the battle ends, proceed around the bend and Blink across the gap.

The next Xel'Naga shrine (3) is just ahead, but an Overseer hovers over the path. Gun it down with your Stalkers and then Blink down the ramp past from the striking Spine Crawler in the pit to the right. Now the cloaked Zeratul can move unhindered to the glowing beacon and find the second fragment of the prophecy.

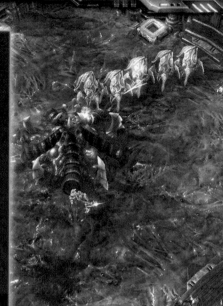

⟶ BONUS: DESTROY THE FIRST HATCHERY.

A large Zerg Hatchery (6) sits in the nearby pit surrounded by Spine Crawlers. In the previous step, you shot down one of two Overseers patrolling back and forth over the pit. Gather your Stalkers and Zeratul near the pit entrance. When the second Overseer approaches, wait until it stops then nail it with Void Prison. Immediately destroy it with your Stalkers. Then pull the Stalkers back and let Zeratul clean out the pit alone.

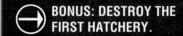

Hatchery Swarm

Keep your Stalkers well away from the Hatchery. When it finally collapses, a swarm of nasty Broodlings is released. They can't detect Zeratul so they'll head straight for the Stalkers.

FOLLOW THE PATH TOWARD THE THIRD XEL'NAGA SHRINE.

Go through the newly opened gate to the edge of the creep. An Overseer patrols back and forth, and further down the path some Mutalisks and Spine Crawlers (K) block the way. Wait until the Overseer gets closest then freeze it with Void Prison and destroy it. Pull your Stalkers back and send Zeratul ahead to nail the Spine Crawlers. Then watch the Mutalisks and wait until one comes forward alone. Have Zeratul freeze it and then blast it with Stalkers. Repeat until you've eliminated all Mutalisks.

Next comes a Baneling challenge. After the path curves northeast up a ramp, a bridge collapses ahead. Rush your Stalkers up the leftmost path (L) so they have the most possible time to fire on the pack of Banelings that rush single-file down the rightmost path. It might require you to Blink the Stalkers across the gap to finish off the Banelings. Note that although Zeratul is invisible to the Banelings, the creatures can splash acid that damages him when they explode, so keep him back.

BONUS: DESTROY THE SECOND HATCHERY.

Here the path splits. Go left (south) to the collapsing chasm and Blink across. This puts you at the edge of another Hatchery pit (6). Stop at the edge of the creep, then move one unit a bit forward. A huge burrowed Ultralisk suddenly pops up to attack! Incapacitate it immediately with Zeratul's Void Prison then take it out with your Stalkers. Keep Zeratul well back from the Spine Crawler next to the Hatchery until you can use Void Prison on that too. Kill it then send Zeratul to hack up the Hatchery. As he does this, Blink your Stalkers back across the chasm so they're safe from the Broodlings released when the Hatchery explodes.

KILL THE UPROOTED CRAWLERS.

Follow the path north. A small batch of Zerglings and Hydralisks pop out of the ground; kill them. Then you find a group of Spine Crawlers (M) caught defenseless on normal ground. (Spine Crawlers can't take root and fight unless they're on creep.) Nail as many as possible before they can scurry into the creep to the east. When the surviving crawlers take root (under a patrolling Overseer), pull back out of their range. Move Zeratul carefully forward and cast Void Prison on the Overseer at its closest point. Then have Zeratul destroy the remaining Spine Crawlers.

SMASH THROUGH THE ZERG DEFENSES.

Push forward to the rocks and smash them to trigger the arrival of High Templar Karass and a phalanx of Zealots. These troops automatically assault the powerful lines of Zerg blocking the way to the shrine. You can't control them, so just follow them into the fight.

The battle is chaotic and wild. Keep your Stalkers behind the line of Zealots but close enough to provide ranged support. Soon a large pack of Zerglings pops from the ground behind your right flank. Zerglings chew up Stalkers quickly, so immediately run your Stalkers around your Zealots to the south, letting Karass' troops and Zeratul screen off the Zerglings.

Now your Zealots automatically assault the line of Spine/Spore Crawlers blocking the gap (N) to the west. From behind the Zealots, concentrate your Stalker fire on the airborne assault (Mutalisks and especially the Brood Lord) that swoops in over the rooted Zerg. Once the flyers are eliminated, focus Stalker fire on the Spore Crawlers. These are the only Zerg cloak-detecting units in the area, so once you knock them out, Zeratul has free rein.

As your troops fight their way through the gap, several Nydus Worms suddenly appear and start disgorging Zerg units. Take Zeratul's advice and rush your Stalkers up the ramp to the high ground on the right (O). On the ridge they're safe from Zerg melee attacks and can direct a withering fire down on the worms.

If the Spore Crawlers are gone, rush Zeratul forward to attack the Nydus Worms, too. Use his Void Prison on them when it's available to stop their flow of units. After the worms, you face a last battery of Spine Crawlers plus a big pair of Ultralisks. Keep fighting until all the Zerg are destroyed.

BONUS: DESTROY THE THIRD ZERG HATCHERY.

Before you send Zeratul onto the beacon at the Xel'Naga shrine (4), you have one last Hatchery (6) to eliminate. First, Blink up onto the ridge revealed to the west of the canyon you just fought down. The Hatchery sits across a narrow chasm with a pair of Spore Crawlers providing detection. Blink your Stalkers across the chasm and knock out at least one of the Spore Crawlers as fast as you can. Then Blink Zeratul across, nail the other Spore Crawler with Void Prison, and destroy it. Now Zeratul can eliminate the last Hatchery under cover of cloak.

VISIT THE LAST SHRINE AND RUN!

Get ready! Once you step into the glowing beacon back at the third Xel'Naga shrine and Zeratul gains the last tablet of the prophecy, all hell breaks loose. The Queen of Blades unleashes a mighty horde and you can do nothing but run to your ship (5). Karass gives you another squad of Stalkers and tries to cover your escape, but he doesn't last long. Hurry through the newly opened gate and follow the path. (Note that arrows on the mini-map point the way.)

Do not stop to fend off pursuers or fight any sentries along the route. Just run! Use Blink to get past each of rock piles that block the path. When you reach the last glowing beacon by the ship, Zeratul escapes and you win the mission.

INTERLUDE: *HYPERION*

Afterwards, check out the research panel in the Lab to see if you've got enough points for new upgrades. Talk to Tychus, Horner, and Tosh (if he's still around) for their perspective on things.

A SINISTER TURN

MISSION OVERVIEW

Zeratul arrives on the archive world of Zhakul to consult with the Preservers about the Xel'Naga prophecy he recovered on Ulaan. Only they can transcribe the fragments. But he soon discovers that the holy mystics have been imprisoned by a strange and powerful entity. Your task here is to fight off the seemingly indestructible creature and his minions while rescuing the three Preservers.

PREREQUISITES

Use the Ihan Crystal after completing "Whispers of Doom."

OBJECTIVES

MAIN

- Power up the abandoned Protoss base.
- Free all 3 Preservers (+3 Zerg Research).

BONUS

- Power up all 3 abandoned structures (+3 Protoss Research).

CREDIT REWARD

None

ACHIEVEMENTS

ACHIEVEMENT	PTS	REQUIREMENTS
A Sinister Turn	10	Complete all mission objectives
Out for Justice	10	Kill all the Protoss
Maar-ked for Death	10	Complete the mission on Hard difficulty in less than 20 minutes

LOCATION: ZHAKUL

Zhakul is an ancient Xel'Naga planet discovered by Protoss wayfarers after the Aeon of Strife. When the Conclave took power on Aiur, all texts and artifacts from the Aeon of Strife were sealed away on Zhakul ... and guarded by three holy Preservers.

ZERATUL'S BRIEFING

I gathered allies and we made our way to the forbidden archive world of Zhakul. There, a triumvirate of mystic Preservers awaited us. And in the shadows, something else was watching ... and waiting.

MISSION

This mission teaches you the fundamentals of playing as a Protoss. Zeratul and his allies discover an abandoned but functional Protoss base (1). Your first objective is to get the place powered up and running. As you do so, you soon find yourself under attack from fellow Protoss warriors.

NEW TECHNOLOGY

ZEALOT

Powerful Protoss melee warrior that can attack ground units.

HIGH TEMPLAR

Psionic master with potent special abilities.

IMMORTAL

Assault strider with shields that deflect high damage attacks. Can attack only ground units.

DARK TEMPLAR

Deadly warrior-assassin. Cloak renders him invisible to enemies without detection.

RESEARCH OPPORTUNITIES

- +3 Protoss Research
- +3 Zerg Research

LEGEND

PRIMARY

1. Start

2. Imprisoned Preservers

5. Guardian base

7. Guardian base

8. Light bridge

9. Guardian base

SECONDARY

3. Abandoned Robotics Facility

4. Abandoned Dark Shrine

6. Abandoned Templar Archives

POWER UP THE PROTOSS BASE.

Select the Probes, the basic worker unit of the Protoss, and set them to work in the mineral fields behind the base. Click on the Nexus, the large building in the middle of the base, and order a few more Probes. (Unlike SCVs, which are "trained" at a Command Center, your Probes are warped in.) As with SCVs, you can set the rally point for arriving Probes right in the mineral fields so they start mining automatically.

Now you need to power up the base. Protoss do this by placing support structures called Pylons. Each Pylon creates an aura of powerful energy that powers up any Protoss building within its radius. To place a Pylon, click on any Probe and select Warp-in Structure, then select Warp-in Pylon (the glowing crystal icon). When you move the cursor onto the map you can see the Pylon's energy radius so you can determine which buildings it will affect.

In this case, the two optimal Pylon locations are indicated on the map for you. Direct a Probe to warp in a Pylon at each spot to power up all six Protoss structures and complete your first objective. Note that the Protoss Pylon, like the Terran Supply Depot, creates your total supply cap number. Once you hit your supply cap, you can't create any more Protoss units until you construct more Pylons.

Now send a Probe over to one of the Vespene gas geysers and warp in an Assimilator atop the geyser. Assign two more Probes to start collecting gas.

BUILD A STRONG BASE DEFENSE.

Zeratul announces that the three Preservers have been imprisoned (their locations appear on your mini-map) and must be freed. But two other tasks should be completed before you set off on any rescue mission. First, you need a well-defended base. The reason: You soon come under attack from a Protoss force called the Zhakul Guardians.

The Guardians are followers of a powerful Zerg-Protoss hybrid creature called Maar, who introduces himself soon enough. Maar draws energy from the three imprisoned Preservers and then sets off slowly across the map to attack your forces.

MAAR'S ICON

Whenever Maar is fully recharged and moving to attack, his location on the mini-map is marked by a pulsing death's-head icon.

Before you do anything else, direct Probes to build two more Photon Cannons, one near each of the existing cannons. Next, select the Gateway near the front of the base and put a few Stalkers and Zealots in the warp queue. Zealots are your front line melee grunts, and Stalkers are ranged units that can hit air or ground targets. Finally, if you have enough resources, select the Forge and start upgrading your weapons. But that should come last.

FIGHT OFF MAAR AND MINIONS.

Maar's troops soon begin their raids on your base. Maar himself moves slowly, and you can easily track his progress across the map. (Look for his pulsing icon on the mini-map.) He may attack any of your installations, including the three outlying buildings you can activate.

Maar looks frightening, but he's actually not that tough to beat. If you keep a battery of 3-4 Photon Cannons plus a few good troops at each of your installations, you can KO Maar fairly quickly. (Note: He will target your cannons and Pylons, so keep a Probe at each location to rebuild after the fight.)

The problem with Maar is that he simply regenerates himself after each battle. He recharges on his platform (2) drawing the Preservers' energy as before, and then comes slowly at you again. The plucky hybrid cannot be terminated until you free all three Preservers by shattering their prisons.

BONUS: POWER UP THE THREE ABANDONED BUILDINGS.

Zeratul also points out a second task: three more functional but unpowered Protoss structures are scattered around the area. If you find and fire them up by building a Pylon near each, you gain the ability to create some powerful new units. You also pick up a Protoss Research point for each building you power up; if you power all three, you complete the mission's bonus objective.

A Robotics Facility (3) sits just southwest of your base; when first powered up it automatically warps in a tough Immortal to join your cause. This facility can warp in more Immortals, heavily armored walkers with a potent ranged attack.

A Dark Shrine (4) sits east of your base; this structure allows you to produce powerful Dark Templars, permanently cloaked units with great melee hitting power. (Zeratul himself is a Dark Templar.) Two warp in immediately after you power up the shrine.

Power up and defend these first two structures as soon as you can. Both new unit types are very useful in this mission. Later, you can find a third abandoned structure, a Templar Archives (6), on the eastern edge of the map. But you'll have to smash through a Zhakul Guardian base (5) to reach it.

SMASH THE GUARDIAN BASE(S).

Start assembling a strike team near your Dark Shrine (4) for the drive to the Preservers platform. Don't sacrifice your base strength for this team; Maar and minions keep raiding your bases through the entire mission. Warp in new troops. Once you gather 3-4 Immortals, 3-4 Dark Templars, a few Stalkers and Zealots, and at least one Probe, send that team southeast to attack the Guardian base (5). Wipe it out!

If you want, you can warp in a new Nexus and start an expansion base here. But first, move the strike team southeast to the Templar Archives and direct a Probe to power it up with a Pylon. This automatically warps in a High Templar, a psionic master with deadly abilities. Now you can warp in a few High Templars back at your Gateway.

Another much larger Zhakul Guardian base (7) sits over in the southwest corner of the map. You can try to wipe it out too, but it's entirely unnecessary to do so. Conserve your forces and get ready for the final move.

LIBERATE THE PRESERVERS.

Good timing can make this last step much easier. Add a few more Immortals and Dark Templars to your strike force and assemble off to the side of the platform leading up to the light bridge (8). Wait until Maar gets knocked out during his current assault on your bases. Once he regenerates again (2), he crosses the light bridge and moves north for his next base assault. Keep your force far enough from the bridge that Maar doesn't spot you; pull back if necessary! Let Maar pass, and then rush your strike force to the bridge.

STAY FOCUSED

After you shatter the first two Preserver prisons, focus all attacks on the third one, ignoring nearby Guardian troops or even Maar. You win the mission the moment the third Preserver prison shatters.

Eliminate the bridge guards quickly and hurry across the light bridge. Plunge through the Zhakul Guardian base (9) and make a beeline to the three Preservers enclosed in their glowing crystalline prisons. Don't engage Guardian troops unless you have enough size to split your force. Concentrate your team's attacks on each successive prison until you bust out all three Preservers. Immortals, in particular, are good at punching through the crystal pods. Once the third Preserver is liberated, you win the mission and Zeratul gets his Xel'Naga prophecy interpreted.

INTERLUDE:
HYPERION

Back in the Lab, see if anything new is available for research on the console. Then proceed to the Bridge. Talk to Horner to hear Raynor's thoughts about Zeratul's new revelations.

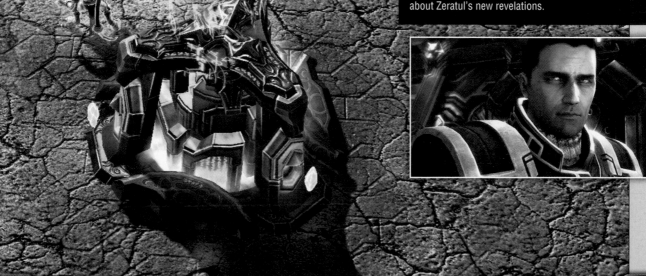

ECHOES OF THE FUTURE

MISSION OVERVIEW

Zeratul faces the unsettling task of tapping into the fading sentience of the Zerg Overmind to extract its insights into the prophecy revelations. The remains of the great Zerg lie on Aiur, the war-ravaged home planet of the Protoss. You must direct Zeratul to each of four massive tendrils connected to the Overmind's cortex. But the Zerg minions guard these desiccated remains with fanatical loyalty.

PREREQUISITES

Use the Ihan Crystal after completing "A Sinister Turn."

OBJECTIVES

MAIN

- Reach the Nexus.
- Guide Zeratul to all 4 Overmind tendrils (+4 Zerg Research).
- Zeratul must survive.

BONUS

- Power the 2 Obelisks (+2 Protoss Research).

CREDIT REWARD

None

ACHIEVEMENTS

ACHIEVEMENT		PTS	REQUIREMENTS
	Echoes of the Future	10	Complete all mission objectives
	Army of One	10	Complete the mission with Zeratul killing 50 Zerg units
	Overmind Dead Body	10	Complete the mission on Hard difficulty in less than 20 minutes

LOCATION: AIUR

Aiur was the home world of the Protoss: a jungle planet with multiple oceans, gleaming cities and ancient temples. The arrival of the Zerg changed everything. Now Aiur's ancient jungles are littered with ash, broken war-machines, and the remains of the dead.

ZERATUL'S BRIEFING

I returned to our ruined homeworld of Aiur. The Zerg infestation still covered much of our beloved world. The desiccated remains of the Overmind were still there, a grim reminder of battles lost … and battles won.

MISSION

Zeratul must probe the Overmind's cortex at each of its four remaining tendrils. You start on a small map with only Zeratul (1) next to his Void Seeker. Hack north through Zerglings, following the creep as it curves east until you reach an old Protoss Observer, which now reveals what's burrowed in the creep: more Zerglings and some Creep Tumors. Slash these as you proceed to the abandoned Protoss base (2) and step into the glowing beacon.

NEW TECHNOLOGY

OBSERVER

Flying spy that can spot burrowed Zerg. Its cloak renders the unit invisible to enemies without detection.

COLOSSUS

Towering battle strider with a powerful area attack can step up and down cliffs. Tall enough to be targeted by anti-air weapons. Can attack ground units.

RESEARCH OPPORTUNITIES

- +2 Protoss Research
- +4 Zerg Research

LEGEND

PRIMARY

1. Start

2. Abandoned Protoss base

3-4. Chokepoints

5. Overmind tendril

7. Abandoned Warp Gate

9. Abandoned Robotics Bay

10. Gas/mineral shards (Colossus-only pickups)

11, 17. Zerg base

12-14. Overmind tendrils

15. Abandoned Robotics Facility

16. Infested Terran base

SECONDARY

6. Abandoned Warp Gate & Obelisk

8. Abandoned Robotics Facility, Obelisk, & Warp Gate

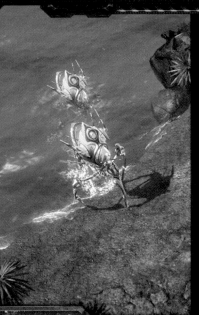

Your arrival "awakens" a pair of ancient Protoss defenders and the map expands. The two Colossi emerge from the lake and take a position up on a low ridge overlooking a chokepoint (3). Leave them on this high ground for now! It gives them a nice targeting location for the early Zergling rushes that will come through the gap below. The Colossus is lethal to Zerglings. Send Zeratul with an Observer north to clear out the creep in the gap.

BUILD YOUR BASE DEFENSE.

The Zerg are relentless and try to swarm the base every few minutes, so you need a good defensive perimeter right away. Put your Probes to work gathering minerals and gas, and get a couple of Pylons in place to power up structures. The Colossi and existing Photon Cannons will suffice to protect the north chokepoint (3) for the first few waves, so focus on getting defenders (including Zeratul) in the eastern gap (4).

Stalkers are weak against Zerglings, so put Zealots in the gap to start. Add extra Photon Cannons when you can. Eventually you want at least one Colossus here, but you'll need a Robotics Facility (which also produces Immortals and Observers) with a Robotics Bay to produce them. Of course, you can build those expensive structures … or you can get them for free! Read the next two sections to see how.

"OBSERVE" THE MAP!

Always send an Observer to scout ahead when you plan to push into a new area. You can see what Zerg are lurking up ahead (including burrowed units) and build the appropriate counter units for your strike force.

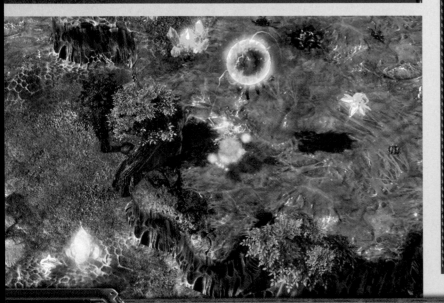

TAP THE FIRST TENDRIL.

The nearest Overlord tendril (5) is on a plateau just northeast of your base. It sits in a nice expansion area: plenty of minerals plus a gas geyser nearby. The only hostiles around the tendril are Zerglings and Roaches, with some Overlords hovering above: no detector units at all. Thus Zeratul can secure this area himself with just the initial Observer as escort to spot burrowed Zerg and Creep Tumors.

Once the area is clear, move Zeratul onto the glowing beacon to tap into the Overmind. Then order a Probe to build a Pylon to power up the abandoned Warp Gate and an ancient Obelisk (6) near the tendril. This frees a squad of Protoss (a High Templar and some Stalkers) who were trapped in the Warp Gate's energy matrix. Instant troops! If you want, you can build another Nexus here and start making Probes to mine the minerals.

POWER UP OLD STRUCTURES

Whenever you find an old Protoss structure, clear the area of any Zerg; use an Observer to make sure you find them all. Then have a Probe build a Pylon to power up the structure. Each abandoned Warp Gate releases a Protoss squad for an instant boost to your force.

BONUS: POWER THE TWO OBELISKS.

The Obelisks you find (6, 8) have no powers. Powering up each Obelisk earns you +1 Protoss Research apiece.

POWER UP MORE ABANDONED FACILITIES.

Other abandoned but functional Protoss structures can be found scattered across this map. Send Zeratul, an Observer, and a Probe heading through the north chokepoint (3) from your main base. Stick to the left (west) edge of the passage, then veer northwest to the bottom of the ramp. Send the Observer up the ramp to reveal a cloak-detecting Zerg Overseer hovering above some Zerglings and Roaches burrowed in the creep. You also see some abandoned Protoss structures: a Warp Gate (7) and a Robotics Facility near another Obelisk (8).

COLOSSAL CREDIT REWARD

Look for gas and mineral shard pickups nestled atop a nearby platform (10). Direct a Colossus to step up and grab them!

The Overseer detects cloaked units, so direct Zeratul to cast his Void Prison ability on it. Now Zeratul has about 10 seconds of invisibility to decimate the surrounding Zerg units. When time is up, rush Zeratul back out of the Overseer's detection range. When Void Prison is fully charged, use it on the Overseer again and mop up ground Zerg. Repeat until the area around the abandoned buildings is clear.

Now bring your Probe up the ramp and build a Pylon to power the Warp Gate (7). More Protoss soldiers (High Templar and Stalkers) are released from the gate's energy matrix and immediately warp in. Cast Void Prison on the Zerg Overseer one more time; the new Stalkers will shoot it down. Build another Pylon to power up the Robotics Facility and Obelisk (8). You can build Immortals now. Protect your new acquisitions, adding more troops and Photon Cannons in the north chokepoint to fight off any Zerg rushes.

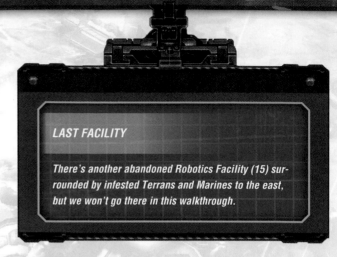

But you want Colossi too, so let's liberate the nearby Robotics Bay (9) as well. It is well guarded: flying Mutalisks and powerful Hydralisks join the usual Zergling swarm, plus a Spore Crawler adds extra detection to the Overseer floating overhead.

Add a few Zealots to your strike squad. Attack carefully, making sure you get the right match-ups: Stalkers hitting Mutalisks and the Overseer; Zealots tackling Hydralisks; and the High Templar decimating Zerglings with blasts of his Psionic Storm. Meanwhile, send Zeratul to kill the Spore Crawler. Once the Overseer and Spore Crawler are down, Zeratul is unseen once more.

When you clear the area, bring in an Observer to reveal the Creep Tumors; destroy them to eliminate creep so you can build Protoss structures on clear ground. Then bring up your Probe and drop a Pylon to power the Robotics Bay. Now you can warp in Colossi!

LAST FACILITY

There's another abandoned Robotics Facility (15) surrounded by infested Terrans and Marines to the east, but we won't go there in this walkthrough.

LAST FACILITY

There's another abandoned Robotics Facility (15) surrounded by infested Terrans and Marines to the east, but we won't go there in this walkthrough.

TAP A SECOND TENDRIL.

You can move around the map in either direction to reach the other three tendrils. We'll move counterclockwise to the next one. Fly an Observer north from your new robotics buildings into the small Zerg base at (11) working the nearby mineral field. It looks scary, but you'll find no detection units whatsoever. If you send Zeratul and some Dark Templars (if you have a Dark Shrine) into the base they can tear it to pieces without taking a scratch. Then you can start another expansion base here if you want.

Now scout ahead to the next tendril (12). Hydralisks, Zerglings, and a big squadron of Mutalisks defend it so you need a good mix of troops, including a healthy squad of Stalkers to shoot down flyers. There's only one enemy detector, an Overseer, but it floats above the tendril at the back of the area, so it's not easy to get your Stalkers in close. You'll have to keep Zeratul and your Observer safely out of the Overseer's detection radius and slug it out using your other troops until your Stalkers can nail the Overseer.

When the way is clear for Zeratul, send him to the glowing beacon to get another reading from the Overmind.

TAP THE THIRD TENDRIL.

Scout ahead to check out the area around the third tendril (13). You'll see that the area is swarming with greenish Banelings: not a pretty sight. But your Stalkers are particularly effective against Banelings. A strike force with 8-10 Stalkers and 2-3 Colossi should do well here. (Banelings are quite lethal to your Zealots, so keep them back.) Remember to use Zeratul's Void Prison to freeze Overseers or Spore Crawlers that can detect cloaked units. Clear the area and move Zeratul onto the third glowing beacon. One more to go!

TAP THE FOURTH TENDRIL.

The Overmind's fourth tendril (14) seems well-guarded too, but here's a trick: the moment Zeratul reaches the glowing beacon, the mission is won. You don't need to fight here. Simply run Zeratul directly to the beacon. The Zerg start to attack, but when you step into the glowing circle they stop. Watch as Zeratul views a shocking message from a most unlikely messenger.

INTERLUDE: *HYPERION*

Chat with Horner on the Bridge to get a perspective on what you just saw in Zeratul's vision. If Tosh is still around the Cantina, he has some thoughts too.

IN UTTER DARKNESS

MISSION OVERVIEW

Zeratul's final vision comes courtesy of the Overmind itself, and it paints a grim, pitiless image of the future. The Protoss must marshal the last of their forces and gather their great heroes in a fortress on Ulnar for a final stand against slavering waves of Zerg. But the irony is that the great Zerg victory will prove to be the final undoing of that race as well.

PREREQUISITES

Use the Ihan Crystal after completing "Echoes of the Future."

OBJECTIVES

MAIN

- Kill 1500 enemy forces (+3 Zerg Research).
- Defend until the last Protoss falls.

BONUS

- Protect the Protoss Archive for 25:00 (+3 Protoss Research).

CREDIT REWARD

None

ACHIEVEMENTS

ACHIEVEMENT	PTS	REQUIREMENTS
In Utter Darkness	10	Complete all mission objectives
Semi-Glorious	10	Kill 250 Zerg units
Blaze of Glory	10	Kill 750 Zerg units

LOCATION: ULNAR

In Protoss legends the planet Ulnar was the mythical last resting place of the gods, the very center of creation from which all life ultimately flows.

ZERATUL'S BRIEFING

Now, friend Raynor, you must see the Overmind's vision of the future. The end of my people … and of all things. This is our fate, should Kerrigan die.

MISSION

This mission is the Overmind's vision of what will come to pass if Kerrigan, the Queen of Blades, is killed. Your singular task is to kill as many Zerg as you can before you get overrun. A massive Zerg encampment is spread around the darkened three-quarters of the map. The Protoss fortress you must defend sits in the southwest quadrant. It features an outer perimeter with high ramparts overlooking three entryways that lead into a central courtyard where the Archive (3) is kept. Your troop production facilities (2) are arrayed further back, behind another fortified wall with two entrance ramps.

NEW TECHNOLOGY

PHOENIX

Air superiority fighter. Its Graviton Beam ability raises a targeted ground unit so other air units can attack it.

CARRIER

Capital ship that releases a swarm of small robot fighters called Interceptors that can hit both ground and air targets.

VOID RAY

Surgical strike craft with a powerful beam attack. Damage output increases the longer the beam remains on target.

MOTHERSHIP

The ultimate Protoss vessel with powerful special abilities. It can attack both air and ground targets. Cloaks nearby units and structures.

LEGEND

PRIMARY

1. Hero rally point

2. Protoss base

4. Rich mineral field

SECONDARY

3. Protoss Archive

RESEARCH OPPORTUNITIES

- +3 Protoss Research

- +3 Zerg Research

GET A GOOD OVERVIEW.

Hectic as this battle is, its basic strategies are fairly straightforward. You start with a well-developed base, plenty of minerals and gas, and a strong garrison of defenders including Colossi, High Templars, Immortals, Stalkers, and Zealots. You have strong batteries of Photon Cannons in place. Your Probes are already harvesting minerals and gas.

First off, you must gear up troop production and keep new Protoss units warping into the field from mission start to mission end. You need a full mix of unit types because Zerg of every stripe will hit you in relentless waves.

Second, you must use the natural advantages presented by your position in the fortress. In particular, the high ground and chokepoints created by the structure let you force the Zerg into unfavorable positions. You can fire down from the relative safety of the heights and slaughter many Zerg as they funnel through the gaps.

Later enemy waves will feature Zerg flyers, however. So you need a strong anti-air presence up on the raised platforms as well, and throughout the base for that matter.

FORTIFY THE PERIMETER.

As the mission opens, quickly add more Probes to your harvesting operations; you need raw materials to pour in as fast as possible. Also send a few Probes out to the courtyard; as the battle rages, you'll want them feverishly replacing lost Photon Cannons. Start a Robotics Bay (for Colossi) and a Dark Shrine (for Dark Templars). Then set rally points out in the courtyard (1) near the front gate for your existing Gateways and Robotics Facilities. Start putting new troops in your warp queues. Be sure to order a good mix of unit types.

Out on the perimeter, deploy your initial allotment of troops. Distribute your Colossi and Stalkers up on the ramparts, with units of both types overlooking all three chokepoints. Group your Zealots into a single melee squad to start, with Zeratul in the lead; start adding Dark Templars to this squad as they become available. Your Immortals and High Templars can stay on the courtyard floor to provide ranged support behind your melee squad.

Important: As soon as possible, get your Probes building Photon Cannons across the mouth of each chokepoint. You want at least four cannons pumping fire into each gap.

MINE THE YELLOW CRYSTAL

One Rich Mineral field (4) sits just outside the fortress gates. It's risky, but you can try putting a Nexus next to it and assign Probes to mine it in the early going. But the Zerg will find it sooner or later and destroy everything. Later, if your in-base mineral field runs dry, you can reroute your Probes out to the Rich Mineral field.

BONUS: PROTECT THE PROTOSS ARCHIVE.

Before the first Zerg arrive, Protoss High Templars ask for time to seal up the Protoss archive in the main courtyard. A countdown timer appears under the Bonus Objectives on the screen: it starts at 25:00 and counts down. When this timer reaches zero, the archive is preserved and retracts safely into a protective vault in the ground.

WELCOME YOUR HEROES!

Also before the first Zerg wave hits, the first of several Protoss heroes arrives to join in the glorious finale of the race. Admiral Urun has rallied the last of the Protoss fleet and flies his custom Phoenix strike craft (labeled onscreen as "Urun") with a wing of other Phoenix fighters into the courtyard. Hotkey this group and hold it in reserve until Zerg flyers start to appear.

DEFEND THE COURTYARD CHOKEPOINTS.

The first three Zerg attack waves consist of a mixed assault group hitting just one courtyard entrance at a time. Each group is led by melee units (Zerglings, Roaches, Hydralisks, then later Ultralisks) followed closely by a flock of Mutalisks (plus Brood Lords and Overseers later). You can see each Zerg wave gather at the base of the chokepoint, so you have some time to rally your troops in response.

DARK FORCES

Build a Dark Shrine and start warping in Dark Templars early in the mission. You'll need them against the hybrid monsters that start attacking after the first few waves.

Other heroes who join you later include Dark Prelate Mohander with a wing of Void Rays; Executor Selendis in a capital ship with her fleet of Carriers; and finally High Executor Artanis in the powerful Protoss Purifier, the "Shield of Aiur," with an escort of Void Rays and Carriers.

Group your melee squad and its support units and rush to meet each attack at the top of the chokepoint ramp, just in front of your line of Photon Cannons; you can do this in the early waves without worrying about defending the other two chokepoints. Make sure your Zealots and Dark Templars form a screen across the top of the chokepoint in order to keep Zerglings and other Zerg ground units bottled up and away from your ranged support units behind the melee line. Cooping up the Zerg on the ramp also makes the splash damage much more effective from your Photon Cannons and Colossi firing down at them. Hammer the Zerglings with Psionic Storm blasts from your High Templars for quick multiple kills. Target Roaches with your Immortals and Stalkers. Get more Colossi up on the ramparts when available.

BASE DEFENDERS

Deploy a mix of defenders and Photon Cannons in the heart of your base too. A few Zerg may break through or fly over your courtyard forces and try to strike your production facilities. Later, Nydus Worms burst up into your base area too.

When the Mutalisks arrive, they generally strike at your troops up on the ramparts first, so fly your Phoenix squadron straight to meet them. Again, an important part of your defense is a strong battery of Photon Cannons covering each entry to the courtyard. The Zerg aggressively target these guns and the Pylons that power them, so keep some Probes in a safe spot in the courtyard, ready to rush forward and rebuild those structures immediately after the current Zerg wave is defeated. Add extra Photon Cannons up on the ramparts when you can.

TAKE DOWN THE HYBRIDS.

The fourth enemy wave hits the front gate with a squad of devastating Zerg-Protoss hybrid monsters. You face two hybrid unit types, the Hybrid Viper and the Hybrid Destroyer. Your best counter against both is Zeratul and a squad of other Dark Templars, but make sure to quickly pop any Overseer that floats in to detect your cloaked units.

Soon the Zerg waves hit different checkpoints only slightly staggered, giving you less time to finish off one group and rush across the courtyard to the next. Eventually the attacks come so close together that you'll have to split your force in two. If Zerg overrun your ramparts, consider consolidating your courtyard forces tightly around the Archive. But try to keep defending the three chokepoints as long as you can.

BE READY FOR WORMS.

Soon the Zerg try a new approach. Nydus Worms start popping up from the ground and disgorging units in the courtyard behind the Templar Archive and, eventually, around the big warp portal up in your base. If Mohander and his Void Rays have arrived yet, set them to blistering worms. Zeratul can gut a worm in three good strikes as well. Keep a Colossus or two in the area to quickly sizzle any Zerglings that sneak amongst your buildings.

KEEP UP THE CAP

Start adding extra Pylons to your base area early in the mission. When you finally fall back from the courtyard you lose all of the Pylons you had there, and your supply cap quickly drops.

FALL BACK ONCE THE ARCHIVE IS SEALED.

If you manage to hold out in the courtyard until the Protoss High Templars finish preserving their civilization's records and seal the Archive, congratulations; now fall back immediately into the main base. Consolidate your forces around the two access ramps and start dropping in as many new Photon Cannons as possible.

The attack waves come faster and much more furiously; you start seeing more hybrids, Ultralisks and Brood Lords. The situation can go south fast if you lose production facilities and can't keep pumping out a steady flow of new troops, so defend your structures well. Use the brief lulls between rushes to survey your defenses and replace what you've lost. Again, you want balance, so build a good mix of troops

KILL 1500 ENEMY FORCES.

Once your kill count goes over 1500 you've "won" the mission, but it's a bittersweet win: the battle continues until your last Protoss unit falls.

INTERLUDE: *HYPERION*

Back in the Lab, check the research panel for any new upgrades that might be available. Then head to the Bridge and chat with Matt Horner.

MAW OF THE VOID

MISSION OVERVIEW

This mission is a brutal slog across a derelict space platform crawling with Protoss defenders. Worse, you may have to sacrifice some new Battlecruisers in order to deactivate powerful Protoss Rip Field Generators. Resources are at a premium here, because you'll need a lot of units to smash your way to the vault holding the final Protoss artifact.

PREREQUISITES

Complete "Supernova."

OBJECTIVES

MAIN

- Clear the landing zone.
- Destroy the vault door.

BONUS

- Rescue the Protoss prisoners (4 groups).

CREDIT REWARD

125,000

ACHIEVEMENTS

ACHIEVEMENT		PTS	REQUIREMENTS
	Maw of the Void	10	Complete all mission objectives
	I Have the Power	10	Destroy all Rip Field Generators
	Master of the Universe	10	Complete the mission without losing a unit inside the Rip Field Generators on Hard difficulty

LOCATION: SIGMA QUADRANT

This mysterious, largely unexplored tract of space is rumored to hold derelict spacecraft of unknown alien origin.

VALERIAN'S BRIEFING

Commander, our mutual friends at the Moebius Foundation have located the last artifact fragment. When this final piece is secured, we can proceed to Char and confront Kerrigan. Good luck, Mr. Raynor. I fear you'll need it.

MISSION

Your goal is to collect the last piece of the mysterious ancient artifact stored on this derelict Xel'Naga world ship. But most of the ship is encased in overlapping Protoss Rip Field Generators that inflict serious damage to any non-Protoss unit within the field. To get across the platform to the artifact, you must deactivate each Rip Field Generator by knocking out its generator. Of course, you need sturdy and powerful units to reach and destroy a generator while taking damage from the Rip Field Generator in the process. Fortunately, this mission introduces your new Minotaur-class Battlecruiser.

BLAST THE FIRST RIP FIELD GENERATOR.

You start with three Battlecruisers hovering near the eastern edge of the Xel'Naga world ship. Target the Rip Field Generator (1) in the center of the platform up ahead using the Yamato Cannons of all three ships. Once the Rip Field Generator goes down, Raynor brings in a full set of base buildings and the map expands.

Your platform has very limited resources and you need expensive Battlecruisers, so scour each platform for pickup items: mineral shards (blue) and crystallized vespene gas (green). Some of these pickups have Tal'darim Protoss guards. Send three cloaked Banshees to eliminate the Protoss on the platform's lower tier then send any ground unit to scoop up the gas and shards.

NEW TECHNOLOGY

BATTLECRUISER

Heavy assault capital ship. Deadly Yamato Cannons inflict massive damage with a single hit.

RESEARCH OPPORTUNITIES

- +4 Protoss Research

NEW UPGRADES AVAILABLE AFTER MISSION

- Missile Pods: Deals heavy damage to all air units in target area.
- Defensive Matrix: Erects a temporary shield that absorbs 200 damage before failing.

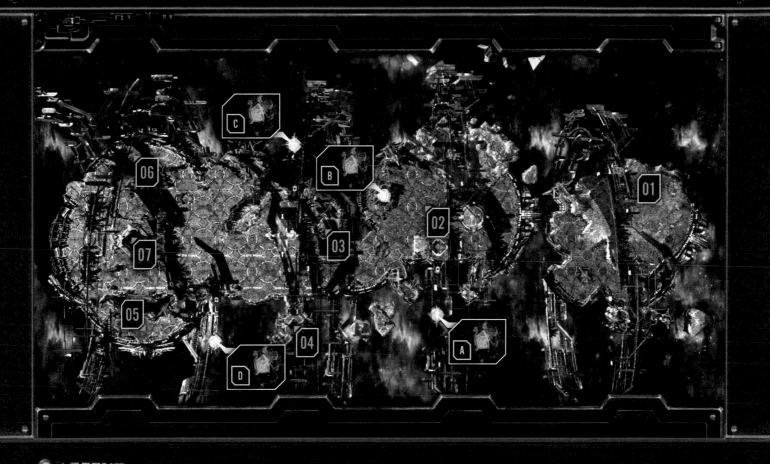

LEGEND

PRIMARY

1. Start

2-6. Rip Field Generators

7. Xel'Naga Vault

SECONDARY

A-D. Tal'darim prisons

BLAST THE SECOND RIP FIELD GENERATOR.

Your main production goal is to build a mighty armada of Battlecruisers that can lay siege across the Xel'Naga world ship knocking out seven more Rip Field Generators and then the Xel'Naga Vault. You want to keep these expensive capital ships intact and avoid replacing lost ones; they suffer heavy damage when traveling through Rip Field Generators. So you want a support squad of 5-6 SCVs grouped for repair with a Medivac to transport them. Don't waste many resources on training other units from this point on. You will gain all the combat allies you need as you cross the platform.

⊖ RED GENERATORS

Each Rip Field Generator is marked with a red square on your mini-map. You can also see the field radius of each generator as a red circle.

Build 2-3 more Battlecruisers and push the fleet west through the next Rip Field barrier. Nail the three highlighted Photon Cannons with Yamato Cannon shots; one shot kills each cannon. If you feel conservative, you can pull each Battlecruiser back out of the Rip Field Generator after it shoots, sending it to your SCVs for repair. When the fleet is back to full health and energy, send the entire fleet through both barriers to the next Rip Field Generator (3) and blast it with Yamato Cannons.

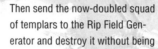

Rip Field Generator Overlap

The Tal'darim Rip Field Generators are set up to overlap; in most cases, each Rip Field Generator is covered by its own field plus at least one other generator's field. So don't assume your Battlecruisers are clear when they destroy a generator. You may need to pull your fleet back out of an overlapping field.

BONUS: RESCUE THE PROTOSS PRISONERS.

Destroying the second generator triggers an exchange with a Protoss Dark Templar who has been imprisoned by the Tal'darim sect. He pledges to join Raynor if you set him free. Four Tal'darim prisons (A-D) appear marked on your mini-map. Attack these green force-field prisons when you reach them to release the prisoners and thus gain allies.

Send a Battlecruiser to smash the nearest prison (A) which floats on a small platform south of the world ship. A ramp automatically connects to the ship so the Dark Templar prisoners can join your side. Because they are Protoss, they can operate without damage within the Rip Field Generators.

NO TEMPLAR RIP

The Protoss prisoners you liberate are unaffected by the Tal'darim Rip Field Generators.

DESTROY THE THIRD RIP FIELD GENERATOR.

Releasing the Protoss detainees from the first prison provides you with an extra benefit. The three Dark Templars released are permanently cloaked. Conveniently, the next Tal'darim prison and the next Rip Field Generator (5) have no cloak detection units near them! So you can walk your Dark Templars right up to attack the prison and free their comrades.

Then send the now-doubled squad of templars to the Rip Field Generator and destroy it without being detected. This friendly Protoss squad can also start clearing the area of other Protoss units and structures. But keep them away from Photon Cannons, which can detect them!

FEND OFF THE MOTHERSHIP.

Destroying the third Rip Field Generator triggers a scary response from the Tal'darim. A huge, powerful, but very slow Mothership appears near the Xel'Naga Vault and slowly moves toward your forces. Array your Battlecruiser fleet to meet it, hitting it with every Yamato Cannon you have. The Mothership warps in Protoss Carriers, cloaks its surrounding units, and can use its Vortex to suck your units out of existence for a period of time, so make sure you have your full fleet spread out and targeting the big ship.

TERMS OF VICTORY

It's not necessary to destroy the Mothership or all of the Rip Field Generators in order to win. The moment you destroy the Archive vault, the mission is successfully completed.

When it takes enough damage, the Mothership warps back to the Xel'Naga Vault, then slowly creeps back toward you. It keeps doing this until you destroy it. If you have 8-10 Battlecruisers in your front line fleet, then your Yamato Cannons can chase the Mothership away quickly before it can cause too much trouble. Once it is finally destroyed, you are in the driver's seat for the rest of the mission.

PUSH YOUR COMMAND CENTER FORWARD TO NEW RESOURCES.

Between visits of the Protoss Mothership, send a Battlecruiser or two north to destroy the Protoss Nexus (near 4). Now you can lift up your Command Center (load up your SCVs into it first!) and fly it there to extract resources when you run out of minerals/gas back on the first island.

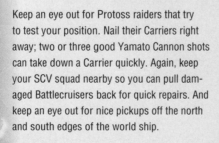

Keep an eye out for Protoss raiders that try to test your position. Nail their Carriers right away; two or three good Yamato Cannon shots can take down a Carrier quickly. Again, keep your SCV squad nearby so you can pull damaged Battlecruisers back for quick repairs. And keep an eye out for nice pickups off the north and south edges of the world ship.

KEEP TAKING OUT GENERATORS.

Once your Battlecruiser fleet grows to 10-12 or bigger, you are a juggernaut. Hit the next two Rip Field Generators (7, 8) and free the remaining prisoners (C, D). Keep your Dark Templar allies scouting ahead and wiping out as many ground units and Pylons as you can.

DESTROY THE VAULT DOOR.

A trio of generators (11, 12, 13) creates overlapping Rip Field Generators over the Xel'Naga Vault (14). These three generators are within reach of your Dark Templar allies, so you can destroy them without damaging your Battlecruisers in the Rip Field Generators, Then turn all of your guns on the vault door to retrieve the last artifact and complete the mission.

INTERLUDE: *HYPERION*

Your victory triggers a cinematic, "Bar Fight" featuring a moment of high-tension in the Cantina. Afterwards check in with Tychus at the Cantina.

THE GATES OF HELL

MISSION OVERVIEW

The invasion of Char begins, but it's more like the Bay of Pigs than a glorious offensive. Zerg flyers and massive ground-based Spore Cannons shatter the vaunted Dominion fleet while your landing turns into a piecemeal slaughter, with isolated Terran drop pods falling into midst of Zerg swarms spread across the volcanic wasteland. Your first task is to keep your small landing zone from being overrun. Then you must build up a strike force big enough to smash through large Zerg hive complexes and rescue General Warfield's isolated attachment.

PREREQUISITES

Complete "Maw of the Void"

OBJECTIVES

MAIN

- Gather a large army (100 Supply).
- Destroy the 3 Nydus Worms to rescue Warfield.

CREDIT REWARD

None

ACHIEVEMENTS

ACHIEVEMENT		PTS	REQUIREMENTS
	Gates of Hell	10	Complete all mission objectives
	The Big Bang Cannon	10	Destroy all the Spore Cannons
	Dominion Roundup	10	Rescue 10 drop pods of Dominion troops on Hard difficulty

LOCATION: CHAR

The ash-world of Char serves as the Zerg swarm's primary hive and base of operations in the Koprulu Sector. Its brutal volcanic landscape is riddled with extended hive colonies and labyrinthine tunnel systems that teem with millions of malevolent Zerg.

NO TURNING BACK

Once you launch The Gates of Hell you cannot leave Char. Any missions remaining on other planets are locked out, including the Zeratul missions accessed via the Ihan Crystal in the Laboratory.

VALERIAN'S BRIEFING

Everything is in motion to begin the final act: the invasion of the primary Zerg hive on Char. Once we begin, there will be no turning back. Ensure that you are fully prepared, commander. Destiny awaits!

MISSION

Just when you thought you were finally taking the battle to the Queen of Blades, you learn that the first attack waves have been decimated, and your tiny group of rebels is essentially alone on Char. This mission starts out as a frantic defense of your tiny foothold (1) on the planet, so bunker down. But you also want some good mobility in the early going; the going is less brutal if you can break out of your base and rescue the Dominion troops arriving in drop pods. Very large Zerg bases sit in the three corners of the map (2, 3, 4), and you should avoid them. But eventually you'll have to push to the southeast through the Zerg-infested base at 5.

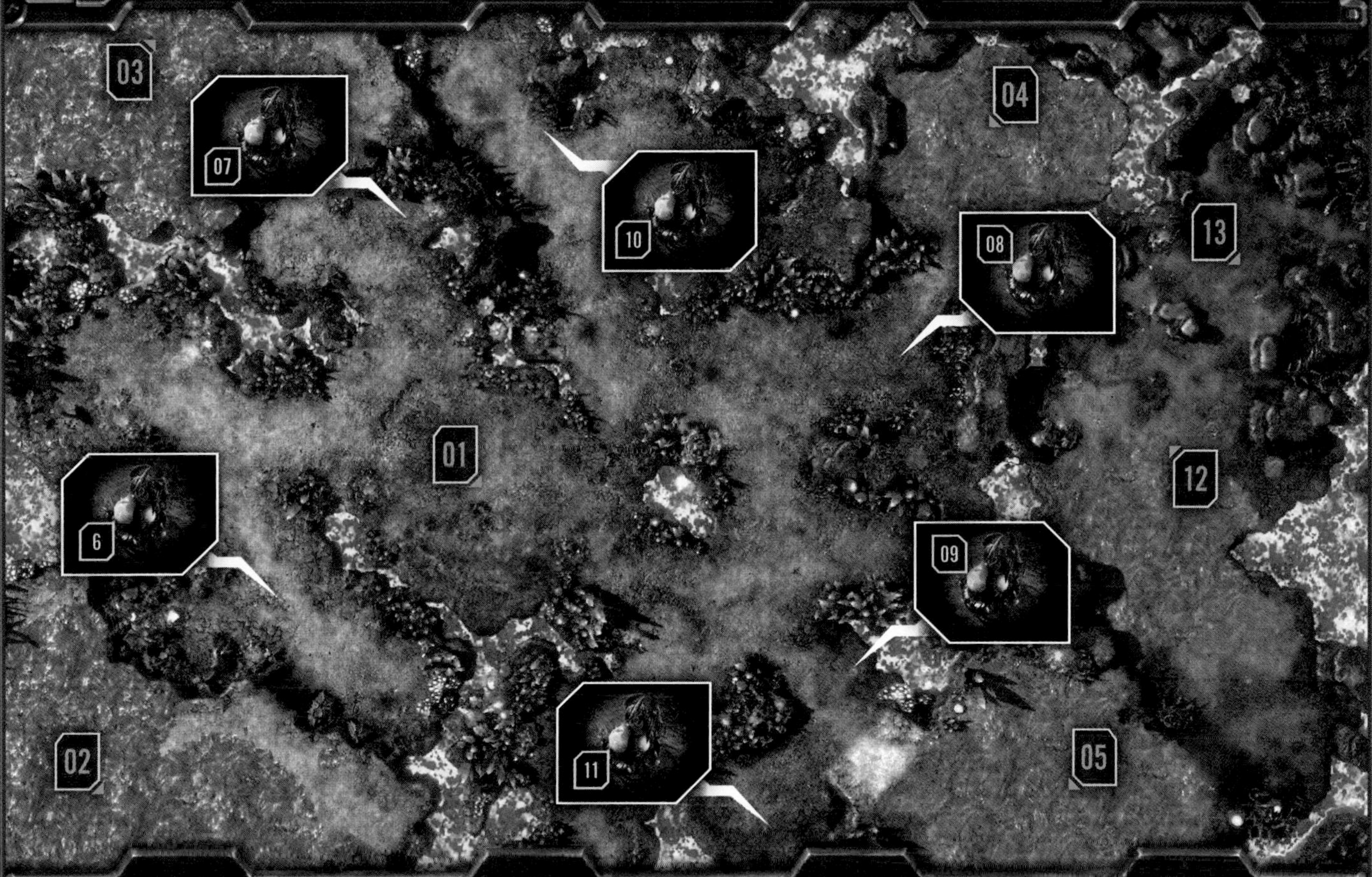

LEGEND

PRIMARY

1. Start

2-4. Zerg hives (avoid)

5. Infested base

10. General Warfield crash site

13. 3 Nydus Worms

SECONDARY

6-11. Spore Cannons

NEW TECHNOLOGY

- None

NO DEPOTS NECESSARY

You start with an automatic Supply limit of 200 for the mission, so you don't need to build any Supply Depots.

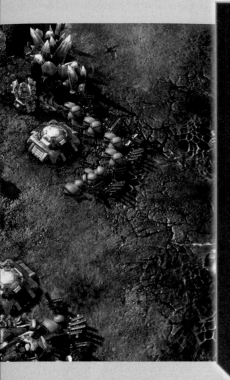

⊖ SET UP A BASE DEFENSE.

Immediately garrison the Bunkers with the Marines you're given at the start and build a Refinery. You have other units already deployed in good defensive spots at mission start, so focus on getting new troops in production. Train more Marines for your Bunkers then add a Tech Lab to your Barracks. If you've researched Perdition Turrets in the Lab, this is the perfect place to build a couple. If not, add a second Bunker to each base entry area. Note that the first Dominion drop pod ferries down a squad of five Marines. If you can rescue them, you have some instant garrison troops for your new Bunkers.

PALLET RICHES

Numerous gas and mineral pallets lie scattered around this map. Be sure to scoop up these instant resources if you venture out to rescue any Dominion troops arriving in drop pods.

BUILD A STRIKE/RESCUE TEAM.

As you defend your base you should be gradually amassing troops for an eventual assault to the southeast. But this strike team can also double as a rescue team for the Dominion battle groups dropping in around the map. (See the next objective.) Pump out Marines, Firebats, Marauders, and a few Medics early. Don't build a Factory or a Starport; these will arrive via Dominion drop pods and become yours if you rescue them.

RESCUE THE TERRAN UNITS/STRUCTURES DROPPING IN.

Both of the previous endeavors (setting up a base defense and building a strike/rescue force) can be expedited if you lend a hand to fellow Terrans falling from the sky. A total of 10 Dominion drop pods land on the map during the mission; all pods contain troops, and two pods even ferry down production facilities. When a drop pod lands, the troops/structures emerge and wait until either you rescue them or the Zerg wipe them out. A "Drop Pods En Route" onscreen counter keeps track of the number of pods yet to arrive.

FLY IN NEW BUILDINGS

Remember that Terran buildings can fly. If you rescue the Factory and Starport that arrive via Dominion drop pods, you can fly them over to your main base location.

These forces can significantly help your cause in the early going. Unfortunately, none of the drop pods land inside your base due to the chaos wrought by the furious Zerg air defenses; you must venture out to rescue them. Horner marks the locations so you can spot them on your map. Only one unit under your control needs to reach a Dominion "drop pod squad" for you to take control of the new troops or buildings. Then you can rush them back to bolster your base defense or beef up your strike force.

FLYERS TO THE RESCUE

A squadron of Vikings plus a Medivac arrives in one of the Dominion drop pods; these crafts can form an effective drop pod rescue team. The Medivac can swoop in to pick up newly arrived troops then ferry them where you want them. The Viking escort can decimate Mutalisks in the air or drop to the ground to eliminate Hydralisks that threaten the Medivacs.

We should note that it's possible to complete this mission without rescuing *any* of the Dominion troops arriving in drop pods, but again, adding them to your force makes the going much easier.

DESTROY ALL THREE NYDUS WORMS.

Hit the worms with everything you've got. Don't waste much firepower on other targets: The moment all three Nydus Worms are destroyed, you liberate Warfield and win the mission. Your victory triggers the spectacular cinematic entitled "Card to Play."

FIGHT YOUR WAY TO GENERAL WARFIELD.

As soon as your Supply exceeds 100 to complete your first objective, you get a distress call from General Warfield. A brief cutscene shows his command ship crash-landing up in the northeast (10). He's trapped behind a large Zerg hive cluster that includes three nasty Nydus Worms (11). Your new objective is to rescue the General. It will take some time, but his contingent can hold out for quite awhile on its own. Don't rush out your strike force before it's ready! Keep rescuing Dominion drop pods until the counter shows that no more pods remain.

SMASH THROUGH THE INFESTED BASE.

A former Terran base now full of Zerg and Infested Marines sits to the southeast (5). When you've built up a strong column with a good mix of units, push up the rock ramp leading into that base and raze it. Be sure to attach a good squad of repair/healer units (SCVs, Medics, Medivacs) to the main strike force. After you clear out the infested area, heal up and head due north to the Nydus Worms.

INTERLUDE: CHAR

Afterwards, you end up on the defensive perimeter with Raynor, Tychus, and General Warfield. But you can click buttons on the bottom of the screen to access important locations.

Talk to Tychus; talk to Warfield. He suggests that you'll have to choose between knocking out the Zerg ground reinforcements or its air support. Finally, click the mission briefing case on the crate in front of Raynor. This brings up the mission selection screen for the next mission.

BELLY OF THE BEAST

MISSION OVERVIEW

Tychus thinks the biggest menace is the Zerg Nydus Worms bursting up unannounced underfoot; Raynor admits that planting charges in their Nydus Network could flood the whole underground system with lava and cripple the Zerg ground effort. General Warfield sees it differently, however. He believes the Zerg flyers are a bigger problem; without adequate air cover, the invasion is doomed. He wants to hit the infested space platform hanging in low orbit, where 80 percent of the Zerg flyers nest.

PREREQUISITES
Complete "The Gates of Hell"

OBJECTIVES
MAIN
- Plant nuclear devices at 3 fissures.
- Run to the extraction point.

BONUS
- None.

CREDIT REWARD
None

ACHIEVEMENTS

ACHIEVEMENT	PTS	REQUIREMENTS
Belly of the Beast	10	Complete all mission objectives
Unbreakable	10	Complete the mission without letting a Hero fall incapacitated
One Shot, Fifty Kills!	10	Raynor must Kill 50 units with a single Penetrator Round in the mission on Hard difficulty

LOCATION: CHAR
Yes, you're still here, and it's not getting any prettier.

VALERIAN'S BRIEFING

We've secured our landing zone thanks to you, Commander. General Warfield believes an attack on the primary hive is suicide under the current conditions . A diversionary attack to cripple part of the Zerg defenses will give us the opportunity that we need.

THE CHAR DECISION

Do you focus on taking out the Zerg air support by landing a strike force on the orbital platform as General Warfield suggests? If so, select ATTACK PLATFORM to proceed to "Shatter the Sky." Completing that mission neutralizes all Zerg Mutalisks and Brood Lords in the final battle.

Or do you take Tychus Findlay's advice and focus on the Nydus Worms, sabotaging their tunnels to secure the ground below you? If so, select SABOTAGE TUNNELS to proceed to "Belly of the Beast." Completing that mission eliminates all Nydus Worms from the final battle.

If you select SABOTAGE TUNNELS, General Warfield graciously defers. Your Adjutant reports that a deep scan has detected three fault lines converging at one spot. Detonating a seismic charge over each fault will tear them open and redirect lava into the adjacent caverns, sealing up the Nydus Worms' underground network. Raynor wants a small, elite force for the job, but Warfield notes that some of his boys took cover in the tunnels, so you may pick up reinforcements down there.

MISSION

This is a tactical squad-based mission that gives you four "Hero" characters, each with a powerful special ability. Raynor carries a lethal sniper weapon; Tychus flings fierce Shredder Grenades; Swann can deploy a deadly flame turret; and Stetmann is equipped with state-of-the-art healing equipment. Along the route you have the option to rescue trapped Dominion soldiers who join your team. One other twist: if the Zerg take out any of your four principal characters, stay and defend the fallen, incapacitated heroes will stand back up after a short amount of time.

SETTING THE FIRST CHARGE

USE RAYNOR'S RIFLE.

Raynor carries a powerful railgun firing the Mark 12 Penetrator Round that can pass through multiple targets in one shot. The round also inflicts fearsome damage of 300, so it's perfect for one-shot kills against big beasts like Nydus Worms.

LEGEND

PRIMARY

1. Start

2-7. Zerg encounters

8. Aberration attack

9. Warfield's men

10. Narrow bridge

11. Chokepoint ambush!

12. Nydus Worms

13. Beacon

MOTION SENSOR

Your squad has a detector that puts a red "!" icon in the dark wherever it senses motion.

A short distance from the start you encounter some Zerg (2) conveniently lined up in a row. Use Raynor's Penetrator Round and target the last Zerg (farthest left) and fire. The round takes out the entire row!

Continue down the cave, moving in short increments until you spot the next Zerg pack (3). Use Raynor's Penetrator Round to target the nearest Spine Crawler, which also eviscerates the Hydralisk in front of it. Have your full squad hold their position and take out the Zerg that come forward. Finally, use another Penetrator Round on the second Spine Crawler.

TO A "T"

Each Hero's special attack is auto-set to the hotkey of "T."

USE TYCHUS' GRENADES.

Move carefully down the tunnel until Tychus complains that Raynor's hogging all the fun. His special attack is tossing a Shredder Grenade, perfect for shredding clustered enemies. Select Tychus and his "Toss Grenade" button, then move the targeting sphere over the clump of Zerglings up ahead (4). The toss knocks out most of them; mop up the few who survive with your full squad and march on.

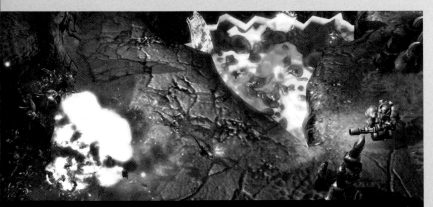

When you get within range of the next Zerg group (5) try a combo attack. First, have Raynor move to his left and line up a shot that picks off multiple targets. Immediately switch to Tychus and toss a grenade just ahead of the onrushing Zerg. Don't rush anyone forward! Two Spine Crawlers are rooted up ahead. Stay back and mop up the last few Zerglings. Then let Raynor pick off each of the Spine Crawlers from a safe distance with Penetrator Rounds.

USE SWANN'S FLAME TURRET.

Note the large number of red "!" icons lurking in the dark (6) down the tunnel to the right. The narrow chokepoint leading to them is a perfect spot to place Swann's special turret called the Flaming Betty. Select it and click to deploy it where you see the glowing green template of the turret. The Zergling horde attacks, but Betty broils them quickly. Toss in one of Tychus' grenades for good measure.

Continue to the next set of red "!" icons (7). It's just a few final Zerg on a ramp. Take them out however you want then move up the ramp to trigger an incoming transmission from General Warfield.

RESCUE WARFIELD'S MEN.

Warfield reports that some of his men are pinned down nearby, and their location (9) appears as a ping on the map. As you pass under the rock arch and approach the "!" icons to the right, get ready to use Raynor's rifle. A powerful Aberration (8) struts out of the darkness and launches powerful melee attacks. Nail it with a Penetrator Round for a quick kill. Then use more rounds to nail the Spine Crawlers in the creep beyond. Now you can climb the slope up to liberate Warfield's men, who join your party.

USE THE CHOKEPOINTS.

Backtrack to the main path and follow it until you reach a narrow rock bridge (10). Not far up the path on the other side, a big swarm of Zerglings are burrowed in the ground, waiting. Have Swann plant a Flaming Betty turret right on the bridge, send any soldier forward to trigger the Zergling rush, then run your man back past the turret. The Flaming Betty exacts a grim toll from the swarm.

KILL THE NYDUS WORMS.

Now you're close to the fissure where you want to place the seismic charge. But as you approach, Nydus Worms burst from the ground (12) and start spewing dozens of Swarmlings. To make matters worse, another brutal Aberration soon bursts from

the ground to attack. Immediately set a Flaming Betty in the gap and array your squad behind it. Have Raynor get a one-shot kill one worm with his Penetrator Rounds; Tychus can kill another worm with a grenade toss. Fend off Zerg waves in the chokepoint until both special weapons regenerate, then nail the other two Nydus Worms with a Penetrator Round and a Shredder Grenade.

PLANT AND DEFEND THE CHARGE.

Send Swann into the glowing green beacon on the ground to plant the nuke. Now you must defend the charge from waves of Zerg until it's armed; an onscreen timer counts down the seconds. Three corridors lead into the area. Place a Flaming Betty in the eastern corridor and have your squad defend the other two corridors. If any of your team is still conscious when the timer hits zero, the squad escapes the blast into the next area.

CHOKES OF FIRE

A Flaming Betty in a narrow corridor is a beautiful thing, especially if the Zerg are on one side and your guys are on the other. When facing big Zerg swarms, retreat through the nearest chokepoint and set up Swann's flame turret behind you in the passage.

A little further ahead you find a narrow pass with two big mobs of Zerg just around both sides. (You can see them on the map.) Use the same tactic: array your troops across the right side of the gap, have Swann plant a Flaming Betty right in the chokepoint, and send a unit forward to lure the Zerg through the pass. Toss a grenade into the swarm as it arrives. You should make quick work of many Zerg.

LEGEND

PRIMARY

1. Start

4-5. Infested horde

6. Burrowed Aberration

7. Banelings

8. Infestors and Nydus Worms

9. Warfield's men

10. Corridor worm-spawned attacks begin

11. Ultralisk & Aberration!

12. Beacon

SECONDARY

2-3. Place turret here

SETTING THE SECOND CHARGE

ROAST THE INFESTED; SNIPE THE INFESTORS.

The defense force in this second cavern is primarily comprised of Infested Terrans and Infested Marines, with a few suicidal Banelings adding acid to the test. Swann's Flaming Betty works wonders against infested troops, which are particularly weak against fire attacks, and Tychus' grenades can tear huge gaps in the clustered hordes. But the key to quick victory is to find and take out the source of the scourge: the big bug-like Infestors who spawn the horde by spitting out Infested Swarm Eggs that hatch into infested folk.

The first infested encounter is just east of your starting point (1). Take a few steps forward and have Swann toss a turret into the narrow entrance (2) to the cave where the infested gather. Keep your troops behind the Betty but push Raynor up next to it so he can spot the Infestor spitting out its eggs back in the cave and nail it with a Penetrator Round. Once the Infestor is dead, the flow of infested troops stops and you can mop up the remaining ones.

Continue down the tunnel and repeat this tactic against the next infested horde, a huge one. The key here is to send a scout forward to alert the horde (4) and lure its initial swarm back to the narrow choke-point (3) where Swann should place a Flaming Betty turret. After you thin out the first big rush of infested troops, use Tychus' grenades to create space to move forward to the Infestor, and then have Raynor pop the big purple bug with a Penetrator Round. Repeat this basic tactic against the next big infested horde (5) as well, placing your Flaming Betty in the narrow passage between the spiky clusters of orange crystals.

FEND OFF THE ABERRATION AND BANELINGS.

Continue down the south passage but be ready for a burrowed Aberration (6) to pop up and attack. One good Penetrator Round puts him out of his howling misery.

Raynor can pop an Infestor with a single Penetrator Round, but only if you spot the beast and then get Jimmy within range. Note also that Banelings tend to line up and attack in a single column, one after another. This sets them up well for a multiple-kill shot; if Raynor fires a Penetrator Round from the right spot, you can take out many Banelings in one shot.

A line of Banelings (7) is ready to make a rush at you next. Try to set up Raynor to fire a Penetrator Round right down their line, taking out multiple Banelings with one shot.

BLOW HOLES

If an infested horde engulfs one of your troops, your guy is essentially stuck in the mud and can't move. Have Tychus toss a Shredder Grenade to blow a bloody hole in the surrounding swarm so the trapped troop can escape and pull back to better ground.

LIBERATE WARFIELD'S MEN.

After you get past the Banelings, a transmission comes in from Warfield: more of his guys (9) are trapped just ahead. More Banelings plus some Infestors and Nydus Worms (8) block the way. But that's not all: once you attack them, more Zerg including an Aberration hit your position from behind. Nail the big units with grenades or Penetrator Rounds, mop up the smaller units, and then push forward to rescue the Dominion troops. They warn you that the cavern ahead is "full of worms." And boy, are they right.

FIGHT THROUGH WORMS TO THE FISSURE.

Now comes a hefty challenge. The second fissure is to the north, but to reach it you must travel through a winding corridor (10). Around each new bend sits a Nydus Worm spawning Zerg swarms that block your path. You must hack your way forward through these slavering swarms until Raynor gets within range of each worm to pop it with a Penetrator Round. (A Tychus Shredder Grenade will work too.)

Whenever there's a brief lull in the worm-spawned flow of Zerg, immediately push your squad forward to gain precious feet of ground. Use Tychus' grenades to create pockets in the swarm too. Just remember to rush forward into each new pocket. If you simply stay put, the Nydus-spawned swarms will overwhelm you eventually.

PLANT AND DEFEND THE SECOND SEISMIC CHARGE.

When you finally reach the fissure, walk Swann into the green glowing beacon to place the charge. Now you have to defend it while it arms. (A countdown timer appears onscreen again.) Place Swann's flame turret just east of the charge to defend it, and then array your squad in the west and southwest gaps. When the Zerg swarms start to hit, fight within range of any Nydus Worm or Infestor and kill it to reduce the number of spawned enemies. But don't stray too far from the nuke!

Once the onscreen timer hits zero, your team escapes to the next area and the seismic charge detonates. Just one more charge to go!

Double Trouble

After you get past the first few Nydus Worms in the winding corridor (11), a massive Ultralisk pops out to hit you from the front while an Aberration de-burrows to hit from the rear! The Ultralisk requires at least two Penetrator Rounds to kill.

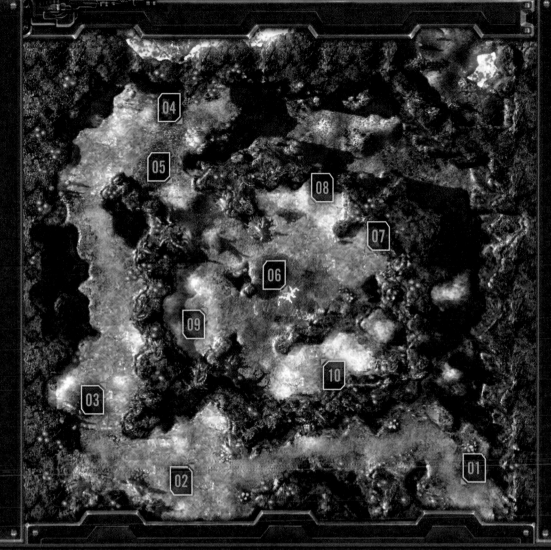

LEGEND

PRIMARY

1. Start

2-3. Zerg Cocoons

4. Omegalisk and Warfield's men

5. Beacon

6. Fissure/charge

7-10. Hatcheries (Zerg Queen)

SETTING THE THIRD CHARGE

HARD-BOIL THE EGGS.

This final complex is filled with dozens of Zerg Cocoons laid by the Zerg Queen. Each cocoon produces a Zerg creature, so you want to destroy as many of these eggs as possible, preferably before they hatch. When you enter the first open cavern to find the cocoon patch (2), the eggs immediately start hatching. Open fire! Wipe out all Zerg and continue on. Stetmann suggests that something may be controlling these eggs.

Follow the same procedure in the next open cavern (3). Watch out for a few Banelings amongst the egg spawn. Don't let them get close! When the second cavern is cleared out, continue up the passage to pick up another transmission from General Warfield.

KILL THE OMEGALISK AND RESCUE YOUR ALLIES.

More Dominion troops are trapped in an enclosure up ahead (4). But these ones face dire prospects: a gargantuan Omegalisk is hammering at the rock barrier they built for protection. If the huge beast breaks through, their chances for survival are slim.

Rush to the third cavern and open fire on the Omegalisk (4) as fast as you can, but direct Swann to place a Flaming Betty turret left of your attack position to fend off Zerg units hatching from nearby eggs. Focus your squad's full firepower on the Omegalisk, including Shredder Grenades and Penetrator Rounds. If you can kill the monster before it breaks through the wall and decimates the trapped Marines, the troops will join your tactical squad.

PLANT THE THIRD NUKE IN THE QUEEN'S LAIR.

Simply send Swann into the nearby beacon (5) to trigger a short scene: as he plants the third seismic charge on the fissure (6), the angry Zerg Queen appears (7) and starts slicing open nearby cocoons to release hungry Zerg.

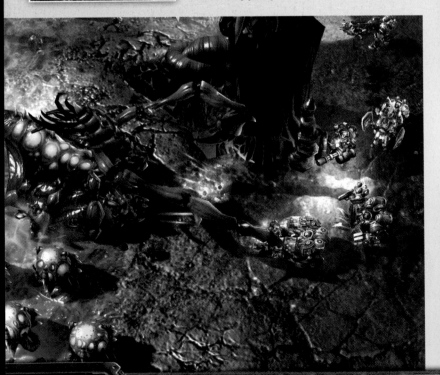

DEFEND THE CHARGE AND CHASE THE QUEEN.

Put down a Flaming Betty next to the seismic charge and then focus all your firepower on the mighty Queen with her massive claws and her Life of 3000. She rushes north into another hatching chamber (8) and starts ripping open eggs to release a variety of Zerg units. Follow her and toss a Tychus grenade when you can at any egg cluster to wipe out a handful of potential foes. Keep heavy pressure on the Queen. After suffering some damage she burrows away for a few seconds.

Rush directly to the hatching chamber at (9) to attack eggs. Hurry! Destroy as many as you can before the Queen pops up there. When she appears, she starts tearing open eggs again, releasing more hostile Zerg! Turn your full guns on her until she takes enough damage to burrow to safety again.

Now send Swann to check on the Flaming Betty protecting the nuke. If its life is expended, immediately place another one there. Meanwhile send the rest of your squad into the hatching chamber to the southwest (9). Smash as many eggs as you can before the Queen emerges from the ground and starts releasing Zerg from the eggs again. Attack her until she disappears one last time. Rush over to the southeast egg chamber (10) and smash eggs, then attack the Queen when she arrives.

KILL THE QUEEN.

Rush back to the seismic charge and get ready. Soon the Queen bursts from the ground. No egg ripping this time: she just wants your hides. When she emerges this time she stuns everyone for a short time. Hit her with everything until she finally falls dead. This triggers a scene: the charge detonates and the lava starts rising. Time to get out!

RUN TO THE EXTRACTION POINT.

Follow the winding path up to the glowing beacon. En route Zerg rise up to block your escape: keep running! Focus only on getting to extraction point as fast as possible. Don't stop to fight. You can have Swann toss a Flaming Betty ahead to occupy Zerg, and Tychus can toss a grenade to clear the path a bit. But the key is to keep moving. All four Heroes must make it to the extraction point in order to complete the mission.

After the cinematic you return to the forward staging area on Char, where you can talk to Tychus or the General. From here you can return to the *Hyperion* if you want. When you're ready to launch the final mission of the Wings of Liberty Campaign, click the mission briefing case on the crate in front of Raynor. This brings up the mission selection screen for the grand finale.

MERCS FOR HIRE

This is your last chance to buy mercenary contracts. You'll face relentless waves of Zerg flyers in the next mission, so we strongly recommend that you hire the Hel's Angels squadron of Vikings, if you haven't already done so; Vikings will be invaluable against all the Brood Lords and flocks of Mutalisks coming at you in "All In." Duke's Revenge (a super-durable Battlecruiser) is also a nice pickup for that same purpose.

If you have the funds, we also suggest you hire the Spartan Company. These dual-purpose Goliaths are very useful at the chokepoints you must defend in "All In." Finally, pick up the contract of the Siege Breakers (Siege Tanks) to defend chokepoints. These elite tanks deal out +66 percent damage compared to your standard issue vehicles.

INTERLUDE: CHAR

Completing "Belly of the Beast" unlocks a stunning cinematic sequence. Raynor returns to the surface to a grim sight, but it's always darkest before the dawn.

After the cinematic you return to the forward staging area on Char, where you can talk to Tychus or the General. When you're ready to launch the final mission of the Wings of Liberty Campaign, click the mission briefing case on the crate in front of Raynor. This brings up the mission selection screen for the grand finale.

SHATTER THE SKY

MISSION OVERVIEW

If you went with General Warfield's advice and selected "Attack Platform" at the mission branch, Raynor deploys a strike force to the orbital platform above Char that serves as a nest for Zerg Mutalisks and Brood Lords. Its superstructure combines several smaller platforms tethered together; each platform's power source is a nuclear fusion reactor kept stable by Coolant Towers. Raynor wants to take out these towers to trigger reactor meltdowns that will obliterate the platforms.

PREREQUISITES

Complete "The Gates of Hell"

OBJECTIVES

MAIN

- Destroy all 4 Coolant Towers.

BONUS

- Destroy the Zerg Leviathan.

CREDIT REWARD

None.

ACHIEVEMENTS

ACHIEVEMENT	PTS	REQUIREMENTS
Shatter the Sky	10	Complete all mission objectives
Demolition Man	10	Complete the mission without losing a unit to a platform explosion
Speed Too!	10	Complete the mission on Hard difficulty in less than 25 minutes

LOCATION: MINING PLATFORM ABOVE CHAR

This old Riksville Mining Operations complex sits in geostationary orbit above Char. It is now a nesting place for Zerg flyers and is heavily defended. Nuclear fusion reactors still power the four docked platforms.

VALERIAN'S BRIEFING

We've secured our landing zone thanks to you, Commander. General Warfield believes an attack on the primary hive is suicide under the current conditions. A diversionary attack to cripple part of the Zerg defenses will give us the opportunity that we need.

MISSION

The orbital platform was built onto an asteroid for mining purposes. Note the distinction between man-made platform flooring and the asteroid's natural rock. When a fusion reactor melts down, anything on the platform flooring above it is destroyed. However, any natural rock area is a safe place to ride out the meltdown.

SECURE YOUR BASE AND GEAR UP PRODUCTION.

First, set up a solid perimeter defense. Zerg raiding parties, some quite strong, will harass your base throughout the mission. Build a Bunker and a Missile Turret (plus an SCV for repairs) at the top of each of the two entrance ramps leading up to your base. Deploy at least one Viking to each ramp as well; occasionally, a Brood Lord flutters up to spit Broodlings at your chokepoint defense, but the canny beast stays out of your turret range so you must fly a Viking forward to kill it. Add a Goliath and at least one Siege Tank in Siege Mode next to each Bunker when you can.

NEW TECHNOLOGY

- None.

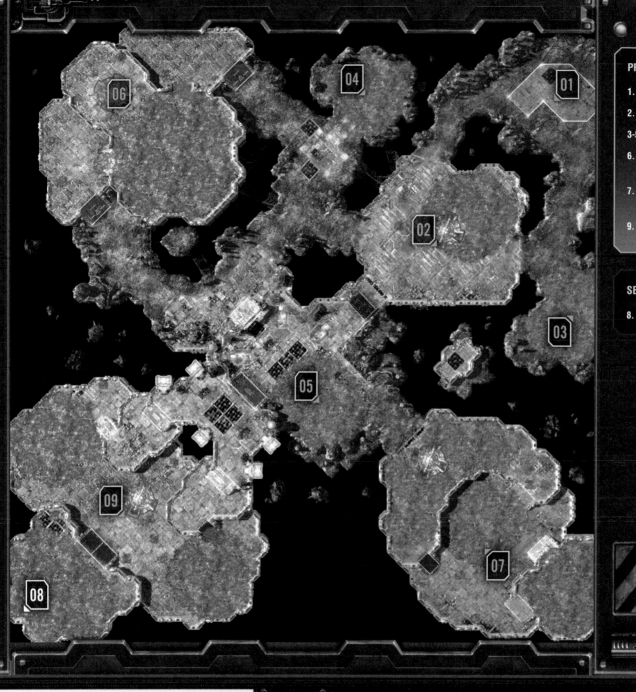

LEGEND

PRIMARY

1. Start

2. Coolant Tower

3-5. Expansion base areas

6. Coolant Tower: Heavy anti-ground defenses

7. Coolant Tower: Heavy anti-air defenses

9. Coolant Tower

SECONDARY

8. Leviathan appears

Now gear up your troop production. You need a strong squadron of Banshees plus some Vikings for support to hit the Coolant Towers on the northeast and northwest platforms (2, 6), so add a Tech Lab to your Starport right away. You also need a powerful ground force of Goliaths, Siege Tanks, and Hellions to smash your way to the Coolant Tower on the southeast platform (7); add a Tech Lab to your Factory for these. And you'll need a strong mixed force to take out the final Coolant Tower (9) on the teeming southwest base.

DESTROY THE NORTHEAST COOLANT TOWER.

The Zerg enclave at the bottom of the ramps from your base is only moderately defended. It features just a few anti-air Spore Crawlers, none of which sit in the route to your primary target, the Coolant Tower (2). Thus Banshees with Viking support makes a good strike team. Add the Battlecruiser that you start the mission with to your assault squadron, too.

Fly this group south, down the rightmost ramp. Cloak your Banshees and kill any ground troops around the bottom of the ramp; target anti-air Hydralisks first. Meanwhile your Vikings can shoot down any Overseers (which can detect cloaked units) or Mutalisks that appear. Then bring in your Battlecruiser too. Don't waste your time attacking Zerg buildings. Fight your way to the Coolant Tower (2) and open fire; drop your Vikings to the ground so they can help destroy it too.

Important: On each mining platform you must make sure your troops have a clear escape route to any patch of solid asteroid rock before you start bombarding that platform's Coolant Tower. Once the tower is destroyed, the reactor melts down in less than a minute (an onscreen timer counts down the seconds); when it does, everything Zerg or Terran on the man-made part of the platform will be incinerated.

So the moment the Coolant Tower crumbles, extract all troops *immediately* from the platform. This is easy if you deployed flyers only, as we suggested for this first platform. If you have ground troops involved, run them to the nearest brown natural soil (here, most likely on the ramps). Again, any troops left on or over the platform will get nuked when the meltdown occurs.

No Attack Move!

Don't use Attack Move to escape the platform once the Coolant Tower is destroyed! Time is tight. You don't want troops engaging with anything during the escape to safe ground.

After the meltdown wipes out the Zerg, you can return to the platform and nab all the gas/mineral pickups left. This gives your economy a quick lift.

OPTIONAL: BUILD EXPANSION BASES.

You need plenty of troops for this mission, so there's a good chance you'll run out of resources at your starting base. Fortunately, you can find three resource-rich areas (3, 4, 5) for expansion that are nearby and fairly easy to reach and secure. All three start out as lightly defended Zerg mining bases. Send in a strong strike force to wipe out the Zerg presence, then either fly in your original Command Center (if your previous base's resources are expended) or build a new one. Put a fully garrisoned Bunker and a Missile Turret in each entrance chokepoint, add another turret or two around the perimeter, and post a few mixed-unit defense troops as well.

DESTROY THE NORTHWEST COOLANT TOWER.

The northwest platform features fearsome ground defenses, including many Ultralisks, Roaches, and Spine Crawlers. It's a very dangerous slog if you try to go in with ground forces. So your best bet is to use the same combo as on the previous platform: cloaked Banshees, with Vikings to protect them. The Vikings should focus on popping Overseers or dropping to the ground in assault mode to kill the few anti-air Spore Crawlers you encounter on this platform.

Again, your target is the Coolant Tower (6); you don't need to raze the entire Zerg base. After the tower is destroyed and the fusion reactor melts down, every Zerg unit or structure on the platform is wiped out. So don't waste time attacking anything that isn't blocking your route to the tower.

DESTROY THE SOUTHEAST COOLANT TOWER.

The southeast platform is packed with anti-air units. Spore Crawlers, Mutalisks, and Hydralisks abound, so invading with a flight-based group can be suicide. Instead, spearhead the assault with ground troops. Use Siege Tanks, Goliaths, and Hellions, with some infantry for cheaper extra firepower, including a strong squad of 10-12 Marines for anti-air support against Mutalisks. Bring in your flying units behind the ground assault once an area is cleared of Spore Crawlers.

Remember that since much of your force is ground-based here, it is important to have a good exit strategy before you blast the Coolant Tower (7). When the tower goes down, keep an eye on the countdown timer as you make a run to safe ground.

BONUS: KILL THE ZERG LEVIATHAN!

Destroying the second Coolant Tower triggers a frightening cinematic: the Leviathan, a colossal Zerg flying creature, starts moving across the map to join the battle. This boss has 2,500 hit points, unleashes a Scourge Swarm, and has a devastating close-range Tentacle attack. It appears on your mini-map as a pulsing white death's-head icon.

The Leviathan starts in the southwest corner of the map and drifts slowly northeast to attack you. Wait until it gets beyond any Zerg-controlled areas and then unleash your Viking squadron on the monster; the Viking's Lanzer Torpedoes are excellent anti-capital ship missiles. A group of 13-14 Vikings can take out the Leviathan fairly quickly; more is better, of course. If you have any Battlecruisers, use them too. Their Yamato Cannon blasts will hasten the Leviathan's demise as well.

DESTROY THE SOUTHWEST COOLANT TOWER.

If you're running short on resources, you can take over the expansion site (5) on the central docking module. Bring in a Command Center and SCVs along with your strike team. Set up Missile Turrets behind your mineral row to fight off Mutalisks and defend your harvesting. Then spend some time beefing up your invasion force.

When you've got a sizeable force of mixed units, get ready to push off toward the final Coolant Tower. Set up some Siege Tanks in Siege Mode along the edge of the docking module to start a bombardment. Then send in the full strike team; throw in everything you've got. Hammer your way straight to that final Coolant Tower and focus your full fury on the structure. The moment you destroy the last tower, you've won the mission, so don't worry about getting off the final platform before the meltdown.

INTERLUDE: CHAR

Completing "Belly of the Beast" unlocks a stunning cinematic sequence. Raynor returns to the surface to a grim sight, but it's always darkest before the dawn.

MERCS FOR HIRE

This is your last chance to buy mercenary contracts from Mr. Hill in the **Hyperion** Cantina. You face a withering ground assault in the final mission so we recommend that you hire any or all of the following mercs if you haven't already done so: Siege Breakers (Siege Tanks), Dusk Wings (Banshees), and Hammer Securities (Marauders).

Duke's Revenge (a single pirate Battlecruiser) is also useful for dealing extra Yamato Cannon damage.

After the cinematic you return to the forward staging area on Char, where you can talk to Tychus or the General. From here you can return to the *Hyperion* if you want. When you're ready to launch the final mission of the Wings of Liberty Campaign, click the mission briefing case on the crate in front of Raynor. This brings up the mission selection screen for the grand finale.

ALL IN

MISSION OVERVIEW

The Dominion engineer corps has transported the fully assembled Xel'Naga artifact to the base of Char's primary hive cluster. Your job is to protect the artifact until it is fully charged and operational. Unfortunately, the device is a veritable Zerg magnet; according to General Warfield, all Zerg in the area will be in a frenzy to reach it. But the artifact can emit a sub-sonic Energy Nova discharge that kills all Zerg within its radius of effect. After the discharge, however, the artifact must recharge for several minutes, so you must use it sparingly.

PREREQUISITES

Complete "Shatter the Sky" or "Belly of the Beast."

OBJECTIVES

MAIN

- Defend the artifact until it is 100 percent charged.

BONUS

- None.

CREDIT REWARD

None.

ACHIEVEMENTS

ACHIEVEMENT	PTS	REQUIREMENTS
All In	10	Complete all mission objectives
Burn and Turn	10	Kill 150 Zerg units with the Artifact in the mission
Aces High	10	Use the Artifact only once in the mission on Hard difficulty.

LOCATION: CHAR

It's a slithering inferno of tusks and tentacles, but somebody's got to face the Queen of Blades. That somebody is you.

CHOICES

You will play a slightly different version of this mission (and hence require different strategies) depending on whose suggestion you followed in the previous mission:

If you agreed with Tychus Findlay and went underground for "Belly of the Beast," you eliminated the Nydus Worm network, so no worms will pop up in your base or elsewhere during "All In."

If you took General Warfield's advice and hit the orbital platform in "Shatter the Sky," you wiped out most of the Zerg flyers and won't see Mutalisks or the dreaded Brood Lords in "All In."

VALERIAN'S BRIEFING

It seems my faith in your abilities has been vindicated, Commander Raynor. Now the final blow must be struck. Use the artifact to neutralize the Queen of Blades and bring this bloodshed to an end.

MISSION

Much of the strategy for this mission is the same whether you got here via "Belly of the Beast" or "Shatter the Sky," but there are a few key differences, mostly related to the type and placement of counter units. The overall goal is to fend off increasingly desperate Zerg attack waves as you defend the artifact while it slowly charges up to 100 percent. However, depending on your choice for the previous mission, what types of Zerg units that hit you and where they hit you will be somewhat different.

UNDERSTAND THE SITUATION.

You start out with a good-sized base that includes every basic structure you need: Barracks, Factory, Starport, Engineering Bay, Armory, and Fusion Core. You have two chokepoints to defend (3, 4) but note that each choke has *two* approach routes coming into it; the first Zerg waves will smash through the side barricades in short order.

NEW TECHNOLOGY

- None.

LEGEND

PRIMARY

1. Start

2. Artifact

3-4. Chokepoints

5. Place Vikings here (for Mutalisk waves)

6. Place mobile defense squads here (for Nydus Worms)

○ = Place Siege Tanks & Missile Turrets here

Note the "Charging" percentage tracker for the artifact up in the corner. You must hold out until the device is 100 percent charged up. You also see a countdown timer for the artifact's Energy Nova cooldown period. Whenever that timer reaches zero, the nova is ready to emit another circular burst of energy that will incinerate any Zerg within its radius.

OCCUPY THE HIGH GROUND.

As the mission opens, you watch a cutscene: the artifact wipes out a huge Zerg assault, so the "Nova Cooldown" period begins. Immediately get your mineral/gas production running, garrison your starting Bunkers with Marines, and add Tech Labs to your Barracks, Factory, and Starport.

First, rush each of the four Siege Tanks you start with to one of the four high-ground overlook points indicated on our map (the green circles) and put all four tanks into Siege Mode. The bombardment your Siege Tanks provide from these raised spots overlooking the chokepoints is critical to your defense. Eventually you want to get at least one companion tank and a Missile Turret at each of those four positions too.

SIEGE MENTALITY

Your Siege Tanks on the perimeter high ground aren't going anywhere. Put them in Siege Mode right away for the added range and power.

Second, rush an SCV and more Marines to each chokepoint (3, 4) and start working on two more Bunkers at each spot. One Bunker should sit near the top of each side ramp initially blocked by barricades. As mentioned earlier, the Zerg will soon pound through these barricades, so you'd better have a Bunker full of Marines ready to greet them.

Third, get a squad ready to face the specific threat based on your choice in the previous mission:

If you completed "Belly of the Beast," you'll face successive waves of Mutalisks throughout this final mission, plus some Brood Lords later. Most Mutalisk waves approach from the northwest, flying directly across the lava lake toward the artifact on the plateau. Eventually you want a Viking squadron and a Battlecruiser or two waiting for them (5). But to start, add two more Missile Turrets, placing them between the two turrets you started out with. Then get some Vikings to that spot as soon as your Starport is ready to produce them.

If you completed "Shatter the Sky," you'll encounter Nydus Worms popping up in your base interior. To counter this, start assembling a mobile strike force of Siege Tanks, Hellions, Marauders and/or Goliaths, plus a squad of 8-10 Marines (with Medic support). Deploy this group right in the middle of your base so it can rush to any Nydus Worm eruption. Eventually you want a second interior group too; when you get it assembled, you can post each group on opposite sides of the base in case of multiple worm incursions.

Finally, get an SCV dedicated to building more Supply Depots. You want to push your Supply cap up to 200 as soon as possible. You'll need a lot of units to mount a defense against the Queen of Blades.

REPAIR TEAMS

Be sure to deploy two SCVs to each important part of your defense perimeter: your tanks on the high ground, your Bunker clusters, and either your air defense squadron on the artifact plateau (if you completed "Belly of the Beast" last mission) or the mobile defense team in your base interior (if you completed "Shatter the Sky" instead).

KEEP BEEFING UP YOUR DEFENSES.

Now you just hunker down and fight. You will suffer losses, but you can minimize these if you get enough firepower to the spots we've described and make sure you've got enough healing units (SCVs, Medics, Medivacs) at each location. Keep your base production queues filled so you can rush in reinforcements when someone goes down. In particular, keep two Siege Tanks up on each of those high overlooks!

SEND VIKINGS OUT TO HIT BROOD LORDS.

If you came to this mission from "Belly of the Beast," most of your Vikings and your Battlecruisers can hover in a stationary position (5) in front of the artifact to fend off the Mutalisk waves. But you need at least one Viking hovering over each chokepoint (3, 4) as well. The reason: Kerrigan sends an occasional Brood Lord to hit the chokes, and the canny beast will keep a safe distance from your Bunkers and other defenders as it spits out its Broodlings. Thus you need a Viking or two to push out and target the Brood Lord.

FIGHT OFF THE KERRIGAN ATTACKS!

Several times during the battle, the Queen of Blades herself has had enough of your impertinence and launches an attack herself. (Your Adjutant always gives you early warning when this happens.) Kerrigan is a "choke-breaker"; she starts up in the main Zerg hive cluster in the northwest and strides across the map to one of the two chokepoints (3, 4) where she starts laying waste to your defenses. You can follow her progress by watching the big death's-head icon moving across your mini-map.

Kerrigan has a damage bar; when it drops to zero, she suddenly burrows and disappears. Wait until she reaches the fork where she must veer to one chokepoint or the other. When you see where she's targeting, send all of your Battlecruisers toward that chokepoint and your mobile base defense team. As she arrives, immediately target her with all of the Yamato Cannons you have available. These blasts take down her health quickly, and the concentrated fire from your chokepoint defenses should force her to burrow away within a few seconds.

MEET THE LEVIATHAN WITH VIKING FURY.

If you came to "All In" from "Belly of the Beast," you face an additional boss threat later in the mission. A colossal Zerg flyer called the Leviathan appears in the northwest and heads toward the artifact. This boss has 2000 hit points, unleashes a Bile Swarm, and has a devastating long-range Tentacle attack. It appears on your mini-map as a pulsing white death's-head icon.

Wait until the Leviathan gets close and then unleash your Viking squadron on the monster; the Viking's Lanzer Torpedoes are excellent anti-capital ship missiles. A group of 13-14 Vikings can take out the Leviathan fairly quickly; more is better, of course. If you have any Battlecruisers, use them too. Their Yamato Cannon blasts will hasten the Leviathan's demise as well. If you don't kill the Leviathan it will spawn more and more Mutalisks/Broodlords; you must deal with it.

HANG ON!

You can do it! Keep funneling new troops to contested chokepoints. The Zerg assault grows more intense as the artifact gets closer to a 100-percent charge. But if you can save an Energy Nova blast for the final few percent of charging, unleashing it at 97 percent or so, you are most likely home free. (Don't use Energy Nova after the artifact charge hits about 75-80 percent; that way you have one more blast available near the end.)

When the artifact charging gauge hits 100 percent, you've won the mission and completed the Wings of Liberty Campaign. Congratulations, and enjoy the powerful final cinematic sequence.

IN A PINCH, UNLEASH THE ENERGY NOVA.

Don't forget that when all seems lost, you may have the artifact's amazing Energy Nova available. Just select the artifact and click the Energy Nova button to unleash the blast. Every Zerg unit within a huge radius suffers immediate damage of 550, which kills almost any Zerg, plus additional damage of 10 per second for the next 30 seconds. It's a good idea to assign a hotkey to the artifact for quick emergencies, especially if one of your chokepoints gets breached.

Remember, however, that after you release the Energy Nova it takes several minutes of cooldown time until you can use it again. So save it for really dire situations.

CHALLENGES

Challenges are a set of single player missions designed to aid your transition from the single player campaign in StarCraft II, Wings of Liberty, into the multiplayer arena on Battle.net.

Alongside the single player campaign and tutorials, the challenges serve as a very useful tool to learn some basic skills that are helpful in multiplayer matches. In general, these challenges are most useful for a new player, or one who is inexperienced in online multiplayer RTS play.

On a surface level, you can simply go after the challenges to get a Gold ranking and move on, but if you look a little deeper, there are some useful concepts to be learned here. Some of the concepts here may be very basic if you are a veteran, but keep an eye out, you might spot a few things that are helpful even if you're experienced.

All of the subjects explored in challenges (and more) are expanded on in the multiplayer strategy section of the guide, but if you don't feel like diving into everything at once (or you're just going after Achievements!), this is a good place to start.

BASIC LEVEL

Basic challenges cover fundamental unit mixes and relationships. Play through these challenges to get a feel for what units you can field effectively against opposing forces from other races. For each of the Basic level challenges, you face three rounds of battle. Each round, there are three different mixes of enemy units to fight, and a different set of units for you to control.

To complete these challenges, you need to create appropriate groups of units to counter each enemy force, and make use of positioning and abilities correctly.

After completing a Basic challenge, you can also retry individual waves to improve your score or simply practice unit control. There's a lot of room here for unit micro to shine, controlling one type of unit or your bonus caster can improve your score, and you can also improve by focus firing properly and moving units around as bait.

UNIT RELATIONSHIPS

The balance between the races is influenced heavily by the strength or weakness of each race's units against each other race at any given tech level. In other words, early in the game, if one of your basic units can handily defeat a basic unit of another race, you can have a strong advantage by scouting your opponent's army, seeing his force mix, and adjusting your own composition.

Similarly, in the midgame, if you can rush to tech for a specific unit that you know your opponents race has a difficult time handling at that stage of the game (requiring either a specific unit to counter, or solid micro and defense to stop), you can gain an advantage by making good use of that unit.

The *concepts* presented here are important. Learning what units work well against other units is the most basic building block of combat strategy in StarCraft II, and from there, you need to build those blocks into *combinations* of units that are effective. In some cases, the relationships are very obvious—anti-air units are almost always strong against air units, but even when the answer is obvious, the details become more about *what* anti-air units (or abilities) to use, and *how many* of them you need.

You don't have to spend hours testing obscure unit mixes in matches with friends to stay on top of the balance in any given patch (though there are players that do exactly that), you can often figure out the basic relationships with simple observation. If a patch changes a unit from bonus Light damage to bonus Armored damage, that's a pretty clear indication of a shift in a units role.

You can expect that players will share information on the effectiveness of units against other races and combinations of units online—though beware of opinions masquerading as fact; watch a replay demonstrating the combo, or test out the mix yourself in several matches. TheoryCraft is an ok game, but StarCraft II is a better one.

In terms of your own personal testing, the best use of your time is to experiment with unit mixes of your personal best race against the race that is giving you the most trouble. You can often find an answer that works best for you specifically, because there are often multiple solutions to any one unit problem you're encountering, and some of those may be more comfortable for you to execute, due to the micro involved, or the build order required.

HEALTH BARS

Visit your options menu and enable health bars to display always—this is a good idea for multiplayer anyway, and these Basic challenges are a good place to practice.

By having health bars visible, you can quickly and easily select and move damaged targets to the back, as well as focus on the most damaged hostile targets to eliminate them quickly.

BONUS UNITS

Each round in the Basic challenges has one or more 'bonus' caster units that can be used to supplement one or two of your combat groups.

Effective use of these bonus units makes some rounds much easier, and allows you to aim for Gold completion by preserving your own units in some encounters.

Experiment with including them in various groups, even after you've completed the challenges, it's a useful way of quickly testing their various abilities against different targets, and seeing how effective they are in various combat situations.

TACTICAL COMMAND

MISSION OVERVIEW

Survive three rounds of Zerg without losing your Supply Depots

OBJECTIVES

MAIN
- Protect all Structures for 3 Rounds (Bronze)

BONUS
- Lose 20 Units or Less (Silver)
- Lose 10 Units or Less (Gold)

ROUND 1

INITIAL FORCES: 10 HELLIONS, 20 MARINES, 1 SIEGE TANK, 2 MEDIVACS 1 GHOST

NORTHWEST: 39 ZERGLINGS

Make use of your Hellions against the Zerglings in the northwest. Practice your 'dancing' by moving them away from the Zerglings, then holding CTRL and right clicking to issue an instant attack-move command.

The Hellion's flamethrower deals area damage in a straight line, and as the Hellions also do bonus damage against Light targets, they will quickly incinerate the Zerglings.

SOUTHWEST: 12 MUTALISK

Send the Marines up this way with the Medivacs to provide healing. Marines can easily take down Mutalisks when backed by Medivacs.

Be sure to focus fire to eliminate the Mutalisks more quickly, Mutalisks become increasingly dangerous in larger numbers, because their attack bounces between targets, acting as a sort of area of effect damage.

EAST: 8 BANELINGS

Banelings deal explosive area effect damage when they make physical contact with an enemy. This damage is greater against Light targets. Set up a single Marauder to take the brunt of the damage, with the Siege Tank in Siege mode behind it to destroy the Banelings before they can get close.

ROUND 2

INITIAL FORCES: 9 MARINES, 9 MARAUDERS, 6 SIEGE TANKS, 2 MEDIVACS, 1 GHOST

NORTHWEST: 9 ROACHES

Roaches are a heavily armored shock force for the Zerg, your Marauders are perfectly suited to counter them, as they are tough enough to stand up to the Roaches, and deal bonus damage against Armored targets.

Be sure to focus fire the Roaches, they'll go down extremely quick.

SOUTHWEST: 17 HYDRALISKS

All five of your Siege Tanks in Siege Mode will quickly devastate the Hydralisks. It only takes two shots from a Siege cannon to kill a Hydralisk, and with splash damage, entire packs fall quickly to massed Siege fire.

Try to spread out your tanks in a line stretching towards the Hydralisks, it will cause your tanks to open fire sequentially, avoiding wasted shots by having all of your tanks open fire simultaneously.

EAST: 1 ULTRALISK

The Ultralisk deals rapid damage in a 180 degree arc in front of them. Send your Marauders to deal bonus Armored damage, and spread them out to avoid suffering excessive area effect damage. Having the Ultralisk attacking only one or two Marauders at a time is ideal.

ROUND 3

INITIAL FORCES: 7 MARAUDERS, 10 HELLIONS, 6 SIEGE TANKS, 5 THORS, 3 MEDIVACS, 10 VIKINGS, 1 GHOST

NORTHWEST: 22 ZERGLINGS, 5 BROOD LORDS

Send a mix of Vikings and Hellions to the northwest to dispatch these targets. The Hellions make short work of the Zerglings, and the Vikings can attack the Brood Lords *immediately* as the attack begins, as the Brood Lords and Zerglings cannot retaliate against air units.

When the fight starts, focus fire the Brood Lords with your Vikings immediately, you can start taking them down before they get in range of your Hellions.

SOUTHWEST: 17 MUTALISKS

Send the Thors as a group to the southwest, their anti-air missiles make short work of the Mutalisks.

EAST: 9 ROACHES, 12 HYDRALISKS

A mix of Siege Tanks and Marauders is your cure for the eastern wave. Put the Siege Tanks in Siege Mode to dispatch the Hydralisks, and focus fire the Roaches with your Marauders to take them down quickly. Bring the Medivacs along to heal your Marauders while they absorb fire.

BONUS UNIT

Your Ghost can be used effectively in the southwest or east, picking off Mutalisks, Hydralisks, or Roaches with Snipe.

PATH OF ASCENSION

MISSION OVERVIEW

You must survive three rounds of Terran assault without losing your Pylons.

OBJECTIVES

MAIN
- **Protect all Structures for 3 rounds (Bronze)**

BONUS OBJECTIVES
- **Lose 20 Units or Less (Silver)**
- **Lose 10 Units or Less (Gold)**

ROUND 1

INITIAL FORCES: 14 ZEALOTS, 9 STALKERS, 5 COLOSSI, 1 SENTRY

NORTH: 13 HELLIONS

Send your Stalkers to the north to deal with the Hellions. While the Hellions will deal some area damage, your Stalkers are physically larger (reducing the number that can be hit at once), and are Armored, not Light, meaning they take no bonus damage from the Hellions.

Note that this matchup is a good lesson in using not what is most effective against your target, but what is least *affected* by your target. That is, while the Stalkers deal no bonus damage against Hellions, they also

suffer no bonus damage, and because of the way Hellions area of effect damage works, they do not take a severe level of damage from the flame shots. Because they have Blink, you can also Blink each Stalker away as it becomes damaged, avoiding excessive losses if you are quick.

NORTHEAST: 55 MARINES

While this seems an overwhelming number of Marines, send your Colossi to the northeast and watch as their Thermal Lances devastate the Terran infantry. Retreat any Colossus that takes excess damage and you can avoid losing any of them.

EAST: 12 MARAUDERS

Send your force of Zealots to the east, they do not suffer bonus damage from Marauders, and can quickly surround and eliminate them.

MICRO MIXUP 1

This fight is a good example of a battle that can play out significantly differently with direct control involved. Before Zealots have Charge, upgraded Marauders that are microed well can 'dance' by shooting them with their slowing grenades, then backing up and firing again. In unrestricted terrain, this allows Marauders to kite Zealots and deal disproportionate damage, far more than they would inflict if they were simply attack moved into battle.

Keep an eye out for fights like this one that change when direct unit micro is involved. Sometimes a fight that is only even at best can be turned in your favor with direct control.

EAST: 3 BATTLECRUISERS

Send your Void Rays and focus fire them—Void Rays deal increasing damage over time, and bonus damage to Armored targets. When focused, they can quickly devastate the toughest enemy targets.

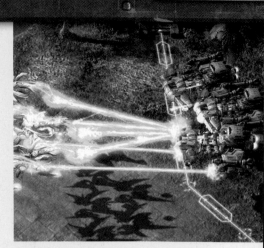

BONUS UNIT

Your Sentry can be effective with Guardian Shield in any direction; Zealots are more fragile, though you may want to screen your Stalkers while they focus fire.

Be sure to create one Hallucination early, either a pair of Zealots, Stalkers, or an Archon, depending on which direction you choose to go. Match up the unit with the incoming damage type. Placing the Hallucination in front of your regular troops guarantees that it will sponge up incoming damage.

BONUS UNIT

Your High Templar can be effective in the north or east, be careful in the northeast, as splash damage from the Siege Tanks is dangerous.

In any direction, Psionic Storm will cause heavy area of effect damage, but if you want to deal a huge amount of focused damage send the Templar north and use Feedback on the Thors. Each Feedback will deal 200 damage, and you can cast it four times!

ROUND 2

INITIAL FORCES: 7 IMMORTALS, 6 VOID RAYS, 7 CARRIERS, 1 HIGH TEMPLAR

NORTH: 10 THORS

Send your Carriers in and once they launch their Interceptors, pull them back slightly. Interceptors can attack Thors from beyond the range at which they can retaliate against the Carriers, allowing you to pick them off from a distance.

Be *sure* to focus fire with your Carriers, or the Thors will deal too much anti-air damage to your Interceptors, and then attack your Carriers directly.

NORTHEAST: 12 SIEGE TANKS

Send your Immortals to the northeast, their Hardened Shields will absorb the punishing ground fire from the tanks, and their heavy bonus Armored damage will quickly reduce them to scrap metal.

ROUND 3

INITIAL FORCES: 8 ZEALOTS, 8 STALKERS, 7 IMMORTALS, 4 ARCHONS, 4 PHOENIX, 3 COLOSSI, 1 SENTRY, 1 HIGH TEMPLAR

Properly targeting and focus firing is very important in this round, particularly in the north and east. The northeast group can generally be managed simply by moving damaged Archons out of range.

NORTH: 5 VIKINGS, 1 BATTLECRUISERS

Focus fire the Battlecruisers with your Stalkers, and have the Phoenix target the Vikings. Once the Battlecruisers drop, you can assist the Phoenix in eliminating any remaining Vikings with the Stalkers.

INEFFICIENT AIR

Phoenix are best against Light targets with little or no armor, as they fire two low damage shots against non Light targets, and if they have armor, that low damage drops even lower.

They can still get the job done even against a non-ideal target, but as is the case here, you may need ground anti-air support to come out of the fight with any reasonable number remaining.

This holds true for Zerg as well, as their Mutalisks and Corruptors are more effective against different targets, but they can still fight against a non-optimal target with the assistance of Hydralisks or Infested Terrans.

NORTHEAST: 14 HELLIONS, 14 REAPERS

These units all have bonus damage against Light targets, so send in your Archons to absorb the punishment and your Colossi to back them up. Between them, both deal heavy area of effect damage and can dispatch all of the targets with ease.

EAST: 6 MARAUDERS, 11 SIEGE TANKS

Send in your Immortals first to soak up fire and dispatch the Siege Tanks, then follow up with your Zealots targeting the Marauders.

Don't try to focus fire the Zealots directly as a whole group, as they are melee range, and need to spread out and surround multiple targets to deal the most damage possible. Selecting a smaller group and focusing does work well however.

> ### BONUS UNIT
>
> The Sentry can be used to Guardian Shield your forces in the north or east (don't forget to use Hallucinate), and you can send the High Templar to either Feedback the Battlecruisers, or Psionic Storm clumped forces in the east or north.
>
> Your Phoenix wing isn't great against Vikings or Battlecruisers, so you may want to send at least one of your bonus units north to help eliminate the opposing forces.

FOR THE SWARM

MISSION OVERVIEW

Divide up your units to protect your Spires for three rounds of attacks

OBJECTIVES

MAIN

- Protect all Structures for 3 Rounds (Bronze)

BONUS OBJECTIVES

- Lose 20 Units or Less (Silver)
- Lose 10 Units or Less (Gold)

ROUND 1

INITIAL FORCES: 10 ZERGLINGS, 21 HYDRALISKS, 4 ULTRALISKS, 1 INFESTOR

WEST: 5 COLOSSI

Send your Ultralisks to dispatch the Colossi, they are large and sturdy units that can shrug off the splash damage dealt by a Colossus. Try to spread them out to avoid suffering any needless extra damage from the Colossus' area attack.

NORTHWEST: 1 IMMORTAL

Immortals have Hardened Shields that are strong against powerful attacks, but have no effect on fast, weak attacks. Send your Zerglings to surround and eliminate the Immortal.

NORTH: 8 VOID RAYS

Void Rays deal heavy, focused damage, and bonus damage against Armored Targets. They are poor against numerous non-Armored targets, so use your Hydralisks to destroy them—be sure to focus fire to dispatch them quickly.

> ### BONUS UNIT
>
> You can make good use of your Infestor's Infested Terran ability to create a group of additional anti-air units against the Void Rays, as well as soaking up some incoming fire.
>
> You can also use Neural Parasite to gain control of a Colossus in the west, cutting down on the number of enemies your Ultralisks must face.

ROUND 2

INITIAL FORCES: 20 ROACHES, 11 MUTALISKS, 2 ULTRALISKS, 1 INFESTOR

WEST: 19 ZEALOTS

While Zealots have comparable stats to your Roaches, you have the advantage of more armor and higher base damage. Focus fire on the Zealots to eliminate them.

NORTHWEST: 5 VOID RAYS

Send your Mutalisks as a group to deal with the Void Rays. Focus fire them to take them down quickly. Void Rays cannot deal with many smaller threats efficiently, giving you an edge in this fight.

NORTH: 9 STALKERS

This number of Stalkers seems overwhelming, but send in your Ultralisks and watch the carnage. Their scything tusks deal heavy area damage, and they have the health and armor to survive the incoming damage.

MICRO MIXUP 2

Here's another good example of a muddy unit relationship. Roaches have similar armor to Stalkers, but shorter range and less movement speed. They deal more damage, but attack slightly slower. Their total health levels are comparable, though they have different methods of regeneration.

In a standup fight with the Stalkers being directly controlled to dance out of range and take shots at straggling Roaches, Stalkers can pick off pursuit one by one. This relationship changes when Roaches acquire their movement speed upgrade, and again if Stalkers acquire their Blink upgrade.

*In many cases, upgrades to a unit will change their power against other units, particularly unique tech upgrades (as opposed to general weapon or armor upgrades, though even those can have a significant impact in some cases). Whenever you compare units, be sure to consider a) what upgrades a unit can acquire and b) how long it takes to **get** those upgrades.*

BONUS UNIT

You can use your Infestor's Fungal Growth in the west. Massed small units are perfect targets for this immobilizing ability, and freezing the Zealots in place while they take damage lets your Ultralisks mop up the mobile ones safely.

Your Roaches are up against a somewhat less ideal target, so you may want to send the Infestor to help them with Infested Terrans—remember, the number of units you lose matters more than the types of units you lose, so an Ultralisk dropping isn't as bad as losing multiple Roaches when going for Gold.

ROUND 3

INITIAL FORCES: 12 ROACHES, 4 ULTRALISKS, 14 CORRUPTORS, 5 BROOD LORDS, 1 INFESTOR

WEST: 11 STALKERS, 2 IMMORTALS

Send your Brood Lords west, and focus fire on the Stalkers to eliminate the only threat to your Brood Lords. Once they are down, you can distract the Immortals from taking out the Spire with the Broodlings that are spawned with each attack.

NORTHWEST: 10 ZEALOTS, 4 ARCHONS

Send your Ultralisks and Roaches, with the Ultralisks out in front of the Roaches to soak up incoming damage. To cut down on damage taken, once the Zealots drop, focus fire the Archons with your Roaches.

NORTH: 4 CARRIERS

Focus fire with your Corruptors to take out the Carriers quickly. Remember to target the Carriers directly, you don't want Corruptors wasting shots on Interceptors.

BONUS UNIT

Send the Infestor northwest to help against the Zealots and Archons. Use Frenzy on the Ultralisks, lock Zealots in place using Fungal Growth, then take control of the Archon and turn its power against the Zealots.

ADVANCED LEVEL

Advanced challenges cover 'caster' units for each race, as well as ability focused normal units. Good use of small numbers of these units is crucial in multiplayer, so learning to control them comfortably is important.

While the Protoss advanced challenge is a straightforward survival battle, both the Terran and Zerg missions have you assaulting prepared bases. Take a moment before the challenge begins to study the terrain and choose your route of attack. The challenges aren't so static that you have to take one 'best' route to achieve a Gold rating, and there is enough flexibility for you to practice ability usage in different areas to test its effectiveness.

COVERT OPS

MISSION OVERVIEW

Kill as many enemies as possible with your starting Terran casters

OBJECTIVES
MAIN
- Kill 100 Enemies (Bronze)

BONUS
- Kill 125 Enemies (Silver)
- Kill 150 Enemies (Gold)

INITIAL FORCES: 11 GHOSTS, 8 RAVENS

You begin this mission with a mixed force of Ghosts and Ravens, as well as 7 armed Nukes for the Ghosts.

Your objective here is to kill as many enemies as possible, making use of the various special abilities of your units. Remember that Ghosts can use Cloak to reach a target and drop a nuke, but you must first kill any Detectors in the area (Spore Crawlers or Overseers).

GHOST USAGE

Your Ghosts are useful for attacking Light enemy units (or any units while cloaked), dropping Nukes on fixed Zerg defenses (or large clumps of enemies), and occasionally for using Snipe to pick off targets.

RAVEN USAGE

Ravens are useful in a normal match for their status as a mobile Detector, and in all situations for their abilities. All three abilities that a Raven possesses are useful; Auto-Turrets and Seeker Missiles can be used to destroy enemies, and Point Defense Drones can protect your units from hostile forces.

When moving as a group and facing light enemy resistance, drop a few Auto Turrets and let your Ghosts clean up the Zerg while they are distracted. If you are facing larger groups of ranged foes, make use of at least one Point Defense Drone to sponge up damage.

If you spot a very large clumped group of enemies, drop a Seeker Missile in the middle of them.

CLEARING THE ZERG

There are pockets of Zerg units and structures scattered all about the map, with the largest concentrations in the north and northeast, where a Hatchery and a Hive provide juicy Drone targets as bonus kills.

Be sure to hotkey your Ghosts and Ravens into two separate groups. When performing more delicate operations with Cloaked Ghosts, try to make use of only one at a time for dropping Nukes, or multiples if you are making a Cloaked attack on enemy Light units.

To wipe out the greatest number of forces, you need to land Nukes on the northwest base, the northeast base, and the center unit clump. Use Nukes to clear out the large Spine Crawler wall in front of the northeast base, then a few more to clear the way to the back of the Hive, wiping out all units and workers in the area.

Between the two groups of workers, the large clump of troops in the center, and the incidental kills you pick up while moving, you should easily pass the Gold mark, as long as you move reasonably quickly.

Remember to use Auto Turrets to distract lone Spine Crawlers, and let your Ghosts finish them off, along with any nearby enemies.

Stealthy Cloak usage is not necessary here to rack up the kills, you mostly want to get in and land Nukes on the largest concentration of units to increase your score as quickly as possible.

That said, once you're comfortable with 'Nuke rushing' the map, spend some time playing around with Cloak, Snipe, Point Defense Drones, and Seeker Missiles. The experience gained here can be quite useful online.

PSIONIC ASSAULT

MISSION OVERVIEW

Kill as many enemies as possible with your starting Protoss casters

OBJECTIVES
MAIN
- Kill 75 Enemies (Bronze)

BONUS
- Kill 150 Enemies (Silver)
- Kill 225 Enemies (Gold)

INITIAL FORCES: 11 SENTRIES, 6 HIGH TEMPLAR

PSIONIC POWER

This mission focuses on the powerful caster units of the Protoss. The High Templar's Psionic Storm, combined with careful usage of Hallucinations and Force Field will lead you to victory.

Remember that you can make use of Sentry Force Fields to block the narrow ramps leading to your starting platform, very helpful for stopping units while they are attacked by your Sentries, and shredded by Psionic Storm.

BLOCKING LINE OF SIGHT

On mixed waves with ranged attackers that do **not** have air units or Reapers mixed in, you need to be sure that you place Force Fields very low on the ramp.

If a hostile unit gets even part of the way up the ramp, they **will** gain line of sight to your units, and any ranged attackers outside will open fire on your units in range.

This is particularly noticeable during the Zealot/Sentry wave, but it can happen on any Terran wave as well if you aren't careful with positioning.

When it comes to Hallucinating units, make use of Archons most frequently, they give the most health of any Hallucinated unit, though if you want *more* units, Zealots or Stalkers are a good choice as well.

WAVES

New waves of units constantly stream in to attack you, beginning in the northeast, then the southeast, and finally the northwest as well. The northeast and southeast both have ramps that can be blocked by a double Force Field, while the northwest is (initially) blocked by Destructible Rocks.

When a wave consists of no Reapers or aerial units, you can use twin Force Fields to shut out the hostile units and pick them off with Sentries and Psionic Storm usage. Be sure to use Force Fields to stop Banelings from getting in range of your units.

Remember that once energy for Psionic Storm runs low (try not to use it more than once per pack if possible), morph the depleted High Templar into an Archon. There isn't time to wait for Energy to regenerate.

With good usage of Force Fields and Hallucinated Archons, you should be able to squeeze out 3 Psionic Storms per High Templar, giving you *eighteen* total storms, that's a lot of damage, as long as you place it carefully.

ENERGY MANAGEMENT

Remember that two Force Fields will block any ramp, and that the Energy cost is the same as a single Hallucination.

Make use of Force Fields when you can block the units completely, and Hallucinations when you cannot (whether due to Reapers, air units, or ranged attackers).

Try to avoid using more than two Force Fields or one Hallucination per wave if at all possible, the longer you stretch out your Sentry Energy supply the better.

As a general rule, let your Sentries do the work, and later, your Archons and Sentries, with only one to two storms used per wave.

Nailing Bronze or even Silver isn't too difficult with good unit control, but Gold requires that you squeeze every bit of efficiency out of your units, so monitor your ability usage carefully.

THE WAVES

Here's an exact listing of what you up to the 21st Wave (and the needed kills to reach Gold).

Should you survive past this point, waves will continue to come at you…how long can you survive?

1. 14 Zerglings (NE)

2. 10 Marines

3. 8 Zerglings, 4 Hydralisks

4. 13 Marines, 1 Marauder

5. 16 Zerglings, 8 Banelings, 1 Roach

6. 10 Marines, 3 Marauders

7. 22 Zerglings (SE)

8. 6 Zealots, 5 Sentries (SE)

9. 10 Reapers (NE)

10. 6 Reapers (SE)

11. 4 Banelings, 6 Hydralisks (SE)

12. 2 Banshees (NE)

13. 4 Stalkers (NE)

14. 10 Reapers, 2 Ghosts (SE)

15. 6 Mutalisks (NE)

16. 10 Marines, 2 Marauders, 2 Vikings (SE)

17. 20 Zerglings (NW)

18. 6 Roaches (NW)

19. 1 Ultralisk (NW)

20. 10 Banelings (NE)

21. 2 Siege Tanks (SE)

INFESTATION

MISSION OVERVIEW

Kill as many enemies as possible with your initial units, you have 5 minutes.

OBJECTIVES

MAIN
- Kill 75 Enemies (Bronze)

BONUS
- Kill 100 Enemies (Silver)
- Kill 125 Enemies (Gold)

INITIAL FORCES: 10 ROACHES (WITH BURROW MOVEMENT UPGRADE), 9 INFESTORS

SWARM PREPARATION

This mission teaches you to make good use of two Zerg units that have the unique ability to move while Burrowed, the Roach and the Infestor. The Infestor is also the Zerg caster unit, and good use of its abilities here is crucial for achieving a Gold rating.

A large Terran base with a few Protoss Colossi defending it is located to the northwest of your position. You need to sneak in and eliminate as many packs of Marines and (eventually) the SCVs mining at the Command Center to rack up a good kill score.

WATCH THOSE RAVENS

Without Ravens present, you can abuse Burrow movement heavily, moving your units freely about the Terran base, avoiding or controlling any dangerous units on your way to the tasty worker line at the back of the base.

Use Infested Terrans to deal with any Ravens you do spot, or simply avoid them entirely.

CONSUMING THE TERRAN

The fastest and easiest way to clear this mission is to use Neural Parasite to gain control of the Siege Tanks and Colossi scattered about the level. Doing so allows you to quickly mop up the Marine packs, and once you gain control of the Siege Tank and Colossus near the Terran Command Center, you can wipe out the SCV line and inflate your kill score greatly.

Use your Roaches as bullet sponges for your Infestors, let them take hits while your Neural Parasite controlled Siege Tank or Colossus destroys any nearby forces. Remember that your Roaches can heal rapidly while Burrowed, so careful micro will allow you to preserve most, if not all of them.

Infestors on the other hand, are quite frail, so be careful about going for the Neural Parasite if there are enemies around.

Fungal Growth also works well for dealing heavy damage to Marine packs, and Infested Terrans can be used to take down hostile Ravens, but try to save Energy for Neural Parasite use whenever possible, controlling all of the area of effect damage dealers on the level will lead you to an easy win.

Once you've knocked off the Gold, experiment with using Fungal Growth and Infested Terrans, as well as Roach Burrow micro for the practice.

> ### ABILITY USAGE
>
> *You can deal with Siege Tanks easily by moving up beside them and having a few Roaches pop up. Remember, Siege tanks in Siege Mode have a minimum range, they cannot fire at units right beside them.*

EXPERT LEVEL

Expert level challenges are focused on more general skills applicable to all races—good hotkey usage, economic buildup, and defending against an early rush.

HARBINGER OF DEATH

Use hotkeys only to kill as many units as possible in 2 minutes 30 seconds.

OBJECTIVES

MAIN

- Kill 50 Enemies (Bronze)

BONUS

- Kill 100 Enemies (Silver)
- Kill 150 Enemies (Gold)

This mission can feel intimidating the first time you tackle it, but it is easily one of the most important challenges. Learning proper group and hotkey usage is *vitally* important for your development in multiplayer, and this is a good basic tutorial. The initial groups that you begin with are actually quite effective in the respective directions they are facing, you simply need to manage them properly by making good use of hotkeys.

GROUP HOTKEYS

The number of groups you need to manage on this challenge is actually far **higher** than what you need to manage to be effective in a multiplayer match. In a normal multiplayer match, you will rarely be dealing with more than three major control groups unless the game goes long (or you're especially fond of raiding groups).

Consider this good practice for cycling between groups and handling multiple fights at once.

Several of the engagements here are relatively fire and forget. The northwest, northeast, and east can all be simply attack-moved to victory, while the Stalkers in the southeast and High Templar in the southwest need their Blink and Psionic Storm directly managed to rack up kills.

Spend some time experimenting on this mission with combat in the various areas, it's good practice for managing a variety of unit mixes and abilities at once.

Try to clear out the northeast or southwest fully, even if you aren't going for Gold, it's still a useful exercise to manage your troops purely with hotkeys.

One last note: while group hotkeys rarely hit the numbers that you see here, **ability** hotkeys, and hotkeys for your production structures are **always** important in every multiplayer match. If you take away anything from this challenge, it is that you should always be using hotkeys for your abilities, unit production, and base management.

And don't freak out if you find this overwhelming or uncomfortable at first, you don't have to master these overnight! Pick a few to learn and work on them, over time, they become muscle memory.

You need to warp in some ground units in the northwest and north-east to get enough kills for Gold. Move a single Warp Prism from the northeast to the northwest, and put them into Phasing mode to allow you to warp in units on the ground.

In the northwest, make use of your Phoenix in a group with some warped in Dark Templar. The Phoenix can deal with the Mutalisks while the ground forces are quickly eliminated by the Dark Templar.

In the northeast, warp in a group of Dark Templar and send them to eliminate ground threats. There are Overseers here that will cause your Dark Templar to be eliminated eventually. If you were trying to clear this area properly, mixing in Stalkers would help, but it isn't necessary for this challenge, as you need to turn your attention to other groups quickly.

In the east, send your Carriers to wipe out the Marines and Missile Turrets. Be sure to enable Autocast of Build Interceptor (hold Alt and press the Interceptor hotkey to enable Autocasting). This will rebuild any Interceptors lost to ranged fire.

In the southeast, Blink your Stalker group up onto the ledge, then down to the lower level in the southeast, picking off Reapers as you go. Finally Blink them up to the small ledge in the southeast to eliminate the last of the Reapers.

In the southwest, keep Guardian Shield activated, and Hallucinate up a few Archons to soak up damage. Once that's done, move around and unleash the pain with repeated Psionic Storms to wipe out the mixed Terran groups.

If you can manage to trigger all of these groups and use their abilities, you should easily clear Gold, and gain some good experience in fighting in multiple areas.

You may want to play through this challenge a few times to practice your hotkey usage, switching between groups and using abilities via hotkeys should be instinctive. In multiplayer matches, you should rarely be clicking on the Command Card.

Selecting an upgrade from an upgrade structure with the mouse usually isn't a problem, but in battle, you should always be using hotkeys to trigger abilities. Similarly, queuing up new units by clicking on them is usually ok, though you should be using their hotkeys while in battle (and always as Zerg!)

OPENING GAMBIT

Build a strong economy and a large army while fighting off early enemy assaults within 18 minutes.

OBJECTIVES

MAIN

- Train 30 Marines
- Train 8 Siege Tanks
- Train 8 Ghosts

BONUS

- 2 Minutes Remaining (Silver)
- 4 Minutes Remaining (Gold)

This mission tests your ability to efficiently build up a base and expand, while creating a sizable military force and repelling hostile raids against your bases. This is a perfect mission for practicing a smooth buildup of workers and military forces, as well as learning to manage expansion creation and development.

You begin with 6 SCVs, 50 Minerals, and a single Command Center, and you must build up a large military within the time limit to hit Gold ranking. To reach Gold, you're going to have to expand early, so try to do so sooner rather than later! Ideally, you should be expanding immediately after the first group, and erecting a Bunker to help hold off the second wave. Rally your newly created units to the ledge overlooking your natural expansion's choke-point, and eventually add Bunkers guarded by SCVs set to Autocast Repair.

Once you get Siege Tech for your Siege Tanks, defense becomes even easier, and you should be on autopilot until your units finish building.

Be sure to get up Refineries at your expansion and put 3 SCVs on each, you don't want to end up gas starved while creating Ghosts and Siege Tanks.

Alongside a Barracks with a Reactor, two Factories and a Barracks with Tech Labs attached can create enough Ghosts and Siege Tanks in time, but you cannot starve yourself of Gas or lose your Ghosts or Siege Tanks. Be sure to protect Ghosts inside Bunkers, and repair Siege Tanks (and Bunkers) with SCVs.

Don't forget to do a worker transfer. Up to 16 workers, your SCVs are highly efficient while gathering Minerals, this drops off as they approach 24 (3 per Mineral patch). To avoid this diminishing returns as long as possible, transfer any excess workers from your main to your expansion, then resume building up workers to max out your production.

Don't Supply cap yourself—keep an eye on it as you pump workers and military units, and periodically build up single, and later, double Supply Depots.

RUSH DEFENSE

Learn how to fight off early rush attacks by Protoss and Zerg forces as a Terran.

OBJECTIVES

MAIN

- Survive the Zergling Rush
- Destroy the Protoss Structures

BONUS

- Lose 16 Units or Less (Silver)
- Lose 9 Units or Less (Gold)

> ### SUPPLY
>
> *Remember you're going to need at least 70 Supply just for your military alone, and if you max out both bases, that's another 60 Supply worth of workers, for 130 total.*
>
> *Your initial Command Center and expansion account for 13 Supply, meaning you still need somewhere near 15 Supply Depots, depending on how many SCVs you wind up creating.*

This challenge is a two-stage battle, as you first have to fight off several waves of Zerglings using only your SCVs, and then you need to fight off a Protoss that has aggressively built into your base with a Photon Cannon and forward Gateways.

This challenge teaches you some very important skills that are critical in a multiplayer match, for any race. Remember, your workers are always a viable fighting unit!

The Zerg will send larger waves as time goes by, including Ultralisks, but as long as you have a few Bunkers erected and Siege Tanks in Siege Mode on your ridge, none of these attacks should even get near your worker lines.

Be sure to use Snipe on your Ghosts to take down any Mutalisks quickly. You can use it on Roaches as well, but your Siege Tanks will usually dispatch them quickly enough.

EXPANSION AND GROWTH

This challenge is perfect practice for exactly the sort of economic, infrastructure, and military buildup that you should *always* be doing while in a multiplayer match.

It's important to take away the lesson from this challenge that you need to build up your economy, military, and infrastructure simultaneously. If you slack in any area, your opponent can pull ahead of you, without having to actually engage you in battle. The economic and infrastructure/tech war might not be as interesting as actual combat, but it is every bit as important as fighting or scouting.

PART 1: ZERGLING RUSH

You begin with 11 SCVs, a single Supply Depot, and your Command Center. Begin building more SCVs (and don't stop building them!).

When Zerglings attack, pull your SCVs from mining and attack the Zerglings. To minimize incoming damage, select a small number of your SCVs and put their Repair ability on Autocast (hold Shift and press the Repair hotkey, or right click on the Repair ability).

ZERGLING BATTLE

Small numbers of Zerglings can easily be defeated by SCVs, and this also applies to small numbers of Zealots.

The key is to surround them, so pulling your workers out from the Minerals and attack moving on open ground is a good idea, to allow the maximum number to surround.

Any SCVs that you have set to Autocast Repair will prioritize repairing over attacking, so be **sure** that you have sufficient SCVs that are actually fighting to kill the Zerglings quickly. You don't want half your SCVs repairing each other while they are chewed up!

The starting timer counts down from 57 seconds; when that hits 0 the Zerglings will spawn and start heading to your base. It takes them about 24 seconds to walk all the way to you Command Center. You must defeat 22 Zerglings in total.

RUSHDOWN

While this challenge can't **really** teach you what it's like to be rushed in a multiplayer match, it does give you a very good grounding in the basics of **defending** from such a rush.

The main point is to simply keep your cool and make use of your defensive advantages. Your units are being produced right where they need to be (by your workers), and your workers can join the battle at any time to tip the scales in your favor.

Losing a few workers to fight off an early attack is **always** the right choice. The alternative is losing your workers (and probably the game). Not much of a decision is it?

A true rush also damages your opponent's economy, and once you become skilled at fending them off, you will find that beating opponents who try to pull these stunts on you fairly easy.

Aggressive early attacks are likely to come at you from any more skilled player, and may not cripple their economy, so it is still important to learn how to fight off attacks when you have little more than your workers and your first few basic units.

Remember, fine unit control matters a lot more when there are **less** units on the field, and even more when you are fighting a critical battle—and there is nothing more critical than a fight in your base in the beginning of the game, where losing it can lose you the match.

PART 2: GATEWAY RUSH

In the second half of this challenge, you begin with 11 SCVs, a Supply Depot, and your Command Center.

A Protoss Probe soon begins warping in Gateways near your base, covered by a Photon Cannon. To complete the challenge, you must build up enough of a military force to forcibly evict the Protoss from your base, while losing as few units as possible.

Get a Barracks and Bunkers up as fast as possible to protect against the attacks, while you build up more Marines to repel the Zealots completely. Because you begin with some Minerals, you can begin creating your initial Barracks immediately. Get two up, while continuing to pump out new SCVs. Don't forget to start a Refinery after you get a few more SCVs out, you'll need the Vespene Gas for a Tech Lab and a Reactor. Once the Barracks finishes, you can then create Bunkers (and an Engineering Bay if you really want an overwhelming advantage).

The first Zealot attack comes at 1:30, and should be right around the time your first Marine is emerging. If you can bait the Zealot, get it to chase your Marine while a second Marine and a Bunker are being created. Once you have two Marines (or one and a Bunker), you can kill the first Zealot easily.

It's also possible to simply mob the Zealot with your workers while a Marine fires, though you will lose workers if you use this method.

After the first Zealot, the Protoss will periodically send groups of Zealots against you. Use your Bunkers to hide your Marines and repair them while under attack by the Zealots. This should easily hold off the first attacks, while you add a Tech Lab and Reactor, and begin to create Marauders and Reapers.

When you have a sufficient force to repel the Zealots easily, push back and destroy their structures. Be sure to take down the Pylons first, before you destroy the Photon Cannon—shutting down the Pylons powers down all remaining Protoss structures in the area, allowing you to destroy the Photon Cannon losing any units (though a large enough group of Marauders can simply attack it directly).

UNIT PRESERVATION

Saving as many workers as possible is always important any time you are rushed or raided, but don't hesitate to take some losses in a multiplayer match to eliminate the threat swiftly.

In this challenge, you can take your time because the goal is saving units, not quickly eliminating the threat.

In a multiplayer match, unit preservation is still important, but time also becomes a factor. Losing a worker or two to quickly kick an early push out of your base is preferable to spending a lot of time and micro to kill the assault without any losses (of course, if you can manage to kill the units quickly **and** save your units, so much the better!).

RUSH DEFENSE

While this Challenge can't accurately replicate the level of micro control a player will use against you online, it does give you a good feel for what an aggressive early push can feel like, and trains you in the proper response techniques.

It is vitally important that you remember that workers can fight back, as defending against very early rushes with all races is fairly simple as long as you remember that simple fact. You may lose a few workers to the rush, but a real rush damages your opponent's economy, so at worst you'll be even, and often in better shape.

The Protoss push is a different type of rush, a forward Gateway (or Barracks) by Protoss or Terran is one way for them to apply heavier pressure to you by shortening the distance between their base and yours for newly created units.

It's important to understand that you are no worse off than even in such a fight however, and the scenario presented here is actually **worse** than most situations you should expect to encounter online—generally, a forward Gateway or Barracks push is a short distance outside your base, giving you the benefit of a potential chokepoint, plus the greater travel time for hostile units.

While there are many new features in StarCraft II, and new units and abilities to play with, for the average player, the most dramatic improvement may well be the matchmaking system built into the new Battle.net. With it, Blizzard has now made it easy for anyone to get into a match, and not just any match, but a *good* match.

Amazingly though, the core aspects of the game; harvesting, base building, and combat, are still entirely intact, and those fundamentals still determine the outcome of a match in StarCraft II as much as they ever did in StarCraft, from the crazy 8 player FFA matches to the highest levels of 1v1 matches played for thousands of dollars.

Some of the best games of StarCraft II multiplayer are those that are tough fights. Interesting matches where you feel like every decision you make could win or lose the game.

We wrote this multiplayer guide to help you to make *good* decisions.

It is impossible to predict what the face of StarCraft II multiplayer will be in a year, much less in twelve, but we believe that the fundamentals will still be important, and that is what we have chosen to focus on.

While build orders will change, stats will be tweaked, abilities will be altered, and the metagame on Battle.net will shift from month to month and patch to patch, the heart of the game will not, and we have tried to share a look at that heart, with a focus on all the fundamental areas of a multiplayer match.

We hope you enjoy the guide and the game! Have fun on Battle.net, and bring some friends. Multiplayer with your buddies is the best multiplayer.

MULTIPLAYER

BATTLENET®

Welcome to the new and improved Battle.net! This upgrade to Blizzard's Battle.net service is a massive overhaul that impacts not just StarCraft II, but all of Blizzard's products.

We've prepared this section to act as a mini-guide to the new Battle.net, so that you can absorb some information about all of the new features that are available specifically in StarCraft II, as well as other features that are shared across all Blizzard titles.

SOCIAL SYSTEMS

Battle.net social functions are fully integrated into all aspects of StarCraft II, whether you are playing online, in the campaign, or simply logged into Battle.net.

From anywhere within StarCraft II, you can access the Friends List. This allows you to quickly:

- Text chat with friends

- Broadcast a text message to all Real ID friends

- Create a chat room with multiple friends

- Invite or join friends into a party, private chat, or game

The text chat functions actually extend beyond StarCraft II—in World of Warcraft and any future Blizzard titles, you can send text chat messages to friends, even in different games. You could, for example, send a message from inside a StarCraft II ladder match to a friend running a Heroic dungeon in World of Warcraft!

THE FRIENDS LIST

Most Battle.net social functions are handled through the friends list, which is a simple window that can be accessed from anywhere within StarCraft II—in the single player campaign, online but not in a game, or while in a match.

From this interface, you can send messages to friends, join games, add new friends, accept invites, and set your online status.

Private chat lobbies can also be created on the fly, so you can create a chat room with one or more of your friends (or accept an invite to one) whenever you want.

THE PARTY

Parties let you quickly get together with your friends and play together online in StarCraft II.

Parties are handled through the party interface, which is not accessible while in-game, but is visible at all times while in Battle.net interface. Party invites can be sent to players anywhere online, in-game or not!

Parties are automatically placed into a private voice chat channel, and the party leader can take the whole party into team ladder matches or join custom games.

PARTY MATCHMAKING

In addition to being able to join ranked team match-making while in a party, Battle.net automatically tracks each group of players you participate in ladder play with!

This means that if you play with several different friends of varying skill levels, over time, Battle.net will automatically try to match you up with other teams who have roughly the same total skill level.

REAL ID AND CHARACTER ID

The friends system on Battle.net operates on two levels of identity. The first level is Character ID—this is simply a 'public' character name that is visible to anyone online. Anyone can add you as a CID friend, and you can add anyone as a friend from their CID.

Character ID level only shows the name of the character—in StarCraft II, this is your non-unique character name.

Real ID is an optional, richer level of identity, as it displays your real name, and can ONLY be shared by adding a friend through an email address. To establish a RID relationship you must accept the invite. You can send or receive and then accept an email invite with a Battle.net email. You can also add RID friends via Friends of Friends or via Facebook.

Character ID

- Can be added by anyone

- CANNOT join in progress to a Character ID friend, must be invited

- Can chat, view profile, and see online status

Real ID

- Can be added through Battle.net email invite and Friends of Friends or via Facebook

- Real name is visible, shows real name and character account you are logged in on World of Warcraft and StarCraft II

- Cross game chat is possible between Real ID friends

- Rich presence info is shared—you will be visible as Online in 2v2 Match on Lost Temple, or Online in a Heroic Dungeon in World of Warcraft!

- Offline status will show when you were last online

- Real ID friends can broadcast text messages to all Real ID friends online

- Real ID friends and broadcasts can be removed or disabled

It is also possible for a party leader to create a Custom Game with their party, and then open the game to the public, which allows you to quickly fill a game with friends before inviting in other players.

Parties cannot normally join games that are smaller than the party size [in other words, you can't join a 2v2 fixed team Automatic Matchmaking (AMM) match, or a 3 player Free For All (FFA) Custom Game with a 4 person party]. You *can* however create a 2v2 Custom Game room with a 4 person party, allowing you to easily play team games with your friends.

It is also possible to join a *larger* AMM match with a smaller party, and Battle.net will find you additional teammates to fill any missing slots.

TEXT CHAT

Text chat is pervasive and available at any time while logged into Battle. net. It is also integrated into the game in both the in-line chat system, and through a separate message window.

This means you can, for example, send a quick message to your party while in a StarCraft II match, or open up a windowed chat with several of your Real ID friends, one in a StarCraft II game, one sitting in Battle.net, and one in a dungeon in World of Warcraft!

CHAT SHORTCUTS

You can even use some basic slash (/) commands in the in-game chat of StarCraft II or World of Warcraft!

Use /r to reply to the last private message you received, or /p to send a quick message to your party!

Chat conversations are automatically stored, so you can start a private chat with one or more friends in the lobby, play a match or two, return to the chat window, and the chat history will remain intact.

IN-GAME CHAT

In-game chat in StarCraft II works as you would normally expect—you can cycle between All chat or Ally chat as usual, or use the shortcut keys to quickly access either chat mode using Enter or Shift-Enter.

In addition, by tapping TAB with the in-game chat open, you can cycle through recent private messages from friends, in case you want to fire back a quick reply.

VOICE CHAT

Voice chat is also available on Battle.net, and is always active during two situations; while in a party, or while on a team in a match.

If you join a larger match as a Party (in other words, your party of 3 joins a 4v4 match), you automatically join the team 'voice chat channel', so that you can hear your allies while in the match. Once the game ends and you are back in the lobby, voice chat automatically reverts to your party only.

Individual players can enable or disable their mic, and adjust the volume level or mute specific players (Battle.net also automatically adjusts player volume so you don't get your ears blown out or have to yell to be heard!).

When a player is speaking, it also pops up their RID or CID name while in a match, so you can quickly tell who on your team is speaking!

TOASTS

At any time while you are logged in, small message toasts will pop up to notify you of friend activity, keeping you in touch with your online buddies.

SAMPLE AUTOMATIC ALERTS

- Friend Online
- Friend Request
- Chat Request
- New Broadcast message

Toasts can be disabled entirely if you would prefer not to be bothered by them.

YOUR PROFILE

Your StarCraft II Battle.net profile is a repository for information about your StarCraft II character. You can check match statistics in various game modes, view your Achievements, check match history, access unlockabel rewards, you can also check out your own or view other peoples profiles.

MATCHMAKING

Automatic Matchmaking (AMM) is a core function of the new Battle.net, with the intention of allowing you (and your friends) to quickly get into satisfying, challenging matches.

Leagues are collections of Divisions: Bronze, Silver, Gold, Platinum, Diamond. On top of the five leagues are two special leagues: Semi Pro and Pro, which will be added after launch.

AMM MODES

Automatic Matchmaking covers 1v1, 2v2, 3v3, 4v4, FFA, and Co-op Vs A.I. gameplay modes.

In addition, for the team based modes (2v2, 3v3, and 4v4), AMM supports both fixed teams, and random teams.

Free for all and Co-op Vs A.I. games use the AMM system, but they do not have the same League and Division system as the other modes (see below), but you can earn FFA and Co-op specific Achievements.

Co-op Vs A.I. are 2vsA.I. or 3vsA.I. matches, where you can team up against the computer in a classic compstomp match!

LEAGUES

A League is a collection of Divisions that are all around the same skill level. In the higher level Leagues, the players are progressively more experienced and skilled at the game.

Practice	Bronze	Silver	Gold	Platinum	Diamond

The Practice League is 'time limited'—players can only be a newbie for so long, and once their account is kicked out of the Newbie League, they cannot return to it.

The Practice League also features special, anti-rush maps, and plays at a slower game speed, to give new players a chance to get used to StarCraft II multiplayer.

The Pro League is a special, invite-only League that gathers the best players from many Divisions.

Playing in the Pro League places certain demands on the players— they must play a certain minimum number of matches, they cannot be inactive for long periods of time, and eventually Pro League replays are automatically uploaded for the community to view.

Fight your way to the top of your Division to gain access to ever-higher Leagues, Tournaments, and possibly the Pro League as well!

PLACEMENT MATCHES

You are given a limited number of placement matches for each game mode. In other words, you can play your placement rounds in 1v1, a different set in 2v2 fixed teams, and yet another in 3v3 random teams.

If you team up with a new player for a 2v2 fixed team match, you will have a new set of placement matches for that specific team.

To begin the matchmaking process, you simply have to select Multiplayer for the first time. Simple select your race and game mode to start playing.

Once you have completed your placement rounds, the matchmaking system automatically places you into a Division and a League. A Division is a collection of 100 players of similar skill, and once inside a Division, you battle with your pool of opponents for the duration of a Battle.net Season. Note that if Battle.net can't find you a player online inside your Division, it *will* look for players of similar skill in other Divisions—but all points earned through play are applied to your personal Division for ranking purposes.

All online players participating in AMM matches compete for position within their Divisions, and at the end of a StarCraft II Season, the top players within each Division are automatically invited to end of season tournaments which will be added later.

DIVISION PLACEMENT

The placement matches are used to determine your initial Ladder position within a given Division. You won't ever be placed within the top, tournament qualifying slots of a Division, but you will be slotted in based on your performance.

It is possible to move up or down from one League to another, if you perform exceptionally well (or poorly) within your Division for an extended period of time. In general, once you are matched into a given League level, you should expect to face challenging, but not insurmountable opponents.

SABBATICAL

If you happen to take a break for a few days (or even weeks), you don't have to worry about your ranking decaying automatically in your Ladders.

You will however, naturally drop down the Ladder as other players do participate in matches, so unless you luck out and end up in the slowest Division on Battle.net, don't expect to reach 1st place, leave for a month, and return to still be in the top slot!

CHECK ME OUT!

You can check the position of any of your friends within their Divisions and Leagues, and compare your rankings.

LEAGUES, DIVISIONS, AND TOURNAMENTS

Leagues and Divisions are essentially the new, automatic form of the StarCraft and Warcraft ladders and tournaments.

By placing you into a small pool of similarly skilled opponents, you can fight your way to the top of your Division Ladder, earning the right to participate in end-of-Season Tournaments, and potentially, rewards (and bragging rights).

Leagues are broader categories of player skill—within any given League, many hundreds and thousands of Divisions will be battling it out, competing for the top spots within a given League level.

THE PRACTICE LEAGUE

For very new players, we strongly recommend that you start in the Practice League, when you log into Multiplayer for the first time.

This places you into a special new players League, where you will battle it out against other green players on special anti-rushing maps, at a slower game speed than the normal League matches.

Note that you *cannot* remain in this newbie League indefinitely. Once you've played enough matches and the system is satisfied that you've improved, you're placed into a Division within a normal League, and you can begin your fight to the top!

SMURFY

Worried about Smurfing accounts? Don't be—ALL online Characters are tied to a single StarCraft II key. Once a given account is experienced enough, they can't get back into the newbie League through any means!

'BONUS POINTS'

World of Warcraft has Rested Experience, StarCraft II has Division bonus points.

Say that you are competing well within your Division, and approaching the top ranks, but then you have to take a break for a week.

If this occurs, you will build up bonus ranking points to your account. Note that bonus points are accrued over time whether you are playing or not, but you may not notice their buildup if you are playing constantly.

When you return and begin to play matches online again, you will begin to earn those bonus ranking points by winning matches. The tougher your opponent, the more bonus points from your pool you earn.

Unlike Rested Experience in World of Warcraft, there is no maximum force bonus points. If you take a long break, you can then play a good number of matches to earn all of your accumulated bonus points. This allows you to stay competitive within your Division as long as you make at least an occasional commitment to play matches!

THE NEW CUSTOM GAME INTERFACE

The old Battle.net Interface (and many other RTS game lobbies) used a game lobby that simply displayed each available game on a giant list.

In other words, if there were 500 hosts who created public games, you would see 500 different games, each with a different player written title.

This made finding a joining a specific map and a specific lobby a bit difficult, especially if you were trying to join as a group of friends.

The new Battle.net Custom Game Interface works differently. When you see a specific map, with specific match settings (2v2 Lost Temple for example), you are actually seeing ALL 2v2, Lost Temple games that have been created, across ALL of Battle.net on a single line entry!

When you join that 2v2 Lost Temple game, Battle.net simply inserts you into a game that has space for you.

If you are in a Party, Battle.net will automatically join your Party into a game that has space (in this case, you and one friend would join the open team of a 2v2 Lost Temple game).

If you are online in a larger party, only games that have maps and settings that can fit your whole party will be visible!

CUSTOM GAMES

Custom Games is an entirely separate section of Battle.net, separate from the AMM system. While the Custom Games Interface does not use automatic matchmaking, it *does* have some very sophisticated interface to help you get into the games you are interested in, whether playing alone, or with your friends in a party.

The Custom Games Interface has two major functions—you can Create a Custom Game room, or you can Join an already existing lobby.

The Custom Games Interface looks somewhat similar to the StarCraft or Warcraft Custom Game Interface—there is a list of available lobbies, and a set of dropdown filters to find a specific map type, game size, or game speed.

However, very much unlike the old Battle.net lobbies, the new Custom Games Interface gives you powerful control over what games are visible, and has a new system for joining or creating a game lobby.

In addition to the new 'room' list, there are also new filtering tools that allow you to quickly find a match on a map of your choice, with settings of your choice. You can even search for a specific map name, or show ONLY new maps.

POPULARITY

Because the Custom Games Interface now 'combines' all game lobbies of a given map and game settings into one single line, this allows Battle.net to show the 'popularity' of a given map based on the rate that a specific map is being played over all of Battle.net.

This means that if a player (perhaps you!) creates a new map, and many people begin to download and create games for it, over time, its popularity will automatically increase, and finding matches on that map will become increasingly easy.

But don't worry if you're a map creator, or you enjoy playing new maps and mods—you can use the filters system to find ONLY new or 'unpopular' maps to try them out.

Fun maps will naturally gain in popularity as time goes by, and the filtering tools guarantee that you can always find something new to play.

FILTERS

Filters are very simple tools that allow you to find specific maps and settings. It is also possible to search for a specific map by name, in addition to any other settings.

Naturally, you can create a lobby with any map and setting that you want, but to find a room with a map and settings you like, you can specify, for example, that you want a 3v3 on a new, custom map.

Filters allow you to sort through all of the various maps that are being offered for play on Battle.net at any time. Because you can automatically download a new map by joining the lobby, you can always find something new to play by using the Filters system.

There are a few unique properties of the new Custom Game lobbies. By default, when you create a Custom Game, it is Private. Once you have configured the settings to your liking (or invited some friends to join you), you can then make the game Public.

Doing so has two effects—first, it allows other, non-friend players to find your game, and second, it removes the ability to kick players from your lobby. If you open your game, you can't start ejecting other players and parties from your lobby!

SPECTATORS

Spectators can be invited into Custom Games to observe a match.

SINGLE PLAYER

Even while playing 'single player', you are still online and connected to Battle.net. The messenger is still active, and it is still possible to receive messages and notifications while playing the Campaign, Co-op vs A.I., or Challenges.

Should you accept a party invite from a Campaign map, it will immediately save your game and let you leave to join a party or game room.

CLOUD FILE STORAGE

Battle.net supports automatic online saving of your campaign progress to your account. Should you log in at a friends house, you can then resume your campaign play from any completed mission save point.

If you explicitly create a saved game, it is stored locally on your hard drive.

EDITOR INTEGRATION

The StarCraft II Editor is fully integrated with the new Battle.net feature set, particularly in the area of Map sharing.

It is now possible to create a custom map in the Editor, set the specific settings you want that map to be played with (for example, 2v2 Teams only), and then publish the map to Battle.net in one of your Profile map slots.

Once published, any other player can view and download your map, and when it is used in a Custom Game on Battle.net, it can *only* be used with the settings you have specified.

ACHIEVEMENTS AND UNLOCKABLE REWARDS

Battle.net incorporates a full featured Achievement system. There are 4450 Achievement Points that you can earn while playing StarCraft II across all of the single and multiplayer modes of the game.

Completing Achievements does more than just earn you points however, you also unlock rewards.

ACHIEVEMENT REWARDS

New Portraits and Decals can be unlocked to your account for completing certain Achievements.

Portraits allow you to customize your online Characters, showing your experience with StarCraft II, and letting you show off the completion of especially difficult Achievements.

Decals are race-specific unlocks that can be applied to your units and buildings of that race—they actually show up in-game!

There are many different Decals available for each race, most unlocked by completing Achievements.

THE SHOWCASE

A special area of your Profile, the Showcase allows you to display both recently earned Achievements, and 'pinned' Achievements that you can send to the Showcase.

Completed an especially grueling multiplayer challenge? Place the Achievement in your Showcase and show the world!

Achievements can be compared to other players—simply browse another users Profile and examine their Achievements and you can see yours side by side, allowing you to easily see what areas of StarCraft II you each like to focus on.

Achievements come in many forms, some must be completed in a series, some have stages of progression before unlocking, others are 'meta' Achievements that unlock upon the completion of several other related (or unrelated) Achievements.

CHARACTER CREATION

Character creation on Battle.net is simple. The first time you log into your new StarCraft II Battle.net account, you are asked to create a Character identity.

THE BATTLE.NET AUTHENTICATOR

Battle.net fully supports the Battle.net Authenticator. This simple device (or phone application) generates a unique numeric key that must be input in addition to your password to authenticate your login.

This extra layer of account security can be very helpful in protecting your Battle.net login from hostile hack attempts.

If you play on a high profile account, or you often play on public computers, strongly consider enabling the Authenticator on your account!

You can create only a single Character on a single Battle.net account, so choose your name wisely!.

You create a character by choosing a character name (any name you want to use), as character names are non-unique. The identifier is simply a single word attached to your Character that allows multiple users on Battle.net to have the same Character name.

NEWS, COMMUNITY, WELCOME, HELP

After you have played a few games, you are greeted by the News and Community Headline feature. From here, you can get basic help for StarCraft II, view the latest news from Blizzard, or jump into Single or Multiplayer.

The Welcome Screen is constantly updated, and changes what is displayed based on your activity within StarCraft II. After you complete the campaign or participate in three non-campaign activities, the Welcome Screen will display an achievement guide, pointing you towards other possibilities to explore.

Expect the Battle.net welcome page to change over time, with new features and options as Blizzard updates Battle.net.

GUEST MODE

This is done simply by selecting Guest Mode from the main menu, and this allows friends or family to play the Campaign, without logging in to your account (or messing with your Achievements or Campaign saves).

It is possible to play StarCraft II while not logged in to your Characters (or while simply playing offline). You can't earn Achievements or rewards while logged off, but the next time you reconnect to Battle.net, any Campaign progress you may have made while offline will automatically resync and be stored online with Battle.net.

PROFILE

Your Profile is your Character's home base. From here, you can view your Achievements, Statistics, Match History, Portraits you have unlocked, Decals you have earned, your Ladder participation.

You can always view other players Profiles while online as well, and examine and download any Maps or Replays they have offered, as well as check out their stats.

HELP!

The Battle.net welcome page also has a small help section with some basic game information—technology trees, unit listings, hotkeys, etc. If you want to quickly check on a simple bit of info, hit the help section!

MP-BEGINNER

EASY TO LEARN, DIFFICULT TO MASTER

Learning to play StarCraft II well is a lengthy process. Don't get frustrated if you don't improve immediately—it takes time to learn the races, time to learn the hotkeys, time to learn good tactics and strategies. To aid your learning process, pick a few points from the list below and focus on implementing them in your next several games. Once you feel comfortable with your new techniques, pick another few tips and repeat the process! Don't try to absorb everything at once, it's simply too much to think about while you're busy managing your bases and your army!

CRITICAL EARLY GAME TACTICS

Each race has a few *very* critical abilities, technologies, or tactics that should almost always be researched or used, no matter the game type you are playing.

SIMPLE EARLY GAME BUILD ORDERS

These are very simple early game builds that can be followed to get you into a decent starting economic and military position.

After your early military structures are built, continue to tech up and ramp up military unit production. Add your second Vespene Geyser harvesting structure as quickly as you can without sacrificing defense.

For the Protoss, reaching Warp Gates is critical, for the Zerg and Terran, they should begin constantly constructing new units once the Barracks and Spawning Pool finish.

Note that these are simple, flexible build orders, they may need to be altered depending on the map and game mode, but use these as a starting place to get your timing down. Once they're second nature, you can begin to experiment with varying the timing and order of buildings.

For all three races, always remember to use your economic boosters! Once you have your build order down and you're managing to a) continue to create workers to max and b) constantly maxing out your Supply with military units, work on adding MULE, Chrono Boost, and Spawn Larvae into your build. Spawn Larvae is especially crucial for Zerg, so try to work on that early!

TERRAN

ORDER	BUILD	SUPPLY COUNT	UNIT-STRUCTURE
1		9/11	Supply Depot
2		12/19	Barracks
3		13/19	Refinery
4		15/19	Supply Depot
5		15/19	Orbital Command

Choose to go infantry (build multiple Barracks, at least one Starport, get Marines, Marauders and Medivacs), mechanized assault (build multiple Factories) or air (build multiple Starports)

CORE UNITS

- Infantry: Marines, Marauders, some Medivacs
- Mechanized: Hellions and Siege Tanks, some Thors
- Air: Vikings or Banshees, some Ravens

ECONOMY

The **most important** phase of the early game is building up your economy to maximum efficiency.

The rule of thumb for gathering resources is that you need about 2.5 workers per Mineral patch, and 3 workers per Vespene Gas geyser.

Because a starting home base usually has 8 Mineral patches and 2 geysers, you want around **24 workers** in total. You can build more workers to harvest Minerals, but you begin to see diminishing returns on your investment. In the midgame, it can be advantageous to build up extra workers to transfer to a new expansion, which can help to get the expansion up and running immediately, and you always want to build replacements when your workers are destroyed.

ORDER	BUILD	SUPPLY COUNT	UNIT-STRUCTURE
1		9/10	Pylon
2		10/18	Use Chrono Boost on Nexus
3		12/18	Gateway
4		13/18	Assimilator
5		14/18	Pylon

Follow your second Pylon with a Cybernetics Core and a second Gateway. Quickly research Warp Gate at the Cybernetics Core, then convert all Gateways to Warp Gates. Two Gateways is sufficient very early, expand to 3 in early-midgame, then 5-6 in mid-late if needed.

Choose a tech path to pursue early – Twilight Council, Stargate, or Robotics Facility.

CORE UNITS

- Infantry: Zealot, Stalker, Sentry (add Immortals for heavy ground)

- Air: Void Rays (use Phoenix for anti-air, add Carriers for heavy air)

- Specialist: High Templar (Psionic Storm for massed armies), Dark Templar (cloak assault)

ORDER	BUILD	SUPPLY COUNT	UNIT-STRUCTURE
1		10/10	Overlord
2			Create Extractor to drop to 9/10, create Drone to reach 10/10, CANCEL Extractor and place on Minerals, wait for Overlord at 11/10
3		12/18	Spawning Pool
4			Continue making Drones as needed, make Queen when Spawning Pool finishes

If you do not quick expand with a second Hatchery, be sure to build a second one inside your main base to increase your Larva generation rate.

Depending on the map size, you may need a pair of Spine Crawlers for base defense near your Drone line. In any case quickly mass Zerglings for early offense or defense.

Choose to head straight for Roaches and an early assault, or tech to Lair (for Hydras or Mutalisks), and research Burrow and upgraded Overlord speed soon after acquiring Lair.

CORE UNITS

- Infantry: Zergling and Roach, or Zergling and Hydralisk (use Baneling against massed ground forces, or to break a walled in chokepoint)

- Air: Mutalisk (use Corruptor for anti-air, add Brood Lords for heavy ground)

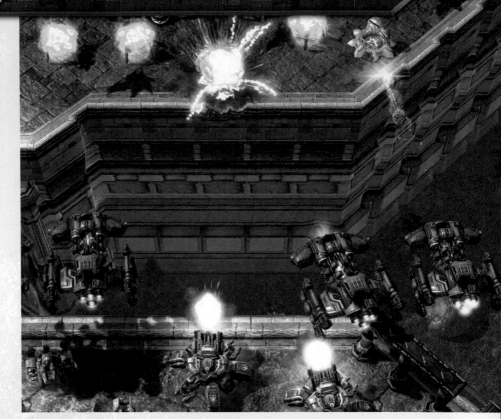

Be sure to transfer 8 workers from your main to your natural expansion to get an immediate surge in income!

For the duration of the early game, *always* have at least one worker building until you reach maximum efficiency at your base. The only time you should delay building a worker is when you have to save up for critical early structures—your Supply producers and your first military buildings.

Note that around 2 workers per Mineral patch (16) is very efficient, and you will continue to see income returns up to 3 workers per (24), but the rate of gathering essentially stops after 24, so don't build more unless you are replacing workers lost in raid, or expanding immediately! This means that a good working base should have from 22 (16 + 6 on gas) to 30 (24 + 6 on gas) workers!

MONITOR YOUR WORKERS

A quick way to see if your base is running at optimal efficiency is to simply CTRL-click a worker, or drag-select your worker line.

A full group selection box in StarCraft II is 24 units, so if you see about a full box, you know your base is running at full speed!

If you see less (or a lot less), get building!

GET THAT GAS

Vespene Gas is vital for all advanced units and technology research, so if you are establishing a new expansion, be sure to get 6 workers working on the gas mines immediately, unless you have a a massive demand for more Minerals immediately.

Don't forget to put your workers back on Gas after running from a worker raid!

ALL RACES

Defend your base!

Wall off the entrance to your base as Terran or Protoss, and build Spine Crawlers to defend your Drones and your Spawning Pool as Zerg.

Don't spend an excessive amount of resources on defensive structures (Bunkers, Missile Turrets, Photon Cannons, Spine and Spore Crawlers) early in the game, but take steps to make sure that early raids by your opponent are more difficult, and that when defending with your army, you have the home field advantage.

Walling off the entrance of your base makes it impenetrable to your enemies (as Terran) or creates a natural chokepoint (as Protoss), both of which give you a natural defensive advantage.

Remember to use Hold Position on your Zealots to block off the chokepoint. Once you have Stalkers in place behind the Zealots, this becomes much more difficult for a light raid to penetrate (and still works effectively against large offensives when your full army is near the chokepoint).

Be sure to have enough Pylons to keep your Gateways covered if you lose a few during an attack!

As Zerg, walling off the entrance to your base isn't possible, but you have the advantage of being able to build Spine Crawlers immediately after your Spawning Pool is constructed.

Be sure to place your Spawning Pool AWAY from the front of your base (behind your Mineral line often works well), and place the Spine Crawlers to cover your Drone line and Spawning Pool. Remember that you can move the Spine Crawlers if necessary!

And remember, your workers have an attack for a reason—use your workers to fend off very early unit attacks. Losing a few seconds of gathering time is vastly preferable to losing multiple workers because you don't have a military unit around!

Be sure to get upgrade your Command Center to an Orbital Command as soon as your Barracks finishes building.

Use the MULE calldown to create a 'super SCV'. Remember that you can target a Mineral patch directly with the MULE calldown, and it will begin harvesting immediately.

Depending on what unit mix you go for, be sure to research Stimpack for infantry, Siege Tech for Siege Tanks, or Cloaking Field for Banshees.

The Nexus special ability, Chrono Boost, allows you to speed up the build time or research time of ANY building by 50%. Use this ability on your Nexus to speed up Probe production, on your Stargates or Robotics Facilities to speed unit production, or on your research structures to speed up key technology research.

Be certain to build a Cybernetics Core and research Warp Gate technology, then upgrade your Gateways to Warp Gates. This allows you to Warp in all Gateway units ANYWHERE you have Pylon power. While Warp Gate is researching, you can Chrono Boost your Gateways to get your early army built faster!

WARP GATES

Remember, not only do Warp Gates let you warp in units anywhere you have Pylon power, they also reduce the build time of any unit created from a Warp Gate.

It is always faster to produce units from Warp Gates over building them from Gateways, as long as you remember to warp them in each time the cooldown wears off!

Note that you *can* Chrono Boost a Warp Gate. Try warping in several units, then Shift all of the Warp Gates, speeding up the next wave!

Build a Queen after your Spawning Pool completes, and use her Spawn Larvae ability on your Hatchery as often as possible.

Quickly upgrade your Hatchery to a Lair and research Burrow, then build your preferred military unit structures.

Be sure to get a second Hatchery and Queen up, either at your main base, or at an expansion, to increase your Larva production rate.

MISTAKES

There are a lot of ways you can misstep when you're first learning to play StarCraft II. This section covers some of the more common errors in play that newer players tend to make.

Don't feel bad if you're guilty of a few of these, learning to recognize what you are doing wrong is part of the progression from newbie to intermediate player.

BUILD QUEUES

Don't max out your build queues as Terran or Protoss early in the game. In other words, on your first Barracks or Gateway, you should be building just enough Marines or Zealots to keep military units coming in, while spending excess resources to continue to build up your worker count and tech up or get more production buildings online.

Once your economy is fully established, you can crank up the unit production, but early on, dumping 250 or 500 Minerals on a full queue of Marines or Zealots is just tying up resources you could be using to build more workers and buildings that are critical in the early minutes of a match.

By the same token, don't max out your Probe or SCV production, instead keep one to two building at all times until you've reached the soft cap for your base.

Similarly, *never* queue up multiple research upgrades early in the game. Research is generally fairly expensive for the early game, and takes a relatively long time to acquire, so having two or more upgrades in a build queue provides you with no battlefield benefit, and wastes resources.

MILITARY PRODUCTION

Related to queueing up too many units (or upgrades) is the error of building too *few* military structures.

While Zerg don't operate by the same rules, Terran and Protoss need to be sure to have enough military structures to build up a military without floating too many resources, and even Zerg need to have enough Hatcheries (and Queen usage) to keep their military flowing.

Having enough military production capability is important both for keeping your resources working for you as military units on the field, and to recover from combat losses sustained while on offense or defense.

TOO MUCH DEFENSE

Bunkers, Missile Turrets, Photon Cannons, and Spine and Spore Crawlers are all defensive structures that are very useful for protecting key chokepoints and worker lines, but they are *not* more useful than minerals spent on mobile military forces.

Particularly early in the game, do not invest heavily in defensive structures, because if you do, and your opponent invests in military, you're not going to have enough mobile troops to fight him off.

Unless you literally wall off your base with defenses (which is a viable tactic), your opponent can simply walk *past* the defenses you've built, and hit your unprotected buildings. Without wasting a huge amount of resources, it is very difficult to protect all areas of your base.

With that said, Zerg are a notable exception in that one or two Spine Crawlers placed near their worker line can be useful to protect against early offensives (as Zerg cannot wall in or block their chokepoint with buildings early in the game), and Terran Bunkers can be 'Scavenged', returning their mineral cost once their usefulness has expired.

RESOURCE FLOAT

'Floating' resources simply means accumulating an excess amount of Minerals and Vespene Gas, without spending it. This is almost always a bad idea—especially early in the game, the only time you want to float *any* resources is if you're saving up to build a specific structure, unit, or technology.

In the mid and late game, unless you're capped at 200/200 Supply and all of your possible research upgrades are building, you still should avoid resource float.

Always, *always* be building up your military forces and expanding.

RESEARCHING EVERYTHING, BUILDING EVERYTHING

In the early game, and in the transition to the midgame, it's important to have a technological and military goal in mind. This could be air units, cloaking units, casters, advanced ground units or a specific research upgrade—whatever the case, you should endeavor to reach that point by the fastest route possible.

What you do *not* want to be doing is building every possible building, and researching every possible upgrade. You simply do not have the resources or, more critically, the time to do this. If you spread out your resources across several tech and military buildings, and then spread them ever further across multiple random upgrades, you're not going to have a large enough military to effectively attack or defend.

Keep a clear goal in mind as you build up and you should find that your military production is much smoother, and you reach your targeted tech much faster!

QUICK EXPANSION

Once your main base is maxed out on worker production (roughly 2.5 workers per Mineral patch, and 3 workers for each Vespene geyser), you can maintain a healthy military production while teching easily.

On the other hand, if you attempt to expand early, you are giving up 300-400 Minerals for another base, plus the cost of Vespene extractors, plus the cost of more workers for the second base. In some cases, this is the right call (team games where you have protection, maps with long ground routes between bases, an early Hatchery expand as Zerg), but as a general rule of thumb, don't expand early.

If you bottle up your opponent with an aggressive offense, or your main base is beginning to run low on resources, you can (or must) expand, and in those situations, you should be sure to secure the expansion grounds with adequate military defenses.

TERRAN EXPANSION

Remember that Terrans can float a Command Center to an island expansion. If the map has island expansions, be sure to utilize these (as Terran) and watch out for them (if your opponent is Terran!).

POOR EXPANSION PLACEMENT

When you place a new base, be sure that the core building is as close as possible to the Minerals and Vespene Gas at the expansion site. Misplacing your structure will result in slower resourcing, as the workers will have to travel farther.

TAKING YOUR EYE OFF THE FIGHT

NEVER take your eye off your army while it is on the offensive. If you have to float some resources or neglect your teching to manage your army instead, do so. Your army wins the game for you, building an extra worker or building does not.

You can still manage your bases by making good use of hotkeys, and as you grow more comfortable with the game, you will increasingly be able to keep your technology and military production going while 'in the field' with your army, but to begin with, your army takes priority over building your base.

Once you make the decision to attack, stay with your army until you either defeat your opponent, destroy a key target, inflict enough damage to his army, or decide to retreat. Once your forces are back on (relatively) safe ground, you can resume building and quickly spend any excess resources that have accumulated.

And remember, when your forces encounter the enemy, attack move your entire force past the enemy army, then control your units after they have engaged the enemy fully.

SPLITTING YOUR FORCES

When you attack (or defend) early in the game, do so with your whole army. Later, you have enough Supply capacity to play around with multiple forces, but early in the game, if you don't commit to an offensive action with your army, you open yourself up to the possibility of total military annihilation.

If you send half your army and your opponent defends with his full army (plus any static defenses), odds are, you're going to lose your entire force, inflicting minimal damage. When your opponent counter-attacks, you won't have enough military to defend successfully.

Moving your whole army does leave your base temporarily defense-less, but you can compensate for this with good scouting—as long as you're aware of the enemy troop movements, you should be safe from a surprise attack.

A few enemy forces might slip through while your army is away, but as long as you don't let a major force in, you can almost always defend against a few troops simply using your workers and a few freshly built troops intelligently.

And remember, when you fight with your full army against your opponents full army, assuming equal control and similar sizes, you will both suffer roughly even losses. Even if you lose your entire army on offense, the damage you deal will give you enough time to rebuild on defense (with a better idea of what to build to counter your opponents troop choices!).

RETREAT!

When you engage your opponents forces, if you see that you are clearly outmatched, or something happens to suddenly shift the balance of an engagement, don't stick around and fight to the bitter end. Losing troops needlessly serves no purpose, and unless you're in the process of de-stroying an absolutely crucial tech structure, it's almost never worthwhile to sacrifice your army to, for example, destroy a few extra workers.

If your army is slower than some (or all) of your opponents army, you will take some losses retreating, but even in that situation, losing some troops is still preferable to losing *all* of your troops.

Remember that retreating is simply another tactical tool; you protect your investment of resources in at least part of your army, you keep an active military to defend your bases with, and you buy time to build up more forces or a technological counter for whatever trouble you ran into on offense.

WE HAVE NOT ENOUGH INTELLIGENCE

Scouting is *critical* in StarCraft II. A good rule of thumb in the early game is to send the worker that builds your first Supply structure to scout out enemy positions (or in the case of Zerg, send your Overlord or a Drone).

Beyond the very early game scouting to determine your opponent's position, it is critical that you maintain a scouting presence at ALL times. While you may not be equipped to process the information you receive from scouting a base as a new player, at the *very* least, you can see where their military is, and where and when it is moving!

Each race has specialized units and abilities for scouting, but for the early game and early-mid game, constantly send out cheap military units to keep tabs on your opponents military movements.

Once you get close to 20 to 30 Supply, send out a triple set of workers, place one at each Xel'Naga tower, one in front of the enemy base, and one a short distance in front of your base. 150 Minerals can save you a lot of pain when you know when and where your opponent's army is moving!

XEL'NAGA WATCHTOWERS

Check your minimap—any blue eye icons you see are Xel'Naga Watchtowers.

When a friendly unit is adjacent to such a tower, you gain a large line of sight to the surrounding area.

Be sure to keep a worker or cheap military unit on these at all times during a match. If you get kicked off by a military unit, sweep them off when you pass by with your army and put up new sentries!

WATCH THOSE HEALTH BARS

By default, holding the **Alt** button shows healthbars over all units on screen. This is very important for micromanaging your army in battle, as you can retreat damaged units, and focus fire weakened enemy units. Pay a visit to the options menu and enable the health display on units at all times—removing a step to making intelligent targeting decisions can save you precious time while micromanaging a battle.

Note that this level of micromanagement in small scale engagements is a somewhat advanced technique, so if you're just starting out, don't worry too much about managing every unit in a fight. But even if you're just starting out, get in the habit of watching unit health bars, so you can get a feel for how various engagements play out, and what you should be targeting, as well as what your opponent is targeting.

DON'T TRY TO LEARN EVERYTHING IN ONE GAME!

It's very easy to be overwhelmed by all of the choices that StarCraft II offers. There are many possible units to build, and many possible technologies to research. Not all are needed in any given game to win. In a very long slugfest of a 4v4, you might actually get all technologies researched, and have units of all sorts, but even then, you still won't necessarily be using every single unit in concert.

You are always Supply limited for the total size of your army, and a more focused mix of units that is controlled well can be far more effective than a haphazard mix of units that are controlled poorly. Instead, pick a few units (any units! Whatever looks appealing to you) and focus on learning in the ins and outs of that particular unit mix.

Because there are so many different variables that can affect a match; map choice, map size, your race, the opponents race, 1v1 or a team game, the skill of the players in the match, even an identical mix of units can have considerably different effectiveness in different matches.

A good rule of thumb is to pick around two core units to make up the bulk of your army, and then supplement that force with another attack 'vector': cloaking, air units, cliff walkers, dropships, casters, etc. If you smoothly build up your economy and keep your military production going the entire time, staying at your Supply cap, you can threaten even any opponent by managing your army well, even if only using a few units out of all the options available to you seems strange.

In some cases, you will run into counters to your chosen mix of units (air units if you're all ground, anti-Armored if your units are all Armored), but learning to build the correct units or technologies in response to these challenges is part of the learning process.

Critically, learning those weaknesses (and their solutions) is part of the process of mastering StarCraft II. Each time you learn (and master) a new way to deal with a threat, you hone your tactical skill, and those lessons stay with you, no matter what race you play, or what unit mixes you experiment with.

MULTIPLAYER INTRODUCTION

There is no magic bullet for winning in StarCraft II. No single strategy, no perfect build order, no level of execution so perfect it is unbeatable. You won't find the secret in these pages, and even if you play constantly, you'll probably still be looking for better ways to win for many years to come.

But that's part of the fun. What we *can* give you are the tools needed to learn, to improve, and to train your StarCraft skills. Of which there are many; how well you control your troops in battle, how aggressively you attack, how skillfully you defend, and how well you read your opponent, to name just a few. StarCraft II, when played competitively against a skilled opponent, demands a lot from you. You need to intelligently choose and execute your chosen build order quickly and precisely, yet still respond to the shifting battlefield circumstances, constantly scout the map and react to the information you acquire, and manage your main base, your expansions, and your army nearly simultaneously!

And of course, playing StarCraft II simply for fun is the best way to play any game, and there are plenty of options to keep you occupied even if your interest in multiplayer is worlds removed from climbing the ladder and playing at 100% all the time.

ONLINE OPTIONS

Take a look at the Battle.net chapter of this guide for some information about the various game modes that you can play while online.

In addition to the automated matchmaking for everything from 1v1 to 4v4 matches, you can actually get into automated games against the AI if you want to simply go compstomping.

You can also create or join custom games, played on any map with almost any settings.

You can still go compstomping with friends, and go smashing huge armies into each other in large free for all and team games, and with the improved features in the map editor and on Battle.net, you can expect to see a profusion of new maps and mods as the community embraces the new tools.

WHAT NEXT?

We're well aware that writing a fixed print strategy guide for a changing online game is in some ways a rather futile task. Trying to pin down a handful of specific tactics for a game that will naturally evolve and change as it is played and patched is somewhere between difficult and impossible.

What we can do is to provide you with solid foundation. A ground of bedrock from which you can naturally improve your play. While it is inevitable that some of the specific numbers on some of the units will change, and even some abilities may see dramatic changes, it is still possible to develop an understanding of the gameplay that will allow you to quickly adapt to any changes, no matter how large or small.

Beyond the specifics of each race's units and buildings, there are certain truisms that apply to any strategy game, StarCraft II included, no matter how the game evolves over time.

A quick and aggressive rush is always dangerous, and smart, sturdy base defense is always critical. Reading your opponent's actions correctly and responding appropriately will always be important, and you can always improve your own skill by speeding up your play and improving how well you manage your own limited time in the heat of battle.

It is our hope that this guide will provide you with a firm grounding for playing StarCraft II in multiplayer, whether your interest is the top of the ladder and really heavy competitive gaming, or simply spending some time with friends and dropping half a dozen nukes on your buddy after you break your alliance.

STARCRAFT USER INTERFACE

TIME

*When we refer to times in StarCraft II, unless otherwise noted, we are referring to the **listed, in-game** times on units, buildings, and abilities.*

We bring up this point because Ladder games in StarCraft II are played at Faster game speed, which runs at 1.4 seconds per 'real' second (that'd be 1.2 for Fast, and 1.0 for Normal!).

Consequently, you will find that units and structures are built more quickly than you might expect, research finishes sooner, and combat is over faster!

Note that when watching a replay, the clock will tick faster as well, so while the speed is faster than real time, you can still use replays to compare relative build times.

Don't let this trip up your build time calculations, you can still easily compare the total length of time it takes to get to a particular unit or technology 'on paper'.

If you really want the actual real world times in a ladder match, just divide the listed times by 1.4 for the exact number, or mentally shave off about 30% for a quick estimate.

The most basic and fundamental aspect of playing StarCraft II is controlling your units and developing your bases successfully.

Doing so efficiently requires understanding what can and cannot be done within the user interface, and there is almost always room to improve your speed when using the UI.

While it is *not* necessary that you have incredibly high Actions per Minute (APM) to play competitively online, it is important that you fully understand all of the options available to you.

CONTROLS

Most controls in StarCraft II should be very familiar to you if you have played any RTS games in the past several years, but just in case, we'll touch on some basics.

MOUSE BASICS

In general, *Left Clicking* selects units, or places abilities, while *Right Clicking* issues context sensitive orders. Right click on the ground to move, right click on an enemy unit to attack it, right click on a Mineral patch with a worker to harvest it, etc.

CONTROL QUEUEING

By holding the Shift key while issuing almost any order in the game, you can queue up multiple actions for any unit or group of units. This is particularly useful for queuing scouting movements, focus firing several enemy units in sequence, or building multiple structures quickly.

Additionally, while a unit or group is selected, any queued commands for the unit are visible onscreen, with green lines for movement orders, red lines for attack orders, and blue lines for patrol orders.

Note that you *can* queue up a hold position or hold fire order, though it may not be immediately apparent that the order has been followed—you have to check the unit's control pane when it has arrived at its destination to verify that it is in hold position or hold fire mode.

SPELL QUEUING

By default, casters in StarCraft II act in 'smartcast' mode, where only a single spell will be cast per click (or hotkey press), and the closest possible caster will cast, or move into range to cast or use an ability.

To cast more than once, you either need to press the ability button or hotkey again, or you need to hold Shift and click multiple times.

Holding Shift after you activate a targeted ability can be useful, because while the spell is on your mouse pointer and Shift is held, you can right click on the minimap safely to move the screen around, without accidentally issuing a movement or attack order.

This is also particularly handy for economic boosting abilities such as the MULE, Spawn Larvae, and Chrono Boost, which you can activate, hold Shift, and then quickly zip around the minimap with right clicks, without worrying about accidentally setting a rally point.

SELECT

Selection is accomplished simply by left clicking on a unit. Double click on a unit to select all units of that type on the screen. This is handy for quickly grabbing all of your workers, or selecting all of one type of military unit.

CTRL-CLICK

Holding Control and clicking on a unit selects all units of that type on screen, just like double clicking a unit.

The benefit of Control clicking over double clicking is precision— you can easily control click a single small unit such as a Zergling or a Marine, where you might miss the double click.

DRAG SELECT

Drag section is simply holding the left mouse button and dragging a banding box around multiple units. You can use this to quickly gather up all units in an area, particularly handy for grabbing all military units on screen.

SHIFT SELECTION

Shift has another function beyond queuing unit orders—while holding Shift, if you click, double click, control click, drag select, or control-group select units, they are either added or removed from your unit selection.

If you hold Shift and select units that are NOT in your current group, they are added to your group, and if you hold Shift and select units that ARE in your current group, they are removed.

Performing this sort of group control seems very basic, but it is actually extremely important.

In general, most military management is handled with a few primary control groups—usually something like your main army group, a secondary group of units (air, cloaked, shuttles, etc), and possibly a third group of casters or other specialists.

Being able to quickly add or remove units from any of those groups is vital, because you should always be building reinforcements for your military, and quickly adding those new units to your existing control groups is important.

Similarly, sometimes you need to pick out a group of units from an existing mixed group of units, and the Shift selection provides you an easy method of doing exactly that.

CONTROL GROUPS

Control groups are how you manage your military, both in terms of groups of units into armies, and your military production structures back in your base.

Control groups are an RTS staple, and a very simple concept—select a group of units (or buildings), hold the CTRL key, and press any number from 1 to 0 on the keyboard.

Once this is done, you can then select that group at any time by simply pressing the number. Pressing the number twice selects the group *and* centers the screen on the group.

Control groups are a simple concept, but they are *extremely* important. Your military units should *always* be grouped, and your primary production structures should *always* be grouped.

BUILDING HOTKEYS

*Remember that you can add new structures to control groups **while** they are building. Have your core structures on 5? Select your newly building expansion and hit Shift-5 to add it to your group key.*

You can even set rally points for core structures and military production structures while they are building.

Have all of your Barracks on 4? Select each new building and hit Shift-4 and then rally them to the same area.

As you gain experience in using control groups, you should also get in the habit of placing your upgrade structures into control groups. You don't need to hit these as often as your primary army groups, or even your production buildings, but it can be helpful both to remember to keep your upgrades flowing, and to avoid losing time hunting for the buildings in your base.

Each race also has an economic boosting unit or building that should also always be grouped—conveniently, for both Terran and Protoss, this is their core structure, but for Zerg, is the Queen, a unit produced from the Hatchery.

BASIC CONTROL GROUPS

Control groups are a highly personal choice—there isn't really a right or wrong way to set up your groups, as long as you use them consistently from game to game.

We're presenting a simple template for your use here, but the specific numbers aren't important, only that you are consistent about what units and buildings are used on what numbers.

- Control Group 1-3: Military Units
- Control Group 4-6: Production Structures
- Control Group 7-0: Upgrade Structures, rarely used units or buildings

As an example, group 1 would be your 'primary army', group 2 would be any units that need special micro attention—air units, ranged units that you need to dance, shuttles, etc. Group 3 would be any casters that need to have their spells used individually, or a secondary military force (for base defense, etc).

For your production structures, you ALWAYS want to have your core structures hotkeyed on one control group for worker production.

Beyond that, be sure that your primary military buildings are hotkeyed. Remember that you can place multiple buildings onto one hotkey, so for Terran and Protoss, you can place all Barracks, all Stargates, etc, onto one hotkey.

If you're comfortable with hitting Tab repeatedly to cycle through subgroups, there is nothing preventing you from placing ALL of your military structures on one hotkey.

In the case of Zerg, your primary military AND worker producing building is always your Hatcheries, and you always want to have all of them grouped for quick larva access.

The Terran Orbital Command and Protoss Nexus both function as their economic boosters, so they don't require a separate control group, but the Zerg must have all of their Queens placed on a control group.

For the final hotkeys, you can group buildings such as the Terran Engineering Bay and Armory, Protoss Forge and Cybernetics Core, and Zerg Evolution Chamber and Spire, to have quick access to your army upgrades.

The main reason to have most of your groups in the 1-6 range is because most StarCraft II hotkeys are located on the left side of the keyboard. If you use custom hotkeys, you can of course simply move the groups around on the keyboard to fit your finger position, but the basics remain the same.

SUBGROUPS

When multiple types of units or buildings are placed into one control group, you gain access to another control function, that of *subgroups*. In essence, each type of unit or building becomes its own 'minigroup' within a single control group, and you can cycle through the subgroups by pressing **Tab**, or backwards by holding Shift and pressing Tab. By default, units with usable abilities are automatically placed at the top of a 'stack' of units in a given control group, so that you can easily utilize their special abilities in combat.

As a rule, you should keep units that are entirely (or even mostly) useful for their abilities in separate control groups, because using their abilities quickly and having instant access to them is important.

For units that have less time critical abilities, or that are relatively 'fire and forget', you can safely have them grouped up with other units, and simply press Tab a few times to cycle to them when you need to use their abilities.

Another point about subgroups—because identical units are automatically grouped together on the control group UI panel at the bottom of the screen, you can easily select or target units inside the panel.

You can left click to select a single unit, or shift-left click to remove a single unit at a time from a control group.

You can also ctrl-click select or shift-ctrl-click deselect one type of unit out of a control group quickly. This is handy if you want to quickly ctrl-click select a group of units to micromanage, or split off into their own control group.

MOVE

Right clicking while you have one or more units selected on open ground issues a move order. Units moving to a point will NOT fight on the way. For this reason, do NOT issue blind movement orders into the fog of war with your army—use Attack Move orders instead, unless you've already scouted or you're very confident about what you're going to encounter!

For scouting, unit repositioning, or dancing ranged attackers, movement orders are useful, just be careful about walking past hostile enemy units with your army blissfully unaware of the danger.

ATTACK

Right clicking on an enemy unit or building issues an explicit attack order to attack that target until it is dead. Your units will NOT respond to other threats, and will chase a moving unit if it flees, as long as it is visible.

For this reason, you should be careful with direct attack orders—if you target your entire army on one fast enemy unit and they move it away, your army will follow while being attacked by any hostile enemy unit nearby!

Issuing explicit attack orders *is* a useful tactic in multiplayer battles, particularly Shift-queueing multiple attack orders on specific enemy units, so that you can quickly focus fire down multiple enemy units, one after another.

This is especially effective with ranged units, and somewhat less so with ground based melee units, who have to maneuver around enemy and friendly units, as well as terrain and buildings to reach their designated target.

ATTACK MOVE

An *attack move* order is issued by pressing **A** for Attack, and then left clicking on the ground (NOT on another unit).

Units that are given an attack move order will move to the target point, and attack any units or buildings in the area, prioritizing hostile military units (or defensive turrets) over normal buildings or workers.

Keep that target priority in mind if you're explicitly raiding workers or a key tech or military building. You need to issue an explicit attack order on your chosen target, instead of an attack move order.

In general, attack move should be your 'default' movement order for your massed army. When your massed army on attack move encounters a hostile force, it will spread out and engage with all forces.

Don't assume that once you've engaged with an attack move order that you can simply ignore the engagement and let it play out—once a battle is started, in most cases, the player who then directly intervenes will either come out on top, or retreat successfully while taking minimal losses.

That said, beginning an engagement with attack move is still usually preferable to simply moving to a point near a hostile force and then having your troops engage, only after they've already begun to take fire.

Attack moving your army into or just beyond your opponent's army also has the advantage of guaranteeing that all available forces *will* get into the battle. If your force is attacked first, and you do *not* issue an attack move order, some of the troops at the back of the pack may simply stand around doing nothing!

One last point—you can issue an explicit attack order against your *own* units or buildings, which obviously, you usually don't want to do. If for some reason you accidentally do something like wall yourself into your base, or trap a created unit from a military structure, you can always destroy the offending structure.

HOLD POSITION

By pressing **H** for Hold Position, you can order a unit to remain stationary, even if a hostile enemy unit comes in range.

Hold Position is very useful for blocking chokepoints, as you can prevent enemy units from 'baiting' your defenders away from their position, to be easily picked off, and creating a breach in your defensive line.

CANCEL

While a building is selected, you can press **Escape** to cancel a queued unit or technology. This is handy if you accidentally overbuild units, if you need to quickly adjust a queue, or if a structure is under attack and likely to be destroyed (no reason to give extra resources away!).

Escape will also cancel a building in production, which is helpful if you misplace a building, but be very careful with this when playing Zerg—accidentally cancelling a morphing Lair or Hive can be a painful setback, and cancelling morphing Larva does *not* return the Larva to you instantly.

Escape will also cancel ability usage, though you can simply right click to do that as well, and the same warnings about Zerg apply (Low Energy Spawn Larvae into Lair cancel is not a pro move).

STOP

Pressing **S** causes units to cease whatever previous orders they were following, and return to a default stationary stance. If you had several orders queued up, they are all cancelled.

Generally, stop isn't needed unless you accidentally do something like order your entire worker line to move to an enemy base! You can use it with aerial or dancing ranged units being given movement orders as a sort of 'pause and fire' command.

PRO TIP!
Mondragon (ToT)
CHRISTOPH SEMKE

Zerg against Terran:

Because players regularly bunker rush in Zerg vs. Terran, I prefer to open with a 14 pool followed by a 14 Gas and an Overlord with 15 Drones. Usually Terran will not dare to rush you and you can easily make another Drone. When your pool finishes you will be at 16/18 supply to make a Queen immediately. Right after the third Overlord pops out, you can start to either make more Drones if you feel safe or start producing Zerglings. With your first 100 Gas you should research Zergling speed and with another 100 Gas you need to upgrade to a Lair, then get Banelings and Hydras. Zerg against Terran is all about a combination of Zerglings/Banelings and Hydras/Roaches.

A unit that is 'stopped' simply returns to its default idle state, military units will still attack enemy units that come into range, a stopped unit is *not* on Hold Position.

BUILD AND ADVANCED BUILD

The Build Basic Structure and Build Advanced Structure (**V**) commands are standard to workers for all three races. 'Basic' buildings are those that are accessible immediately with no prerequisites, or very early structure requirements. Advanced buildings are typically those that provide access to your higher tier and higher tech units and upgrades.

PRO TIP!
Mouz.White-Ra
OLEKSII KRUPNYK

Specific tactics with units:

1. If your Terran opponent produces nothing but land units, a Protoss Sentry will help defend against them. When they rush you, have your Sentry cast a Guardian Shield to reduce the damage your units take from enemy shots.

2. Use Phoenixes to quickly decimate enemy workers. Also, in a large-scale fight, decide which enemy units pose the most danger and decommission them with your Phoenix's Graviton Beam.

3. If you use Immortals, try to target their ranged attacks only on armored enemy units (such as Siege Tanks, Marauders, Roaches, Stalkers, Colossi, etc.) to inflict maximum damage.

4. When you upgrade your Colossi's shooting range, they can annihilate the enemy's forces from a distance while staying out of harm's way. Approach, shoot and retreat to inflict maximum damage without taking any yourself. Works like a charm!

5. When launching an offensive, make sure that all your units charge the enemy at the same time, and, ideally, from several sides. This will ensure a simultaneous attack, for a few seconds render useless those enemy units that stay in the rear, and hopefully tip the scales in your favor.

GATHER

Gather is a specific command available only to the worker units for each race. All workers collect Minerals or Vespene Gas from extractors built on the raw Vespene Gas nodes.

For reference, you want about 2.5 workers per Mineral patch, and 3 for each Vespene geyser.

Right clicking on a Mineral or Vespene geyser with a worker issues a gather command.

REPAIR

Available only to the Terran SCV worker, the Repair command allows SCVs to repair any structure or Mechanical unit. Repair can be Autocast, right click on the Repair command to automate repairs for any unit in range of the SCV.

Consider keeping 3 or 4 SCVs around on Repair duty, particularly at the chokepoint at the front of your base, or in position near key Missile Turrets or Siege Tanks.

SCVs set to Autocast Repair are also helpful to bring along with an offensive force that has Medivacs, Siege Tanks, Thors, Battlecruisers, or other expensive, important Mechanical units accompanying your troops.

REPAIR SPEED

SCVs (and MULEs) don't repair at a fixed rate. Instead, they repair at a speed that is dependant on the **build time** of a unit or building.

In other words, a Battlecruiser will take you longer to repair than a Hellion, and a Supply Depot will be faster than a Planetary Fortress.

You can use multiple SCVs to speed up this process, and the increase is completely linear—5 SCVs will repair a unit or structure 5 times as fast as a single SCV.

The cost for repairing a unit or structure is equal to 25% of the original price, if it is nearly fully destroyed, proportionally less if it is only partially damaged.

RALLY POINTS

All production buildings have the ability to set a Rally Point, a specific point on the map where new created units will travel once created.

You can rally any military building or core structure by simply right clicking anywhere on the map.

For worker production, rally points can be placed directly on Minerals or Vespene geysers to make them gather instantly after creation. Rallying your first core structure on your Minerals should be the first action you take in every game after putting your first workers to work.

ZERG RALLY POINTS

Zerg are unique in that they have **two** rally points for their only unit producing building, the Hatchery.

It is possible to set both a worker rally point **and** a military rally point for any Hatchery that you control.

Simply right click on a Mineral patch or Vespene geysyer to set the worker rally point, then right click anywhere on open ground to set the military rally point.

Any non-worker units will always travel to the military rally point.

Be mindful that Overlords count as military units, so be careful about sending your floating Supply into the field accidentally!

In general, these rally points should be located somewhere in your initial base, or just outside the base at your natural expansion, if you have one.

In some cases, in longer games, you might want to rally your troops to a midpoint on the map, especially if you have a large number of military production buildings, and it can also be useful for air units, as they can swiftly travel to a location closer to the action.

Be careful about rallying your units out in the open, especially in un-scouted territory, you don't want to have your reinforcements picked off while traveling across the map.

LAST EVENT

Pressing the Space Bar snaps the camera to the last 'event' that has occurred. This can be a unit under attack or a technology research completing.

Multiple recent events are queued up, so you can tap the Space Bar repeatedly to cycle between recent attacks on your units or buildings, or multiple buildings that have completed research, so that you can queue up another research project.

In addition, recent events are shown on the left of the screen briefly, and you can click on an event to center the screen on it.

CYCLE BASES

Tap the **Backspace** key to cycle through all of your placed core struc-tures—handy for cycling between your bases and expansions.

SHOW HEALTH/AUTOCAST TOGGLE

Holding the Alt key toggles the display of all unit and building health bars onscreen. This is very helpful for picking out targets to focus fire, or units of your own to move away from the front line—remember that a unit with 1 health still does just as much damage as a unit at full health.

You can also toggle an Autocast ability, such as Repair or Create Inter-ceptor by holding Alt while pressing the hotkey of the Autocast ability.

FOLLOW

While not an explicit command on the command panel, or a hotkey, by default, if you right click on a non-transport *friendly* unit with a non-transport military unit, the selected units will automatically attempt to follow the friendly unit as it moves.

Be careful with this command in combat though, if the unit dies, the units that were on follow will simply stop moving, so if you were expecting them to follow your army, you could end up with some units left behind!

Transport units have a different behavior, and they will move to pick up a friendly unit, or if right clicked on by another unit, that unit will enter the transport.

CAMERA FOLLOW

While we're speaking about following behavior—you can left click and hold on a unit portrait to center the screen on the unit *and* to follow it as it moves.

Not the most crucial of commands, but if you want to track a transport or other air unit while it flies, this is a decent method of doing so.

SHOW HEALTH BARS

Under the options menu, you can set health bars to be enabled when units are selected, or turn them on at all times.

We strongly recommend that you enable health bars **always**, as this makes picking out focus fire targets and targets to retreat much faster than having to hold alt during every engagement.

THE MINIMAP

The minimap is a simple but crucial aspect of the UI. Always visible in the bottom left of the screen, the minimap is useful both for quickly jumping around the map by left-clicking on it, but also for receiving early warning of enemy movement while you are busy elsewhere. You should always be keeping an eye on the minimap, particularly later in the game when you have more scouts and scouting units scattered around the map giving you line of sight.

Note that you can set the minimap to display team colors instead of player colors by pressing ALT-F (in other words, you can make it *always* show red for hostile units, rather than the color the other player has selected.) This is particularly useful in team games, where you need to keep an eye on multiple enemy forces.

In team matches, you can also ping the minimap by ALT-left-clicking in it to indicate an enemy attack, a rallying point, or a target for your teammates to focus on.

ADVANCED CONTROLS

The basic controls provide the foundation for controlling all of your units and managing your bases, but it isn't always immediately clear exactly *how* you should be using all of these various options.

Here are some examples, to give you a feel for what you can (and often should) be doing with these various options.

ARMY GROUPING

The most crucial use for the various unit selection and control options is constantly maintaining a sizable army on one or more control groups. As a general rule, you want your main group of forces on your primary group hotkey, and any specialist units on secondary or tertiary groupings.

There are several quick ways to assemble your army, the first is rallying your newly produced troops to one common area in your base. You can then easily drag select the whole mass of troops (if they are a mix of units) or ctrl-click on one (if you've made a bunch of a single type of unit).

Ctrl-clicking on single unit types is also helpful if you're maintaining multiple groups for your army.

Say you're playing Terran and building Marines and Marauders as your core ground force, with Medivacs as your support unit. You already have some Marines and Marauders out in the field on group 1, and your Medivacs on group 2.

Assuming you had rallied all of the newly created units into the same pile in your base, you could quickly add the new troops to your first group by drag selecting all the Marines and Marauders onscreen.

Doing so will add all of the Marines and Marauders to an unassigned group. You then press shift-1 to add the new group into control group 1, and your main force is ready to go.

The process for the second group is identical: ctrl-click on a Medivac to add all of the Medivacs to a group, then press shift-2 to add the new members to group 2, and move out.

You could of course double click on a unit instead of ctrl-clicking, but ctrl-clicking is slightly more precise, and speed and precision are both helpful when you may be in battle elsewhere at the same time you are trying to add these new units to the fight.

With practice these key combinations should become second nature, and the entire process should take no more than a few seconds at most.

GROUP CREATION AND ADDITION

There are actually two ways to create a control group, and one way to add units to a control group.

While you have a group of units (or buildings) selected, you can:

1. Press CTRL and a number from 1-0, this will create a group with the currently selected units. If another control group was previously in that numbered slot, the new group will overwrite it.

2. Press Shift and a number from 1-0. This will add the currently selected units to the control group. This is very handy for adding new units to an existing army group. If no group is in that number, a group will be created.

3. Right click on one of the control group tabs at the bottom of the UI. Similar to ctrl-grouping, this will overwrite any units already in that numbered group. You cannot hold shift and add units via this right click method.

MULTIGROUP SELECTION

A single unit or building can actually belong to more than one control group at the same time.

For example, if you have a group of Zealots and Stalkers, you could have all of them on control group 1, but then also put the Stalkers on control group 2, giving you the ability to quickly select all of them and target an aerial threat, or to dance them around melee attackers and make good use of Blink.

This multigroup selection is most useful when you want to move your entire army as one force, but still have the ability to quickly select a subset of the army and gain precision control.

PROTOSS WARP AND ZERG MORPH

There are two peculiarities of unit creation unique to the Protoss and Zerg.

For the Protoss, you can Warp in units from Warp Gates. These units build on the battlefield at an accelerated rate, but while they are Warping in, they cannot move or fight.

*They can, however, be added to control groups **and** can be issued movement orders.*

For example, if you have a ground force in group 1 already, you can quickly move the screen to a nearby Pylon, Warp in a mix of units, drag select all of them, then hit shift-1 to add them to your army instantly.

The important point here is that you can still issue a movement order, even while the units are Warping in—when they finish the Warp, they will immediately move to join the rest of the group!

Similarly, for Zerg units that are Morphing (Banelings or Brood Lords), they too will remember any movement orders given to the group, and because you can Morph units that are already part of a control group, it's actually a bit easier to manage the 'new' additions to your army, as you don't have to re-add them to the group (unless you want to split them off of course!).

BUILDING MANAGEMENT

Building management is considerably simpler than controlling your units in battle, and even easier than managing your control groups well, but it is still very important.

As with your units, you want to have your primary production buildings hotkeyed at all times. The specific hotkeys don't matter, but as long as you have your core buildings on one hotkey (and your Queens on another, for Zerg), as well as all of your main military buildings, and your upgrade structures on another set of hotkeys, you're in good shape.

Having your core buildings hotkeyed allows you to quickly build (and re-build) workers, even while managing your units in battle, and even more critically, having your military buildings hotkeyed allows you to begin rebuilding your forces as you suffer losses in battle.

Done well, and you can have an equal (or larger!) group of troops waiting for you when you retreat, or waiting for your enemies if they push to your base.

BUILDING QUEUES

All production buildings, even research buildings, have the ability to queue up to 5 units or technology upgrades at a time.

It's worth noting that except in rare cases, if you find yourself queuing up many units or upgrades at once and you *still* aren't spending your resources fast enough, you probably don't have enough military buildings (or Hatcheries, for the Zerg).

Don't let this happen to you, always build more production structures to keep pace with your economy—if you don't, you won't be able to build (or rebuild) your military fast enough to fight with your opponent on equal terms.

There are a few specific exceptions to building queue, one being the Terran Reactor, which allows a building to have *two* queues of 5 units, producing 2 at a time from the same building.

Another is the Zerg method of troop production, which relies on Larva creation from the Hatchery, and has a significantly different flow than 'normal' building queues (though Zerg still have queues for their various upgrades).

Finally, Protoss Warp technology allows units to be built 'in advance' with a cooldown after the unit is created, rather than by queuing individual ground units in single military buildings.

Having your upgrade structures hotkeyed is less vital than the other production buildings, but it is still helpful to be able to quickly check on research progress, as well as queue up new upgrades without having to hunt down the buildings in your base.

BUILDING WAYPOINTS

Remember to constantly adjust waypoint locations for your production buildings as the match progresses.

Early in the match, rallying your troops to your initial base makes good sense, but once you expand to your natural expansion, having your troops rally at the chokepoint or entrance to your expansion is usually a better idea.

Later in a match, you might have your military buildings (or at least your air forces) rallying to a point further forward on the map, giving your reinforcements a headstart on joining the battle at the frontlines.

Forward rallying is particularly useful if you're pushing your opponent's hard and have them contained, but you haven't quite cracked their defenses.

Just be careful not to over-commit and have no forces in range of your bases should you be hit by a raid.

For your core buildings, you should move the worker rally points to quickly build up an expansion, or rebuild at a base that was raided and lost a lot of workers.

WORKER MANAGEMENT

One very handy way to make use of control groups, command queuing, and StarCraft II's smart unit behavior is to maintain a group of workers on a single hotkey throughout the game. You'll have to adjust this group from time to time as you move workers between bases, place them on Gas, or lose them to raids, but the basics are simple.

Select a group of 4-6 or so workers on your Mineral line. Place them on a new control group. This doesn't have to be an easily accessible number, though if you have room on your 'main' hotkey bank, go ahead and place them in easy reach.

Whenever you need a new structure (or structures) built, select this group of workers and queue up the construction of whatever you need built, ending the orders with a shift-right click order to return to Mineral gathering.

The workers will automatically a) send out only as many workers are needed and b) send one worker to each construction project, all of them returning to gather more Minerals when they have completed their tasks.

What's even more impressive about this behavior is that if you form this worker group out of workers from a few locations (say, your main base and a more distant expansion), it will *always* send the closest worker to complete the building.

This is very handy for quickly erecting defensive structures at several of your bases simultaneously. Without having to individually select each worker for each building, or have one or two workers trying to build up many buildings, you can quickly and easy construct multiple defensive buildings and know that they'll then return to work when you're finished.

Note that this smart behavior isn't dependant on having the workers on one hotkey, you can always just drag select a group of nearby workers on a Mineral line and then issue the orders—again, only as many workers as are needed will be sent, and as long as you end the string of build orders with a shift-right click back on the Minerals, they'll promptly return to work.

PRO TIP!
Live Hydralisk
KIBONG KOOK

Protoss Ground Unit Features

Zealot: Indispensible units from early to late or end game. You should increase the movement speed of Zealots through Charge from the Twilight Council after an expansion.

Sentry: Very strong units when attacking with Stalkers or Zealots. In particular, the double effect of Force Field and Guardian Shield grants an enormous advantage.

Stalker: The Zealot is a close proximity fighter, while Stalker is a long-range fighting unit. Stalkers can be used in "best counter" attacks or when you need to stop retreating enemies.

High Templar: You can still win what appears to be a hopeless battle if you use Psionic Storm on 2-3 medium units.

Dark Templar: Being invisible to enemies without detection, Dark Templar can be used when you want to take back or check expansions.

Immortal: The Immortal is a high-value unit that should be used after the middle of the game. No matter the strength of an attack, the amount of damage is limited by an Immortal's Hardened Shell, so you can attack strong units head on.

Colossus: It ignores terrain and does splash damage, nuff' said. The disadvantage is that they are tall enough to be shot by air to air units. Make sure they have air defense units with them like Sentries or Stalkers, etc.

IDLE WORKERS

Another very helpful feature of the StarCraft II UI is the Idle Worker button. Located at the bottom left of the hud, pressing F1 or clicking once on this button will select a single idle worker. Pressing F1 or clicking on the button repeatedly will cycle through all idle workers.

Conveniently, the shift and ctrl modifiers work for this button. If you hold shift and press F1 repeatedly, you will add idle workers to a new group. Hold ctrl and press F1 and you will instantly add ALL idle workers to a group!

This is very useful for gathering up workers who aren't producing for you, and getting them back to work, either gathering, building, or repairing.

CONTROL IN COMBAT

Unit control in combat is one of the most vital skills you can learn in StarCraft II, possibly the most vital, and it also often an area that is least comfortable for new players in multi, because they're so concerned about building up their base properly that they manage their army poorly (or worse, not at all!).

Don't worry though, basic battle management really isn't difficult, and just by sticking to a few simple basics, you can get your combat control up to an acceptable level very quickly.

MANAGE THE FIGHT

The first and most important of all battle management techniques in StarCraft II is also the easiest—*never take your eyes off your army in battle!*

As you grow more proficient in your control of the game, there will be times when it is acceptable to shift your view to your bases for a few seconds, but when you're still learning, once you commit to an attack (or defense) with your army, don't stop watching the fight until the fighting is over and you have either won, retreated, or your opponent has retreated.

Yes, you're going to allow some resources to accumulate while you are fighting, and yes, you may not get some upgrades researching or new buildings built, but this is far, far less costly than losing your entire army in battle because your opponent was watching the fight while you were not.

Buildings and technologies do not win matches in StarCraft II—units do. Remember that, and you're on the right path.

GROUP CONTROL

Assuming that you have your army units hotkeyed (and you should!), managing them in combat is as simple as ensuring that they are all engaged (hold A and left-click to attack move them), and then monitoring their performance in the battle as it unfolds.

Remember that you can quickly select all units of a single type by ctrl-clicking on them, either on the map, or in the group pane at the bottom of the UI. This is handy if you need to reposition or retreat a subset of your army.

Another very handy UI component for managing your army is the group pane. Because you aren't clicking on 3d models in the world who are moving around (and falling in battle!), you greatly reduce the chance of a missclick or accidental order.

Use the group pane for selecting units, and remember you can ctrl-click on a unit in the pane to select all of that unit type, or shift-ctrl-click to remove a unit type from the group.

Once your army is engaged, you need to keep an eye on the fight and make sure that your units are fighting efficiently. If your melee troops are getting bunched up, pull part of the group away from the back of the pack and move them around.

If your aerial units or transports are drifting close to enemy anti-air units or fixed defenses, move them back.

If you have Burrowing units that are getting heavily damaged, you can easily click on their portraits in the group UI pane as they go red and hit burrow to conceal them from enemy attack (as long as your opponent doesn't have detection present!).

Similarly, if you have ranged units, or large, tough units that are being focus fired (or simply damaged by unfocused attacks), it is often worthwhile to move them quickly out of range, then back in again. Be careful with this level of control however, because while it can be useful, interfering with too many units in a fight while your opponent continues to attack with his forces can result in heavy losses.

If your army is on attack-move in an enemy base and you see that part of your force is attacking non-critical buildings, move them to engage enemy forces, workers, or to focus on a key enemy building.

When your general combat units are engaged, you should keep your casting units selected, and ready to use their abilities at a moments notice. If you have no casting units (or their abilities have already been used), you should turn your attention to units that benefit the most from direct control.

Many ranged units (particularly if they are faster than your opponent's ground force) can be microed to 'dance' out of range and fire. Simply select the units, right click repeatedly to move them out of range, and occasionally pause to attack ground to make them pause and attack enemies in range, then return to moving them out of range.

FOCUS FIRING

Focus firing is simply the act of attacking a single enemy unit (or building) with all (or even most) of your army simultaneously. The benefit to focus firing (or queuing up multiple focus fire targets with shift) is that you can potentially decrease your opponent's damage output faster than he decreases yours.

A unit with 1 health deals just as much damage as a unit at full health, so if you kill his units faster than he kills yours by focus firing, even if he starts with roughly equal troops, you will win the fight handily.

There are a few downsides to focus firing however.

The first is that pathfinding can cause you to lose significant damage while your units attempt to move into range to attack, and this can cost you a fight if you over-manage your troops. In general, ranged troops are better for focus firing than melee troops, and aerial units are better than ground units (as they don't have to deal with terrain issues).

The second occurs if your opponent spots you focus firing, he can pick the unit out that you are targeting and retreat it. It may not save the unit, but it forces you to waste even more time.

INDIVIDUAL UNIT MICRO

When people think about micromanagement in RTS games, and particularly in StarCraft, they often think about it in terms of controlling individual units in battle.

The truth is that outside the very highest levels of play, trying to control all of the units individually in your army is not only extremely difficult (bordering on impossible for very large groups), it is often only of minor effectiveness, *and* it can pull your attention away from other aspects of a match that demand your time—controlling the *rest* of your army, controlling secondary assaults, maintaining your base and tech development, watching your scouting, and so on.

A good rule of thumb for individual unit micro is that when the number of troops in an engagement is less, individual unit micro matters *more* than it does when larger forces are clashing.

This is particularly relevant in the very early stages of the game, when an early rush or raid may consist of no more than 6 units, and controlling your units well is vital to deal the maximum damage possible, or to prevent as much damage as possible.

In larger conflicts, your unit micro should typically be confined to using caster abilities intelligently, ensuring units with large bonus damage are hitting their preferred target, and possibly dancing with ranged units or moving damaged targets out of enemy range.

PRO TIP!
Mondragon (ToT)
CHRISTOPH SEMKE

Zerg against Protoss:

Protoss regularly uses a two gate Zealot rush strategy. In this case, I opt for the same opening as I do versus Terran. Open with a 14 pool, 14 Gas, 15 Overlord but instead of making the 16th Drone save the Larva and make Zerglings. Make a Queen right after the Spawning Pool is finished and as soon as possible research the speed upgrade. Against Protoss you must be really careful because before Zerglings have their speed upgrade they are very weak vs. Zealots. Tech up speed right away, then scout what Protoss is doing. You will always be okay to make a second hatch at your natural expansion: expansions for Zerg are mandatory.

SPECIFIC MICRO SITUATIONS

Some examples of when you should be worrying about direct, immediate, and fast unit micro:

- You have a mixed force of ground forces and you spot a wave of Banelings rolling towards you. Quickly move non-Light units to the front to sponge up the damage while retreating your Light units to avoid taking bonus blast damage. Don't have non-Light units? Quickly split up your ground force and move each group away from the other to minimize the damage received.

- You have a mixed ground force with some anti-air units, and your opponent attacks with a group of air units. Quickly select the anti-air only units and focus fire them against individual air units to destroy them as fast as possible. Send in the ground only units to provide additional targets for the air units, if your opponent isn't careful, they'll target units that cannot damage them, saving your anti-air units.

- Your worker line is attacked by a raid, and you only have limited defensive forces present. Quickly select all of your workers and run away from the raid, while moving your defensive forces up. Micro them as carefully as possible to hold off the raid while your army returns to rescue your base.

- There are an almost countless number of specific scenarios that can crop up during a match in StarCraft II, but the important point is to recognize when ALL of your attention needs to be on microing units, and not on other aspects of the match.

- Quickly analyzing what is at stake during a battle can help you to recognize those situations—being forced to retreat after losing a few units on offense is a far less dire situation than losing the match if you lose a fight at the chokepoint to your main base.

USE THE SHORTCUTS!

*Remember whenever you get into battle, you **always** want to be using hotkey shortcuts, and mouse shortcuts.*

Instead of clicking on Stimpack, press T.

Instead of double clicking on a Zergling, hold ctrl and click it.

Instead of trying to find units onscreen to use their abilities, select their group and hit Tab a few times to select their subgroup, or ctrl-click on them in the group UI pane.

When adding newly built units to your army hotkey, instead of selecting the group, holding shift and selecting the new units, then pressing ctrl-#, simply select the new units and press shift-# to add them quickly.

PRO TIP!
Mondragon (ToT)
CHRISTOPH SEMKE

Hotkey Techniques for Zerg:

What I like to do is to put my main-producing Hatcheries, such as my main Hatchery and my natural expansion Hatchery, on the Hotkey '5' and hotkey the Drones to the specific Mineral line (main hatch to main Minerals and expansion hatch to expansion Minerals) and rally the units to the expansion. Whenever I take my second, third, or fourth expansion I hotkey my third Hatchery on hotkey '6', my fourth on '7', and my fifth on '8'. When I think that I have an adequate Drone count at my second expansion, which is close to my natural expansion, usually I add them to my main hotkey '5' and set the rally point between my natural and my second expansion.

If I take, for example, another natural and main position as an expansion for my third and fourth expansion, I hotkey them on one hotkey, be it '6' or '7'. It depends on the situation with my second expansion, but usually by then I already included my second expansion in my hotkey '5' so I'll group my third and fourth expansion (if it is a main and natural of another starting position) on hotkey '6'. Hotkey '0' and '9' are always my two Queens which remain on Hotkey '0' and '9' throughout the whole game. Hotkey '1', '2', '3', and '4' are reserved for unit groups and I try to design the specific groups how I need them the most vs. the specific races. Usually I hotkey Hydras or Roaches on '1' to target bigger units that are a threat to my Zerglings and Banelings and hotkeys '2' through '4' with a mixture of Zerglings, Banelings, and maybe a few other Hydras/Roaches.

USEFUL INFO

RANGES

On a normal monitor, the screen is roughly 24 Range from left to right, and about 18 Range from top to bottom.

On a widescreen monitor, the screen is roughly 28 Range from left to right, and 18 Range from top to bottom.

Keep these numbers in mind, and you can get a feel for the actual screen distance of any given weapon's listed range.

ATTACK AND MOVEMENT SPEEDS

A few points about this: First, we list the actual, internal attack and movement speeds in the Races chapter, but these numbers *will* change as Blizzard patches the game.

Second, in most cases you don't need to worry too much about the specifics of a unit with 0.8 attack speed vs 1 attack speed—it's enough to know what a specific unit is strong or weak against. It's usually much more important to know when a unit can outrun another one.

ACCELERATION

*A few units in the game have **acceleration** on their movement. That is, rather than going from a dead stop to full speed, they have a brief period (typically less than a second) before they reach their full movement speed.*

The only units in StarCraft II with acceleration are the aerial units and the worker units for each race.

Because air units (and workers) do take a moment to reach full speed, it's important that you start their movement towards (or away from) hostile units slightly more quickly than ground units.

The acceleration delay isn't much, but it can be the difference between losing a transport or key early air unit and getting away safely.

COMBAT MECHANICS

Combat in StarCraft II is very simple—the damage displayed by a unit minus the armor of the target is exactly the amount of damage done, for every attack.

Some units deal bonus damage to certain unit types (Light, Mechanical, etc), and every unit in the game has one or more unit type.

Some units do deal area of effect damage, and there are a fair number of abilities from the caster units of each race that can deal splash damage to multiple targets.

Note that abilities that deal damage typically completely ignore armor.

Some units have *multiple attack*s with their weapon. That is, for a single attack time period, they will instantly strike 2 or more times.

This is important when it comes to fighting armored units, as units with multiple attacks are *weaker* against heavily armored targets than units with a single strong attack. For example, if a unit hits twice for 5 damage per attack on a unit with 2 armor, it will deal 6 damage total, while a unit with a single 10 damage attack will deal 8 damage.

Keep that armor reduction in mind when it comes to both unit upgrades, and unit selection.

HEALTH AND SHIELDS

All units in the game have a Health score, but only Protoss units and buildings have Shields.

Zerg units regenerate health automatically, while Protoss shields begin to regenerate if they are out of combat for 10 seconds.

Terran units do *not* regenerate automatically, but their mechanical units can be repaired by SCVs (or MULEs), and their biological units can be healed by making use of the Medivac.

Zerg units *and* buildings regenerate 0.2734 per second (about 16 a minute), while Protoss Shields recharge at 2 per second, but they must have taken no damage for 10 seconds before the recharging begins.

Burrowed Roaches regenerate at an additional 5 per second, and when upgraded, an additional 10 per second. Zerg natural regen *does* apply to Roaches, so Burrowing Roaches heal at a very high rate. If your opponent has no detection, it is always better to Burrow wounded Roaches.

Terran SCVs repair at a rate based on the build time of the unit or structure they are repairing. That is, a nearly fully damaged Battlecruiser will take 110 seconds to fully repair by a single SCV.

Each additional SCV cuts the repair time to a fraction of the original build time (five SCVs will repair five times as fast!). The cost for repairing a unit or structure damaged almost fully is 25% of the original price, proportional to the amount of damage taken.

Medivacs heal 3 life per Energy, at a rate of 3 life every third of a second, so they heal 9 and drain 9 Energy per second.

Terran buildings that are heavily damaged begin to burn down at 3 per second when damaged beyond 33%. They will burn and collapse if left unrepaired!

ENERGY

For units (or structures!) that make use of Energy, the maximum amount of Energy for a given unit is always 200.

In most cases, freshly created units begin with 50 Energy. A fair number of units also have upgrades to give them a slightly higher starting Energy total.

All units that have Energy regenerate it at a fixed rate of 0.5625 per second, or just shy of 34 Energy per minute. It takes about four and a half minutes for a newly created unit to reach full Energy.

Because many units that have Energy have an upgrade that grants them an additional 25 Energy when they are created, you can think of that upgrade as saving you 45 seconds of waiting for each unit that you produce!

Those upgrades tend to be more useful in the mid-game however, when your econ can support pumping out multiple casters simultaneously. Early on, just get those units onto the field!

ENERGY REGENERATION IN SECONDS		
Energy Goal	Normal Speed	Faster Speed
25 Energy	44.44	31.74
50 Energy	88.89	63.49
75 Energy	133.33	95.24
100 Energy	177.78	126.98
125 Energy	222.22	158.73
150 Energy	266.67	190.48
175 Energy	311.11	222.22
200 Energy	355.56	253.97

UNIT TYPES

A unit's 'type' determines what bonus damage works against it, and in a few cases, what abilities.

There are 7 unit types in StarCraft II multiplayer.

- Light
- Armored
- Biological
- Mechanical
- Psionic
- Massive
- Structure

In most cases, units tend to have bonus damage against Light or Armored units. A few have bonuses against Massive, Biological, or Structure.

Structure, obviously, only applies to Buildings. Again, a few units have special attacks or damage against buildings only.

Note that because all Structures are also Armored, any unit with bonus damage against Armored is a good candidate for raiding buildings.

GROUND

Ground units form the bulk of your army in the early and mid game. Some ground with a ranged weapon can attack air units, important for defending against aerial assaults.

AIR

Air units have very powerful mobility, as they can travel anywhere on the map, unrestricted by changes in elevation, choke points, water, or even open space!

Some air units are purely air to ground or air to air, some can attack both freely.

CLIFF WALKERS

There are two special units, the Terran Reaper and the Protoss Colossus that can move up and down cliff faces to reach ledges. They are not actual flying units (they cannot traverse open space, water, or fly over buildings or obstructions), but they do have superior mobility in comparison to standard ground units.

You can utilize this mobility to harass worker lines and stage quick raids on key technology buildings.

Note that the Colossus can actually walk over normal sized ground units freely!

CASTER

Caster units are special units that provide the bulk of their utility through special abilities. Many do not even have a standard attack at all, and can only contribute to the fight by using their abilities.

Because caster units require individual control to utilize effectively, they place an additional micromanagement demand on your army while it is in the field.

Casters are also high value targets for your opponent, so they must be watched carefully, lest they are picked off without having a chance to use their abilities.

Many caster abilities are very powerful when used correctly, and even a small number can turn the tide of a fight.

CLOAKED

Cloaked units are powerful units that are almost completely invisible to your opponent. Without some form of cloak detection, the only visible indication of a cloaked unit is a slight shimmering on the screen when the unit moves.

Zerg units cannot cloak, but they gain the ability to Burrow, allowing them to dig into the ground. While burrowed, Zerg units are functionally cloaked. They can only be spotted by a detector unit. Unlike other cloaked units, burrowed units cannot attack, move, or use abilities, the only exceptions being the Roach and the Infestor which can move while burrowed.

Cloaked units *can* be fought with some splash damage attacks, and some special abilities as well. If you don't have immediate access to a Detector unit, it is occasionally possible to improvise and fight off a cloaked attack by making use of area of effect abilities or units.

DETECTOR

Detector units are crucial for fighting cloaked troops, in the same way that anti-air units are critical for fighting off air units.

Each race has at least one unit that can detect, and usually some form of special ability that can also be used as a temporary solution.

DETECTOR UNITS AND ABILITIES		
Terran	Protoss	Zerg
Raven	Observer	Overseer
Missile Turret	Photon Cannon	Spore Crawler
Orbital Command Scanner Sweep	N/A	Infestor Fungal Growth
Ghost EMP	N/A	N/A

BASE MANAGEMENT

Managing your bases is an important skill to master, and when building (or expanding) any base, you should ask yourself a few quick questions.

- What are you building?
- Why are you building it?
- Is your base adequately defended?

Obviously, any new base has to start with a single core structure, but beyond that, you should have a clear goal in terms of production, resource, and defensive goals.

YOUR FIRST BASE

Building up your initial base properly is extremely important, and in tight 1v1 matches, making the wrong decisions can win the game for your opponent before the fighting even begins.

Your early priorities should be as follows:

1. Maximize your economy
2. Get your military production going
3. Tech towards your chosen units and research
4. Place your structures carefully

ECON

Building up your economy is quite simple, and we've gone over the various goals numerous times, but to recap: Get from 16 to 24 workers on Minerals, and 6 workers on Vespene Gas, leaving you with anywhere from 22 to 30 workers total.

Workers reach peak efficiency at 2 workers per Mineral patch, and suffer some diminishing returns up to 3 workers per patch, so the initial 16 and 6 on Gas are the most important.

The simple rule of thumb for your workers in the early game is to always build one to two new workers as Protoss or Terran, or to morph one or more new Drones as Zerg, any time you are *not* spending the resources on either new military units, or new buildings.

In the case of your early build up, it is very important that you occasionally delay worker production to get your first military structures up, and to make sure that you always have troops being created. Don't worry about 'falling behind' on econ while you're doing this.

While it is true that an opponent who fast expands and does nothing but pump workers will have an economic advantage over a more balanced build that pushes military as a first priority, when you scout your opponent doing just that, you simply rush them immediately with your troops. Money in the bank and workers don't fare well against troops on the field.

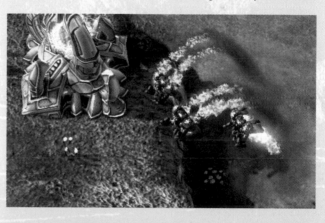

No Gas, 2 Gateways

Without Chrono Boost at your Nexus, build 12 or 13~14 Probes, then produce Zealots using Chrono Boost. This allows you to attack with a quick Zealot rush in the early game.

If it is a smaller map you might be able to finish your opponent off in the early game. Or, if you prefer to gather Minerals at the beginning, this build can be an effective strategy to force a Zerg player into producing many Zerglings.

 PRO TIP!
Garimtoi
KIM DONGSU

This is more dangerous in StarCraft II, because the Queen can spawn additional Larvae and you can be easily overwhelmed by wave after wave of Zergling attacks. This build is particularly good for opponents who prefer to build an early natural expansion. If a Zerg player starts off by producing 6 Zerglings at the beginning and begins to extract Gas early then you need to be flexible, limit Zealot production between 1~3 and go up the tech tree right away.

ECONOMIC BOOSTERS

Remember that each race has an economic unit or ability that **must** *be utilized constantly to maintain economic parity with your opponent.*

If you manage your booster more efficiently than your opponent, you **will** *pull ahead in economic and military production, giving you an edge when the fighting starts.*

THE RUSH, TECH, BALANCE TRINITY

There are, broadly speaking, three different routes you can take with your economic and military development in the early game.

You can rush, building your military structures very early and pushing troops out very early, then attacking your opponent immediately. This sacrifices your early economy in favor of speed.

You can boom, quickly expanding or prioritizing worker buildup and quickly building structures to reach a chosen unit or technology. This sacrifices troop development in favor of a stronger economy and quicker buildup to a specific unit.

Or you can go for a balanced build, producing early military units constantly, while building up your workers simultaneously.

As a general rule, without interference (or proper scouting!) a rush will beat a tech build, a boom build beats a balanced build, and a balanced build will beat a rush.

These are generalities, and the specifics vary depending on the racial matchup and the map you are playing on, but it's a good rule of thumb worth keeping mind.

Because **builds** *(even moreso than units) tend to be somewhat rock-paper-scissors in their nature, this is why we stress scouting as such a critical component in your development as a StarCraft II player.*

If you scout your opponent very early and spot a Spawning Pool at 6 workers, you know your opponent is rushing with several Zerglings, block your choke and get your military units building!

If you scout and spot an early expand or very light military, get your troops out and rush his worker line.

And if you scout and see a 'normal' buildup, you know you need to keep an eye on your opponent and see what he builds so you can tailor your response to his development.

MILITARY

The second crucial goal is to get your early military structures up, and to begin producing troops. Once you start, you don't ever stop!

Early game units in StarCraft II don't become obsolete (partly due to upgrades available later, partly simply due to unit design), so there is rarely a good reason to stop producing basic units even in the mid and late game.

The other important point here is that you need to get into the habit of constantly pumping out troops, all throughout the game, while managing your econ, scouting, and fighting. Make troops! Make more troops! Hit your Supply cap, build more Supply, make more troops!

For Terran and Protoss, you should always have one to two units queued up in each military building, for the duration of the early game. If you have to delay a worker for a few seconds to make sure your early Gateways and Barracks are working, do so.

Zerg function a bit differently, as your larva production limits your troop creation early, and you're forced to choose between a Drone or a military unit. For this reason, it is crucial that you get a Queen early, and begin to utilize Spawn Larvae. Zerg also need a second Hatchery soon after, to keep up with the production potential of the Terran and Zerg.

Nonetheless, just as with Terran and Protoss, make sure that you're getting early military units out. Getting hit by an aggressive opponent when you have nothing but Drones is a good way to lose the match.

Be *sure* that your Queens are hotkeyed and that you are utilizing Spawn Larvae on your Hatcheries every single time it is up.

Remember to build *enough* military structures as Terran and Protoss to build up an army in a reasonable amount of time. Early in the game, this can be two Gateways or Barracks, but later, as your economy fills out, you should always add more military buildings so that you can spend resources faster, and recover from losses in battle more quickly.

Finally, we've mentioned this before, but it bears repeating—for the Terran and Protoss, never fully queue up units (or research!) in any structure in the early game. Build units one to two at a time, and use the extra resources to build more structures!

Once you hit the mid-game, and any time when you are going on offense, it is totally acceptable to dump all of your resources into your production buildings and then let them run while you fight, but never do this while you are managing your base directly!

TECH UP!

Beyond the early game buildup of workers and basic military forces, you have to progress into the midgame by building towards a specific unit (and usually some attendant technologies).

It is crucial that you have a plan for what you are going to tech for, before you even start building the necessary buildings, because it determines your build order beyond the first 30 Supply or so (and for specific early game builds, can influence when or if you build Gas, and how many military buildings you create).

Once you have chosen your desired unit and techs, build directly towards the structures you need, and don't waste any resources on other buildings. Focus is critical.

If you decide to go Banshees as Terran, go straight for double Starport with attached Tech Labs, and start pumping those Banshees while Cloak researches, don't stop to get a Tech Lab on your Factory and research Siege Tech.

If you decide to go Mutalisk as Zerg, decide if you can skip Roach production and immediately build the Lair and Spire.

If you decide to go Dark Templar as Protoss, build the Twilight Council and the Dark Shrine as quickly as possible, don't detour by building Stargates or the Robotics Facility.

The key point here is to hit your chosen unit and technology as fast as possible, so that when it hits the field, you can inflict the maximum possible damage to your opponent, possibly ending the match immediately if they aren't prepared for your assault.

As a general rule, teching for an aerial or cloaking unit (burrowing, in the case of the Zerg) is a solid basic strategy, and a good place to begin.

CHOOSING THE RIGHT TECH

The tech that you build towards should be dictated by the racial matchup, the map you're playing on, and what your scouting reveals about your opponent's development.

Even the unit mix of your basic troops needs to be determined by the racial matchup and the current metagame on Battle.net.

Because there are quite a few factors that we can't predict that will affect how each race will **often** build up, we can't give you any bullet proof rules for exactly what you should build in any given matchup (and as Blizzard patches the game, and the metagame shifts, what is correct one month likely will not be the next!).

The key points remain the same however—scout early, scout often. Build towards units that are strong against your opponent's race, and don't hesitate to change your strategy if it isn't working for you over the course of several games.

UPGRADES

Don't forget about upgrades!

Each race has access to basic structures that unlock global upgrades for all military units. These upgrades generally take the form of level 1, 2, and 3 versions of offensive and defensive bonuses (online you'll often see these referred to as +1, +2, and +3, though this isn't entirely accurate in terms of damage bonuses, see the sidebar on upgrade rules!).

For the Terran, they can upgrade Barracks units (from the Engineering Bay), or Factory or Starport units (from the Armory).

The Protoss can upgrade ground troops and all shields from the Forge, or air units from the Cybernetics Core.

The Zerg can upgrade ground melee or ranged attacks and armor from the Evolution Chamber, and air attacks and armor from the Spire.

The upgrade structures for each race also unlock defensive Detector structures for each race, useful for protecting your initial bases chokepoint, and your worker lines at your main base and expansions.

PRO TIP!
Mouz.White-Ra
OLEKSII KRUPNYK

Hot key suggestions

I assign 1, 2, 3 and 4 to units, depending on my build orders.

1 - Drone, Zealots

2 - Stalkers, Immortals

3 - Observer or air unit

4 - The rest

6 - Nexuses

0 - Gateway

9 - Robotics Facility

8 - Stargate

You can put all buildings under a single hot key, and then just click on the right building in the bar when you need to speed up construction or upgrade with a Chrono Boost.

WHEN TO UPGRADE

As a general rule, you should have your upgrade structure built and working either just *before* or just *after* the first major skirmish. You can try for a quick upgrade before you fight, to give your units an edge in battle, or you can let the upgrade run so that your reinforcements will be tougher when you re-engage your opponent.

Some offensive pushes rely on the added punch from an upgrade that considerably changes combat dynamics. When an offensive upgrade changes the number of hits it takes to kill a basic enemy unit with one of your own basic units, it can significantly affect the outcome of a fight.

If you are going for a fast tech or defensive build, you may want to get an early upgrade structure so that you can get a few defensive structures built to help hold the line while you rush for your chosen tech or unit.

Remember that upgrades act as a force multiplier—the more troops you have on the field, the more effective a single upgrade is (conversely, having many upgrades with few troops is extremely *in*effective).

For this reason, it's important to have upgrades running from the early-mid game to the late game constantly, so that by the late game, your troops are fully upgraded.

Because there are so many potential upgrades for each race, and they take so long to research, you may want to add a second (or even third!) upgrade structure going into the mid or late game.

While the upgrades are somewhat expensive to insert into an early build, they are very inexpensive later in the game, and having several running at once won't excessively strain your economy after you have expanded.

If you are going for a very specific build that involves a lot of one general troop type (Infantry as Terran, ground units as Protoss, or air units as Zerg, for example), building double upgrade structures and pushing upgrades that affect only those units can be effective—just be wary of overcommitting on troops that your opponent's race has a good answer for.

UPGRADE RULES

The general rule of thumb for combat upgrades is that they increase the raw damage a unit deals by about 10%

Each race can upgrade their units attacks up to three times.

For units that deal 1 to 14 damage, they get +1 for each level of upgrade you purchase. However, units that deal 15 to 24 damage per attack will get +2 from that same level of upgrade, and so on.

For example, the Protoss Zealot deals 8 damage, hitting twice per attack. Purchasing the Ground Weapons Level 1 upgrade makes them hit for 9 damage twice (from 16 to 18 damage per attack).

The Protoss Immortal on the other hand, deals 20 damage per shot, with an additional +30 damage against Armored targets. The same Ground Weapons Level 1 upgrade provides +2/+3 damage.

That single upgrade pushes the Immortals damage to 22 against a non-Armored target, or 55 against an Armored target!

The Terran Battlecruiser hits for 6 (against aerial targets) or 10 (against ground targets), so it only gets +1 damage per upgrade level—but it also has an *extremely* fast attack speed, attacking nearly 5 times per second. One upgrade adds a lot of damage over time!

Upgrades range from +1 to +5 in strength, per level, so units that deal more than 50 damage in an attack (eg. Banelings vs Structures, Siege Tanks in Siege Mode) will not get more than a +5 bonus per level.

Online, you will often hear about upgrades in terms of a +1, +2, or +3 upgrade, but don't mix those up with the damage bonus a unit is receiving—a single upgrade level can provide more than +1 point of damage!

In the Races section, you can see how a weapon upgrade level will affect a given units damage, but remember the 10% rule—even if the numbers change in the future, you can quickly get an idea of how much damage an upgrade will add.

And don't forget about attack speed! Some units may not deal high damage per attack, but due to the number of attacks (Carriers) or the attack speed (Battlecruisers, upgraded Zerglings), they can deal a lot of damage very quickly.

Armor (or Shield) upgrades are much simpler. A level 1, 2, or 3 upgrade provides 1, 2, or 3 total points of armor (or shielding), no tricks there!

Armor (or Shield) upgrades are best against units with multiple attacks, or low damage, high speed attacks.

SPECIAL UPGRADES

In addition to the 'normal' damage and armor upgrades that each race has access to, every race also has access to special technologies that benefit one specific troop type, or a limited number of troops.

Special upgrades are typically purchased either from the building the unit is enabled (for Zerg), an attached Tech Lab (for Terran), or at a special technology building (for Protoss).

These upgrades tend to make the unit considerably more effective, and allow early-game units to remain effective even into the late game.

Any time you are fielding a considerable number of a basic unit type, you should *always* purchase the upgrades for that unit. Marine and Marauder Stimpacks, Zealot Charge, or Zergling movement and attack speed upgrades are all very effective.

For more specialized units, or caster units, you should consider how many of that unit you will be fielding. Buying upgrades for units that you use very few of is generally a waste of time and resources, and you're never going to have enough of either in a close match to buy upgrades for every unit.

Pick out complementary upgrades that support your overall army composition, and research them as quickly as possible. And remember—units first, upgrades later. Better to have one Siege Tank on the field than to have Siege Tech and no tanks to use it!

INVISIBLE UPGRADES

Because the effects of normal combat upgrades are 'hidden', players often do not notice their impact on combat, or forget about researching them.

*Don't make this mistake—in larger mid-game battles, if two roughly even armies clash, the force that has more upgrades **will** win without outside interference, and even if one side micros their troops well, without upgrades, they are fighting at a painful disadvantage.*

The effects of Stimpacks, Psionic Storm, or Metabolic Boost for Zerglings are all visible and obvious, but the effects of Level 2 Air attack upgrades on a pack of Mutalisks aren't quite as visible—you only know that your workers and ground forces sure are dying fast!

BUILDING PLACEMENT

Finally, the last of your early buildup considerations is simply that of placing the buildings in your base intelligently.

For the Terran and Protoss, you should almost always wall off the choke-point entrance to your base.

Terran can literally wall off the entrance, because their Supply Depots can lower, and their military buildings can liftoff!

Protoss cannot, but they can place Pylons and Gateways in such a way that only a single square gap is left—allowing a single Zealot to hold off any number of troops, and at a really narrow choke, a single Sentry Forcefield can block the entrance completely.

As Zerg, you don't have this option, but you should be sure to place your early structures behind your Mineral line, where your Queen, military units and Spine Crawlers can protect them. Losing your Spawning Pool to the first push from your opponent because you put it at the front of your base is not a good thing!

Beyond your initial buildings, be sure to place new Supply buildings at the outer edges of your base. The first couple should go towards the 'front' edges of your base, where they can provide line of sight and early warning of incoming enemies.

Many maps have your first base on a raised platform, so placing Supply buildings on the edges can give you free recon around the outskirts of your base. Even on maps where this is not the case, it is still a good habit, as you can receive early warning of incoming aerial assaults or drop ships.

The rest of your supply buildings should go around the edges of your base until you have full line of sight to your entire base. You should *never* be surprised by a stealthy drop at the back of your base, and rarely surprised by any aerial assault. Far better to lose one supply building than to lose your worker line to a fast raid from air units, a drop, or cliffwalkers that you didn't spot in time!

Zerg obviously don't have Supply buildings, but you can use Overlords for the same purpose. Spread them around the outskirts of your base to get full vision of incoming troops.

Overlords also have the benefit of flight, which means that on maps where your base is *not* on a ledge, Zerg actually have the scouting edge, as their Overlords can see incoming units faster than Terran or Protoss.

When it comes to placing buildings that aren't part of your frontal wall-in, their placement is *generally* less important, just be sure to avoid placing key technology structures directly in the path from your front entrance to your worker line. You don't want to lose a Fusion Core, Fleet Beacon, or Greater Spire first in a battle!

Against Terran, one consideration is dealing with Scanner Sweeps. Because Orbital Command scans have a limited radius, you can often hide key tech buildings by placing them at the edges of your base.

There's no guarantee your opponent won't randomly scan that section of your base, but if you always place your buildings in a clump in the middle of your base, they *will* spot your tech buildings with a single sweep. Denying your opponent free intel is always a smart move.

WALLING IN

A 'wall in' is simply using buildings to create a 'wall' at the frontal chokepoint to your base, preventing enemy ground units from penetrating your base. This is useful both to force a battle at a chokepoint in your favor defensively, and for denying your opponent easy recon into your base with early ground scouts.

Remember that you can also block the entrance of your base with troops on hold position. In cases where you might not wish to wall in (Protoss vs Terran) or where you simply cannot wall in (Zerg early game), you can simply use early units on hold position at the chokepoint of your base as a means of preventing early scouts or raids from getting to your worker line, or scouting your technology development.

Each race also has means of fighting from behind even a full wall-in. As Terran, you can float your buildings out of your base to establish an expansion. As Protoss, you can warp new units in at an external Pylon or Warp Prism power field, meaning the only unit that can't escape your base if it is completely blocked is the Immortal. The Zerg can easily travel between bases or around the map via their Nydus Network.

While on offense, all races can of course bypass a wall-in with aerial units, making them useful to bypass choked off entrances. Cliffwalkers can bypass *most* wall-ins, though not all.

TERRAN

As Terran, there is no reason at all not to block the entrance to your base, as *all* of your units are ranged attackers, so you can easily defend from behind the wall, and you can simply lower a Supply Depot or raise a Barracks to walk out!

Not only that, the Bunker gives +1 range to units inside it, so if you really need a defensive edge, a Bunker with a few SCVs repairing it as part of your wall can be extremely difficult for your opponent to break.

Once Siege Tanks and Missile Turrets are added, the Terran wall starts looking more like a fortress—though in most cases, you don't need to go to that extreme to protect your base!

DEFENSIVE BUILDINGS

Defensive structures are the one category of building where it *does* matter where you place them, and each building placement should be carefully considered for maximum effectiveness.

Each race has access to different defensive structures. For the Terran, they have the Bunker, Missile Turret, Sensor Tower, and Planetary Fortress, the Protoss have the Photon Cannon, and the Zerg have the Spine and Spore Crawlers.

Emphasizing their defensive strength, the Terran also have access to two upgrades that improve their structure armor and ranges, as well as the ability to repair defensive buildings during or after battle with SCVs, and Bunkers that can be salvaged, removing them from the battlefield and refunding their purchase price.

As a general rule, the two most important areas to protect are your worker line, and your chokepoint. Placing key tech buildings in range of these defenses is often a good idea.

Be careful about over-fortifying your chokepoint however, because a chokepoint is only useful until it is broken, and once your enemy breaks through (or bypasses it!), any fixed defenses placed there are essentially useless.

Defending your worker line is almost always a smart move, as any good opponent who breaks into your base is going to make straight for your workers.

If you do have choke defenses set up and your opponent bypasses them to hit your workers, you can always run your workers away to the chokepoint, but this then leaves your core structure at risk of destruction.

PROTOSS

For the Protoss, because your Zealot is a melee unit, walling in against Terran may not always be quite as desirable, as it can restrict your ability to get your Zealots into contact with his ranged forces as quickly as possible.

But even there, you still prevent his troops from moving into your base, which can be useful for stopping a worker raid, and buying time for your army to return to your base. Just beware of having your frontal buildings being picked off by the ranged Terran force.

Against Protoss or Zerg, having a tight chokepoint allows you to block the entrance with just a few Zealots, while your Stalkers and Sentries deal their damage from behind to any incoming Zealots or Zerglings.

On maps with a ramp chokepoint or a narrow base entrance, be sure to utilize the Sentry Forcefield, as it can block off the entrance completely, and remember, if your opponent has no line of sight into your base, they *cannot* fire at your units or buildings.

On any map with a ramp, if you Forcefield the ramp before their troops get up it (or even if a few do, they can be taken out quickly), any remaining troops outside can be taken out by your ranged troops, and they can't do anything about it until the Forcefield wears off.

ZERG

Zerg of course, cannot wall in their base in the early game, so careful building placement and good troop control is vital for defending against early attacks.

You *do* get the benefit of faster unit movement on Creep, the Queen is a good anti-rush early unit, and your Spine and Spore Crawlers can move around if needed.

By the midgame, you should have Creep spread all over your bases, and once this has occurred, you *can* block off the ground entrance to your base with Spine Crawlers. Because you can simply uproot them and move them away, this isn't a bad delaying tactic to protect an expansion until your army can arrive to help defend.

Defending your worker line is very useful, as it may ward off light raids, and give you the defensive edge needed to kick out a roughly equal force with your military plus new reinforcements as they come onto the field in your base.

The only downside to fixed defenses at your worker line is that once the Minerals (and later Gas) are mined out, they're usually wasted money, because your opponent no longer has a reason to hit that area of your base.

Remember that defensive structures aren't going to fend off anything but the lightest of raids on their own—they act as a defensive bonus for your army when you *are* fighting on the defensive. They can also buy you some time to retreat your workers and get your army back to your base before you start losing key buildings.

In situations where your army might not match up favorably in an open field battle, fighting on the defensive with the benefit of defensive structures can provide you the edge you need to win, possibly decisively enough that you can then either counter-attack, or at least immediately expand while you rebuild your military.

DETECTORS

Each race has access to a defensive structure that acts as a Detector, unlocked by building their basic upgrade structure.

Detectors are very important to build in response to scouting that shows the development of Cloaking technology, and are almost always needed against Zerg, due to their ability to Burrow any ground unit.

Detectors can be built early, but all Cloak and Burrow technology arrives no sooner than early-mid game, so unless you need the structures for defensive purposes, they do not always need to be part of your initial build order—just don't forget about them come midgame!

USEFUL INFO

Economics in StarCraft II are simple, but difficult to manage perfectly.

Ideally, you want to have your resources zeroed at all times—in other words, you're spending resources as quickly as you are gathering them. In practice, this isn't always possible, as your attention is split between combat and growth, but at all times while playing, you should be aiming to operate your economy as efficiently as possible. A huge surplus of Minerals and Vespene Gas does nothing for you when the enemy army comes rolling into your base. Make sure your resources are working for you on the battlefield!

MILITARY AND ECONOMIC GROWTH

One of the most common mistakes of new players to StarCraft II is *not building enough*. That means enough workers, and almost always, enough military units.

The resources in StarCraft II are finite, but they are not so limited that you are punished harshly for losing units in battle. You're *expected* to lose many units while on offense and defense, and still have enough left over to continue to rebuild and expand.

Remember: Never stop building military units. Units in StarCraft II never become obsolete, the lowly Marine, Zergling, or Zealot are dangerous all the way into the end-game. Don't lose sight of massing your basic troops into a fighting force in favor of trying to tech to high tier units.

Similarly, don't stop building workers until your base is 'maxed out' and producing at peak capacity.

If you're having trouble spending your resources on your army fast enough (having units queued up in Terran or Protoss military units is usually bad!), be sure to build more military buildings, or for the Zerg, more Hatcheries (and make use of your Queen Spawn Larvae ability!).

You should be able to constantly dump your resources into a fresh wave of reinforcements, either growing your total army, or quickly replenishing from losses suffered in combat.

Your goal should always be aiming for 200 Supply and a gigantic, maxed out army!

ECONOMY NUMBERS

The key numbers to remember for worker management are simple—2 to 3 workers per Mineral patch, 3 workers per Vespene Geyser.

For most main bases, this translates to 16 to 24 workers on Minerals, and 6 workers per Geyser, meaning 22 to 30 workers per base. High Yield expansions often have less Mineral patches, usually 6, so you only need 12 to 18 workers there.

Because workers reach high efficiency at 2 per Mineral patch, having 16 workers running on two bases is preferable to hitting 24 in your main before you send those extras to your expansion.

QUICK ECON CHECK

Remember, the fastest way to check your current econ is to simply ctrl-click on a worker. If you see that you have about a full selection box of three rows (24 units), your base is running near peak efficiency, and you can stop building workers there.

If you want to check Gas, just drag select the two visible miners and wait—if you see a third, unselected worker pop out, you know you have three. If you don't see the third, get another worker on Gas!

Also remember that 2 workers per Mineral patch is near peak efficiency, so if you see that you have two full rows of workers in a selection, plus a few extras on Gas, your base is still in good shape, particularly an expansion.

When you expand, if you are running a maxed out base (26-30 workers or so), be sure to transfer over 8 workers immediately, they'll provide an immediate surge in income.

In terms of gather rates, take a look at the chart to see what sort of income per minute we're talking about. Remember, these numbers could easily change through patches, but the fundamentals remain the same. Whatever the optimal number of workers ends up being, try to keep your bases running around those numbers!

As you can see, going past 3 workers per Mineral patch provides no real benefit—the *only* time you should ever be building more workers past that point is if you're planning on sending the extras to a new expansion. But even then, don't build the extras if you need more military or structures, save the cash and send 8 workers instead.

The difference between 16 and 24 workers is roughly 200 Minerals a minute on a normal Mineral patch, but those 8 workers on a fresh expansion will pull in more than double that amount!

Until diminishing returns, workers gather at 60 Minerals per minute, or about 86 per minute at a High Yield patch. The Terran MULE gathers at a massively accelerated rate of 270, but has a limited duration.

TIME AGAIN

In StarCraft II Ladder matches, the game is played on Faster game speed, which is 1.4 seconds per real second, or about 30% faster than the displayed build times in-game!

Consequently, you can expect to to harvest resources more quickly than the listed times per minute here.

WORKER GATHER RATE, NORMAL MINERALS

Worker Count	Income Per Minute
8	480
12	690
16	940
20	1030
24	1140
28	1130
32	1150

WORKER GATHER RATE, HIGH YIELD MINERALS

Worker Count	Income Per Minute
8	686
12	994
16	1134
20	1176
24	1204
28	1260
32	1218

WORKER GATHER RATE, VESPENE GAS

Worker Count	Income Per Minute
3	164
6	328

Unit Tactics:

Always have two Queens available as early as possible in every matchup. The units that are used literally every matchup at some point are Hydras. In combination with Zerglings, Banelings and Roaches, Hydras are the best combination available vs. Terran. Against Terran, the most important unit is Banelings. Without a very high count of Banelings you will not be able to beat any decent Terran player. Thus you must make sure to have a lot of Banelings and use them wisely. A good start is 50 or more Banelings for the first big battle(s) in combination with Hydras and Zerglings. Banelings are especially good vs. Marines, but not against Marauders or Hellions. Good

Terran players try to place their Marauders or Hellions in front of the Marines in order to take the hits of Banelings. Banelings do extra damage to light units such as Marines, which is why it is very important to use them vs. Marines. If possible you should try to target Marauders with Hydras because they are most dangerous vs. Zerglings and Banelings and use the Banelings against Marines. After winning the first big battle you should start your Hive tech and mix in Broodlords for the second big battle.

VESPENE GAS

Gathering Vespene Gas is very straightforward, but it bears special mention that because your Vespene income is so sharply limited, and it is required for *all* high tier units and all research, Vespene quickly becomes the limiting factor of your economy for your military production in the mid and late game.

It is entirely worthwhile to setup an expansion that only harvests Gas in the mid or late game. At worst you lose 750-900 Minerals if the entire base is wiped out, worthwhile if you can get at least two real time minutes of production out of it.

While you should always get both Vespene Geysers in your main base producing, exactly how fast you start that production depends heavily on your initial build.

A rush build might skip Gas entirely, a more moderate build will usually get one Geyser fully operational first, and a booming tech build will generally go for double Gas fairly quickly. All builds should eventually get both geysers running full speed!

SUPPLY

Supply is the way StarCraft II represents the resources needed to field a large military force.

For the Terran, they require Supply Depots to provide for their army, while the Protoss use Pylons to power their forces, and the Zerg swarm make use of Overlords to control their minions. In each case, every new Supply structure (or unit) provides 8 more Supply for your army, up to a maximum of 200.

The core structures for each race also provide supply, with the Command Center giving 11, and the Hatchery and Nexus providing 10. Hatcheries give additional 2 supply, while additional Command Centers and Nexus give the full 11 and 10, respectively. Remember that Terran SCVs have to be present to build their structures, so they get the extra Supply point to compensate for this disadvantage.

Be very careful about supply capping yourself, you always need room to grow your military and economy to keep pace with your enemy. Destroying Supply can be an effective offensive tactic, as it allows you to stall the enemies rebuilding of losses taken, while you can keep the pressure on them. This is particularly noticeable against Zerg with air units, as they have to explicitly build anti-air defenses or units to deal with this form of harassment.

While your early game build order should be very tight, and include the first 2-3 Supply producers as part of the build, once you get beyond the first 30-40 Supply, you can respond to your Supply needs more organically, simply building up new Supply producers as needed.

Remember to use your Supply producers as 'base scouts', and spread them around your base to give full line of sight.

Beyond that, you can use them to wall in your worker line, wall in defensive structures, or even shield more valuable tech buildings. In the mid and late game, it's always better to lose a few Supply producers than it is to lose a key tech building.

There's also nothing stopping you from using them as fairly cheap 'scouts' by dropping a few at key points around the map, though be wary of wasting too many Minerals on this tactic early in the game.

As long as you don't stall your military and economic growth early in the game, occasionally hitting your cap in the midgame is rarely crippling, as you can quickly build multiple Supply producers, and they all build fairly rapidly.

A good rule of thumb is that whenever you hit a new, higher Supply cap, you should be pushing out with your army while new Supply producers build. As you suffer losses, you can replace them while in the field, and by the time you retreat, you should have an even larger force waiting for you at home!

EXPANSION

Expanding from your initial base to other Mineral Fields with new Vespene Geysers is absolutely vital in StarCraft II.

While you can certainly finish a game before your base runs dry, planning on certain victory in every match is a dangerous strategy, and if anything goes wrong, or your opponent expands before you do and you don't stop him, you're going to run into trouble.

WHEN AND WHERE

You cannot survive on a single base in an extended multiplayer match without running out of resources, so creating new expansions is critical in any extended match.

Expanding more than your opponent can also provide you with an insur-mountable economic advantage, as you can build a larger army, research more technology, and replace combat losses more quickly.

Each race has slightly different requirements for the timing of their expansions, and different means of expanding.

Most often, the best (and safest) time to expand is when your opponent is on the defensive. If you are in the process of an attack, or you know you have your opponent contained, you can expand much more freely than if your opponent is in the field with his army.

For the Zerg, on some maps it is often desirable to expand immediately as the game begins. The Terran can construct a Command Center, load it with SCVs, and simply float to a new expansion site. Protoss have the least early/safe options for expansion, but they still need to expand soon after the first major skirmish in a match, if at all possible.

Be careful about building an unprotected expansion if your opponent is using air units or dropships, as they can quickly reach and destroy the expansion.

Most expansions should be protected with at least a few defensive structures, as they can prevent a light harassing force from eliminating your workers. They usually can't stop a dedicated assault from an army, but they can give you enough time to get your own army in place to repel the assault.

Expanding to your 'natural' expansion (that is, an expansion right outside your main base entrance) is almost always a good idea, as you can defend your natural almost as easily as your main, simply by massing your newly created troops at your expansion. At such short ranges, you can easily move between your expansion and your main for defense as necessary.

EXPANSION MATH

Resources in StarCraft II are finite. Mineral Patches hold 1500 Minerals each, while Vespene Geysers hold 2500 each.

As a result, you cannot remain at your main base indefinitely. If your opponent expands before you, the additional income will allow them to tech faster, build faster, and recover from losses faster—you will usually lose the fight if it becomes drawn out.

Therefore, you *must* expand to new bases, and preferably you should do so *before* your main base runs dry on Minerals.

Having multiple bases bringing in resources at once allows you to deploy your strongest units on the field, in numbers that can do serious damage, in addition to being able to Supply cap yourself with a strong mix of basic unit types without straining your econ, all while researching upgrades and technologies.

Your main base and expansions typically start with 8 Mineral patches and 2 Vespene Geysers, while High Yield Mineral expansions typically have only 6 Mineral patches.

Consequently, your main base and expansions can provide you with 12000 Minerals and 5000 Gas, while High Yield expansions only have 9000 Minerals (but they are gathered considerably faster than normal Minerals).

You will typically begin to mine out your main base of Minerals in about 10-12 minutes real time (on Faster game speed) and the Gas will be depleted around 13-16 minutes (slightly more or less depending on how quickly you get your extractors up and running).

Because of this fact, you should generally be expanding at the latest near the 10 minute mark, and if you can get away with expanding earlier, do so.

THESE TIMES AREN'T EXACT!

True—remember, your early build order will dictate how fast you ramp up your worker production, and how fast you get your Gas.

Additionally, each race's economic booster works slightly differently, and there's no way to account for raids on your worker line, which can and will occur early.

Use the figures as a ballpark, you can always watch your replays to see exactly how fast *you* mine out your base in a typical game, and then use that information to plan your expansion timing.

Another point is that these timings could easily change in the future due to patch changes, so if (when!) they do, use the updated numbers to do some calculation yourself—you don't need militant precision, but having a good feel for what the timing windows are can help your gameplay.

Most skirmishes tend to begin around the 5+ minute mark, which gives you around a 5 minute window for expansion, which *is* enough time, as long as you exploit it.

PRO TIP!
Live Hydralisk
KIBONG KOOK

Tips on Resource Management

If you are a beginner, you need to know that 20-24 is the maximum number of Probes needed to extract Minerals and 3 is the maximum for each Vespene Gas resource.

ALL THE WEALTH IN THE WORLD

Once you have two (or more!) bases running at full speed, your economic power increases substantially.

To make use of this economic power, it is *vital* that you expand your military production. This means two things; more expensive units, and *more* units.

The first can be accomplished simply by teching to higher tier units and building them, but the second requires more production structures (or in the case of the Zerg, more Hatcheries).

Be sure to get more military buildings on the field as your expansions ramp up, and to add more Hatcheries as Zerg (and never stop using Spawn Larvae!).

It is also important that you expand your military production because if you don't, and you *do* start building higher tier units, you can choke off your production.

High tier units are both expensive *and* slow to build, and it's the 'slow to build' part that can cause you serious problems.

WE HAVE NOT ENOUGH MILITARY UNITS

It's hard to give a rule of thumb for exactly how many military buildings you should have at any given stage of the game, but in general, you want at least 2-3 in the early game for Terran or Protoss, and at least two Hatcheries as Zerg (with Queens).

When you approach the midgame, and especially after you expand, you **must** increase that military output, moving up to 4-6 buildings as Terran or Protoss, though Zerg can move to three or more Hatcheries a bit later if Spawn Larvae is used well.

Specific early game builds can radically change your early military development, but it is always the case in the midgame, that if you expand and do not have enough production, and your opponent *does*, you will get overrun.

If your opponent has more military production, assuming roughly equal economies, they will be able to replace their losses, and build to a higher Supply cap more quickly than you.

PRO TIP!
Mouz.White-Ra
OLEKSII KRUPNYK

Protoss vs Terran

Immortals can be transported in a Warp Prism and act as a nasty little distraction at the Terran's base. Disembark the Immortal and start killing their workers and destroying buildings. Don't forget to get away as soon as enemy infantry approaches.

SAVE THE WORKERS

Your workers *are* your economy. When your opponent hits your base or your expansions and goes for your workers, you need to respond.

In almost all situations, the correct course of action is to simply drag select all of your workers, and run them away from the enemy army, towards the closest friendly military force, or defensive structures. If there aren't any friends nearby, then just run them away period! It is always better to lose *time* harvesting than it is to lose *workers* harvesting.

You will take losses when your opponent performs a worker raid, but by responding quickly, you can save the majority of your workers at any base or expansion, which greatly aid your economy in the long run.

Very early in the game, or in especially desperate situations, it is entirely acceptable to use your workers to attack enemy units. When you are facing very small numbers of units, your workers can tie up the enemy troops in melee while your few military units finish them off.

For very small numbers of enemy troops, your workers alone may be able to finish the job! However, always go for running away first, combat second, unless you simply cannot run from your attackers.

Don't forget that Terran SCVs can repair one another, even while under attack, and Zerg Drones can Burrow to hide from attackers without a Detector present.

Remember that workers are helpless against aerial pursuit, so be sure to get up anti-air defenses in the midgame when you know your opponent is building up a substantial air force—you can't have your army on defense for the entire match if you hope to win, and anti-air defenses can buy your workers the time you need to get your troops back in time.

ECONOMY BOOSTERS

Each race has access to a unit, building, or ability that allows you to enhance your harvesting power. Each of the economy boosters also have some additional utility that can be helpful in non-economic situations as well.

For Terran and Zerg, the boosters can be built after building your initial military building (Barracks, or Spawning Pool), for Protoss, their Nexus acts as their booster.

Try to make use of your boosters constantly, but particularly just before you make an assault or get involved in heavy defense. You may not have time mid fight to return to your base, and keeping your economy moving while you're busy is important.

PROTOSS CHRONO BOOST

The Protoss Nexus has the ability to use the Chrono Boost ability. Chrono Boost boosts the production or research speed of a targeted building by 50% for 20 seconds.

Chrono Boost takes 25 Energy to cast, so you are limited in how often you can boost buildings in the early game. Later, once you expand, you will have more Energy to spend on your military buildings, and indeed, once you have two (or more) Nexus, you should *always* be Boosting your Stargates or Robotics Facilities.

In the very early game, you should generally save Chrono Boost to speed out your Probes in groups of two. Each Boost provides just enough of a speed boost to power out two Probes quickly.

Once you hit your first major econ threshold (16 Probes), you should transition to boosting your Gateways while your Warp Gate research is under way, to aid in getting out a sizable army.

Later in the game, you can certainly use Boost on Warp Gates, but the speed benefit provided by Warp Gate alone is sufficient to maintain a good size army, as long as you're diligent about warping in new units every time your Warp Gates refresh.

If you are in a situation where you need more ground units *now*, don't hesitate to mass warp a full group, then Boost all of the Warp Gates to speed their cooldowns.

Also in the mid-game, be sure to boost all researching technologies, and check the buildings periodically to refresh the Boost as it wears off.

When building Probes for a new expansion, you can quickly and easily use Chrono Boost on your Nexus by selecting them all (on a single hotkey!) and casting Chrono Boost directly onto all of your Nexus buildings through the unit selection panel!

CHRONO BOOST

Chrono Boost is a highly flexible ability, and deciding where to use the Nexus energy is a difficult decision, even moreso than the Terran MULE/Scanner Sweep, and much moreso than the Queen Spawn Larvae ability/Creep Tumor tension.

Make a point of experimenting with Chrono Boost in different builds, and deciding what you need to speed up.

Where you use Chrono Boost matters most in the very early game, on your starting build, as you have to decide between Boosting your Probe production, or Boosting your early military output.

In the midgame, after your economy is established, and you have more than one Nexus, it is easier to simply concentrate on constantly Boosting your military structures and ongoing research.

However you decide to utilize Chrono Boost, be sure to *use* it! It is far better to have your Nexus energy zeroed out constantly on a slightly sub-optimal target than to have that energy sitting and doing nothing for you!

ZERG QUEEN

The Zerg Queen is a defensive unit as much as an economic and military caster unit.

The Queen has a weak ground attack and a solid long range anti-air attack. While the Queen is not especially quick moving, it can help to protect your base during the early game.

The Queen has three powers, including the ability to build a Creep Tumor, heal a Biological unit or building, or to Spawn Larvae on a Hatchery.

Early in the game, two Queens provide a very effective anti aerial harassment force, as they can use Transfusion on one another to heal any damage suffered, and easily fight off an early air unit or two.

When fighting off ground forces, use the Queens short ranged melee attack to good effect, by hiding her in your worker line like a good mother!

SPAWN LARVAE

Spawn Larvae is the Queen's economic power, though it can potentially boost either the Zerg military OR economy. Spawn Larvae must target a Hatchery, Lair, or Hive.

Once a building has been hit with Spawn Larvae, it spawns 4 new Larva after 40 seconds. You cannot use Spawn Larvae again on the same building until the Larva have spawned.

It is vitally important that you hotkey all of your Queens and use Spawn Larvae on your Hatcheries each and every time the larva spawn.

Normally a Hatchery only generates 1 new Larva every 15 seconds, so Spawn Larvae provides a very significant production boost. There is a hard cap of 19 for any Hatchery, Hive, or Lair.

A Hatchery that has more than 3 Larva due to Spawn Larvae usage will *not* generate Larva normally, but there is no limit on how many Larva you can create.

Whenever possible, you should be using up ALL Larva at ALL of your Hatcheries, while using Spawn Larvae, to maximize your overall Larva generation rate.

CREEP TUMOR

Creep Tumor lets you create a small burrowed structure anywhere on friendly Creep. Once created, the new tumor begins spreading Creep automatically, just as a Hatchery or Overlord does. Because it is burrowed, your opponent must use a Detector to locate and destroy it.

Creep Tumors have the ability to spawn a single new Creep Tumor, so even one Creep Tumor could potentially cover the entire map with Creep if not dealt with!

You can use Creep Tumors to extend the area that you can build defensive structures, and to provide a larger area for your units to get the Creep movement speed bonus. If you place a Creep Tumor on the Creep generated by an Overlord, you can then move the Overlord away and leave the tumor to maintain the Creep patch.

Because Creep automatically grants line of sight, by the time you reach the midgame, if you have been diligent with spreading Creep Tumors, you can have your bases and the area out in front of your bases completely covered in Creep. This makes it impossible for your opponent to make a frontal assault without you spotting him, *and* your units have a speed bonus, giving you an edge in battle. At the latest, once you have a second Queen and Hatchery up, you should delay a pair of Spawn Larvae to get two Creep Tumors up, and then use those Tumors to continuously spawn new ones, spreading the creep across the map.

TRANSFUSION

The Queen's final ability allows you to give an instant and large heal to a single target, be it a unit or building, as long as it is Biological.

Few units are worth using this expensive ability on, though Brood Lords or Ultralisks are tough enough to make the heal worthwhile.

It can also be used in a pinch to keep a key structure standing, such as your Lair or Hive, or a Spine or Spore Crawler, perhaps just long enough for your army to get in position, or to win an even battle.

Using Transfusion early can also help to fight off aerial attacks, by healing a Queen or Spore Crawler, helpful before you get Hydralisks or a Spire on the field.

> ### AERIAL DEFENSE
>
> *Zerg mobile anti-air is nonexistent until Tier 2, and the Spore Crawler requires an Evolution Chamber to build.*
>
> *Consequently, a pair of Queens can act as decent defense against early aerial Overlord harassment.*
>
> *By using your two Queens in concert, along with Transfusion, you can scare away light raids of air units, before you have access to Hydralisks, Spire units, or have Spore Crawlers created.*

TERRAN ORBITAL COMMAND

The Orbital Command is an upgrade to a Command Center that gives it several new abilities.

CALLDOWN: MULE

The MULE is a special type of SCV that can gather Minerals much more quickly than a standard SCV. You can target the MULE anywhere that you have line of sight. It is possible to use a MULE as a free mobile scout if you wish, though you do give up the economic benefit if you do so.

You can target a MULE directly onto a Mineral Field and it will automatically begin harvesting and return to the nearest Command Center. If you happen to miss the Minerals, or if you call it down to scout briefly, you can always order it to harvest directly at any time.

SCOUTING

It is almost impossible for us to overstate how important scouting is in StarCraft II. In any match between roughly even players, the person who scouts more will have a *tremendous* advantage.

Scouting lets you see what your opponent is building so that you can build an appropriate counter. Scouting warns you of early rushes, or early expansions. Scouting keeps eyes on your opponent's army, and lets you know when and where it is moving.

Scouting *wins games*.

Scouting is one of the single most important skills that you must develop to play StarCraft II effectively. There's a reason we're dedicating an entire section of this book to scouting, it is that important.

Because certain units are hard counters to others, and some are quite strong against others, knowing what your opponent is building, and what they *will* be building is extremely important.

It is also extremely important that you stay on top of your opponent's army movement, so that you know where it is, and if it is moving, where it is headed.

The only way to gain this knowledge is to scout constantly. Using your basic worker unit is a great early game scouting technique. Zerg can make use of single Zerglings for the same purpose, as they are even cheaper than a single worker.

Each race also has access to many units and abilities that allow you to keep tabs on your opponent, and the Xel'Naga Towers on each map are also crucial for keeping line of sight to a large portion of the map.

MULES cannot harvest Vespene Gas (though they can Repair in a pinch! Use an MULE drop and Repair to fix up a damaged unit in the field or a key structure!).

MULEs harvest at an amazing 270 Minerals per minute (more on a High Yield!), compared with 60 per minute for a normal worker.

SCANNER SWEEP
Using the Scanner Sweep allows you to temporarily gain line of sight to any area on the map, as well as reveal any cloaked units within the affected area for the duration of the scan.

The Scanner Sweep is a very powerful advantage for the Terran player, as it allows you to have near perfect reconnaissance of an enemy base throughout the course of the game.

Because you can wall-in so easily as a Terran, this allows you to choose your tech path in response to your opponent's build, or to exploit a weakness that you see in their defenses.

If your opponent is using cloaked units, you can use the scan to temporarily reveal them, but it is not a permanent solution if your opponent is heavily relying on cloaked units—be sure to complement your sweeps by building Missile Turrets and Ravens.

WATCH YOUR ENERGY
Be careful with Scanner Sweep usage early in the game.

Getting as many MULEs on the field as possible is important for your early economic development, and every scan you use costs you a lot of potential Mineral income!

Once you have a second Orbital Command up and running, you can be more free with your scans, but that may not be until well into the midgame, as building a Planetary Fortress at an expansion is a common move, meaning you'll be relying on the lone Orbital Command at your main for some time.

CALLDOWN: EXTRA SUPPLIES
Extra Supplies allows you to boost the Supply generated by a Supply Depot by 8. Generally, you should be saving the Energy to use on MULEs and Scanner Sweeps, but if you accidentally cap your Supply, or if an enemy drops you under your Supply cap, you can use this ability to temporarily fix the problem.

Continuously scout your opponent throughout the course of the game, and make periodic sweeps of all expansion sites. Keeping an eye on their base is important, as it allows you to see what tech they are pursuing, how large their army is, and if their army is absent or moving.

Scouting is especially vital to spot when your opponent is going for air or cloaking units. It might just save you from a quick loss if you build a counter quickly enough.

XEL'NAGA WATCHTOWERS
Scattered around most maps, these ancient Xel'Naga artifacts can be located and secured.

When ANY friendly ground unit is standing near a tower, you gain a large spherical line of sight in the area.

This free line of sight bonus is extremely useful, and on any map with towers, you should *always* send a few cheap units out to secure the towers.

When you are about to make an offensive push, consider sending a small raiding force to clear all towers of hostile enemy presence, or at the very least, clear any towers you know you must pass with your army and replace the sentries.

SCOUTING TECHNIQUES

The most basic scouting is simply using your workers as scouts. They cost 50 Minerals, only use one Supply, and can build a forward building if needed.

For the Terran, single Marines work as well, and for the Zerg, single Zerglings are ideal, as they cost 25 Minerals, less Supply, and can burrow!

Your first scout should usually head out just after your first Supply producer finishes, usually around 9 or 10 Supply. Getting that quick scout out is important on larger maps to locate your opponent's base, and still important on 1v1 maps to spot an early rush or expansion.

SCOUT HARASSMENT

Place your first worker scout on your opponent's natural expansion. If they are going for a quick expand, they'll have to chase off your worker, which can result in wasted time before the expansion goes up.

You can also perform annoying harassment on SCVs building early structures with your scouting worker, forcing your opponent to pull a worker off to deal with you.

Just don't get so involved with scout antics that you mess up your own build order.

Beyond the early game, you want to get a unit at each Xel'Naga tower on the map, *and* one or more units near your opponent's base and in the midfield between your base.

Consider that for the investment of 150-200 Minerals, 3-4 Supply, and a few seconds of micro, you can have immediate early warning of any incoming military force. Not much of a price is it?

TERRAN INTEL

Terran have strong, solid recon ability, and their knowledge of the opponent's build with Scanner Sweep should be fully abused.

Because Terran have excellent defensive power, making full use of their recon to scout your opponent while keeping your own build hidden can cause serious problems for your enemy if they are Protoss or Zerg!

ORBITAL COMMAND SCANNER SWEEP

Terran have perhaps the single strongest recon ability in the game, the Scanner Sweep. This ability allows you to instantly scan any area on the map, granting temporary line of sight in the area.

This ability has military applications as well, allowing your ranged units to fire on units atop cliffs, and it can temporarily reveal cloaked or burrowed units in an area, giving you a quick answer to cloak or burrow tech from your opponent.

However, its main strength is the ability to instantly scout your opponent's base throughout the match.

While expending too much Energy early in the game can harm your economic development by taking away from MULE production, carefully timed scans in concert with normal scouting can give you perfect knowledge of your opponent's build.

Canny players will attempt to avoid your scans by hiding tech buildings at the edges of their base, so try to scan various areas of the base each time you sweep—don't just drop it on top of their core structure each time!

Make use of the knowledge gained by using Scanner Sweep to respond to any tech that your opponent is developing. If he's going for cloaking units, get Ravens, Missile Turrets, Ghosts, or another Orbital Command! If he's going air, be sure you have your own air units ready, or a good supply of Missile Turrets, Marines and Thors to deal with them.

SENSOR TOWERS

Another unique defensive benefit of the Terran is the Sensor Tower. Once created, it projects a large radius of sensor coverage, instantly warning you of any hostile units that enter its perimeter with flashing red indicators on both the main screen and the minimap.

Sensor Towers can provide early warning of any attack on your base from non cloaked units, giving you time to prepare yourself for the assault.

There are a few caveats to the power of the Sensor Tower. The first is that your opponent can see the Sensor radius! Any time you place a Sensor Tower, they know you have one up, and they know exactly where it is.

This normally isn't a bad thing, but be careful about putting up Sensor Towers at expansions, you don't want to alert them to your expansion until they find it on their own!

Another point to be careful about—a smart opponent will bait you by placing units inside the Sensor range, then hitting you with a second force from a different direction. Don't become blind to other threats just because you can see some hostile units in range of the tower!

You can pull tricks with Sensor Towers as well however—build one up at an expansion site and wait with your army nearby, if they move to hit it, attack!

REAPERS

Reapers are solid, cheap scout units, as they can Cliffwalk, allowing them to hop onto otherwise inaccessible terrain and provide recon.

While later in the game, air units can do the same, Reapers are cheap, and easily accessible early in the game. Placing a *few* Reapers on key ledges can be a useful tactic, just don't go overboard, or you're wasting Supply.

RACIAL SCOUTING

Every race has access to a variety of useful scouting units, abilities, and technologies. Knowing how to use all of the tools at your disposal to gain an intelligence advantage over your opponent is critically important.

AERIAL SCOUTS

For all races, air units make the best 'normal' scouting unit. For this reason, we're concentrating on non-aerial units in this section.

Once you reach air tech and the midgame, you can utilize air units for fast scouting of expansions and enemy movements quite easily.

Placing a few air units on patrol is also a good idea, as they can cover a wide swath of terrain easily, just don't use your first crucial air units for this duty, they need to be in combat!

The Reaper speed upgrade makes them an even better recon unit, but don't waste the resources on the upgrade for scouting unless you're planning on maintaining a Reaper harass force in the midgame.

HELLIONS

In addition to being great worker raiders, Hellions are excellent mobile scout units. If you want to quickly scout all expansions on a map, using Hellions to do so is your fastest option before you get air units.

Hellions also make good patrollers—place one or two on patrol routes out in front of your bases, and you'll have a very good chance of spotting any incoming forces (as well as quickly killing scouting workers).

PROTOSS INTEL

Of the three races, Protoss are unfortunately cursed with the least impressive overall reconnaissance ability.

Protoss have no global specials like the Scanner Sweep, and no general recon benefits like Zerg Creep, Overlords, or burrowed Zerglings.

In exchange however, Protoss do get a very strong mid and late game scout in the form of the Observer, and the fastest air unit in the Phoenix, giving them excellent aerial recon.

Because Protoss lack easy early game methods of scouting your opponent, be sure to make use of Probe scouts. It is important that you maintain a line of sight web by having Probes out on the field and at Xel'Naga towers until your midgame scouting comes into play.

STALKER BLINK

Stalkers on their own are reasonably speedy units that make decent scouts, but once they acquire Blink, they become excellent units for recon.

Even if you lack an air unit to grant line of sight to an enemy base on a ledge, you can always make a frontal feint attack and then use Blink to get past the defenders. Losing the Stalker isn't important here (and you may not anyway, depending on how fast your opponent is), you just need to get a unit inside the enemy base and see what they are building.

Blink can also be used in concert with air units to place Stalkers up on ridges that normal ground units can't reach, though because they are a ranged unit, your opponent will know they are there when they pass them!

SENTRY HALLUCINATE

The illusory units created by Hallucination function exactly like their normal counterparts, which means that if you create an illusionary Phoenix, it scouts just as well as the real thing!

Illusionary units deal no damage, but they do provide line of sight, so you can use a fake Phoenix to check your opponent's build, and to provide line of sight up ledges, great for attacking your opponent's main up a ramp, or for blinking Stalkers onto otherwise inaccessible ledges.

Hallucinated units don't have the duration to act as permanent aerial patrolling scouts, so instead, use them for base recon and forward recon when attacking with your army.

OBSERVER

The Observer is a slow to build and Gas costly unit, but it is an amazing scout—the Observer is a flyer that is *permanently* cloaked *and* it is a Detector.

PROTOSS

Consequently, in the mid to late game, you can potentially have the entire map covered in Observers, and even a diligent opponent who scouts out your Observers and actively attempts to eliminate them will still probably miss a few (not to mention the time and effort it takes to hunt them down).

Building at least a few Observers in the midgame is always a good idea, because Protoss have no other form of mobile cloak detection, so they are vital against Zerg to fight Burrow, and still important against Terran or Protoss to deal with Ghosts, Banshees, and Dark Templars.

Don't feel that you always have to build Observers in every match early, you can get by with Photon Cannons on defense, but do make a point of picking up at least a single Robotics Facility in the midgame.

DARK TEMPLAR

While hardly a traditional scouting unit, Dark Templars permanent cloaking certainly gives them an edge in the recon department.

Be careful to place stationary Dark Templar scouts on Hold Position, so that they don't run off and attack the first hostile unit they spot. If an army passes directly over them, they'll still take a swipe, so be sure to place them slightly off to the side if you're watching a commonly travelled path.

You can also use Dark Templar to scout enemy bases or expansions, just be wary of enemy Detectors. But in spite of the risks, the resource cost for a single Dark Templar is hardly excessive, so if you're planning on building Dark Templar anyway, use them to the fullest, in combat and in scouting!

ZERG INTEL

ZERG

Zerg have several fantastic recon advantages over the other races—their Overlords can fly, ALL of their ground have access to Burrow, and Creep Tumors provide free line of sight (and movement speed bonuses!) as the Creep spreads across the map.

Remember that burrowed units have about half the line of sight of a unit above-ground (though Infestors keep their full line of sight while burrowed).

Once you gain access to Burrow, place a single burrowed Zergling at every expansion site, and scatter a few across the map at key chokepoints between your bases.

Be careful with Overlords—once you have the Overlord speed upgrade, they are somewhat more mobile, but don't use your core Supply producing Overlords as military scouts, you can get into serious trouble if several die rapidly, forcibly capping your Supply.

BASE SCOUTING

Each race has a different ability to defend their own base from recon, and to scout your opponent's base.

As with general scouting, all races can scout the enemy base with air units once they have access to them, but until you have air units, you have to use your other options.

TERRAN

With Scanner Sweep, you can *always* scout your opponent's base and see what he is teching for. Be careful not to overuse this early over your MULE production, but as you approach the mid game, make use of scans to see what tech route your opponent is taking.

On defense, with your ability to wall in freely, you can often keep enemy ground units completely out of your base, preventing your opponent from scouting you without another way in.

QUEEN CREEP TUMOR AND CREEP
The Queen can spawn a Creep Tumor for 25 Energy, creating a burrowed structure that then automatically spreads Creep.

Creep Tumors can only be placed on existing Creep, but the Creep generated by an Overlord works just as well as the creep created by any building!

Each Creep Tumor can spawn one new Creep Tumor, so this allows you to constantly expand the 'borders' of your Creep, out from your base into the midfield.

Because Creep provides both line of sight and a speed boost to Zerg ground units, getting several Creep Tumors up and running just past the early game is always a good idea.

Creep Tumors are vulnerable to an enemy who brings a detector along with them on a military push, but they are cheap to rebuild in the midgame, and when they've provided you with early warning of the attack and faster movement to respond to it, consider it a fair trade!

OVERLORD AND OVERSEER
The basic Overlord is a solid scouting unit due to its aerial nature, but you need to be careful not to lose your Overlords to aggressive scouting.

Overseers, on the other hand, are instantly available once you have upgraded to a Lair, and act as Detectors, in addition to having faster movement speed than Overlords, *and* the ability to spawn Changelings for even more recon.

Overseers should accompany your mobile military force if you know or suspect your opponent is making use of cloaking units, and always against Zerg to kill burrowed units.

Be sure to research the Overlord speed upgrade as quickly as possible, it is very cheap, and the movement speed increase for both Overlords and Overseers is very important, both for scouting, and for the safety of your Supply!

CHANGELING
The Overseer can create Changelings for the cost of 50 Energy. These mutable creatures transform into a Marine, Zealot, or Zergling automatically whenever they come into range of a hostile unit.

With this new decoy unit, you can then move into your opponent's base to scout, or move along near his army to keep tabs on his movement.

Changelings are vulnerable to detectors, and observant opponents *will* spot your changelings and destroy them—but don't worry about that, Changelings are essentially free recon. Use them as such!

BURROW
Burrow allows ALL Zerg ground units to function as hidden scouts. While any unit can do this, Zerglings are especially well suited because of their extremely low cost and good movement speed.

By choking off your base entrance with buildings and units on Hold Position, you can protect the interior of your base from ground scouts almost as easily as Terran.

For enemy base scouting, Protoss lack any early non-ground means of doing so. Keep tabs on your opponent's army with your early offensive pushes and your scouting Probes.

Thankfully, no matter which tech tree you choose to pursue for the midgame, you gain access to base scouting—Hallucinate for Sentries, Stargate gives air units, Robotics Facility gives Observers, and Twilight Council gives you access to Blink.

Zerg have no means at all of walling off their base in the early game and it is somewhat expensive and messy to do in the midgame, though possible.

Consequently, you have to rely on your military force to repel any adventurous scouts early in the game. The movement speed boost you gain on creep can help, but be sure to place key tech buildings like the Spire as far from the front of your base as possible, to try to hide their presence as long as possible.

For enemy base scouting, Overlords provide early and immediate access to any enemy base, just accept that a dedicated scouting Overlord is probably going to get shot down, and choose when to send it for the most information gain.

Once you reach Lair tech, you gain Overlord speed, and you have access to Overseers and Changelings, both of which are useful for base recon, and can be used no matter what unit path you are pursuing.

Ground Weapons Upgrades

PRO TIP!
Garimtoi
KIM DONGSU

You can construct Forges, upgrade one step of ground weapons, then attack during the time window that you have an upgrade advantage. In order to supplement the late ground forces and timing due to Forges, you should produce Phoenix frequently from Stargates. An early unexpected attack could break you. A good combination of units to support this build is Immortal, Zealot/Stalker or Zealot/Immortal units. Through scouting with your Phoenix, you can figure out your opponent's build order and make your own strike force the perfect counter.

CONTINUOUS SCOUTING

Scouting tends to be one of the most difficult areas of the game for new players to focus on, partly because processing the information can be difficult, and partly because it feels like it draws away valuable attention from your base development or military management.

While this is true, the value of the information gained is so crucial that we believe incorporating early recon and constant scouting into your builds is just as vital as your initial economic and military buildup.

Managing your scouts is lower priority than microing your military (AL-WAYS prioritize your military), but any time you have a lull in the fighting, do a quick scout check, replace any Xel'Naga sentries you lost, and get a new scout in front of your opponent's base, possibly scanning for new expansions as well.

It is easy to forget about scouting in the mid and late game, even if you did remember to do the initial base scout, but don't do that! Keep up your recon all throughout the game.

By the late game, each race should have a strong network of intelligence, and you should *always* know where your opponent has expansions, and where his main military force is.

You can't always keep track of enemy aerial units perfectly, or small raiding forces, but you should never lose sight of your opponent's main army, and you should absolutely never allow your opponent to have a 'free' expansion that you never scout or threaten!

BASE DEFENSE

We've touched on this topic before, but as it relates to scouting, having full line of sight in and around your base is very important for responding quickly to worker raids.

All races have access to various units and abilities that are ideal for hitting worker lines, and all good players *will* hit your worker lines, sooner or later.

You can't stop these raids, but what you can do is minimize the damage that they deal, and one of the ways you go about doing that is by having full line of sight in your base.

Make sure that you use your Supply producers to spread line of sight around your base. Just doing this simple step alone can save your workers from getting hit by an aerial assault or cliffwalker attack, as you can spot the incoming forces in time to retreat your workers while your military comes back to help.

It's better to lose a core structure and rebuild it than it is to lose your entire worker line *and* your core structure!

Beyond getting line of sight on the full extent of your bases, it is also important to have scouts on the outskirts of your base. We've already touched on the importance of covering the Xel'Naga towers and the corridor of space between your bases and your opponent's bases, but it is also worthwhile to maintain a few patrolling units on the outskirts of your bases.

Later in the game, when you can afford to spare them, one or two air units on patrol on the obvious 'backdoor' air approaches to your expansions can also help to protect against worker raids in the mid and late game.

Another point about having full base line of sight—in any base that is on an elevated ledge, your ranged units can make use of the line of sight to attack incoming troops as they try to move to the entrance to your base. On some maps, this can provide you with a very useful damage advantage in the coming battle.

SCOUT! SCOUT! SCOUT!

We really can't say enough about scouting. Perhaps because scouting isn't as obviously 'part of the game' in the same way that building your base or fighting with your military are, many players tend to neglect scouting.

Don't make that mistake—consider scouting to be every bit as important as your economic buildup, your military buildup, and your fighting. Not only that, scouting is *easier* than any of those skills!

Try to grow your scouting skills alongside every other aspect of your play. We promise it will pay a generous return on your investment!

In a match where you really nail your recon on top of your build order and combat, and your opponent does *not* scout, it can almost feel like cheating.

- You always know what your opponent is teching for, so you always build the right counters.

- You know if your opponent is rushing or quick expanding, so you know to defend or to attack early.

- You know what army makeup you are facing, so you know makeup to use in response.

- You know where your opponent's army is, so you're never surprised, and you can ambush it at any time.

- You know when and where your opponent is expanding, so you know where to attack.

- You spot a weak army and attack with a superior force.

- You spot incoming raids coming before they hit your worker line, so you get away with minimal losses.

PRO TIP!
Live Hydralisk
KIBONG KOOK

Tips for Smart Gaming

Practice to produce and attack at the same time: Many players only produce units when they need to produce and only attack when it is time to attack. In particular when they attack, they get lost in the beautiful game that is StarCraft II. StarCraft II is not a movie.

You should defend and produce as many units as possible during your attack so that you can counterattack after defending. If you produce units at the same time you are attacking, you can suppress opponents properly.

Collect Minerals & Gas and spend them: If you are losing the game, look at your hands. What are they doing? Keep yourself busy collecting resources and using them to produce units in the best way possible.

Protoss can also have advantages if you minimize the entrance by structures: Usually Terran players block entrance by buildings and open or close the entrance so that they can minimize the damage from small units in early game, such as a Zealot Stalker rush and Zerg Zergling.

As a Protoss player you can minimize your entrance with Pylons and Gateways. You can create one Zealot or Sentry against enemy rushes in early game. If it is not possible to build a unit at the moment, you can build an additional Pylon to block the entrance completely to buy extra time.

When you are attacking and feel uncomfortable just leaving your base empty, which can be a target for Zergling/Baneling, a good way to seal the entrance is to place a Pylon . If you upgrade to a Warp Gate, allowing you to summon to the Pylon, you can produce as many units as you want.

OFFENSIVE STRATEGY

Finally, we come to the fighting.

It might seem strange to have the discussion of combat tactics and strategy last, but while combat is a obviously an important part of the game, your base development, economy and military buildup, and scouting are all pillars that prop up your military.

- Without a strong economy, you cannot produce enough military to fight.
- Without a strong infrastructure, you cannot replace losses fast enough to recover from a defeat.
- Without strong technology, you cannot defeat your opponent's technology.
- Without strong scouting, you will not know when or where to attack or defend.

Now, with that said, we'll begin with the first and most important rule for battles in StarCraft II.

NEVER TAKE YOUR EYES OFF THE FIGHT

We've said this before, and we'll say it again—once the combat starts, all of your attention must be on the fight.

All of the preparation that goes into creating your military is wasted if you throw away your military force because you were too busy putting up another building, creating another worker, or scouting the map.

The instant you hear a combat alert, immediately hit the Spacebar, double tap your army hotkey, click the minimap, or click on the alert.

From that point on, your attention must be fully focused on the battle until you win or lose, and depending on how decisively you won or lost, whether you should push or retreat.

PRO TIP!
Mouz.White-Ra
OLEKSII KRUPNYK

Protoss vs Zerg

When your Zealots gain +1 to attack, they become a lot more effective against Zerglings. Killing one now takes two strikes instead of three.

WHY GO ON OFFENSE?

With few exceptions, it is always preferable to be on the offensive than the defensive. Keeping pressure on your opponent keeps him occupied, and can prevent him from expanding or attacking you. Fully containing your opponent can allow you to expand with impunity.

Playing offensively also has the benefit of built in scouting. Because you have units with eyes on the enemies troops (and often base), you can usually make use of the information while your opponent is busy fending you off to tech towards a weakness in his forces, or to build a defense for a tech he is pushing towards.

Against a roughly even opponent, it is rare that any single early skirmish is going to win the match for you, but even if you suffer slightly greater losses and your opponent counter attacks, you still have time to rebuild your forces and make use of choke points and wall ins to defend yourself.

In the mid and late game, all-in offensive pushes are more risky, as unit production often reaches a point where if you suffer heavy losses in comparison to your opponent, their counter-push will have more units than you can defend against, even with defensive advantages.

Learning when to make a mid or late game attack is part experience, and part scouting. In some cases, you simply have to make an educated guess about the comparative strength of your armies and go for the kill.

If your opponent has an obvious weakness to your army (little or no anti air, little or no detection, poorly placed base defenses, an undefended choke point), press the attack.

Similarly, if you've discovered that your opponent's micro is generally inferior to yours in a straight fight, or your casters are inflicting disproportionate casualties, use that edge to push when your forces are roughly numerically equal.

COMBAT TIPS

You can use flying units to grant line of sight to higher ground—this is particularly useful when you have ranged units on a lower level, and an opponent is defending a narrow ramp chokepoint with units from above.

Cloaked or aerial units are ideal for gaining line of sight to high ground, though some special abilities can also be used for temporary reconnaissance on high ground.

Focus firing with air units or longer ranged units is more effective than with melee units or short ranged units.

WHEN TO ATTACK

Immediately!

Most newer players tend to hesitate to attack, fearing to leave their base undefended while the army is away, but this is (in most cases) an unfounded fear.

RUSH RUSH

Just how fast should you attack? On any smaller map, where the distance between your bases is low, try building your first military building early, and sending your very first military unit straight to your opponent's worker line.

Seem crazy? You'd be surprised how often you can get several worker kills for free at the start of a match against an opponent who did not build their military immediately.

You don't even need to cripple your economy or go for a pure rush build to do this either. Just hit them immediately. If you see they've walled off or do have troops already, no problem, back off (free scouting!).

With good scouting, you will have early warning of any significant ground assault from your opponent, and with few exceptions, there are very few early raiding units (and no aerial units) that can inflict critical damage to your base or workers early in the game.

Additionally, early raiding units means that your opponent has less main troops at home, and they have to make a decision about which force to micro (and if they ignore their main army in favor of raiding, you're going to wipe out their army fast and have time to return and deal with the raiders).

In the mid and late game, there are more dangerous raiding troops present, but by that point, you should have expansions up, and more options of your own for defense while your army is away.

When you have a sizable offensive force, make a push. As long as you don't over commit yourself, you really have nothing to lose. You may suffer some losses, but your opponent will as well, and psychologically, you can put them on the back foot by being the aggressor.

This may cause your opponent to hesitate to attack or expand, or possibly to waste time and resources on building unnecessary base defenses.

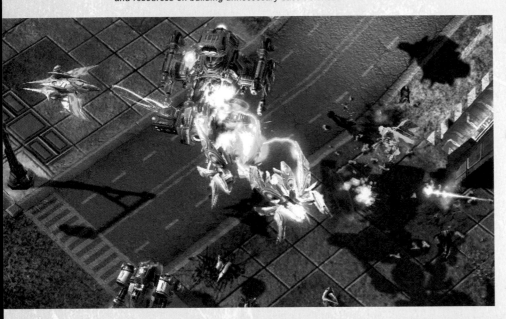

MY ARMY IS TOO SMALL!

Another common reason for hesitation to attack among newer players is the feeling that their army is somehow 'too small'.

*Remember, as long as you've been following all of the economic and infrastructure advice we've given, you will **not** be at an economic disadvantage.*

As a result, the army that you can build will be just as large (or larger) than your opponent's, unless they are choosing to produce troops at the expense of their economy or technology (and if you're scouting well, you'll know that too!).

It is generally a good time to attack just after a new unit or technology hits the field. Push with Ghosts against Protoss, with Colossus against Terran or Zerg, with Roaches after Burrow finishes, and so on.

You don't even have to wait for a higher tech unit either, mass up basic troops and push! Hit your opponent with Marines and Marauders just as Stimpacks or Stimpacks and Level 1 Weapons research finishes. Push with Zealots or Zealots and Stalkers with a lone Sentry just as Ground Weapons Level 1 finishes. Push with Zerglings and Roaches when Zergling speed arrives. Opponent walled in? Hit when Banelings are ready.

Scouting in advance of an attack is always a good idea, but you should already have a scout network in place across the map before your first attack (even if it's just a few workers!), so you aren't surprised by the enemy army half way across the map (or worse, hitting your base while you hit his).

Always aggressively push with your army if you are reasonably certain you can escape with no or minimal losses.

PRO TIP!

Garimtoi
KIM DONGSU

3 Gateways, 1 Robo, Zealot, Sentry, Immortal combination

This build is the simplest and most straightforward strategy for Protoss to beat Zerg. This strategy is focused on Immortals which are particularly powerful against Roaches—taking advantage of Sentry's Force Field and Guardian Shield. The biggest disadvantage of this build is that it is very vulnerable to an air force counter like Mutalisks. You need to be aggressive early when you have 2 Zealots and 4 Sentries. This early attack should induce a Zerg player to produce Burrowed Roaches or Zerglings, thereby reducing the production of Mutalisks. Immortals are the key unit in the build but this means that if Immortals are removed, then the build is useless. Another disadvantage is that it is vulnerable to Zerg if the match turns into a production race as Protoss has slow production times.

TYPES OF ATTACKS

Attacking through multiple vectors (ground, air, cloak), can also force a response from your opponent. If they don't have an answer to your air or cloak attack, you may well win the game right there. If not, it is still likely that you will inflict enough damage to pay for the cost of teching to that particular air or cloaking unit.

Air units are particularly notable as an offensive force, as they *must* be dealt with. Once air to ground forces reach a point of critical mass, they can begin to take on even dedicated anti-air ground units, and once that happens, static base defenses can crumble, and anti-air can be picked off due to the superior mobility of the aerial units.

Caster units are another valuable tech to attain, because as a general rule, casters are at their most dangerous when accompanying your army in small numbers—even 2-3 caster units, used well, can act as a force multiplier, greatly increasing the danger of your army.

Just be careful not to go straight for casters if you can't deal with an opposing air or cloak tech!

It is important that you use the intelligence gained from scouting to determine if it is safe to push in the mid and late game. You need to know what types of units your opponent is using, as it can affect the safety of a push.

As an example, an army of slow units against your opponent's army of faster units (or worse, faster ranged units) is not a safe push.

If your opponent is fielding Speedlings, Hellions, Zealots with Charge or Stalkers with Blink in the early engagements, be careful about over committing on offense with slower units, as you can easily lose the bulk of your army trying to retreat if the fight does not go in your favor.

Another dangerous situation is pushing when you know your opponent has a reasonably well defended base, and a sizable air force. Either air to ground aerial units, or drop ships of some sort. Make sure you have enough anti-air defenses and troops at your base to fend off the attack, or you may suffer serious damage at your main base while your army is out in the field.

PRO TIP!
Mouz.White-Ra
OLEKSII KRUPNYK

Controlling single units or small groups

Managing small groups is easiest because it takes less control than when you wage a full-scale battle. You can see your attack objective priorities and focus on them quickly. In a large battle it can be difficult to select units from the whole crowd that you want to target and kill first. So, try to use all your units' magical abilities first, and then focus on destroying select targets.

CONTAINMENT

Containment is simply the act of locking your opponent in their base and preventing them from expanding. If you can contain your opponent (even if you can't quite break through his army and defenses), you are free to expand.

Once your expansions are up and running, no matter his level of defenses, you will vastly outnumber and outproduce your opponent, and even with perfectly managed defenses, your opponent will run out of resources and eventually be unable to replace losses.

Containment can be as simple as parking your army outside his base at his natural expansion, or as elaborate as forward-building turrets and military structures.

Generally, those resources are better spent on expansion, teching, and unit production at home, but there's nothing stopping you from spending some resources on strengthening a contain if you do get extra expansions running—you have the income, use it!

CONTAINMENT ESCAPE

Be wary of containing Terran players on a map with island expansions. Terrans can construct a Command Center and simply fly it out of their base, expanding safely even while contained.

Similarly, Zerg can use a Nydus Canal and an Overlord to expand out of their base without needing to use the front door.

Protoss lack those easy options, but they can build Warp Prisms from a Robotics Facility and simply transport Probes to another base.

Remember, keep scouting the interior of their base and expansion sites on the map, you need to know what they are using to break out, or if they have broken out, to where!

Be wary of escape attempts by your opponent when they are contained—you can almost always expect that your opponent will quickly tech to whatever unit or ability they think will work to get them out of their base, and this can often be air units, so watch for hits at your main base.

Scouting the interior of their base while they are contained is even more important than it normally is, because you need to see what tech they are choosing to respond with. If you're aware of their answer before they can deploy it in force, you likely have the game already won.

One last point—don't be afraid to back off on a contain if you can't maintain it. If you see that your opponent has built a good counter to your containing force, retreat before you suffer serious losses, while you build a counter of your own.

The time that you gained to freely expand once or twice will pay off with faster economic growth, which you can then use to hit your opponent again, even if they managed to make you back off and get an expansion of their own.

  PRO TIP!
Garimtoi
KIM DONGSU

The Race in Absolute and Relative Numbers

In case of the battle of Zerg vs. Terran, it is a "selected centralized" battle. There are best counter units for every unit in Zerg vs. Terran: Zerglings/Banelings are the best counter unit against Terran Biological; Roach/Infestor are the best counter unit to the Terran Mechanical; Hydralisks are the best counter unit against Banshees. In short, victory in a Zerg vs. Terran match depends on how well you understand your enemy's strategy, and how well you can play the best counter units against your enemy units.

The key to unlocking many strategies is the Mutalisk. Zerg Mutalisks acts as the deciding factor in a battle of counters.

In the battle of Protoss vs. Zerg, the balance tips in the Zerg's favor with the combination of Spine Crawler/Mutalisk. This is not because the Protoss player cannot block the combination of Spine Crawler and Mutalisk, but because Protoss has no way of following Zerg's mobility and maneuverability with this combination. The Protoss player cannot block all of the Zerg's expansions while still defending against Mutalisks.

Basically, Spine Crawler/Mutalisks are a must have. It may be tough to survive until Mutalisks can support from the air, but, if you do, the Zerg will begin to win the fight. Build about 12 free Drones; don't remove any from Minerals or Gas, then check your enemy's strategic build with an Overlord or Overseer. With those numbers, you can be easily Morph from Larvae anything you need.

One of the most popular builds for Terran is Mechanical. It is easy to operate and there are not many Zerg units you can build to counter a Mechanical order. In Terran Mechanical, the Hellion is the key unit. The best way of preventing the Hellion's attack is to block the route of Hellion's movement with Spine Crawlers. Once you can minimize the damage from Hellions, you can dominate the match by using the superior numbers advantage of the Zerg. Of course, Mutalisks are not highly effective as a counter unit against Terran Mechanical, but the reason why they are so important is because they are the only unit that doesn't allow the player to use the natural Terran build order. It really doesn't matter if Mutalisks cause any damage or not. Their presence changes the game.

DEALING WITH DEFENSES

Always remember that static defenses are fairly easy to bypass with your army. If you feel that you have the numeric advantage on the ground, even if your opponent has some defenses built, push into their base and take some damage to bypass the fixed defenses.

While Zerg can pick up and move Spine Crawlers, neither Protoss nor Terran have this luxury, and even Spine Crawlers are fairly slow to be moved, slower than you can move your ground army around to hit a Drone line or a specific tech building.

If your opponent is *really* walling off their base with a great number of fixed defenses, simply contain him and expand. But when you must break through an enemy defensive wall, each race has several units and abilities that are particularly useful for destroying, disabling, or bypassing enemy defenses.

Note that air units are always useful for bypassing fixed ground defenses, but enemies will usually build anti-air fixed defenses in greater numbers at their frontal chokepoint, and at their worker lines. You need a significant critical mass of air units to destroy these defenses fast enough to avoid retaliation by the nearby enemy army.

Cloaked units are generally *not* great units to use for bypassing defenses, as fixed defenses all give Detection, so if your opponent is walled off, save the cloaked units for containment and general combat in the field or on defense. If your opponent isn't diligent about placing them however, you can bypass them, or possibly hit a more lightly defended expansion by first destroying the detectors, then using your cloaked units to raid the expansion.

Cliffwalkers, of course, are quite useful for bypassing fixed defenses and raiding, and both the Reaper and Colossus pull double duty because the Reaper deals bonus damage to structures, and the Colossus can get a range upgrade to outrange fixed defenses.

Reapers are unfortunately too fragile to use as direct defense breakers, but if you are making a push with your army, having a few Reapers mixed in can certainly help.

DESTROYING DEFENSE

Terran	Protoss	Zerg
Siege Tank	Immortal	Baneling
Ghost Nuke	Colossus with range upgrade	Brood Lord
Battlecruiser	Carrier	Ultralisk

BYPASSING DEFENSE

Terran	Protoss	Zerg
Reaper	Stalker Blink	Roach Burrow
Ghost Cloak	Colossus	Infestor Burrow
N/A	Dark Templar	Nydus Canal

PRO TIP!
Garimtoi
KIM DONGSU

The Race in Absolute and Relative Numbers Cont.

If you didn't take any damage from Hellions in the early game and you produced Mutalisks, then it is better to explore the enemy base now. If they stick with the Mechanical strategy you can fight them with Roach/Infestor. Roaches movement while Burrowed allow them to move closer and closer to the enemy, perhaps even forcing them to panic. After dominating the game by consistently expanding and with the Roach/Infestor unit combination, you can turn to Brood Lords or Ultralisks for the win.

If the enemy starts Mechanical then switches to Biological, you only have to convert your production to Zergling/Baneling. When you play against a Terran Biological build order, it is recommended that you have at least 30 Banelings. It is always good to have more Banelings. They are a disposable unit. Roaches, even when half-dead, are a great menace.

Queens should always generate Creep Tumors between the main base and the natural expansion.

PRO TIP!
Live Hydralisk
KIBONG KOOK

Unit Combination and Strategy

If you only produce Zealots thinking they are powerful, you can lose if your enemy produces the correct unit combination. You need to produce a lot of units while keeping in mind the best counters.

The combinations of Zealot/Sentry, Zealot/Sentry/Stalker, and Stalker/Sentry are powerful groups that can thwart a variety of enemies.

Zealot/Sentry: In this build, Zealots attack from the front and Sentries defend at the rear. This is a good combination to use when you fight in early game. With this combination you can produce more units effectively, particularly in regards to resources. When you use Sentry you should use Force Fields to divide and conquer.

Force Fields are a good way of preventing retreating enemies from escaping. It is very likely that a match victory might depend on how to use Sentry Force Fields in an early battle.

An appropriate counter combination for Zealot/Sentry is Marine/Marauder combination, or Zergling/Baneling.

Depending on the situations, you can produce a large number of fictitious units using Sentry Hallucination ability and make them take a role in reducing damage and embarrassing enemies.

Zealot/Immortal/Sentry Combination: In this strategy, Zealots block and attack from the front, while Immortals attack from the back and a Sentry uses Guardian Shield and Force Field from the side. This is a pretty good counter combination for almost any ground unit heavy army.

An appropriate counter can be a large army of Zerg Roaches or a Terran Marauder/Tank combination. When your enemy uses many small units, however, this combination can still work if you can micro manage the combat.

Colossus/Stalker/Sentry/Zealot: This is the strongest and most common combination for Protoss ground units. Zealots can resist damage in the front lines, while Colossi use their superior splash damage at the back. Sentries use Guardian Shields and use Force Fields. While Stalkers protect Colossus from air to air attacks. This is a strong combination that you can maintain until the end of the game.

Zealot/Stalker/Sentry/High Templar: This is good flexible combination. You don't need to particularly think about whether your enemies are air or ground units. You can cope with any enemy unit with this build and you might win a losing game depending how you use the Psionic Storm ability of the High Templar.

UNIT COUNTERING

StarCraft II has few hard counters, and many situational ones. While air units and cloaked units are special cases that can fully counter ground forces without anti-air or armies that lack detection, most units have a slight damage bonus against a specific unit type, or no obvious counter in their raw statistics.

A lot of unit countering comes down to certain basic attributes and properties of a unit.

BASIC UNIT COUNTERS	
Unit Property	**Strong against**
Air to ground	Ground units without anti-air
Cloak	Units or buildings with no detection
Ranged	Melee units, units with less range
Fast	Slower units
Bonus damage	Units vulnerable to the bonus damage
Area of effect damage	Large clumped armies, armies fighting in choke points

The interplay between cloaked, air, and ground units is a fundamental aspect of the tech tree war. If you can reach and utilize air or cloak technology before your opponent, you can often inflict enough damage to seal a victory, either immediately, or later in the match as a result of the damage done.

Softer counters, as between fast and slow units, ranged and melee, bonus damage against specific unit type, or area of effect damage is all much more situational. Fighting at a disadvantage can be crippling, but it may not matter if, for example, you have a significantly stronger economy and can win against the soft counter to your army composition through sheer numbers (or intelligent micro and ability or terrain usage).

AIR AND CLOAKING

Aerial units and Cloaking (or burrowing) units are key units in the tech tree war.

If you have air or cloak technology before your opponent, you can often inflict serious damage until they manage to counter with air units of their own, heavy anti-air ground forces, or enough Detectors to protect their force.

When fighting with aerial forces, you should have one of two goals, either striking your opponent's bases and expansions where he cannot retaliate, or supporting your army on the attack, focus firing enemy air to air and ground to air units. If you finish off your opponent's anti-air capability, he must retreat, or you will win the fight.

AERIAL DEFENSE

To defend against air forces, you need two things—anti-air ground troops in your army, and fixed defenses on your worker lines.

With few exceptions (small island expansions for example), you **cannot** fully defend your bases against air attacks with fixed defenses without wasting a lot of resources.

As a result, don't try. Defend your **workers** with fixed defenses, and simply run your workers away to the nearest anti-air turret or friendly ground force when you get hit by air units.

You will lose some workers and buildings to aerial raids, but as long as you respond quickly to them, the damage should be both minor and temporary.

While building up an air force of your own, your army must also maintain a good number of anti-air units, because once your opponent goes air, he will be targeting your anti-air units in any ground fight.

Remember also that air units are generally slower to build and more expensive than their ground counterparts, so if your opponent is investing heavily in air forces, his ground army will be proportionally weaker—push his expansions and his main base with your ground force if he's busy raiding with his air force!

CLOAK DEFENSE

Cloaking units are much more limited in number than air units. Only the Terran Ghost and Banshee, and the Protoss Dark Templar, Observer, and Mothership have access to cloaking.

The Zerg have access to cloaking for literally their entire ground force in the form of Burrow, so it is very important that you get up detection at your Mineral lines and with your army as you approach the midgame.

Protoss cloaking is permanent, while Terran cloaking relies on Energy, so it is temporary.

If you know a cloaked attack is coming, be sure that you have Detectors ready, preferably in advance.

If you do get hit by a cloaked force without Detectors built, don't panic. Withdraw your workers, and start building detector buildings in several places at once, preferably out of sight of your opponent. You can then build new ones in range of those while your workers or army wait near the Detector.

Mobile Detectors are more expensive and slower to build for the Terran and Protoss than the Zerg, who gain quick access to the Overseer at the Lair tech level. Consequently, expect to face Overseers quickly if you go for cloaking tech.

Against Terran or Protoss, you can often contain effectively with cloaked forces until they get their mobile detectors build. Use the time gained to expand!

Cloak (and burrow) works similarly, in that once cloaking hits the field, your opponent must field detectors with his army in order to safely attack.

For this reason, you should always focus on killing enemy detectors with their army when they are out in the field. Just like the anti-air war, if you kill his detectors and still have cloaking units in the fight, your opponent *must* retreat.

When attacking an enemy base, Detector structures provide vision for the defender, so don't expect cloaking to act as an instant-win when attacking bases, but even there, if you focus on taking down the detectors in battle as a priority, you can give your cloaked units free reign to deal damage until more detectors can be built.

There are two special types of 'cloaked' units, the Zerg Overseer's Changeling, and the Protoss Sentry's Hallucinations that can both be spotted by any Detector.

PRO TIP!
Mouz.White-Ra
OLEKSII KRUPNYK

Protoss vs Protoss

If you and your opponent have about the same number of Zealots, victory will go to whoever makes his/her Zealots attack at the same time. To ensure this, line then up in straight line.

ANTI-AIR GROUND UNITS		
Terran	Protoss	Zerg
Marine	Stalker	Hydralisk
Ghost	Sentry	Queen
Thor	Photon Cannon	Spore Crawler
Missile Turret	Archon	N/A
Bunker	N/A	N/A

AIR TO AIR UNITS		
Terran	Protoss	Zerg
Viking	Phoenix	Mutalisk
Battlecruiser	Void Ray	Corruptor
N/A	Carrier	N/A

CLOAKING UNITS		
Terran	Protoss	Zerg
Ghost	Dark Templar	Any Burrowed Ground Unit
Banshee	Mothership	N/A

DETECTOR UNITS AND ABILITIES		
Terran	Protoss	Zerg
Raven	Observer	Overseer
Missile Turret	Photon Cannon	Spore Crawler
Orbital Command Scanner Sweep	N/A	Infestor Fungal Growth
Ghost EMP	N/A	N/A

TARGETING THE WEAKEST LINK

Whenever you are fielding cloaking or air units with your army and fighting away from the enemy base, you should always try to target your opponent's mobile Detectors or anti-air units. If you can destroy them all, you can force a retreat by your opponent, or you are guaranteed to wipe out his army.

UNIT SPEED

Fast and slow (particularly fast ranged units against slower melee units) interactions come down partly to micromanagement, and partly to the battlefield. If you are defending a chokepoint with slow units and have no intent to pursue your opponent, the speed isn't an issue.

On the other hand, if you are attempting to come to grips with a group of faster units that are being directly micromanaged to stay out of reach, you can potentially lose your whole force.

This is also true of retreating from a losing battle. Speed gives you the ability to disengage, retreat, and return to fight again safely. If your army is slower, retreating will cause you to suffer much heavier losses.

This does not mean you should never attack with a slower force, simply that you should be aware of the risk before you commit to an attack.

NOTABLE FAST UNITS		
Terran	Protoss	Zerg
Reaper with upgrade	Stalker with Blink	Zergling with upgrade
Hellion	Phoenix	Mutalisk

RANGED AND MELEE

There are only a handful of pure melee units in the game, the Protoss Zealot, and the Zerg Baneling, Zergling and Ultralisk.

There are also a few very short ranged units, the Zerg Roach and the Protoss Archon, that behave similarly to melee units in some respects.

As a general rule, melee units need wide, open ground to fight at maximum effectiveness, while ranged units prefer fighting at chokepoints or from high ground.

Note that for purposes of ranged units, a wall of melee units in front can be just as good as a chokepoint!

When melee (or very short range) units attack an enemy force, they will deal the most damage when they have the room to move up and surround enemy units.

One side-effect of this behavior is that *physically larger* ground forces are *more* vulnerable to melee units in the open, as they have more area for melee units to surround and attack them from.

MELEE UPGRADES

Both the Zealot and Zergling have movement speed upgrades that greatly increase their effectiveness. Be sure to pick up these upgrades either early, or as you go into the midgame, depending on your build order.

The Ultralisk has upgrades as well, but given its placement in the tech tree, fast upgrades are less vital than for the Zergling and Zealot, who tend to play a large role in early and midgame battles.

Consequently, this battle comes down almost entirely to terrain and micromanagement. If you can hit your opponent's ranged force out in the open, you can fight at full effectiveness, while if you can bottle up your opponent's melee forces at a chokepoint with your ranged force, you can inflict massive damage while the melee units struggle to break through.

High ground is also very valuable for ranged units—remember, enemy units cannot return fire to units on higher ground without line of sight, and melee units can't return fire period.

RANGE FOCUS

Ranged units can make the best use of focus fire. Focus firing with melee troops in larger engagements is generally a bad idea, because while they are struggling to reach your designated target in melee, your opponent's ranged troops are hammering away freely.

In any mixed engagement of troops, try to control (at least) your longest range ranged troops and focus fire down key targets in your opponent's army—highly dangerous units that are on the field in smaller numbers, or casters.

If there are no high value targets, focus firing enemy units is fine as well.

BONUS DAMAGE

Units with bonus damage are a natural and obvious counter to units that are weak to that bonus damage. They are especially effective If your opponent is massing an army that is almost exclusively one unit type.

However, with the obvious out of the way, it is worth knowing that just because you have a force of troops with bonus damage against most (or even all) of your opponent's army, that does *not* mean you will win 100% of the time.

Numbers, upgrades, micromanagement, flying or cloaking, and terrain all play a significant role in any battle, and bonus damage is simply an advantage, not a guarantee.

Always take advantage of bonus damage when you can, but don't rely on it to win the fight for you without your intervention!

BUILDING BASHING

Note that all structures are Armored, in addition to their Structure type, so units with a bonus against Armored targets are always a bit better against buildings (or a lot better, in the case of the Protoss Immortal).

The Terran Reaper and Zerg Baneling and Ultralisk have special attacks that are strong specifically against Structures.

PRO TIP!
Garimtoi
KIM DONGSU

4 Gateways, Zealot, Sentry combination

This strategy is easier than 3 Gateways and 1 Robo build. You extract enough Gas for 1 Gateway, construct a Cybernetics Core, add 3 Gateways, and produce only Zealots and Sentries.

This build order is repetitive. It is easy to use for a quick attack, but has some substantial disadvantages. If you start from the 2 Gateways build you can be aggressive, but will tech up slowly, allowing the Zerg player more time. On the other hand, if you start from the 1 Gateway build, you will tech up fast, but you give preemptive strikes to the Zerg. In particular, you should be careful of enemy attacks in the early game if you start from 1 Gateway build. You will have to deal with upgraded Zerglings or Zergling/Baneling units. To protect from them, you should wall off the entrance to your base by building Pylons, Gateways, and Cybernetics Cores.

Quickly scout the enemy base and see when their Gas timing is. If you scout the enemy base and find that they are constructing Spawning Pools and Gas extractors, you can be fairly confident that they will attack early. If they speed up extracting Gas, you should produce Sentries as soon as you have 100 Gas and keep watching the entrance to your base carefully.

If you build structures properly, you can defend the entrance with 1~2 Zealots. If there are only Zerglings, divide them into three groups with the Sentry's Force Field to reduce the number of enemies. If there are Zergling/Baneling units, you should use the Force Field to block the Banelings completely. If the Banelings get through, be cautious in the deployment of your units. You should spread them out to the maximum to reduce damage from the Banelings.

If, when you scout early, your opponent is gathering Minerals with less units, then you don't need to fear a Zerg rush. You could counter if you have 4~6 Sentries. If you go out to attack, take 1~2 Probes and construct Pylons along the way to increase the speed of reinforcements. It is amazing to beat the enemy with those forces and quite a feat, but it is very rare. When you go out, block the entrance with Pylons to prevent a Zergling's counterstrike in advance. When you block the entrance, just summon 1 Sentry inside: a Force Field and additional units summoned are enough to block them.

If your opponent's armies are massing in the center, then you must induce them to attack to reduce the Zerglings. Use the above strategies to block off your base and separate the Zergling from the other forces. Keep fighting until the Zerglings are all killed or when you feel you are not in danger, then move forward slowly to the enemy base. The important thing is not to kill the enemy outright, but to reduce their forces while increasing yours. I call this 'rolling the units'. If you keep your units alive, the size of your army gets bigger just like a snow ball. Use Force Field to prevent Zerglings from approaching; spread Roaches out and reduce them little by little using Force Field. Keep reducing the enemy forces and increasing your units, when you are ready for the final push use your Force Fields differently: do not separate them using the Force Field but rather block their escape.

The highly skilled Protoss players in StarCraft could be identified by their Zealot control; highly skilled Protoss players in StarCraft II are identified by their Sentry Force Field control skills.

PRO TIP!
Mouz.White-Ra
OLEKSII KRUPNYK

Protoss Build Order

Protoss vs Zerg (Air attack)

This strategy works on all 1v1 maps, but can also be used on large maps as long as your Zerg opponent starts off close by. Once the game starts, go to your Nexus and begin producing Probes.

Then use the following build order:

Limit 9 – build a Pylon.

Limit 11 – use Chrono Boost to speed up Probe production.

Limit 13 – build Gateway and send one Probe exploring.

Limit 13 – use Chrono Boost to speed up Probe production.

Limit 15 – order an Assimilator.

Limit 16 – use Chrono Boost to speed up Probe production.

Limit 16 – build a Pylon.

Limit 19 – build a Cybernetics Core.

Limit 19 – use Chrono Boost to speed up Probe production.

Limit 20 – produce a Zealot.

Limit 24 – build a Stargate.

Limit 25 – build a Pylon.

Limit 26 – order a second Assimilator.

Limit 26 – produce a second Zealot.

Limit 28 – build a Forge.

Limit 29 – order a Void Ray and speed up their production (use Chrono Boost).

Limit 32 – build Zealot #3.

Limit 34 – build another Pylon.

Limit 34 – order a Photon Cannon at the choke point (if you anticipate that your Zerg opponent is making a lot of Zergling s or Roaches, order one or two extra Photon Cannons). Send the Void Ray toward the Zerg. Try to find and kill any Overlords along the way.

Limit 34 – order a Phoenix.

Limit 36 – produce another Zealot.

Limit 38 – speed up the Phoenix production (use Chrono Boost).

Limit 39 – order another Phoenix.

BIO BLOB

The Protoss Archon is unique in that has a damage bonus against all Biological targets. Naturally, this makes it most dangerous against the Zerg, good against Terran players massing Barracks troops, and least effective against the Protoss unless they are massing Zealots heavily.

TERRAN BONUS DAMAGE	
Unit	**Vs.**
Marauder	Armored
Reaper	Light Ground, Structure
Ghost	Light, Nuclear Strike
Hellion	Light Ground
Siege Tank	Armored Ground
Thor	Light Air
Viking	Armored Air

PROTOSS BONUS DAMAGE	
Unit	**Vs.**
Stalker	Armored
Immortal	Armored Ground
Phoenix	Light Air
Archon	Biological

ZERG BONUS DAMAGE	
Unit	**Vs.**
Baneling	Light, Structure
Ultralisk	Structure, Armored Ground

AREA OF EFFECT ATTACKS

With few exceptions, area of effect attacks don't start showing up until the midgame, generally after the first few skirmishes have already been fought.

However, this works out well, because area of effect damage is most effective against *large* clumps of troops, and those packs generally don't arrive until the midgame and later.

Once armies reach large sizes, you should *always* be fielding some form of AoE mixed in with your army. Their effectiveness is multiplied by the number of enemies they can hit with each attack.

If your opponent is not using AoE of their own, you are very likely to come out of any major battle in the mid or lategame with a significant advantage in remaining troops, possibly enough to cripple an expansion, or simply finish off your opponent.

AREA OF EFFECT ATTACKS		
Terran	**Protoss**	**Zerg**
Siege Tank Siege Mode	Archon	Baneling
Ghost EMP Round	High Templar Psionic Storm	Infestor Fungal Growth
Nuclear Strike	Colossus	Mutalisk (minor)
Raven Seeker Missile	N/A	Ultralisk
Hellion	N/A	N/A

UNIT MIXES

Unit mixing is a very basic and simple tactic. You build two complementary unit types (either due to resource cost, tech tree placement, or unit role), and add a third support unit in smaller numbers to supplement your army (or in the case of the Zerg, add a third unit in swarming numbers).

Such mixes form the core of any military force, and while the exact composition varies from game to game (and army to army), the principle is a simple and effective one: Maximize your unit production, build an overwhelming force, and push on your opponent.

PRO TIP!
Mouz.White-Ra
OLEKSII KRUPNYK

Protoss Build Order Cont.

Next comes a crucial moment when your Void Ray reaches the Zerg's base. Start off by pouncing on the Queen, and then use the newly arrived Phoenix to lift it in the air so it can't fight back or get away. After you're done with the Queen, shoot up all the Overlords around you. If they manage to send their first Hydralisks your way, make quick work of them by lifting them in the air with your newly arrived Phoenixes.

Even if the Zerg repels your attack, you'll have a strong advantage when you come at them a second time with all your land and air armies.

As an alternative, build a second Nexus and launch your attack a bit later, with more force.

Specific tactics with units:

1. If your Terran opponent produces nothing but land units, a Protoss Sentry will help defend against them. When they rush you, have your Sentry cast a Guardian Shield to reduce the damage your units take from enemy shots.

2. Use Phoenixes to quickly decimate enemy workers. Also, in a large-scale fight, decide which enemy units pose the most danger and decommission them with your Phoenix's Graviton Beam ability.

3. If you use Immortals, try to target their ranged attacks only on Armored enemy units (such as Seige Tanks, Marauders, Roaches, Stalkers, Colossi, etc.) to inflict maximum damage.

4. When you upgrade your Colossi's shooting range, they can annihilate the enemy's forces from a distance while staying out of harm's way. Approach, shoot and retreat to inflict maximum damage without taking any yourself. Works like a charm!

5. When launching an offensive, make sure that all your units charge the enemy at the same time, and ideally from several sides. This will ensure a simultaneous attack, for a few seconds render useless those enemy units that stay in the rear, and hopefully tip the scales in your favor.

COMMON EARLY MIXES

 TERRAN

Marines and Marauders form the core of any solid Terran infantry force. Both are increasingly effective in larger numbers, both benefit from Stimpacks, and both are further boosted by the addition of Medivacs.

Terran Marines also benefit from a durability upgrade that increases their staying power in battle, further magnifying the impact of Medivac healing.

 PROTOSS

Zealots and Stalkers are the heart of the Protoss ground army, and both have upgrades to boost their mobility, allowing the Zealots to get into melee quickly, and the Stalkers to aggressively pursue or quickly retreat as needed.

The addition of the Sentry provides more solid range damage, ranged protection, instant choke point generation, and decoy targets to inflate overall army health.

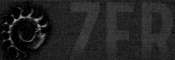 ZERG

Zerglings and Roaches form a strong initial ground force for the Zerg, though Hydralisks can replace or supplement Roaches later in the game. Zerglings are an omnipresent and cheap threat, while Roaches provide a tough core to the army, and Hydralisks become an increasingly dangerous ranged threat as their numbers grow.

Zerglings can be morphed into Banelings at any time to provide a strong area of effect and building demolition force, strengthening the utility of any Zerg ground offensive.

A word of caution—while mixed forces are effective, trying to mix *too many* units is often a mistake. It takes too much time and investment of resources to create the necessary structures to support many different units in the early and midgame, and if you try to spread your army out over many units early, you are going to find yourself facing an enemy army that has less *types* of units, but *many more* of those units.

Don't hesitate to deviate from the early game mixes of units once you're into the midgame and past the early skirmishes, but don't lose games because you didn't build enough troops!

RUSHING

Rushing, in all its myriad forms, is simply committing to a powerful early offensive against your opponent. The specifics vary depending on the races in the match (and the map and starting locations), but the basics are simple: build a strong military early, at the expense of your economy, and rush your opponent before they are prepared to deal with such a large force early in the game.

Rushing is distinct from early game attacks or harassment which you should *always* be engaging in, or expecting to defend against. Such early attacks rarely have severe economic repercussions for either player, as-suming roughly equal skill.

Committing fully to an early rush typically puts you well behind in the teching game if your opponent manages to fend off your rush, and may also put you behind on worker count, further damaging your ability to compete effectively in the transition to midgame.

Rushing does have certain advantages however. It always results in the quickest possible victories. It can handily defeat an opponent who is quickly teching or expanding at the expense of their early game military. And it can force you to learn better unit micro to make the best use of your units, which are that much more precious when you are depending on them fully for an early victory.

An unsuccessful rush that still deals heavy economic damage is an acceptable outcome. You are still on roughly even ground when you rebuild, and your opponent may well be shaken from the aggressive early attack.

Remember that your first priority target is *always* the enemy workers, unless you know you can defeat his few military forces entirely and then finish off the workers.

Rushing is generally most effective on smaller maps, where the distances between bases are short, and all but useless on large maps. The longer your troops have to travel to hit the enemy worker line, the less effective the rush is going to be.

Experiment with rushing while you are learning to play the game, it is very important that even if you don't always rush, you understand how to do so, and what it's weaknesses are, the better to enable you to fight off enemy rushes.

RUSH DEFENSE

While walling in is the best defense against an early attack, a true rush will sometimes hit before a wall in is complete, and Zerg do not have the option to wall in.

Early scouting is critical for detecting a rush build. If you see that a rush is coming, get your military units building immediately.

When the enemy troops hit, don't forget that your workers can (and often must) fight to win the battle.

*A few military units might not be enough to fight off your opponent's early rushing troops, but your military units, plus your workers, plus your producing units and workers **can** do so, if controlled correctly!*

And don't worry about suffering losses against an early rush—your opponent has damaged his economy to rush you, so as long as you don't take excessive losses, you should be at no worse than even, and often in better shape.

PUSHING

Simply fighting your opponent's army and winning isn't enough to win the game. You have to destroy your opponent's buildings (or make them concede), and while winning skirmishes is important, it is equally impor-tant that you know when to capitalize on a victory and inflict economic or technological damage on your opponent.

If you can push into their base with even damaged remnants from a fight you barely won, inflicting heavy damage to a worker line or taking down a key technology or unit producing building can give you the edge you need to finish the fight.

When you make a push with your army, *always* have a goal in mind. Simply getting into a fight with your opponent's army is not why you are attacking! If you can attack your opponent's workers and buildings and leave without even fighting the opposing army, do so! By the time he rebuilds from the damage, you will often have a larger army, and can crush his force in battle.

Your first priority should be killing enemy workers to slow your op-ponent's economy. If he is alert and runs the workers away, and your troops are too slow to effectively chase them, go for a building instead.

Taking down your opponent's core structure can stall his economic recovery significantly, and taking down a key technology building can stall his ability to build a critical new unit.

In most cases, unless you broke through with overwhelming numbers, you aren't going to be able to stay long enough to do more than kill some workers or possibly one building. Once this is accomplished, if you see that your opponent has rallied enough to beat you back, retreat your forces—better to save the money and fighting power, and group them up with fresh reinforcements.

On the other hand, if you see that you may just barely take down a key building, stay put, even if it costs you your army. Losing a few troops and denying your opponent a crucial unit or technology is almost always worth the price.

PRIORITY TARGETS

Always have a target in mind when you hit your opponent's main base or an expansion.

- #1: Destroy his workers. This slows and damages his economy. Good players will run their workers away quickly, so if you can't chase them down easily, proceed to the next target.

- #2: Destroy his core structure. This prevents harvesting, forces a rebuild, and generally damages his economy.

- #3: Destroy a key technology building. This can delay the appearance of a crucial new unit for your opponent, allowing you to exploit the weakness with units of your own.

If you cannot accomplish any of those goals, retreat!

Note that, generally speaking, targeting Supply producers, military buildings, or fixed defensive buildings usually isn't an effective use of your time.

The reason for this is that while raiding Supply buildings can be useful, and taking down fixed defenses to prepare for a major assault is helpful, once you are actually past his army and his defenses, you want to strike at the heart of his economy, and then at his technology base.

Hitting Supply after you have *already* won the fight against his army doesn't help much, as he is nowhere near his Supply cap. Unless you can manage to destroy ALL of his Supply before he can rebuild or send reinforcements, in which case you should have enough time to win the game anyway!

If for some reason you have not fought his army, targeting his Supply can stop his troop building temporarily, but unless you damage his economy, this is very temporary (and not especially costly) damage.

Similarly, fixed defenses are there to slow or stop your army on the assault, once past them, you can either ignore them entirely, or only destroy the ones that are protecting the workers, core structure, or the tech building you want to destroy.

Military buildings are a special case. For both the Terran and the Protoss, they tend to be tough buildings, and it's usually better to use your damage on softer, more critical targets.

For the Zerg however, taking down certain military structures can be quite useful. Because the Zerg use single buildings to enable unit production at all of their Hatcheries, destroying a lone Greater Spire shuts down *all* of their air capability, and requires a long time to recreate and re-upgrade.

PRO TIP!
Live Hydralisk
KIBONG KOOK

Tips for Smart Gaming

Don't forget to capture the Xel'Naga Towers located in the map. If your units touch the Xel'Naga Towers, you can learn when you will be attacked and the unit combination of your enemy more quickly.

In the early game, capture the Towers with Probes, then use your units to secure them. Even though players know the Tower's function, they don't actually use in real time. The more you learn to use the Xel'Naga Towers, the more you will win.

Do not attack in a line: When you go to attack you should not just give the orders to attack the enemy base and watch the scene, instead you should keep on checking whether your units are going to the right direction to attack or not. When you see a war movie, you can see armies making camps and attacking at the same time or you can see them fighting a guerilla war somewhere in the enemy base to turn their attention to attack. Just like that, if you use the same strategies in your game, you can find it more exciting and double the fun.

RAIDING

Raiding is simply a high speed attack where your goal is to get in and get out as fast as possible, doing as much damage as possible in the shortest amount of time possible.

As a general rule, raiding forces are small, and are secondary to your main army. A large enough raiding force is no longer a raid, it is an army on the attack!

Because raiding forces are smaller, they must be carefully controlled. And always remember that retreat, not engagement, is your only response to incoming enemy troops.

Each race has units that are well suited to this role, either due to speed, mobility, or special abilities.

In most cases, raid targets have identical priorities to a normal army penetration: workers, then technology or core structure buildings.

All three races also have access to transport tech that can allow them to drop a ground army in the back door and then escape again before a reaction force can arrive.

Remember, once you hit your opponent with your raid, you're on the clock. Deal as much damage as you can before his reinforcements show up, then get out!

TERRAN

Terran have excellent raiding options at all tech levels, which is very useful, given their ability to wall in and defend their bases effectively.

You can use the Terran raiding power to contain your opponent, or to damage lightly defended expansions and force him to make difficult decisions about whether it is safe to push out with his army.

Early in the game, you can make use of the Reaper. This cliff jumping unit deals excellent damage to both light units and buildings. While you can't tackle buildings with a pair of Reapers very early in the game, you *can* take apart a worker line with frightening efficiency if your opponent does not immediately retreat his workers and counter-attack with a ranged unit or a worker/melee unit combination.

In larger packs, later in the game and with their speed upgrade, Reapers become very dangerous raiding units, as they can take down buildings in seconds, and then easily escape before a reaction force can arrive.

The almighty Terran Nuke can also be used as a 'raid' of sorts, with a cloaked Ghost. However, you should be aware that landing the Nuke against an alert opponent is difficult, as an enemy's first reaction to hearing the launch warning is going to be to check their army first, and then each of their worker lines.

Ideally, you want to launch a Nuke from cloaked concealment (or on a ledge after being dropped off by a Medivac) as you hit your opponent with your army (or in team games, while your teammates hit your target). A distracted opponent may miss the launch warning window, and a Nuke will kill all workers and deal heavy damage to nearby buildings.

A small group of cloaked Ghosts can also work as worker raiders purely on the strength of their cloaked attack and Sniper Round ability, but Ghosts are very expensive in Gas costs, so be careful about risking their lives on worker raids!

From the Factory, Hellions are another great worker raider, as they are an extremely fast ground unit, and deal area of effect damage in a straight line. A handful of Hellions can shred a worker line (and they don't do badly against Zealots, Zerglings, or Marines either).

Because Hellions lack the Reaper cliff jumping ability, you can't break through a walled in base with Hellions, but you can hit expansions easily, and you can also harass your opponent if he has a slow moving army, as Hellions are almost impossible to catch if controlled well.

Lastly, the Starport opens several raiding options, including the Viking, which in addition to being the core Terran air to air unit, can also transform to a ground walker to harass workers (or in a pinch, contribute to a ground battle).

Vikings are an expensive raiding option, but if you are building Vikings to deal with aerial threats anyway, be sure to make use of their raiding potential.

The Terran Banshee is both a dangerous cloaked air to ground threat *and* a strong raiding unit. Building Banshees and researching cloak forces your opponent to build detectors in his base, or you can destroy his workers (and his base) at your leisure.

Be careful with Banshee raids once those defenses go up, as they are fragile, and better used alongside your army at that point (though you can and should still probe for weaknesses at expansions, a large enough group of Banshees can take down a few lone Detector building easily).

Finally, the Raven can work as a worker raider due to its Auto-Turret ability. A few Ravens with enough Energy can fly in and drop several Auto-Turrets right in a worker line, then fly away.

There are a few issues with Auto-Turret raids however—first, they take valuable Energy away from the Raven's other abilities, all of which are useful and important in battle with your main army.

Second, an alert opponent can simply run the workers away from the Auto-Turrets, which cannot pursue, and unless you dropped an extreme number of turrets, they won't be able to destroy the core structure at the expansion.

And finally, Ravens are expensive, slow to build, and are a critical mobile Detector for the Terran army. Still, if you have Ravens idling and getting close to maximum Energy, don't hesitate to pay an unwelcome visit to your opponent's expansions!

PROTOSS

Protoss do not excel at raiding, but they do have some units that can work quite well for hitting worker lines, and the Dark Templar and Void Ray are amazing units for quickly destroying core structures or tech buildings.

Most Protoss raiding options arrive in the mid-game, with Stalker Blink, Dark Templar, Colossus, Phoenix groups, or the Void Ray after it has its speed upgrade.

Stalkers with Blink make great raiding units, as they are already fast, and Blink allows them to escape almost any pursuit attempt.

In addition, with line of sight granted by Protoss aerial units, the Observer, or Hallucinated air units, the Stalker can Blink onto ledges, giving them mobility on par with cliffjumper units.

Be sure to make use of Blink not only to get onto enemy bases that are up on ledges, but also to escape pursuit by Blinking onto raised ledges where pursuing armies cannot attack due to line of sight. Some maps are more friendly to this tactic than others, so be sure to look over the map and pick out possible escape routes.

Dark Templar can be a powerful raiding unit, but you usually only get one clean shot at your opponent's main base—after the first hit, you can expect Detectors to be built throughout the base. You may still be able to hit expansions, but be careful about sending your full Dark Templar force in alone, losing a large number of them is very costly, when they could be contributing more effectively as part of your ground army.

It is a good idea to pick out a key structure to destroy with your first Dark Templar assault, rather than simply going for workers, as Dark Templar have very high damage output. A small group of them can destroy a core structure or a tech building in seconds, giving them enough time to escape without suffering heavy losses.

The Colossus, as a cliffwalker, can be a solid raiding unit, but you must be *very* careful about raiding with your Colossi, as they are expensive, slow to build, and more dangerous in greater numbers—losing even one on a raid is a foolish use of resources.

With that warning in mind, in some situations, you may be able to hit an opponent's expansions from high ground, depending on the map you are playing. Take a look at the terrain and see if there are any easy to reach ledges that overlook enemy expansions and have no quick route for enemy ground forces to retaliate against your Colossus.

Once your opponent has built up air units to counter the Colossus, don't risk unsupported worker raids, use other units for that job, and keep your Colossus with your main army.

Finally, Protoss air has some reasonably effective raiding options.

Groups of Phoenix with their Graviton Beam ability can simply lift up workers and pop them in midair. To accomplish this with reasonable speed, you need a good sized group of Phoenix.

As with Terran Vikings, Phoenix are most important for their air to air potential, and are too expensive to be built purely as raiders, but if you are building them anyway, don't hesitate to use their raiding ability to pick off workers (or isolated and expensive enemy ground units!)

The Void Ray is generally too slow to raid without its speed upgrade, but the first few you get on the field before your opponent has a substantial anti-air force should be used to strike at your opponent immediately.

Because of the way Void Rays deal damage, they are best used for downing structures. A small group of Void Rays can destroy a core structure with frightening speed, and once you have the movement speed upgrade for your Void Rays, they become more viable as high speed building raiders.

Void Rays aren't amazing at worker raiding, even with their speed upgrade, as your opponent can simply run his workers away before the Void Rays can charge up their beams fully. However, they make up for it with their danger to enemy core structures and tech buildings.

ZERG

Zerg lack many units with unusual special abilities, but in spite of this, they still have several types of unit that are quite effective at raiding.

First, the lowly Zergling, once it receives its speed upgrade, becomes a lightning fast, cheap, and expendable worker raider. Zerglings become even more dangerous once their attack speed upgrade arrives, and with a few ground damage upgrades, a cheap pack of Zerglings can destroy workers and escape with amazing speed.

Enough Zerglings can even destroy buildings with great speed, but that leads us to our next option, the Baneling.

Banelings are good at blowing up workers, and they are amazing at building demolition. 10 Banelings can instantly deal *800* damage to a building, not counting damage upgrades.

However, keep in mind the cost involved in Baneling use, as each Baneling costs you 50/25, so those 10 Banelings are 500/250. For most tech and military structures, this is much more expensive than the building you can destroy, but in some cases, it can be worthwhile.

If your opponent's tech building is his only means of dealing with your particular army composition, by all means, destroy it! Losing out on the resource exchange and winning the war is always a good trade.

In most other cases, you should either be using a small number of Banelings to destroy a worker group, or saving them for taking down defensive structures or in combat with your army.

Both Roaches and Infestors, with their ability to move while burrowed, can make excellent expansion raiders. Simply move in while burrowed, pop up, and either eat the workers, or drop a Fungal Growth to do the work for you. As with other cloaked units, be careful about attempting multiple burrowed raids, you can expect detectors to be in place after the first hit.

Finally, the mighty Mutalisk is an excellent aerial raider. With both anti-air and anti-ground, it can fend off air or ground units in small numbers easily, and with its high movement speed, Mutas can hit worker lines and retreat before a counter-attack can arrive.

Unless you are focusing all of your Gas on your ground army, picking up at least a few Mutalisks for raiding purposes can usually pay for itself fairly easily.

TRANSPORTS

The last type of raid is that of the drop, as in 'dropships', though the type of transport used differs significantly for each race.

Excepting the Nydus Canal, each transport unit can carry up to 8 cargo size worth of units, see the Races section of the guide for the exact size of any given unit (in most cases, they're about what you would expect, a Thor or Colossus takes up more room than a Marine or Zergling!)

Transports aren't especially durable units, so sending them into a combat zone is a good way to lose your raiding force very quickly.

Generally, transport raids should be kept small, no more than 2 full transports with possibly a decoy transport or two accompanying the loaded ones.

The Terran Medivac has an average movement speed, and the benefit of healing any infantry that it carries.

The Zerg Overlord suffers from the slowest movement speed of all transports, but Zerg should usually be using the Nydus Network for transport raids and inter-base transit. If you are using Overlords, be sure to send extras, they are the cheapest transports with the most health.

The Protoss Warp Prism is slightly more fragile than the others, but has the greatest movement speed after being upgraded, and has the ability to create a Pylon power field, allowing for Protoss units to be warped in anywhere on the map.

RACIAL TRANSPORTS			
Unit	Health	Speed	Cost
Medivac	150	2.75	100/100
Warp Prism	100/40	2.5 (3.37)	200
Overlord	200	0.46 (1.87)	100
Nydus Worm	200	N/A	100/100

TERRAN

Terran drops can make use of several forces effectively.

A mixed group of Marines and Marauders with Stimpacks can quickly rip apart a worker line, and easily destroy nearby buildings.

A few Ghosts, carefully placed, can make use of Nukes, or infiltrate cloaked and pick off targets with their normal attack and Snipe, or land a free EMP on a Protoss force before a major engagement.

Siege Tanks, placed on a ridge overlooking an expansion (or a battlefield) can be extremely annoying for your opponent to dislodge, and they will instantly devastate a worker line if you want to do a hit and run.

Thors on a ridge near a battle location can make use of their 250mm cannons and high damage output without threat of ground retaliation—typically most useful on defense, when you know your opponent will be attacking you.

PROTOSS

Protoss drops have the significant benefit of the Warp Prism's power field, allowing you to warp in *any* Gateway units that you have access to.

Sending a single unloaded Warp Prism to an expansion and then warping in four Dark Templar can be a very unwelcome surprise for your opponent.

High Templar also make excellent worker raiders when used as a drop, even two Psionic Storms will devastate a worker line. Remember that you can't warp in High Templar and use Psionic Storm unless you have researched Khaydarin Amulets, you have to bring High Templar that have already been built and have enough Energy.

In cases where you don't want to risk so much Gas on a raid, simply warping in a small group of Zealots can inflict reasonable damage on a worker line, particularly once you have Charge researched to chase down fleeing workers.

Finally, loading a Warp Prism with a pair of Immortals and then dropping them off and warping in some ground units can act as an expansion wrecking force—Immortals deal very heavy building damage.

ZERG

Zerg are unusual in that their normal transport does not need to be utilized to perform a 'drop', instead, you can build Nydus Worms *anywhere* on the map that you have line of sight, from a centrally located Nydus Network.

As a Nydus Worm can disgorge an entire Zerg army in an enemy base in moments, this is a significant threat for your opponent.

Because both the Nydus Network and the Nydus Worms are cheap to build, you should take full advantage of this mid-game mobility, not just for 'drop' backdoor attacks, but also as a movement network between all of your bases.

For raiding purposes, be careful about sending too many units through a Nydus Worm—while you can load the network quickly, unloading units is *not* instant, and having half your army trapped on the other side of a destroyed Nydus Worm is a great way to lose a match.

However, don't hesitate to send your normal raiding units through a Nydus network, and using Zerglings once they have their upgrades make for a cheap and effective backdoor attack on workers (and sometimes even tech buildings, depending on where your opponent's army is).

Remember that Nydus Worms can be placed anywhere you have line of sight (they do not require Creep to be placed), so any Overlord, Overseer, Changeling, or air unit can quickly get you the line of sight you need to create a transit node.

Finally, just because you have access to the Nydus Network does not mean that you can't use Overlord transports. Overlords are cheap and relatively durable compared to the other transports, though slower, so you can easily mix a swarm of empty Overlords with the actual transports, providing cover for an Overlord drop, which can be useful if your opponent lacks significant anti-air in his army.

DANGER DROPS

Medivac/Warp Prism/Nydus or Overlord attacks can be very effective, but full force transport attacks are also *very* expensive. Before you embark on a campaign of using drops against your opponent's in every match, take a look at the economics involved.

A simple single Warp Prism drop of 2 Immortals accompanied by a warp in of 4 Zealots costs *1100* Minerals and 300 Gas. You better get your money's worth from that attack!

Similarly, a Terran drop of two Medivacs with full Marine/Marauder loads is 1000 Minerals and 300 Gas.

A less extreme, more economical backdoor attack is 12 Speedlings from a Nydus Canal, but that still costs 450 Minerals and 300 Gas.

As a general rule, you should make drop attacks with *less* forces that are more carefully controlled.

Ideally, you inflict damage (kill workers, then destroy a tech building), and *get out*. If you can deal damage without suffering losses, you've had a successful raid.

If you can deal heavy damage and suffer full losses, it may be a worthwhile trade, but try to avoid suicidal drops, they're expensive, they tie up your attention, and they distract from your army buildup and management.

TRANSPORT DANCING

Because transports are aerial units, if you are facing a ground-only army, be sure to abuse the ability to pick up your expensive ground units and simply move them out of harms way.

Transports are also useful for moving strong units that are *slower* than the transport, just be very careful about moving transports near a battle loaded with expensive units.

If your opponent retaliates to your drop with ground-only units, not only can you safely escape with your transports at any time, you can drop off and pick up dangerous units like Siege Tanks or Immortals to deal free damage, until your opponent can get anti-air into the mix.

Remember that you can load units by right clicking with the transport on a unit, or right clicking on the transport with a unit.

You can unload units by clicking on their portraits in the transport, or by using the Drop All command.

Load and Drop commands can both be queued with Shift, so you can set up a roundabout route for your transports to take to reach an enemy base, and automatically drop off your troops when they arrive.

Note that you should never leave a drop totally unattended, but when simply moving workers or troops between relatively safe areas, queuing up the transit can save you some time and attention.

AIR POWER

We've touched on some of the utility that air units bring to your offensive arsenal: bypassing chokepoints, worker raiding, recon, line of sight, containment, and forcing your enemy to invest in anti-air.

Air units have powerful mobility, as they completely ignore all terrain, and they make excellent scouts, as they can act as spotters anywhere on the map, providing line of sight up ramps for your ground army.

In addition, air units make a strong addition to your main army, as they provide offensive firepower with the added bonus of being completely immune to attacks from many units.

Once air units hit the field in any significant numbers, anti-air defenses and mobile anti-air units become just as important as Detectors are for dealing with cloaked forces.

Air units can also act as strong containment units, just as cloaked units do, because even if your opponent has enough fixed anti-air to repel your force, you can still keep him bottled up until he builds up enough mobile anti-air troops to move out with his army.

In situations where your opponent is fielding air units, you need to make sure your worker lines are covered with at least a few anti-air defenses, and then get your anti-air units built up in your main army to allow you to attack safely.

When you are fielding air units with your army, targeting your opponent's anti-air in battle is critical, and you should build your army to have a greater percentage of units strong against your opponent's anti-air.

It's always preferable to be the first player to field air units, as you can force your opponent to spend resources on anti air defenses, while you can expand, and because there are only a limited number of ground based anti-air units, you'll have a good idea of what your opponent is building.

Air to air battles are a messy affair. Generally, he who has the largest econ wins. A stronger economy and a larger production base allows you to outproduce your opponent's air force and win a battle of attrition.

Once one player establishes aerial dominance with a critical mass of air units, it becomes very difficult to retake the skies with smaller groups of air units.

Because air to air fights lack the terrain factor, pure numbers and up-grades tend to matter a lot more. Whenever possible, engage in air to air battles with your anti-air ground units or defensive structures nearby to tip the battle in your favor.

A few caster abilities can also play a significant role in the air battle, as some can be used against air units to good effect.

It is possible to feint with air units, by creating a few and raiding with them, you can force your opponent to overreact and build anti-air defenses, and to change their army composition to include more anti-air ground forces.

Unlike cloaking units, which have a single mobile Detector answer from each race, air units can change the makeup of an opponent's army, and by building units that are strong against the anti-air units, you can win the ground battle handily by making your opponent overreact to an aerial threat.

Without exception, air units require Gas to build, and usually a lot of it, so you are most often Gas limited when building a large number of air units. This can result in the creation of a disproportionate number of the basic Mineral units for each race (Marine, Hellion, Zealot, and Zergling) to fill out your ground army.

If your opponent is heavily investing in air units and you see the shift in his ground force due to Gas starvation, be sure to adjust your troop makeup to compensate.

Striking at your opponent's Gas extractors with raids can also stall the production of new air units, giving you another way to win a battle against an air force.

ANTI-AIR ABILITIES		
Terran	Protoss	Zerg
Ghost Sniper Round	High Templar Psionic Storm	Infestor Fungal Growth
Ghost EMP Round	Mothership Vortex	Overseer Infested Terran
Raven Seeker Missile	N/A	Infestor Neural Parasite
Raven Point Defense Drone	N/A	N/A

COMBAT POSITIONING

The position of your army before a battle begins can have a significant impact on the outcome, before the shooting even starts.

Melee or very short range units tend to be most affected by terrain, as they are at their strongest when they have room to maneuver and surround enemies.

Longer range units do well with a front line of close range or tough troops, and also do very well behind chokepoints where they can focus fire, or on high ground where they can attack freely without retaliation.

Good scouting is vital for positioning your army in an advantageous location before a battle starts.

Whenever possible, try to engage your opponent's army where your army can make use of its strengths to the fullest. Whether this means from behind a wall-in at your base, or out in the open field in front of your expansion, always try to fight where all of your troops can deal the most damage possible.

The one time you cannot do this is when you are on the attack at an opponent's base, and depending on the defenses present, you may need to create a few siege breaker units to penetrate the blockade.

When possible, try not to engage with your opponent's main army while in an enemy base. Using attack move in a base can result in some of your units attacking buildings (though they will prioritize hostile military units in range), and the accidental reduction in firepower can be dangerous or fatal.

Even if you properly micro your troops to engage, your enemy has no such handicap, and can be assured that his troops will be focused 100% on killing yours.

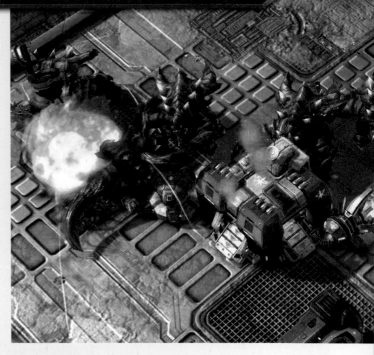

Note that while StarCraft II has no explicit formations for groups of units, there do tend to be 'natural' formations that arise when combat starts, based purely on the ranges of units.

Longer range units naturally tend to be towards the back of a battle, and enemy caster units are often near the rear of an attack as well.

For this reason, if you can manage to hit an enemy army from behind as it attacks your base (or a decoy force), you can often inflict crippling losses in terms of resource cost by hitting expensive casters and long range units from the rear first, before tackling the shorter range, cheaper units at the front.

Be sure that you wait until the enemy army attacks if you're trying to hit it from behind. Until an army is actually engaged, it has no front or back, and is usually a giant blob of units! (which, incidently, is often the best time to make use of area of effect attacks or abilities).

Protoss Tip

PRO TIP!
Garimtoi
KIM DONGSU

A Protoss vs Zerg match can be divided into three phases: early, middle, and end game.

In the early game, it is important to make good use of Force Field to defend and counter Zergling or Zergling/Baneling. Middle game mainly consists of one big battle in the main enemy base, using Force Field and Guardian Shield. In end game, you have a variety of battles in huge scales, focusing on Colossi and High Templar, etc.

In StarCraft II, at the very moment you encounter your enemy, your hands should be already hitting the "F" button of the Sentry continuously.

When the battle seems to be headed for an extended engagement, concentrate on a Colossus/Stalker build order, or a Stalker/Immortal or Zealot/Templar combination.

RETREATING

When it becomes clear that you are not going to win a fight, or that you are not going to win a fight without heavy losses, *retreat*. Fighting to the bitter end earns you *nothing* in StarCraft II.

There are only a few cases where it is acceptable to throw away troops, and in battle with your opponent's army is not one of them. Remember, the goal of an attack is to cripple your opponent's economy or destroy key tech buildings, and the winning condition for a match is destroying all enemy buildings. Fighting a losing battle against your enemy army fulfills none of those goals, so when it is clear that you are no longer in a favorable fight, get out!

In essence, you always want to be a bully when fighting and a coward when confronted. Hit your opponent where he is weakest, and run when he is stronger.

HOW DO YOU KNOW IF A FIGHT IS FAVORABLE?

1. Does your opponent have cloaked units? If so, do you have a detector with your army?

2. Does your opponent have air units? If so, do you have enough anti-air?

3. Is your opponent fighting from behind a wall-in? Do you have means of breaking the wall?

4. Does your opponent have dangerous casters? Do you have your own casters, or a means of killing his?

If you answered no to any of those questions, the fight probably isn't one you want to engage in. Back up, create a solution to your problem, then re-engage.

When it comes to a straight up slugfest, there's no substitute for experience. You simply have to get your hands dirty to begin to recognize when one army has the upper hand over another.

Given all the variations in maps, race combinations, possible army compositions, and possible upgrade combinations, you're looking at hundreds (or thousands) of potential matchups, and knowing with certainty that one army can beat another is borderline impossible—and that's not counting micro skill, which differs from player to player.

With that said, if you and your opponent have been maxing out your economy and spending resources constantly from the same number of bases, you can expect your forces to be roughly similar in overall size, if not in effectiveness, depending on exactly what units and upgrades have been built and researched.

You should never feel that your opponent has somehow managed to get a leg up on your before a fight begins, unless you *know* that he has an expansion running somewhere that you don't know about.

Don't be afraid of the army you can't see, be afraid of the army right in front of you.

If you've maintained economic parity, you will always have at *least* an even chance in a straight fight, and often better than even if you've scouted well and built your army appropriately.

PRO TIP!
Live Hydralisk
KIBONG KOOK

Protoss Air unit Features

Phoenix: An air to air only unit, the Phoenix also has a clever skill that allows them to "lift" ground units.

Void Ray: This unit can cause massive damage; the longer it focuses fire on a target, the more damage it does. It is slow to move but good for attacking stationary buildings. With one or two units you can destroy an enemy's main base in short order.

Carrier: Never just build one Carrier; multiple Carriers are essential as this capital ship is very deadly when battling in numbers. The Carrier has good health and makes quick work of weak ground or air units. Don't forget to train more Interceptors.

Mothership: The Mothership in the middle to end game, can hide and summon in your Protoss forces for a surprise attack. Moves very slowly.

ATTACK MOVE TO VICTORY

One last word about fighting in StarCraft II.

We've touched on this issue before, but in essence, when fighting, you should a) be moving your army as one large group and b) when the fighting starts, you should be engaging by attack moving your army into or just past your opponent's army.

Doing so guarantees that all of your combat units will be in the fight, and only *after* this has been done should you begin to micro abilities, individual groups of units, single units, focus fire targets, and so on.

In some cases, you may want to begin an engagement by using a few caster abilities, which is totally acceptable, just make sure that your whole army follows up with an attack (partly because sending lone, un-cloaked casters out to cast on an enemy army is a good way to get shot).

In smaller fights, you want to micro the entire group carefully, this is most noticeable in early engagements or raids, but when it comes to army vs army fights, trust in your units to do their work—too *much* of the wrong micro in a battle can be very damaging (eg, directing all of your Zealots to focus fire a unit at the back of a large fight will result in them trying to run around hostile enemy units that are happily tearing them up).

When it comes to microing specific forces in a larger battle, your priorities should be

1. Utilizing caster abilities

2. Using unit special abilities

3. Focus firing with long ranged units

In some cases, you can also retreat units that are being focus fired to draw your opponent's troops away while the remainder of your troops continue to attack the overly aggressive enemy.

Some units also have specific demands for your attention—Siege Tanks need to be sieged and unsieged as the fight moves, Hellions make best use of their speed when directly controlled, Stalkers with Blink must be controlled specifically, Roaches with Burrow must be microed to regenerate, and so on.

Others are much more fire and forget—Marines and Marauders can be stimmed and sent to attack move, only worrying about focus fire once they are fighting. Zealots with Charge or Zerglings with upgrades can be sent in on attack move to quickly hit the enemy line and start dealing damage.

Making good use of caster abilities from the Ghost, Raven, Sentry, High

PRO TIP!
Live Hydralisk
KIBONG KOOK

End Game

In end game, you can produce whichever units you want because you have a lot of resources coming in from many expansions. This is not the case in the early game. You have limited Minerals and Gas, so scout your opponent and build units that will counter your opponent.

Templar, and Infestor can all have a dramatic impact on the outcome of a battle, and learning to incorporate the use of these units into your army is important—as with upgrades, caster abilities act as a force multiplier for your army.

When choosing focus fire targets, sometimes you want to eliminate the most dangerous units in the enemies army first (air units, cloaked units, Detectors, anti-air units, single strong high tech units, casters, etc). Other times you may want to focus fire units with bonus damage, eg. focusing your Immortals on enemy Armored targets to deal the most damage possible.

Careful micro in large fights is very effective, but when you are just starting to learn how combat plays out in StarCraft II, remember—attack move it and forget it. Gradually increase your direct control of fights as you become more comfortable with the interactions of various units on the battlefield, and you can squeeze more efficiency out of each combat unit on the field.

PRO TIP!
Garimtoi
KIM DONGSU

3 Gateways, Fast Expo

This build order is similar to the previous one. The difference is that you summon a Nexus at your natural expansion right after having creating 1~2 Sentries. Your game can be very defensive, but if the Zerg player invests Zerglings and Roaches instead of Drones in the early game the Zerg user will be in trouble. If you choose to go into a long race as a Protoss player, you should think about producing almost all your units. With Sentry's Force Field and Guardian Shield you can focus on defense, while making an effort to dominate the air by producing Phoenix from 1~2 Stargates. Also, make Colossi to counter the huge Zerg rushes that will come. Wait for a chance to finish them until you have 3~4 Colossi. As Zerg will also be trying to finish it with one big rush, you should carry out yours sensitively and boldly.

DEFENSE

Defense is an extremely important part of your game. Every time your opponent makes a push on your main base or an expansion, you have to repel or destroy the invaders, preferably while suffering minimal damage to your army, your economy, and your base itself.

While defense is generally easier than offense, there are certain tactics that can help you no matter which race you are playing.

DEFENSE AND SCOUTING

It should go without saying, but when fighting a defensive battle, or when playing defensively in general, scouting becomes *more* important than when on offense, not less!

You need to know what your opponent is doing, and especially if he is attempting to expand. One of the largest dangers of sitting on defense is giving your opponent free reign to expand uncontested.

You also need to know what your opponent is teching towards, and where he is attacking you, because you can be assured that if you are sitting on defense with your army, your opponent will build siege breaking or bypassing tech and attack you, it's just a question of where and when, and being surprised while waiting on defense is not a winning strategy.

CHOKE POINTS

Funneling your opponent's ground forces into a narrow area is one of the easiest ways of defending against a ground force. This is true for all types of ground units, but especially true against melee or short range units; Zealots, Zerglings, Roaches, even Hellions to some extent.

When defending your base, you usually have the luxury of a single entrance to your base. On some maps, this may be a very narrow ramp, which is extremely easy to block off with buildings or troops set to Hold Position.

If the entrance is a bit wider, you may need to build more buildings across the open space to compress the opening.

Expansions typically have more access points than your main base, but many maps have a 'natural' expansion that is located right outside your main base, and may have a chokepoint that can be protected fairly easily.

Making use of ranged units behind a frontal wall of sturdier troops or buildings is the perfect combination for defending a chokepoint.

Area of effect abilities and units are also very powerful at defending chokepoints, as your opponent's force has no other option but to pass through the killing zone to reach your army.

Out in the field, you may not be able to make use of choke points, which is one reason why retreating to defend is often a better idea than engaging an enemy force you are uncertain you can defeat in a straight open field battle.

Protoss vs Zerg (Quick Nexus)

PRO TIP!
Mouz.White-Ra
OLEKSII KRUPNYK

Beating Zerg is too hard a task with a weak economy, so you should try to capture a second resource stack as soon as possible. After you order the first Pylon (near your expansion) and scout, place a Forge to close off the choke point as much as possible. The third building should be a Nexus. 50% of the time the Zerg will try to kill you or get through to your main base, so put down enough buildings so that no ugly little Zergling squeezes through. The benefit will be twofold since the Zerg is probably building Zerglings instead of workers. Your goal is simply to fend off their attack.

HIGH GROUND

While high ground in StarCraft II doesn't provide any mechanical benefit to your troops (ie, you don't gain a damage or evasion bonus for fighting from high ground), you **do** get the benefit of line of sight blocking.

Because units **must** have line of sight to attack, if you have ranged units of any type stationed on high ground, and your opponent cannot see that high ground, or get some sort of aerial scout or Scanner Sweep to spot your troops, you fire down freely on enemy forces without retaliation.

Enemy melee or very short ranged units can't retaliate against forces on high ground, even if they **do** have line of sight.

This makes units such as the Reaper, Colossus, or Stalkers with Blink very annoying to fight against, and any army using transports can drop off dangerous ranged units like Siege Tanks on otherwise unreachable high ground.

Make use of high ground on defense whenever possible. If there are routes that your opponent's ground force **must** take to reach your bases, station units on the ledges around that route and deal as much damage as possible before they can come to grips with your army.

In some cases, the enemy ground army may not be able to reach your forces on high ground at all, so unless they have air units or another way to attack your units, they may be forced to retreat and build an answer to your threat.

WALLING IN

As we mentioned in the base management section, walling in is simply blocking off the entrance to your choke with buildings, creating a wall that must be destroyed before an offensive ground force can break through.

Walling in is a typical tactic for Terran, and a common one for Protoss. Zerg lack the ability to do early game wall-ins (though they can wall in around the midgame due to Creep spread by Creep Tumors).

A wall allows your ranged units to fire at enemy units from behind a shield of buildings that can soak up much more damage than your early troops.

By adding a few defensive structures to a wall, you can make it disproportionately costly for your opponent to break through. Use Bunkers, Missile Turrets, and Photon Cannons at a wall to create a difficult obstacle for your enemy.

Keep in mind that while a wall-in can help to fend off early attacks, all armies gain access to means of bypassing chokepoints (or breaking through them) by the midgame at the latest, and Zerg actually have access to the earliest siege busting in the game with the Baneling.

A good wall-in should be used to defend with your army and then to counter-attack, or to buy you time to build a key technology, don't expect a wall to hold off a determined opponent indefinitely.

RAID RESPONSE

Having a small group of fast moving ground units or air units on a separate hotkey is a good idea if you know or suspect your opponent will attempt to raid your bases.

A small force may not be able to repel a full force aerial assault, or even a heavy drop, but it can buy you time for your forces to return to your base in time.

PATROLLING BASE DEFENSE

Making use of the Patrol command is particularly useful for Raid response, and you can make good use of it in two ways.

The first is to place several cheap military units on patrol around the outskirts of your base. The early warning these guards provide can alert you to an incoming enemy force, and give you more time to respond to a raiding force or aerial assault.

The second is to have a small secondary guard force of military units. It must be large enough to repel a very light raid or drop, but not large enough to significantly weaken your offensive force. Put this group on patrol in or very near your main base or your most important expansions.

Such a group will instantly pick up and attack any hostile raid force, and buy you even more time to get your main army back to defend. In some cases, you may be able to repulse a weak attack simply with the show of force from your 'rear guard' of military units.

The specific units you use for base patrol duty vary from race to race, but generally, units that have anti-air capability are a good choice, as they can help to protect against drop attacks, or aerial assaults.

Fast units or aerial units also make good picket troops, as they can spot incoming forces over a wider area of terrain.

The most important part about dealing with a raid is to not panic—get your workers to safety by quickly selecting them all with drag select or ctrl-click, move them to an area with friendly troops, or at the very least, away from the hostile forces.

Then micromanage your defensive troops until your army can return to provide relief. If you're still pumping out troops, be sure to move their rally points so they can group up before they get taken apart by the massed enemy forces—it's better to lose a few buildings or workers and retaliate in force than to lose all of your military units as they build *and* several buildings and workers.

RESOURCES

Spend the extracted resources as quickly as you can to produce units. If you have a lot of resources but not units, how will you attack or defend? In StarCraft II, you cannot exchange Minerals and Gas for cash, so make sure to create as many units as you can and win battles.

RACIAL RESPONSE

Protoss and Zerg have significant advantages for responding to raids—both can get military units on the field very quickly in response to a raid.

Protoss can warp in as many Gateway units as they have Warp Gates almost instantly, and Zerg can immediately begin building reactionary troops from all of their Hatcheries simultaneously, all rallied to the base under attack.

Zerg can also make use of the Nydus Network in the midgame to instantly ferry troops from one base to another, giving them a frightening level of mobility, as a new Nydus Worm can be created instantly beside a Zerg army, allowing it to travel from any point on the map to a friendly base in seconds.

*Remember when warping in units as Protoss to warp them in **away** from the enemy units—warping them beside enemy troops is a good way to lose the units before they have a chance to fight. If one wave of troops isn't enough to repel the attack, Chrono Boost your Warp Gates and wait for a second wave of warps before counter-attacking.*

Terran lack this fast military response ability, but they do have quite a few unique abilities.

Terrans can lift off buildings against ground forces, the Command Center and Planetary Fortress can bunker SCVs, their SCVs can repair each other and buildings, and they have defensive upgrades and more defensive structures than either the Protoss or the Zerg (and a Planetary Fortress that can defend itself!).

Remember that Terran Bunkers can be salvaged to return their full cost at any time, so don't hesitate to spread a few Bunkers around your bases, they are useful for fighting off attacks with just a few infantry, they can hide SCVs, and you can salvage them once they are no longer needed.

After the raid has been repelled, rebuild any lost buildings and get your workers back to work—don't forget to get 3 workers on each Vespene Geyser, it's easy to place them all on Minerals and forget about the Gas.

WORKER OVERBUILDING

Past 3 workers per Mineral patch, workers provide no economic benefit.

*However, if your worker lines are being raided heavily and constantly, and fixed defenses and a picket force simply aren't enough to stop worker harassment, you **can** build past the 3 worker mark, in an effort to keep your economy running at full speed even after a raid.*

However, don't do this overbuilding in the early or even early-mid game, you simply can't afford to waste the resources on units that take up Supply and provide you with literally no other benefit.

It's prudent to build some defenses to protect against raids, but don't fall into a besieged mentality—don't give your opponent free reign to expand while you spend an excessive amount of time and resources building up against another raid that may not come.

Similarly, never over-commit mobile military units to base defense because of a raid—your military **must** be used on offense to threaten, contain, and destroy your opponent's military and expansions, or you simply will not win a match.

PRO TIP!
Garimtoi
KIM DONGSU

2 Stargates

This build is appropriate when there is a long rush distance, or when you face a Zerg player who blocks an early rush attack the correct way. Just like 3 Gateways and Robotics Facility, or the 4 Gateways build, you must defend your entrance properly with 1 Gateway tech build in the early game, and produce 3~5 Phoenix from 2 Stargates to beat the Queen and as many Overlords as you can. You won't be able to finish with Phoenixes, so you should begin to hunt Drones while avoiding Spore Crawlers or Hydralisks. After the 2 Stargates are complete, construct Pylons near the enemy base and build 4 Gateways, then attack. This method easily transitions into a long race build order because you will know the location of your opponent's units and can expand safely. Continually scout the enemy base to see whether they are building Spires or not. Beware, because Overlords can spread Creep, you opponent could be secretly building Spires and 8~10 Mutalisks will devastate this build. I recommend that you not produce Void Ray as they have low mobility but high price.

WATCH YOUR WORKERS

There are three different ways you can be attacked by your opponent. He can hit your army, your base, or your workers.

Your army or your base are much better for you than your workers, as both give you a bit of time to respond. Buildings have plenty of hit points, and troops will fight back and you can suffer a few losses and still win a battle.

Your poor workers however, have no defenses, and are very weak, especcially against mid and late game raiding forces. It is *very* important that you develop a fast reaction to worker raids. The instant you see or hear your workers come under attack, drag select all of them and move them away from the enemy units.

You are going to take losses, this is unavoidable—don't worry about that, the point is to avoid losing ALL of your workers, rather than just some.

Workers that aren't harvesting are costing you *current* income, but they aren't costing you any future income, and it's better to suffer a stall in unit production than a stall in unit production *and* the cost and time of rebuilding your worker force.

Improving your reaction time to worker raids can *really* help you out in tough fights against an evenly matched opponent.

DEFENSE WITH A PURPOSE

It is important that when you are defending, it has a purpose. Simply having your army idling in your base while your opponent builds up and expands (or worse, bottles you into your own base) is not an effective tactic.

You generally need standing troops for two reasons, either to protect against a known incoming force, or to protect against any attack while you tech to a specific unit or upgrade.

If you are **not** defending to tech up, you should have your force on the offense, or at the very least, out protecting a fledgling expansion.

Scouting is critical when you are sitting on defense. If you hole up in your base with your army, you lose sight of your opponent, and you lose the ability to react effectively to the threats that they can present.

If you spend resources and tech upgrades creating a powerful ground force and your opponent blindsides you with an air force instead of a ground push, you're going to be hurting badly.

If you aren't defending to stop an incoming attack or to tech up quickly, you generally only want to be building up defensively if you lost an offensive engagement and you need the proximity to your base to turn the tide when they make a push against you.

RACE SPECIFIC DEFENSE

While general defensive strategies tend to apply to all races, each race certainly has specific units and abilities that are of particular use while fighting on defense.

TERRAN

Terran SCVs can repair any structure, or mechanical unit in the Terran army, and they do so for a very reasonable price (25% of the original cost of the unit or building, for fully repairing a unit or building).

SCVs also multiply their building speed with each SCV added to a repair job, so having multiple SCVs repairing a key structure on defense is always a good idea.

SCVs set to Autocast Repair also make great patrolling rebuilders. You can put a small group of SCVs on patrol near your army rally point, and any time you return from battle with damaged mechanized units, the SCVs will quickly patch them up to full health.

Terran are the only race that have an upgrade that provides an armor bonus to their *buildings*. Be sure to pick up this upgrade as you head for the midgame, it makes your buildings much more durable against low damage, fast attacking enemy units, and also magnifies the impact of repairing defensive structures.

Terran also have an upgrade that increases the range of their Missile Turrets, the Planetary Fortress, and both of the Raven's special abilities, the Auto-Turret and Point Defense Drone.

Finally, Terran have an upgrade that increases the cargo capacity of Bunkers by 2, and Command Center and Planetary Fortresses by 5.

All of these upgrades are useful on defense (and in the case of Bunker armor and cargo space, potentially on offense as well). Be sure to grab them as you approach the midgame, as they are all quite cheap.

As far as units go, the Siege Tank, Thor, Ghost, Banshee, and Raven can all be quite helpful on defense. Siege Tanks with Siege Mode active are a powerful defense against enemy ground assaults on your bases, and many players will hesitate to push an attack against a base that has Siege Tanks positioned near its chokepoint. The Thor has very strong anti-air capability, and a powerful ability that can destroy any tough opposing ground unit instantly (and it deals pretty heavy ground damage as well). Thors also have a large amount of health, and are prime targets when on defense to be repaired by a group of SCVs. The Ghost and Raven can make good use of their special abilities on defense, while the Ghost and Banshee can utilize their cloaking technology to punish any enemy push that doesn't have enough mobile Detectors with them.

Ghost EMP and Sniper Round are both helpful on defense (EMP is devastating against enemy Protoss ground forces), and the Raven Point Defense Drone and Seeker Missile are both very powerful defensive tools, as they can shut down your opponent's ranged damage, or deal massive damage to bunched up armies.

Ghost Nukes are generally too slow to use against an attacking force—save them for siege breaking or hitting worker lines against a distracted opponent.

Terran defensive buildings include the Bunker, the Missile Turret, and the Sensor Tower. All three are cheap and useful, and the Bunker can be salvaged, returning its cost in full. This makes early bunkers a very useful defensive building, as you can build a few as part of your wall, then simply salvage them when you're ready to push and you want the resources back. Bunkers require infantry inside them to actually deal any damage, but even a single Marine hidden inside can make your opponent hesitate to attack—he doesn't know how full that Bunker is!

Remember that SCVs can hide inside a bunker in a pinch, useful for fleeing from a worker raid.

Missile Turrets act as both your anti-air structure, and as your stationary Detector. Be sure to get Missile Turrets up in the mid-game near your worker lines and chokepoints.

Sensor Towers provide instant information on incoming enemy forces, so you should never be surprised by an incoming army while you have a tower active.

BURNING BUILDINGS

Terrans do have one unusual defensive **dis**advantage. Specifically, when any of their buildings drops below 33% health, they begin to burn down, at a rate of 3 health per second.

You can stop this burning by repairing with an SCV, but keep it in mind, if you don't start repairs on a critically damaged structure fast enough, it will burn down automatically!

Those contractors were maybe a bit too cheap.

PROTOSS

While Protoss lack many explicitly defensive upgrades or units, they do have several powerful abilities useful for defense.

First, the Protoss ability to warp Gateway units into existence anywhere in a Pylon power field is a very powerful defensive tool. Because unit creation with Warp Gates is 'front loaded', you can have the units *now* and wait for the cooldown after, rather than waiting for the units to build in the first place. Remember that you can Chrono Boost a Warp Gate on cooldown to speed up its recharge.

When warping in units on defense, do *not* warp them in near the enemy army, warping units are vulnerable while they warp in. Warp them in either near your troops, or out of line of sight of the enemy army, and wait until they finish warping in (5 seconds) to group them up and join the battle.

The High Templar's Feedback can be useful if your opponent brings dangerous casters, but Psionic Storm is downright lethal if your opponent has to push through a chokepoint to hit your base.

The Sentry's Guardian Shield, Force Field, and Hallucinate are *all* useful on defense, and Force Field can outright stop an attack for 15 seconds if you have a ramp chokepoint that can be blocked. With any ranged units present, your opponent's army will simply have to suffer the hits until the Force Field wears off (and then you cast another).

With enough Sentries, you can create a chokepoint *anywhere* on a map, even out in the open.

Hallucinate is useful in many situations, but on defense, simply creating extra decoy defenders forces your opponent to waste time in combat targeting useless illusions. Generally, Force Field should be used first, but if you have sufficient Sentries with enough Energy, a large hallucinated force can be created, tipping the scales in your favor—just be careful about using Hallucinate if your opponent has mobile Detectors with his army.

Guardian Shield is much more fire and forget, much like the Terran caster abilities—use it against Terran armies to greatly reduce Marine damage, and use it against Protoss or Zerg armies consisting of large numbers of Stalkers, Sentries, Roaches, or Hydralisks.

Finally, the Protoss Mothership is a very powerful defensive unit (and of course, offensive!). With its ability to perform a Mass Recall on your army and Vortex most of an enemy army out of existence, it can instantly tip the scales of a defensive fight, not to mention its ability to cloak your entire army and base!

As far as the Protoss units and buildings go, few of them are as explicitly defensive in nature as the Terran force. Dark Templar can be useful on defense, if you can destroy your enemies mobile Detectors, you force his ground army to retreat—though beware, this won't work if part of his offensive force is aerial. Protoss Photon Cannons act as anti ground and anti-air turrets *and* stationary Detectors, so they are quite useful both for protecting worker lines and chokepoints.

Zerg have almost no explicitly defensive options in their army, but they do have several unique advantages that still make their base defense quite strong.

First, Zerg Creep increases the movement speed of all Zerg ground forces by 30%. This allows you to respond more quickly to any attack on Zerg home turf, and in the case of the already fast speed enhanced Zerglings, they become a lightning fast raid reaction force. Be sure to spread Creep around your bases with Creep Tumors from your Queens, it can pay off in the midgame on defense.

Next, all Zerg ground units have access to Burrow once you reach Lair tech. Drones can instantly burrow to hide from a raiding force, and your army can burrow to wait for reinforcements either en route or being created at your Hatcheries.

And speaking of traveling, the Nydus Network is an extremely powerful defensive tool. By creating a Nydus Network that spans all your bases, you can instantly move your army from the frontlines to any base simply by creating a Nydus Worm near your army.

Remember that it takes time to spawn a new Nydus Worm, and that Worms are more fragile than the Nydus Network, so be sure to create actual Networks in your bases, and save the Worms for moving your army in from the field.

The Zerg Queen is an important early-game defensive unit. With both a short ranged ground attack and a reasonably strong anti-air attack, the Queen can be very helpful in fending off early pushes or raids. In addition, once you have two Queens up, they can make use of their Transfusion ability to heal one another, extending their combat surviv-ability. Remember that a Queen can burrow to hide from an attack if necessary, Queens are slow to build and vital to the Zerg econ and military, so don't throw them away on defense whenever possible!

All of the Zerg Infestor's abilities are useful on defense, and a small group of Infestors with enough Energy and burrow can stall a larger enemy force long enough for reinforcements to arrive.

Neural Parasite can be very useful for grabbing key enemy units and doesn't expose your Infestors to direct retaliation.

The Overseers' Infested Terran ability can spawn enough units to fight off a small enemy force. A small group of Infested Terrans can be used to freeze a group of raiders in place, giving your workers time to escape.

Zerg defensive structures consist of the Spine and Spore Crawlers. The Spine Crawler is anti-ground only, while the Spore Crawler is anti-air only, and acts as your Detector. Unlike other stationary Detectors however, the Spore (and Spine) Crawlers can move! By 'uprooting' your Crawlers, your defensive structures temporarily transform into a mobile unit, but while uprooted Spore Crawlers lose Detection. While not es-pecially fast, this can be extremely useful to concentrate your defensive structures wherever they are most needed! Crawlers can survive off Creep and uprooted, but are extremely slow. You should only move them short distances between bases if you need to do so.

Finally, the Zerg method of unit creation from their Hatcheries is well suited to responding to a defensive need, as all of your accumulated Larvae can be converted into an army that is generated simultane-ously, as long as you have the resources for it.

TRAINING

If you've made it this far, you should have more than enough material to chew on and practice on Battle.net, but we'd like to leave you with a few thoughts about focusing your training to improve your skills.

There are several distinct areas of StarCraft II play that can see great progress with just a bit of time invested in training them specific

UI AND HOTKEYS

The most basic area of the game is almost one of the most important. You *must* learn to control your base and your troops with the least amount of effort.

Making good use of all of the UI features available to you lets you spend more time on interesting and important decisions, and less time getting new military units into groups, using your economic boosters, building structures, or checking on your economy.

In battle, UI mastery is vital, you need to be able to control your troops well, and control them quickly. Once the fighting starts in a StarCraft II match, it doesn't take long to finish! The less time it takes you to execute orders in battle, the better.

BUILD ORDER TIMING

Build orders will be constantly tweaked and fiddled with for years to come, but the important point here is simple: develop an early game build order that you are comfortable with, and execute it perfectly every match.

You might have a slightly different build order for a given racial matchup, and you might be experimenting with a new build order, or a tweak to an existing one, but the point remains the same: your early build should be smooth and automatic.

ECONOMIC AND MILITARY GROWTH

Getting your economy up and running is critically important, and learning when to expand your military growth and to claim new expansions are all critical aspects of any StarCraft II match.

Simply knowing how many workers you should have in a given base is an important first step, and learning to build up your military and your military production smoothly will *always* help you in *any* match.

Never forget to develop anti-air and anti-cloak technology in the midgame.

SCOUTING

We've said it over and over, and we won't stop now: You *must* learn to scout constantly, until it is an automatic reflex.

When you start feeling uncomfortable because you haven't seen what your opponent has been doing in the last 30 seconds, you'll know you're feeling uncomfortable for all the *right* reasons.

COMBAT CONTROL

Controlling your troops in battle is obviously a vital skill, but trust us, for your early matches, building up a good sized military that has been properly upgraded and sending it as a single large group on attack move is a great place to begin.

And one more time, don't take your eyes off your army when you begin an assault or a defensive battle!

As you gain experience, you should be practicing finer and finer details of combat micro. Practice dancing with ranged units, especially fast ranged units. Remember, you can right click to move around. Focus fire key targets in battle. Use ranged units in larger engagements, always focus fire in smaller engagements. Retreat units that are being focused to draw your opponent's army out of position. Utilize caster abilities the instant a fight begins, and throughout the battle as needed. Make use of unit special abilities, as the fight begins if they are fire and forget, or throughout the fight if they require constant attention. Make use of the mobility of fast units, cliffwalkers, and air units to harass and destroy your opponent's army.

In small, early game engagements, don't forget to use your workers to fight, SCV repair, Bunkers, Command Center load, Zealot hold position, and your Queen to fight off early game raids.

Practice raids of all sorts. Raid with very few units, try transport and Nydus backdoor raids. Practice aerial raids. Go for the workers and core structures first, later, learn what tech buildings to target to cripple your opponent's build.

Practice fast, aggressive pushes. Don't wait for your opponent to hit you, get out there and fight. You may lose games this way, but by seeing why you lost, you can refine your offensive timing and control, and gradually develop your offensive skills.

Not every battle should begin in the midgame, and each time a new technology hits the battlefield, there is a window of opportunity for you to inflict the most damage before your opponent can create a counter. Be the player pushing that advantage!

PRO TIP!

Garimtoi
KIM DONGSU

The Race in Absolute and Relative Numbers

The most difficult situation for a Zerg player is keeping Hellions in check in early game, then following the Terran player's switch to a Biological build after going for an early expansion. A new or uninformed Zerg player will have difficulty in making the right counter combination. In this case, the answer is to have superior resource gathering.

The Zerg is a race where 'quantity' is most important, regardless of whether the quantity is absolute or relative.

SPARRING

*Unit micro and combat is the one area of StarCraft II that you **cannot** practice alone. You can build up a base, expand, and practice build orders alone, but you can't practice real combat (even against the AI, which does not behave like a human in battle!).*

Because you will build up your base every single match that you play, it is easy to have a very polished build order execution and early game, but a very weak mid or late game, and poor to average unit control—not due to lack of skill, but simply due to lack of practice!

The best way to remedy this is to practice in private matches with friends. Experiment with unit combinations. Test out abilities. See what units should be microed directly in a battle for maximum effectiveness. Practice dancing.

*With unlimited resources to build units, you can try out all sorts of battles, large and small, with all types of units and upgrade combinations, and you can do so **much** more quickly than you could by simply playing matches normally.*

If you don't have a sparring partner handy, try to get into larger matches on Battle.net. 2v2, 3v3, 4v4, or FFA games all have very different buildup and combat than 1v1 games, and they can be a good chance to experiment with different army sizes, and good practice for expanding aggressively and managing a large economy and military infrastructure.

Also, expect custom maps to show up online that will let you participate in army battles with little or no base management. These can be very useful training tools for practicing your unit control!

REPLAYS

Finally, replays are one of the most useful tools that you can use for improving your game.

- Lost a match? Watch the replay and find out why. Don't understand why you lost? Post the replay online and ask for advice.

- Losing to a specific tactic? Ask around online and find replays from players beating it.

- Having trouble with a specific racial matchup? Look for replays from good players fighting that specific match.

- Want to learn different styles of play? Find replay packs from top players and examine how they execute their chosen strategies.

Replays are most useful for seeing **why** you lost a match, and indeed, you can usually learn more from a loss than a win. In cases where you are examining a close match that you did win, see if you can spot the key mistake (or mistakes) that your opponent made that let you win.

If they are simple execution errors, they may not be valuable, but if they expose a racial weakness or a timing weakness in a particular racial matchup, you can make use of that information in the future.

In the very best matches, neither player makes significant errors. It tends to come down more to racial matchups and the timing and usage of specific units and abilities. When you reach that level of play, and are up against opponent's of equal caliber, you should be sharing your own replays!

Remember: StarCraft II will constantly change over time due to patches and expansions, so learning is a constant process. If you take a long break and return to the game, you may find that old tactics and strategies no longer work, due balance changes, or simply due to the shifting metagame on Battle.net.

REPLAY FEATURES

Replays in StarCraft II have all of the basic featuers you'd expect in any modern RTS, including time controls and different player viewpoints, but they also have two very useful and unique features.

The first is a dropdown box in the top left of the screen that lets you monitor anything from the production of each player to their income levels.

You can use these displays to see exactly what each player is building at each stage of a game, how strong their economy is, and how and where their resources are invested.

The second useful and extremely impressive feature is the ability to **rewind** replays. Once you have watched a replay to any point, you can then rewind it to any earlier point in the replay!

This is fantastically useful for carefully examining a very close game, as you can skip around in a replay to any point and see how an early decision impacts the match later.

CONTROLLING EVERYTHING

One of the most difficult aspects of SC2 multiplayer is figuring out what you should focus your attention on. A common mistake for new players is to spend too much time on details that simply do not matter in the larger overall battle.

Remember that your attention is the most valuable resource in StarCraft II, far more than Minerals or Vespene Gas. Where you choose to spend your personal resources in any given match is the most important decision you can make.

No player can perfectly manage every aspect of a StarCraft II match, and it is the process of learning to give your attention to the **most important** detail at any given moment that improves your skills.

In any given game of StarCraft II, you must:

- Hit your build order perfectly
- Build up your economy and military and supply constantly
- Increase your military production
- Upgrade your units
- Expand to new bases
- Scout constantly
- Raid enemy workers
- Fight battles with your military while microing the troops in those fights.

It is a bit much to take in all at once! But those are all the areas that you must manage in a match of StarCraft II.

When you are still learning to play the game, we strongly recommend that you simply pick one area and focus on it until you are comfortable with it.

Over time, as you learn to manage each of the aspects of a match, you will find that certain processes that were at first overwhelming are now automatic. As each area of the game becomes more muscle memory and less active thought, you can focus your attention more keenly on areas that separate new players from intermediate players, and intermediate players from experts.

Remember: sticking to a plan, even if it turns out to be a bad one, is better than simply randomly building units and buildings and hoping to win the eventual battle with your opponent. When you **are** executing a plan, even if it ends badly, you can watch a replay and figure out what went wrong, then adjust your tactics and try again!

TERRAN ARMY

The Terran army is flexible and complex,
much like the humans that populate known Terran space.

Their army has the advantage of strong defenses, allowing you to more easily defend your base against early attacks, and to protect your expansions with sturdy Bunkers, watchful turrets, and powerful Siege Tanks. Humans are an adaptable race, and their selection of units reflects this trait. Even their buildings may have multiple abilities, along with unique traits not found in the Protoss or Zerg structures. Most effective Terran armies consist of a complimentary mix of units, along with a handful of specific support units, designed to either assist the primary combat troops, or to cripple your opponent's army.

TERRAN ADVANTAGES

Terrans have several unique racial benefits; taking full advantage of them will help you in any battle with the Terran force.

Defensive Upgrades

The Terran army is the only race in the game to have access to specific defensive upgrades that benefit their structures. Purchased from the Engineering Bay, these upgrades increase the durability and cargo capacity of your structures, as well as the range of Terran turrets.

Defensive Structures

Where Protoss have one defensive building and Zerg have two, the Terran have access to *three*, and a Command Center upgrade that transforms an expansion into an armored fortress with a powerful cannon!

The Terran Bunker is especially notable, as it is useful and powerful on defense or offense, and can greatly increase the strength of even small numbers of infantry when fighting against a superior force.

Repair

Terran SCVs can repair all Mechanical units and structures, greatly increasing their durability while defending, and allowing for field repairs of mechanized armies.

Lift Off

All Terran military buildings and the Command Center and Orbital Command can literally lift off, slowly flying through space with built in thrusters.

Terran buildings don't move especially fast while lifted, but this allows you to easily buy time against an enemy ground force, and you can use the ability to lift off to expand freely to island expansions, or use large, sturdy buildings as slow moving scouts for your army.

Terran also have the completely unique ability to expand freely to an island expansion without having to build a transport of any kind. In fact, it is even possible to load up your initial 5 SCVs and move to a different starting location if you wish to do so!

Pop-up Supply Depots

The Terran Supply Depot can be raised or lowered into the ground. This allows friendly ground forces to pass it, while blocking out hostile enemy forces. You can make use of this (in combination with lift off) to create a wall of buildings at your base chokepoint to prevent enemy ground forces from getting inside your base to scout or raid.

Modular Buildings

Terran military structures can have Tech Labs or Reactors attached to them, and any military structure can make use of any Tech Lab or Reactor.

Terran Reactors allow any military building to produce two basic units at a time, while Tech Labs enable more advanced units, and access to research upgrades for the attached military structure.

You can make use of lift off in combination with the modularity of Terran military buildings to your advantage—create a Tech Lab or Reactor early on a Barracks. You can then lift it off and let your first Factory or Starport that hits the field make use of it immediately!

Finally, Terran Command Centers can be upgraded into Orbital Commands, which have powerful economic and recon abilities, or the Planetary Fortress, a tougher Command Center that cannot lift off, but has heavier armor and a turret mounted cannon!

Scanner Sweep

Terran reconnaissance is unsurpassed, with the ability to instantly scan any area on the map, you can keep tabs on enemy base buildup, and instantly reveal Cloaked or Burrowed units in a pinch.

TERRAN DISADVANTAGES

Upgrades

Terran have three distinct upgrade lines, requiring them to spend more money and time to fully upgrade their army.

Because your Barracks, Factory, and Starport units all use a different weapon and armor upgrade line, your army will be overall more effective if you focus on building an army from troops belonging to one of the three production lines.

Never hesitate to build units from any production line, but do try to research the *most* upgrades for the units you will be fielding in the greatest numbers.

Another issue with Terran upgrades is that many Terran units have crucial abilities locked with upgrades—Stimpacks, Siege Tech, Cloak, Yamato Cannon, etc., all are vital for their respective units, and must be acquired as soon as possible. This raises the Gas cost and time commitment for fielding any one particular unit at full effectiveness.

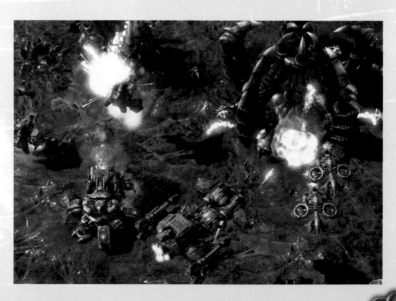

Burn Down

Terran structures will begin to burn down at 33% health, at a rate of 3 per second. Be sure to repair any heavily damaged buildings, or they will burn down!

Military Production Speed

Terran military production can be the slowest of the three races, because in spite of their Reactor technology, Zerg can produce waves of units from all of their Hatcheries simultaneously, while Protoss can warp in units nearly instantly with a bonus to their production speed, and use Chrono Boost to further boost the speed of their reinforcements. To compensate, you must *constantly* produce new units from your military structures.

Complexity

Terran have by far the most complex army in terms of ability management. With two exceptions, every unit in their army has at least one activated ability (and the two without activated abilities require direct micro to perform well!).

Even Terran military production is more complex than Protoss or Zerg, as each of their buildings can have three states (unmodified, Tech Lab, or Reactor), requiring the usage of Tab for cycling through subgroups when you are handling multiple military buildings on one hotkey.

TERRAN UNIT ROLES

The Terran have three units that benefit from strong dancing micro, the Marauder, Reaper, and Hellion can all be used to good effect against slower enemy forces.

Almost the entire Terran army benefits from careful focus fire micro, as *all* of their units are ranged. (Outside their two workers, the SCV and MULE.)

- The Terran mobile Detector is the Raven, while their stationary Detector is the Missile Turret. Orbital Command Scanner Sweep and Ghost EMP both act as temporary Detector abilities. (Note that a Ghost's EMP only reveals cloaked units that suffer Shield damage.)

- The Terran Siege Tank in Siege Mode, the Hellion, and the Raven Seeker Missile provide the Terran with area of effect damage. And technically, the Nuke is the ultimate in area of effect damage!

- Terran anti-air comes from the Marine, Ghost, Thor, Viking, Battlecruiser, Missile Turret, and (in a pinch) the Raven Auto-Turret or Seeker Missile.

- Terran siege breakers are the Siege Tank in Siege Mode, Battlecruiser Yamato Cannon and the Ghost Nuke.

- Terran air has very average movement speeds, but quite a bit of flexibility, with more choices available than either the Protoss or Zerg.

UNIT MIXES

Marines and Marauders work quite well together, and even better with Medivacs or Ghosts added as support units. Be sure to pick up Stimpacks.

Marauders and Hellions make a very dangerous ground force, as both Hellions and Marauders can dance effectively, and between the two, both Light and Armored units suffer bonus damage. Just watch out for enemy air!

A small group of SCVs should accompany any significant Mechanical force while on offense, their ability to Repair can greatly increase the durability of your tough units such as the Thor and Battlecruiser, and extend the lifespan of your lighter Mechanical units.

INFANTRY UPGRADES

All Infantry Weapon and Armor upgrades can be purchased at the Engineering Bay.

VEHICLE UPGRADES

All Vehicle Weapon and Armor upgrades can be purchased at the Armory.

AIR UPGRADES

All Air Weapon and Armor upgrades can be purchased at the Armory.

LEGEND

Minerals		Supply		
Vespene Gas		Build Time		

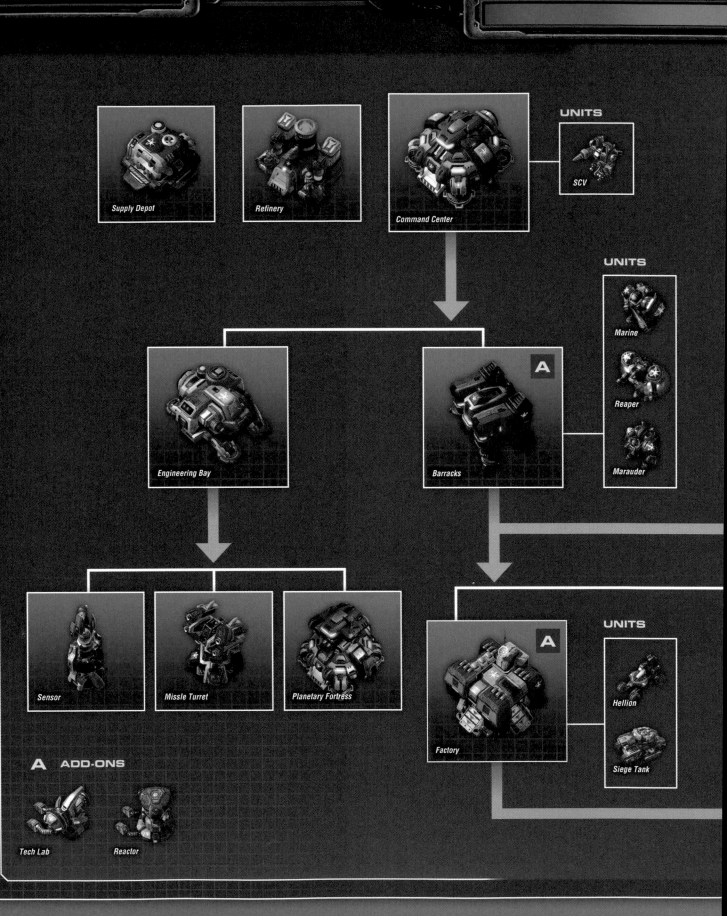

UNITS

SCV

Supply Depot

Refinery

Command Center

UNITS

Marine

Reaper

Marauder

Engineering Bay

Barracks **A**

Sensor

Missle Turret

Planetary Fortress

UNITS

Factory **A**

Hellion

Siege Tank

A ADD-ONS

Tech Lab

Reactor

TERRAN TECH TREE

Orbital Command

Bunker

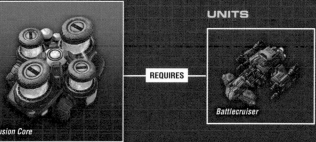
Fusion Core

UNITS

REQUIRES

Battlecruiser

Ghost Academy

REQUIRES

UNITS

Ghost

Starport

UNITS

Banshee · Raven · Viking · Medivac

Armory

REQUIRES

UNITS

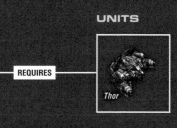
Thor

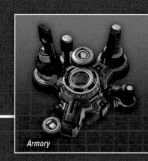

SCV

COST:

 50   0   17   1

BUILT FROM:	BUILD REQUIREMENTS:	UPGRADES:
Command Center	NONE	NONE

The ability to repair is one of the Terran army's main strengths. SCVs can repair defensive Missile Turrets and Bunkers, buildings used to block choke points, or mechanized units, all while under attack, giving Terran buildings much greater durability in battle.

Multiple SCVs can (and should) be used to repair critical structures under attack. This forces your opponent to deal with the SCVs directly, and in many cases, you can then simply micro an SCV under fire away and return when they shift targets.

To repair a fully damaged structure or unit, it costs 25% of the original cost—not a bad deal, and if your repair target is lightly damaged, the cost is proportionally less.

Multiple SCVs increase the rate of repair in a totally linear manner—ten SCVs repairing an Orbital Fortress under attack are ten times as fast as a single SCV—and there is no additional cost for repairing more quickly!

WEAPON STATISTICS

Weapon	Damage	Attacks	Attack Speed	Range	Targets
Fusion Cutter	5	1	1.50	Melee	Ground

UNIT STATISTICS

Health	Energy	Armor	Movement Speed	Acceleration	Line of Sight	Size
45	No	0	2.81	Yes	8	1

UNIT TYPE

Light	Armored	Biological	Mechanical	Psionic	Massive	Structure

The Space Construction Vehicle is a sturdy builder unit with the unique ability to repair structures and mechanical units—including other SCVs!

REPAIR
Hot Key: R

Effect: Repairs damaged Mechanical units or Structures at the cost of resources

Cost	Range	Radius	Autocast
Resources	0	0	Yes

MULE

COST:

BUILT FROM:	BUILD REQUIREMENTS:	UPGRADES:
Orbital Command	*Orbital Command*	**NONE**

MULEs only last for 90 seconds, but while active, they harvest Minerals at an amazingly accelerated rate, greatly boosting Terran Mineral income while active.

Consequently, all available Orbital Command Energy should be used on MULEs as much as possible, as using Scanner Sweep drains your own economy each time it is used.

Remember that you can create a MULE directly on a Mineral patch to begin harvesting instantly, and a MULE can also be called down *anywhere* you have line of sight. While generally Scanner Sweep is a more effective scout, you could use a MULE as a ground scout if you really wanted to.

MULEs *can* repair friendly Mechanical units and structures, so you could call down a MULE on the battlefield to fix a critical unit if needed.

MULEs cannot harvest Vespene Gas, only Minerals (whether Rich Mineral or normal).

WEAPON STATISTICS

Weapon	Damage	Attacks	Attack Speed	Range	Targets
None					

UNIT STATISTICS

Health	Energy	Armor	Movement Speed	Acceleration	Line of Sight	Size
60	No	0	2.81	Yes	8	1

UNIT TYPE

Light	Armored	Biological	Mechanical	Psionic	Massive	Structure

The Terran MULE isn't a traditional worker, as it is created by making use of the Orbital Command Center's Calldown: MULE ability.

🔧 REPAIR
Hot Key: R

Effect: Repairs damaged Mechanical units or Structures at the cost of resources

Cost	Range	Radius	Autocast
Resources	0	0	Yes

MARINE

COST: 50 0 25 1

BUILT FROM:	BUILD REQUIREMENTS:	UPGRADES:
Barracks	NONE	Barracks Tech Lab

The Marine is a solid basic unit, one that becomes extremely dangerous in large groups, as its ranged attack allows for powerful focus fire, something the Zealot and Zergling cannot manage as easily.

In exchange however, the Marine is quite weak individually, and very vulnerable to area of effect damage. Keep your marines away from splash damage or area attacks such as Siege Tanks, Colossi, or Baneling packs.

The Marine works well in large groups, but it works even better when it is part of a mixed ground force.

Because Marines are cheap and only cost Minerals, it is strongly recommend that you have at least one Barracks with a Reactor *constantly* producing Marines, basically throughout the entire game. Quickly replenishing the frequent losses Marines suffer is very important.

WEAPON STATISTICS

Weapon	Damage	Attacks	Attack Speed	Range	Targets
C-14 Gauss Rifle	6 (+1)	1	0.86	5	Air/Ground

UNIT STATISTICS

Health	Energy	Armor	Movement Speed	Acceleration	Line of Sight	Size
45 (55)	No	0	2.25 (3.37)	No	9	1

UNIT TYPE

Light	Armored	Biological	Mechanical	Psionic	Massive	Structure

The Terran Marine forms the core of the Terran ground force, weak individually, strong in numbers.

UPGRADES		COST			EFFECT
Upgrade	Requirement				
Stimpack	None	100	100	140	Grants Marines and Marauders Stimpack ability
Combat Shield	None	100	100	110	Gives Marines +10 Health

COMBAT SHIELD

Combat Shields provide a much needed health increase for all marines, giving them slightly more than 22% bonus health. Given Marines low starting health, if you're planning on using Marines in any significant numbers, be sure to pick up this upgrade.

Combat Shields are lower priority than Stimpacks, but should be picked up soon after if you are using a ground force with Marines mixed in. Combat Shields are also important because they act to counteract the initial damage of Stimpack usage.

Combat Shields are particularly important to keep pace with enemy upgrades and higher tech units as the game progresses, as they can allow your Marines to survive one or two more hits in battle.

STIMPACK
Hot Key: T

Effect: Boosts movement and attack speeds by 50%

Cost	Range	Radius	Autocast
10 Health	0	0	No

Stimpacks boost Marine movement and attack speed by 50%, and increase their threat level significantly.

If you're using Marines in any significant numbers, you should *always* make acquiring Stimpacks an early game priority, possibly even delaying your first major push until they finish researching.

Stimpacks do deal damage to Marines, but the increased damage output is almost always worth it. Unless you're re-pelling a light base raid, in any sort of real engagement, you should always trigger Stimpacks as you begin the fight.

MARAUDER

COST:

 100   25   30   2

BUILT FROM:	BUILD REQUIREMENTS:	UPGRADES:
Barracks	*Attached Tech Lab*	*Barracks Tech Lab*

A strong anti-Armored unit, the Marauder also slows units hit with its Concussion Grenades, allowing retreating units to be picked off with ease, and many ground units to be kited and killed with dancing micro. Concussion Grenade hits slow enemy units by 50%, so it is not difficult to dance Marauders out of range of enemy units, especially if you outnumber them.

The Marauder's grenades are anti-ground only, so a force consisting of only Marauders is vulnerable to aerial assault. When mixed with Marines, Marauders compliment the Marines anti-air and good massed focus fire damage with their stronger defenses and slowing grenades.

If your opponent is massing a large force of Armored units and shows no signs of going air, increase the percentage of Marauders in your ground force to compensate. Marauders have no problems dealing with almost any roughly cost-equivalent ground force if it consists of mostly Armored units.

Take advantage of the Marauder's slowing attack—you can kite hostile units that are melee only or too short ranged to bring their fire to bear while you constantly micro your Marauders out of range.

WEAPON STATISTICS

Weapon	Damage	Attacks	Attack Speed	Range	Targets
Concussive Shells	10 +10 vs Armored (+1/+1)	1	1.50	6	Ground

UNIT STATISTICS

Health	Energy	Armor	Movement Speed	Acceleration	Line of Sight	Size
125	No	1	2.25 (3.37)	No	10	2

UNIT TYPE

Light	Armored	Biological	Mechanical	Psionic	Massive	Structure

The burly Marauder provides some much needed backbone to the Terran infantry.

UPGRADES		COST			EFFECT
Upgrade	**Requirement**				
Stimpack	None	100	100	140	Grants Marines and Marauders Stimpack ability
Concussive Shells	None	50	50	60	Upgrades the Marauder weapons to slow down opponents

STIMPACK
Hot Key: T

Effect: Boosts movement and attack speeds by 50%

Cost	Range	Radius	Autocast
20 Health	0	0	No

Stimpacks do double duty for the Terran army, boosting not only the Marines, but also all Marauders. As with Marines, Marauders receive a 50% movement and attack speed boost while the drugs are active.

Marauders take slightly more damage per use, but they have larger health pools to begin with, so this is less of an issue than it is for Marines. This upgrade is very important if you are planning on using Marauders in any significant numbers.

CONCUSSIVE SHELLS

Effect: Slows targets by 50% for 1.5 seconds

Cost	Range	Radius	Autocast
Passive	6	0	No

REAPER

COST:

 50   50   45   1

BUILT FROM:	BUILD REQUIREMENTS:	UPGRADES:
Barracks	Attached Tech Lab	Tech Lab

Reapers deal heavy damage to all structures, and a small group of them left unhindered can level a base in very short order. A large group of them can destroy a key structure so quickly that a response force cannot stop them.

Reapers cliffjumping should be exploited to the fullest—on any map that has many small ledges, you can hide Reapers from enemy ground forces easily, attacking them from above, or simply escaping retaliation and waiting to strike again. On many maps, their cliffjumping also allows them to raid main bases very early in the game, and rushing straight for Reapers to hit your opponents economy early is a viable tactic.

In the mid-game and later, you need to be very careful with Reaper groups, not because they are excessively expensive, but because they are both slow to build and very frail. Their inability to target air units also renders them at risk from any mobile air force that your opponent fields, as their cliffjumping can no longer protect them.

Reapers can also be fairly effective against enemy units that are slower than them, *if* they are carefully microed to take advantage of their speed and cliffjumping. They're too fragile to simply attack move and hope for the best.

WEAPON STATISTICS

Weapon	Damage	Attacks	Attack Speed	Range	Targets
P-45 Gauss Pistol	4 +5 vs Light (+1/+0)	2	1.10	4.5	Ground

UNIT STATISTICS

Health	Energy	Armor	Movement Speed	Acceleration	Line of Sight	Size
50	No	0	2.95 (3.84)	No	9	1

UNIT TYPE

Light	Armored	Biological	Mechanical	Psionic	Massive	Structure

The Reaper deals excellent damage to light units of all types, and due to their Jet Packs, they can perform lightning raids on lightly defended expansions.

UPGRADES		COST			EFFECT
Upgrade	Requirement				
Nitro Packs	None	100	100	100	Increases Reaper movement speed by 0.89

NITRO PACKS

Reaper Nitro Packs permanently increase Reaper movement speed. This makes them even more dangerous for lightning raids against expansions, worker lines, and key tech buildings.

If you are planning on using Reapers in significant numbers throughout the game, be sure to pick up this upgrade, but otherwise, don't spend the resources or Tech Lab time on it early in a match.

JET PACK

Effect: Allows Reapers to jump up and down cliffs

Cost	Range	Radius	Autocast
Passive	0	0	No

Hot Key:

G

GHOST

COST:

 150 150 40 2

BUILT FROM:

Barracks

BUILD REQUIREMENTS:

Ghost Academy

Attached Tech Lab

UPGRADES:

Ghost Academy

The Ghost is generally most effective when used in small numbers to supplement an existing army, as they are too fragile, expensive, and time consuming to develop to be used in isolation.

The Ghost also has access to the mighty Tac Nuke Strike, allowing the Terran forces to call down nuclear fire on their foes.

In some cases, you may not want to not deploy Ghosts to the field until you have researched Cloak. Nukes are optional (though not actually very expensive to equip!), but Cloaking gives Ghosts increased survivability, giving you time to make full use of their abilities.

The other major benefit is delaying your opponent's time to react to the Cloak, if they don't have Detection of some sort on the battlefield, your Ghosts cannot be stopped, and you *will* get full use out of their abilities (not to mention being able to simply pick off any enemies who can't spot them).

Ghosts are expensive units in terms of Gas cost, especially if you purchase their upgrades. Consequently, you should field small numbers of them as support for your primary army, don't try to build a force consisting solely of Ghosts!

WEAPON STATISTICS

Weapon	Damage	Attacks	Attack Speed	Range	Targets
C-10 Canister Rifle	10 +10 vs Light (+1/+1)	1	1.50	6	Air/Ground

UNIT STATISTICS

Health	Energy	Armor	Movement Speed	Acceleration	Line of Sight	Size
100	Yes	0	2.25	No	11	1

UNIT TYPE

Light	Armored	Biological	Mechanical	Psionic	Massive	Structure

The Terran Ghost is a specialist unit, capable of utilizing powerful Cloaking technology, and equipped with several potent special abilities.

UPGRADES		COST			
Upgrade	Requirement				EFFECT
Personal Cloaking	None	150	150	120	Grants Ghost Cloak ability
Moebius Reactor	None	100	100	80	Increases Ghost starting Energy by 25
Arm Silo with Nuke	None	100	100	60	Arms Silo with a Tactical Nuke

PERSONAL CLOAKING

Personal Cloaking enables the Ghost's ability to Cloak. In some situations, you may want this researched before you field any Ghosts, but in others, it is perfectly acceptable to field Ghosts without any Cloak technology, as they can accompany your army and still have time to utilize their abilities.

MOEBIUS REACTOR

The Moebius Reactor increases the Ghost's initial Energy by 25. This may not sound like much, but Energy regenerates quite slowly in StarCraft II, and the extra initial Energy allows you to make use of more Ghost abilities.

Don't pick this upgrade up early, but if you are using Ghosts throughout a match, do research it before you have built too many Ghosts.

ARM NUKE

In order for a Ghost to launch a Nuke, a Ghost Academy must first be armed with one! Each Ghost Academy can store a single Nuke, so if you find yourself using them heavily, building more than one as you head into the mid game is advisable.

Abilities

SNIPER ROUND
Hot Key: R

Effect: Deals 45 damage to a Biological target. Ignores Armor.

Cost	Range	Radius	Autocast
25 Energy	10	0	No

With its low Energy cost and fairly high damage output, Snipe allows you to pick off Biological targets with considerable speed if you have more than one Ghost making use of this ability.

Even 2 to 3 Ghosts in a battle can make short work of targets such as Terran Marines, Zerg Hydralisks or Mutalisks, or Protoss High or Dark Templar.

CLOAK
Hot Key: C

Effect: Cloaks Ghost while active

Cost	Range	Radius	Autocast
25 Energy, 0.9 Energy per second	0	0	No

The Ghost's Cloak allows it to move within range of an unaware army and make full use of its abilities. Against an army or base without Detection present, the Ghost is free to pick off helpless troops or workers without fear of retaliation.

Because a Ghost's Cloak takes Energy both to activate and to maintain (25 to activate, 0.9 per second), it should only be used for brief periods of time, just before using its other abilities on an enemy army, or while scouting in enemy terrain.

Once your opponent begins fielding mobile Detectors, and building Detectors in their bases, be very careful about sending out Ghosts unescorted, Cloaked or no.

EMP ROUND
Hot Key: E

Effect: Deals 100 Shield damage, drains all Energy, reveals Cloaked units for 10 seconds

Cost	Range	Radius	Autocast
75 Energy	10	1.5	No

The Ghost's EMP is a devastatingly powerful weapon against the Protoss army, as it deals heavy damage to Shields within its area of effect. The total damage dealt by a single EMP on a clustered Protoss force is immense, and Ghosts should *always* be fielded against the Protoss army.

The EMP deals 100 Shield damage against any Protoss units or buildings caught in the blast radius.

EMP is also useful against certain other targets, as it also drains targets within its area of effect of ALL Energy, as well as temporarily revealing any Cloaked Protoss units drained of Shields.

Some key non-Protoss targets that EMP can be useful against include Banshees (very effective), any enemy casters (Ghosts, Ravens, Infestors, High Templar), and Thors or Battlecruisers, to disable their ability to use their powerful weaponry.

TAC NUKE STRIKE
Hot Key: N

Effect: After 20 second launch time, deals 300 damage +200 vs Structures

Cost	Range	Radius	Autocast
Build Nuke at Ghost Academy	9	8	No

Calling in a Nuke is free, but it must first be built at the Ghost Academy.

Once a Nuke is prepared, you can designate a target for the nuclear strike, but once set, the Nuke will not launch for 20 seconds—and when you call in a Nuke, your opponent *immediately* receives an audible alert.

While there is a large graphic visible to you while a Nuke is lined up to launch, your opponent will *only* be able to see a small red dot indicating the point of impact. Because your opponent will immediately begin looking for that dot when they hear 'Nuclear Launch Detected', you must choose your target carefully.

Enemy armies are rarely a good target for a Nuke, as that is the first place most players will check. Enemy worker lines *can* be good targets, but it is usually best to distract your opponent first, by attacking or raiding just before you call in the Nuke (worker lines are the second important target players will usually check!).

Nukes *are* quite good against static defenses. If your opponent has bunkered down behind a wall of defensive structures, a Nuke or two can easily clear the way for your army, and structures can't dodge a Nuke like armies or workers!

HELLION

COST:

 100 0 30 2

BUILT FROM:	BUILD REQUIREMENTS:	UPGRADES:
Factory	NONE	*Factory Tech Lab*

The Hellion deals its damage by projecting a burst of flames in a straight line at its target—anything along the line is damaged, so groups of Hellions can tear apart clustered groups of enemy Light units. Because Hellions lack significant damage against non-Light targets, they are a poor choice for destroying structures or fighting against mixed ground forces.

Hellions should be used (and abused) for their speed, and power against Light units. If your opponent is massing their basic troop type (Marines, Zealots, or Zerglings), Hellions can shred such one dimensional armies.

Otherwise, make use of Hellions for their speed (which makes them a useful scout), and their worker raiding potential (which forces your opponent to defend their expansions or suffer constant worker losses).

Keep in mind that using Hellions against enemy forces effectively requires constant micro attention, or they will be destroyed easily. Except in cases where they are being used to fight off mass basic troops, you should rarely field more than small groups of Hellions for scout, patrol, and raiding duty.

WEAPON STATISTICS

Weapon	Damage	Attacks	Attack Speed	Range	Targets	Radius
Infernal Flamethrower	8 +6 vs Light (+1/+1)	1	2.50	6	Ground	6 (in a straight line ONLY)

UNIT STATISTICS

Health	Energy	Armor	Movement Speed	Acceleration	Line of Sight	Size
90	No	0	4.25	No	10	2

UNIT TYPE

Light	Armored	Biological	Mechanical	Psionic	Massive	Structure

The Hellion is a fast moving raider, excellent for hitting enemy worker lines, or harassing slow moving armies.

UPGRADES

Upgrade	Requirement				EFFECT
Infernal Pre-Igniter	None	150	150	110	Increases Hellion flamethrower damage by +10 vs Light

INFERNAL PRE-IGNITER

The Infernal upgrade to the Hellion's flamethrower massively increases its damage output against Light units. With this upgrade, even a few Hellions can nearly instantly destroy a fully developed worker line, causing serious economic damage in seconds. If you are planning on raiding with Hellions heavily, consider picking this upgrade up, as it makes even a few Hellions very dangerous to workers.

As an added benefit, it also makes Hellions even more lethal against all types of Light military units, which is particularly useful against basic troops from all races, and quite good against the Zerg Hydralisk, a dangerous midgame Light unit that often shows up in large groups.

SIEGE TANK

COST:

 150   125   45   3

BUILT FROM:	BUILD REQUIREMENTS:	UPGRADES:
Factory	Attached Tech Lab	Factory Tech Lab

While in normal tank form, Siege Tanks deal good damage against Armored targets, and when transformed into Siege Mode, Siege Tanks deal heavy area of effect damage against any ground units. Siege Tanks are a fairly expensive unit in terms of Gas, so you should expect to field them in relatively limited numbers, always accompanied by the rest of your army when on offense. Siege Tanks are the first Factory unit that is durable enough to be worth repairing in battle, and especially on defense. Consider bringing a few SCVs along with your army if you are making use of the Siege march.

When fighting against buildings or ground armies consisting largely of Armored units, you may want to keep your tanks in tank mode, as they will deal good damage over time, and keep the benefit of mobility to advance, retreat, or focus fire as needed.

On defense, or when making a Siege push against an enemy base, be sure to make use of the strength of Siege Mode. Even a few Siege Tanks in Siege Mode can be a powerful addition to a base's defenses, so even if you skip them in the early game, try to pick up a few later in the match to protect your bases.

Siege Tanks are also a very viable unit for Medivac dropship assaults. Place a few Siege Tanks on an unreachable ledge overlooking an enemy base or army and put them into Siege Mode.

WEAPON STATISTICS

Weapon	Damage	Attacks	Attack Speed	Range	Targets	Radius
90mm Cannons	15 +10 vs Armored (+2/+1)	1	1.04	7	Ground	0
Crucio Shock Cannon	60 (+5)	1	3.00	13 (2 Minimum)	Ground	1.25*

*(deals full damage out to 0.46, half damage to 0.78, and quarter damage to 1.25)

UNIT STATISTICS

Health	Energy	Armor	Movement Speed	Acceleration	Line of Sight	Size
160	No	1	2.25	No	11	4

UNIT TYPE

Light	Armored	Biological	Mechanical	Psionic	Massive	Structure

The mighty Terran Siege Tank is a powerhouse ground defender, and a dangerous weapon on offense.

UPGRADES		COST			EFFECT
Upgrade	**Requirement**				
Siege Tech	None	100	100	80	Grants Siege Tanks Siege Mode

SIEGE TECH

Siege Tech unlocks the ability for all Siege Tanks to make use of Siege Mode.

You should *always* acquire Siege Tech if you are planning to builld more than a handful of Siege Tanks, as even a few tanks in Siege Mode while on defense can make attacking your base with a ground army extremely costly for your opponent.

Note that Siege Mode has a longer range than the Siege Tanks line of sight. If you can spot for them with an aerial or scout unit, they can fire at targets at a very great distance. If you really need to get a few shots off, you can use Scanner Sweep to spot for your tanks, but try not to do this unless really necessary, as the Energy and economic cost is high.

Siege Mode also has the disadvantage of having a *minimum* range. If enemy units move into close contact with a Siege Tank, it can no longer fire at them. Worse, Siege Mode knows no friends—it can and will inflict splash damage on your own units, so if an enemy moves units into contact with a tank, your other tanks can destroy it with Siege fire!

THE SIEGE MARCH

When on offense with multiple Siege Tanks, you can take advantage of their huge range while in Siege Mode to make a particularly difficult to stop push into enemy territory.

When you have scouted out the position of the enemy base and army, you can move your army and its Siege Tanks just outside of visual range of your opponent.

At this point, deploy one Siege Tank in Siege Mode, move forward a short distance, deploy a second, and repeat, until you make contact with the enemy in range of your last deployed Siege Tank.

If the enemy army pursues, retreat, leading them into the line of already deployed Siege Tanks.

If they do not, move up the rear Siege Tanks and place them into Siege Mode in range of the enemy army or enemy base.

Your opponent has no choice but to deal with your army and deployed Siege Tanks, or watch as his base is slowly ground down by the incessant pounding of the Crucio cannons.

Abilities

SIEGE MODE/TANK MODE
Hot Key: E/D

Effect: Transforms the Siege Tank to or from Siege Mode

Cost	Range	Radius	Autocast
4s Cooldown	0	0	No

Once Siege Mode has been researched, Siege Tanks can transform between Siege and Tank mode at any time. Note that there is a 4 second transformation delay, so try to set up Siege Tanks *before* a battle begins, and be sure to de-siege them if you expect that you will need to retreat.

THOR

COST:

 300   200   60   6

BUILT FROM:	BUILD REQUIREMENTS:		UPGRADES:
Factory	Armory	Attached Tech Lab	Factory Tech Lab

The Thor is expensive unit, second only to the Battlecruiser on cost, and slow to build, so it is best used in small numbers alongside your ground army, providing anti-air coverage and strong fire support.

Thor anti-air causes small area splash damage, making it ideal for repulsing packs of tightly clustered Light enemy air units (notably Mutalisk harassment packs!)

As a very durable unit, the Thor is well suited to protection by SCVs, they can keep a Thor standing much longer in battle than other than any other Terran Mechanical unit besides the Battlecruiser.

The Thor is a very straightforward unit, it simply increases the overall power of your ground army, shielding it with strong anti-air support, and greatly increasing your ability to take down tough enemy ground units or bases quickly with the Thor's 250mm Strike Cannons.

WEAPON STATISTICS

Weapon	Damage	Attacks	Attack Speed	Range	Targets	Radius
Thor's Hammer	30 (+3)	2	1.28	7	Ground	0
Javelin Missile Launchers	6 +6 vs Light (+1/+1)	4	3.00	10	Air	0.5

UNIT STATISTICS

Health	Energy	Armor	Movement Speed	Acceleration	Line of Sight	Size
400	Yes	1	1.88	No	11	8

UNIT TYPE

Light	Armored	Biological	Mechanical	Psionic	Massive	Structure

The Thor is a intimidating walker unit, armed with devastating ground cannons and lethal anti-air missiles.

UPGRADES		COST			EFFECT
Upgrade	Requirement				
250mm Strike Cannons	None	150	150	110	Fires at a single target, stunning it and dealing 500 damage over 6 seconds

Cost	Range	Radius	Autocast
150 Energy	7	0	No

When activated, these cannons deal 500 damage over 6 seconds to any ground target in range. The Thor becomes stationary for the duration of the barrage, so be careful not to activate this ability against weak ground units if the Thor is in danger of being surrounded.

The Thor's Strike Cannons are ideal for taking down dangerous enemy ground units such as enemy Thors, the Protoss Colossus, or Zerg Ultralisks. Enemy Siege Tanks or Protoss Archons are also good candidates for demolition.

Weaker enemy targets usually aren't worth the use of Energy, and you may want to save the cannons for destroying an enemy expansion quickly. Even two Thors firing their cannons at a core structure alongside a handful of ground troops will level the building in seconds.

VIKING

COST:
 150   75   42   2

BUILT FROM:	BUILD REQUIREMENTS:	UPGRADES:
Starport	NONE	NONE

The Viking excels in its dual role as both an anti-air aircraft and light ground raider. Because it can transform, it can slip past anti-air defenses, or fly in from behind a worker line and land to deal rapid damage to another players economy.

Vikings are too fragile and expensive to be used as a primary ground army unit, but in a tight situation, you can certainly land and lend their firepower to a close battle.

When you know an enemy is going for an air force, Vikings should be part of your defense, as they are far cheaper and faster to build than the Battlecruiser, and work well together with your Missile Turrets, Marines, and Thors to fend off enemy air attacks.

WEAPON STATISTICS

Weapon	Damage	Attacks	Attack Speed	Range	Targets
Lanzer Torpedos	10 +4 vs Armored (+1/+0)	2	2.00	9	Air
Gatling Cannon	12 (+1)	1	1.00	6	Ground

UNIT STATISTICS

Health	Energy	Armor	Movement Speed	Acceleration	Line of Sight	Size
125	No	0	2.25 (Ground) 2.95 (Air)	No (Ground) Yes (Air)	10	2

UNIT TYPE

Light	Armored	Biological	Mechanical	Psionic	Massive	Structure

Exemplifying the Terran army's flexibility, the Viking is a modular spacecraft that can transform between its airborne form, and a ground walker mode.

Abilities

 ASSAULT MODE/FIGHTER MODE
Assault Hot Key: D / Fighter Hot Key: E

Effect: Transform between Air and Ground modes

Cost	Range	Radius	Autocast
3s Cooldown	0	0	No

Vikings can transform between air and ground mode at any time. Be aware that there is a 3 second delay on the transformation, so if you are performing a Viking raid and expect your opponent to retaliate, be sure to leave *before* his troops show up and start shooting your Vikings.

Because the Viking can transform, it can take advantage of enemy units that can only attack air or ground units, and it can avoid units that are purely anti-air, such as the Missile Turret, Protoss Phoenix, or Zerg Corruptor. In the case of the Missile Turret, you can actually land and destroy them without retaliation if there are no other enemy forces nearby!

MEDIVAC

COST:
 100 100 42 2

BUILT FROM:	BUILD REQUIREMENTS:	UPGRADES:
Starport | NONE |
Starport Tech Lab |

This strong support unit can be used as both infantry support, and quick evacuation from the front lines if the battle turns sour, in addition to its uses as a transport for constructing island expansions or raiding poorly defended bases from unusual angles.

Adding a handful of Medivacs to a Terran infantry force greatly increases the survivability of the army while using Stimpacks, and allows you to heal surviving units to full health after a battle has finished.

Medivacs default to Autocasting their Heal ability, so all you need to do to make them work for you in a battle is have them near your infantry—they'll automatically move around and heal damaged units.

One point about Medivacs accompanying your ground force—be careful when moving your army around as a group, if you accidentally right click on a friendly unit (or on a Medivac) your Medivacs will attempt to pick up the unit, or your units will attempt to enter the Medivac.

You may want to keep your Medivacs on a separate group hotkey, even if they are part of your main army hotkey, to allow you to move them away from the frontlines in a fight—Heal has enough range to restore your infantry from the back lines.

WEAPON STATISTICS

Weapon	Damage	Attacks	Attack Speed	Range	Targets
NONE					

UNIT STATISTICS

Health	Energy	Armor	Movement Speed	Acceleration	Line of Sight	Size
150	Yes	1	2.75	Yes	11	8

UNIT TYPE

Light	Armored	Biological	Mechanical	Psionic	Massive	Structure

The Medivac is an upgraded Dropship, capable of both transporting and healing units.

UPGRADES		COST			EFFECT
Upgrade	Requirement				
Caduceus Reactor	None	100	100	80	Increases starting Medivac Energy by 25

CADUCEUS REACTOR

The Caduceus Reactor increases starting Medivac Energy by 25. If you are planning on making heavy use of Medivacs alongside an infantry army, be sure to pick up this upgrade. It is reasonably priced and researches fairly quickly, and it gives your Medivacs more staying power in fights when they are built.

Abilities

+ HEAL
Hot Key: E

Effect: Heals friendly Biological targets 9 Life per second

Cost	Range	Radius	Autocast
1 Energy per 3 Life	4	0	Yes

Heal restores 9 health per second to friendly Biological targets, at a cost of 3 Energy per second.

The Medivac defaults to Autocasting Heal, and will target any unit within a range of 4, so even a few Medivacs can easily cover your entire ground force with healing. Though there's rarely any reason to do so in a larger battle, you can micro the targeting of Heal manually if needed.

RAVEN

COST:

 100 200 60 2

BUILT FROM:	BUILD REQUIREMENTS:	UPGRADES:
Starport	*Attached Tech Lab*	*Starport Tech Lab*

The Raven is a pure caster unit, in that it has *no* normal weapon attack. All of its utility and power comes through the use of its abilities, so Ravens *must* be microed and controlled carefully in battle. With upgrades, the Raven gains a powerful area of effect attack, lethal against massed enemy armies.

The Raven also acts as the mobile Detector for the Terran army, so when facing enemy Cloaked or Burrowed forces on offense, Ravens must be brought with your army to safely make a push.

In situations where you are relying on your Ravens for their Detection, rather than their abilities, be sure to build at least one or two extra, as they are expensive and slow to build, and you can expect your opponent to mark them as a priority target.

As casters, Ravens are best used in support of an existing army, though they can harass enemy expansions with their Auto-Turrets, and once outfitted with Seeker Missiles, can also be used to make hit and run attacks against clumped enemy armies if you are careful.

WEAPON STATISTICS

Weapon	Damage	Attacks	Attack Speed	Range	Targets
NONE					

UNIT STATISTICS

Health	Energy	Armor	Movement Speed	Acceleration	Line of Sight	Size
140	Yes	1	2.25	Yes	11	

UNIT TYPE

Light	Armored	Biological	Mechanical	Psionic	Massive	Structure

The Terran Raven is a powerful support craft, outfitted with an array of advanced autonomous offensive and defensive equipment.

UPGRADES		COST			EFFECT
Upgrade	Requirement				
Corvid Reactor	None	150	150	110	Increases Raven starting Energy by 25
Durable Materials	None	150	150	110	Extends duration of Raven Auto Turrets, Seeker Missiles, and Point Defense Drones
Seeker Missile	None	150	150	110	Enables Raven Seeker Missile

CORVID REACTOR

The Corvid Reactor increases Raven starting Energy by 25. As with the Ghost and Medivac, if you are planning on fielding many Ravens throughout a match, pick up this upgrade—but you should get your first few Ravens onto the field before spending the time and resources to research this upgrade, the Gas cost nearly pays for a Raven.

DURABLE MATERIALS

The Durable Materials upgrade increases the lifespan of Auto-Turrets, Point Defense Drones, and Seeker Missiles. Save this upgrade for last though, as it has the least direct impact on the performance of your Ravens.

While Point Defense Drones already have a long enough lifespan to do their work (usually running out of Energy or being destroyed well before they expire naturally), and Seeker Missiles usually don't need the extra duration to hit their mark, Auto-Turrets do benefit from this upgrade, increasing their damage potential over the course of a longer battle, or making them more dangerous as a base raiding tool.

SEEKER MISSILE

The Seeker Missile research unlocks the ability for Ravens to make use of their powerful area of effect missile.

Abilities

AUTO-TURRET
Hot Key: T

Effect: Creates an automated defensive turret that lasts for 180 seconds

Cost	Range	Radius	Autocast
50 Energy	3	0	No

The Raven can drop remote sentry turrets with this ability, which will instantly begin firing on any hostile unit in range. You *can* direct the fire of these turrets yourself, should you wish to focus fire them on a particular target.

Individually, Auto-Turrets are not especially strong, but because even a few Ravens can quickly create a turret field, either in support of your army, or to perform a worker raid on an enemy expansion, they can be quite effective.

Don't expose your Ravens to risk when dropping turrets in battle. Either throw them out in front of your army and then engage, or drop them after the battle begins, while enemy anti-air units are too busy being shot by your army to deal with your Ravens without direct enemy intervention.

Auto-Turrets can act as instant anti-air, as their cannons can fire at ground or air targets, useful for defending against an enemy air raid when your army isn't around to help.

SEEKER MISSILE
Hot Key: R

Effect: Launches a guided missile dealing 100 damage on impact

Cost	Range	Radius	Autocast
125 Energy	9	2.4	No

The powerful Seeker Missile is one of the Terran army's best answers to massed enemy forces. Seeker Missiles travel out from the Raven and then gradually accelerate towards your chosen target. Seeker Missiles *can* be evaded by fast enemy troops, though your opponent must be attentive to the launch, and correctly pick out the targeted unit to run with.

A very alert opponent could potentially direct a Seeker Missile back onto your own forces, though don't expect this to happen often.

In general, if you can get off even two well placed Seekers targeted at the heart of your opponents army, you can inflict grievous casualties, usually enough to turn the tide of battle in your favor.

Seeker Missiles *can* be used as worker destroyers, but given their power and expense, they are usually best saved for assisting your army in battles against your opponent's primary force.

You should always acquire Seeker Missiles in the mid to late game for your Ravens, they can turn the tide of battle in your favor when facing massive enemy forces.

Seeker Missiles are particularly strong against Zerg ground armies, Terran infantry armies, and massed air units of any sort other than Battlecruisers or Carriers.

POINT DEFENSE DRONE
Hot Key: D

Effect: Destroys incoming projectile attacks

Cost	Range	Radius	Autocast
100 Energy	3	0	No

POINT DEFENSE DRONE TARGETS		
Terran	**Protoss**	**Zerg**
Marauder	Stalker	Queen (air attack only)
Viking (air attack only)	Phoenix	Mutalisk
Banshee	Photon Cannon	Corruptor
Battlecruiser	N/A	Hydralisk
Thor (air attack only)	N/A	Spore Crawler
Missile Turret	N/A	N/A
Reaper (building attack only)	N/A	N/A

The Point Defense Drone is an *amazing* defensive ability, and can turn a close battle into a decisive victory for your forces against certain enemy units. The Point Defense Drone is deployed much like an Auto-Turret, though it is a stationary air structure once placed, unlike the ground based Auto-Turret.

Once placed, the Drone will automatically shoot down enemy projectiles—each Drone can destroy up to 20 projectiles (Drones are deployed with 200 Energy, and each shot intercepted costs 10 Energy). The Point Defense Drone will shoot down anything that qualifies as a 'projectile' ranged attack.

Keep in mind that the Point Defense Drone will automatically shoot down any projectile in its range, so large masses of ranged attackers will overwhelm its defense—but you can deploy more than one Drone in a large battle, to help absorb more damage.

Be wary of Battlecruisers, their rapid attacks will quickly deplete the energy of your Drones.

Against smaller numbers of enemy troops that are affected by the Point Defense, even one or two Drones can completely nullify any incoming damage, resulting in a crushing victory for your forces.

Always deploy a Point Defense Drone before engaging in any major battle with your opponent's army, the Drones can significantly increase the effective health of your army.

BANSHEE

COST:

 150 100 60 3

BUILT FROM:	BUILD REQUIREMENTS:	UPGRADES:
Starport	Attached Tech Lab	Attached Tech Lab

Once upgraded, it becomes both a very dangerous raiding and combat unit.

Even without cloaking, your first Banshees on the field can often safely perform raids against undefended worker lines—just don't throw any early Banshees away on raids or in battle, they're relatively fragile and become much more dangerous in groups with cloak.

Banshees have no anti-air capability, so until you have cloak, be very careful with your Banshees if your opponent has air units on the field that can hunt down and destroy your Banshees.

Banshees also cannot last long against fixed anti-air defenses or armies until they reach critical mass, and carefully protecting your Banshees until they reach that point is important.

Remember that Banshees can be repaired by SCVs. After a raid or combat action, be sure to return them to base to be fully repaired before you send them out again.

WEAPON STATISTICS

Weapon	Damage	Attacks	Attack Speed	Range	Targets
Backlash Rockets	12 (+1)	2	1.25	6	Ground

UNIT STATISTICS

Health	Energy	Armor	Movement Speed	Acceleration	Line of Sight	Size
140	Yes	0	2.75	Yes	10	

UNIT TYPE

Light	Armored	Biological	Mechanical	Psionic	Massive	Structure

The Banshee is an air to ground gunship, with access to sophisticated cloaking technology.

UPGRADES		COST			EFFECT
Upgrade	Requirement				
Cloaking Field	None	200	200	110	Enables Banshee Cloak

CLOAKING FIELD

This research grants Banshees the ability to Cloak. It should always be acquired soon after you field your first Banshees, as they become considerably more dangerous with it.

Cloaking Field research is both expensive and fairly time consuming, so try to get a few Banshees on the field before you begin the research, unless you are planning to surprise your opponent with a single massed attack of Cloaked Banshees.

Abilities

CLOAK
Hot Key: C

Effect: Cloaks Banshee

	Cost	Range	Radius	Autocast
	25 Energy, 0.9 Energy per second	0	0	No

Cloaking activation requires 25 Energy, and drains Energy at 0.9 per second, so freshly created Banshees cannot be cloaked for long. Be sure not to toggle Cloak on and off—approach your target, activate Cloak, then get in and get out before you deactivate it. You want to give your Banshees as much time as possible out of combat to regenerate Energy, and wasting it by turning Cloak on and off several times is a poor use of time.

Once you begin using cloaked Banshees, expect your opponent to respond with Detectors, both mobile and fixed. Once those Detectors are on the field, you need to pick your targets carefully.

With enough Banshees, you can destroy fixed Detectors or anti-air structures quickly, but Banshees alone can do nothing to the mobile Detectors that each race can field.

Try to strike against lightly defended expansions, and when your opponents bases are too heavily defended, use your Banshees with your main army to add more firepower to an offensive push. If your army can take out mobile enemy Detectors, your Banshees can easily rout their ground force.

BATTLECRUISER

COST:

 400 300 90 6

BUILT FROM:

Starport

BUILD REQUIREMENTS:

Fusion Core *Attached Tech Lab*

UPGRADES:

Fusion Core

The Battlecruiser is a heavy air unit, expensive and slow to build and to move, but packing a punch when it arrives.

Battlecruisers are costly and slow to produce, so each should be used carefully. If your opponent has large amounts of mobile anti-air or air units, do not send Battlecruisers off on their own, move them with your main army.

Battlecruisers are the toughest single unit in the Terran army, so they should always be repaired by SCVs, both in the field in battle, and when at rest on defense or after an offensive push.

Battlecruisers can provide the final knockout punch to an enemy in the mid to late game, but be careful about tying up your Starport production completely with Battlecruisers if your opponent is already fielding many air units or cloaked units, you may need Vikings or Ravens on the field more than a few Battlecruisers.

WEAPON STATISTICS

Weapon	Damage	Attacks	Attack Speed	Range	Targets
ATA Laser Battery	6 (+1)	1	0.23	6	Air
ATS Laser Battery	10 (+1)	1	0.23	6	Ground

UNIT STATISTICS

Health	Energy	Armor	Movement Speed	Acceleration	Line of Sight	Size
550	Yes	3	1.4	Yes	12	

UNIT TYPE

Light	Armored	Biological	Mechanical	Psionic	Massive	Structure

The massive Terran Battlecruiser is a capital class spacecraft, wielding immense firepower against air or ground targets, and utilizing the devastating Yamato Cannon.

UPGRADES		COST			EFFECT
Upgrade	Requirement				
Weapon Refit	None	150	150	60	Enables Battlecruiser Yamato Cannon
Behemoth Reactor	None	150	150	80	Increases starting Battlecruiser Energy by 25

WEAPON REFIT

Researching Weapon Refit equips all Battlecruisers with the Yamato Cannon, be sure to have this researching while your first Battlecruisers are being built!

BEHEMOTH REACTOR

Behemoth Reactors grant Battlecruisers 25 more starting Energy. Because Yamato Cannon takes a massive 125 Energy to fire, this upgrade can allow your newly created Battlecruisers to use the cannon almost 45 seconds sooner than without it.

Assuming you can spare the resources, it is worth acquiring the reactor once you begin Battlecruiser production.

Abilities

YAMATO CANNON
Hot Key: Y

Effect: Charges for 3 seconds, then fires. Deals 300 damage

Cost	Range	Radius	Autocast
125 Energy	10	0	No

The mighty Yamato Cannon deals *300* damage to a single target, though it requires 3 seconds for the cannon to warm up and fire. Once it is launched, the cannon blast cannot be dodged (short of an army being Mass Recalled by a Mothership with the shot in the air!).

The strength of the Yamato Cannon is ideal for dispatching extremely strong enemy units such as opposing Battlecruisers, Carriers, the Mothership, the Colossus, and Thor.

Because the Yamato Cannon is a siege ranged ability, it can also be used to destroy most fixed enemy defenses in a single shot, clearing the way for your ground army to make a final push—but don't waste a Yamato shot on structures if the enemy army has more critical targets.

TERRAN BUILDINGS

Terran structures are modular and upgradable, offering more flexibility at the cost of increased complexity.

TERRAN STRUCTURE NOTES

SCV Auto-loading
The Terran Command Center and Planetary Fortress have a range of 6 for using the Load SCV command.

Salvaging
Terran bunkers can be salvaged, returning their full Mineral cost.

Burning Buildings
Heavily damaged Terran buildings begin to burn down slowly, if they are not repaired by an SCV, they eventually self-destruct.

Buildings begin to burn at 33% health and burn at 3 health a second.

Lift Off
Several Terran buildings have the ability to actually launch from the ground and become both mobile and aerial. The Command Center, its Orbital Command upgrade, and all three core military buildings (Barracks, Factory, Starport) can perform a Lift Off. Unsurprisingly, your buildings don't move particularly quickly while in the air, but it provides several interesting tactical and strategic options.

In the heat of a fight, you can lift off a building to protect it from ground only units completely.

You can also use the flight to move Command Centers to distant expansions relatively safely (especially expansions normally only accessible via drop-ship for other races).

Note that the Planetary Fortress upgrade removes the ability for the Command Center to lift off.

Want a durable and cheap aerial scout? Float a military structure to provide line of sight for your Siege Tanks, or for your army up a ramp.

> **BUILDING TYPES**
>
> *All Terran structures are Armored, Mechanical, Structure.*

BUILDING UPGRADES

All Terran unit producing buildings (the Command Center, Barracks, Factory, and Starport) can be upgraded to improve or modify their construction capabilities.

Command Center Upgrades

Command Centers can be upgraded to either an *Orbital Command* or a *Planetary Fortress*.

The Orbital Command upgrade is vital for economic support and cloak detection, while the Planetary Fortress provides increased armor and a heavy automated turret built into the structure of the Command Center.

Barracks, Factory, Starport Upgrades

All of the military structures can be upgraded with either a *Reactor* or a *Tech Lab*. Once built, a Reactor or Tech Lab remains where it is placed beside the parent building.

This also allows you to swap building upgrades—you can construct a Tech Lab or Reactor on an early Barracks, lift off the Barracks, then build (or lift off) a new Factory or Starport to use the Tech Lab or Reactor, instantly granting you access to advanced units or double speed basic unit production.

The Reactor

The Reactor provides a second build queue in the building it is attached to, creating units two at a time. Only basic units can be constructed, but this allows you to greatly speed up the production of basic military units.

Building		Units available
	Barracks	Marine
	Factory	Hellion
	Starport	Viking, Medivac

The Tech Lab

An attached Tech Lab grants access to the advanced military units available in the building, as well as providing upgrades for those units.

Building		Units Added	Upgrades Available
	Barracks	Marauder, Reaper, Ghost	Combat Shield, Stimpacks, Nitro Packs, Concussive Shells
	Factory	Siege Tank, Thor	Infernal Pre-igniter, Siege Tech, 250mm Strike Cannons
	Starport	Raven, Banshee, Battlecruiser	Caduceus Reactor, Corvid Reactor, Durable Materials, Seeker Missile, Cloaking Field

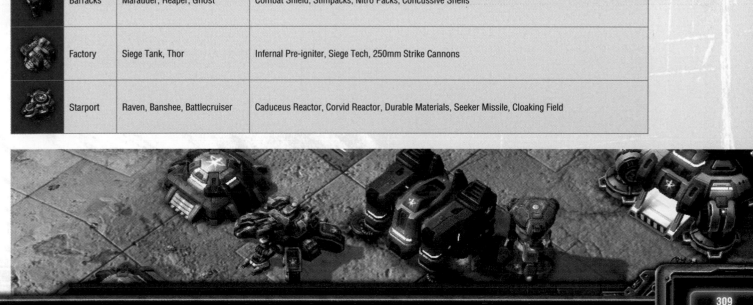

COMMAND CENTER

Hot Key: C

COST:
 400   0   100

BUILDING STATISTICS		
Health	Armor	Energy
1500	1	

BUILD REQUIREMENTS:

NONE

The Command Center is the Terran core structure, producing SCVs to power your economy.

The Command Center has the ability to load up to 5 SCVs, either for defense against worker raids, or to use in a new base after you move a lifted Command Center to an expansion.

The Command Center is unique among core structures in that it can be upgraded to either an Orbital Command or a Planetary Fortress, providing either economic boosts or defenses.

BUILDING PRODUCTION			COST			
Unit	Requirement					
SCV	None	50	0	1	17

BUILDING UPGRADES		COST			EFFECT
Upgrade	Requirement				
Orbital Command	Barracks	150	0	50	Unlocks Scanner Sweep, MULE, and Extra Supplies, loses SCV cargo space
Planetary Fortress	Engineering Bay	150	150	50	Increases building armor, adds defensive turret, cannot lift off

ORBITAL COMMAND

Hot Key: B   UPGRADE

COST:
 150   0   35

BUILDING STATISTICS		
Health	Armor	Energy
1500	1	Yes

BUILD REQUIREMENTS:

Command Center

Barracks

The Orbital Command is the economic booster for the Terran race, and should be built *immediately* after your first Barracks. The Orbital Command provides access to the Calldowns for the critical MULE robotic miner, Extra Supplies, and the powerful recon ability of Scanner Sweep.

Orbital Command Energy is limited, so you must decide between using MULEs constantly to boost your economy, or saving Energy for Scanner Sweeps.

If your opponent fields Cloaked or Burrowed units before you have Ravens out in the field and Missile Turrets in your base, you can make use of Scanner Sweep as a temporary solution.

The Orbital Command *can* lift off, but it *cannot* store SCVs.

BUILDING PRODUCTION			COST			
Unit	Requirement					
SCV	None	50	0	1	17

BUILDING ABILITIES					
Calldown: MULE					
	Cost	Range	Radius	Effect	Autocast?
	50 Energy	Unlimited	0	Creates a MULE harvester for 90 seconds	No
Calldown: Extra Supplies					
	Cost	Range	Radius	Effect	Autocast?
	50 Energy	Unlimited	0	Increases the Supply output of a Supply Depot by 8	No
Scanner Sweep					
	Cost	Range	Radius	Effect	Autocast?
	50 Energy	Unlimited	13	Reveals Cloaked and Burrowed units for 12 seconds	No

PLANETARY FORTRESS

Hot Key: P   UPGRADE

COST:
 150  150 50

BUILDING STATISTICS		
Health	Armor	Energy
1500	3	

WEAPON STATISTICS					
Weapon	Damage	Attacks	Attack Speed	Range	Targets
Ibiks Cannon	40	1	Normal 2	6	Ground

The Planetary Fortress is a powerful defensive upgrade to the Command Center, adding more armor and a hard hitting turret that can repel light ground raids.

BUILD REQUIREMENTS:

While adding a second Orbital Command will increase your potential income and ability to use Scanner Sweep more freely, in some cases, a Planetary Fortress may be preferable.

Command Center

At expansions where you expect to be raided often, particularly at hi-yield Mineral expansion sites that are often open to attack from multiple angles, a Planetary Fortress can act as its own defender against light ground raids. The extra armor can also buy time for your army to return, particularly when the Fortress is repaired by SCVs—a Fortress being repaired by multiple SCV can be *extremely* difficult for an opponent to destroy, especially when you simply hide the SCVs when they are targeted.

Engineering Bay

Planetary Fortresses *can* store SCVs, but they *cannot* lift off.

The range of the turret on the Planetary Fortress can be upgraded by purchasing Hi-Sec Auto Tracking at an Engineering Bay.

BUILDING PRODUCTION		COST			
Unit	Requirement				
SCV	None	50	0	1	17

THE SUPER BUNKER

For the cost of 550 Minerals and 150 Gas, you can have yourself a super bunker named the Planetary Fortress anywhere on a map.

While this isn't the cheapest or fastest defense you can create, where else can you get a unit for that price that has 1500 health, 3 armor, a 40 damage attack, can store SCVs, can be repaired by SCVs and costs 0 Supply?

If there's a chokepoint you absolutely must hold against a ground assault, consider building an 'extra' Planetary Fortress!

REFINERY

Hot Key: R

COST:
 75 0 30

BUILDING STATISTICS		
Health	Armor	Energy
500	1	

The Refinery is the Terran structure for extracting Vespene Gas.

BUILD REQUIREMENTS:

Unlike the Protoss or Zerg extractors, when a Refinery is finished building, the SCV that built it will automatically begin harvesting, unless you have given it another order. Consequently, you only need to place two more SCVs on a Refinery to get it running at full speed.

NONE

SUPPLY DEPOT

Hot Key: S

COST:
100 0 30

BUILDING STATISTICS		
Health	Armor	Energy
350	1	

BUILD REQUIREMENTS:

The Supply Depot is, unsurprisingly, the Terran source of Supply for its army.

Supply Depots also have the advantage of being able to retract into the ground, allowing friendly ground units to pass, and then raising them again, closing the 'door' to hostile ground forces.

NONE

BUILDING ABILITIES					
Raise/Lower					
Cost	Range	Radius	Effect	Autocast?	
1s Cooldown	0	0	Raises or Lowers a Supply Depot to allow ground units to pass	No	

ENGINEERING BAY

Hot Key: E

COST:
 125   0   35

BUILDING STATISTICS		
Health	Armor	Energy
850	1	

The Engineering Bay contains all upgrades for Terran infantry forces, as well as the special Terran defensive upgrades.

The Engineering Bay is also necessary for the construction of Missile Turrets, so be sure to build one *before* you have need of them!

BUILD REQUIREMENTS:

NONE

ARMORY

Hot Key: A

COST:
 150   100   65

BUILDING STATISTICS		
Health	Armor	Energy
750	1	

The Armory contains all upgrades for Terran Factory and Starport units, and is necessary for the construction of the Thor, as well as more advanced infantry upgrades at the Engineering Bay.

You should have an Armory under construction once you begin recruiting Factory and Starport units in significant numbers, for increased access to upgrades, and for the ability to create the Thor.

BUILD REQUIREMENTS:

Factory

BUILDING UPGRADES		COST			EFFECT
Upgrade	Requirement				
Infantry Weapons Level 1	None	100	100	160	Increases Infantry weapon damage
Infantry Weapons Level 2	Armory	175	175	190	Increases Infantry weapon damage
Infantry Weapons Level 3	Armory	250	250	220	Increases Infantry weapon damage
Infantry Armor Level 1	None	100	100	160	Increases Infantry armor
Infantry Armor Level 2	Armory	175	175	190	Increases Infantry armor
Infantry Armor Level 3	Armory	250	250	220	Increases Infantry armor
Hi-Sec Auto Tracking	None	100	100	80	Adds +1 Range to Auto-Turrets, Missile Turrets, Planetary Fortresses and Point Defense Drones
Neosteel Frame	None	100	100	110	Increases Bunker Cargo Space by 2, Command Center and Planetary Fortress Cargo Space by 5
Building Armor	None	150	150	140	Increases all Terran building armor by 2, including Auto Turret and Point Defense Drone

BUILDING UPGRADES		COST			EFFECT
Upgrade	Requirement				
Vehicle Weapons Level 1	None	100	100	160	Upgrades vehicle damage
Vehicle Weapons Level 2	None	175	175	190	Upgrades vehicle damage
Vehicle Weapons Level 3	None	250	250	220	Upgrades vehicle damage
Vehicle Armor Level 1	None	100	100	160	Upgrades vehicle armor
Vehicle Armor Level 2	None	175	175	190	Upgrades vehicle armor
Vehicle Armor Level 3	None	250	250	220	Upgrades vehicle armor
Ship Weapons Level 1	None	100	100	160	Upgrades spacecraft damage
Ship Weapons Level 2	None	175	175	190	Upgrades spacecraft damage
Ship Weapons Level 3	None	250	250	220	Upgrades spacecraft damage
Ship Armor Level 1	None	150	150	160	Upgrades spacecraft armor
Ship Armor Level 2	None	225	225	190	Upgrades spacecraft armor
Ship Armor Level 3	None	300	300	220	Upgrades spacecraft armor

REACTOR

Hot Key: C

COST:

 50 50 50

BUILDING STATISTICS		
Health	Armor	Energy
400	1	

BUILD REQUIREMENTS:

Reactors can be built from any Barracks, Factory, or Starport, and an attached Reactor allows the creation of two basic military units at a time.

Barracks   Factory   Starport

TECH LAB

Hot Key: X

COST:

 50 25 25

BUILDING STATISTICS		
Health	Armor	Energy
400	1	

BUILD REQUIREMENTS:

The Tech Lab can also be built from any Barracks, Factory, or Starport, and when attached, it allows the creation of more advanced military units, as well as research for units from the attached building.

Remember that the Reactor and Tech Lab can be 'shared' by lifting off and moving military structures around.

Barracks   Factory   Starport

BUILDING UPGRADES		COST			EFFECT
Upgrade	Requirement				
Stimpacks	Barracks Tech Lab	100	100	140	Enables Marines and Marauders to use the Stimpack ability
Combat Shield	Barracks Tech Lab	100	100	110	Marines gain +10 life
Concussive Shells	Barracks Tech Lab	50	50	60	Marauder weapons now slow down opponents
Nitro Packs	Barracks Tech Lab	100	100	100	Increases the movement speed of Reapers
Infernal Pre-Igniter	Factory Tech Lab	150	150	110	Increases Hellion flamethrower damage by +10 vs Light
Siege Tech	Factory Tech Lab	100	100	80	Enables Siege Tanks to deploy into Siege Mode
250mm Strike Cannon	Factory Tech Lab	150	150	110	Allows Thors to use the 250mm Shock Cannons ability
Caduceus Reactor	Starport Tech Lab	100	100	80	Increases the starting energy for Medivacs by 25
Corvid Reactor	Starport Tech Lab	150	150	110	Increases the starting energy for Ravens by 25
Durable Materials	Starport Tech Lab	150	150	110	Extends the duration of Auto-Turrets, Seeker Missiles, and Point Defense Drones
Seeker Missile	Starport Tech Lab	150	150	110	Enables Ravens to use the Seeker Missile armament
Cloaking Field	Starport Tech Lab	200	200	110	Enables Banshee Cloak

BUNKER

Hot Key: U

COST:

 100   0   30

BUILDING STATISTICS

Health	Armor	Energy
400	1	

BUILD REQUIREMENTS:

Barracks

The Bunker is unique to the Terran army, and unlike the Protoss or Zerg, who have autonomous defensive turrets, the Bunker must be manned by Terran infantry. Cheaply and quickly built by an SCV, a Bunker can hold up to 4 capacity worth of infantry, or 6 after being upgraded with a Neosteel Frame at the Engineering Bay.

Bunkers can also be salvaged, returning their full Mineral cost to you—as a result, you should make use of Bunkers on both offense and defense, as you can simply salvage any Bunker that is no longer needed, with no wasted resources.

While inside a Bunker, infantry units are granted +1 range, and when protected within the Bunker, are considerably more durable as well.

Bunkers used as part of a wall in become particularly difficult for an opponent to destroy if you make use of SCVs to repair them, and the same tactic can work on offense as well, when Bunkers are used as part of a containment or slow push into an enemy base.

Remember that SCVs can hide inside of a Bunker to escape from a raiding force!

Because Bunkers must be manned by infantry units to actually attack your opponent, they should only be manned when you *know* your opponent is attacking. Trying to fill every Bunker you build to capacity will starve your offensive army of its full potential early in the game.

However, in exchange, the Bunker can have *much* more firepower than any turret created by the Protoss or Zerg, and Stimpacks can be used by Marines or Marauders inside!

BUILDING ABILITIES

Salvage

	Cost	Range	Radius	Effect	Autocast?
	5 seconds	0	0	Returns 100% of Bunker construction cost, CANNOT be cancelled once activated	No

MISSILE TURRET

Hot Key: T

COST:

 100   0   25

BUILDING STATISTICS

Health	Armor	Energy
250	0	

WEAPON STATISTICS

Weapon	Damage	Attacks	Attack Speed	Range	Targets
Longbolt Missile	12	2	0.86	7	Air

The Terran Missile Turret is their Detector structure as well as their anti-air building. Turret range can be upgraded by purchasing Hi-Sec Auto Tracking at the Engineering Bay.

Once you reach the mid game, Missile Turrets should be placed near your worker lines and chokepoints, to act as protection against aerial and cloaked raids.

Missile Turrets are cheap and fairly quick to build, so if you spot enemy air, cloaked, or burrowed units while scouting or on offense, you can often have them prepared before your opponent attacks.

If it becomes necessary to build Missile Turrets while *under* attack, be sure to build them out of range (and preferably) out of sight of the attacking force, to provide an area of Detection and anti-air protection that you can then build out from.

BUILD REQUIREMENTS:

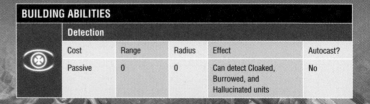

Engineering Bay

BUILDING ABILITIES

Detection

	Cost	Range	Radius	Effect	Autocast?
	Passive	0	0	Can detect Cloaked, Burrowed, and Hallucinated units	No

SENSOR TOWER

Hot Key: N

COST:

 125 100 25

BUILDING STATISTICS		
Health	Armor	Energy
200	0	

BUILD REQUIREMENTS:

Engineering Bay

The Sensor Tower is unique to the Terran army, and provides a large (30 radius) constant sensor scan, instantly alerting you on the minimap and in the fog of war of enemy units within its range. The Sensor Tower's radius appears on your *enemy's* minimap as well, so be careful about building them at fresh expansions before they are defended (unless you are attempting to bait your enemy into attacking a nonexistent expansion).

Sensor Towers are cheap to add to any base, though you shouldn't waste the Gas on them early in the game—use your worker scouts instead for early recon.

If you're willing to lose some of them, you can create a Sensor Tower network in the midgame to provide constant updates on the enemy army's position, but expect your opponent to destroy undefended towers if you create too many to protect with your army.

BUILDING ABILITIES

	Radar				
	Cost	Range	Radius	Effect	Autocast?
	Passive	30	0	Reveals hostile unit movement within its range, even in the Fog of War	No

TERRAN MILITARY TIERS

Terran military units are unlocked sequentially, a Barracks must be built to create a Factory, and a Factory must be constructed to build a Starport.

BARRACKS

Hot Key: B

COST:

 150 0 65

BUILDING STATISTICS		
Health	Armor	Energy
1000	1	

BUILD REQUIREMENTS:

NONE

The Barracks produces all Terran infantry units. A Barracks should be created soon after you hit 10 Supply, enabling the upgrading of your Command Center to an Orbital Fortress.

Early in the game, you should have at least two Barracks constantly producing units, though you can make use of one or three depending on your chosen build order. In the mid-game or later, you should add a third and possibly fourth Barracks if you are producing large numbers of infantry.

Remember to create additional Tech Labs or Reactors using your early Barracks for Factories or Starports under construction. You can lift off your Barracks and recreate its own Tech Lab or Reactor without slowing down your infantry production dangerously after your initial force is created.

BUILDING PRODUCTION			COST			
Unit		Requirement				
	Marine	None	50	0	1	25
	Marauder	Attached Tech Lab	100	25	2	30
	Reaper	Attached Tech Lab	50	50	1	40
	Ghost	Attached Tech Lab, Ghost Academy	150	150	2	40

BUILDING UPGRADES		COST			EFFECT
Upgrade	Requirement				
Reactor	None	50	50	50	Enables double build queue
Tech Lab	None	50	25	25	Enables Marauders, Reapers and Ghosts with Ghost Academy

FACTORY

Hot Key: F

COST:

 150 💣 100 🕐 60

BUILDING STATISTICS		
Health	Armor	Energy
1250	1	

BUILD REQUIREMENTS:

Barracks

The Factory constructs all Terran mechanized units.

The Hellion only requires Minerals to build, so it can be used effectively fairly early in a match, but both the Siege Tank and Thor are Gas heavy units, so they require a fully running Gas economy from at least one base to support, and from two bases if you want to produce them in large numbers.

You can use a single Factory with a Reactor if you simply want to add Hellions as a raiding force to your army, or as a complement to your Marauders, otherwise, a single Factory with a Tech Lab followed by a second when your economy can support it is sufficient for producing Siege Tanks and Thors in reasonable numbers in the early to midgame.

As with Barracks, be sure to add more Factories later in the game if you find yourself building great numbers of mechanized units.

Remember that building Thors will tie up a Factory's construction queue for a considerable amount of time, be sure that you have all the Hellions or Siege Tanks that you need on the field before beginning to build them, or create additional Factories to keep production running.

BUILDING PRODUCTION			COST			
Unit		Requirement	🪨	💣	🔷	🕐
	Hellion	None	100	0	2	30
	Siege Tank	Attached Tech Lab	150	125	3	45
	Thor	Attached Tech Lab, Armory	300	200	6	60

BUILDING UPGRADES		COST			EFFECT
Upgrade	Requirement	🪨	💣	🕐	
Reactor	None	50	50	50	Enables double build queue
Tech Lab	None	50	25	25	Enables Siege Tanks, Thors with Armory

STARPORT

Hot Key: S

COST:

 150 💣 100 🕐 50

BUILDING STATISTICS		
Health	Armor	Energy
1300	1	

BUILD REQUIREMENTS:

Factory

The Starport generates all Terran air units.

A single Starport with an attached Reactor can easily support your early game Viking and Medivac needs, but once you require greater numbers of advanced Starport units, you typically need two Starports with attached Tech Labs running simultaneously.

Advanced Terran air units and their attendant upgrades are very Gas heavy, so you usually need at least two bases supplying Gas to support two or more Starports while still producing a sizable ground force. If you're willing to sacrifice some ground power, you can create a larger advanced air army earlier in a match.

As with the Thor, later in a match, Battlecruisers can tie up Starport construction queues for a long period of time, if you need other air units, make sure you have the extra Starports to support all needed production.

BUILDING PRODUCTION			COST			
Unit		Requirement	🪨	💣	🔷	🕐
	Viking	None	150	75	2	42
	Medivac	None	100	100	2	42
	Raven	Attached Tech Lab	100	200	2	60
	Banshee	Attached Tech Lab	150	100	3	60
	Battlecruiser	Attached Tech Lab, Fusion Core	400	300	6	90

BUILDING UPGRADES		COST			EFFECT
Upgrade	Requirement	🪨	💣	🕐	
Reactor	None	50	50	40	Enables double build queue
Tech Lab	None	50	50	30	Enables Banshees, Ravens, Battlecruisers with Fusion Core

GHOST ACADEMY

Hot Key: G

COST:
 150   50   40

BUILDING STATISTICS		
Health	Armor	Energy
1250	1	

The Ghost Academy is a secondary military structure, enabling the recruitment of the Ghost at Barracks with a Tech Lab attached.

Ghost upgrades are also researched here, and Nukes are armed at the Ghost Academy.

Remember that you can arm one Nuke for each Ghost Academy you build, should you actually need more than one at a time!

BUILD REQUIREMENTS:

Barracks

FUSION CORE

Hot Key: C

COST:
 150   150   65

BUILDING STATISTICS		
Health	Armor	Energy
750	1	

The Fusion Core is a secondary military structure that unlocks the Battlecruiser for construction at your Starports with an attached Tech Lab.

Upgrades for the Battlecruiser, including the critical Yamato Cannon are also researched here.

BUILD REQUIREMENTS:

Starport

BUILDING UPGRADES		COST			EFFECT
Upgrade	Requirement				
Personal Cloaking	None	150	150	120	Grants Ghosts the Cloak ability
Moebius Reactor	None	100	100	80	Increases Ghost starting Energy by 25
Arm Silo with Nuke	None	100	100	60	Allows Ghosts to designate Nuke targets

BUILDING UPGRADES		COST			EFFECT
Upgrade	Requirement				
Weapon Refit	None	150	150	60	Enables Battlecruiser Yamato Cannon
Behemoth Reactor	None	150	150	80	Increases Battlecruiser starting Energy by 25

PROTOSS ARMY

The Protoss are a powerful psychic race, inscrutable in their motives, ancient and technologically advanced. While their numbers are limited, the Protoss make up for this with sophisticated weapons of war.

Protoss units are individually powerful, making even small groups of Protoss units a dangerous combat force, and Protoss psionic abilities give them access to devastating abilities such as the feared Psionic Storm.

The Protoss army consists of many autonomous robotic forces, as well as machines purpose-built for battle. The two factions of their race, the High and the Dark Templar have joined one another in support of the war effort, and now the Psionic warrior Zealots are accompanied by the agile Stalkers.

Even a small army of basic Protoss units forces can be effective, and large groups of their more advanced units are exceptionally devastating and difficult to stop.

PROTOSS ADVANTAGES

Protoss have many advantages stemming from their mastery of sophisticated technology and psionic power.

Powerful Units

Protoss units are almost all individually stronger than Terran or Zerg units. At equal or greater numbers, they can often easily win a battle, and against superior forces, they can still manage to fight on even terms.

Chrono Boost

The Protoss economic booster, Chrono Boost, is distinct from the Terran or Zerg abilities, as it can be used to boost not only the Protoss economy, but also their military production and research speed.

This ability grows in power over the course of the game, as less Energy needs to be spent on speeding Probe production, and more used for speeding army production and research.

Shields

All Protoss units and buildings are protected by powerful energy barriers. These Shields form an extra layer of defense on top of the health of any Protoss unit or structure.

Protoss Shields also regenerate automatically—if 10 seconds pass without a Protoss unit or structure taking damage, their Shields begin to recover at a rate of 2 per second. While this will not help you directly in battle, it *is* helpful when retreating a damaged force from battle, or after recovering from an enemy push.

Lightly damaged buildings will suffer no permanent health damage at all, and even severely damaged units will often have full powered Shields before the next major battle begins.

Protoss air units in particular benefit from Shields, as they can perform hit and run attacks, falling back as their Shields begin to fail and giving them time to recover.

Pylon Power

The Protoss Supply structure is the Pylon, and these special crystals also create a Pylon Power Field in a radius around each Pylon. This power field is necessary to power *all* Protoss structures, as well as their defensive Photon Cannon.

New structures must be created within this field, but in exchange, new structures (and units!) can be warped into existence at great speed once a power field has been created.

WE REQUIRE MORE POWER

The Protoss Nexus, Assimilator, and Pylon do not require a power field to create.

Warp Technology

Protoss are masters of a sophisticated warping technology. With their ability to warp in units and structures, they can create an entire functional base from a single Probe, and create a ground army literally out of thin air.

Unlike the Terran SCVs (who must build each structure by hand) or the Zerg Drone (which is consumed with the creation of a new building), Protoss Probes can warp in a structure and then return to work immediately while the structure finishes warping into existence.

A single Probe can create an entire expansion, a line of Photon Cannons, several Pylons, or a whole new military production line in seconds, and all of the new structures will warp in nearly simultaneously.

In addition, once Warp Gate research has been unlocked at the Cybernetics Core, all Protoss Gateways can be converted to Warp Gates.

Once this has been done, *all* Gateway units can be warped into existence *anywhere* that you have a Pylon power field. Units that are warped in are 'created' in 5 seconds, no matter their original Gateway build time. As if that wasn't enough, every unit has a speed bonus applied to its creation (the cooldown of a Warpgate is 10 seconds faster than the creation of a unit from a Gateway normally!).

The Protoss transport, the Warp Prism, can also create small Power Fields, either to temporarily power base structures, or to create a field anywhere on the map for Warp Gate usage.

Split Tech Tree

The Protoss tech tree is unusual in that after the Cybernetics Core has been constructed, any of three different branches of their tech tree become immediately accessible.

This allows you to progress down the Templar, Air, or Robotics paths, either in response to your opponent's army choices, or to force a response *from* your opponent. Fielding the right answer to your opponents army can give you a decisive advantage on the battlefield.

It is important to take advantage of this tech tree flexibility by making a decision about the route to take, and executing it as quickly as possible— there's a limited window of opportunity to inflict maximum damage with a tech unit before your opponent can stabilize the fight, and the faster you acquire your chosen tech units, the better your chances of exploiting that window.

Permanent Cloaking

As masters of Cloaking technology, Protoss units that have access to Cloak are *permanently* cloaked. They require no Energy to maintain, and do not have to activate or deactivate their Cloak like Zerg Burrow.

The Dark Templar and Observer are permanently cloaked, while the Mothership cloaks *all* friendly units near it.

The Mothership

The Protoss Mothership is a super unit, unique among all races. Only a single Mothership can be fielded at any time, it is the single most expensive unit in the game, with the greatest technology requirement and longest build time.

In exchange, the Mothership is a powerful combat unit that *must* be dealt with swiftly by your opponent once it hits the field, or it can end a match alongside your army, as it cloaks your entire military force (and any friendly buildings in the area). If your opponent loses his Detectors in battle and cannot destroy the Mothership quickly enough, destruction is soon to follow.

Photon Cannons

The Protoss defensive structure is an all in one turret—the Photon Cannon can attack air units, ground units, *and* serves as a Detector. Make use of this flexibility by placing a few near your worker lines and key chokepoints, and you can rest assured that any cloak, burrow, or aerial raid will quickly be spotted and attacked, giving you time to respond.

PROTOSS DISADVANTAGES

Expensive Units

As a counter to their individual power, Protoss units are also the most expensive units of any race. Each loss is more painful for the Protoss than the Terran or (especially) the Zerg.

Make good use of your troops on offense or defense, you cannot afford to throw Protoss units away, and responding quickly to hard counters (air, cloak, or burrow technology) is extremely important.

Pylon Power

Ironically, the same Pylon Power Field that is a useful benefit for the Protoss when warping in structures and units is a *disadvantage* when it comes to fighting your opponent's army off in a close fight inside your bases.

When Pylons powering your military structures or Photon Cannons are destroyed, those structures or defenses power down, crippling your ability create reinforcements or fight off your opponent's force.

It is very important that you create redundant power fields to cover your military production structures, because Pylons are the weakest structure in a Protoss base, and intelligent enemies will target your Pylons *first* if they see a single Pylon powering all of your Gateways or Photon Cannons!

Split Tech Tree

Another double edged sword, the flexibility offered by the split tech tree can also cause problems for you if it is not used carefully.

Scouting your opponent properly is *vital* for choosing which tech tree to pursue, because you do not have the resources early in the game to easily create the structures and units from multiple trees simultaneously.

As a match progresses into the mid game, be sure to build the additional structures in response to your opponent's military, and your changing needs. Having rapid access to your full unit selection is well worth the cost, and isn't a burden once your economy is working at full speed.

Reconnaissance

Protoss have the weakest scouting ability of all three races in the early game. It is vitally important that you make good use of Probe scouts to cover Xel'Naga Towers, and create a line of sight corridor to your opponent's base.

Due to the nature of the Protoss tech tree, it is very important that you periodically scout your opponents base (assuming it isn't walled off!), to ensure that you are making the right tech decisions.

Once you get access to Hallucinate, Blink, the Observer, or air units, your recon becomes considerably stronger.

EMP

Finally, while it is rare that any single unit or ability in StarCraft II is useful against every possible unit in an army, the Terran Ghost's EMP bears special mention, because it is *exactly* that against ALL Protoss forces.

If your opponent is fielding Ghosts (and if he knows you're playing Protoss, you should expect them!), you need to make them a priority target. A single or double EMP strike can strip the Shields from your entire army, leaving them painfully vulnerable in the ensuing battle.

On offense, if you are hit by an EMP, but you at least have the option of retreating and allowing your Shields to recover, but on defense, you have no such luxury, and you must engage in battle.

Killing the Ghost after the EMP has hit your army won't help you in the current fight, but it at least forces your opponent to build more, and they are costly units in terms of Gas.

Good recon is *vital* for stopping a push accompanied by Ghosts. If you see your opponent pushing towards your bases with Ghosts in his army, try to send out a strike force to kill the Ghosts before they reach your base, or to at least bait out an early EMP.

It is better to lose a few units assassinating enemy Ghosts than it is to lose your army in battle!

The trickiest part about dealing with the Ghost is that while Protoss have their own powerful area of effect ability with Psionic Storm, the Ghost's EMP arrives on the battlefield long before you can research Psionic Storm.

Once Ghosts have Cloak, you need Observers to locate them in battle, though your opponent can't keep his Ghosts cloaked at all times, so again, if you can hit them before they cloak while on offense, you can eliminate their danger.

High Templar Feedback can strip the Energy from a Ghost, but High Templar are too slow and fragile to land a Feedback before an EMP goes off in most normal engagements (which then drains their Energy, stopping the Feedback). Once Psionic Storm research is finished, you at least have parity in the area of effect war (as long as you get off the storms before the EMP hits!).

Dark Templar work well for pre-fight assassination, unless the enemy army has Ravens present, but you will usually see an instant Scanner Sweep (or EMP!), so don't expect the Dark Templars to return from their mission!

A few Stalkers with Blink or Zealots with Charge can also act as a mobile Ghost-killing force. Phoenix can also make use of Graviton Beam to lift off a Ghost before it can cast, but don't try to perform a lift in isolation with a mass of Marines nearby!

Finally, the last option you have is simply trying to bait out the EMP. A skilled opponent won't use the EMP on small numbers of troops, but if you can spare even half of your army and your Photon Cannons, you can have a fighting chance on defense. Being hit with an EMP and repulsed on offense is not an immediate loss (back off!), but having your entire army's Shields and Energy stripped on defense can cost you a match.

Consider researching Hallucinate early and making use of the decoys to bait an EMP, at the very least you will drain Energy from MULEs due to Scanner Sweep usage, and until Ravens arrive, at least some EMPs will be wasted on fake units.

PROTOSS UNIT ROLES

The Protoss Stalker benefits from dancing micro, particularly once Blink has been researched.

Stalkers, Sentries and Immortals are all good candidates for focus firing, and the Void Ray is especially devastating when focused on single strong targets or structures.

The Protoss mobile Detector is the Observer, and their stationary Detector is the Photon Cannon. They have no temporary means of revealing Cloaked or Burrowed units, but Psionic Storm can damage undetected units, Forcefield can block them, and Vortex can temporarily remove them from a battle.

The Colossus and Psionic Storm provide area of effect damage for the Protoss army.

Protoss anti-air is available from the Stalker, Sentry, Archon, Phoenix, Void Ray, Carrier, Mothership, Photon Cannon, and if carefully aimed, Psionic Storm.

Protoss siege breakers are the Colossus with range upgrade, the Carrier, and Mothership Vortex.

Protoss air is very strong, it has the benefit of the fastest unit in the game with the Phoenix, the strongest focused damage from the Void Ray, and the powerful Carrier and Mothership as finishers.

UNIT MIXES

Zealots, Stalkers, and Sentries all work well together as a ground force. The composition of this mix should be changed depending on the mix that your opponent is using. As an example, Zealots and Sentries using Guardian Shield are strong against many Marines, while Stalkers (when microed carefully) with Sentries are effective against massed Roaches. If your opponent is using a mixed force, you will likely need to mix yours as well.

Remember to upgrade your core units; Charge, Blink, and Hallucinate all greatly increase the power of Zealots, Stalkers, and Sentries.

Many Protoss units are specialists, and small numbers should be added to your core ground force, depending on what you scout your opponent using. High and Dark Templar, Archons, Immortals, and Colossi are all very effective when supplementing an existing ground force.

PROTOSS GROUND UPGRADES

All Protoss Ground upgrades are purchased from the Forge, in addition, all Protoss shields can be upgraded from the Forge. Shielding upgrades affects all Protoss units and structures.

PROTOSS AIR UPGRADES

All Protoss Air upgrades are purchased from the Cybernetics Core.

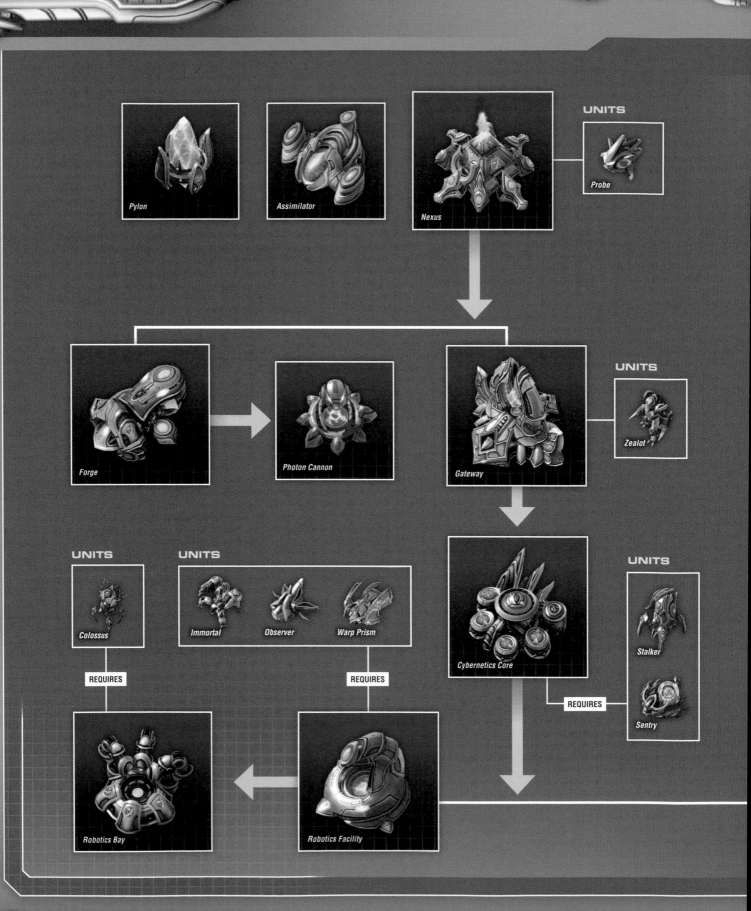

UNITS

Pylon

Assimilator

Nexus

Probe

UNITS

Forge

Photon Cannon

Gateway

Zealot

UNITS

Colossus

UNITS

Immortal

Observer

Warp Prism

Cybernetics Core

UNITS

Stalker

REQUIRES

REQUIRES

REQUIRES

Sentry

Robotics Bay

Robotics Facility

PROTOSS TECH TREE

UNITS

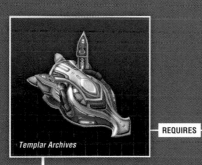

Templar Archives

Archon

High Templar

REQUIRES

Dark Shrine

UNITS

REQUIRES

Dark Templar

UNITS

Fleet Beacon

REQUIRES

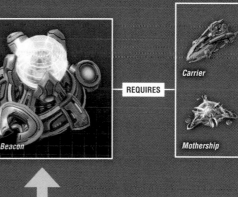

Carrier

Mothership

Twilight Council

Starport

UNITS

Pheonix

Void Ray

PROBE

COST:

 50   0   17   1

BUILT FROM: | **BUILD REQUIREMENTS:** | **UPGRADES:**

Nexus

NONE

As with the other workers, while this unit is weak defensively and offensively, it is absolutely vital for your victory on the battlefield.

The Probe's unique power is the ability to construct multiple buildings at once. While the Terran SCV must construct each building individually, and the Zerg Drone is destroyed in the process of building a single building, a lone Probe can build an entire base almost simultaneously, resources permitting!

The Protoss Probe warps in new buildings. When you construct a building, the cost is paid immediately. Once a building begins warping in, it automatically finishes once it has reached full health and shields. If you cancel a structure before it has fully built, 75% of the resources spent are refunded.

It is possible to queue up multiple buildings very easily with a Probe (the Terran SCV can do so, but it is a slower process, Zerg Drones cannot).

You do need to be careful with this ability. While it is powerful, building multiple structures while under attack is a good way to lose a lot of resources quickly. Your opponent can target the buildings that are warping in and destroy them easily while they are at low health and shields.

Because you can warp in many buildings at once, the Probe is also powerful due to its ability to create a nearly fully functioning expansion almost immediately. Only Photon Cannons cannot be placed during the initial warp of the Nexus, Assimilators, and Pylons. Once the Pylons have finished, you can easily finish the job by warping in several Photon Cannons to protect the fledgling expansion.

WEAPON STATISTICS

Weapon	Damage	Attacks	Attack Speed	Range	Targets
Particle Beam	5	1	1.50	Melee	Ground

UNIT STATISTICS

Health	Shields	Energy	Armor	Movement Speed	Acceleration	Line of Sight	Size
20	20	No	0	2.81	Yes	8	1

UNIT TYPE

Light	Armored	Biological	Mechanical	Psionic	Massive	Structure

The Probe is the basic worker unit for the Protoss army.

GATHERER

ZEALOT

COST:

 100 0 38 2

BUILT FROM:	BUILD REQUIREMENTS:	UPGRADES:
Gateway	NONE	*Twilight Council*

When upgraded with Charge, they gain increased movement speed *and* gain the ability to charge nearby units, greatly increasing their lethality against ranged or fast moving units.

Zealots are more than a match for Zerglings in close combat individually, but it is important that you engage Zerglings in a chokepoint, or at the very least, with the Zealots back to a nearby wall. This prevents the Zerglings from surrounding the Zealots and bringing their full potential damage to bear. When blocking off a chokepoint or ramp leading into your base (or any area you are defending), make use of Hold Position to lock your Zealots in place. They'll still attack any Zealots or Zerglings that come into range, but you will still have to watch out for Marines engaging them.

You can expect Zealots to slice through Marines fairly quickly if they can close the distance, but be wary of attacking massed Marines unsupported. Once a critical mass of Marines is reached, focused fire can down Zealots very quickly. Zealots can be kited by Marines, though they are equivalent speed without Charge or Stimpacks.

Because Zealots only cost Minerals, it is important that you build them throughout a match and mix them with your other, more Gas heavy units to produce a solid mix of ground forces.

WEAPON STATISTICS

Weapon	Damage	Attacks	Attack Speed	Range	Targets
Psi Blades	8 (+1)	2	1.20	Melee	Ground

UNIT STATISTICS

Health	Shields	Energy	Armor	Movement Speed	Acceleration	Line of Sight	Size
100	50	No	1	2.25 (2.75)	No	9	2

UNIT TYPE

Light	Armored	Biological	Mechanical	Psionic	Massive	Structure
	Armored	Biological				

The iconic Zealot is a powerful psionic warrior, and the toughest of the basic starting units for all of the races.

WARP GATE

UPGRADES		COST			EFFECT
Upgrade	Requirement				
Charge	None	200	200	140	Grants Zealot Charge ability and increases movement speed

CHARGE

Charge grants a movement speed increase to all Zealots, and an automatically triggered charge that rushes Zealots into melee range at great speed. With Charge, Zealots can get into melee range almost instantly, which allows you to close the gap with almost any ground unit. Charge should always be researched if you are fielding Zealots in any significant numbers, it greatly increases their combat power.

This is particularly important against ranged units, or units with a faster base movement speed. Because Charge increases Zealot movement speed *and* gives them an actual charging move, they become substantial more mobile.

Because Zealots are both tough and cheap units, once you research Charge, they remain useful throughout the game. Their only substantial weakness once Charge is researched are air units, or aoe attacks that can damage a pack of them.

Abilities

CHARGE
Hot Key: C

Effect: Causes the Zealot to charge at a nearby enemy ground unit

Cost	Range	Radius	Autocast
10s Cooldown	5	0	Yes

STALKER

COST:

 125   50   42   2

Hot Key:
S

| BUILT FROM: | BUILD REQUIREMENTS: | UPGRADES: |

Gateway

Cybernetics Core

Twilight Council

When upgraded with Blink, Stalkers become a powerful harassing unit, and can use their Blink to move up and down differing levels of elevation, as long as they have line of sight. They also provide early anti-air for the Protoss force.

Stalkers are perfect against early units that Zealots are too slow to effectively engage, and because they are ranged, they benefit from the ability to effectively focus fire your opponents units.

Stalkers are vital if you know your opponent is going for any sort of serious air assault, both for protecting your base from raids, and for providing mobile anti-air to a mixed ground force.

While Stalkers deal less damage individually than Zealots, they are slightly more durable, and their mobility and potential for focus fire attacks keep them roughly on par in terms of potential effectiveness.

Stalkers are also important if your opponent is massing Armored units in their ground force, their focused bonus damage can help to turn to the tide of battle.

WEAPON STATISTICS

Weapon	Damage	Attacks	Attack Speed	Range	Targets
Particle Disrupters	10 +4 vs Armored (+1/+0)	1	1.44	6	Air/Ground

UNIT STATISTICS

Health	Shields	Energy	Armor	Movement Speed	Acceleration	Line of Sight	Size
80	80	No	1	2.95	No	10	2

UNIT TYPE

Light	Armored	Biological	Mechanical	Psionic	Massive	Structure

The armored Stalker is a fast moving combat walker unit armed with a reasonably strong ranged attack.

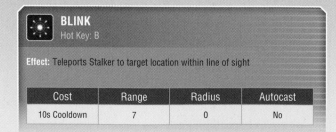

UPGRADES

UPGRADES		COST			EFFECT
Upgrade	Requirement				
Blink	None	150	150	110	Grants Stalkers Blink ability

BLINK

Blink grants an activated ability to all Stalkers to teleport a short distance. This ability has a 10 second cooldown, which can allow you to endlessly dance away from melee, short ranged, or slower units. With careful micro, it greatly extends the lifespan of any Stalker on the frontline of a conflict.

In addition, Blink allows for rapid mobility when chasing a fleeing enemy, and (with proper line of sight), allows for teleportation onto higher ground, useful for attacking an enemy base from an unexpected direction, or escaping a ground force. On some maps, it is even possible to blink across chasms or open space.

If you're planning on using Stalkers in any significant numbers, Blink is a vital upgrade, as it greatly extends their tactical options, substantially increasing their utility, but remember that it also demands direct micro to have any impact on the outcome of a battle.

Abilities

BLINK
Hot Key: B

Effect: Teleports Stalker to target location within line of sight

Cost	Range	Radius	Autocast
10s Cooldown	7	0	No

SENTRY

COST:

 50  100 42 2

BUILT FROM:	BUILD REQUIREMENTS:	UPGRADES:
Gateway	Cybernetics Core	Cybernetics Core

The Sentry is more fragile than the other Protoss ground units, and has a high Gas cost, so it is usually best used mixed in smaller numbers with a larger force of other ground units.

The Sentry is a support caster unit. It has a reasonably strong ranged attack that can hit air or ground units, but it is much less durable than the Zealot or Stalker.

The Sentry's support abilities are all very useful in many situations.

WEAPON STATISTICS

Weapon	Damage	Attacks	Attack Speed	Range	Targets
Disruption Beam	6 (+1)	1	1.00	5	Air/Ground

UNIT STATISTICS

Health	Shields	Energy	Armor	Movement Speed	Acceleration	Line of Sight	Size
40	40	Yes	1	2.25	No	10	2

UNIT TYPE

Light	Armored	Biological	Mechanical	Psionic	Massive	Structure

The Sentry is the earliest caster unit that the Protoss can access, though it is also a solid combat unit as well.

WARP GATE

UPGRADES		COST			EFFECT
Upgrade	Requirement				
Hallucination	None	100	100	110	Grants Sentry the Hallucination ability

HALLUCINATION

Researching Hallucination unlocks the ability for your Sentries. Typically, you should research Warp Gates at your Cybernetics Core first, but do quickly pick up this research once Warp Gates have completed if you are making use of Sentries in any significant numbers.

FORCE FIELD
Hot Key: F

Effect: Creates a Force Field that blocks ground unit movement for 15 seconds

Cost	Range	Radius	Autocast
50 Energy	9	?	No

Force Field creates a roughly circular energy barrier on the ground, preventing ground units from moving through it. Force Field *can* be placed atop ground units (friendly or enemy), and it will displace them.

Force Fields can be placed atop one another, so you can create an overlapping barrier of fields that can block a large stretch of terrain, with sufficient Sentries and Energy.

Force Field is a very powerful defensive tool for the Protoss, and it is especially potent against melee units. It allows you to create choke points instantly, and in some cases, can also be used to block some (or all!) of an enemy force in or out of an area (often a base).

Because Protoss units tend to be superior in a one on one fight to most other ground units, setting up a situation where you have numerical superiority, or limited frontage at a chokepoint is very advantageous for the Protoss army.

Use Force Field to block off ramps leading into your bases, to constrict existing chokepoints, to cut off the retreat of a fleeing force, to separate an enemy army, or to protect your own force while retreating.

When you only have limited Energy for Force Field creation, you should make use of existing chokepoints on the map to maximize the power of the ability.

Force Fields can also be used to disrupt enemy formations, making it difficult for them to focus fire effectively on your army.

GUARDIAN SHIELD
Hot Key: G

Effect: Reduces incoming ranged damage by 2 for 15 seconds

Cost	Range	Radius	Autocast
75 Energy	0	4	No

Guardian Shield creates a large spherical aura of protection around a Sentry. Friendly units inside this barrier take 2 less damage from any enemy ranged attack.

This makes the Guardian Shield extremely strong against the Terran army, as not only is their entire army ranged, it severely cuts the damage output of their basic unit, the Marine.

Guardian Shield is still useful against Zerg and Protoss forces, as they both field a variety of ranged units as well, though it obviously helps less against high damage units, and not at all against Zealots, Dark Templar, Zerglings, Banelings, Broodlings, or Ultralisks.

Guardian Shield is a very fire and forget ability. Any time you engage in battle, activate Guardian Shield, then worry about microing your various units. If necessary, move the Sentry slightly to cover more of your army. Extra Sentries can make use of Guardian Shield to protect larger armies. Guardian Shield does not stack with itself, and doesn't protect stuctures, only units!

HALLUCINATION
Hot Key: C

Effect: Creates an illusionary Protoss unit that lasts 60 seconds

Cost	Range	Radius	Autocast
100 Energy	0	0	No

Hallucination must be researched from the Cybernetics Core before it can be used by your Sentries. Hallucination creates temporary illusory units. These units deal no actual combat damage, and take double the damage of a real unit, but they can be used to bolster the apparent size of your army, fake out your opponent with a specific tech unit, scout with a fast air unit, or simply increase the total effective health of your army.

Without a Detector, Hallucinations appear to be real units to your opponent, and his troops and defenses will automatically fire at them. Mixing in Hallucinations with your army is useful both for the psychological effects (your opponent may see a certain tech unit and waste time and resources building a counter, or they may react differently to an apparently larger army) and its practical combat effects.

Because Hallucinations can provide line of sight, creating a fast unit such as the Phoenix and using it to scout or sight for your army is very helpful.

A mass of basic units in your army created via Hallucination is also very useful, as your enemy cannot distinguish between a Hallucinated unit and a normal unit without a source of Detection.

At the very least, you force your opponent to expend resources on bringing a source of Detection to the battle, and if they don't, they're going to expend part of their army's offensive power on destroying harmless illusions, handing you an easy victory in battle.

Be careful about using Hallucination to create high-tech units too early in the game. If your opponent ignores the obvious fake units, you don't gain any effective health bonus in combat.

Hallucinations are generally a bit less useful on offense than defense, as your opponent will usually have fixed Detectors in their base. Even so, with their limited range, your Hallucinations will likely still absorb fire from enemy forces in the confusion of battle, and on defense, your opponent must bring mobile Detectors, or your Hallucinations will absorb damage freely.

Even if your opponent is diligent in covering their Detector needs to counter Hallucination usage, you can still make use of the scouting power by creating illusionary Phoenix.

Hallucination is expensive to use, and its combat uses require several Sentries creating a good sized group of illusions to be more effective than a smaller number using Guardian Shield and Force Fields well.

If you *do* have a moderate sized group of Sentries with full Energy bars, don't hesitate to make use of Hallucinate for a major push or defense, it can significantly increase the durability of your army.

HIGH TEMPLAR

Hot Key:
T

COST:
 50   150   55   2

BUILT FROM:	BUILD REQUIREMENTS:	UPGRADES:
Gateway	Templar Archives	Templar Archives

The High Templar is a dedicated caster unit, with no basic attack, it relies instead on the power of its abilities and Psionic Storm to cripple and destroy foes of the Protoss.

High Templars are expensive, slow, and weak, so they must be protected by a standing army, or used defensively to protect your bases from raids. High Templar are priority targets for your opponent, so you can expect them to be focus fired and picked off if left unattended.

High Templars can inflict grievous damage to an opposing army, so even if they are taken out, as long as you get a few well placed Storms on the field, they can still be well worth their cost.

Two High Templar can merge to form an Archon, so even after they have expended their Energy, they can be used to create a powerful ground unit to add to your army.

WEAPON STATISTICS

Weapon	Damage	Attacks	Attack Speed	Range	Targets
NONE					

UNIT STATISTICS

Health	Shields	Energy	Armor	Movement Speed	Acceleration	Line of Sight	Size
40	40	Yes	0	1.87	No	10	2

UNIT TYPE

Light	Armored	Biological	Mechanical	Psionic	Massive	Structure

The High Templar is the most powerful Protoss caster unit, with access to the lethal Psionic Storm ability.

WARP GATE

UPGRADES		COST			EFFECT
Upgrade	Requirement				
Psionic Storm	None	200	200	110	Grants High Templar Psionic Storm ability
Khaydarin Amulet	None	150	150	110	Increases High Templar starting Energy by 25

PSIONIC STORM

High Templar do not have access to their signature ability immediately, it must be researched, which is both expensive and slow. Once you have built a Templar Archives, this upgrade should be your first priority.

KHAYDARIN AMULET

The Khaydarin Amulet increases the starting Energy of newly created High Templar by 25. Unlike the Energy upgrades for other caster units, this one is *extremely* important for High Templar, as it allows newly warped in High Templar to immediately cast Psionic Storm. Without it, they have to wait to build up the Energy necessary.

This should still be researched after Psionic Storm, but it is absolutely worth acquiring, particularly since High Templar tend to be expended quickly—they get off their storms and then either morph into an Archon, or are killed by enemy forces due to their slow speed.

FEEDBACK
Hot Key: F

Effect: Drains all Energy from a target, dealing damage equal to the Energy lost

Cost	Range	Radius	Autocast
50 Energy	9	0	No

Feedback drains all Energy from an enemy unit, dealing damage equivalent to the Energy drained.

Feedback is particularly useful for targeting enemy units that cannot dump their Energy quickly or have a large impact on the battlefield, such as the Thor, Medivac, Banshee, Raven, Battlecruiser, Mothership and Overseer.

Ghosts, Sentries, High Templar, and Infestors are all viable targets, but all of them have the ability to quickly dump their Energy on the battlefield, and High Templar are generally too slow to move into range and cast Feedback in time to stop them from casting from the back lines of a battle.

In most cases, you should save Energy for Psionic Storm usage, but against key units that can affect the outcome of a battle (eg, Thors vs Colossus, Battlecruisers vs Carriers, Ravens or Overseers when you have Dark Templar or the Mothership on the field), Feedback may be the right choice.

PSIONIC STORM
Hot Key: T

Effect: Deals 80 damage over 4 seconds.

Cost	Range	Radius	Autocast
75 Energy, 3s Cooldown	9	1.5	No

The powerful Psionic Storm deals 80 damage over 4 seconds to all units in an area, ground, air, cloaked, or burrowed. Psionic Storm can shred an opponent's army in seconds, but an alert opponent will immediately move his troops out of range of the storm. This is still desirable in battle, because your own forces will continue to attack, while his take damage and move to evade the damage.

Psionic Storm has a 3 second cooldown from a single High Templar, and multiple Psionic Storms DO NOT stack, so you should either spread storms around your opponents army, or wait for the first to elapse before casting a second in the same area.

Be careful with storm, you can kill your own units, so it is best used against enemy ranged units, or on their army before it spreads out and their melee or short ranged units hit the front of your army.

Psionic Storm can be effective against packs of air units as well, but be careful with your placement of the storm—when targeting air units, you need to place the storm where the *base* of the air unit is, not where the 3d model of the unit is on your screen (aim low!).

To aid with targeting, while you have Psionic Storm activated, but before you place it, any enemy units that will be hit by the storm are highlighted in red with your cursor. Use this indicator to quickly check your placement before hitting a group of air units.

Psionic Storm can be used for worker raids in concert with Warp Prisms, but High Templar are generally too expensive and important for army battles to be used in this role.

ARCHON WARP
Hot Key: C

Effect: Sacrifices two Templar to create an Archon

Cost	Range	Radius	Autocast
12s Merge Time	0	0	No

DARK TEMPLAR

Hot Key:

D

COST:

 125 125 55 2

BUILT FROM:	BUILD REQUIREMENTS:	UPGRADES:
Gateway	Dark Shrine	NONE

Perfect for raids or combat support, Dark Templars are rather frail if spotted without their cloak. Fielding Dark Templars will *immediately* cause your opponent to begin building Detectors in his base, and adding mobile Detectors to his offensive army. If he does not, Dark Templar can quickly win you a fight by assassinating the enemy army, worker line, and core structure.

Even once your opponent begins to field Detectors in larger numbers, Dark Templar remain a viable and dangerous part of your army, as they still deal extremely high damage per hit—just be sure to keep them mixed in with your army, not used for raids on their own, where they can be picked off.

With Dark Templar as part of your army, when your enemy is on offense, he *must* field mobile Detectors with his force, or use his temporary detection methods to reveal your Dark Templar. If you can destroy the enemy mobile Detectors, they must either retreat immediately or suffer crippling ground losses.

For this reason, Dark Templar work very well as a containment threat when mixed in your army. Your opponent may be able to hold the line with fixed Detectors at his bases, but this gives you the ability to freely expand around the map.

WEAPON STATISTICS

Weapon	Damage	Attacks	Attack Speed	Range	Targets
Warp Blades	45 (+5)	1	1.69	Melee	Ground

UNIT STATISTICS

Health	Shields	Energy	Armor	Movement Speed	Acceleration	Line of Sight	Size
40	80	No	1	2.81	No	8	2

UNIT TYPE

Light	Armored	Biological	Mechanical	Psionic	Massive	Structure
	Armored		Mechanical		Massive	Structure

The Dark Templar is a permanently cloaked warrior, armed with a vicious psi-blade.

WARP GATE

Two Dark Templar can be morphed into Archons, but their total cost per Archon is higher than that of a High Templar morph, and they may be more effective in Dark Templar form as part of your army.

Still, if you need Archons for fighting air units or massed biological armies, don't hesitate to morph them.

THE DARK TEMPLAR REVEAL

When you strike with your first Dark Templar, carefully choose a target in your opponent's base, or make a push with your army with the Dark Templar mixed into your force.

You want to deal the most damage possible before your opponent responds to the threat with Detectors near his worker line, choke points, and with his army.

A skilled opponent will often scout your Dark Shrine before Dark Templar hit the field, so be sure to keep them with your army, don't send them out alone if your opponent knows they are coming.

PERMANENTLY CLOAKED

Effect: Dark Templar are always Cloaked

Cost	Range	Radius	Autocast
Passive	0	0	No

ARCHON WARP
Hot Key: C

Effect: Sacrifices two Templar to create an Archon

Cost	Range	Radius	Autocast
12s Merge Time	0	0	No

OBSERVER

Hot Key: B

COST:

 50 100 40 1

BUILT FROM: Robotics Facility

BUILD REQUIREMENTS: NONE

UPGRADES: Robotics Bay

Once you have access to Observers, you should gradually create a network of them covering the area around your opponent's bases, and eventually at all potential expansion sites and areas around your bases.

Even an alert opponent traveling with mobile Detectors with his army will rarely manage to catch every Observer that you place throughout the mid and late game, and for Observers in particularly crucial locations, you should always replace them even if they are destroyed.

Observers must accompany your army on offense when facing enemy cloaked or burrowed troops, and if you are forced back to your base by the threat of a cloaked or burrowed foe, hold your army near your Photon Cannons until you can get a Robotics Facility up and running.

Be sure to bring multiple observers with your air or ground armies if your opponent is being alert about dispatching your Observers in combat. They are difficult to target, but depending on how heavily your opponent is relying on Cloak or Burrow, they may explicitly target them in every engagement.

WEAPON STATISTICS

Weapon	Damage	Attacks	Attack Speed	Range	Targets
NONE					

UNIT STATISTICS

Health	Shields	Energy	Armor	Movement Speed	Acceleration	Line of Sight	Size
40	20	No	0	1.87 (2.81)	Yes	11	

UNIT TYPE

Light	Armored	Biological	Mechanical	Psionic	Massive	Structure

The Protoss Observer is a permanently cloaked aerial scout, a nearly perfect reconnaissance unit.

ROBOTICS

UPGRADES

Upgrade	Requirement	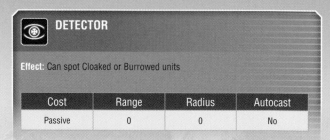		
Gravitic Boosters	None	100	100	80

EFFECT Increases Observer movement speed

GRAVITIC BOOSTERS

Gravitic Boosters increase Observer movement speed significantly. Before they upgrade, they will lag behind your armies, but after the upgrade, they can keep up with even your faster units, and can respond more quickly to mobile cloaked or burrowed threats.

This is definitely an optional upgrade early in a match, but don't hesitate to pick it up in the midgame.

DETECTOR

Effect: Can spot Cloaked or Burrowed units

Cost	Range	Radius	Autocast
Passive	0	0	No

PERMANENTLY CLOAKED

Effect: Observers are always Cloaked

Cost	Range	Radius	Autocast
Passive	0	0	No

WARP PRISM

Hot Key:
A

COST:
 200   0   50   2

BUILT FROM:	BUILD REQUIREMENTS:	UPGRADES:
Robotics Facility	NONE	Robotics Bay

When in Phasing Mode, the Warp Prism radiates a power field. Warp Gate units can be warped into this power field just as a normal Pylon field, and it can be used to power buildings that have been shut down due to a loss of a nearby Pylon.

The Warp Prism is the most fragile of the various racial aerial transports, but its double duty as transport and mobile Pylon makes it a useful addition to your army, and with its speed upgrade, it can move Immortals or Colossus around the battlefield rapidly, as well as responding to threats or creating offensive forces via Warp Gates.

Because a Warp Prism can both carry units *and* allow them to be warped in, the Protoss backdoor capability is second only to the Zerg's Nydus Network.

Just be careful about the costs involved—Protoss units are expensive, and carrying a load of Immortals or Colossus and warping in more units to protect them is a *very* expensive attack.

WEAPON STATISTICS

Weapon	Damage	Attacks	Attack Speed	Range	Targets
NONE					

UNIT STATISTICS

Health	Shields	Energy	Armor	Movement Speed	Acceleration	Line of Sight	Size
100	40	No	0	2.5 (3.37)	No	10 (11 while in Phase mode)	8

UNIT TYPE

Light	Armored	Biological	Mechanical	Psionic	Massive	Structure

The Warp Prism is a very powerful support aircraft, as it acts as both a transport and a mobile Pylon.

ROBOTICS

UPGRADES		COST			EFFECT
Upgrade	Requirement				
Gravitic Drive	None	100	100	80	Increases Warp Prism movement speed

GRAVITIC DRIVE

This upgrade greatly increases the Warp Prism's movement speed. If you find yourself using Warp Prisms heavily either for transport or for warping, be sure to pick up this upgrade, it increases their survivability and responsiveness.

Abilities

PHASING MODE
Hot Key: E

Effect: Creates an area of Pylon Power

Cost	Range	Radius	Autocast
2s Cooldown	0	3.75	No

While in Phasing Mode, Warp Prisms project an area of Pylon power that can be used to power Protoss buildings, allow a Probe to create advanced structures, or warp in units from your Warp Gates.

Remember that with a single Probe on board, a Warp Prism allows you to create expansions anywhere on a map, including at island sites, and lets you build Photon Cannons before your Pylons finish building!

IMMORTAL

COST:

 250   100   55   4

BUILT FROM:	BUILD REQUIREMENTS:	UPGRADES:
Robotics Facility	NONE	NONE

An Immortals Hardened Shields provide resistance from any high damage attack, making them ideal for facing opposing Immortals, Siege Tanks, or Thors. Few Zerg units deal high individual damage for their shields to be a significant benefit, but they are still strong against the uncommon Ultralisks.

These formidable walkers have very high Health and Shields, and deal heavy damage, especially against Armored Units, though they have no defense against air units, so be sure to escort them with anti-air units if your opponent is fielding an aerial force.

Immortals are ideal for dealing with massed enemy Armored units. If your opponent begins fielding a disproportionate number of their early armored unit (Marauders, Stalkers, or Roaches), even a few Immortals can punch a hole in their army with little difficulty.

Mixing in a number of Immortals with any Protoss ground force gives the army real backbone, as the Immortals require a heavy beating to destroy.

Immortals are ideal for leading the assault on heavily defended positions, and even a small number can quickly reduce enemy structures to rubble (or organic sludge, in the case of the Zerg).

WEAPON STATISTICS

Weapon	Damage	Attacks	Attack Speed	Range	Targets
Phase Disrupters	20 +30 vs Armored (+2/+3)	1	1.45	5	Ground

UNIT STATISTICS

Health	Shields	Energy	Armor	Movement Speed	Acceleration	Line of Sight	Size
200	100	No	1	2.25	No	9	4

UNIT TYPE

Light	Armored	Biological	Mechanical	Psionic	Massive	Structure

The Immortal is a ground unit, with powerful Phase Disrupters that devastate Armored targets and structures.

ROBOTICS

Immortals are weakest against masses of smaller units. Zerglings, Marines, or even Zealots can all surround and destroy the large Immortal, or overwhelm them with low damage that bypasses their Hardened Shields.

Given their cost and build time, it is painfully expensive to constantly replace Immortal losses on the battlefield, so be sure to accompany them with your army and protect them.

Abilities

 ### HARDENED SHIELDS

Effect: Reduces any damage above 10 to 10 if Shields are active

Cost	Range	Radius	Autocast
Passive	0	0	No

DAMAGE REDUCTION

Terran	Protoss	Zerg
Marauder	Stalker	Roach
Siege Tank	Dark Templar	Baneling
Thor	Archon	Hydralisk
Viking	Immortal	N/A
Banshee	Colossus	Ultralisk
N/A	Photon Cannon	Brood Lord
N/A	N/A	Spine Crawler

Hardened Shields reduce any damage above 10, down to 10. Though this damage reduction helps against units that deal any damage above 10, it is most useful against units that deal a *lot* more than 10 damage.

This benefit requires that the Immortal has remaining Shield strength to function, once the Shields are depleted, the damage reduction no longer takes place.

Pay attention to the composition of your opponents army (or the expected composition) before you field Immortals in any significant numbers.

Hardened Shields also essentially ignore the effects of upgrades on enemy unit damage against Immortals.

COLOSSUS

COST:

 300   200   🕐 75   6

BUILT FROM:	BUILD REQUIREMENTS:	UPGRADES:
Robotics Facility	Robotics Bay	Robotics Bay

Several Colossi in a group can devastate a clumped up ground army in seconds. The Colossus is so tall that it can walk up and down cliff edges easily, allowing it to escape from ground pursuit, or strike against enemy worker lines from an unassailable position. Unfortunately this height also allows it to be attacked by air units, which it cannot defend itself against.

The Colossus becomes increasingly dangerous as more are grouped together. One is a serious threat early in the game, two can be lethal, and three or more will vaporize almost any ground army in seconds.

While powerful, the Colossus is vulnerable to attacks from air *and* ground weapons, and against enemies that have multiple attacks (Thor, Battlecruiser, Queen, etc.). This also means that attacks that are normally anti-air only (Missile Turret, Phoenix, etc.) can hit the Colossus.

The Colossus is the only other unit in the game besides the Terran Reaper with cliffwalking, and it has an additional advantage—it's tall legs allow it to actually walk over ground units!

Make use of this mobility in battle to reach a nearby ledge and fire down at hostile units, your Colossus cannot be blocked by normal sized ground units.

WEAPON STATISTICS

Weapon	Damage	Attacks	Attack Speed	Range	Targets	Radius
Thermal Lance	15 (+2)	2	1.65	6 (9)	Ground	1.25 in a line perpendicular to the Colossus (2.5 wide total)

UNIT STATISTICS

Health	Shields	Energy	Armor	Movement Speed	Acceleration	Line of Sight	Size
200	150	No	1	2.25	No	10	8

UNIT TYPE

Light	Armored	Biological	Mechanical	Psionic	Massive	Structure

The Colossus is an extremely powerful anti-ground walker, with a scything beam of energy that deals heavy area of effect damage in a straight line.

ROBOTICS

The Colossus deals its area of effect damage by firing its twin Thermal Lances in a line perpendicular to the facing of the Colossus. When the lances hit, they project damage out to a range of 1.25 to the left and right of the point of impact (so a line 2.5 range long in total).

This makes the Colossus *more* effective against smaller targets, where it can strike more per shot. It is also more effective against targets with lower maximum health levels, as they cannot stand up to the continuous area of effect damage.

UPGRADES		COST			EFFECT
Upgrade	Requirement			🕐	
Extended Thermal Lance	None	200	200	140	Increases Colossus weapon range

EXTENDED THERMAL LANCE

The range upgrade for the Colossus increases its range to 'siege range', that is, outside the range at which fixed defenses can respond to its attacks. This can force an enemy to respond to a push containing upgraded Colossus in the same way that the Terran Siege Tank can strike from beyond the range of fixed defenses.

The extended range also makes the Colossus even more dangerous on maps where it can make use of ledges to strike at your opponent's army while avoiding retaliation from enemy range units that can't quite reach it.

If you're making use of Colossus extensively, pick up the upgrade, but wait until you get first several Colossus on the field if you're low on Gas, it's an expensive and slow to research upgrade.

Abilities

CLIFF WALK

Effect: Allows Colossus to walk up and down cliffs

Cost	Range	Radius	Autocast
Passive	0	0	No

PHOENIX

COST:

 150 100 45 2

BUILT FROM:	BUILD REQUIREMENTS:	UPGRADES:
Stargate	NONE	NONE

Its high speed makes the Phoenix an excellent scout, in addition to its role of air superiority.

The Phoenix's Graviton Beam can lift a targeted ground unit into the sky to be picked apart by its brethren in the air. This is excellent for disabling high value, high power ground targets such as Siege Tanks, Immortals, Ghosts, High Templar, or Infestors.

The Phoenix is also a threat to the Zerg Queen, you can slow a Zerg's economy by lifting and killing the Queen with a pack of Phoenix.

Phoenix should be used primarily to stop an opponent from massing Light air units, but a large group of them can be used to support your army by making good use of Graviton Beam.

You can use the Phoenix to pick off enemy workers, but this is an expensive option in terms of Energy costs, and it is usually better to go for disabling dangerous enemy units in battle once your opponent's air force has been neutralized. The Phoenix is a poor choice for dealing with non-Light air units, as its relatively weak double attack is ineffective against targets with natural armor. Use the Void Ray instead!

Remember that the Phoenix's speed means that it can *always* retreat from an unfavorable situation. If you see a fight you can't win, leave. The Phoenix is also fast enough to 'dance' in the air, and you can micro individually damaged Phoenix out of a fight to regenerate their shields.

WEAPON STATISTICS

Weapon	Damage	Attacks	Attack Speed	Range	Targets
Ion Cannons	5 +5 vs Light (+1/+0)	2	1.10	4	Air

UNIT STATISTICS

Health	Shields	Energy	Armor	Movement Speed	Acceleration	Line of Sight	Size
120	60	Yes	0	4.25	Yes	10	

UNIT TYPE

Light	Armored	Biological	Mechanical	Psionic	Massive	Structure

The Phoenix is a pure anti-air spacecraft, and one of the fastest units in the game.

STARGATE

Abilities

GRAVITON BEAM

Hot Key: G

Effect: Suspends a non-Massive ground unit in the air, disabling it

Cost	Range	Radius	Autocast
50 Energy	4	0	No

The Phoenix Graviton Beam can lift any non-Massive unit from the ground, completely disabling it for several seconds.

The Phoenix that is using the beam cannot attack its target, but any *other* Phoenix in the area certainly can, and if used in an army battle, all of your anti-air units can target the suspended unit as well.

Make good use of Graviton Beam when you have few Phoenix by lifting enemy casters first, and with larger numbers of Phoenix, by lifting as many dangerous targets as possible.

VOID RAY

Hot Key:
V

COST:

250   150   60   3

BUILT FROM:	BUILD REQUIREMENTS:	UPGRADES:
Stargate	NONE	*Fleet Beacon*

The Void Ray deals damage by doing first 5 then 10 damage per second. Every five seconds that the Prismatic Beam is active, it increases its damage by one stage. For another five seconds after it stops firing, it will maintain its charge level. The beam is best used against tough Armored enemy targets.

Remember that against an Armored target, those values become 5 then 25 damage per second!

The upgrade levels for the Void Ray are also distinct, as it gains first +1/+1 damage, then +1/+3 to its base damage. Fully upgraded Void Rays are extremely powerful!

WEAPON STATISTICS

Weapon	Damage	Attacks	Attack Speed	Range	Targets
Prismatic Beam	5(+1)/10(+1) + 0(+0)/15(+2) vs Armored	1	0.60	6	Air/Ground

UNIT STATISTICS

Health	Shields	Energy	Armor	Movement Speed	Acceleration	Line of Sight	Size
150	100	No	0	2.25 (3.375)	Yes	10	

UNIT TYPE

Light	Armored	Biological	Mechanical	Psionic	Massive	Structure

The Void Ray is an unusual aerial unit, armed with a Prismatic Beam that charges up over time and can deal damage to ground or air targets.

STARGATE

UPGRADES		COST			EFFECT
Upgrade	Requirement				
Flux Vanes	None	150	150	80	Increases Void Ray movement speed and acceleration

FLUX VANES

This upgrade increases both Void Ray movement speed and acceleration, moving them from average speed to one of the faster air units in the game, and granting them more mobility in battle.

Because Void Rays can fire while on the move, this can significantly increase the danger of your Void Rays, both because of their ability to respond to enemy movements in battle, and the increased ability to project threat across the map.

You should *always* purchase this upgrade when fielding Void Rays in any significant numbers.

Abilities

PRISMATIC BEAM PRE-CHARGE

If you're willing to sacrifice a bit of shielding on a building while defending with Void Rays, you can actually charge up the Prismatic Beam by shooting your own units or structures.

Because the Prismatic Beam retains its charge for 5 seconds, you need to time this trick very carefully to coincide with an enemy attack.

Just don't go trying to pull off this stunt with 6 fully upgrade Void Rays. your building won't survive the attempt.

 PRISMATIC BEAM

Effect: Increases Void Ray damage the longer it remains on a single target

Cost	Range	Radius	Autocast
Passive	0	0	No

As a result of this weapon's behavior, it is best used against slow moving, high health targets, or against enemy structures. Even a small group of Void Rays can level a structure or heavy target in seconds, but they are very poor against numerous weaker, non-Armored targets.

Close range anti-air or ground unit, best vs slow moving units or buildings, as it deals more damage the longer the beam is held on target.

The Void Ray is also unique in that it can fire its beam while moving—this means that it can pursue enemy targets, whether ground or air, and continue to deal damage *and* charge up its beam level.

CARRIER

Hot Key: C

COST:
 350 250 120 6

BUILT FROM:	BUILD REQUIREMENTS:	UPGRADES:
Stargate	*Fleet Beacon*	*Fleet Beacon*

Carriers do not attack directly, but instead launch waves of lethal Interceptors to attack targets continuously. Carriers launch with 4 Interceptors, and can be equipped with up to 8. Carriers are the top tier air unit for the Protoss, and outside the Mothership and Battlecruiser, are easily one of the strongest single units in the game.

Carrier Interceptors will launch from a range of 8, but once targeted, the parent Carrier can then move *anywhere* within a range of 12 and the Interceptors will continue to attack their target.

This makes Carriers extremely dangerous for base siege operations, as well as effective in battle, as even a few can cover the enemy force in cloud of Interceptors, while remaining safely out of range of enemy anti-air units.

A Carrier with a full load of Interceptors also has one of the highest damage outputs over time in the game, so even a few can turn the tide of battle once on the field.

Carriers tend to be immediately focus fired by enemy units once they are fielded, and as they are slow to move, expensive, and slow to produce, it is important that you make use of their maximum range to deal damage. Protect them from ground troops by keeping them hovering over inaccessible terrain while Interceptors do their work.

STARGATE

WEAPON STATISTICS

Weapon	Damage	Attacks	Attack Speed	Range	Targets
Interceptors	5 (+1)	2	1.00	8 (12)	Air/Ground

UNIT STATISTICS

Health	Shields	Energy	Armor	Movement Speed	Acceleration	Line of Sight	Size
300	150	No	2	1.87	Yes	12	

UNIT TYPE

Light	Armored	Biological	Mechanical	Psionic	Massive	Structure

The awesome Carrier is a capital class spacecraft, capable of sieging bases or providing aerial cover for armies.

UPGRADES		COST			EFFECT
Upgrade	Requirement				
Graviton Catapult	None	150	150	80	Carriers launch Interceptors more quickly

INTERCEPTORS

Interceptors cost 25 Minerals and 8 seconds to produce, have 40 Health and 40 Shields, they have a speed of 7.5, no armor, and are Light and Mechanical.

Interceptor Shields regenerate like any Protoss unit, but their Health is not restored when they are docked, so a Carrier's complement of Interceptors can be worn down by continuous anti-air fire, and must be periodically replaced.

GRAVITON CATAPULT

The Graviton Catapult upgrade increases the speed at which Carriers launch their Interceptor force. Normally, a Carrier takes 0.5 seconds per Interceptor to launch, meaning they take 4 seconds to ramp up their damage output with a full load of Interceptors.

With this upgrade, the launch times are shortened to 0.125 each for the first four Interceptors, and 0.25 each for the last four. This means that 4 Interceptors hit the field in half a second, the same speed as it took one to launch before the upgrade! The last 4 launch in a single second, meaning the entire Interceptor force is on the field in 1.5 seconds.

As a result, this greatly increases the initial damage that a Carrier can deal—important for taking out threats to the Carrier more quickly, and increasing its ability to strike at fixed defenses and retreat swiftly, before the Interceptors are picked off by anti-air fire.

This is a worthwhile upgrade, but don't delay the creation of your first few Carriers to wait for it if you are tight on Gas.

Abilities

 TRAIN INTERCEPTOR
Hot Key: I

Effect: Builds Carrier Interceptors, up to a maximum of 8

Cost	Range	Radius	Autocast
25 Minerals, 8s	0	0	Yes

Using this ability adds a single Interceptor to the Carrier's internal build queue. Up to 8 Interceptors can be held, and this ability can be turned on Autocast, to automatically rebuild Interceptors lost in battle.

If your economy can support it (and if it can't, you shouldn't be building Carriers!), you should always have this ability on Autocast.

ARCHON

COST:

 2 DARK OR HIGH TEMPLAR 12 ⬛ 4

BUILT FROM:	BUILD REQUIREMENTS:	UPGRADES:
Dark or High Templar	NONE	NONE

A manifestation of Protoss fury on the battlefield, the Archon lashes out with powerful Psionic Shockwaves that can strike air or ground units, deal splash damage, and deal bonus damage to Biological units. Consequently, the Archon is one of the best units that the Protoss army can field against the Zerg—their entire army *and* their bases are Biological!

Note that a Ghost's EMP will strip 100 Shield away, not the full amount, so Archons can still deal effective damage against massed Marines. This is particularly important if you are using Archons while waiting for Psionic Storm research to complete.

Against the Protoss army, the Archon is somewhat less useful, unless your opponent is fielding large numbers of Zealots or Dark Templar. Archons have very powerful shields and next to no health. Whenever possible, remove partially damaged Archons from a battle and let them regenerate their shields.

Morphing High Templar who have fully expended their Energy in battle is often a wise move, as it increases your army strength more quickly than waiting for the High Templar to regenerate their Energy. Remember, any damaged High or Dark Templar morphed into an Archon immediately gain the full shield total of an undamaged Archon.

WEAPON STATISTICS

Weapon	Damage	Attacks	Attack Speed	Range	Targets	Radius
Psionic Shockwave	25 +10 vs Biological (+3/+1)	1	1.75	2	Air/Ground	1

UNIT STATISTICS

Health	Shields	Energy	Armor	Movement Speed	Acceleration	Line of Sight	Size
10	350	No	0	2.81	No	9	4

UNIT TYPE

Light	Armored	Biological	Mechanical	Psionic	Massive	Structure

Formed by combining any two High or Dark Templars, or one High and one Dark Templar, the Archon is a powerful psionic entity.

SPECIAL

MOTHERSHIP

COST:

 400 400 160 8

BUILT FROM:	BUILD REQUIREMENTS:	UPGRADES:
Nexus	Fleet Beacon - No Mothership Present	NONE

Once you have constructed a Fleet Beacon, it can be built from any Nexus.

The Mothership is the slowest and most expensive unit in the game, and it is also the most individually powerful. With a huge health and shield total, inherent armor, and a strong attack against air or ground units, the Mothership is a dangerous unit on its own, but its true power is its ability to permanently cloak *all* friendly units or structures near it, ground or air.

If your opponent does not have enough Detectors and cannot take down the Mothership when you make a push with it, they cannot stop your invisible army from destroying their army and their base.

The cost of this power is speed, as the Mothership is one of the slowest units in the game. Making a Mothership push with your army is a slow process on any map with a great distance between bases, giving your opponent time to build more Detectors or anti-air units.

If left unescorted, the Mothership can deal solid damage to a force sent to destroy it, but it can and will be taken down with ease if left alone.

Don't expect the Mothership to last long in a frontal assault either, as your opponent will target it with his entire anti-air force and any special abilities that can damage it.

WEAPON STATISTICS

Weapon	Damage	Attacks	Attack Speed	Range	Targets
Purifier Beam	6 (+2)	6	2.21	7	Air/Ground

UNIT STATISTICS

Health	Shields	Energy	Armor	Movement Speed	Acceleration	Line of Sight	Size
350	350	Yes	2	1.4	Yes	14	

UNIT TYPE

Light	Armored	Biological	Mechanical	Psionic	Massive	Structure

The Protoss Mothership is a unique and powerful spacecraft. Only one Mothership may be built at any time.

SPECIAL

Abilities

CLOAKING FIELD

Effect: Cloaks friendly units and structures near the Mothership

Cost	Range	Radius	Autocast
Passive	0	5	No

The Mothership's Cloaking Field permanently cloaks all friendly units and buildings with a radius of 5. The Mothership itself is *not* cloaked.

VORTEX
Hot Key: V

Effect: Removes all units in target area from the battlefield for 20 seconds

Cost	Range	Radius	Autocast
100 Energy	9	2.5	No

Vortex is an extremely strong ability that removes ALL units in an area of the battlefield from the fight for 20 seconds. Note that the Mothership cannot remove itself with Vortex, but it can certainly suck an opposing Mothership into the Vortex. You can use Vortex to instantly cut your opponents army into two parts, giving you a crushing numeric advantage in a straight fight.

Note that a swift opponent can intentionally move his remaining army *into* the Vortex—removing your opponents entire army gives you (at most) 20 seconds to deal damage to surrounding defenses before the entire army returns at once.

MASS RECALL
Hot Key: R

Effect: Teleports all friendly units in the target area to the Mothership

Cost	Range	Radius	Autocast
100 Energy	Unlimited	6.5	No

Mass Recall instantly teleports all friendly units in a targeted area to the Mothership. If you want to keep the Mothership on defensive duty in one of your bases, Mass Recall guarantees that you can immediately respond to any major push with your entire army, and the Mothership alone can handle light raids.

If you don't want to send the Mothership on offense for any reason, leaving it on defense with enough Energy for a Mass Recall can let you strike out with your army freely, without worrying about retaliation at your base—just watch out for a well placed EMP or Feedback that can strip your Mothership of the ability to use Mass Recall!

PROTOSS BUILDINGS

Protoss structures are unique in that they are warped onto the battlefield by a Probe anywhere inside a friendly Pylon Power Field.

Other than their method of creation, Protoss structures are considerably less complex than Terran structures, they have no special abilities outside the Nexus and Warp Gate, and no modular upgrades of any kind.

PROTOSS BUILDING SHIELDS

All Protoss buildings have shields, just as their units do, and while no Protoss building begins with stronger than normal shields, ALL Protoss buildings benefit from shield upgrades researched at the Forge.

BUILDING TYPES

All Protoss structures are Armored or Structure.

MILITARY STRUCTURES

PROTOSS MILITARY STRUCTURES

The Protoss have three core lines of military structures—the Gateway produces most of their ground force, the Stargate produces air units, and the Robotics Facility produces additional robotic ground units and their recon and transport units.

All three structures have additional support facilities that can be constructed to unlock additional units and upgrades.

NEXUS

Hot Key: N

COST:

 400   0   100

BUILDING STATISTICS		
Health	Shields	Armor
750	750	1

BUILD REQUIREMENTS:

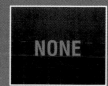

NONE

The Nexus is the basic Protoss base structure, necessary for producing Probes and harvesting Minerals and Vespene Gas.

The Nexus also acts as the construction facility for the mighty Protoss Mothership.

The Protoss Nexus immediately has access to Chrono Boost, the Protoss race's economic and military booster ability. Note that unlike other caster 'units' in the game, the Nexus is created with no initial Energy. Early in the game, you must often decide between using Chrono Boost to speed up the production of more Probes, or to speed up the production of military units or key research. However, Chrono Boost grows *more* powerful the more Nexus core structures you have on the field, and more powerful again once your economy has been built up and you have no more need for speeding worker production. With more Energy available and less targets that need that Energy, you are free to focus Chrono Boost exclusively on speeding up your military production and research.

Protoss already have powerful late-game armies, and with the ability to speed up their production and development, the mid and late game Protoss army is one to be feared, both for the speed at which it can be created, and the speed at which it can be rebuilt—and each time it is rebuilt, it is tougher as a result of faster upgrades.

BUILDING PRODUCTION		COST			
Unit	Requirement				
Probe	None	50	0	1	17
Mothership	Fleet Beacon	400	400	8	120

BASIC

BUILDING ABILITIES					
Chrono Boost					
	Cost	Range	Radius	Effect	Autocast?
	25 Energy	Unlimited	0	Target Production or Research building operates 50% faster for 20 seconds	No

ASSIMILATOR

Hot Key: A

COST:

75   0   30

BUILDING STATISTICS		
Health	Shields	Armor
450	450	1

BUILD REQUIREMENTS:

NONE

The Protoss Assimilator must be built over a Vespene geyser, and allows the collection of Vespene Gas by Probes.

The Assimilator has more total health than either the Terran or Zerg extractors, rendering it a slightly stronger structure against Gas raids. Because the Protoss army is so expensive in terms of Gas cost per unit, this is a helpful perk.

BASIC

PYLON

Hot Key: E

COST:

 100   0   25

BUILDING STATISTICS		
Health	Shields	Armor
200	200	1

BUILD REQUIREMENTS:

NONE

Protoss Pylons serve as both the Supply increasing structure for the Protoss, and as a source of power for their buildings. Pylons radiate a power field that powers other Protoss buildings and allows for the warping in of new Protoss structures and units from the Warp Gate. Protoss buildings MUST be powered by Pylon power, or they cease functioning, the only exceptions being the Nexus and the Assimilator.

Remember that placing Pylons out on the map towards your opponents base opens up the ability to warp in units from your Warp Gates and get them to your opponents base much faster than you would be able to normally.

BASIC

CYBERNETICS CORE

Hot Key: Y

COST:

150   0   50

BUILDING STATISTICS		
Health	Shields	Armor
550	550	1

BUILD REQUIREMENTS:

Gateway

The Cybernetics Core is a critical technology building, as it unlocks the ability to create structures from any of the three branches of the Protoss tech tree, as well as unlocking the Stalker and Sentry at the Gateway. You should always create a Cybernetics Core early in any build, both to unlock access to your higher tech structures, and to quickly acquire Warp Gate research.

Warp Gate tech should be researched immediately after a Cybernetics Core is created, and your Gateways transformed as soon as possible to accelerate your ground army production rate (as well as the ability to warp in units at forward Pylons closer to your opponent).

The Cybernetics Core also allows the research of weapon and armor upgrades for your air forces.

MILITARY

BUILDING UPGRADES		COST			EFFECT
Upgrade	Requirement				
Hallucination	None	100	100	110	Grants Sentries the Hallucination ability
Warp Gate	None	50	50	140	Grants Gateways the Warp Gate upgrade
Air Weapons Level 1	None	100	100	140	Upgrades Protoss air unit weapons
Air Weapons Level 2	Fleet Beacon	175	175	170	Upgrades Protoss air unit weapons
Air Weapons Level 3	Fleet Beacon	250	250	200	Upgrades Protoss air unit weapons
Air Armor Level 1	None	150	150	140	Upgrades Protoss air unit armor
Air Armor Level 2	Fleet Beacon	225	225	170	Upgrades Protoss air unit armor
Air Armor Level 3	Fleet Beacon	300	300	200	Upgrades Protoss air unit armor

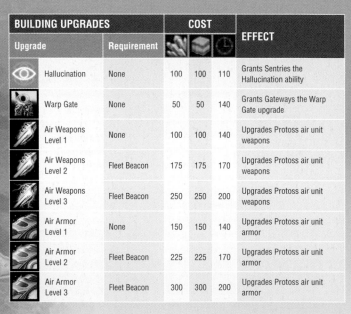

FORGE

Hot Key: F

COST:
 150   0   45

BUILDING STATISTICS

Health	Shields	Armor
400	400	1

The Forge allows the research of Protoss ground unit weapon, armor, and shield upgrades, as well as unlocking the ability to construct Photon Cannons.

Multiple Forges should be used to more quickly research ground upgrades if you are focusing on a ground army, or if you want to upgrade Shields for all of your units and structures simultaneously.

BUILD REQUIREMENTS:

NONE

MILITARY

BUILDING UPGRADES

Upgrade	Requirement	COST			EFFECT
		🪨	📦	🕐	
Ground Weapons Level 1	None	100	100	140	Upgrades Protoss ground unit damage
Ground Weapons Level 2	Twilight Council	175	175	190	Upgrades Protoss ground unit damage
Ground Weapons Level 3	Twilight Council	250	250	220	Upgrades Protoss ground unit damage
Ground Armor Level 1	None	100	100	140	Upgrades Protoss ground unit armor
Ground Armor Level 2	Twilight Council	175	175	190	Upgrades Protoss ground unit armor
Ground Armor Level 3	Twilight Council	250	250	220	Upgrades Protoss ground unit armor
Shields Level 1	None	200	200	140	Upgrades the Shields of all Protoss units and buildings
Shields Level 2	Twilight Council	300	300	190	Upgrades the Shields of all Protoss units and buildings
Shields Level 3	Twilight Council	400	400	220	Upgrades the Shields of all Protoss units and buildings

PHOTON CANNON

Hot Key: C

COST:
 150   0   40

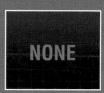

BUILDING STATISTICS

Health	Shields	Armor
150	150	1

WEAPON STATISTICS

Weapon	Damage	Attacks	Attack Speed	Range	Targets
Photon Cannon	20	1	1.25	7	Air/Ground

The Photon Cannon is the Protoss defensive structure. It requires Pylon power to function. In comparison to the Terran and Zerg defensive structures, it has the benefit of acting as an all-in-one answer to ground, air, or cloaked units, but it is reliant on Pylon power to function.

Because the Photon Cannon is one of only two ways Protoss can gain access to Detection, building a Forge fairly early if you expect cloaked or burrowed units from your opponent is an important defensive measure. You won't have time to build a Forge and multiple cannons when your base is under attack by Dark Templar, Banshees, or burrowed Roaches or Infestors.

BUILD REQUIREMENTS:

Forge

DEFENSIVE

BUILDING ABILITIES

	Detector				
	Cost	Range	Radius	Effect	Autocast?
👁	Passive	0	0	Can spot Cloaked, Burrowed, or Hallucinated units	No

GATEWAY

Hot Key: G

COST:

 150　　 0　　 65

BUILDING STATISTICS		
Health	Shields	Armor
500	500	1

The Gateway allows the construction of the majority of Protoss ground forces aside from the Colossus and the Immortal. New units for the Gateway are unlocked by building the Cybernetics Core, or structures down the Twilight Council branch of the Protoss tech tree. Gateways have a very unique and important special ability to transform to and from a Warp Gate, with the research of Warp Gate technology from the Cybernetics Core.

Once converted, a Warp Gate no longer has a standard unit build queue, but instead it can warp in units anywhere on the map inside a Pylon Power Field (including one created by a Warp Prism). This is an extremely powerful special ability, and in most cases, you should always immediately convert all Gateways into Warp Gates once the technology has been acquired. When you warp in a unit, the Warp Gate used to create the unit goes into a cooldown timer, and cannot be used to Warp in another unit until it expires.

The cooldown is dependant on the unit created, but it is actually faster than building the unit normally. A unit created via Warp has a 10 second faster cooldown than it would to build normally.

A Zealot created normally would take 33 seconds to create, while one warped in would have a cooldown timer of 23 seconds *after* it has been warped in. You get the unit up front, a faster cooldown after, *and* Warp Gates can be Chrono Boosted, speeding up their cooldown timers even further.

The only downside to using Warp instead of a normal build queue is that you must be vigilant about Warping in new units constantly, whenever the cooldown elapses. If you do not, you can fall behind a Terran or Zerg who is constantly pumping out new units.

Conveniently, all Warp Gates have a default hotkey of W, and you can simply get in the habit of tapping the Warp Gate hotkey every 20 to 30 seconds in a match and warping in new units as needed.

BUILD REQUIREMENTS:

NONE

BUILDING PRODUCTION			COST			
Unit		Requirement				
	Zealot	None	100	0	2	38
	Sentry	Cybernetics Core	50	100	2	42
	Stalker	Cybernetics Core	125	50	2	42
	High Templar	Templar Archives	50	150	2	55
	Dark Templar	Dark Shrine	125	125	2	55

MILITARY

BUILDING UPGRADES		COST			EFFECT
Upgrade	Requirement				
Transform to Warp Gate	Cybernetics Core Warp Gate research	0	0	10s	Upgrades Gateway to Warp Gate

TWILIGHT COUNCIL

Hot Key: C

COST:

 150 100 50

BUILDING STATISTICS		
Health	Shields	Armor
500	500	1

BUILD REQUIREMENTS:

Cybernetics Core

Building the Twilight council unlocks the first of three possible tech routes, and grants you access to research to upgrade your Zealots with Charge or your Stalkers with Blink, as well as stronger ground weapon, armor, and shield upgrades for the Protoss army from the Forge.

Once constructed, the Twilight Council allows you to further specialize into the High or Dark Templar aspects with the creation of a Templar Archives or Dark Shrine.

MILITARY

BUILDING UPGRADES		COST			EFFECT
Upgrade	Requirement				
Charge	None	200	200	140	Grants Zealot Charge ability and increases movement speed
Blink	None	150	150	110	Grants Stalkers Blink ability

TEMPLAR ARCHIVES

Hot Key: T

COST:

 150 200 50

BUILDING STATISTICS		
Health	Shields	Armor
500	500	1

BUILD REQUIREMENTS:

Twilight Council

The Templar Archives allows you to build High Templar at your Gateways, and contains key research to upgrade them as well, including the powerful Psionic Storm and an upgrade to their starting Energy.

The Templar Archives also indirectly unlocks the Archon unit, as two High Templar can be merged into an Archon.

MILITARY

BUILDING UPGRADES		COST			EFFECT
Upgrade	Requirement				
Psionic Storm	None	200	200	110	Grants High Templar Psionic Storm ability
Khaydarin Amulet	None	150	150	110	Increases High Templar starting Energy by 25

DARK SHRINE

Hot Key: D

COST:

 100 250 100

BUILDING STATISTICS		
Health	Shields	Armor
500	500	1

BUILD REQUIREMENTS:

Twilight Council

The Dark Shrine lets you draw on the power of the Dark Templar for your armies, potent permanently cloaked assassins. Once created, Dark Templar can be built from the Gateway.

Two Dark Templar can be merged into an Archon, just as their High Templar brethren, and if you have one High and one Dark Templar, they can also be merged into an Archon. Whenever possible, try to conceal the construction of this structure from your opponent, Dark Templar are most effective when they arrive with no warning (preferably warped in from a Warp Gate in one large group).

MILITARY

STARGATE

Hot Key: S

COST:

 150 150 60

BUILDING STATISTICS		
Health	Shields	Armor
600	600	1

The Stargate unlocks the path to Protoss air units, and it allows the construction of the air-to-air Phoenix and the versatile Void Ray.

Remember to Chrono Boost production of units from this structure whenever possible.

BUILD REQUIREMENTS:

Cybernetics Core

BUILDING PRODUCTION		COST			
Unit	Requirement				
Phoenix	None	150	100	2	45
Void Ray	None	250	150	3	60
Carrier	Fleet Beacon	350	250	6	120

MILITARY

FLEET BEACON

Hot Key: F

COST:

 300 200 60

BUILDING STATISTICS		
Health	Shields	Armor
500	500	1

The Fleet Beacon allows the construction of the mighty Carrier at your Stargates, as well as research upgrades for the Void Ray and Carrier.

A Fleet Beacon also allows the Protoss Mothership to be created at a Nexus.

BUILD REQUIREMENTS:

Stargate

MILITARY

BUILDING UPGRADES		COST			EFFECT
Upgrade	Requirement				
Flux Vanes	None	150	150	80	Increases Void Ray movement speed and acceleration
Graviton Catapult	None	150	150	80	Carriers launch Interceptors more quickly

ROBOTICS FACILITY

Hot Key: R

COST:
 200 100 65

BUILDING STATISTICS		
Health	Shields	Armor
450	450	1

The last of the Protoss armies three military production structures, the Robotics Facility allows you to create two vitally important Protoss support units, the Observer and the Warp Prism, as well as two powerful robotic ground units, the Immortal and Colossus.

BUILD REQUIREMENTS:

Cybernetics Core

BUILDING PRODUCTION		COST			
Unit	Requirement				
Observer	None	50	100	1	40
Warp Prism	None	200	0	2	50
Immortal	None	250	100	4	55
Colossus	Robotics Bay	300	200	6	75

MILITARY

ROBOTICS BAY

Hot Key: B

COST:
 200 200 65

BUILDING STATISTICS		
Health	Shields	Armor
500	500	1

A Robotics Bay unlocks the impressive Colossus walker at the Robotics Facility, and allows for research into upgrades for most of the units at the Facility, including movement speed boosts for the Observer and Warp Prism, and a siege range upgrade for the Colossus.

BUILD REQUIREMENTS:

Robotics Facility

MILITARY

BUILDING UPGRADES		COST			EFFECT
Upgrade	Requirement				
Gravitic Boosters	None	100	100	80	Increases Observer movement speed
Gravitic Drive	None	100	100	80	Increases Warp Prism movement speed
Extended Thermal Lance	None	200	200	140	Increases Colossus weapon range

ZERG ARMY

The Zerg army isn't an army at all, but a ravenous, numberless, ferocious biological terror.

The vast hordes of the Zerg swarm are a terrible threat to the Terran and Protoss forces. Zerg 'armies' consist of large groups of few unit types. Effective Zerg swarms consist of large groups of complementary units, controlled well in battle.

Because the Zerg can produce any type of unit from any of their Hatcheries, Zerg can afford to lose units in an uneven battle, and then produce a new mix of units that effectively counters whatever troops their opponent is fielding.

ZERG ADVANTAGES

Zerg are the most straightforward of all three races. They have no complex building system like the Terran, and fewer activated abilities than either the Terran or the Protoss.

As a result, it is easy to utilize their strengths in battle: Large armies with many expendable troops that are relatively easy to control. Lose some troops to the wrong enemy force? No problem, make the right force back at home immediately.

Unit Production

Unlike the Terran or Zerg, who create their units from military structures, almost all the Zerg units are produced from Larva spawned at their Hatcheries, only the Queen is created at a Hatchery. As a result, Zerg can instantly shift their production to create any unit available to them, always building a new mix of units best suited to exploit any weakness in an opposing army.

This also allows Zerg to dump floating cash after (or during!) a battle into a new army *extremely* quickly, and that army will all be generated simultaneously, in one giant flood, where Terran or Protoss must wait for their units to rebuild one by one.

After a battle where both players take heavy losses, Zerg can have a new swarm on the field and en route to an enemy base to finish the fight with frightening speed.

The Zerg can also respond to a raid (or even a direct army offensive) against ANY of their bases by quickly building units in response, and not just any units, but the exact units needed to counter whatever forces are attacking you.

The Queen

The Zerg Queen acts as their economic booster unit, as well as a very useful early game defensive unit. With constant usage of Spawn Larvae, the Queens can keep the Zerg Larva count high enough on all of their Hatcheries that they can rebuild instantly from any serious losses suffered in combat—resources become the constraining factor for the Zerg military, rather than production capacity.

Controlling your early game Queens well can help to fend off any early rushes before the Zerg military is fully established, at which point the ability to create a new military force from any base allows you to respond to raids with instant force.

Creep

Zerg Creep is the organic mass spread by many of their structures across the ground. Terran and Protoss players cannot build structures on it (though Zerg buildings *must* be placed on Creep), and it provides automatic line of sight anywhere it spreads.

In addition, Zerg ground forces receive a 30% speed boost while moving on Creep, greatly aiding their ability to respond to a hostile force in their bases. The Queen's Creep Tumor ability allows you to spread Creep outside of your bases, as does the Overlord's Generate Creep ability.

Between the line of sight and speed benefits, by the midgame, no army can enter Zerg territory without being spotted, and then having a sped up army en route to intercept.

The Hatchery, Lair, Hive, Nydus Worm, and Creep Tumors produce Creep.

Burrow

All Zerg ground units can Burrow once the technology has been researched at any Lair. Burrow allows you to spread cheap Zergling scouts all over the map, to hide Queens or Drones from enemy raids, and to hide your army from an enemy offensive force that lacks a mobile Detector.

Two units, the Roach and the Infestor, can actually move while burrowed, allowing them to harass or destroy enemy forces or bases lacking detection.

Target your opponent's mobile Detectors while in battle and they will have a difficult time destroying your army when you can always burrow to wait for reinforcements!

Burrow can also be used to spring nasty ambushes on your enemy's army. Burrowed Banelings can detonate under an enemy force, and burrowed Zerglings can instantly get into melee with your opponent's forces if they do not spot the burrowed units.

Hide your Baneling/Zergling force ahead of your army, bait your opponent into following, then detonate the Banelings and spring the Zerglings up to devour the tasty, tasty casters and rear line units when his army engages yours.

Regen

While minimal, Zerg units and structures automatically regenerate about 16 health a minute. If you do pull back from a fight or suffer light damage on defense, your units will be at least partially restored before you engage in battle again, and structures will recover from light raids.

Broodlings

One interesting quirk of Zerg 'architecture' is its Biological nature. When a Zerg structure is destroyed, swarms of angry Broodlings spawn and attack any hostile ground units in the area.

Your Hatchery will create 9 Broodlings, while any other structure will create 6. Spine and Spore Crawlers, Nydus Worms, and Extractors do not spawn Broodlings when destroyed. Broodlings won't stop a serious assault, but they can help in a very close battle. These Broodlings are identical in strength and duration to those spawned by a Brood Lords attack.

Early Siege Breaking

While Zerg lack the ability to wall in early in the game, they do have the benefit of the earliest unit that can easily *break* a wall in.

The Baneling deals a massive 80 damage to structures, and even a few can break a hole in an opponent's wall in (not to mention dealing heavy damage to any clumped Light troops in the area). Ground melee damage upgrades also grant Banelings an additional +5 damage to their structural damage, on top of boosting their explosion damage against troops.

Make use of this perk by breaking into an expansion or main base that your opponent thinks is safely protected and send a force of expendable Speedlings through the gap to hit his worker line.

Recon

Zerg have arguably the best reconnaissance ability in the game, lacking only the Terran ability to instantly scan an area of the map.

Between Overlords, Creep, Burrow, Overseers, and the Changeling, it is very easy for Zerg to spread a network of vision all over the map, instantly alerting you to any enemy army movement, and allowing you to respond quickly with your production advantage to any enemy army technology.

Nydus Network

In addition to their speed boost on Creep, and their ability to create any unit from any Hatchery, the Zerg also have access to the strongest transport ability of any race.

Zerg can create a Nydus Network in any base on Creep, and then create Nydus Worms from that single Network anywhere on the map where you have line of sight. This can be used to move armies between bases to respond to attacks, to recall an army from the field for defense, or to attack an enemy from behind their base's chokepoint.

Simplicity

Zerg unit production is the easiest of all three races—put your Hatcheries on one hotkey, rally them wherever you want, and you're done!

Any Hatchery can produce any unit you have access to, so you can immediately build any mix of units from a single hotkey, compared with the Terran who can have three subgroups for a single type of military structure on a hotkey, or the Protoss who must monitor Warp cooldowns, their other military structures, and Chrono Boost usage to maintain full speed unit production.

Zerg also benefit from the simultaneous unit production—Terran and Protoss build queues will empty at different rates, so they must be constantly monitored to maintain peak military production. Zerg can 'store' production with Spawn Larvae, and production time is not lost in the same way that it is when a build queue is idle for the Terran or Protoss. Literally the only maintenance you need to worry about to maintain your unit production is making use of Spawn Larvae from the Queen every time it is available.

Similarly, Zerg armies are simpler to handle than either Terran or Zerg. Zerg have less activated abilities, less casters, and less abilities period than either the Terran or Protoss.

ZERG DISADVANTAGES

Queen Vulnerability

Continuing the trend of double edged benefits, the Zerg Queen is a strength for the Zerg force, but she is also a vulnerable target for enemy raids. The Queen is slow to build and slow to move, and losing Queens will hamper your military and economic output considerably. Remember to use Burrow, and protect your queens with fixed defenses if your opponent is targeting them with raids.

Lack of Abilities

Zerg lack the more numerous ability and caster options available to Terran and Protoss forces. This slightly limits their options for fine unit micro in battles. On the upshot, this does free more mental time to control your forces well in battle!

No Early Wall-Ins

The Zerg lack the ability to wall in their base early in a match. This makes them more vulnerable to scouting and raiding by basic ground forces early in the game.

In the midgame, with proper Creep Tumor usage (or earlier, if you're willing to delay Spawn Larvae, or make use of Generate Creep from an Overlord), you can create a wall of Spine or Spore Crawlers at a chokepoint.

Be sure to make use of your large armies to block chokepoints and ramps to your base—your army itself can act as a living wall to prevent early scouting when you aren't on the offensive with your army.

Very early in the game, remember that you can use your first Zerglings alongside your Queen AND your workers to fight off a rush. Hide the Queen in your workers and use her ranged attack to help defend, while you run units away from enemy forces, or surround them with Zerglings and workers.

Critical Structures

While Zerg military production is a strong benefit of the race, they are very vulnerable to base raids that hit their technology buildings. Losing a Spire means you cannot build any more air units until it is rebuilt, and losing a Greater Spire is even more painful, given the extended build time.

If your opponent can destroy the structure that has a crucial unit for countering his force, it can put you in a very difficult situation while you build a replacement. Don't hesitate to create 'backup' structures in the midgame at your other bases (or even in your main!) if you are concerned about your opponent hitting your key tech buildings.

Similarly, losing a Hatchery at an expansion due to a push is doubly painful for the Zerg, as not only do you lose the income, you also lose the additional military production. Remember to build additional Hatcheries in a defended base if you are concerned about the safety of your expansions.

Overlords

Overlords make great scouts, but if your opponent is aggressive about getting air units on the field, they can become a Supply liability. Be *sure* to protect your largest Overlord group with a small web of Spore and Spine Crawlers in the midgame. Your Hydralisks and air forces cannot always stop your opponent from hitting your Overlords, and having all of them floating undefended in one area (or even spread about the map) is a great way to end up painfully Supply capped.

While you can easily rebuild Overlords, this cuts into your military production, and if you don't defend them well, your opponent will continue to pressure them.

Consider Overlords that you have out in the fields scouting as 'extras', and be sure to slightly overbuild your Supply cap to compensate for losses if your opponent is actively taking down your Overlords in the field.

Remember that several Overlords can also create a temporary "highway" of Creep between two critical bases, giving your army stronger mobility to respond to enemy threats or to attack or retreat more quickly. Just don't expect Overlords used to make a path to your opponents base to survive a push by your opponent!

Area of effect damage

Because Zerg armies are large swarms of units, they are especially vulnerable to enemy area of effect damage. Terran Siege Tanks in Siege Mode, Raven Seeker Missiles, and the Protoss Colossus, Archon or Psionic Storm are all painful units to face with a large massed army.

When your opponent begins to field area of effect damage against you, be sure to prioritize the destruction of those units first. Taking a few losses to destroy them before a full battle begins is well worth it, the cost of the units lost in a suicide mission is almost always lower than the cost of your units being slaughtered from area of effect damage.

Make use of your superior recon to spot these threats early and eliminate them, either with suicidal Zerglings with their Speed upgrade, a Mutalisk hit and run, or burrowed Baneling, Roach or Infestor attacks. In a late game battle, Brood Lords or Ultralisks have the range or durability to dispatch the ground based area of effect threats, though neither can harm a Raven.

Opposing Zerg can present a similar though lesser threat with Banelings or Fungal Growth (or more rarely, the Ultralisk). Unlike the Terran or Protoss options however, these are relatively limited—a Siege Tank or Colossus can continue to detonate or fry your army indefinitely.

ZERG UNIT ROLES

Zerg have several units that benefit from direct micro. Speedlings are strong candidates for precise control against slower units. The Roach is designed for burrowing micro. Mutalisk groups are fast enough to hit and run, and can threaten air or ground targets.

Zerg Hydralisks are prime candidates for focus firing, though Roaches and Speedlings can be effective as well, depending on the terrain during an engagement. All Zerg air units benefit from focus fire control, but especially the Mutalisk when raiding.

The Zerg mobile Detector is the Overseer, and their stationary Detector is the Spore Colony. Fungal Growth works as a temporary Detector ability.

Banelings, Infestor Fungal Growth and the Ultralisk are the Zerg sources of area of effect damage.

Zerg anti-air is provided by the Hydralisk, Mutalisk, Corruptor, Queen, and Spore Colony. Infestor Infested Terrans, Fungal Growth or clever Neural Parasite use can help in a tight situation.

Zerg siege breakers are the Baneling and Brood Lord, though the Ultralisk also works as a sort of organic shield when breaking through a defensive position.

Zerg's air power is defined by the flexibility of the Mutalisk. Fast moving, dangerous in large numbers, and useable as anti-air or anti-ground, it is a strong threat to any opponent. The Corruptor provides the Zerg with a means of dealing with heavy enemy air units, and the Brood Lord is most useful as a siege breaker, or to strengthen your ground army in a direct army battle.

UNIT MIXES

Zerg unit mixes should *always* respond to the composition of the enemy army. Take advantage of your unit creation method by scouting what your opponent is using and build (or rebuild!) the best mix of units to combat it.

Is an opponent using Siege Tanks or Colossus? Swap out your Zerglings for Roaches and Mutalisks or Corruptors. Enemy using masses of Zealots or Marines? Break out the Banelings. Lots of air? Hydralisks and Mutalisks or Corruptors.

With that said, as a general rule, Zerglings should be part of any ground unit mix. With upgrades, they are by far your cheapest source of damage output, and are very dangerous in numbers, plus they can be upgraded to Banelings to quickly deal with massed Light units or defensive structures.

Besides the Zergling, your two other primary ground units should be Roaches or Hydralisks. Roaches provide you with a sturdy combat force, while Hydralisks are effective against any target in large numbers.

Banelings should be added when you spot your enemy fielding many Light units, and a few Ultralisks are almost always useful as part of any ground army if the game goes long enough for you to produce them.

ZERG UNIT TIERS

Unlike Terran or Protoss military structures, new Zerg units are unlocked by creating structures that enable specific units to be morphed from any Hatchery.

These unit-enabling structures are 'gated' to the evolution of your Hatchery. Tier one units are available immediately, then tier two requires a Lair and tier three requires a Hive. Some upgrades are restricted to tiers two or three as well (eg, Zerglings have upgrades in all three tiers).

ZERG TIERS	
Tier	Units Available
Hatchery	Zergling, Baneling, Roach, Queen, Overlord, Drone
Lair	Hydralisk, Mutalisk, Corruptor, Infestor, Overseer
Hive	Ultralisk, Brood Lord

ZERG GROUND UPGRADES
All Zerg ground upgrades are researched at the Evolution Chamber.

ZERG AIR UPGRADES
All Zerg Air upgrades are purchased from the Spire or Greater Spire.

BURROW
All Zerg ground units can Burrow once it has been researched at a Lair.

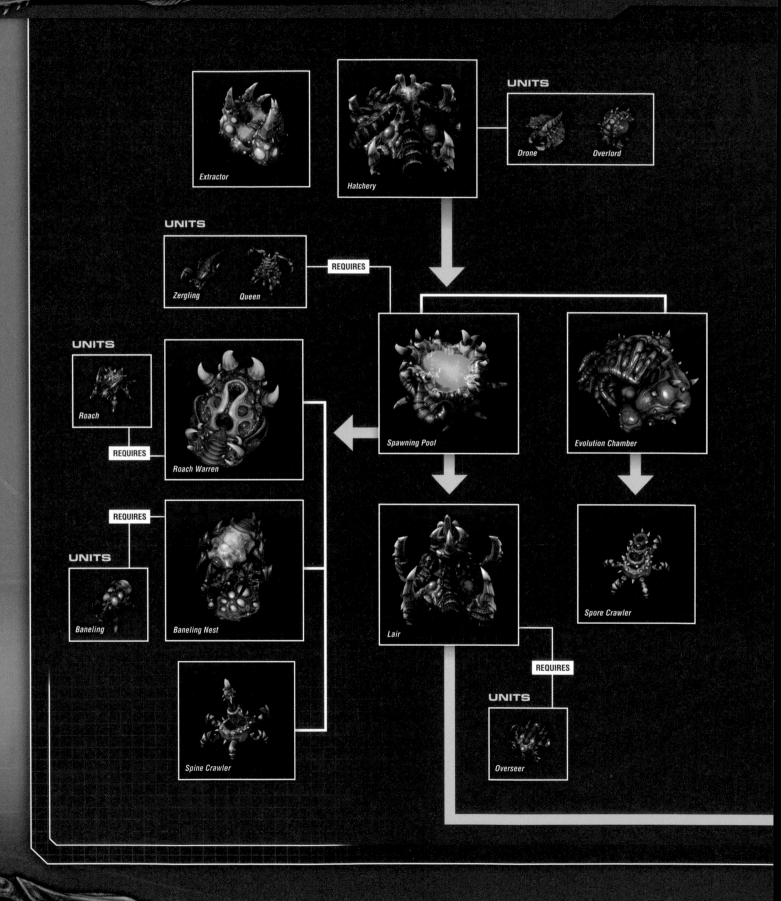

Extractor

Hatchery

UNITS

Drone

Overlord

UNITS

Zergling

Queen

REQUIRES

UNITS

Roach

Roach Warren

REQUIRES

REQUIRES

UNITS

Baneling

Baneling Nest

Spine Crawler

Spawning Pool

Evolution Chamber

Lair

Spore Crawler

REQUIRES

UNITS

Overseer

ZERG TECH TREE

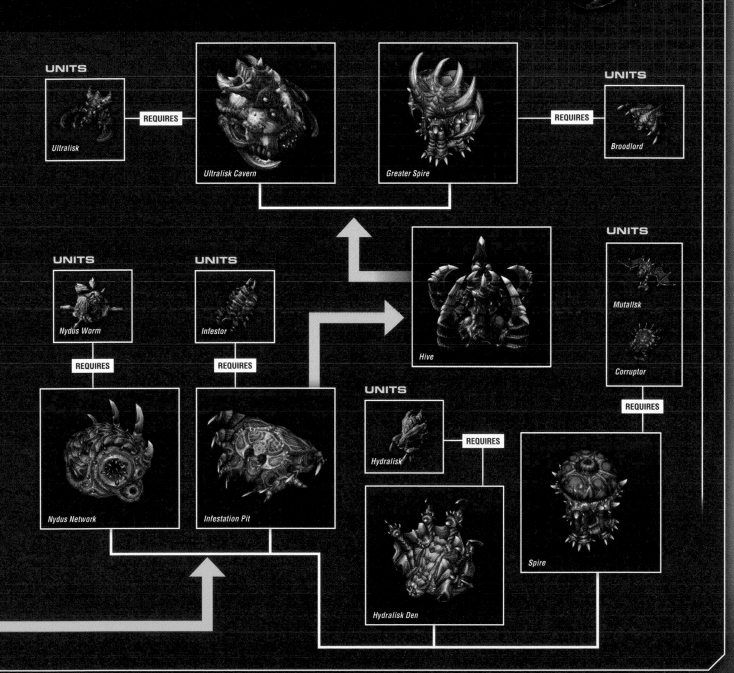

UNITS

Ultralisk

REQUIRES

Ultralisk Cavern

Greater Spire

UNITS

Broodlord

UNITS

Nydus Worm

UNITS

Infestor

UNITS

Mutalisk

Corruptor

REQUIRES

REQUIRES

Hive

REQUIRES

Nydus Network

Infestation Pit

UNITS

Hydralisk

REQUIRES

Spire

Hydralisk Den

DRONE

COST:

 50 0 17 1

BUILT FROM:	BUILD REQUIREMENTS:	UPGRADES:
Hatchery	NONE	NONE

Unlike Terran SCVs or Protoss Probes, Drones are consumed when they create a new structure. To compensate for this, Zerg structures tend to be slightly less expensive than their Terran or Protoss counterparts.

Drones have one other peculiarity. Because they are produced from the same pool of Larva as all Zerg military units, early in the game, you must choose between creating an early military force, or building up your econ to its maximum level more quickly.

Drones gain access to Burrow along with all other Zerg ground units, allowing them to easily hide from a worker raid that lacks Detection. Remember to create new Drones as you use them up to create new structures!

WEAPON STATISTICS

Weapon	Damage	Attacks	Attack Speed	Range	Targets
Claws	5	1	1.50	Melee	Ground

UNIT STATISTICS

Health	Energy	Armor	Movement Speed	Acceleration	Line of Sight	Size
40	No	0	2.81	Yes	8	1

UNIT TYPE

Light	Armored	Biological	Mechanical	Psionic	Massive	Structure

Drones are the basic worker for the Zerg force.

HATCHERY

QUEEN

COST:

 150   0   50   2

BUILT FROM:

Hatchery

BUILD REQUIREMENTS:

Spawning Pool

UPGRADES:

NONE

The Queen should be the first unit produced after your Spawning Pool is finished, and each of your Hatcheries should have a dedicated Queen nearby at all times.

ALL of your Queens should be placed on a single hotkey, allowing you to quickly cycle through your bases and make use of Spawn Larvae every single time it can be used.

The Queen is also a helpful unit for repelling very early raids or rushes. Placed in your worker line, she can make good use of her short ranged ground attack and her stronger (and longer ranged) anti air attack to protect your workers.

Working in concert, your Queen, your Drones, and your first Zerglings can usually manage to repel an early ground attack, if controlled well. Two Queens can also work together by using Transfusion and their anti-air attacks to repel an early air raid on your base or your Overlords until you can get Spore Crawlers and Hydralisks or Spire units on the field.

WEAPON STATISTICS

Weapon	Damage	Attacks	Attack Speed	Range	Targets
Talons	4 (+1)	2	1.00	3	Ground
Acid Spines	9 (+1)	1	1.00	7	Air

UNIT STATISTICS

Health	Energy	Armor	Movement Speed	Acceleration	Line of Sight	Size
175	Yes	1	1.5	No	9	2

UNIT TYPE

Light	Armored	Biological	Mechanical	Psionic	Massive	Structure

QUEEN MANAGEMENT

A very simple method of maintaining Spawn Larvae usage is to hotkey your Queens and Hatcheries onto the same hotkey.

Remember to keep a separate hotkey with just your Hatcheries grouped, so that you still create units quickly.

The Queen is the Zerg's economic booster unit, vital to Zerg military production.

HATCHERY

SPAWN LARVAE
Hot Key: V

Effect: Generates 4 Larva Cocoons on targeted Hatchery

Cost	Range	Radius	Autocast
25 Energy	0	0	No

The Queen's Spawn Larvae ability creates 4 Larva on a targeted Hatchery that spawn after 40 seconds. Because Larva are normally generated (up to a maximum of 3) every 15 seconds, this is a significant increase in the Larva generation rate for a single Hatchery.

If Spawn Larvae creates Larva in excess of the 3 that are normally generated by a Hatchery, no further Larva will be naturally generated until the Larva count drops below 3 again.

If you *really* want to be maximally efficient with Zerg, you will always fully deplete your Hatcheries of Larva each time Spawn Larvae triggers, to allow natural Larva generation to resume, though in practice this is very difficult simply due to economic constraints.

SPAWN CREEP TUMOR
Hot Key: C

Effect: Creates a Creep Tumor on targeted Creep space, spreads Creep out to 9 radius

Cost	Range	Radius	Autocast
25 Energy, 15s Cooldown	0	0	No

Queens can create Creep Tumors, burrowed structures that spread Creep automatically. Each Creep Tumor can also spawn one new Creep Tumor, so over time, a single Tumor created by a Queen can cover the area in front of your bases with Creep, giving your units a movement speed bonus, and spreading line of sight around, providing early warning of enemy offensives.

Creep Tumors are visible while being created, so don't drop them near a hostile enemy force.

Note that Creep Tumors are not burrowed while they are being created, so don't drop them near a hostile enemy force, even if they lack a Detector!

TRANSFUSION
Hot Key: T

Effect: Heals 125 Health on targeted Biological unit or structure

Cost	Range	Radius	Autocast
50 Energy	7	0	No

Tranfusion is a quick and strong (125 point) heal that can be used on any friendly Biological target. A Queen cannot use Transfusion on herself, but Transfusion can be crost-cast by a *second* Queen.

Transfusion is most useful in early skirmishes, where healing a Queen or critical Spine or Spore Crawler can win a battle for you. It can also be used to save a critical tech structure from falling—two Queens casting Transfusion on a Spire under attack just might save your Muta production.

OVERLORD

COST:
 100   0   25   0

BUILT FROM:	BUILD REQUIREMENTS:	UPGRADES:
Hatchery	NONE	*Lair*

Due to their nature as a mobile aerial unit, Overlords are also extremely useful as scouts, and placed carefully, can provide line of sight between your base and the enemy base, with minimal risk from ground forces.

Once enemy aerial units hit the field, it is very important that your core group of Overlords are protected by several Spore Crawlers and possibly Spine Crawlers. You can 'hide' your Overlords in a far corner of the map, but an opponent determined to hunt your Overlords will check your bases, and if he doesn't see them there, will begin to sweep the map to find them. It is usually better to keep them near the protective reach of friendly defensive buildings.

Overlords can also generate Creep in small patches, handy to provide speed for a Zerg army. It can also allow the creation of a Creep Tumor by a Queen, a Nydus Network (instead of a Nydus Worm, remember, the Network is more durable and creates Creep of its own), or a Spine or Spore Crawler anywhere on the map.

With upgrades, Overlords gain movement speed (very important, as they are normally painfully slow), and the ability to transport units. Overlord transport is generally unnecessary due to the excellent Nydus Network transport system, but it can be useful in some situations, such as placing ground units on otherwise unreachable high ground, or performing a drop against an enemy force that lacks anti-air.

WEAPON STATISTICS

Weapon	Damage	Attacks	Attack Speed	Range	Targets
NONE					

UNIT STATISTICS

Health	Energy	Armor	Movement Speed	Acceleration	Line of Sight	Size
200	No	0	0.46 (1.87)	Yes	11	8

UNIT TYPE

Light	Armored	Biological	Mechanical	Psionic	Massive	Structure

The floating Overlord is the Zerg's Supply producing unit.

HIVE

UPGRADES		COST			EFFECT
Upgrade	Requirement				
Pneumatized Carapace	Lair	100	100	60	Increases Overlord and Overseer movement speed
Ventral Sacs	Lair	200	200	130	Allows Overlords to transport units

PNEUMATIZED CARAPACE

This upgrade increases the speed of Overlords and Overseers. After Burrow, this technology should be immediately researched, as it increases both the scouting potential and survivability of your Overlords and Overseers.

VENTRAL SACS

Ventral Sacs allow Overlords (and not Overseers) to transport units. This upgrade is rarely needed, but if you do see a reason to use it, pick it in advance of your need, it takes a long time to research.

GENERATE CREEP

Hot Key: G

Effect: Generates a Creep field while active

Cost	Range	Radius	Autocast
None	0	5	No

While active, this ability spawns a pool of Creep with a radius of 5. The Overlord must remain stationary while channeling this ability, so either use it quickly to create another Creep generating structure, or accept that you may lose the Overlord while using it as a temporary Zerg highway creator.

Remember that an Overlord can move while this ability is active—it will stop creating Creep until it is stationary again, then resume dumping Creep on the battlefield.

MORPH TO OVERSEER

Hot Key: V

Effect: Mutates Overlord to Overseer

Cost	Range	Radius	Autocast
50 Minerals, 100 Gas, 17s	0	0	No

Morphing an Overlord to an Overseer is the quickest creation of a mobile Detector of any race in the game. This substantially weakens Cloak or Burrow tech against a Zerg, but don't grow complacent—you can expect that a determined opponent will target your Overseers directly.

OVERSEER (DETECTOR)

COST:

 50   100   17   0

BUILT FROM:	BUILD REQUIREMENTS:	UPGRADES:
Overlord	Lair	Lair

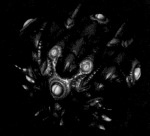

Overseers are excellent recon units, as they can create Changelings, mutable creatures that assuming the shape of enemy units. Dropping a Changeling in or around an enemy base is a great way to get easy intelligence on enemy tech development or their army position.

Overseers benefit from the same movement speed upgrade as Overlords.

WEAPON STATISTICS

Weapon	Damage	Attacks	Attack Speed	Range	Targets
NONE					

UNIT STATISTICS

Health	Energy	Armor	Movement Speed	Acceleration	Line of Sight	Size
200	Yes	1	1.87 (2.75)	No	11	

UNIT TYPE

Light	Armored	Biological	Mechanical	Psionic	Massive	Structure

Overseers are mutated Overlords that gain movement speed and Detection, but lose the ability to transport units or generate Creep puddles.

LAIR

UPGRADES		COST			EFFECT
Upgrade	Requirement				
Pneumatized Carapace	Lair	100	100	60	Increases Overlord and Overseer movement speed

SPAWN CHANGELING
Hot Key: C

Effect: Creates a Changeling

Cost	Range	Radius	Autocast
50 Energy	0	0	No

Changelings are temporary units that automatically assume the shape of an enemy Marine, Zealot, or Zergling, depending on the race of the enemy force they move in range of. Any enemy unit within 12 range will trigger the transformation.

An alert opponent can detect a changeling simply by clicking on it (or by spotting the one unit that isn't responding to their selection commands).

However, this isn't a major problem—Changelings are entirely expendable. Use them to scout the interior and exterior of enemy bases, and you can make good use of the intelligence gathered in your inevitable next wave of unit creation.

INFESTED TERRAN SPAM

Make use of Shift-queueing to rapidly cast Infested Terrans. Hold Shift, press the Infested Terran hotkey, and then rapidly left click on a target area while still holding Shift.

Done correctly, you should see a continuous stream of Infested Terran cocoons springing up, and once they are all launched, you can fly your Overseer out to a safe distance.

INFESTED TERRAN
Hot Key: T

Effect: Spawns a single Infested Terran unit that lasts for 30 seconds or until killed

Cost	Range	Radius	Autocast
100 Energy	0	0	No

Overseers have the ability to spawn individual Terran Marines that have been corrupted by the Swarm to temporarily fight for you.

Infested Terrans can be very helpful either to supplement your army's strength in battle and since they can fire at air or ground units, they can also work as anti-air in a pinch. Infested Terrans can also perform worker raids on enemy expansions. If you know your opponent lacks anti-air defenses you can send in a group of Overseers to drop a few Infested Terrans to harass their worker line.

Don't hesitate to throw out some Infested Terrans as a fight begins, or just before a battle begins. Having your enemy shoot at Infested Terran cocoons before they spawn is still preferable to having them shoot at your units, and the delay gives your Zerglings, Banelings, Roaches, and Ultralisks time to close the distance.

CONTAMINATE
Hot Key: E

Effect: Target structure cannot train units for 30 seconds

Cost	Range	Radius	Autocast
75 Energy	3	0	No

Contaminate, will stop all unit production or research that a building is doing at the time. That production isn't cancelled but is paused for the duration of the Contaminate debuff. There are some interesting cases though when Contaminate is used on specific buildings.

Contaminate can be used on the Zerg Hatchery/Lair/Hive to stop Larvae generation. Also, if used on a Hatchery that has had Spawn Larvae cast on it by a Queen, the duration of Spawn Larvae will be momentarily paused for the duration of Contaminate.

Contaminate also pauses unit production and research of any Protoss unit building structure however, Warp Gates can still warp in units even with the debuff.

All production and research for Terran units is also halted including the production of Nukes at Ghost Academies however, Orbital Commands can still summon MULE's. Terran structures lose the ability to take off and land when affected by the ability Contaminate.

DETECTOR

Effect: Can spot Cloaked, Burrowed, and Hallucinated units

Cost	Range	Radius	Autocast
Passive	0	0	No

ZERGLING

COST:

 50 (PER 2)   0   24   1/2

BUILT FROM:	BUILD REQUIREMENTS:	UPGRADES:
 Hatchery	Spawning Pool	Spawning Pool

Zerglings become significantly more dangerous with their upgrades researched. They are affectionately referred to as 'Speedlings' with their Speed upgrade researched.

Groups of Zerglings should accompany your ground army at all times, unless your enemy is fielding units that are especially hostile to the long and healthy life of your Zerglings. Keep Zerglings away from enemy Siege Tank lines, Colossus, or Archons. They also fare poorly against Banelings

WEAPON STATISTICS					
Weapon	Damage	Attacks	Attack Speed	Range	Targets
Claws	5 (+1)	1	0.70 (0.59)	Melee	Ground

UNIT STATISTICS						
Health	Energy	Armor	Movement Speed	Acceleration	Line of Sight	Size
35	No	0	2.95 (4.69)	No	8	1

UNIT TYPE						
Light	Armored	Biological	Mechanical	Psionic	Massive	Structure

Zerglings are the cheapest and weakest of all the common basic Zerg units, but also the most numerous, as they are created two at a time from a single Larva.

HATCHERY

UPGRADES		COST			EFFECT
Upgrade	Requirement				
Metabolic Boost	None	100	100	110	Increases Zergling movement speed
Adrenal Glands	Hive	200	200	130	Increases Zergling attack speed by 20%

METABOLIC BOOST

This upgrade increases Zergling ground speed to make them the fastest ground unit in the game, *especially* on Creep. This makes Zerglings much more dangerous, as they can rapidly surround large enemy units and tear them apart. They also become much more dangerous for quick worker raids, Nydus raids, or the assassination of key enemy units.

This upgrade should always be purchased, though you can delay the purchase of it if you are using the Gas for an early Lair upgrade.

ADRENAL GLANDS

Adrenal Glands increase Zergling attack by speed by roughly 20%, greatly increasing their damage output, especially if you have researched melee damage upgrades by the time you acquire this technology.

Adrenal Glands are a Hive level tech, and they should always be researched when you gain access to them, they make large groups of Zerglings even more cost effective in battle.

MORPH TO BANELING
Hot Key: E

Effect: Mutates Zergling to Baneling

Cost	Range	Radius	Autocast
25 Minerals, 25 Gas, 20s	0	0	No

BANELING (MUTATION)

COST:

 25 25 20 1/2

BUILT FROM:	BUILD REQUIREMENTS:	UPGRADES:
Zergling	Baneling Nest	Baneling Nest

Banelings are the earliest unit that any race has access to that can destroy enemy structures with reasonable speed. This makes them perfect for breaking a hole in an enemy wall-in early in a match.

They are also extremely dangerous against massed basic troops from any race, as they receive a large bonus to their splash damage against Light units—Marines, Zealots, and Zerglings all fall to Banelings quickly.

Once Burrow is acquired, Banelings can detonate while burrowed, allowing you to create living land mines. Try placing small groups of burrowed Banelings just outside an enemy base, or your own base, where you know an enemy ground army will travel. Even if you miss the window of opportunity to detonate them below ground, you can always unburrow them and hit the rear of your opponent's army (or his undefended base!). Never hesitate to make use of Banelings because they are a suicidal unit. The damage they can inflict when used well always makes them worth their cost.

WEAPON STATISTICS

Weapon	Damage	Attacks	Attack Speed	Range	Targets
Volatile Burst	20 +15 vs Light (+2/+2)	1	0.83	Melee	Ground

UNIT STATISTICS

Health	Energy	Armor	Movement Speed	Acceleration	Line of Sight	Size
30	No	0	2.5 (2.95)	No	8	2

UNIT TYPE

Light	Armored	Biological	Mechanical	Psionic	Massive	Structure

Banelings are mutations of Zerglings, explosive suicide units that can deal very heavy damage to large groups of ground units.

HATCHERY

UPGRADES		COST			EFFECT
Upgrade	Requirement				
Centrifugal Hooks	Lair	150	150	110	Increases Baneling movement speed

CENTRIFUGAL HOOKS

This upgrade increases the movement speed of Banelings. This is very helpful as army sizes get larger, as it allows more of your Banelings to reach a sizable enemy force intact to deal their explosive damage.

It is also very important when attacking a heavily defended position, as every second counts when your Banelings will be taking fire from most of the enemy force while targeting a structure. Be sure to pick up this upgrade if you find yourself using Banelings in any significant numbers, though it is rarely needed early in a match.

EXPLODE

Hot Key: X

Effect: Causes the Baneling to detonate immediately

Cost	Range	Radius	Autocast
0	0	2.2	No

Causes a Baneling to detonate immediately. Banelings will normally detonate on contact with an enemy unit, but you can force an explosion, particularly useful when you have Banelings burrowed beneath an enemy force.

ATTACK STRUCTURE

Hot Key: C

Effect: Force the Baneling to attack a structure, can be Autocast, deals 80 (+5) damage to structures

Cost	Range	Radius	Autocast
0	0	0	Yes

By default, Banelings will prioritize enemy units over structures. If you force attack a structure, they will detonate on the building, and if you wish, you can also set this ability to Autocast, so that they will hit enemy buildings while attacking a wall-in.

Be careful about leaving this ability on Autocast if you're attacking the interior of a base, your Banelings will happily detonate themselves on the nearest hostile enemy structure, whatever its strategic value, usually inflicting minimal damage to multiple structures.

ROACH

COST:

 75   25   27   2

Hot Key:
R

BUILT FROM:	BUILD REQUIREMENTS:	UPGRADES:
Hatchery	Roach Warren	Roach Warren

Roaches regenerate at 5 health per second while burrowed, and later when upgraded, at 15 health per second while burrowed! Against an enemy without a source of Detection, Roaches are nearly unkillable without massed focus fire.

Roaches deal good damage against any target, but they are a *very* short ranged unit, so they function best when the terrain is unrestricted and they can surround their enemies. Given that Roaches are one of the larger Zerg ground units, this means that you should avoid fighting in narrow chokepoints with a large Roach force whenever possible.

Roaches are always a good choice for leading your force into battle, as they are durable enough to take fire from an enemy army and remain standing. Just watch out for enemy air units or heavy anti-Armored damage, both of which are dangerous to Roaches.

Roaches also benefit greatly from Zerg ground armor upgrades, as they begin with 1 armor. Due to their inherent armor and regeneration, additional armor can render enemy units that deal low damage with fast attack speed or have multiple attacks extremely ineffective against your Roaches.

WEAPON STATISTICS

Weapon	Damage	Attacks	Attack Speed	Range	Targets
Acid Saliva	16 (+2)	1	2.00	3	Ground

UNIT STATISTICS

Health	Energy	Armor	Movement Speed	Acceleration	Line of Sight	Size
145	No	1	2.25 (3) - 1.4 Burrowed	No	9	2

UNIT TYPE

Light	Armored	Biological	Mechanical	Psionic	Massive	Structure

*The Zerg Roach is a frontline assault specialist, with a good health total, built in armor, and **incredible** healing ability while burrowed.*

HATCHERY

UPGRADES		COST			EFFECT
Upgrade	Requirement				
Glial Reconstitution	Lair	100	100	110	Increases Roach movement speed
Tunneling Claws	Lair	150	150	110	Enables Roaches to move while burrowed. Increases the life-regeneration rate of burrowed Roaches.

GLIAL RECONSTITUTION

This upgrade increases Roach movement speed. This is very helpful for Roaches, given their short attack range, and it also speeds them up enough to perform some dancing micro against slower units without longer range (notably Zealots early in a match).

If you are fielding Roaches in significant numbers, be sure to pick up this upgrade, though you may want to research Tunneling Claws first, unless the map is large and travel speed is an issue.

Glial Reconstitution is unlocked at Lair level.

TUNNELING CLAWS

Unlocked at Lair level, Tunneling Claws allow your Roaches to move while burrowed. They move more slowly than they would aboveground, but the benefit of stealth can often outweigh the need for speed.

Against enemy expansions that lack fixed Detectors, this allows you to make an unseen approach to a worker line, pop up, and destroy an entire enemy worker line in seconds.

You can also make use of Tunneling Claws to harass a mobile enemy army, burrowing and moving away from any targeted area of effect damage that they may use against the Roaches.

Tunneling Claws are a worthwhile investment if you are planning on fielding Roaches extensively, they greatly increase Roach's tactical flexibility, and force your opponent to focus on building Detectors or suffer heavy damage.

This Lair level upgrade to the Roach massively increases their regeneration, granting them 15 health regen per second while burrowed. Needless to say, this upgrade should be purchased immediately when your Lair finishes building if you are using Roaches in your army.

RAPID REGENERATION

Effect: Causes Roaches to regenerate rapidly while Burrowed

Cost	Range	Radius	Autocast
Passive	0	0	No

ROACH BURROW MICRO

Once you have access to Burrow with a significant number of Roaches in your offensive force, you should always be watching their health bars in battle.

Either watch the group selection pane and burrow them as their icons turn orange or red, or turn on health bars in the options menu and watch their health level in the battlefield view.

As you burrow each damaged Roach, your remaining Roaches aboveground will automatically begin to receive greater focus fire, so after you have burrowed a few of your Roaches, burrow all of your Roaches momentarily, then unburrow the whole group to 'reset' the fight, eliminating any focus fire advantage your opponent might have gained.

Without Detection, your opponent cannot stop this micro, they can only delay the inevitable destruction of their base and army. Just don't waste so much time trying to conserve a few Roaches that you give them time to build Detectors!

HYDRALISK

COST:

 100 50 33 2

BUILT FROM: **BUILD REQUIREMENTS:** **UPGRADES:**

Hatchery *Hydralisk Den* *Hydralisk Den*

Hydralisks are effective against any enemy unit, air or ground, their only real significant weaknesses are area of effect damage or enemies with high bonus Light damage.

In smaller numbers, Hydralisks are less lethal, but still very useful. Hydralisks make a fine main army anchor unit, and they complement the short range of Roaches and Zerglings well if you are creating a mixed force.

Hydralisks are not a fantastic unit for dancing micro on offense, due to their average speed, but they do focus fire well, particularly once their range upgrade has been researched. On Creep, you may be able to dance away from some slower units, so be sure to make good use of the speed boost.

Hydralisks are the *only* ground unit for the Zerg with anti-air capability outside the Queen, so if you are facing enemy air units, you need to decide if you will respond with Hydralisks or Spire units. Given that the Hydralisk Den builds considerably faster than the Spire, you may wish to place one as insurance, in case you do need a quick anti-air force.

WEAPON STATISTICS

Weapon	Damage	Attacks	Attack Speed	Range	Targets
Needle Spines	12 (+1)	1	0.83	5 (6)	Air/Ground

UNIT STATISTICS

Health	Energy	Armor	Movement Speed	Acceleration	Line of Sight	Size
80	No	0	2.25	No	9	2

UNIT TYPE

Light	Armored	Biological	Mechanical	Psionic	Massive	Structure

The Hydralisk is a moderately strong ranged attacker that becomes extremely dangerous in large numbers.

LAIR

UPGRADES

Upgrade	Requirement	COST			EFFECT
Grooved Spines	None	150	150	80	Increases Hydralisk attack range

GROOVED SPINES

This upgrade increases Hydralisk range by 1. This may not seem like much, but it considerably increases Hydralisk power, as it lets them target air units from a greater distance, focus fire more effectively in battle, and force shorter ranged enemy units to cover more ground to damage them.

Always acquire this upgrade if you are planning to field Hydralisks as part of your army.

INFESTOR

Hot Key:

F

COST:

 100 150 50 2

BUILT FROM:	BUILD REQUIREMENTS:	UPGRADES:
Hatchery	Infestation Pit	Infestation Pit

Infestors are slow moving and individually weak, but they have the unique ability to move while burrowed, shared only with the Roach—and they do not require an upgrade to do so!

The Infestation Pit is also required to upgrade to Hive level tech, so you will always have access to these units going into the midgame—don't hesitate to make use of them sooner however, they can be very effective if controlled well.

Even small numbers of Infestors can create large groups of Infested Terrans, which act as a free supplement to your army, or a useful raiding force. Fungal Growth helps to damage and delay enemy armies, and Neural Parasite can be used to disable enemy casters or other dangerous ground units.

WEAPON STATISTICS					
Weapon	Damage	Attacks	Attack Speed	Range	Targets
NONE					

UNIT STATISTICS						
Health	Energy	Armor	Movement Speed	Acceleration	Line of Sight	Size
90	Yes	0	2.5 (2 Burrowed)	No	10	2

UNIT TYPE						
Light	Armored	Biological	Mechanical	Psionic	Massive	Structure

The Infestor is the lone Zerg caster unit, with several interesting abilities to support your army in battle and harass your opponent's forces.

LAIR

UPGRADES		COST			EFFECT
Upgrade	Requirement				
Pathogen Glands	None	150	150	80	Increases Infestor starting Energy by 25
Neural Parasite	None	150	150	110	Controls target unit until Infestor is killed, Channeled ability

PATHOGEN GLANDS

Pathogen Glands increase Infestor starting Energy by 25. As with all other caster upgrades of this nature, it is most useful if you are planning on fielding large numbers of Infestors throughout a match.

FRENZY

Hot Key: Y

Effect: Increases targeted units damage by 25% and makes them immune to slow or stun effects

Cost	Range	Radius	Autocast
25 Energy	9		No

NEURAL PARASITE

Hot Key: E

Effect: Target unit is controlled by the Infestor until one of them dies, or the Infestor relinquishes control. The Infestor cannot take any other action while controlling an enemy unit.

Cost	Range	Radius	Autocast
100 Energy	9	0	No

Neural Parasite allows an Infestor to actually *gain control* of an enemy unit! As long as the unit is in range of the Infestor, the control is permanent, until the Infestor is killed (or you kill the unit yourself).

While active, the Infestor is paralyzed and unable to act, though you can cancel the control should you need to retreat your Infestor. Don't expect Infestors making use of Neural Parasite in a large army battle to last long, your enemy will likely focus fire them quickly.

In some cases however, that may not matter—use burrow movement to get in range of key enemy units, wait until the battle has begun, then pop up and take control of them. There is little more satisfying in a match as Zerg than gaining control of an enemy High Templar and using Psionic Storm on their own army!

In smaller battles, if you see that the troop numbers are low enough, a small group of Infestors can also win you a battle simply by gaining control of several enemy units, tipping the fight in your favor. After an enemy is driven off or defeated, you can kill units under control by attacking them directly, no need to release them!

FUNGAL GROWTH

Hot Key: F

Effect: Immobilizes units in target area, dealing 36 damage over 8 seconds and revealing Cloaked or Burrowed units for 8 seconds, also prevents units from Burrowing

Cost	Range	Radius	Autocast
75 Energy	9	2	No

Finally, the Infestor's Fungal Growth ability is an area of effect snare that prevents enemy units caught in it from moving or burrowing. In addition, it reveals cloaked or burrowed units in an area, *and* it deals light damage over time to the trapped units.

Fungal Growth is especially effective in army battles when used alongside Hydralisks, though it can also be helpful with Roaches if your opponent has many Zerglings or Zealots.

However, Fungal Growth is useful even against enemy ranged units—it prevents movement, which means your opponent cannot effectively make use of focus fire, and while on auto-attack, enemy units cannot shift their position to acquire new targets.

In larger battles where you may not have the time to move your army, simply fire multiple Fungal Growth at the enemy mass, the damage dealt to large groups is well worth the Energy, and your opponent will still lose some of their combat damage due to immobile units.

Fungal Growth can work in concert with Infested Terrans for responding to aerial raids, your Infestors can freeze and damage packs of enemy air units, even if they are cloaked. Make use of Fungal Growth to reveal enemy cloaked or burrowed units if you don't have an Overseer handy.

PARASITE QUIRKS

A few oddities about Neural Parasite. First, you gain access to any activated ability your opponent may have researched, or that is inherent to the unit. So you will have, for example, Psionic Storm on a High Templar or EMP on a Ghost, if Psionic Storm has been researched (or the Ghost has enough Energy to activate EMP).

Your unit will not have access to passive upgrades (or Nukes, sorry!). This means that a fully upgraded +3/+3 Marine will become +0/+0 when you gain control of it, and it will lose its Combat Shield passive health bonus as well!

MUTALISK

COST:

 100 100 33 🔲 2

BUILT FROM:

BUILD REQUIREMENTS:

UPGRADES:

Hatchery

Spire

NONE

Their weapon is the Glaive Wurm, a unique attack that bounces between units, dealing full damage to its first target, then less to a second, and a small amount to a third.

In addition, Mutalisks can target air or ground units, making them a dangerous threat to any enemy force, and they become increasingly deadly when used in large numbers. Even in smaller groups, Mutalisks are still extremely useful, as they have one of the highest speeds of any air unit, making them an ideal unit for worker raiding, and base or army harassment.

Once your Mutalisks are on the field, you should be using them to *constantly* strike at your opponent's workers and bases. Even if they build fixed defenses, keep the pressure on by striking at structures that aren't protected.

If your opponent responds with their anti-air ground army, just leave the area— your Mutalisks are easily fast enough to run! You can then strike at expansions or use your ground army to force a response from your opponent, and then return to harassing his base with your Mutalisks.

Because Mutalisks become more dangerous in larger groups, be careful not to throw away Mutalisks on raids. Losing a few to deal heavy worker damage is acceptable, but don't get involved in battles against enemy anti-air units unless you know you can pick them off in isolation.

LAIR

WEAPON STATISTICS

Weapon	Damage	Attacks	Attack Speed	Range	Targets
Glaive Wurm	9/3/1 (+1)	1	1.53	3	Air/Ground

UNIT STATISTICS

Health	Energy	Armor	Movement Speed	Acceleration	Line of Sight	Size
120	No	0	3.75	Yes	10	

UNIT TYPE

Light	Armored	Biological	Mechanical	Psionic	Massive	Structure

The Mutalisk is a powerful and versatile air unit.

Should an enemy respond with their anti-air units and send them at you in small numbers, rather than a large group, aggressively attack them with your Mutalisks. Enough Mutalisks can easily pick off lone Marines, Stalkers, or Hydralisks, and if your opponent loses too many, you may be able to strike directly at their army with your Mutalisks.

There are few serious threats to a large group of Mutalisks, but there are a few things you should watch out for. Mutalisks are very vulnerable to the sources of area of effect damage that can target them. Seeker Missiles, Psionic Storm, Archons, and Fungal Growth can all cause heavy losses to a Mutalisk pack. Avoid fighting near these threats.

Mutalisks also do not have the health to stand up to fixed anti-air defenses. Once your opponent has built up several anti-air turrets near their worker lines, be cautious about raiding them unless you are sure you have enough Mutalisks to destroy the turrets or workers and escape quickly.

Mutalisks are also relatively poor against enemy capital air units— Battlecruisers and Carriers are sturdy and deal high damage, and are less effected by the Mutalisks bouncing attack in the same way that large groups of smaller air units are.

Mutalisks attack will deal 9, then 3, then 1 damage after each bounce, before upgrades.

MUTALISK HARASSMENT

One odd disadvantage to heavy Mutalisk usage isn't one related to their stats, but rather simple player behavior.

Mutalisks are a Gas heavy unit, and leaving only Minerals to create an army of Zerglings is unlikely to protect your base from a serious enemy ground push. Don't starve your ground army of Gas completely!

It is easy to forget about your ground force while you are raiding with Mutalisks and building more Mutalisks to replace losses suffered while raiding.

The danger of this behavior is that if your opponent realizes what you are doing, they will simply push with their ground army, and if you haven't been maintaining the growth of your own ground army, they can crush your ground force and then hit your base.

If you respond quickly enough with your Mutalisks, you may be able to fend them off in combination with a smaller ground force, but whatever you do, don't get caught in a situation where your army is losing a battle at home and by the time you return with your Mutalisks, your army is already lost.

Doing so essentially hands your opponent victory, as he's only had to fight half of your force with his full army, and that will usually leave him with enough troops to fight off your Mutalisks as well.

Mutalisks are powerful, and strong harassment with them can keep many players bottled up on defense while you expand, but calm opponent's will often respond to harassment by making a direct ground push against your expansions or main base. Be ready for this!

CORRUPTOR

COST:

 150   100   40 2

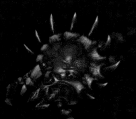

BUILT FROM:	BUILD REQUIREMENTS:	UPGRADES:
Hatchery	Spire	NONE

Corruptors are the Zerg answer to heavy air units, as they deal bonus Massive damage, perfect for destroying enemy Battlecruisers, Carriers, or Colossus (they also deal bonus damage to Brood Lords, but as Brood Lords have no anti-air, Mutalisks can accomplish that task as well).

Corruptors are also helpful for base siege, both because of their Corruption ability, and because they can eventually be morphed into Brood Lords, providing you with a siege range anti-ground air unit.

Unless you see a need for Brood Lords (or Corruption), Mutalisks should be built as your air unit for dealing with other enemy air threats, Corruptors are much less effective in battles against non-Massive targets.

WEAPON STATISTICS

Weapon	Damage	Attacks	Attack Speed	Range	Targets
Parasite Spore	14 +6 vs Massive (+1/+1)	1	1.90	6	Air

UNIT STATISTICS

Health	Energy	Armor	Movement Speed	Acceleration	Line of Sight	Size
200	Yes	2	2.95	Yes	10	

UNIT TYPE

Light	Armored	Biological	Mechanical	Psionic	Massive	Structure

The Corruptor is a pure anti-air flying unit, with the unique ability to corrupt enemy units, temporarily increasing the damage they take.

AIR

UPGRADES		COST				EFFECT
Upgrade	Requirement					
Morph to Brood Lord	Greater Spire	150	150	34	2	Mutate Corruptor to Brood Lord

CORRUPTION
Hot Key: C

Effect: Damage taken by target enemy unit increased by 20% for 30 seconds

Cost	Range	Radius	Autocast
75 Energy	6	0	No

MORPH TO BROOD LORD

Performing this morph requires Hive tech and a Greater Spire. Brood Lords are powerful siege units, and if you need them, have several Corruptors on the field ready to transform when a Greater Spire finishes.

Hot Key:
U

ULTRALISK

COST:

 300 200 70 6

BUILT FROM:	BUILD REQUIREMENTS:	UPGRADES:
Hatchery	*Ultralisk Cavern*	*Ultralisk Cavern*

Ultralisks are the last ground unit that Zerg gain access to and are second only in cost and build time to the Brood Lord. Ultralisks are *very* durable units, in contrast to most Zerg ground forces, making them ideal for leading the assault against enemy armies and bases.

Only a few are needed, as their huge size can be a liability when fighting in constricted terrain, but those few can shrug off damage (especially area of effect damage) that would cripple your primary army.

Ultralisks have several upgrades that increase their power, but you should generally only go after these upgrades if you know the game will be stretching into the late game—even a few Ultralisks without upgrades can break a defensive line when accompanied by your army.

WEAPON STATISTICS
Weapon	Damage	Attacks	Attack Speed	Range	Targets	Radius
Ram	75 (+5)	1	1.67	1	Ground (structures only)	0
Kaiser Blades	15 +25 vs Armored (+2/+2)	1	0.86	1	Ground	1.5

UNIT STATISTICS
Health	Energy	Armor	Movement Speed	Acceleration	Line of Sight	Size
500	No	1	2.95	No	9	8

UNIT TYPE
Light	Armored	Biological	Mechanical	Psionic	Massive	Structure

HIVE

Ultralisks are huge and powerful ground units, their scything tusks capable of causing serious damage to massed ground armies, while their powerful Ram attack does heavy damage against buildings.

UPGRADES		COST			EFFECT
Upgrade	Requirement				
Chitinous Plating	None	150	150	110	Grants Ultralisks +2 Armor

CHITINOUS PLATING

Chitinous Plating adds +2 armor to Ultralisks, increasing their combat durability against enemy units with low damage, fast attacks, or multiple attacks. This is especially notable against each races basic unit, the Marine, Zealot, and Zergling are all greatly impacted by this upgrade.

This upgrade is useful, but again, not immediately vital, Ultralisks have plenty of health when they hit the field initially.

BROOD LORD (MUTATION)

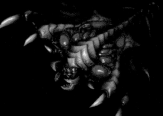

COST:

  150   150   34   4

BUILT FROM:	BUILD REQUIREMENTS:	UPGRADES:
Corruptor	Greater Spire	NONE

The Brood Lord's attack is unique in that it deals damage at long range *and* spawns Broodlings when it impacts, dealing a bit of extra damage as the ravenous creatures feast on nearby enemy units.

Brood Lords are painfully slow, and have no defenses against enemy air units, so they should always be escorted by your ground or air army. Ideally, morph Brood Lords when your Corruptors are already in position for you to attack an enemy base.

Because Brood Lords can attack from such a long distance, and deal very heavy damage, if your opponent is sitting on defense, you can destroy their defenses and eventually their army from a safe range. Fielding Brood Lords *forces* your enemy to engage your army if you make a direct frontal assault.

Brood Lords can also be used to hit a base from an area where your opponent cannot respond with ground forces. If you have air superiority, feel free to take this route with your attack, just be careful that your Brood Lords are not hit with an unexpected enemy air attack while your own Hydralisks cannot move to defend them.

A sufficient force of Mutalisks and Corruptors can protect a Brood Lord assault against a base away from any ground chokepoint or ground forces, but this is an extremely Gas heavy, late game combination of units.

WEAPON STATISTICS

Weapon	Damage	Attacks	Attack Speed	Range	Targets
Broodling Strike	20 (+2)	1	2.50	9.5	Ground

UNIT STATISTICS

Health	Energy	Armor	Movement Speed	Acceleration	Line of Sight	Size
225	No	1	1.4	Yes	12	

UNIT TYPE

Light	Armored	Biological	Mechanical	Psionic	Massive	Structure

The Brood Lord is a powerful siege flyer, with long range attacks that can destroy fixed emplacements and provide strong support for your ground army.

HIVE

SWARM SEEDS

Effect: Creates Broodlings when the Brood Lord hits a target

Cost	Range	Radius	Autocast
Passive	0	0	No

Each time a Brood Lord's attack hits a target, it spawns a pair of Broodlings. These Broodlings will automatically attack any nearby enemy units.

BROODLING

COST:

 0   0   0   0

BUILT FROM:	BUILD REQUIREMENTS:	UPGRADES:
Brood Lord	NONE	NONE

Broodlings only appear on the battlefield under a few situations, the first being when created by the Brood Lord's Swarm Seeds, and the second being when a Zerg structure is destroyed.

Several Broodlings spawn from the remains of Zerg organic structure, quickly swarming the offending units that destroyed their home. 9 Broodlings appear from a destroyed Hatchery, Lair, or Hive, while 6 appear from any other structure that is not an Extractor, Nydus Worm, Spine or Spore Crawler.

WEAPON STATISTICS

Weapon	Damage	Attacks	Attack Speed	Range	Targets
Needle Claws	4 (+1)	1	0.65	Melee	Ground

UNIT STATISTICS

Health	Energy	Armor	Movement Speed	Acceleration	Line of Sight	Size
30	No	0	Fast 3.83	No	7	

UNIT TYPE

Light	Armored	Biological	Mechanical	Psionic	Massive	Structure

Broodlings are small weak Zerg units, more of a form of aggressive larva than a true offensive combat mutation.

SPECIAL

INFESTED TERRAN

COST:

BUILT FROM: **BUILD REQUIREMENTS:** **UPGRADES:**

Overseer

NONE NONE

Infested Terrans can be directly controlled after creation, so feel free to use them to focus fire a specific target, or ignore them and let them deal damage and soak up attacks meant for your normal troops, though they only last for 30 seconds on the battlefield after they are created.

WEAPON STATISTICS

Weapon	Damage	Attacks	Attack Speed	Range	Targets
Infested Gauss Rifle	8 (+1)	1	0.86	5	Air/Ground

UNIT STATISTICS

Health	Energy	Armor	Movement Speed	Acceleration	Line of Sight	Size
50	No	0	1	No	8	1

UNIT TYPE

Light	Armored	Biological	Mechanical	Psionic	Massive	Structure

Spawned by Overseers, these corrupted Marines are nearly identical to normal Terran Marines.

SPECIAL

CHANGELING

Hot Key:
C

COST:

BUILT FROM:	BUILD REQUIREMENTS:	UPGRADES:
 *Overseer*	NONE	NONE

Changelings transform into a Zealot, Zergling, or Marine when they get within 12 range of an enemy race's unit.

Changelings last for a significant 150 seconds, plenty of time to scout out an enemy base or army.

WEAPON STATISTICS

Weapon	Damage	Attacks	Attack Speed	Range	Targets
NONE					

UNIT STATISTICS

Health	Energy	Armor	Movement Speed	Acceleration	Line of Sight	Size
5	No	0	2.25	No	8 (9 as Zealot or Marine)	1

UNIT TYPE

Light	Armored	Biological	Mechanical	Psionic	Massive	Structure

Changelings are created by Overseers, and act as a covert scouting unit for the Zerg.

SPECIAL

 DISGUISE

Effect: Transforms Changeling into a nearby Zergling, Zealot, or Marine

Cost	Range	Radius	Autocast
None	???	0	Yes

ZERG BUILDINGS

Zerg structures are unique in that rather than having unit producing buildings, they create unit-enabling structures that allow any Zerg Hatchery to produce units.

The downside to this model is that if an enemy destroys a key unit-enabling structure, none of your Hatcheries can produce that unit any longer. Combined with Zerg's inability to wall in their bases easily early in the game, and it is crucial that you defend your key tech structures.

Early military enablers should be placed behind your Mineral line, where your Queen, workers, and early Zerglings can defend them.

Later in a match, you should protect your important structures such as the Spire with Spine or Spore Crawlers, as your opponent's will target your military structures during raids. For especially important structures in a late game match, don't hesitate to build a backup structure!

ZERG UPGRADES

Zerg ground upgrades are purchased at the Evolution chamber, while air upgrades come from the Spire.

BUILDING TYPES

All Zerg structures are Armored, Biological, Structure.

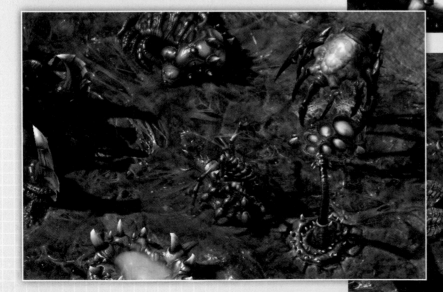

HATCHERY

Hot Key: H

COST:

🪨 300   🔵 0   🕐 100

BUILDING STATISTICS		
Health	Armor	Energy
1250	1	

BUILD REQUIREMENTS:

NONE

The Hatchery is the hub of all Zerg unit production, as well as the key to unlocking higher tiers of Zerg technology. Hatcheries can be mutated first into a Lair, and later into a Hive. A Lair requires a Spawning Pool, and a Hive requires an Infestation Pit.

Hatcheries (and their upgrades) produce 1 Larva every 15 seconds. Each Larva can always be morphed into a Drone or Overlord, and can also be morphed into any military unit that you have created the enabling structure for. Hatcheries store up to 3 Larvae at most, the only way to generate more than 3 (or to generate Larvae more quickly) is to make use of the Queen's Spawn Larvae ability. When a Hatchery has more than 3 Larvae due to Spawn Larvae use, it will not automatically generate more until it drops below 3 Larvae again.

Your military and economic production is limited by the number of Hatcheries you have, and the efficiency with which you make use of Spawn Larvae.

Interestingly, once at least one Hatchery has been upgraded to a Lair, *any* Hatchery can research Lair level upgrades. Be sure to take advantage of this if you have multiple Hatcheries to acquire Burrow and Pneumatic Carapace simultaneously.

You should always have *all* of your Hatcheries on one hotkey, and all of your Queens on another, allowing you to quickly produce any needed units, and to quickly cast Spawn Larvae on your Hatcheries as new Larvae are created.

Zerg need a second Hatchery up and running (preferably with an attendant Queen) as they progress towards the midgame to keep up with opposing Terran or Protoss army production, and in a late game match, you may have many more created.

Once a Spawning Pool has been built, any Hatchery can produce Queens.

BUILDING PRODUCTION		COST			
Unit	Requirement				🕐
Queen	Spawning Pool	150	0	2	50

BUILDING UPGRADES		COST			
Upgrade	Requirement	🪨	🔵	🕐	EFFECT
Lair	Spawning Pool	150	100	80	Mutates Hatchery to Lair

HATCHERY

HATCHERY

QUICK EXPANSION

Because a Hatchery costs 350 (300 + the 50 for a Worker), it is slightly cheaper to expand early with the Zerg than the Terran or Protoss.

An aggressive early play with the Zerg is to expand to their natural expansion almost immediately as the game begins. On larger maps, your opponent may not be able to muster a large enough military to stop you from pulling off this immediate expansion.

The additional Larva production, and eventually, economy can benefit you greatly in the midgame if you can perform this successfully.

In situations where you are not comfortable with expanding immediately, it is still important that you eventually add a second Hatchery to your main base for Larva production!

EXTRACTOR

Hot Key: E

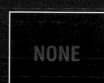

COST:

🪨 25   🔵 0   🕐 30

BUILDING STATISTICS		
Health	Armor	Energy
500	1	

BUILD REQUIREMENTS:

NONE

The Zerg Extractor is necessary to harvest Vespene Gas from a Geyser. Due to the low Gas cost of early Zerg units, you can occasionally get away with delaying Extractor creation to build up a healthy Mineral income, but don't delay if you're planning on upgrading to Lair level and going for Hydralisks or Mutalisks quickly.

SPAWNING POOL

Hot Key: S

COST:
 200 0 65

BUILDING STATISTICS		
Health	Armor	Energy
750	1	

BUILD REQUIREMENTS:

Hatchery

The Spawning Pool enables the mutation of Zerglings, and is a critical early game structure, as important to the Zerg as an early Barracks or Gateway for Terran or Protoss armies.

The Spawning Pool is also vital as it unlocks the Queen at your Hatchery, a must for Spawn Larvae and helpful for early defense. The Spawning Pool also unlocks the Spine Crawler, the Zerg's defensive anti-ground turret. Unlike Terran or Protoss, who must build a separate upgrade structure to unlock their early turrets, Zerg gain access to theirs immediately.

Try to place your Spawning Pool behind your Mineral line, to give it the most protection by your Queen and workers.

All Zergling upgrades are purchased at this structure.

HATCHERY

BUILDING UPGRADES		COST			EFFECT
Upgrade	Requirement				
Metabolic Boost	None	100	100	110	Increases Zergling movement speed
Adrenal Glands	Hive	200	200	130	Increases Zergling attack speed by 20%

EVOLUTION CHAMBER

Hot Key: V

COST:
 75 0 35

BUILDING STATISTICS		
Health	Armor	Energy
750	1	

BUILD REQUIREMENTS:

Hatchery

The Evolution Chamber holds all ground upgrades for the Zerg. Zerg ground forces all benefit from armor upgrades, but you must choose between melee or missile upgrades. Melee upgrades improve Zerglings, Banelings, Broodlings, and Ultralisks, while missile upgrades help Roaches and Hydralisks.

Creating an Evolution Chamber also unlocks the Spore Crawler, giving you access to your fixed Detector and anti-air turret. Multiple Evolution Chambers should be used if you are investing heavily in a Zerg ground army, to speed the research of multiple upgrades.

HATCHERY

BUILDING UPGRADES		COST			EFFECT
Upgrade	Requirement				
Melee Attacks Level 1	None	100	100	160	Upgrades all Zerg melee attacks
Melee Attacks Level 2	Lair	150	150	190	Upgrades all Zerg melee attacks
Melee Attacks Level 3	Hive	200	200	200	Upgrades all Zerg melee attacks
Missile Attacks Level 1	None	100	100	160	Upgrades all Zerg missile attacks
Missile Attacks Level 2	Lair	150	150	190	Upgrades all Zerg missile attacks
Missile Attacks Level 3	Hive	200	200	200	Upgrades all Zerg missile attacks
Ground Carapace Level 1	None	150	150	160	Upgrades the armor of all Zerg ground units
Ground Carapace Level 2	Lair	225	225	190	Upgrades the armor of all Zerg ground units
Ground Carapace Level 3	Hive	300	300	200	Upgrades the armor of all Zerg ground units

ROACH WARREN

Hot Key: R

COST:

 150 0 55

BUILDING STATISTICS		
Health	Armor	Energy
850	1	

BUILD REQUIREMENTS:

Spawning Pool

The Roach Warren enables the mutation of Roaches, and contains all upgrades for Roaches. The Roach Warren only costs Minerals to create, so if you are delaying your Extractors, you can still create the Warren in preparation for Roach production.

HATCHERY

BUILDING UPGRADES		COST			EFFECT
Upgrade	Requirement				
Glial Reconstitution	Lair	100	100	110	Increases Roach movement speed
Tunneling Claws	Lair	150	150	110	Enables Roaches to move while burrowed and increases life-regeneration rate of burrowed Roaches

BANELING NEST

Hot Key: B

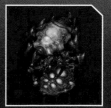

COST:

 100 50  60

BUILDING STATISTICS		
Health	Armor	Energy
850	1	

BUILD REQUIREMENTS:

Spawning Pool

The Baneling Nest enables mutation of Banelings from Zerglings, and provides upgrades for Banelings.

HATCHERY

BUILDING UPGRADES		COST			EFFECT
Upgrade	Requirement				
Centrifugal Hooks	Lair	150	150	110	Increases Baneling movement speed

SPINE CRAWLER

Hot Key: C

COST:

 100   0   50

BUILDING STATISTICS		
Health	Armor	Energy
300	2	No

BUILD REQUIREMENTS:

Spawning Pool

Spine Crawlers are the Zerg's anti-ground turret. They deal solid damage to any hostile ground units in range, and because they are unlocked immediately after building a Spawning Pool, can be used to help fend off an early game rush.

The Spine Crawler is unique among structures, as it can actually uproot itself and move! Spine Crawlers will suffer health degeneration if they move off of Creep, but they can be moved between your main and your natural without suffering much damage. Remember that while Spine (and Spore) crawlers can move, they can only root onto Creep, not open ground.

The mobility of Spine Crawlers allows you to respond to enemy attacks against any structure in your base, though you should generally build early structures near your worker line, so that early Spine Crawlers can provide coverage for your worker line and structures.

HATCHERY

SPORE CRAWLER

Hot Key: A

COST:

 75   0   30

BUILDING STATISTICS		
Health	Armor	Energy
400	1	No

BUILD REQUIREMENTS:

Evolution Chamber

Spore Crawlers are the Zerg's anti-air turret, and their 'fixed' Detector. As with the Spine Crawler, Spore Crawlers are not actually fixed at all, as they can uproot and move around.

This is very helpful on defense, both to provide protection against enemy air if you are not using Hydralisks or Mutalisks, and because it gives you mobile Detection for base defense, even if you don't have an Overseer handy.

Spore Crawlers have more health than Missile Turrets, Photon Cannons, or even the Spine Crawler, as well as a strong and fast anti-air attack. They are ideal for defending against aerial harassment of your Overlords or worker lines.

HATCHERY

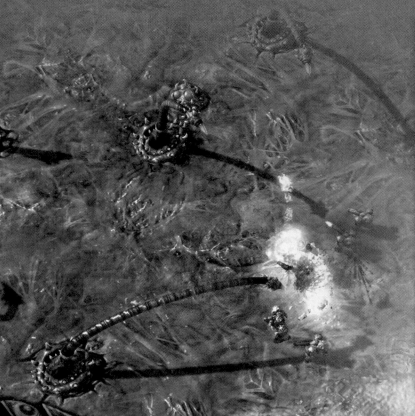

LAIR

Hot Key: L

COST:
 150   100 80

BUILDING STATISTICS		
Health	Armor	Energy
1800	1	

The Lair is upgraded from a Hatchery. This upgrade increases the health of the structure, and unlocks several very useful research options, including the critical Burrow upgrade.

BUILD REQUIREMENTS:

Spawning Pool

BUILDING PRODUCTION		COST			
Unit	Requirement	🥩	🔵	🔺	⏱
 Queen	Spawning Pool	150	0	2	50

BUILDING UPGRADES		COST			EFFECT
Upgrade	Requirement	🥩	🔵	⏱	
Hive	Infestation Pit	200	150	100	Mutates Lair into Hive
Burrow	None	100	100	100	Grants all Zerg ground units the ability to Burrow
Pneumatized Carapace	None	100	100	60	Increases Overlord and Overseer movement speed
Ventral Sacs	None	200	200	130	Allows Overlords to transport units

BURROW

Burrow should be researched immediately after reaching Lair tech, unless you have an immediate pressing need for Gas on another structure or tech.

Once researched, all of your ground units gain access to burrow, granting protection for your workers or Queen raids, better scouting, and improved offense with Banelings, Roaches, Infestors, and your ground army as a whole.

Burrow *forces* your opponent to invest in Detectors, or they hand you a significant advantage.

HYDRALISK DEN

Hot Key: H

COST:
 100   100 40

BUILDING STATISTICS		
Health	Armor	Energy
850	1	

This Den unlocks Hydralisks for mutation. As Zerg's only anti-air ground unit, the Hydralisk Den should be built if you are not making use of a Spire, to prepare for an aerial threat if Hydralisks are needed.

Hydralisk upgrades are purchased at the Hydralisk Den.

BUILD REQUIREMENTS:

Lair

BUILDING UPGRADES		COST			EFFECT
Upgrade	Requirement	🥩	🔵	⏱	
Grooved Spines	None	150	150	80	Increases Hydralisk attack range

INFESTATION PIT

Hot Key: I

COST:
 100 100 50

BUILDING STATISTICS		
Health	Armor	Energy
850	1	

The Infestation Pit enables the mutation of Infestors, and unlocks the ability to upgrade a Lair to a Hive.

Infestor upgrades are purchased at this building.

BUILD REQUIREMENTS:

Lair

SPIRE

Hot Key: S

COST:
 200 200 100

BUILDING STATISTICS		
Health	Armor	Energy
600	1	

The Spire is the slowest of all Zerg military structures to be created, so it should be built early if you are planning on creating air units.

Be sure to protect your Spire, a Spire lost to a raid is painfully slow to replace. The Spire allows the mutation of Mutalisks and Corruptors, and holds upgrades for all Zerg air units.

A Spire can be mutated into a Greater Spire at the Hive level, enabling the mutation of Brood Lords from Corruptors.

BUILD REQUIREMENTS:

Lair

BUILDING UPGRADES		COST			EFFECT
Upgrade	Requirement				
Neural Parasite	None	150	150	110	Allows Infestors to use Neural Parasite
Pathogen Glands	None	150	150	80	Increases Infestor starting Energy by 25

BUILDING UPGRADES		COST			EFFECT
Upgrade	Requirement				
Mutate into Greater Spire	Hive	100	150	100	Allows Corruptors to mutate into Brood Lords
Flyer Attacks Level 1	None	100	100	160	Upgrades the attacks of all Zerg air units
Flyer Attacks Level 2	Lair	175	175	190	Upgrades the attacks of all Zerg air units
Flyer Attacks Level 3	Hive	250	250	220	Upgrades the attacks of all Zerg air units
Flyer Carapace Level 1	None	150	150	160	Upgrades the armor of all Zerg air units
Flyer Carapace Level 2	Lair	225	225	190	Upgrades the armor of all Zerg air units
Flyer Carapace Level 3	Hive	300	300	220	Upgrades the armor of all Zerg air units

NYDUS NETWORK

Hot Key: N

COST:

 150   200   50

BUILDING STATISTICS		
Health	Armor	Energy
850	1	

BUILD REQUIREMENTS:

Lair

The Nydus Network is the Zerg's transportation structure. Once built, Zerg units can enter it as though it were a mobile transport, and exit from any other Nydus Network on the map. Any Nydus Network has the ability to spawn a Nydus Worm, a special transport structure anywhere on the map. Nydus Worms are cheap to create, and build quickly, but thcy can't be placed In the fog of war, and they are more fragile than the Nydus Network itself.

Note that while units enter a Nydus tunnel quickly, they do not unload instantly. Keep this in mind when attempting to move your army in response to an attack, having the Network destroyed with half your army stranded can cause a crushing defeat in battle.

Nydus Worms can be used to send a backdoor force to attack an opponent's base, or built beside your army in the field to allow them to instantly return to base. With multiple Nydus Networks and Worms spread around the map, the Zerg ground army has a frightening amount of mobility.

Try to create a Nydus Network at each of your bases (remember, the Worms are much less durable), and make use of Worms to move your army on offense, or to recall it from the field for base defense.

NYDUS WORM

Hot Key: N

COST:

100 100 20

BUILDING STATISTICS		
Health	Armor	Energy
200	1	

BUILD REQUIREMENTS:

Nydus Network

Created by a Nydus Network, the Nydus Worm acts as an entry point to the Nydus tunnel network, and can be created anywhere on the map where you have line of sight.

Make use of your Overlords, Overseers, Burrow, Changelings, air units, and burrowed Roaches or Infestors to create the line of sight you need to place a Nydus Worm. Remember that you can always place a Nydus Worm near your army to move it quickly to another Nydus Network or Worm.

Offensively, you can use Nydus Worms to bypass enemy chokepoints, but remember that the Nydus Worm has a construction time, and if spotted, can be easily destroyed. Don't let your whole army be stranded in enemy territory—base raids should be done with a small expendable force, unless you are certain that you can break your opponent with an army push from behind.

Nydus Worm, unlike the Network itself, produce Creep. This can give you a small speed benefit on offense, or when retreating units through a swarm. In an exceptionally rare situation, you could even construct a Worm near friendly structures that had lost their Creep due to the destruction of a Hatchery or Creep Tumor to prevent degeneration.

BUILDING ABILITIES

	Summon Nydus Worm				
	Cost	Range	Radius	Effect	Autocast?
	100 minerals, 100 gas, 20s	Unlimited	0	Creates a Nydus Worm at target location within line of sight	No

HIVE

Hot Key: H

COST:

 200 150 100

BUILDING STATISTICS		
Health	Armor	Energy
2500	1	

Upgraded from a Lair, the Hive gains another increase in health, and unlocks the final level of upgrades and structures for the Zerg force. Hives gain no additional research or production options over a Lair (though any upgrades you did not research at Lair level can still be found here).

BUILD REQUIREMENTS:

Infestation Pit

BUILDING PRODUCTION		COST			
Unit	Requirement				
Queen	Spawning Pool	150	0	2	50

ULTRALISK CAVERN

Hot Key: U

COST:

150 200 65

BUILDING STATISTICS		
Health	Armor	Energy
600	1	

The Ultralisk Cavern allows you to build the large and powerful Ultralisk. It is the largest and most powerful Zerg ground unit; all of it's upgrades are purchased here.

BUILD REQUIREMENTS:

Hive

BUILDING UPGRADES		COST			EFFECT
Upgrade	Requirement				
Chitinous Plating	None	150	150	110	Grants Ultralisks +2 Armor

BUILDING UPGRADES		COST			EFFECT
Upgrade	Requirement				
Pneumatized Carapace	None	100	100	60	Increases Overlord and Overseer movement speed
Ventral Sacs	None	200	200	130	Allows Overlords to transport units

GREATER SPIRE

Hot Key: G

COST:

 100   150   100

BUILDING STATISTICS		
Health	Armor	Energy
1000	1	

BUILD REQUIREMENTS:

Hive

Mutated from a Spire, the Greater Spire allows Brood Lords to be mutated from Corruptors, in addition to the mutation of Mutalisks and Corruptors.

As with a Spire, upgrades for your air units can be purchased from here.

As with the Spire, the Greater Spire has a very long build time, and should be carefully protected.

HIVE

CREEP TUMOR

Hot Key: C

COST:

 0   0   15

BUILDING STATISTICS		
Health	Armor	Energy
50	0	

BUILD REQUIREMENTS:

Queen

Used to spread Creep, Creep Tumors remain hidden and thus unattackable unless detected. Zerg ground forces receive a 30% speed boost while moving on Creep, so take advantage of Creep Tumors' ability outside of your bases.

SPECIAL

BUILDING UPGRADES		COST			EFFECT
Upgrade	Requirement				
Flyer Attacks Level 1	None	100	100	160	Upgrades the attacks of all Zerg air units
Flyer Attacks Level 2	Lair	175	175	190	Upgrades the attacks of all Zerg air units
Flyer Attacks Level 3	Hive	250	250	220	Upgrades the attacks of all Zerg air units
Flyer Carapace Level 1	None	150	150	160	Upgrades the armor of all Zerg air units
Flyer Carapace Level 2	Lair	225	225	190	Upgrades the armor of all Zerg air units
Flyer Carapace Level 3	Hive	300	300	220	Upgrades the armor of all Zerg air units

BUILDING ABILITIES					
Spawn Creep Tumor					
Cost	Range	Radius	Effect		Autocast?
15s	10	9	Creates a new Creep Tumor, can only be used once		No

CREEP TUMORS

Creep tumors are not built in the traditional way other Zerg buildings are built. They are first spawned instantly by the Zerg Queen for a cost of 25 energy.

Each Creep Tumor then has the ability Spawn Creep Tumor to propagate itself but can only use it once resulting in a creep chain that can effectively cover a map.

MAPS

Maps are the battlegrounds of StarCraft II. Every match is played out on one of many, many possible battlefields. Learning to adapt to new maps, and to fully exploit the features on any map are very important skills to master.

We've prepared this chapter as an overview of the features common to all StarCraft II maps, as well as a more detailed look at a few specific maps, to give you a better idea of what you should be looking for and thinking about when you are playing on a new map for the first time.

The huge range of possible Race matchups, number of players, and team setups all create a tremendously varied gameplay experience on even a single map.

Over the course of the life of StarCraft II, there will be dozens (if not hundreds) of new maps created and used for the online Leagues and Ladders. In addition, you can expect there to be thousands (possibly tens of thousands) of new maps created for Custom Game play.

Needless to say, knowing how to navigate on *any* map is an important skill to develop.

MAP FEATURES

We begin with a discussion of features that are common to all StarCraft II maps. You can expect to see these features on almost any official Blizzard map, and many fan made custom maps will make use of some or all of them as well.

STARTING LOCATIONS

The most basic feature of a map is the starting positions for each player. The starting locations are shown on a thumbnail of the map while it is loading, so if you have never played on a map before, use the thumbnail as a guide.

Be sure to send your first worker scout out to explore the starting positions on a map. When playing on a 1v1 map with only two starting positions, you know where your opponent is (though you should still see what he is doing!), but on any larger map, you need to scout out the location of all opponent's, and sooner is better than later.

MAP SIZES

Maps in StarCraft II vary from small 1v1 maps with little space between bases to sprawling 8 player maps with many starting bases and many expansion sites.

The size of a map should have a significant impact on your build order and military strategy, as larger maps give more time for technological development, and increase the value of high speed and aerial units.

Conversely, smaller maps make rushes more dangerous, and typically require an earlier focus on basic military development. The distance between bases increases the strength of a defending army relative to the attackers, because a defender can continue to build up forces while the offensive force travels across the map.

Transport units, air units, high speed units, and speed upgrades are all important for making offensive actions against enemies that are distant from your military production centers.

MINERALS AND VESPENE GAS

The number of players also affects the 'size' of a map, in that more players shrinks the available number of expansion sites available to any one player, so a 2v2 on an 8 player map will feel larger than a 4v4 on the same map.

All maps have Mineral patches and Vespene Geysers on them, the source of your economic power. By default, Mineral patches have 1500 Minerals each, and Vespene Geysers have 2500 Gas that can be extracted.

The number of starting locations isn't tied to the size of a map. That is to say, while most of the time, an 8 player map will be physically large, there is nothing preventing a map being created that is 1v1 but very large, or 4v4, but very small.

There are special Rich Minerals that are a yellow-gold in color instead of the usual blue, and provide more Minerals per harvest.

Expansions that contain Rich Minerals typically have less total patches (often 6 instead of 8), but they provide you with a larger boost to your income over time than a normal expansion site. Because they provide more Minerals per harvest, they are also mined out more quickly than a normal Mineral site.

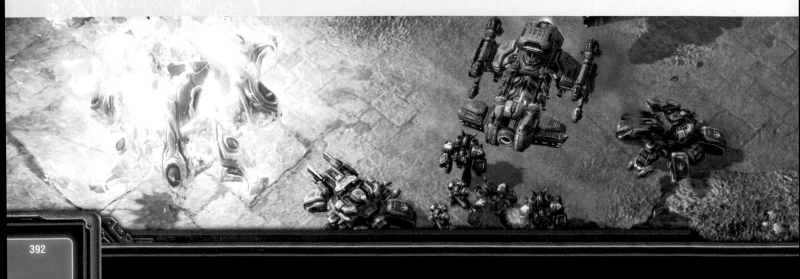

TERRAIN FEATURES

Terrain has a significant impact on the way that a match plays out, as the interaction between units and terrain affects the outcome of a battle.

Intelligent use of terrain features can allow you to make the best use of the strengths of your troops, and to minimize the strengths of your opponent's army.

HIGH GROUND

Terrain in StarCraft II can have multiple levels. To travel between terrain levels, ground units must travel up or down a ramp to change height levels. Ramps are often very narrow and easily blocked at a players starting base location, but may be wider (sometimes much wider) at other areas on a map.

High (or low) ground provides no direct combat benefit to units in StarCraft II, but high ground has a natural benefit in terms of line of sight, which *can* affect the strength of ranged units.

Units in StarCraft II *cannot* fire on a unit they do not have line of sight. If you have a group of ranged units on a higher terrain level than your opponent's forces, and they do not have a unit on the same level, you can freely shoot at his forces, and he cannot retaliate. He will see the units as they fire at him, but he cannot respond in kind. The one exception is if a flying unit is attacking from high ground. It is revealed and can be fired upon.

You can make very good use of this when defending a base that is on a higher level. If you can block your opponent from getting any ground units onto the same level (or kill any that do), you easily repel an attack.

When attacking an enemy who has the high ground advantage, be sure to get line of sight on the higher level as quickly as possible. Either make use of special recon abilities, use air units, or sacrifice some ground forces to get that line of sight established.

Many maps have bits of terrain that are on a higher level, but are *not* normally accessible to ground units. You can still take advantage of these by making use of the transport units that your race has access to. Use transports to place friendly ranged units up on the high ground, and if your opponent has units or buildings in range, you can attack them without any fear of retaliation.

Naturally, your mobility in such locations is restricted, so your opponent can simply move his units out of range, but if he has structures that *are* still in range, there's nothing he can do to stop you from destroying them without transports or air units of his own.

The Terran Viking can land on otherwise inaccessible high ground and attack enemy forces nearby, while the Protoss Stalker can Blink to high ground if you can get line of sight to it. Zerg can place Nydus Worms on high ground in line of sight that has enough space for the Worm and troops.

Make use of inaccessible high ground with transports on defense to attack units moving toward your base, and on offense, to harass an opponent's army or damage their base.

THE FOG OF WAR

When a match begins, you can see the geography of a map, but your line of sight is grayed out and blocked by the Fog of War where you do not have units or structures—which is almost everywhere as a match begins.

As your units are sent around a map, you are given temporary line of sight in range of those units, and if you place a unit near a Xel'Naga Tower, you are given a large spherical line of sight bonus in a radius around the tower.

Enemy units or structures can be hidden in the Fog of War, so it is vital that you have scouts constantly moving out in the map on the path between your bases, so that you can spot an enemy army when it moves, and find any expansion bases.

Aerial units and special recon abilities are also very useful for lifting the Fog of War, as they can provide information on an incoming air assault from your opponent, or spot incoming troops without them knowing you are aware of their advance.

Remember to spread your Supply producers around the outer edges of your base, you should have full line of sight all around your base well before an enemy can hit you with an aerial assault, and the extra warning can save your workers.

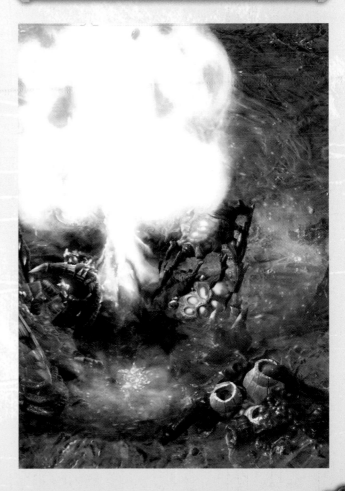

OPEN GROUND

Open ground is simply any area on a map that has wide, flat, unrestricted terrain. These open areas are most useful for melee and short ranged units, so that all of them can get into contact with your opponent's troops and deal maximal damage.

Open ground is also useful for very fast moving units that are good at dancing away from your opponent's troops while pausing momentarily to attack. The more space you have to perform this back and forth combat, the less chance you have of getting stuck on terrain and taking damage or losing units.

Depending on the composition of your army, open ground can be friend or foe.

CHOKE POINTS

In contrast to open ground, chokepoints are areas where the terrain constricts to provide less room for ground troops to move through. This can be due to high or low ground that creates valleys or ridges, or water (or open space!) that creates a natural barrier for ground troops.

Chokepoints are typically most useful on defense, and are extremely useful for long ranged units, that can focus fire on shorter ranged or melee troops stuck in the chokepoint.

Chokepoints are also even more powerful for the defender in situations where the terrain opens up on one side of the choke, so your entire army can be spread around the opening, able to attack your opponent's force as it moves through, while part of their force is stuck on the other side of the choke, unable to contribute.

Chokepoints also magnify the impact of area of effect attacks, as they naturally clump ground units into tight packs where you can inflict heavy damage with your area of effect attacks. Siege Tanks, burrowed Banelings, Colossi, and other abilities and units can all deal devastating damage to units trapped in a choke.

It is possible to hold a chokepoint with a small number of troops if managed well, but remember that a chokepoint cannot be defended effectively if your opponent has units or abilities that outrange your defenders. If this happens, either retreat, or push through the choke and attack his longer ranged units.

On offense, you should always consider whether a given chokepoint must be assaulted. If it is unnecessary, or it can be avoided, don't do so. Consider if you can make use of cliffwalkers, air units, transports, or alternate routes to avoid the choke.

If you absolutely cannot bypass a chokepoint, make use of your siege breakers and special abilities that are most effective against stationary defenders. Long range units, area of effect damage, and most caster abilities are all useful for assaulting a defended area.

In some cases, such as a wall-in protecting a chokepoint, remember what your goal during the assault is—if you only want to bypass the chokepoint to hit a worker line, punch a hole and do exactly that, don't stay to fight at the choke once it is opened.

CHOKEPOINT ABUSE AND AVOIDANCE

Remember, on defense, use chokepoints to increase the power of your army, but learn to recognize situations where your opponent can bypass or damage your units holding a chokepoint, and either withdraw your units, or attack his aggressively.

On offense, learn to recognize when you can bypass a chokepoint entirely, and if you must break it, figure out exactly why you are doing so, and head for that target as soon as the choke is broken.

If your opponent makes use of temporary abilities or abilities dependant on Energy to make a choke assault more dangerous, attack to bait the abilities out, then simply retreat! Energy regenerates very slowly, you can wear down a defender's reserves with constant pressure. Remember that retreat is often a safer option for the attacker than the defender.

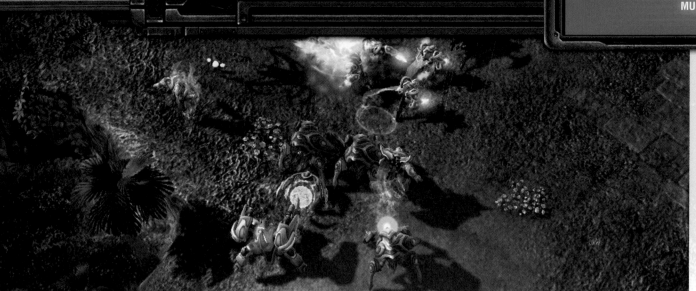

ISLANDS

On some maps, due to terrain features, 'islands' may be created. These may not be islands in the traditional sense—they might be platforms floating in open space, on lava, or even on the rooftops of a megacity, but for convenience, we refer to any isolated bit of terrain as an island. As a general rule, you shouldn't expect to encounter many island-only maps in the normal Battle.net Ladder rotation, but maps that have varying numbers of islands do exist.

A map that has *only* islands demands transport technology, and air superiority becomes *extremely* important, as losing control of the air means all of your defenseless transports are at risk. Maps that have many islands also requires transport technology, though ground forces become more important, as they can protect a greater amount of terrain. Anti-air ground units should be a priority, just as they are on island only maps, and units strong against your opponent's anti-air units are also useful for ground assaults.

Finally, a map with only a few islands may not require transports at all, depending on their strategic importance—most often, a few isolated islands are designed as potential expansion sites.

DEALING WITH ISLANDS

Terrans have a special advantage on maps with many (or even any) islands, as they can lift off and fly their Command Center, Orbital Command, and any military structures from one island to another. This isn't a fast process, but it can be done relatively quickly between adjacent islands.

Zerg can make use of their Nydus Network to move a ground army between islands quickly, but the Networks must be protected carefully, losing one mid-fight can result in a split army and a crushing defeat.

Protoss can make use of Probes in Warp Prisms to project power by using the power field of the Warp Prism to quickly warp units or buildings onto an island.

EXPANSIONS

Another common feature on all maps is expansion sites. An expansion is simply a location on a map with (usually) 8 Mineral patches and 2 Vespene Geysers. Many maps have a 'natural' expansion for each player starting location that is located immediately beside their initial position, and can usually be fairly easily defended.

You will also occasionally see Rich Mineral expansions that have 6 Rich Minerals and 2 Vespene Geysyers. Rich expansions are almost always in exposed or awkward positions (occasionally with destructible debris blocking ideal core structure placement).

Knowing where the expansions are located is important both for your own expansion, and to locate the likely position of enemy expansions. As a general rule, expanding to locations close to your main base is safest, simply because any new military units you produce will then have a shorter trip to protect the base, but you can certainly expand to an unusual position, especially on a larger map.

ISLAND EXPANSIONS

Island expansions are a bit more difficult to reach (except for Terrans), and are therefore more easily defensible, as you can build anti-air fixed defenses and know that you'll have protection against the one form of attack that can definitely reach you.

Be wary of Zerg Nydus Worm attacks, Stalkers Blinking to your island, transports, and of course, aerial assaults.

Still, if you can manage it, securing an island expansion can be very useful, as it requires that your opponent make a special effort to eliminate it.

SPECIAL FEATURES

Some features are less common, but still encountered on many maps.

RICH MINERALS

Already discussed, Rich Minerals have a normal amount of Minerals present (1500 per patch), but are *harvested* at a faster rate than normal Minerals. Most Rich Minerals are located at expansion sites that are more dangerously exposed or centrally located on a map.

XEL'NAGA TOWERS

Xel'Naga Towers are important reconnaissance tools. Any friendly unit standing near a Xel'Naga Tower gains line of sight in a large radius around the tower.

You should always try to have a friendly unit stationed at each Xel'Naga Tower on a map. Don't waste resources fighting over Towers if your opponent sends a few military units, just clear out the Towers when you make an offensive push with your army and place new sentries once they are eliminated.

Some maps have no Towers, some have a few, and some have many, but on any map that does have the Xel'Naga Towers, be sure to make use of them!

VISION BLOCKERS

Vision Blockers block line of sight from units behind it, in the same way that high ground would, but you can simply move your units through it.

Consequently, you can hide scouts or your army behind Vision Blockers, and unless your opponent explicitly places a unit or structure in position near the Vision Blockers, they will not see your units even if they move within line of sight range.

Air units always have line of sight over Vision Blockers, no matter its elevation.

DESTRUCTIBLE DEBRIS

Several maps have destructible rocks (or other bits of debris) placed to block rear routes into bases, or obstruct expansion sites. Destructible debris has 2000 health and any units with bonus damage to Armored units or Structures will do bonus damage against debris.

On many maps, destroying the debris and attacking your opponent's base from the rear access point is a good idea, but expect your opponent to place a Supply structure (or Overlord) near the rocks, and to spot your push. You may still be able to take down the debris safely if you have enough ranged units, which forces your opponent to defend two access points to his base—always good for you.

In other situations, such as rocks at expansions, you can either clear them out, or not worry about the loss of efficiency and simply place your core structure nearby where your workers can still harvest at a reasonable pace.

Debris typically act as a temporary barrier, preventing an early backdoor rush attack, but become a defensive liability in the midgame, as armies become strong enough to clear out rocks quickly. If there are *any* destructible debris piles near your base that provide a rear entrance, be sure to keep line of sight on them at all times to alert you to an enemy ground push.

DETAILED MAP COVERAGE

We picked out a few representative maps to give you an overview of the various map features as they appear on actual StarCraft II ladder maps. In the future, you can expect to see many, *many* more maps added to the game, but the same basic map features and considerations apply.

Once you learn the general structure of a StarCraft II map, you can play on any StarCraft II map.

 Rich mineral patches are harvested at a faster rate than normal mineral patches. They are typically located in more dangerous areas.

Island expansions can provide a powerful position that is both difficult to attack and easy to strike your opponent.

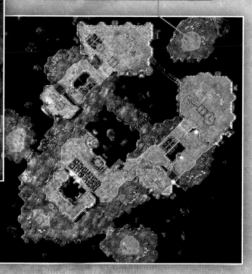

High ground has a natural benefit in terms of line of sight, which can affect the strength of ranged units.

 Destructable Rocks offer 2000 health points of temporary protection to your base from attacking ground forces.

Xel'Naga Towers are typically located near the center of maps, and provides line of sight in a large radius around the tower to whoever controls it.

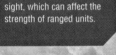 The life blood of any army; look for natural mineral expansions around the map to maintain your economy. Never leave them unprotected!

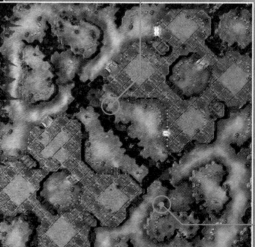

Vision Blockers block line of site from units behind it, but you can move your units through it.

Choke Points magnify the impact of area of effect attacks, as they naturally clump ground units into a tight pack.

MAP FEATURES

PLAYERS: 1V1
TERRAIN FEATURES
- High Ground
- Ramps
- Choke Points

SPECIAL FEATURES
- Rich Minerals
- Xel'Naga Towers
- Vision Blockers
- Destructible Debris

01 Two Rich Mineral expansions are located in the northwest and southeast, and both are blocked by Destructible Rocks. The Rich Mineral expansions are also located on lower ground, down a ramp, making them vulnerable to attacks from above.

02 There are two more regular expansions located at the north and south edges of the map, each beside the Rich Mineral expansions, though their positions are much more exposed and open to attack then the natural expansions.

03 Each main base is located on raised high ground and has a single narrow ramp leading up to it in addition to the blocked backdoor ramp, and a natural expansion located immediately down the ramp.

04 Both bases have a backdoor ramp that is blocked by Destructible Rocks, and the ramp itself is shielded by a wall of Vision Blockers. Be sure to place an early Supply Depot, Pylon, or Overlord here to monitor enemy attempts to break into your rear entrance.

05 The natural expansion has a somewhat constricted choke point leading into it, so an early expansion and defense at the choke point can work well.

06 In the center east and west, a pair of raised platforms have Xel'Naga Towers that can be controlled, giving good line of sight in front of either base.

07 The center of the map provides three lanes to travel between bases, with the center lane dipping down to a lower level of terrain. Try not to fight in the center on the lower level if possible, move around and use the side lanes when moving through the middle.

08 The Vision Blockers that stretches across the north and south center lanes can obscure your view of enemy units if fighting in the center of the map, be sure to send a scout through first to avoid walking into an enemy army behind it if you don't control the towers.

BLISTERING SANDS

There is a decent amount of open ground in the middle of the map, if you need open space to fight effectively, try to force a battle in the open, either by attacking your opponent's army when he pushes, or by baiting out his defensive force when on offense.

STEPPES OF WAR

MAP FEATURES

PLAYERS: 1V1

TERRAIN FEATURES
- High Ground
- Ramps
- Choke Points

SPECIAL FEATURES
- Rich Minerals
- Xel'Naga Towers
- Vision Blockers
- Destructible Debris

Steppes of War is another 1v1 map, but it is distinct from Blistering Sands in that the two initial bases are a very short distance from one another, making early game rush tactics much more viable.

When playing on maps such as this, building up an early military and blocking your ramp are much more important than on a map with more distance between your initial bases. Consider focusing more on early basic units and production structures to repel a rush, and to create a sizable military force to pressure your opponent early.

Remember that your workers may be vital in stopping an early rush, if you get hit and you don't yet have enough military units, either run your workers around while waiting for units to finish, or use them to attack the invaders in concert with your early units.

Zerg obviously cannot block their ramp immediately, so make good use of your early Zerglings, and your Queen alongside your workers to fend off early attacks. In some situations, a carefully placed Spine Crawler can help to hold off an attack as well.

01 Both bases are located on the highest terrain level, with a natural expansion located immediately outside the starting positions. This natural has a fairly broad ramp that descends into the center, the lowest level on the map.

02 There are four more expansions on raised platforms around the map, two on the east and west, and two in the northwest and southeast. All of these expansions are blocked by Destructible Rocks, though the expansions on the east and west can be accessed by a second, unblocked ramp.

03 Finally there are two Rich Mineral expansions in the north and south, both on the same level as the natural expansions, and both exposed to attack from a ramp leading to the center, and through some Vision Blockers leading to the twin Xel'Naga Towers on the map.

04 The two Xel'Naga Towers are located immediately behind Vision Blockers, so having line of sight with them is useful for spotting enemies on the other side of the grass.

05 There are more Vision Blockers in the center of the map, on the east and west side of the middle. Securing the towers or keeping scouts spread along the route to the enemy base is important to avoid missing an enemy army moving behind the cover of the Vision Blockers.

06 Expanding to your natural is reasonably safe on this map once you have a decent military force, as you have a relatively constricted ramp that allows you to defend from higher ground for a moment, but be careful about early expansion, an early military push can destroy a premature expansion.

Terran players can float a Command Center to the north or south expansions that are completely blocked by Destructible Rocks. Remember that they aren't truly island expansions—a dedicated opponent can break through the rocks and hit your expansion.

07 The expansions beside your natural on the east and west can either be protected by blocking off the one ramp that they have open immediately and leaving the rocks intact, or destroying the rocks so that your army from your main base and natural expansion can respond more quickly to an attack.

When engaging in battle on this map, either make use of the open ground on the lowest level in the center, or try to fight at the tops of the various ramps on the level to gain a slight edge from the high ground. Be mindful of the Vision Blockers when fighting on the bottom level, it can break line of sight and cause your units to stop attacking if the opponent is dancing troops or retreating.

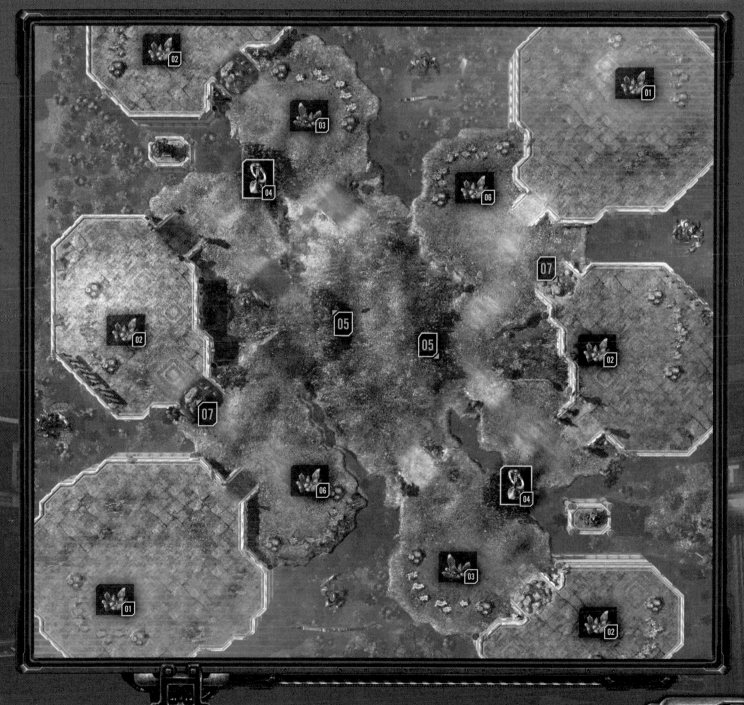

LOST TEMPLE

MAP FEATURES

PLAYERS: 2V2
TERRAIN FEATURES
- **High Ground**
- **Ramps**
- **Choke Points**

EXPANSIONS
- **Island Expansions**

SPECIAL FEATURES
- **Rich Minerals**
- **Xel'Naga Towers**
- **Vision Blockers**
- **Destructible Debris**

Lost Temple is a flexible 4 player map, playable in 1v1, 2v2, or FFA.

In all matches on this map be sure to scout your opponent (or opponents) early to identify their starting positions.

01 Each player begins on a raised platform with a narrow ramp leading down to a natural expansion. The four starting plateaus are located with two to the northeast and two the southwest, each separated from one another by a wide chasm.

02 All four bases have a natural expansion down the narrow ramp that opens up into a relatively wide gap that leads to the center of the map. If you want to constrict it further, you must construct buildings to shrink the chokepoint.

03 Finally, there are two island expansions in the northwest and southeast, and two Rich Mineral expansions also in the northwest and southeast, connected to the center of the map. The Rich Mineral expansions are blocked with Destructible Rocks that must be cleared out for optimal harvesting.

04 The center of the map has four small raised platforms that can be utilized by cliffwalkers or transported units, and there are also raised ledges overlooking all four expansions and the Rich Mineral expansions. The raised ledges can also just barely get line of sight on the island expansions, should you wish to transport units up to attack the island expansions from a distance.

05 Two Xel'Naga Towers in the center of the map provide good line of sight for spotting armies moving in or out of any base, and four walls of Vision Blockers obscure line of sight around the center platforms, making securing those towers (or scouting behind them) important when fighting around the middle of the map.

Most of the center of the map is flat open ground, so if your army prefers fighting in the open, hit your enemy before he reaches your natural expansion or main base ramp, or attempt to draw out his army if he is defending.

It is generally safest to expand first to your natural expansion and then to an island expansion, though you can certainly attempt to claim either another base, or the closer Rich Mineral expansion if you feel you have your opponent sufficiently contained.

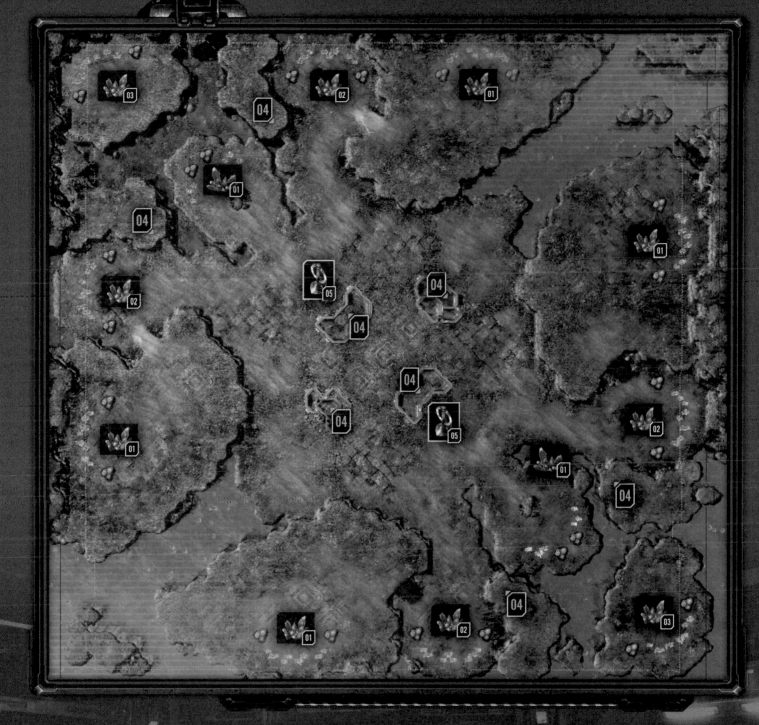

Remember that a Terran can easily float a Command Center to either island expansion relatively quickly, and be sure to check the islands in the midgame if you are facing a Terran. An over-eager Terran might even lift off and set down on an island immediately, if this occurs, prepare for an aerial assault and expand quickly.

Depending on starting positions, you may have an opponent immediately across from you on the diagonal, so watch for transport or aerial attacks, they can hit your base very quickly. Be sure to place Supply structures at the edges of your base plateau to gain line of sight on any incoming forces, air or ground.

TWILIGHT FORTRESS

MAP FEATURES

PLAYERS: 2V2
TERRAIN FEATURES
- High Ground
- Ramps
- Choke Points

SPECIAL FEATURES
- Rich Minerals
- Xel'Naga Towers
- Vision Blockers
- Destructible Debris

Twilight Fortress is, as the name implies, a 'fortress' style map. It is distinct from a 4 player map such as Lost Temple in that it is built intentionally for 2v2 matches. The four starting locations are split, two in the northeast and two in the southwest.

MAP STYLES

There are many many possible maps that can and will be created over time, but these four representative maps give you a good idea of the various basic types of maps you can expect to see in a 1v1 or 2v2 situation.

1v1 maps may be very small, making rush offense and defense very important or midsize, allowing for more teching or fast expansion.

Larger maps that are playable in 2v2 or even bigger team games demand scouting in 1v1 matches, and may result in longer games with more expansions and more high tier units and technologies being used in battle.

2v2 fortress style maps focus on economic and military production as well as quickly teching to high tier units and assembling large armies. Denying enemy expansion while expanding with your team, area of effect abilities, support units, upgrading your troops quickly, and good use of strong high level units become very important in the large brawls these maps create.

Maps with island expansions require that you make use of them, or at least scout them to deny their use by your opponent, and securing Rich Mineral expansions typically requires exposing yourself to some risk.

Xel'Naga Towers are important on any map, and being aware of where high ground, ramps, and chokepoints are located are all important, as well as any Vision Blockers that can interfere with an open field battle.

Most battles in the midfield will be fought on or around the 'expansion platforms' in the center. Whenever possible, try to have your forces on one of the platforms and force your opponent's to attack from below.

Because of the high economy given by this map, exploiting it is important. You want to build up your economy and ramp up your military production as quickly as possible. Double pump upgrades from multiple upgrade structures, create extra military structures, and quickly raise your Supply cap as you pump out troops.

01 Not only that, the entire northeast and southwest base areas are on a large raised plateau with a single large broad ramp leading into the base at the center between the bases. Both starting locations have a natural expansion located on the plateau, not far from the starting location.

As a result, in a 2v2 match, your first expansion is essentially 'free'. You should expand very early and build up a powerful economy while teching for higher tier units immediately.

Because of the distance between the bases, any push should involve both players acting in concert with all of their forces, unless you are very confident in your offensive and defensive player splitting their efforts.

02 Expansions are plentiful on this map, with eight normal expansions located in the center of the the map, four on raised platforms in the middle, and two more each in the west and east, also on raised platforms.

Rich Mineral expansions are located on lower levels in the north and south, with a single Destructible Rock at each, blocking one of the two wide ramps leading down to the lower level.

03 If you do find a need for expansion, consider taking the Rich Mineral expansions first, or the two expansions on the raised platform to the east or west.

The center map expansions are somewhat more difficult to defend, simply because any enemy army marching from base to base will pass right through the central platforms, whereas the side expansions require an explicit decision from your opponent's to attack.

04 There are four Xel'Naga Towers on this map, two on the center platforms closest to the center, and two on the east and west platforms, also facing towards the center.

Try to secure these towers even if you are not expanding, and be sure to place scouts around your opponent's base, you need to know when they are pushing, and where.

05 There are several patches of Vision Blockers on this map, though they do not play a significant role in most battles. A small patch covers each Xel'Naga Tower (be sure to sweep them when you pass with an army, or your units will miss single troops stationed there), and there are longer strands at the north and south ends of the map, just above the Rich Mineral expansions.

Try to coordinate with your teammate and pick a unit mix that complements one another, while focusing on units or abilities that work best against your opponent's races. Be very careful about allowing your teammate to engage in battles alone, fighting a 2v1 situation is rarely favorable.

The specific units used aren't as important as quickly massing up a substantial army before you attack. If your opponent's delay their army buildup, or constrain their military production by not getting enough military structures (or Hatcheries) down, you may simply roll over them in the first major battle.

Raiding is possible on this map, but don't waste significant resources trying to raid their main base while their army is at home, instead, try to keep an eye on their expansion efforts and swiftly destroy any expansion they try to make.

When you expand, be sure to protect your fledgling expansion with military units. If you can out-expand your opponent's, even if they *do* build up a sufficient military force, your stronger economy will allow you to rebuild more quickly, and outlast your enemy as their resources run dry in their main base.

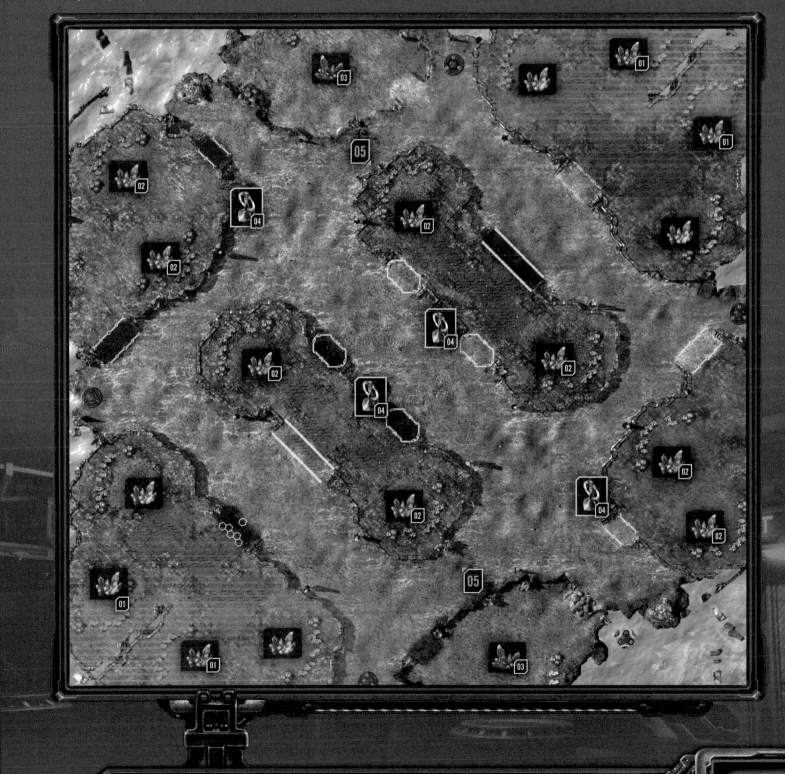

MAP GALLERY

1V1

AGRIA VALLEY

CROSSFIRE

JUNGLE BASIN

1v1

SCRAP STATION

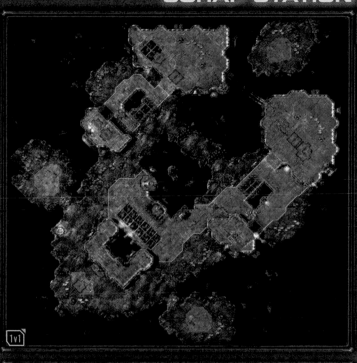

1v1

JUNK YARD

1v1

1v1

WORLD SHIP

DESERT OASIS
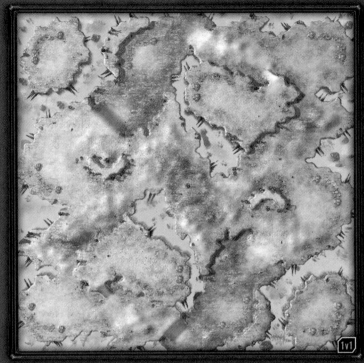

INCINERATION ZONE
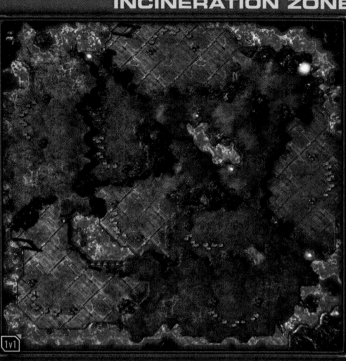

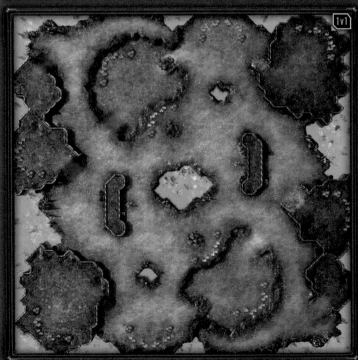
XEL'NAGA CAVERNS

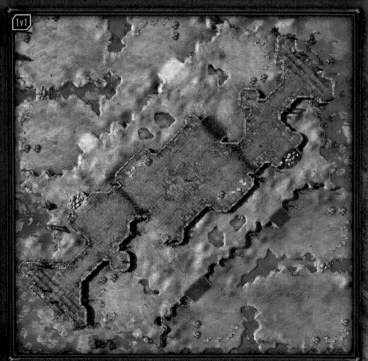
BURIAL GROUNDS

1V1V1 2V2

ELYSIUM

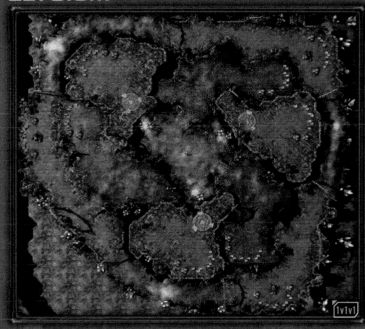

DELTA QUADRANT

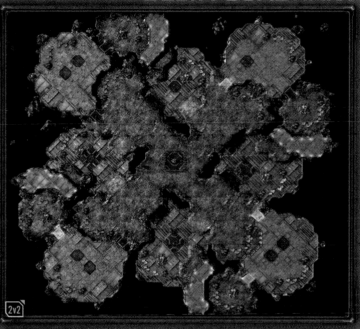

ARID WASTES

DEBRIS FIELD

DISCORD IV

HIGH ORBIT

KULAS RAVINE

METALOPOLIS

MONOLITH RIDGE

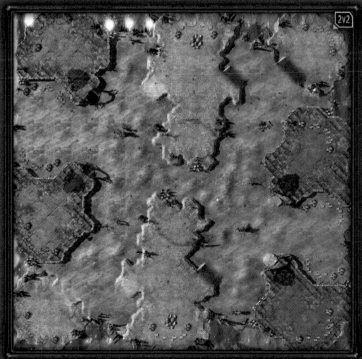

NEW ANTIOCH

RED STONE GULCH

2v2

2v2

NIGHTMARE

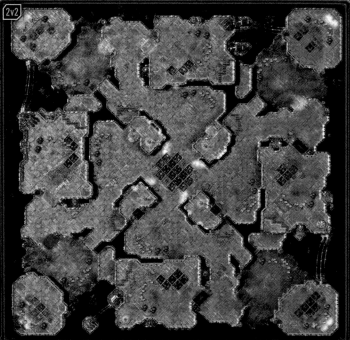

2v2

TERMINUS

3V3

FRONTIER

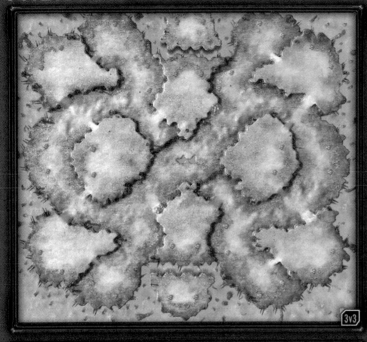

QUICKSAND

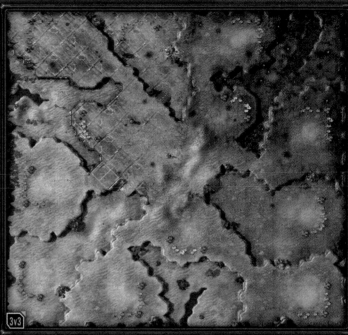

THE BIO LAB

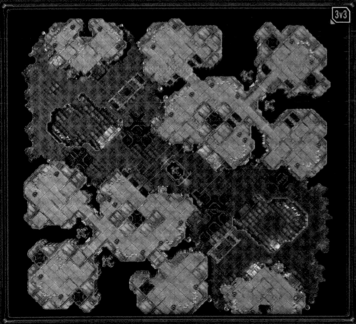

ULAAN DEEPS

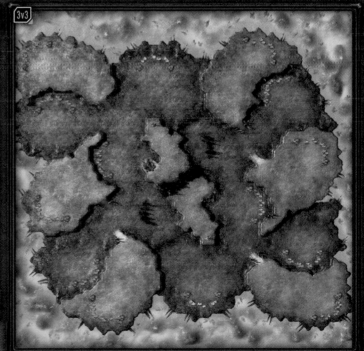

MONSOON

3v3

TECTONIC RIFT

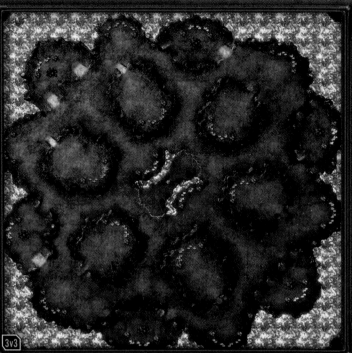

3v3

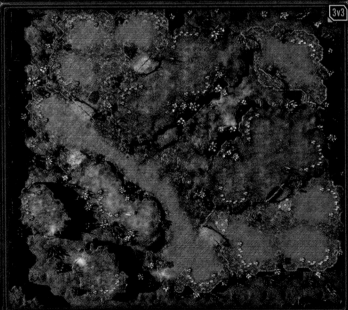

3v3

TYPHOON

4V4

ABYSS

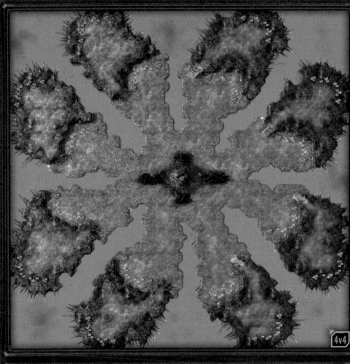

EXTINCTION

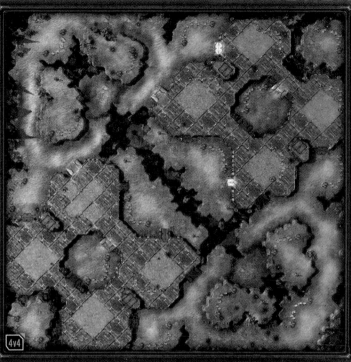

FORBIDDEN PLANET

HIGH GROUND

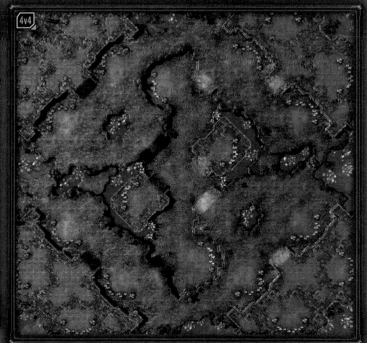

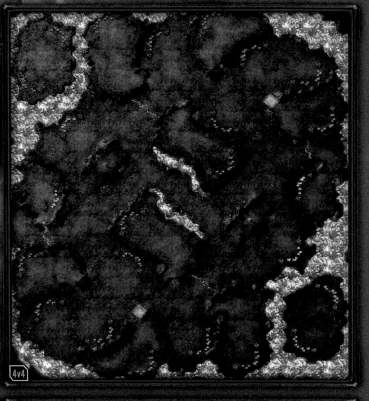

LAVA FLOW

4v4

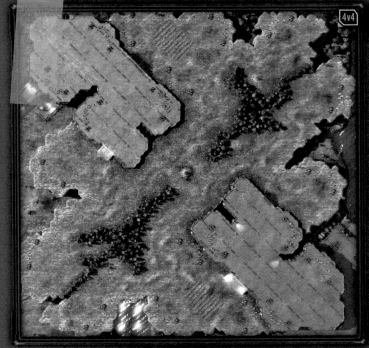

MEGATON

4v4

4v4

OUTPOST

SAND CANYON

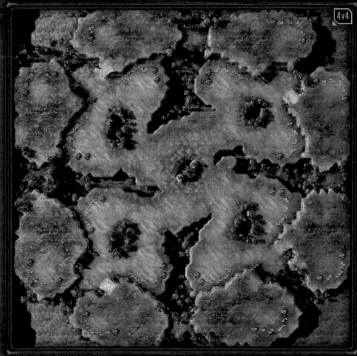

TEMPEST

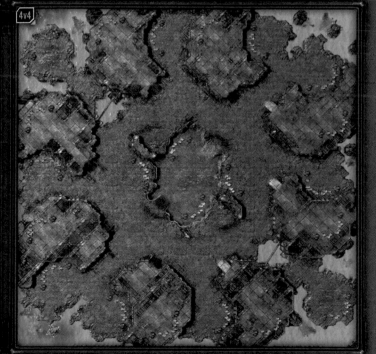

TOXIC SLUMS

LAST WORDS

And there you have it. Many, many hours of work (and play!) went into creating this guide, and those hours are a tiny, tiny fraction of the time the Star-Craft II team poured into this game over the long years of its development. We know many fans have been waiting for just as long (or longer!) to get their hands on this game, and figuring out how to best respect that love for the series (and still get the book done on time!) has been a tricky process, to say the least.

We'll try to answer some of your questions about what we did (or did not!) cover, dear reader, by casting our own psionic gaze into the future and predicting some likely queries.

Why didn't you include more build orders?

We discussed this at some length. Ultimately, we decided that very specific build orders are too 'fragile' to stand the test of time. Each time a patch shifts the cost, build time, or position in a tech tree of any unit, ability, or structure, it disrupts a fixed build order.

While wc have the vestigial openings in the Early Game section of the book, we choose not to provide many specific opening builds for each race. This was an intentional omission, not an accidental one. Instead, our intent was to provide you with the information you need to create your *own* build orders, and to understand your opponents when you watch replays or discuss builds on forums.

No matter which race you're playing, you always have certain specific requirements for any build: You have to develop your economy, you have to develop your military, and then you want to hit your opponent as hard as possible where they are weakest.

It's the 'where they are weakest' part, that is always subject to change. The specific weaknesses that various races showed during the beta testing of StarCraft II are all but guaranteed to be changed or removed by the time you are holding this guide in your hands.

The timing window for a specific push might be no more than one or two minutes on a map of a specific size in one specific racial matchup.

Trying to fill the guide with tables that covered the build order for such a specific push were all but guaranteed to be useless to you by the time you picked up this book and hopped online.

As a rule, very experienced players tend to play one race as a 'main', in the same way that a World of Warcraft player has one 'main'. One of the reasons for this is that developing builds to answer builds from other races is a very specific and *constantly* evolving process, and trying to learn those specific timings and builds is hard enough for one race, much less three.

There was never one perfect build in StarCraft, and we're not expecting that to change in StarCraft II.

Specific builds tend to be useful against specific races on specific maps. Blindly teching for a certain unit is usually a very bad idea, but when you've played fifty matches on one patch against one race, you *know* that the unit you're teching for is *always* useful against that race, and it is therefore a safe build to execute.

In some cases, you may be able to execute a build up to a certain point, but then you have to respond to what your opponent is building. That demands that you scout or push at certain specific timings to discover which path your opponent has taken, which then determines how you respond.

So, to boil it down to a quick answer for a complex problem: Trying to cover every possible build would be impossible, but pointing you at the means of discovering those builds for yourself and learning to respond to them seemed like a much wiser direction to take.

THE BUILD ORDER BUILDER

One other thought on the Build Order issue. It's easy to overcomplicate a build, when they're really quite simple.

Try this out: pick a unit or upgrade (any unit, any upgrade), doesn't matter which.

Now figure out the specific tech path you have to take to reach that unit or upgrade. There's your build order for your base.

Now remember that you have to a) build workers and b) build military to defend yourself while you tech to the unit or upgrade and finally c) push with your created military immediately when you reach your chosen unit or upgrade.

A+B determines how much Supply you're going to need to build while teching.

B is always flexible, in any build. The question becomes how effectively can you defend yourself until your chosen unit or upgrade hits the field, and when it does, how much damage can it inflict alongside the army you have been building? Optimizing the build becomes a matter of figuring out exactly when to build Gas, when to build Supply, and when to delay worker or military production to get a new structure on the field to reach your chosen unit. The optimization is easily done through repetition, but the initial portion is really that simple.

If you want to eyeball a build in comparison to another race's common build, simply add up the build times of all the tech buildings and research times involved to get a quick rough answer.

You can use that method to quickly determine that Battlecruisers really aren't a great answer to an aggressive Hydralisk push! (If this changes in a patch, let us know so we can eat our collective hats. Come to think of it, if your random teammate in a 2v2 says 'just defend while I tech to Carriers', you have our permission to pummel him).

In some cases you might be looking at something more specific. Can you field more Archons or Colossus vs Zerg, and how quickly does it take to reach either? Is the eventual access to Psionic Storm worth losing immediate access to Observers if he develops Burrow movement for his Roaches? What if he goes Mutas?

Those deeper questions are where builds begin to branch and diverge. On one map, Archons might be the right choice, because there are many chokepoints and Psionic Storm will eventually be even more deadly, while on another, there are really convenient ledges overlooking every base and likely battlefield, and your Colossus will be even more difficult for the Zerg to deal with.

If you're playing against a Terran player with access to EMP, suddenly Archons start looking a lot less appealing. And so it goes.

An effective build is also very dependant on what is popular on Battle.net in any given month for each race, and what League level you are playing in. The techniques players are fond of in Bronze aren't the same as in Diamond or Platinum, and techniques that work better or worse against different levels of player can heavily influence the effectiveness of a given build.

Oh and trust us, if you're already investing this much thought into your build orders, you'll soon be moving up through the Leagues (and annoying your more casual friends by being That Guy Who Always Wins FFA Friday).

Q Why did you write more about general strategy than specific races?

While we think that picking one race and focusing on it is the best way to improve rapidly (and at the highest levels of play, almost mandatory to compete), at all levels of play, advice that applies to *all* races and *all* maps and *all* situations is more useful to more players.

In cases where a specific race's units or abilities affected the discussion of a topic, we always tried to include mention of all the various ways one aspect of the game might be different for each race (eg. Worker income for all races is the same, outside the MULE, but the means in which each race can scout effectively are quite different).

Another issue is simply that the fundamentals of playing StarCraft II well are identical for every race, though the specific *execution* of those fundamentals may be slightly different.

And finally, of all the sections in the guide, the racial sections are the most prone to becoming outdated over time as Blizzard patches the game in response to balance issues, gameplay tweaks, bugfixes, changing ladder maps, tournaments, new ladder seasons, and so on.

We figured that investing more time and energy in writing solid basic strategy would be more helpful than writing more about specific unit or ability use that may change over time (and change dramatically in some cases).

With that said, we're not expecting Marines to sprout wings and gain a fireball ability (or at least, not until custom maps start showing up on Battle.net, in which case we do expect that), so many of the overviews we have written should hold up for a good long stretch of time.

Where's my editor manual? I want to create Defense of the Xel'Naga Tower!

A detailed guide to the StarCraft II editor would be, literally, another book entirely.

A few points about the editor: First, creating a map in it for 'normal' StarCraft II play is as easy as any Blizzard editor has ever been. Pick a tileset, paint out your map, raise and lower terrain, place starting locations and resources, play!

Second, the StarCraft II editor is *very* powerful. Those of you with a background in either programming or game scripting and modding will be happy with the power at your fingertips. We're fully expecting to see not just 'custom maps', but some outright 'custom games' created, using StarCraft II as an engine, rather than a 'StarCraft II content creator'.

The new features of Battle.net's Custom Game support are downright cool, and it has become a *lot* easier to share your editor creations with a very, very large audience.

You guys totally didn't cover every map that shipped with the game!

Quite true. This wasn't due to lack of access either, but again, a decision about what to include. While a big gallery section with screenshots of 50 maps might be pretty cool looking, we'd rather give you 50 pages of advice.

Over time, the maps available on Battle.net for the ladder matches are going to change, as Blizzard responds to the desires of players, and their own internal mandate to create interesting new situations for all racial matchups, in all modes of play.

If you play StarCraft II for several years, you're going to end up playing dozens or *hundreds* of maps, all of which won't even exist at the time of this guides printing.

The basics of features define a map won't change over time (at least, not until we see a new StarCraft II expansion…), so having a good grasp on how map features can be used is always a useful skill, no matter what map you're playing on.

TIRED OF LIFE ?

call 777-303
for assignments to first wave
marine landing teams !!

ACHIEVEMENTS

LIBERTY CAMPAIGN

Name	Pts	Mar Sara Missions	Portrait Reward
Liberation Day	15	Complete all objectives in the "Liberation Day" mission.	
Raynor's Back	10	Kill 5 enemy units in the "Liberation Day" mission with Raynor on Normal difficulty.	
Down with Mengsk	10	Kill every enemy unit in the "Liberation Day" mission on Hard difficulty.	
The Outlaws	15	Complete all objectives in "The Outlaws" mission.	
Cash Reward	10	Collect all Mineral and Gas Pallet pickups in "The Outlaws" mission on Normal difficulty.	
Be Quick or Be Dead	10	Complete "The Outlaws" mission on Hard difficulty in less than 10 minutes.	
Zero Hour	15	Complete all objectives in the "Zero Hour" mission.	
Hold the Line	10	Complete the "Zero Hour" mission on Normal difficulty without losing or salvaging a building.	
The Best Defense...	10	Destroy 4 Zerg Hatcheries in the "Zero Hour" mission on Hard difficulty.	
Mar Sara Mastery	20	Complete all the Mar Sara mission achievements.	Adjutant Portrait

Name	Pts	Colonist Missions	Portrait Reward
The Evacuation	15	Complete all objectives in "The Evacuation" mission.	
Handled with Care	10	Complete "The Evacuation" mission on Normal difficulty without losing a Transport Truck.	
Sacrifice Nothing	10	Complete "The Evacuation" mission on Hard difficulty without losing or salvaging a building.	
Outbreak	15	Complete all objectives in the "Outbreak" mission.	
28 Minutes Later	10	Complete the "Outbreak" mission on Normal difficulty before the 5th night.	
Army of Darkness	10	Destroy 15 infested buildings at night time in the "Outbreak" mission on Hard difficulty.	
Safe Haven	15	Complete all objectives in the "Safe Haven" mission.	
You Shall Not Pass	10	Save 4 Colonist Outposts in the "Safe Haven" mission on Normal difficulty.	
My Precious!	10	Save 3 Colonist Outposts in the "Safe Haven" mission on Hard difficulty.	
Haven's Fall	15	Complete all objectives in the "Haven's Fall" mission.	
Outpatient	10	Protect 3 settlements from the Zerg infestation in the "Haven's Fall" mission on Normal difficulty.	
House Call	10	Protect 5 settlements from the Zerg infestation in the "Haven's Fall" mission on Hard difficulty.	
Colonist Mastery	20	Complete all the Colonist mission achievements.	Dr. Ariel Hanson Portrait

Name	Pts	Covert Missions	Portrait Reward
The Devil's Playground	15	Complete all objectives in "The Devil's Playground" mission.	
Red Lobster	10	Kill the Brutalisk with lava in "The Devil's Playground" mission on Normal difficulty.	
Reaper Man	10	Locate all of Tosh's Crew in "The Devil's Playground" mission on Hard difficulty.	
Welcome to the Jungle	15	Complete all objectives in the "Welcome to the Jungle" mission.	
Appetite for Destruction	10	Prevent the Protoss from killing a SCV in the "Welcome to the Jungle" mission on Normal difficulty.	
It's So Easy	10	Prevent the Protoss from capping a Tal'darim Altar in the "Welcome to the Jungle" mission on Hard difficulty.	
Breakout	15	Complete all objectives in the "Breakout" mission.	
Cool Hand Tosh	10	Complete the "Breakout" mission without Tosh dropping below 100 life on Normal difficulty.	
Jailhouse Rock	10	Complete the "Breakout" mission on Hard difficulty in less than 25 minutes.	
Ghost of a Chance	15	Complete all objectives in the "Ghost of a Chance" mission.	
Dominate Tricks	10	Complete the "Ghost of a Chance" mission using Dominated units to kill at least 15 enemy troops on Normal difficulty.	
Total Protonic Reversal	10	Kill every enemy unit in the "Ghost of a Chance" mission on Hard difficulty.	
Covert Mastery	20	Complete all the Covert mission achievements.	Gabriel Tosh Portrait

Name	Pts	Rebellion Missions	Portrait Reward
The Great Train Robbery	15	Complete all objectives in "The Great Train Robbery" mission.	
Bully the Bullies	10	Kill the Marauder kill team in "The Great Train Robbery" mission on Normal difficulty.	
Silver Streak	10	Complete "The Great Train Robbery" mission without letting a train pass by on Hard difficulty.	
Cutthroat	15	Complete all objectives in the "Cutthroat" mission.	
Minesweeper	10	Kill 25 total units with Vulture Spider Mines in the "Cutthroat" mission on Normal difficulty.	
Solitaire	10	Don't train additional SCVs before purchasing Hans contract in the "Cutthroat" mission on Hard difficulty.	
Engine of Destruction	15	Complete all objectives in the "Engine of Destruction" mission.	
Kicking Asgard	10	Destroy the Loki in the "Engine of Destruction" mission on Normal difficulty.	
Ragnarok & Roll	10	Don't let the Odin drop below 30% of its total life in the "Engine of Destruction" mission on Hard difficulty.	
Media Blitz	15	Complete all objectives in the "Media Blitz" mission.	
Seek & Destroy	10	Destroy an enemy Barracks, Factory, and Starport in the "Media Blitz" mission during the sneak attack on Normal difficulty.	
Blitzkrieg	10	Complete the "Media Blitz" mission on Hard difficulty in less than 20 minutes.	
Piercing the Shroud	15	Complete all objectives in the "Piercing the Shroud" mission.	
Lock and Load	10	Locate all 13 weapon pickups in the "Piercing the Shroud" mission on Normal difficulty.	
Not so Brutalisk	10	Kill the Brutalisk on the "Piercing the Shroud" mission without losing a unit to the Brutalisk on Hard difficulty.	
Rebellion Mastery	20	Complete all the Rebellion mission achievements.	Matt Horner Portrait

Name	Pts	Artifact Missions	Portrait Reward
Smash and Grab	15	Complete all objectives in the "Smash and Grab" mission.	
Rock Solid	10	Complete the "Smash and Grab" mission on Normal difficulty without losing a unit to a Protoss Stone Guardian.	
Hit & Run	10	Complete the "Smash and Grab" mission on Hard difficulty in less than 15 minutes.	
The Dig	15	Complete all objectives in "The Dig" mission.	
Drill Hard	10	Kill 20 enemy units with the laser drill in "The Dig" mission on Normal difficulty.	
Yippee-ki-yay...	10	Destroy all the Protoss structures in "The Dig" mission on Hard difficulty.	
The Moebius Factor	15	Complete all objectives in "The Moebius Factor" mission.	
Alive Inside!	10	Locate all the Moebius survivors in the "The Moebius Factor" mission on Normal difficulty.	
Hard Core	10	Complete the "The Moebius Factor" mission before Kerrigan destroys 6 Abandoned buildings on Hard difficulty.	
Supernova	15	Complete all objectives in the "Supernova" mission.	
Cool Running	10	Complete the "Supernova" mission on Normal difficulty without losing a unit to the flame wall.	
Shock N' Awe	10	Complete the "Supernova" mission with 75 cloaked Banshee kills on Hard difficulty.	
Maw of the Void	15	Complete all objectives in the "Maw of the Void" mission.	
I Have the Power	10	Destroy all Rip Field Generators in the "Maw of the Void" mission on Normal difficulty.	
Master of the Universe	10	Complete the "Maw of the Void" mission without losing a unit inside the Rip Field on Hard difficulty.	
Artifact Mastery	20	Complete all the Artifact mission achievements.	Tychus Findlay Portrait

LIBERTY CAMPAIGN

Name	Pts	Prophecy Missions	Portrait Reward
Whispers of Doom	15	Complete all objectives in the "Whispers of Doom" mission.	
Stalker Delight	10	Complete the "Whispers of Doom" mission on Normal difficulty with 3 or more Stalkers.	
Merely a Flesh Wound	10	Complete the "Whispers of Doom" mission on Hard difficulty without suffering Health Damage to Zeratul.	
A Sinister Turn	15	Complete all objectives in the "A Sinister Turn" mission.	
Out for Justice	10	Kill all the Protoss in the "A Sinister Turn" mission on Normal difficulty.	
Maar-ked for Death	10	Complete the "A Sinister Turn" mission on Hard difficulty in less than 25 minutes.	
Echoes of the Future	15	Complete all objectives in the "Echoes of the Future" mission.	
Army of One	10	Complete the "Echoes of the Future" mission with Zeratul killing 50 Zerg units on Normal difficulty.	
Overmind Dead Body	10	Complete the "Echoes of the Future" mission on Hard difficulty in less than 20 minutes.	
In Utter Darkness	15	Complete all objectives in the "In Utter Darkness" mission.	
Semi-Glorious	10	Kill 250 additional Zerg units in the "In Utter Darkness" mission on Normal difficulty.	
Blaze of Glory	10	Kill 750 additional Zerg units in the "In Utter Darkness" mission on Normal difficulty.	
Prophecy Mastery	20	Complete all the Prophecy mission achievements.	Zeratul Portrait

Name	Pts	Final Missions	Portrait Reward
Gates of Hell	15	Complete all objectives in the "Gates of Hell" mission.	
The Big Bang Cannon	10	Destroy all the Spore Cannons in the "Gates of Hell" mission on Normal difficulty.	
Dominion Roundup	10	Rescue 10 drop pods of Dominion troops in the "Gates of Hell" mission on Hard difficulty.	
Belly of the Beast	15	Complete all objectives in the "Belly of the Beast" mission.	
Unbreakable	10	Complete the "Belly of the Beast" mission without letting a Hero become incapacitated on Normal difficulty.	
One Shot, Fifty Kills!	10	Kill 50 units with a single Penetrator Round in the "Belly of the Beast" mission on Hard difficulty.	
Shatter the Sky	15	Complete all objectives in the "Shatter the Sky" mission.	
Demolition Man	10	Complete the "Shatter the Sky" mission without losing a unit to a platform explosion on Normal difficulty.	
Speed Too!	10	Complete the "Shatter the Sky" mission on Hard difficulty in less than 25 minutes.	
All In	15	Complete all objectives in the "All In" mission.	
Burn and Turn	10	Kill 150 Zerg units with the Artifact in the "All In" mission on Normal difficulty.	
Aces High	10	Use the Artifact only once in the "All In" mission on Hard difficulty.	
Final Mastery	20	Complete all the Final mission achievements.	Valerian Portrait

Name	Pts	Story Mode	Portrait Reward
Mar Sara Missions	10	Complete the Mar Sara missions in the Wings of Liberty campaign.	
Dr. Ariel Hanson Mission	10	Complete the Dr. Hanson story line in the Wings of Liberty campaign.	
Gabriel Tosh Missions	10	Complete the Tosh story line in the Wings of Liberty campaign.	
Matt Horner Missions	10	Complete the Horner story line in the Wings of Liberty campaign.	
Zeratul Mission	10	Complete the Zeratul story line in the Wings of Liberty campaign.	
Ihan Crystal	10	Acquire an Ihan Crystal.	
The Artifact	10	Collect all 5 Xel'Naga Artifacts.	
Wings of Liberty	10	Complete the Wings of Liberty campaign.	Raynor Civilian Portrait
Stay Awhile and Listen	10	Start a converstaion with all the main characters.	
Couch Surfer	10	View 10 television news broadcasts.	Lockwell Portrait
Nice Suit	10	Find out why Tychus Findlay is always in a Marine suit.	
Dead Man's Hand	10	Find out what Matt Horner won playing poker.	
Terra-tron Terrorized!	10	Beat the Terra-tron in the "Lost Viking" arcade machine.	
Lost Viking	[30]	Score [250,000/500,000/750,000] points on the Lost Vikings arcade machine.	
Base Tech Master	10	Purchase 8 Base upgrades from the Armory Console.	
Infantry Tech Master	10	Purchase 10 Infantry upgrades from the Armory Console.	
Vehicle Tech Master	10	Purchase 10 Vehicle upgrades from the Armory Console.	
Starship Tech Master	10	Purchase 10 Starships upgrades from the Armory Console.	
Dominion Tech Master	10	Purchase 4 Dominion upgrades from the Armory Console.	
Band of Legends	10	Purchase all Mercenary contracts.	Hill Portrait
Zerg Xenobiology	10	Complete 5 Zerg Research Console projects.	
Protoss Xenobiology	10	Complete 5 Protoss Research Console projects.	
Wings of Liberty: Hard	[50]	Complete [5/10/15/20/25] Wings of Liberty campaign missions on Hard difficulty.	
Wings of Liberty: Brutal	[50]	Complete [5/10/15/20/25] Wings of Liberty campaign missions on Brutal difficulty.	
Liberty Completionist: Normal	15	Complete all 29 Wings of Liberty campaign missions on Normal difficulty.	Warfield Portrait
Liberty Completionist: Hard	15	Complete all 29 Wings of Liberty campaign missions on Hard difficulty.	Arcturus Mengsk Portrait
Liberty Completionist: Brutal	15	Complete all 29 Wings of Liberty campaign missions on Brutal difficulty.	Sara Kerrigan Ghost Portrait
Hurry Up, It's Raid Night	10	Complete the Wings of Liberty campaign under 8 hours of total played mission time.	
Master Mechanic	20	Complete all the Armory Console upgrade achievements.	Swann Portrait
Master Technician	20	Complete all the Research Console upgrade achievements.	Stetman Portrait

COMBAT

Name	Pts	Economy	Reward
Training Day	10	Train 10 Marines during the first 320 seconds of a single Melee game.	
Zergling Rush	10	Morph 20 Zerglings during the first 255 seconds of a single Melee game.	
Zealot Push	10	Warp in 5 Zealots during the first 250 seconds of a single Melee game.	
Fast Expand	10	Expand during the first 225 seconds of a Melee game.	
Erector Time	10	Build a Factory during the first 270 seconds of a Melee game.	
Warp In Time	10	Warp in a Twilight Council during the first 275 seconds of a Melee game.	
It's Morphing Time	10	Morph a Lair during the first 285 seconds of a Melee game.	
The Rich Get Richer	10	Deplete 10 Rich Yield Mineral fields in a single Melee game.	
Just A Scratch	10	Repair 1,000 life on ally buildings in a single Melee game.	
City Builder	20	Complete all the Economy achievements.	

Name	Pts	League Combat	Reward
Yamato Master Blaster	10	Kill 20 units with Yamato blasts in a single League game.	
Professionals Have Standards	10	Kill 20 units with Snipe Rounds in a single League game.	
Infested Terror	10	Kill 30 units with Infested Terrans in a single League game.	
Beep, Beep, Boom!	10	Kill 6 units with a single Seeker Missile in a League game.	
Would you kindly…	10	Kill 5 units with a single Neural Parasited unit in a League game.	
Unbreakable!	10	Kill 40 units with a single unit in a single League game.	
Auto-kill	10	Kill 20 SCVs using Auto-Turrets in a single League game.	
Raining Blood	10	Kill a fully-loaded transport in a League game.	
Nuclear Launch Detected	10	Kill 15 units with a single Nuke in a League game.	
Terran Macro Master	10	Have 9 Terran units training simultaneously in a League game.	
Protoss Macro Master	10	Have 9 Protoss units training simultaneously in a League game.	
Zerg Macro Master	10	Have 21 Zerg units training simultaneously in a League game.	
Warp In Madness	10	Warp in 100 units with Warp Gates in a single League game.	
Centurion Queen	10	Create 100 Larva with Queens in a single League game.	
Neighborly Help	10	Heal 300 life on ally units in a single League game.	
The Flying Healbus	10	Heal 5,000 life with Medivacs in a single League game.	
Frugal Fighter	10	Regenerate 500 shields on a single unit without taking friendly fire in a League game.	
A Roach's Life	10	Regenerate 500 life on a single Roach without taking friendly fire in a League game.	
Shroom Absorption	10	Absorb 1,000 damage with hallucinations in a single League game.	
Counter Proof	10	Attack for 20 seconds with no counter-attacks in a League game.	
Carnage Hall	10	Destroy 4 Command Centers, Hatcheries, or Nexus in a single League game.	
Denied	10	Destroy an enemy Command Center, Nexus, or Hatchery while it is under construction in a League game.	
Hot Pickup	10	Load a Dropship with a unit that is under attack in a League game.	
MULE X'ing	10	Calldown 30 MULE's in a single League game.	
Big Brother is Watching	10	Hold a Xel'Naga Tower for 5 consecutive minutes in a League game.	
Meet the Spy	10	Keep a Changeling alive within sight of enemies for 3 consecutive minutes in a League game.	
War Econ.	10	Win a League game without exceeding 1,000 unspent minerals or 1,000 unspent gas.	
SCII Designer	10	Win a League game without exceeding 30 seconds of total idle harvester time.	
Supreme Being	20	Complete all the League combat achievements.	

Name	Pts	Melee Combat	Reward
I see Dead Units	10	Kill 10 cloaked or burrowed units in a single Melee game.	
Psionic Death	10	Kill 20 units with a single High Templar as a Zerg player in a Melee game.	
Meatgrinder	10	Kill 50 supply worth of units within 30 seconds in a Melee game.	
The Back Door	10	Warp in 50 units in a single Melee game using Phase Prism power.	
Zerglot	10	Train a Zealot while playing as Zerg in a Melee game.	
Distorted Reality	10	Capture 50 enemy units in a single Vortex in a Melee game.	
To The Shadows I Run	10	Use Blink to save a Stalker in a Melee game.	
Can't Touch This!	10	Dodge a Raven Seeker Missile in a Melee game.	
Fire Fighter	10	Save 8 burning Terran structures in a single Melee game.	
One-Finger Discount	10	Cancel construction of a building that is being destroyed by an opponent in a Melee game.	
Just an Illusion	10	Control 15 Hallucinations at once in a Melee game.	
Welcome Back Commander	20	Complete all the Melee combat achievements.	

EXPLORATION

Name	Pts	Guide One	Portrait Reward
Challenge Accepted	10	Complete 3 Challenge missions with a Bronze rating or higher.	
Comp Stomp Novice	10	Win 3 Custom Games against any A.I. opponents.	
Co-op Stomp 3	10	Win 3 Co-Op vs. A.I. games.	
Medal of Combat	20	Complete all the Guide One achievements.	Tiger Marine

Name	Pts	Guide Two	Portrait Reward
Challenge Accepted, Too!	10	Complete 6 Challenge missions with a Bronze rating or higher.	
Comp Stomp Terran	10	Win 3 Custom Games against any A.I. opponents playing as Terran.	
Comp Stomp Protoss	10	Win 3 Custom Games against any A.I. opponents playing as Protoss.	
Comp Stomp Zerg	10	Win 3 Custom Games against any A.I. opponents playing as Zerg.	
Qualified for Action	10	Play enough qualifying games to get placed in a Quick Match league.	
Medal of Valor	20	Complete all the Guide Two achievements.	Panda Marine

Name	Pts	Guide Three	Portrait Reward
Challenge Completed	10	Complete all the Challenge missions with a Bronze rating or higher.	
Free-For-All Crusher	10	Kill a total of 100 enemy units in Free-For-All Quick Match game.	
Play Replay	10	Watch any Battle.net Replay.	
Flying Solo	10	Win 5 1v1 league Quick Match games.	
That's Teamwork	10	Win 5 Team league Quick Match games.	
Medal of Honor	20	Complete all the Guide Three achievements.	Wolf marine

Name	Pts	Challenges Missions	Portrait Reward
Tactical Command	[30]	Score the rank of [Bronze/Silver/Gold] in the "Tactical Command" challenge mission.	
Path of Ascension	[30]	Score the rank of [Bronze/Silver/Gold] in the "Path of Ascension" challenge mission.	
For the Swarm	[30]	Score the rank of [Bronze/Silver/Gold] in the "For the Swarm" challenge mission.	
Covert Ops	[30]	Score the rank of [Bronze/Silver/Gold] in the "Covert Ops" challenge Mission.	
Psionics Assault	[30]	Score the rank of [Bronze/Silver/Gold] in the "Psionic Assault" challenge Mission.	
Infestation: Bronze	[30]	Score the rank of [Bronze/Silver/Gold] in the "Infestation" challenge Mission.	
Harbinger of Death	[30]	Score the rank of [Bronze/Silver/Gold] in the "Harbinger of Death" challenge Mission.	
Opening Gambit	[30]	Score the rank of [Bronze/Silver/Gold] in the "Opening Gambit" challenge Mission.	
Rush Defense: Bronze	[30]	Score the rank of [Bronze/Silver/Gold] in the "Rush Defense" challenge Mission.	
Solid Gold	20	Obtain the rank of Gold in all the Challenge Missions.	Spectre Portrait

QUICK MATCH

Name	Pts	1v1 League	Reward
Solo Terran	[80]	Win [10/25/50/100/200/500/1000/1500] 1v1 league Quick Match games as Terran.	
Solo Zerg	[80]	Win [10/25/50/100/200/500/1000/1500] 1v1 league Quick Match games as Zerg.	
Solo Protoss	[80]	Win [10/25/50/100/200/500/1000/1500] 1v1 league Quick Match games as Protoss.	
Solo Random	[80]	Win [10/25/50/100/200/500/1000/1500] 1v1 league Quick match games as Random.	
Solo Hot Streak	[20]	Win [3/5] 1v1 league Quick Match games in a row.	
Solo Zen Master	10	Win 1000 Solo league Quick Match games as each race option.	

Name	Pts	Team League	Reward
Team Terran	[80]	Win [10/25/50/100/200/500/1000/1500] Team league Quick Match games as Terran.	
Team Zerg	[80]	Win [10/25/50/100/200/500/1000/1500] Team league Quick Match games as Zerg.	
Team Protoss	[80]	Win [10/25/50/100/200/500/1000/1500] Team league Quick Match games as Protoss.	
Team Random	[80]	Win [10/25/50/100/200/500/1000/1500] Team league Quick Match games as random.	
Team Hot Streak	[20]	Win [3/5] Team league Quick Match games in a row.	
Team Zen Master	10	Win 1000 Team league Quick Match games as each race option.	

Name	Pts	Competitive	Reward
FFA Gladiator	10	Kill a total of 5000 enemy units in Free-For-All Quick Match Games.	
FFA Destroyer	10	Win a Free-For-All Quick Match game as each race option.	
FFA Wins	[80]	Win [5/10/25/50/100/200/400/800] Free-For-All Quick Match game.	
League Qualifier	10	Qualify for league Quick Match in each of following modes: 1v1, 2v2, 3v3, 4v4	
Two-way Dominant	10	Win a 2v2 league Quick Match game playing all race possibilities .	
Three-way Dominant	10	Win a 3v3 league Quick Match game playing all race possibilities.	
Competitive Zen Master	10	Complete the following "Competitive" Quick Match achievements.	

CUSTOM GAME

Name	Pts	Medium A.I.	Reward
Terran A.I. Romp	[40]	Win [10/25/50/100] solo evenly matched Custom Games as Terran against Medium A.I. opponents.	
Zerg A.I. Romp	[40]	Win [10/25/50/100] solo evenly matched Custom Games as Zerg against Medium A.I. opponents.	
Protoss A.I. Romp	[40]	Win [10/25/50/100] solo evenly matched Custom Games as Protoss against Medium A.I. opponents.	
Random A.I. Romp	[40]	Win [10/25/50/100] solo evenly matched Custom Games as Random against Medium A.I. opponents.	
Medium FFA	10	Win a Free-For-All Custom Game against 7 Medium A.I. opponents.	
Medium Blitz	10	Win a 1v1 Custom Game against a Medium A.I. opponent under 5 minutes.	
Medium A.I Crusher	10	Complete all the Medium A.I achievements.	

Name	Pts	Hard A.I.	Reward
Hard A.I. Romp	[40]	Win [10/25/50/100] solo evenly matched Custom Games against Hard A.I. opponents.	
Hard FFA	10	Win a Free-For-All Custom Game against 7 Hard A.I. opponents.	
Hard Blitz	10	Win a 1v1 Custom Game against a Hard A.I. opponent under 5 minutes.	
3v3 Mix vs Hard A.I.	10	Win a 3v3 Custom Game with Hard A.I. allies using all three races against Hard A.I opponents.	
3v3 vs Hard A.I. Mix	10	Win a 3v3 Custom Game with Hard A.I. allies against all three races of Hard A.I opponents.	
4v4 Kin vs Hard A.I.	10	Win a 4v4 Custom Game with Hard A.I. allies using the following race combinations against Hard A.I. opponents.	
4v4 vs Hard A.I. Kin	10	Win a 4v4 Custom Game with Hard A.I. allies against the following race combinations using Hard A.I. opponents.	
Hard A.I. Crusher	10	Complete all the Hard A.I. achievements.	

Name	Pts	Very Hard A.I.	Reward
Very Hard A.I. Romp	[40]	Win [10/25/50/100] solo evenly matched Custom Games against Very Hard A.I. opponents.	
Very Hard FFA	10	Win a Free-For-All Custom Game against 7 Very Hard A.I. opponents.	
Very Hard Blitz	10	Win a 1v1 Custom Game against a Very Hard A.I. opponent under 5 minutes.	
3v3 Mix vs Very Hard A.I.	10	Win a 3v3 Custom Game with Very Hard A.I. allies using all three races against Very Hard A.I opponents.	
3v3 vs Very Hard A.I. Mix	10	Win a 3v3 Custom Game with Very Hard A.I. allies against all three races of Very Hard A.I opponents.	
4v4 Kin vs Very Hard A.I.	10	Win a 4v4 Custom Game with Very Hard A.I. allies using the following race combinations against Very Hard A.I. opponents.	
4v4 vs Very Hard A.I. Kin	10	Win a 4v4 Custom Game with Very Hard A.I. allies against the following race combinations using Very Hard A.I. opponents.	
Very Hard A.I. Crusher	10	Complete all the Very Hard A.I. achievements.	

Name	Pts	Insane A.I.	Reward
Insane A.I. Romp	[40]	Win [10/25/50/100] solo evenly matched Custom Games against Insane A.I. opponents.	
Insane FFA	10	Win a Free-For-All Custom Game against 7 Insane A.I. opponents.	Predator Portrait
Insane Blitz	10	Win a 1v1 Custom Game against an Insane A.I. opponent under 5 minutes.	
3v3 Mix vs Insane A.I.	10	Win a 3v3 Custom Game with Insane A.I. allies using all three races against Insane A.I opponents.	
3v3 vs Insane A.I. Mix	10	Win a 3v3 Custom Game with Insane A.I. allies against all three races of Insane A.I opponents.	
4v4 Kin vs Insane A.I.	10	Win a 4v4 Custom Game with Insane A.I. allies using the following race combinations against Insane A.I. opponents.	
4v4 vs Insane A.I. Kin	10	Win a 4v4 Custom Game with Insane A.I. allies against the following race combinations using Insane A.I. opponents.	
Insane A.I. Crusher	10	Complete all the Insane A.I. achievements.	

Name	Pts	Outmatched	Reward
Outmatched: 2 Medium A.I.	10	Win a 1v2 Custom Game with no Allies against 2 Medium A.I. opponents.	
Outmatched: 3 Medium A.I.	10	Win a 1v3 Custom Game with no Allies against 3 Medium A.I. opponents.	
Outmatched: 4 Medium A.I.	10	Win a 1v4 Custom Game with no Allies against 4 Medium A.I. opponents.	
Outmatched: 2 Hard A.I.	10	Win a 1v2 Custom Game with no Allies against 2 Hard A.I. opponents.	
Outmatched: 3 Hard A.I.	10	Win a 1v3 Custom Game with no Allies against 3 Hard A.I. opponents.	
Outmatched: 4 Hard A.I.	10	Win a 1v4 Custom Game with no Allies against 4 Hard A.I. opponents.	
Outmatched: 2 Very Hard A.I.	10	Win 1v2 Custom Game with no Allies against 2 Very Hard A.I. opponents.	
Outmatched: 3 Very Hard A.I.	10	Win 1v3 Custom Game with no Allies against 3 Very Hard A.I. opponents.	
Outmatched: 4 Very Hard A.I.	10	Win 1v4 Custom Game with no Allies against 4 Very Hard A.I. opponents.	
Outmatched: 2 Insane A.I.	10	Win a 1v2 Custom Game with no Allies against 2 Insane A.I. opponents.	
Outmatched: 3 Insane A.I.	10	Win a 1v3 Custom Game with no Allies against 3 Insane A.I. opponents.	
Outmatched: 4 Insane A.I.	10	Win a 1v4 Custom Game with no Allies against 4 Insane A.I. opponents.	
Outmatched Crusher	10	Complete all the Outmatched achievements.	

CO-OP VS A.I.

Name	Pts	Medium A.I.	Rewards
Co-op Stomp Medium	10	Win [10/25/50/100/250] Co-op vs. A.I. games against medium A.I. opponents.	
2v2 Co-op Streak: Medium	10	Win [5/10/15] 2v2 Co-op vs. A.I. games in a row against Medium A.I. opponents.	
3v3 Co-op Streak: Medium	10	Win [5/10/15] 3v3 Co-op vs. A.I. games in a row against Medium A.I. opponents.	
2v2 Co-op Stomp Coverage: Medium	10	Win a 2v2 Co-op vs. A.I. game as all possibilites against Medium A.I.	
3v3 Co-op Stomp Coverage: Medium	10	Win a 3v3 Co-op vs. A.I. game as all possibilites against Medium A.I.	
Gosu Comp Stomp Medium	10	Complete all the Medium A.I. achievements.	

Name	Pts	Hard A.I.	Rewards
Co-op Stomp: Hard	[50]	Win [10/25/50/100/250] Co-op vs. A.I. games against Hard A.I. opponents.	
2v2 Co-op Streak: Hard	[30]	Win [5/10/15] 2v2 Co-op vs. A.I. games in a row against Hard A.I. opponents.	
3v3 Co-op Streak: Hard	[30]	Win [5/10/15] 3v3 Co-op games in a row against Hard A.I. opponents.	
2v2 Co-op Stomp Coverage: Hard	10	Win a 2v2 Co-op vs. A.I. game as all possibilites against Hard A.I.	
3v3 Co-op Stomp Coverage: Hard	10	Win a 3v3 Co-op vs. A.I. game as all possibilites against Hard A.I.	
Gosu Comp Stomp: Hard	10	Complete all the Hard A.I. achievements.	

Name	Pts	Very Hard A.I.	Rewards
Co-op Stomp: Very Hard	[50]	Win [10/25/50/100/250] Co-op vs. A.I. games against Very Hard A.I. opponents.	
2v2 Co-op Streak: Very Hard	[30]	Win [5/10/15] 2v2 Co-op vs. A.I. games in a row against Very Hard A.I. opponents.	
3v3 Co-op Streak: Very Hard	[30]	Win [5/10/15] 3v3 Co-op games in a row against Very Hard A.I. opponents.	
2v2 Co-op Stomp Coverage: Very Hard	10	Win a 2v2 Co-op vs. A.I. game as all possibilites against Very Hard A.I.	
3v3 Co-op Stomp Coverage: Very Hard	10	Win a 3v3 Co-op vs. A.I. game as all possibilites against Very Hard A.I.	
Gosu Comp Stomp: Very Hard	10	Complete all the Very Hard A.I. achievements.	

Name	Pts	Insane A.I.	Rewards
Co-op Stomp: Insane	[50]	Win [10/25/50/100/250] Co-op vs. A.I. games against Insane A.I. opponents.	
2v2 Co-op Streak: Insane	[30]	Win [5/10/15] 2v2 Co-op vs. A.I. games in a row against Insane A.I. opponents.	
3v3 Co-op Streak: Insane	[30]	Win [5/10/15] 3v3 Co-op vs. A.I. games in a row against Insane A.I. opponents.	
2v2 Co-op Stomp Coverage: Insane	10	Win a 2v2 Co-op vs. A.I. game as all possibilites against Insane A.I.	
3v3 Co-op Stomp Coverage: Insane	10	Win a 3v3 Co-op vs. A.I. game as all possibilites against Insane A.I.	
Gosu Comp Stomp Insane	10	Complete all the Insane A.I. achievements.	

Name	Pts	Race A.I.	Rewards
Terran Command	[50]	Win [10/25/50/100/250] Co-op vs. A.I. games as Terran against Medium A.I. opponents.	
Protoss Command	[50]	Win [10/25/50/100/250] Co-op vs. A.I. games as Protoss against Medium A.I. opponents.	
Zerg Command	[50]	Win [10/25/50/100/250] Co-op vs. A.I. games as Zerg against Medium A.I. opponents.	
Random Command	[50]	Win [10/25/50/100/250] Co-op vs. A.I. games as Random against Medium A.I. opponents.	
Supreme Command	10	Complete all the Race A.I. achievements.	

FEATS

Name	Pts	Single Player	Reward
The Scenic Route	0	Kill all the Zerg in "The Devil's Playground" mission on Normal difficulty.	
You'ze So Crazy!	0	Kill all the Protoss in the "Welcome to the Jungle" mission on Normal difficulty.	
Monster Mash	0	Use the A.R.E.S to Kill the Brutalisk in the "Piercing the Shroud" mission on Normal difficulty.	
Devoted Fan	0	Purchase StarCraft 2 Wings of Liberty Collector's Edition	Raynor Marine/Tauren Marine / Night Elf Banshee/Diablo Marine DECALS Alliance Symbol /Horde Symbol/Diablo Skull
Hot Shot	0	Finish a Qualification round with an undefeated record.	

Razer™ Spectre™ Starcraft® II
Gaming Mouse

COMING SOON

www.razerzone.com

OFFICIAL STRATEGY GUIDE

Please be advised that the ESRB ratings icons, "EC", "E", "E10+", "T", "M", "AO", and "RP" are trademarks owned by the Entertainment Software Association, and may only be used with their permission and authority. For information regarding whether a product has been rated by the ESRB, please visit www.esrb.org. For permission to use the ratings icons, please contact the ESA at esrblicenseinfo@theesa.com.

ISBN: 978-0-7440-1128-9

Printing Code: The rightmost double-digit number is the year of the book's printing; the rightmost single-digit number is the number of the book's printing. For example, 10-1 shows that the first printing of the book occurred in 2010.

13 12 11 10   4 3 2 1

Printed in the USA.

BLIZZARD ACKNOWLEDGEMENTS

Licensing
Mark Almeida
Gina Pippin
George Hsieh

StarCraft II Team
Tony Hsu
Claudio Gentilini
Kristoffer Barcarse
David Kim
Matthew Cooper
Kaeo Milker
Samwise Didier
Chris Sigaty
SC2 Level Designers

Quality Assurance
Nathan LaMusaga
Tim Jones
Kelly Chun
Shon Fu
Michael Chen
Jung Hwan Kim
Richard Duran
Michelle Lee
Jimmie Jaimes
Thomas Floeter
Dan V. Nguyen
Jason Briggs

Battle.net
Jason Chayes
Jack Chen
Greg Canessa
Yong Woo
Alex Sun
Jeremy Craig

Creative Development
Zachariah Owens
Skye Chandler

Localization
William Barnes
Richard Honeywood
Megumi Arai
Andrew Vestal
Frederic Baudet
Ines Rubio
Pablo Martin
Katharina Reiche
Stefan Schmitt
Andrea Tüger
Tristan Lhomme
Christelle Bravin
Alexander Lyubov
Ana Alfageme
Cristina Figallo
Joonho Lee
Jong Hyuk Lee
Minjin Lee
Sanghak Jeon
Sunggyu Lim
Wonyoung Choi
David Florez
Wolfram Sack
Marc Wehbe

Marketing
Erik Jensen
Marc Hutcheson
Kevin Carter

BRADYGAMES ACKNOWLEDGEMENTS

KEITH: Thanks to Brian, Areva, Dan, and David. The best looking team a guy could work wth! Special thanks to Nathan Rushton for helping me take some great multiplayer shots. You're a sexy beast!

BRIAN: We did what we thought couldn't be done. This team, this band of yes, envisioned our selves a giant monolith of a book and delivered. Three separate books, six languages, pro-tips, map stand, all out day one with game launch. Sisyphus laughed at us.

We are proud of this book; it represents more than a year's work for all of us and it totally rocks. Thank you to all who stood together to get it done, but especially: Gina, George, Rick, Phil, David W., Leigh, Keith, Areva, Dan, David B. These people made me look like I actually knew what I was doing, and believed me when I said we could do it.

AUTHOR ACKNOWLEDGEMENTS

RICK BARBA

Rick would like to thank the fantastic folks at Blizzard who made my 36 days on-site in Irvine a homey experience, relatively speaking. They welcomed me, offered me catered food nightly, and never ridiculed me for being old, which I am. Special thanks to Tony Hsu for his generous help, patience and availability; this guide owes him a tremendous debt of gratitude. Thanks also to my buddies George Hsieh and Gina Pippin for working out flawless logistics, and for their warm hospitality. Thanks to my man Pedro at the Doubletree Inn for keeping the Makers Mark fresh in my glass. Finally, heartfelt thanks to my daily co-workers: co-author Phil, truly one of the sharpest game gods I know, and a hell of a good guy despite all that multiplayer blood on his hands; Keith Lowe, dude, thanks for taking all those gorgeous shots, and what a gorgeous book, great seeing you; and then there's Mister Shotton: He Is Who Is. The fellow I'd want watching my back in an alley knife fight, without a doubt. Thanks, guys.

PHILLIP MARCUS

The Starcraft II project has been one of the most difficult projects I've worked on in over ten years of guide writing, and easily the longest. In a way, that is entirely appropriate, as the game has been in development even longer. The Starcraft II team at Blizzard has been slaving away at this game for many, many years. You will see the result of that fine polish right around the same time you're holding this book in your hands.

This guide was the result of a very hard working team, and I have to thank my co-author, Rick Barba, for being a fantastic working partner, and my editor and designer, Brian Shotton and Keith Lowe, for handling the massively huge manuscript behind this guide with patience and good grace.

At Blizzard, I want to thank Gina Pippin and George Hsieh for always being welcoming and accomodating, even when the team was exceptionally busy. And of course, the Starcraft II and ESports teams were both fantastic, giving their time to answer the most fiddly of questions. Tony Hsu, Claudio Gentilini, Matthew Cooper, David Kim, as well as Robert Simpson, CW Jung, Stephen Chang, Joong Kim, Eric Yco, Susana Monroy, and others, who answered questions in passing or in detail!.

Finally, a special thanks to the beta testers for Starcraft II. You probably didn't know it at the time, but you helped in the final stages of tweaking for this guide, both in matches that I played against you, and the huge number of replays and videos that the community shared online.

BRADYGAMES STAFF

PUBLISHER
DAVID WAYBRIGHT

EDITOR-IN-CHIEF
H. LEIGH DAVIS

LICENSING DIRECTOR
MIKE DEGLER

INTERNATIONAL
BRIAN SALIBA

CREDITS

TITLE MANAGER
BRIAN SHOTTON

TRANSLATIONS MANAGER
DAVID B. BARTLEY

LEAD DESIGNER
KEITH LOWE

DESIGNER
DAN CAPARO

PRODUCTION DESIGNER
AREVA